To the peaceful application of
remote sensing technology to earth
resource monitoring and management.

PREFACE

This book has been prepared primarily for use in introductory courses in remote sensing. Engineers, soil scientists, foresters, range managers, geologists, geographers, oceanographers, land planners, meteorologists, archaeologists, water resource managers, biologists—anyone involved in measuring, studying, and managing earth resources—should find it valuable as both a textbook and as a reference. It focuses on remote sensing systems and illustrates their utility in a diverse range of data gathering applications.

The book provides a broad, yet not superficial, introduction to the subject of remote sensing. No book can cover all aspects of the theory and practice of remote sensing and most textbooks on the subject are either narrowly focused, dealing with particular sensors or applications, or are multiauthored compendia. This book is a two-person effort aimed at *synthesizing* the subject of remote sensing so that the student might become equipped to understand and apply the appropriate aspects of remote sensing technology to his or her discipline.

We have made every attempt to be clear, concise, thorough, and objective. We have gone beyond the "black box" approach, yet we have written a book for upper division students studying earth resource management, not for electronics experts or theoretical mathematicians. All the "classical" elements of aerial photographic interpretation and photogrammetry are described, but we also introduce the concepts of interpreting images from nonphotographic sensors—both visually and through the application of digital image processing techniques.

After presenting the basic physical principles on which remote sensing is based, the first half of this book concentrates on photographic remote sensing techniques. We treat the tools of the photographic trade (cameras, films, and so on), then provide a general introduction to the airphoto interpretation process. This introduction includes sample applications of airphoto interpretation in specific mapping tasks, such as land use/land cover mapping (including geographic information system design concepts), wetlands mapping, and geologic and soil mapping. We also discuss, in very general terms, the application of airphoto interpretation to the fields of agriculture, forestry, range management, water resources, urban and regional planning, wildlife ecology, archaeology, and environmental assessment. An entire chapter is devoted to terrain evaluation via airphoto interpretation.

v

The metric aspects of dealing with airphotos are covered in our discussion of photogrammetry, which includes a description of how to make reliable measurements from aerial photographs and consideration of how topographic mapping is accomplished through the use of stereoplotter instruments. We also discuss the preparation and characteristics of orthophotography, along with the process of planning a photographic mission.

Our treatment of photographic remote sensing procedures concludes with discussion of the radiometric characteristics of aerial photographs. This involves the details of how to radiometrically calibrate aerial photography and make image density measurements.

The second half of the book deals with the principles of acquiring and interpreting data collected by nonphotographic sensors. We describe thermal scanners, multispectral scanners, and radar systems. As with our discussion of photographic techniques, we illustrate how images produced from these systems are interpreted in various application areas. The book concludes with treatment of the subject of digital image processing.

There is enough material in this book for it to be used in many different ways, in many different course settings. These include courses in remote sensing, photo interpretation, photogrammetry, and digital image processing. Some courses may omit certain chapters and use the book in a one-semester or one-quarter course; the book may also be used in a two-course sequence. We have attempted to design the book with these two different potential uses in mind.

Where pictures were important in formulating the text, we used pictures. Where principle was more important than detail, we sacrificed detail. The International System of Units (SI) is used throughout the book and tables of SI units frequently used in remote sensing are included inside the back book cover. Numerical examples are given where appropriate. At the end of each chapter a selected bibliography appears that includes works specifically cited plus other books and articles recommended for additional reading on various topics.

Those familiar with the previous edition of this book will note that the second edition follows the same general organizational structure as its predecessor. However, we have made many additions and changes that are aimed at both updating and improving the coverage of the first edition. For example, we have devoted an entirely new chapter to digital image processing. This has permitted us to greatly expand our discussion of digital image rectification and restoration (preprocessing), enhancement, classification, and data merging. We have also increased our emphasis on the intimate relationship between remote sensing and geographic information systems (GISs). We describe and illustrate this relationship in several locations throughout the book.

Other changes made in this edition include new or updated material on *sensors* such as the Large Format Camera, the Optical Bar Camera, solid-state array cameras, color infrared video cameras, forward-looking infrared systems, linear array multispectral scanners, the Advanced Imaging Spectrometer, the Thermal Infrared Multispectral Scanner, the Shuttle Imaging Radar systems, light detection and ranging systems, the Landsat Thematic Mapper, the SPOT High Resolution Visible sensors, and the NOAA Advanced Very High Resolution Radiometer.

New or increased coverage is also included that deals with such *concepts* as modulation transfer functions, imaging spectrometry, vegetation indices, geobotany, digital classification accuracy assessment, intensity−hue−saturation color transformations, and spatial feature manipulation through Fourier analysis. This edition also contains several new line drawings and photographic illustrations—including several additional color plates. The bibliography for each chapter has been greatly expanded and the various acronyms frequently used in remote sensing have been incorporated into the index. To the fullest extent possible, we have also implemented the numerous suggestions made by instructors and professionals who have used the first edition of this book.

Although we have discussed remote sensing systems ranging from handheld 35 mm cameras to earth orbiting satellites, we have limited the scope of this book to *electromagnetic* remote sensing of *earth resources*. Consequently, there is a multitude of remote sensing systems and application areas we do not treat. At the same time, remote sensing is such a dynamic field that some of what we present here may soon be outdated. Nonetheless, this book should enable the student to understand the business of stepping back—figuratively speaking—with image in hand and studying the broader perspective of our earth, its resources, and their environment.

The authors express their sincere thanks to the many individuals who have contributed to this edition. Specifically, we are grateful to Professor Roger M. Hoffer, of Purdue University, whose thorough review of the original draft of this entire manuscript and numerous suggestions were extremely valuable. Likewise, the suggestions made by the publisher's formal reviewers of the manuscript were very helpful. Portions of the second edition manuscript were also reviewed by the following (some of whom also supplied illustrations): Professor Sean Ahearn, Professor Marvin Bauer, Mr. William Johnson, and Mr. Douglas Meisner, University of Minnesota, Saint Paul, Minnesota; Mr. Robert Barker and Ms. Nadine Binger, SPOT Image Corporation, Reston, Virginia; Dr. John Ford, NASA Jet Propulsion Laboratory, Pasadena, California; Professor Paul Hopkins, College of Environmental Science and Forestry, State University of New York, Syracuse, New York; Professor Thomas Lo, University of Alabama, University, Alabama; Mr. David Meyer and Mr. Wayne Miller, USGS EROS Data Center, Sioux Falls, South Dakota; Mr. Ronald Ondrejka, ITEK Optical Systems, Lexington, Massachusetts; Professor Frank Scarpace, University of Wisconsin, Madison, Wisconsin; Dr. Susan Till, Canada Centre for Remote Sensing, Ottawa, Canada; and Dr. Earl J. Tullos, Jr., EOSAT Corporation, Lanham, Maryland.

Special illustration materials and suggestions were provided by Mr. Carey Erdman, ITEK Optical Systems, Lexington, Massachusetts; Dr. Donald Morris-Jones, Environmental Research Institute of Michigan, Ann Arbor, Michigan; Dr. Michael Kobrick, NASA Jet Propulsion Laboratory, Pasadena, California; Professor Richard Dahlberg and Professor Donald Luman, Northern Illinois University, DeKalb, Illinois; Professor Lee Miller, University of Nebraska, Lincoln, Nebraska; Dr. Robert Ryerson, Canada Centre for Remote Sensing, Ottawa, Canada; and Mr. Larry Seidl and Dr. Peter Weiler, University of Wisconsin, Madison, Wisconsin.

The authors also thank the many graduate and undergraduate students at the University of Wisconsin−Madison who made valuable contributions to this edition.

Specifically, we acknowledge the assistance of William Bergen, Robert Best, Martin Buchheim, W. Joseph Carper, Chi-farn Chen, Jennifer Dungan, Witold Fraczek, Gary Jedlovec, Richard Lathrop, Jr., Gordon Maclean, Robert Merideth, and Carol Wessman.

We are also grateful to the various individuals, instrument manufacturers, government agencies, and commercial firms who provided background materials and many of the illustrations used in this book.

And finally, special recognition is due the authors' families, who provided 2 years of patient understanding and encouragement while this edition was in preparation.

Thomas M. Lillesand
Ralph W. Kiefer

CONTENTS

CONCEPTS AND FOUNDATIONS OF REMOTE SENSING

1.1 INTRODUCTION

Remote sensing is the science and art of obtaining information about an object, area, or phenomenon through the analysis of data acquired by a device that is not in contact with the object, area, or phenomenon under investigation. As you read these words you are employing remote sensing. Your eyes are acting as sensors that respond to the light reflected from this page. The "data" your eyes acquire are impulses corresponding to the amount of light reflected from the dark and light areas on the page. These data are analyzed, or interpreted, in your mental computer to enable you to explain the dark areas on the page as a collection of letters forming words. Beyond this, you recognize that the words form sentences, and interpret the information that the sentences convey.

In many respects, remote sensing can be thought of as a reading process. Using various sensors we remotely collect *data* that may be analyzed to obtain *information* about the objects, areas, or phenomena being investigated. The remotely collected data can be of many forms, including variations in force distributions, acoustic wave distributions, or electromagnetic energy distributions. For example, a gravity meter acquires data on variations in the distribution of the force of gravity. Sonar, like a bat's navigation system, obtains data on variations in acoustic wave distributions. Our eyes acquire data on variations in electromagnetic energy distributions

This book is about *electromagnetic* energy sensors that are currently being operated from airborne and spaceborne platforms to assist in inventorying, mapping, and monitoring earth resources. These sensors acquire data on the way various earth surface features emit and reflect electromagnetic energy and these data are analyzed to provide information about the resources under investigation.

Figure 1.1 schematically illustrates the generalized processes and elements involved in electromagnetic remote sensing of earth resources. The two basic processes involved are *data acquisition* and *data analysis.* The elements of the data acquisition process are energy sources (*a*), propagation of energy through the atmosphere (*b*), energy interactions with earth surface features (*c*), re-transmission of energy through

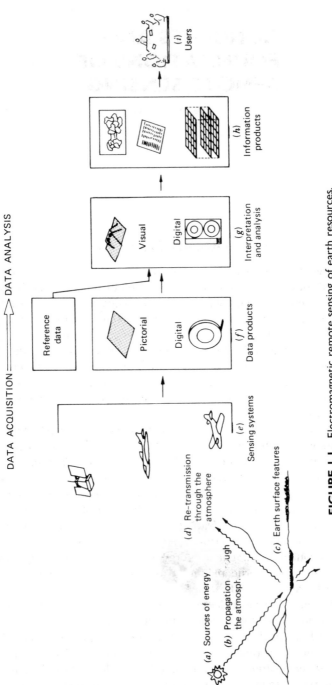

FIGURE I.I   Electromagnetic remote sensing of earth resources.

the atmosphere (*d*), airborne and/or spaceborne sensors (*e*), resulting in the generation of sensor data in pictorial and/or digital form (*f*). In short, we use sensors to record variations in the way earth surface features reflect and emit electromagnetic energy. The data analysis process (*g*) involves examining the data using various viewing and interpretation devices to analyze pictorial data, and/or a computer to analyze digital sensor data. Reference data about the resources being studied (such as soils maps, crop statistics, or field-check data) are used when and where available to assist in the data analysis. With the aid of the reference data, the analyst extracts information about the type, extent, location, and condition of the various resources over which the sensor data were collected. This information is then compiled (*h*), generally in the form of hard copy maps and tables, or as computer files that can be merged with other "layers" of information in a *geographic information system (GIS)*. Finally, the information is presented to users (*i*) who apply it to their decision-making process.

In the remainder of this chapter, we discuss the basic principles underlying the remote sensing process. We begin with the fundamentals of electromagnetic energy, then consider how the energy interacts with earth surface features. We also treat the role that reference data play in the data analysis procedure. These basics will permit us to conceptualize an "ideal" remote sensing system. With that as a framework, we consider the limitations encountered in "real" remote sensing systems. At the end of this discussion, the reader should have a grasp of the general concepts and foundations of remote sensing.

1.2   ENERGY SOURCES AND RADIATION PRINCIPLES

Visible light is only one of many forms of electromagnetic energy. Radio waves, heat, ultraviolet rays and X-rays are other familiar forms. All this energy is inherently similar and radiates in accordance with basic wave theory. As shown in Figure 1.2, this theory describes electromagnetic energy as traveling in a harmonic, sinusoidal fashion at the "velocity of light," *c*. The distance from one wave peak to the next is the *wavelength* λ, and the number of peaks passing a fixed point in space per unit time is the wave *frequency ν*.

From basic physics, waves obey the general equation

$$c = \nu\lambda \qquad\qquad (1.1)$$

Since *c* is essentially a constant (3 × 10⁸ m/sec), frequency *ν* and wavelength λ for any given wave are related inversely, and either term can be used to characterize a wave into a particular form. In remote sensing, it is most common to categorize electromagnetic waves by their wavelength location within the *electromagnetic spectrum* (Figure 1.3). The most prevalent unit used to measure wavelength along the spectrum is the *micrometer* (μm). A micrometer equals 1 × 10⁻⁶ m. (Tables of units used frequently in this book are included inside the back cover.)

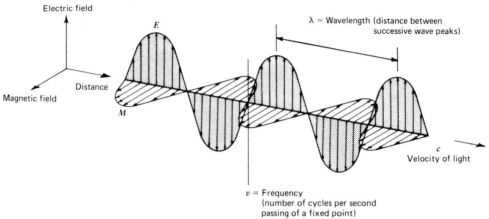

FIGURE 1.2   An electromagnetic wave. Components include a sinusoidal electric wave *(E)* and a similar magnetic wave *(M)* at right angles, both being perpendicular to the direction of propagation.

Although names are generally assigned to regions of the electromagnetic spectrum for convenience (such as ultraviolet and microwave), there is no clear-cut dividing line between one nominal spectral region and the next. Divisions of the spectrum have grown out of the various methods for sensing each type of radiation more so than from inherent differences in the energy characteristics of various wavelengths. Also, it should be noted that the portions of the electromagnetic spectrum used in remote sensing lie along a continuum characterized by magnitude changes of many powers of 10. Hence, the use of logarithmic plots to depict the electromagnetic spectrum is quite common. The "visible" portion of such a plot is an extremely small one, since the spectral sensitivity of the human eye extends only from about 0.4 μm to approximately 0.7 μm. The color "blue" is ascribed to the approximate range of 0.4 to 0.5 μm, "green" to 0.5 to 0.6 μm, and "red" to 0.6 to 0.7 μm. *Ultraviolet* energy adjoins the blue end of the visible portion of the spectrum. Adjoining the red end of the visible region are three different categories of *infrared* (IR) waves: *near-IR* (from 0.7 to 1.3 μm), *mid-IR* (from 1.3 to 3 μm), and *thermal IR* (beyond 3 μm). At much longer wavelengths (1 mm to 1 m) is the *microwave* portion of the spectrum.

Most common sensing systems operate in one or several of the visible, IR, or microwave portions of the spectrum. *Within the IR portion of the spectrum, it should be noted that only thermal IR energy is directly related to the sensation of heat; near and mid-IR energy is not.*

Although many characteristics of electromagnetic radiation are most easily described by wave theory, another theory offers useful insights into how electromagnetic energy interacts with matter. This theory—the particle theory—suggests that electro-

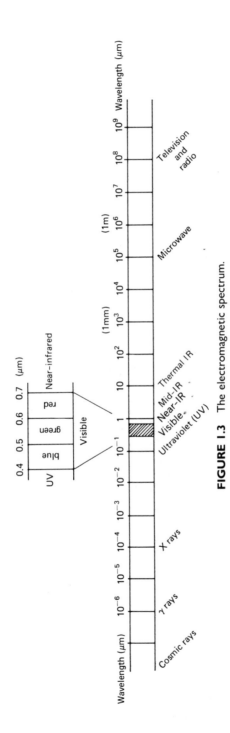

FIGURE 1.3   The electromagnetic spectrum.

magnetic radiation is composed of many discrete units called *photons* or *quanta*. The energy of a quantum is given as

$$Q = h\nu \tag{1.2}$$

where
Q = energy of a quantum, Joules (J)
h = Planck's constant, 6.626×10^{-34} J sec
ν = frequency

We can relate the wave and quantum models of electromagnetic radiation behavior by solving Eq. 1.1 for ν and substituting into Eq. 1.2 to obtain

$$Q = \frac{hc}{\lambda} \tag{1.3}$$

Thus, we see that the energy of a quantum is inversely proportional to its wavelength. *The longer the wavelength involved, the lower its energy content.* This has important implications in remote sensing from the standpoint that naturally emitted long wavelength radiation, such as microwave emission from terrain features, is more difficult to sense than radiation of shorter wavelengths, such as emitted thermal IR energy. The low energy content of long wavelength radiation means that, in general, systems operating at long wavelengths must "view" large areas of the earth at any given time in order to obtain a detectable energy signal.

The sun is the most obvious source of electromagnetic radiation for remote sensing. However, *all* matter at temperatures above absolute zero (0°K, or −273°C) continuously emits electromagnetic radiation. Thus, terrestrial objects are also sources of radiation, though it is of considerably different magnitude and spectral composition than that of the sun. How much energy any object radiates is, among other things, a function of the surface temperature of the object. This property is expressed by the *Stefan−Boltzmann Law*, which states that

$$M = \sigma T^4 \tag{1.4}$$

where
M = total radiant exitance from the surface of a material, Watts (W) m^{-2}
σ = *Stefan−Boltzmann constant*, 5.6697×10^{-8} W m^{-2} °K^{-4}
T = absolute temperature (°K) of the emitting material

The particular units and the value of the constant are not critical for the student to remember, yet it is important to note that the total energy emitted from an object varies as T^4, and therefore increases very rapidly with increases in temperature. Also, it should be noted that this law is expressed for an energy source that behaves as a *blackbody*. A blackbody is a hypothetical, ideal radiator that totally absorbs and reemits all energy incident upon it. Actual objects only approach this ideal. We further explore the implications of this fact in Chapter 7; suffice it to say for now that the energy emitted from an object is primarily a function of its temperature, as given by Eq. 1.4.

Just as the total energy emitted by an object varies with temperature, the spectral distribution of the emitted energy also varies. Figure 1.4 shows energy distribution curves for blackbodies at temperatures ranging from 200 to 6000°K. The units on the ordinate scale (W m^{-2} μm^{-1}) express the radiant power coming from a blackbody per 1 μm spectral interval. Hence, the *area* under these curves equals the total radiant exitance, M, and the curves illustrate graphically what the Stefan–Boltzmann Law expresses mathematically: The higher the temperature of the radiator, the greater the total amount of radiation it emits. The curves also show that there is a shift toward shorter wavelengths in the peak of a blackbody radiation distribution as temperature increases. The *dominant wavelength*, or wavelength at which a blackbody radiation curves reaches a maximum, is related to its temperature by *Wien's Displacement Law*,

$$\lambda_m = \frac{A}{T} \tag{1.5}$$

where
λ_m = wavelength of maximum spectral radiant exitance, μm
A = 2898 μm °K
T = temperature, °K

Thus, for a blackbody, the wavelength at which the maximum spectral radiant exitance occurs varies inversely with the blackbody's absolute temperature. We observe this phenomenon when a metal body such as a piece of iron is heated. As the object becomes progressively hotter, it begins to glow and its color changes successively to shorter wavelengths—from dull red, to orange, to yellow, and eventually to white.

The sun emits in the same manner as a blackbody radiator whose temperature is about 6000°K (Figure 1.4). Many incandescent lamps emit radiation typified by a 3000°K blackbody radiation curve. Consequently, incandescent lamps have a relatively low output of blue energy and they do not have the same spectral constituency as sunlight. We observe this when using flashbulbs for indoor photography when daylight, or outdoor, film is used. With clear flashbulbs, the resulting photography would appear "yellowish" because flashbulbs are incandescent light sources and hence have low blue energy output. By using blue tinted flashbulbs, we can compensate for this inherent spectral imbalance.

The earth's ambient temperature (that is, the temperature of surface materials such as soil, water, and vegetation) is about 300°K (27°C). From Wien's Displacement Law, this means the maximum spectral radiant exitance from earth features occurs at a wavelength of about 9.7 μm. Because this radiation correlates with terrestrial heat, it is termed "thermal infrared" energy. This energy can neither be seen nor photographed,

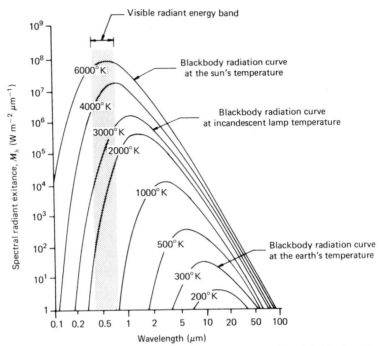

FIGURE 1.4   Spectral distribution of energy radiated from blackbodies of various temperatures. (Note that spectral radiant exitance, M_λ, is the energy emitted per unit wavelength interval. Total radiant exitance, M, is given by the area under the spectral radiant exitance curves.)

but can be sensed with such thermal devices as radiometers and scanners (described in Chapter 7). By comparison, the sun has a much higher energy peak that occurs at about 0.5 μm as indicated in Figure 1.4. Our eyes—and photographic film—are sensitive to energy of this magnitude and wavelength. Thus, when the sun is present, we can observe earth features by virtue of *reflected* solar energy. Once again, the longer wavelength energy *emitted* by ambient earth features can be observed only with a nonphotographic sensing system. The general dividing line between reflected and emitted IR wavelengths is approximately 3 μm. Below this wavelength, reflected energy predominates; above it, emitted energy prevails.

Certain sensors, such as radar systems, supply their own source of energy to illuminate features of interest. These systems are termed "active" systems, in contrast to "passive" systems that sense naturally available energy. A very common example of an active system is a camera used with flashbulbs. The same system used in sunlight becomes a passive sensor.

1.3   ENERGY INTERACTIONS IN THE ATMOSPHERE

Irrespective of its source, all radiation detected by remote sensors passes through some distance, or *path length*, of atmosphere. The path length involved can vary widely. For example, space photography results from sunlight that passes through the full thickness of the earth's atmosphere twice on its journey from source to sensor. On the other hand, an airborne thermal sensor detects energy emitted directly from objects on the earth, so a single, relatively short atmospheric path length is involved. The net effect of the atmosphere varies with these differences in path length and also varies with the magnitude of the energy signal being sensed, the atmospheric conditions present, and the wavelengths involved.

Because of the varied nature of atmospheric effects, we treat this subject on a sensor-by-sensor basis in other chapters. Here we merely wish to introduce the notion that the atmosphere can have a profound effect on, among other things, the intensity and spectral composition of radiation available to any sensing system. These effects are caused principally through the mechanisms of atmospheric *scattering* and *absorption*.

Scattering

Atmospheric scattering is unpredictable diffusion of radiation by particles in the atmosphere. *Rayleigh scatter* is common when radiation interacts with atmospheric molecules and other tiny particles that are much smaller in diameter than the wavelength of the interacting radiation. The effect of Rayleigh scatter is inversely proportional to the fourth power of wavelength. Hence, there is a much stronger tendency for short wavelengths to be scattered by this scattering mechanism than long wavelengths.

A "blue" sky is a manifestation of Rayleigh scatter. In the absence of scatter, the sky would appear black. But, as sunlight interacts with the earth's atmosphere, it scatters the shorter (blue) wavelengths more dominantly than the other visible wavelengths. Consequently, we see a blue sky. At sunrise and sunset, however, the sun's rays travel through a longer atmospheric path length than during midday. With the longer path, the scatter (and absorption) of short wavelengths is so complete that we see only the less-scattered, longer wavelengths of orange and red.

Rayleigh scatter is one of the primary causes of "haze" in imagery. Visually, haze diminishes the "crispness," or "contrast," of an image. In color photography, it results in a bluish-gray cast to an image, particularly when taken from high altitude. As we see in Chapter 2, haze can often be eliminated, or at least minimized, in photography by introducing, in front of the camera lens, a *filter* that does not transmit short wavelengths.

Another type of scatter is *Mie scatter*, which exists when atmospheric particle diameters essentially equal the energy wavelengths being sensed. Water vapor and dust are major causes of Mie scatter. This type of scatter tends to influence longer wavelengths compared to Rayleigh scatter. Although Rayleigh scatter tends to dominate under most atmospheric conditions, Mie scatter is significant in slightly overcast ones.

A more bothersome phenomenon is *nonselective scatter*, which comes about when the diameters of the particles causing scatter are much larger than the energy wavelengths being sensed. Water droplets, for example, cause such scatter. They commonly have a diameter in the range 5 to 100 μm and scatter all visible and near- to mid-IR wavelengths about equally. Consequently, this scattering is "nonselective" with respect to wavelength. In the visible wavelengths, equal quantities of blue, green, and red light are scattered, making fog and clouds appear white.

Absorption

In contrast to scatter, atmospheric absorption results in the effective loss of energy to atmospheric constituents. This normally involves absorption of energy at a given wavelength. The most efficient absorbers of solar radiation in this regard are water vapor, carbon dioxide, and ozone. Because these gases tend to absorb electromagnetic energy in specific wavelength bands, they strongly influence "where we look" spectrally with any given remote sensing system. The wavelength ranges in which the atmosphere is particularly transmissive of energy are referred to as *atmospheric windows*.

Figure 1.5 shows the interrelationship between energy sources and atmospheric absorption characteristics. Figure 1.5*a* shows the spectral distribution of the energy emitted by the sun and by earth features. These two curves represent the most common sources of energy used in remote sensing. In Figure 1.5*b*, spectral regions in which the atmosphere blocks energy are shaded. Remote sensing data acquisition is limited to the nonblocked spectral regions, called "atmospheric windows." Note in Figure 1.5*c* that the spectral sensitivity range of the eye (the "visible" range) coincides both with an atmospheric window and the peak level of energy from the sun. Emitted "heat" energy from the earth, shown by the small curve in (*a*), is sensed through the windows at 3 to 5μm and 8 to 14μm using such devices as *thermal scanners*. *Multispectral scanners* sense simultaneously through multiple, narrow wavelength ranges that can be located at various points in the visible through the thermal spectral region. *Radar* and *passive microwave systems* operate through a window in the region 1 mm to 1 m.

The important point to note from Figure 1.5 is the *interaction* and the *interdependence* between the primary sources of electromagnetic energy, the atmospheric windows through which source energy may be transmitted to and from earth surface features, and the spectral sensitivity of the sensors available to detect and record the energy. One cannot select the sensor to be used in any given remote sensing task arbitrarily; one must instead consider (1) the spectral sensitivity of the sensors available, (2) the presence or absence of atmospheric windows in the spectral range(s) in which one wishes to sense, and (3) the source, magnitude, and spectral composition of the energy available in these ranges. Ultimately, however, the choice of spectral range of the sensor must be based on the manner in which the energy interacts with the features under investigation. It is to this last, very important, element that we now turn our attention.

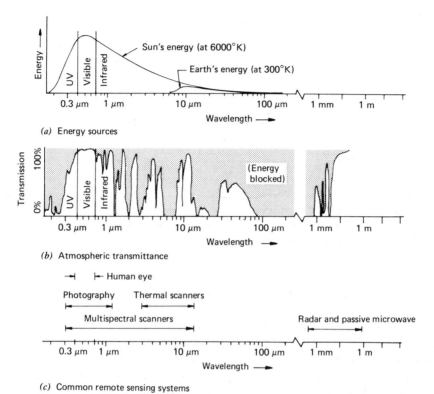

FIGURE I.5   Spectral characteristics of (a) energy sources, (b) atmospheric effects, and (c) sensing systems. (Note that wavelength scale is logarithmic.)

I.4   ENERGY INTERACTIONS WITH EARTH SURFACE FEATURES

When electromagnetic energy is incident on any given earth surface feature, three fundamental energy interactions with the feature are possible. This is illustrated in Figure 1.6 for an element of the volume of a water body. Various fractions of the energy incident on the element are *reflected, absorbed,* and/or *transmitted.* Applying the principle of conservation of energy, we can state the interrelationship between these three energy interactions as

$$E_I(\lambda) = E_R(\lambda) + E_A(\lambda) + E_T(\lambda) \tag{1.6}$$

where E_I denotes the incident energy, E_R denotes the reflected energy, E_A denotes the absorbed energy, and E_T denotes the transmitted energy, with all energy components being a function of wavelength λ. Equation 1.6 is an energy balance equation

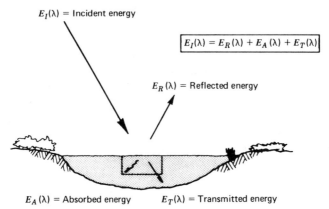

FIGURE 1.6   Basic interactions between electromagnetic energy and an earth surface feature.

expressing the interrelationship among the mechanisms of reflection, absorption, and transmission.

Two points concerning this relationship should be noted. First, the proportions of energy reflected, absorbed, and transmitted will vary for different earth features, depending on their material type and condition. These differences permit us to distinguish different features on an image. Second, the wavelength dependency means that, even within a given feature type, the proportion of reflected, absorbed, and transmitted energy will vary at different wavelengths. Thus, two features may be indistinguishable in one spectral range and be very different in another wavelength band. Within the visible portion of the spectum, these spectral variations result in the visual effect called *color*. For example, we call objects "blue" when they reflect highly in the blue portion of the spectrum, "green" when the reflect highly in the green spectral region, and so on. Thus, the eye utilizes spectral variations in the magnitude of reflected energy to discriminate between various objects.

Because many remote sensing systems operate in the wavelength regions in which reflected energy predominates, the reflectance properties of earth features are very important. Hence, it is often useful to think of the energy balance relationship expressed by Eq. 1.6 in the form

$$E_R(\lambda) = E_I(\lambda) - [E_A(\lambda) + E_T(\lambda)] \tag{1.7}$$

That is, the reflected energy is equal to the energy incident on a given feature reduced by the energy that is either absorbed or transmitted by that feature.

The geometric manner in which an object reflects energy is also an important consideration. This factor is primarily a function of the surface roughness of the object. *Specular* reflectors are flat surfaces that manifest mirrorlike reflections, where the angle of reflection equals the angle of incidence. *Diffuse* (or *Lambertian*) reflectors are rough surfaces that reflect uniformly in all directions. Most earth surfaces are neither perfectly specular nor diffuse reflectors. Their characteristics are somewhat between the two extremes.

Figure 1.7 illustrates the geometric character of specular, near-specular, near-diffuse, and diffuse reflectors. The category that characterizes any given surface is dictated by the surface's roughness *in comparison to the wavelength of the energy incident upon it*. For example, in the relatively long wavelength radio range, rocky terrain can appear smooth to incident energy. In comparison, in the visible portion of the spectrum, even a material such as fine sand appears rough. In short, when the wavelength of incident energy is much smaller than the surface height variations or the particle sizes that make up a surface, the surface is diffuse.

Diffuse reflections contain spectral information on the "color" of the reflecting surface, whereas specular reflections do not. *Hence, in remote sensing, we are most often interested in measuring the diffuse reflectance properties of terrain features.*

The reflectance characteristics of earth surface features may be quantified by measuring the portion of incident energy that is reflected. This is measured as a function of wavelength and *is called spectral reflectance*, ρ_λ. It is mathematically defined as

$$\rho_\lambda = \frac{E_R(\lambda)}{E_I(\lambda)} = \frac{\text{energy of wavelength } \lambda \text{ reflected from the object}}{\text{energy of wavelength } \lambda \text{ incident upon the object}} \times 100$$

where ρ_λ is expressed as a percentage.

A graph of the spectral reflectance of an object as a function of wavelength is termed a *spectral reflectance curve*. The configuration of spectral reflectance curves gives us insight into the spectral characteristics of an object and has a strong influence on the choice of wavelength region(s) in which remote sensing data are acquired for a particular application. This is illustrated in Figure 1.8, which shows highly generalized spectral reflectance curves for deciduous and coniferous trees. (In this discussion, we use the terms deciduous and coniferous somewhat loosely, referring to broad-leaved

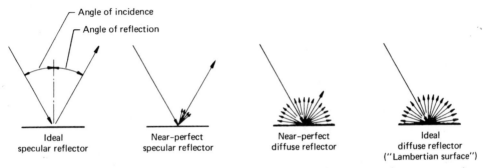

FIGURE I.7   Specular versus diffuse reflectance. (We are most often interested in measuring the diffuse reflectance of objects.)

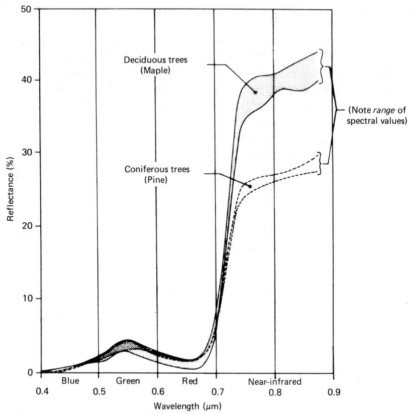

FIGURE 1.8 Generalized spectral reflectance envelopes for deciduous (broad-leaved) and coniferous (needle-bearing) trees. (Each tree type has a range of spectral reflectance values at any wavelength.) (Adapted from [17].)

trees such as oak and maple as deciduous, and needle-bearing trees such as pine and spruce as coniferous.) Note that the curve for each of these object types is plotted as a "ribbon" (or "envelope") of values, not as a single line. This is because spectral reflectances vary somewhat within a given material class. That is, the spectral reflectance of one deciduous tree species and another will never be identical. Nor will the spectral reflectance of trees of the same species be exactly equal. We elaborate upon the variability of spectral reflectance curves later in this section.

In Figure 1.8, assume that you are given the task of selecting an airborne sensor system to assist in preparing a map of a forested area differentiating deciduous versus coniferous trees. One choice of sensor might be the human eye. However, there is a potential problem with this choice. The spectral reflectance curves for each tree type overlap in most of the visible portion of the spectrum and are very close where they do not overlap. Hence, the eye might see both tree types as being essentially the same shade of "green" and might confuse the identity of the deciduous and coniferous trees.

Certainly one could improve things somewhat by using spatial clues to each tree type's identity, such as size, shape, site, and so forth. However, this is often difficult to do from the air, particularly when tree types are intermixed. How might we discriminate the two types on the basis of their spectral characteristics alone? We could do this by using a sensor system that records near-infrared energy. A camera loaded with black and white infrared film is just such a system. On black and white infrared photographs, deciduous trees (having higher infrared reflectance than conifers) generally appear much lighter in tone than do conifers. This is illustrated in Figure 1.9, which shows stands of coniferous trees surrounded by deciduous trees. In Figure 1.9*a* (visible spectrum) it is virtually impossible to distinguish between tree types, even though the conifers have a distinctive conical shape whereas the deciduous trees have rounded crowns. In Figure 1.9*b* (near-infrared), the coniferous trees have a distinctly darker tone. On such an image, the task of delineating deciduous versus coniferous trees becomes almost trivial. In fact, if we could somehow electronically scan this type of image and feed the results to a computer in terms of image tone, we might "automate" our entire mapping task. Many remote sensing data analysis schemes attempt to do just that. For these schemes to be successful, the materials to be differentiated must be spectrally separable.

Experience has shown that many earth surface features of interest can be identified, mapped, and studied on the basis of their spectral characteristics. Experience has also shown that some features of interest cannot be spectrally separated. Thus, to utilize remote sensing data effectively, one must know and understand the spectral characteristics of the particular features under investigation in any given application. Likewise, one must know what factors influence these characteristics.

Spectral Reflectance of Vegetation, Soil and Water

Figure 1.10 shows typical spectral reflectance curves for three basic types of earth features: healthy green vegetation, dry bare soil (gray-brown loam), and clear lake water. The lines in this figure represent *average* reflectance curves compiled by measuring a large sample of features. Note how distinctive the curves are for each feature. In general, the configuration of these curves is an indicator of the type and condition of the features to which they apply. Although the reflectance of individual features will vary considerably above and below the average, these curves demonstrate some fundamental points concerning spectral reflectance.

For example, spectral reflectance curves for healthy green vegetation almost always manifest the "peak-and-valley" configuration illustrated in Figure 1.10. The valleys in the visible portion of the spectrum are dictated by the pigments in plant leaves. Chlorophyll, for example, strongly absorbs energy in the wavelength bands centered at about 0.45 and 0.67 μm. Hence, our eyes perceive healthy vegetation as green in color because of the very high absorption of blue and red energy by plant leaves and the very high reflection of green energy. If a plant is subject to some form of stress that interrupts its normal growth and productivity, it may decrease or cease chlorophyll production. The result is less chlorophyll absorption in the blue and red bands. Often the red reflectance increases to the point that we see the plant turn yellow (combination of green and red).

FIGURE 1.9   Low altitude oblique aerial photographs illustrating deciduous versus coniferous trees, June 29, 1970. *(a)* Panchromatic photograph recording reflected sunlight over the wavelength band 0.4 to 0.7 μm. *(b)* Black and white infrared photograph recording reflected sunlight over the wavelength band 0.7 to 0.9 μm.

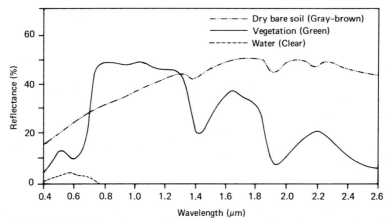

FIGURE 1.10 Typical spectral reflectance curves for vegetation, soil, and water. (Adapted from [27].)

As we go from the visible to the near-infrared portion of the spectrum at about 0.7 μm, the reflectance of healthy vegetation increases dramatically. In the range from about 0.7 to 1.3 μm, a plant leaf typically reflects 40 to 50 percent of the energy incident upon it. Most of the remaining energy is transmitted, since absorption in this spectral region in minimal (less than 5 percent). Plant reflectance in the range 0.7 to 1.3 μm results primarily from the internal structure of plant leaves. Because this structure is highly variable between plant species, reflectance measurements in this range often permit us to discriminate between species, even if they look the same in visible wavelengths. Likewise, many plant stresses alter the reflectance in this region and sensors operating in this range are often used for vegetation stress detection. Also, multiple layers of leaves in a plant canopy provide the opportunity for multiple transmittance and reflectance. Hence, the near-infrared reflectance increases with the number of layers of leaves in a canopy, with the reflection maximum achieved at about eight leaf layers [6].

Beyond 1.3 μm, energy incident upon vegetation is essentially absorbed or re-flected, with little to no transmittance of energy. Dips in reflectance occur at 1.4, 1.9, and 2.7 μm because water in the leaf absorbs strongly at these wavelengths. Accord-ingly, wavelengths in these spectral regions are referred to as *water absorption bands*. Reflectance peaks occur at about 1.6 and 2.2 μm, between the absorption bands. Throughout the range beyond 1.3 μm, leaf reflectance is approximately inversely related to the total water present in a leaf. This total is a function of both the moisture content and the thickness of a leaf.

The soil curve in Figure 1.10 shows considerably less peak-and-valley variation in reflectance. That is, the factors that influence soil reflectance act over less specific spectral bands. Some of the factors affecting soil reflectance are moisture content, soil texture (proportion of sand, silt, and clay), surface roughness, presence of iron oxide, and organic matter content. These factors are complex, variable, and interrelated. For example, the presence of moisture in soil will decrease its reflectance. As with vegetation, this effect is greatest in the water absorption bands at about 1.4, 1.9, and 2.7 μm (clay soils also have hydroxyl absorption bands at about 1.4 and 2.2 μm). Soil moisture content is strongly related to the soil texture: coarse, sandy soils are usually well drained, resulting in low moisture content and relatively high reflectance; poorly drained fine textured soils will generally have lower reflectance. In the absence of water, however, the soil itself will exhibit the reverse tendency: coarse textured soils will appear darker than fine textured soils. Thus, the reflectance properties of a soil are consistent only within particular ranges of conditions. Two other factors that reduce soil reflectance are surface roughness and content of organic matter. The presence of iron oxide in a soil will also significantly decrease reflectance, at least in the visible wavelengths. In any case, it is essential that the analyst be familiar with the conditions at hand.

Considering the spectral reflectance of water, probably the most distinctive characteristic is the energy absorption at near-infrared wavelengths. In short, water absorbs energy in these wavelengths whether we are talking about water features per se (such as lakes and streams) or water contained in vegetation or soil. Locating and delineating water bodies with remote sensing data are done most easily in near-infrared wavelengths because of this absorption property. However, various conditions of water bodies manifest themselves primarily in visible wavelengths. The energy/matter interactions at these wavelengths are very complex and depend on a number of interrelated factors. For example, the reflectance from a water body can stem from an interaction with the water's surface (specular reflection), with material suspended in the water, or with the bottom of the water body. Even with deep water where bottom effects are negligible, the reflectance properties of a water body are not only a function of the water per se but also the material in the water.

Clear water absorbs relatively little energy having wavelengths less than about 0.6 μm. High transmittance typifies these wavelengths with a maximum in the blue-green portion of the spectrum. However, as the turbidity of water changes (because of the presence of organic or inorganic materials) transmittance—and therefore reflectance—changes dramatically. For example, waters containing large quantities of suspended sediments resulting from soil erosion normally have much higher visible reflectance than other "clear" waters in the same geographic area. Likewise, the reflectance of water changes with the chlorophyll concentration involved. Increases in chlorophyll concentration tend to decrease water reflectance in blue wavelengths and increase it in green wavelengths. These changes have been used to monitor the presence and estimate the concentration of algae via remote sensing data. Reflectance data have also been used to determine the presence or absence of tannin dyes from bog vegetation in lowland areas, and to detect a number of pollutants, such as oil and certain industrial wastes.

Many important water characteristics, such as dissolved oxygen concentration, pH, and salt concentration, cannot be observed directly through changes in water reflectance. However, such parameters sometimes correlate with observed reflectance. In short, there are many complex interrelationships between the spectral reflectance of water and particular characteristics. One must use appropriate reference data to correctly interpret reflectance measurements made over water.

Our discussion of the spectral characteristics of vegetation, soil and water has been very general. The student interested in pursuing details on this subject, as well as factors influencing these characteristics, is encouraged to consult the references [6,27] from which our discussion has been adapted.

Spectral Response Patterns

Having looked at the spectral reflectance characteristics of vegetation, soil, and water, we should recognize that these broad feature types are normally spectrally separable. However, the degree of separation between types is a function of "where we look" spectrally. For example, water and vegetation might reflect nearly equally in visible wavelengths, yet these features are almost always separable in near-infrared wavelengths.

Because spectral responses measured by remote sensors over various features often permit an assessment of the type and/or condition of the features, these responses have often been referred to as *spectral signatures*. Spectral reflectance and spectral emittance curves (for wavelengths greater than 3.0 μm) are often referred to in this manner. The physical radiation measurements acquired over specific terrain features at various wavelengths are also referred to as the spectral signatures for those features.

Although it is true that many earth surface features manifest very distinctive spectral reflectance and/or emittance characteristics, these characteristics result in spectral "response patterns" rather than in spectral "signatures." The reason for this is that the term *signature* tends to imply a pattern that is absolute and unique. This is not the case with the spectral patterns observed in the natural world. As we have seen, spectral response patterns measured by remote sensors may be quantitative but they are not absolute. They may be distinctive but they are not necessarily unique.

Although the term *spectral signature* is used frequently in remote sensing literature, the student should keep in mind the variability of spectral signatures. This variability might cause severe problems in remote sensing data analysis if the objective is to identify various earth feature types spectrally. However, if the objective of an analysis is to identify the condition of various objects of the same type, we may have to rely on spectral response pattern variability to derive this information. This pertains to such applications as identifying stressed versus healthy vegetation within a given species. Therefore, it is extremely important to understand the nature of the ground area one is "looking at" with remote sensor data, not only to minimize unwanted spectral variability, but also to maximize this variability when the particular application requires it.

We have already looked at some characteristics of objects per se that influence their spectral response patterns. *Temporal effects* and *spatial effects* can also enter into any given analysis. Temporal effects are any factors that change the spectral characteristics of a feature over time. For example, the spectral characteristics of many species of vegetation are in a nearly continual state of change throughout a growing season. These changes often influence when we might collect sensor data for a particular application.

Spatial effects refer to factors that cause the same types of features (for example, corn plants) at a given point in *time* to have different characteristics at different geographic *locations*. In small area analysis the geographic locations may be meters apart and spatial effects may be negligible. When analyzing satellite data, the locations may be hundreds of kilometers apart where entirely different soils, climates, and cultivation practices might exist.

Temporal and spatial effects influence virtually all remote sensing operations. These effects normally complicate the issue of analyzing spectral reflectance properties of earth resources. Again, however, temporal and spatial effects might be the keys to gleaning the information sought in an analysis. For example, the process of *change detection* is premised on the ability to measure temporal effects. An example of this process is detecting the change in suburban development near a metropolitan area by using data obtained on two different dates.

An example of a useful spatial effect is the change in the leaf morphology of trees when they are subjected to some form of stress. For example, when a tree becomes infected with Dutch elm disease, its leaves might begin to cup and curl, changing the reflectance of the tree relative to healthy trees that surround it. So, even though a spatial effect might cause differences in the spectral reflectances of the same type of feature, this effect may be just what is important in a particular application.

In addition to being influenced by temporal and spatial effects, spectral response patterns are influenced by the atmosphere. Regrettably, the energy recorded by a sensor is always modified to some extent by the atmosphere between the sensor and the ground. We will indicate the significance of this effect on a sensor-by-sensor basis throughout this book. For now, the student should simply realize that the atmosphere is another influence that tends to make spectral response patterns measured by sensors relative rather than absolute.

1.5   DATA ACQUISITION AND INTERPRETATION

Up to this point, we have discussed the principal sources of electromagnetic energy, the propagation of this energy through the atmosphere, and the interaction of this energy with earth surface features. Combined, these factors result in energy "signals" from which we wish to extract information. We now consider the procedures by which these signals are detected, recorded, and interpreted.

The *detection* of electromagnetic energy can be performed either photographically or electronically. The process of photography uses chemical reactions on the surface of a light sensitive film to detect energy variations within a scene. Photographic systems offer many advantages: they are relatively simple and inexpensive and provide a high degree of spatial detail and geometric integrity.

Electronic sensors generate an electrical signal that corresponds to the energy variations in the original scene. A familiar example of an electronic sensor is a video camera. Although considerably more complex and expensive than photographic systems, electronic sensors offer the advantages of a broader spectral range of sensitivity, improved calibration potential, and the ability to electronically transmit data.

By developing a photograph, we obtain a *record* of its detected signals. Thus, the film acts as both the detecting and the recording medium. Electronic sensor signals are generally recorded onto magnetic tape. Subsequently, the signals may be converted to an image form by photographing a TV-like screen display of the data, or by using a specialized film recorder. In these cases, photographic film is used only as a recording medium.

In remote sensing, the term *photograph* is reserved exclusively for images that were *detected* as well as recorded on film. The more generic term *image* is used for any pictorial representation of image data. Thus, a pictorial record from a thermal scanner (an electronic sensor) would be called a "thermal image," *not* a "thermal photograph," because film would not be the original detection mechanism for the image. Because the term *image* relates to any pictorial product, all photographs are images. Not all images, however, are photographs.

We can see that the data interpretation aspects of remote sensing can involve analysis of pictorial (image) and/or digital data. *Visual interpretation* of pictorial image data has long been the workhorse of remote sensing. Visual techniques make use of the excellent ability of the human mind to qualitatively evaluate spatial patterns in a scene. The ability to make subjective judgments based on selective scene elements is essential in many interpretation efforts.

Visual interpretation techniques have certain disadvantages, however, in that they may require extensive training and are labor intensive. In addition, *spectral characteristics* are not always fully evaluated in visual interpretation efforts. This is partly because of the limited ability of the eye to discern tonal values on an image and the difficulty for an interpreter to simultaneously analyze numerous spectral images. In applications where spectral patterns are highly informative, it is therefore preferable to analyze *digital*, rather than pictorial, image data.

The basic character of digital image data is illustrated in Figure 1.11. Though the image shown in (*a*) appears to be a continuous tone photograph, it is actually composed of a two-dimensional array of discrete *picture elements* or *pixels*. The intensity of each pixel corresponds to the average "brightness" or *radiance* measured electronically over the ground area corresponding to each pixel. A total of 320 rows and 480 columns of pixels are shown in Figure 1.11*a*. Whereas the individual pixels are virtually impossible to discern in (*a*), they are readily observable in the enlargements shown in (*b*) and (*c*). These enlargements correspond to subareas located in the vicinity of the "×" in (*a*). A 19 row × 27 column enlargement is shown in (*b*) and a 10 row × 15 column enlargement is included in (*c*). Part (*d*) shows the individual *digital number* (DN) corresponding to the average radiance measured in each pixel shown in (*c*). These values are simply positive integers that result from quantizing the original electrical signal from the sensor into positive integer values using a process called *analog-to-digital* (A-to-D) signal conversion (Section 7.12).

Typically, the DN's constituting a digital image are recorded over such numerical ranges as 0 to 63, 0 to 127, 0 to 255, 0 to 511, or 0 to 1023. These ranges represent the set of integers that can be recorded using 6-, 7-, 8-, 9-, and 10-bit binary computer coding scales, respectively. (That is, $2^6 = 64$, $2^7 = 128$, $2^8 = 256$, $2^9 = 512$, and $2^{10} = 1024$.) In such numerical formats, the image data can be readily analyzed with the aid of a computer.

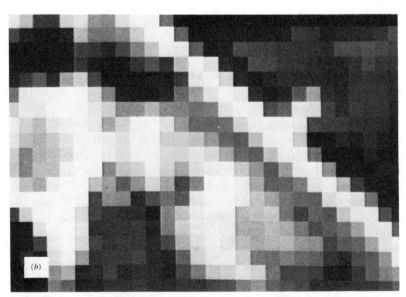

FIGURE 1.11 Basic character of digital image data. (a) Original 320 row × 480 column digital image. (b) Enlargement showing 19 row × 27 column area of pixels in vicinity of "x" in (a). (c) 10 row × 15 column enlargement. (d) Digital numbers corresponding to the radiance of each pixel shown in (c).

54	40	31	27	27	28	39	51	52	50	45	25	24	24	23
55	37	37	35	31	27	26	35	58	66	38	13	17	21	19
56	40	39	45	39	32	27	26	36	52	50	28	14	13	14
52	39	33	42	49	48	36	31	26	33	51	51	31	16	16
42	34	24	30	60	67	49	33	27	28	31	47	51	35	24
26	29	26	44	76	76	49	37	33	30	29	29	44	52	44
14	31	36	50	85	70	36	37	38	30	25	29	28	40	52
20	31	39	51	72	56	35	35	37	35	31	27	29	31	36
21	26	36	46	58	49	37	35	36	37	34	33	26	29	30
21	20	29	43	54	53	40	31	30	32	30	29	24	22	27

(d)

FIGURE 1.11 (continued)

The use of computer assisted analysis techniques permits the spectral patterns in remote sensing data to be more fully examined. It also permits the data analysis process to be largely automated, providing cost advantages over visual interpretation techniques. However, just as humans are somewhat limited in their ability to interpret spectral patterns, computers are somewhat limited in their ability to evaluate spatial patterns. Therefore, visual and numerical techniques are complementary in nature, and consideration must be given to which approach (or combination of approaches) best fits a particular application.

1.6   REFERENCE DATA

As we have indicated in the previous discussion, rarely—if ever—is remote sensing employed without the use of some form of *reference data*. The acquisition of reference data involves collecting measurements or observations about the objects, areas, or phenomena that are being sensed remotely. These data can take on any of a number of different forms and may be derived from a number of sources. For example, the data needed for a particular analysis might be derived from a soil survey map, a water quality laboratory report, or an aerial photograph. They may also stem from a "field check" on the identity, extent, and condition of agricultural crops, land uses, tree species, or water pollution problems. Reference data may also involve field measurements of temperature and other physical and/or chemical properties of various features.

Reference data are often referred to by the term *ground truth*. This term is not meant literally, since many forms of reference data are not collected on the ground and can only approximate the truth of actual ground conditions. For example, "ground" truth may be collected in the air, in the form of detailed aerial photographs used as reference data when analyzing less detailed high altitude or satellite imagery. Similarly, the "ground" truth will actually be "water" truth if we are studying water features. In spite of these inaccuracies, ground truth is a widely used term for reference data.

Reference data might be used to serve any or all of the following purposes:

1. To aid in the analysis and interpretation of remotely sensed data.
2. To calibrate a sensor.
3. To verify information extracted from remote sensing data.

Hence, reference data must often be collected in accordance with the principles of statistical sampling design.

Reference data can be very expensive and time consuming to collect properly. They can consist of either *time-critical* and/or *time-stable* measurements. Time-critical measurements are those made in cases where ground conditions change rapidly with time, such as in the analysis of vegetation condition or water pollution events. Time-stable measurements are involved when the materials under observation do not change appreciably with time. For example, geologic applications often entail field observations that can be conducted at any time and that would not change appreciably from mission to mission.

One form of reference data collection is the ground-based measurement of the reflectance and/or emittance of surface materials to determine their spectral response patterns. This might be done in the laboratory or in the field, using the principles of *spectroscopy*. Spectroscopic measurement procedures can involve the use of a variety of instruments. Often, a *spectroradiometer* is used in such measurement procedures. This device measures, as a function of wavelength, the energy coming from an object within its view. It is used primarily to prepare spectral reflectance curves for various objects.

In laboratory spectroscopy, artificial sources of energy might be used to illuminate objects under study. In the lab, other field parameters such as viewing geometry between object and sensor are also simulated. More often, therefore, *in situ* field measurements are preferred because of the many variables of the natural environment that influence remote sensor data that are difficult, if not impossible, to duplicate in the laboratory.

In the acquisition of field measurements, spectroradiometers may be operated in a number of modes, ranging from hand-held to helicopter or aircraft mounted. Figure 1.12 illustrates a highly portable instrument that is well suited to hand-held operation. This particular system acquires a continuous spectrum by recording data in 256 bands simultaneously. The spectral output goes to a microprocessor-based controller that records data on a built-in tape deck, and also displays and communicates the data in a standard computer-compatible format.

Figure 1.13 shows a multiband *radiometer* that measures radiation in a series of discrete spectral bands, rather than over a continuous range. This particular device operates in eight spectral bands, seven of which match those used by the Thematic Mapper sensor onboard the Landsat satellites (Section 9.8). The instrument is shown here suspended from a truck-mounted telescoping boom. Mounted in this manner, the radiometer can be driven to multiple field locations where spectral response measurements can be made quite conveniently. All data are again stored using a microprocessor-based data logger (located in the cab of the truck).

Using a radiometer to obtain spectral reflectance measurements is normally a three-step process. First, the instrument is aimed at a *calibration panel* of known, stable reflectance. (This step is illustrated in Figure 1.13.) The purpose of this step is to quantify the incoming radiation or *irradiance* incident upon the measurement site. Next, the instrument is suspended over the target of interest and the radiation reflected by the object is measured. Finally, the spectral reflectance of the object is computed by ratioing the reflected energy measurement in each band of observation to the incoming radiation measured in each band. Normally, the term *reflectance factor* is used to refer to the result of such computations. A reflectance factor is defined formally as the ratio of the radiant flux actually reflected by a sample surface to that which would be reflected into the same sensor geometry by an ideal, perfectly diffuse (Lambertian) surface irradiated in exactly the same way as the sample.

Another term frequently used to describe the above type of measurement is *bidirectional reflectance factor*: one direction being associated with the sample view-

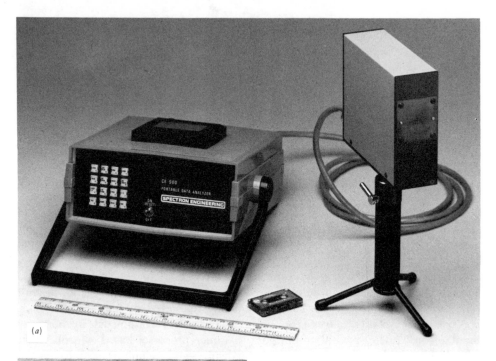

(a)

(b)

FIGURE 1.12 Spectron Engineering SE590 portable radiometer. (a) Microprocessor data logger, tape cassette, and detector head. (b) Unit shown in field operation. (Courtesy Spectron Engineering.)

FIGURE 1.13 Barnes Model 12-1000 Modular Multiband Radiometer. Unit shown viewing calibration panel to quantify incoming radiation. Telescoping boom is subsequently rotated and extended over target to measure reflected radiation.

ing angle (usually 0° from normal) and the other direction being that of the sun's illumination (defined by the solar zenith and azimuth angles). In the bidirectional reflectance measurement procedure described above, the sample and the reflectance standard are measured sequentially. Other approaches exist in which the incident spectral irradiance and reflected spectral radiance are measured simultaneously. Information on these techniques and other aspects of field spectroscopy may be found in references cited in the Selected Bibliography at the end of this chapter [6, 7, 10, 15, 16].

1.7 AN IDEAL REMOTE SENSING SYSTEM

Having introduced some basic concepts, we now have the elements necessary to conceptualize an ideal remote sensing system. In so doing, we can begin to appreciate some of the problems encountered in the design and application of the various real sensing systems examined in subsequent chapters.

The basic components of an *ideal* remote sensing system are shown in Figure 1.14. These include the following:

1. *A uniform energy source.*   This source would provide energy over all wavelengths, at a constant, known, high level of output, irrespective of time and place.

2. *A noninterfering atmosphere.*   This would be an atmosphere that would not modify the energy from the source in any manner, whether that energy were on its way to the earth's surface or coming from it. Again, ideally, this would hold irrespective of wavelength, time, place, and sensing altitude involved.

3. *A series of unique energy/matter interactions at the earth's surface.*   These interactions would generate reflected and/or emitted signals that not only are selective with respect to wavelength, but also are known, invariant, and unique to each and every earth surface feature type and subtype of interest.

4. *A super sensor.*   This would be a sensor, highly sensitive to all wavelengths, yielding spatially detailed data on the absolute brightness (or radiance) from a scene as a function of wavelength, throughout the spectrum. This super sensor would be simple and reliable, require virtually no power or space, and be accurate and economical to operate.

5. *A real-time data handling system.*   In this system, the instant the radiance versus wavelength response over a terrain element were generated, it would be processed into an interpretable format and recognized as being unique to the particular terrain element from which it came. This processing would be performed nearly instantaneously ("real time"), providing timely information. Because of the

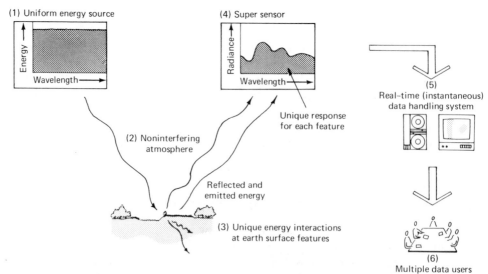

FIGURE I.14   Components of an ideal remote sensing system.

consistent nature of the energy/matter interactions, there would be no need for reference data in the analysis procedure. The derived data would provide insight into the physical—chemical—biological state of each feature of interest.

6. *Multiple data users.* These people would have knowledge of great depth, both of their respective disciplines and of remote sensing data acquisition and analysis techniques. The same set of "data" would become various forms of "information" for different users, because of their wealth of knowledge about the particular earth resources being sensed. This information would be available to them faster, at less expense, and over larger areas than information collected in any other manner. With this information, the various users would make profound, wise decisions about how best to manage the earth resources under scrutiny and these management decisions would be implemented—to everyone's delight!

Unfortunately, an ideal remote sensing system as described above does not exist. Real remote sensing systems fall far short of the ideal at virtually every point in the sequence outlined.

1.8 CHARACTERISTICS OF REAL REMOTE SENSING SYSTEMS

Let us consider some of the basic shortcomings common to all real remote sensing systems in order to better understand their general operation and utility. Regarding the elements of the ideal system we have developed, the following general shortcomings of real systems should be recognized:

1. *The energy source.* All passive remote sensing systems rely on energy that is either reflected and/or emitted from earth surface features. As already discussed, the spectral distribution of reflected sunlight and self-emitted energy is far from uniform. Solar energy levels obviously vary with respect to time and location, and different earth surface materials emit energy to varying degrees of efficiency. While we have some control over the nature of sources of energy for active systems, the sources of energy used in all real systems are generally nonuniform with respect to wavelength and their properties vary with time and location. Consequently, we normally must calibrate for source characteristics on a mission-by-mission basis, or deal with *relative* energy units sensed at any given time and location.

2. *The atmosphere.* The atmosphere normally compounds the problems introduced by energy source variation. To some extent, the atmosphere always modifies the strength and spectral distribution of the energy received by a sensor. It restricts "where we can look" spectrally and its effects vary with wavelength, time, and place. The importance of these effects, like source variation effects, is a function of the wavelengths involved, the sensor used, and the sensing application at hand. Elimination of, or compensation for, atmospheric effects via some form of calibration is particularly important in those applications where repetitive observations of the same geographic area are involved.

3. *The energy/matter interactions at the earth's surface.* Remote sensing would be simple if every material reflected and/or emitted energy in a unique, known way. Although spectral response patterns (signatures) play a central role in detecting, identifying, and analyzing earth surface materials, the spectral world is full of ambiguity. Radically different material types can have great spectral similarity, making differentiation difficult. Furthermore, the general understanding of the energy/matter interactions for earth surface features is at an elementary level for some materials and virtually nonexistent for others.

4. *The sensor.* At this point, it should come as no surprise that an ideal "super sensor" does not exist. No single sensor is sensitive to all wavelengths. All real sensors have fixed limits of *spectral sensitivity*. They also have a limit on how small an object on the earth's surface can be and still be "seen" by a sensor as being separate from its surroundings. This limit, called the *spatial resolution* of a sensor, is an indication of how well a sensor can record spatial detail.

   The choice of a sensor for any given task always involves trade-offs. For example, photographic systems generally have very good spatial resolution characteristics, but they lack the broad spectral sensitivity obtainable with nonphotographic systems having poorer spatial resolution characteristics. Similarly, many nonphotographic systems (and some photographic systems) are quite complex optically, mechanically, and/or electronically. They may have restrictive power, space, and stability requirements. These requirements often dictate the type of *platform*, or vehicle, from which a sensor can be operated. Platforms can vary from stepladders to space stations. Depending on the sensor/platform combination needed in a particular application, the acquisition of remote sensing data can be a very expensive endeavor.

5. *The data handling system.* The capability of current remote sensors to generate data far exceeds the current capacity to handle these data. This is generally true whether we consider "manual" image interpretation procedures or computer assisted analyses. Processing sensor data into an interpretable format can be—and often is—an effort entailing considerable thought, instrumentation, time, experience, and reference data.

   While much data handling can be done by machines (computers and other electronic or mechanical devices), human intervention in data processing is and will continue to be essential to the productive application of remote sensor data.

6. *The multiple data users.* Central to the successful application of any remote sensing system is the person (or persons) using the remote sensor data from that system. The "data" generated by remote sensing procedures become "information" only if and when someone understands their generation, knows how to interpret them, and knows how best to use them. A thorough understanding of the problem at hand is paramount to the productive application of any remote sensing methodology. Also, no single combination of data acquisition and analysis procedures will satisfy the needs of all data users.

   Whereas the interpretation of aerial photography has been used as a practical resource management tool for nearly a century, other forms of remote sensing are relatively new, technical, and "unconventional" means of acquiring information. These more recently developed forms of remote sensing have had relatively few satisfied users until recently. However, as new applications continue to be developed and implemented, increasing numbers of users are becoming aware of the potentials, *as well as the limitations*, of remote sensing techniques. As a result, remote sensing has become an essential tool in many operational programs involving resource management, engineering, and exploration.

I.9   THE STATUS OF REMOTE SENSING

The student should now begin to appreciate that successful application of remote sensing is premised on the *integration* of multiple, interrelated data sources and analysis procedures. No single combination of sensor and interpretation procedure is appropriate to all resource inventorying and environmental monitoring applications. In fact, *many inventorying and monitoring problems are not amenable to solution by means of remote sensing at all*. Among the applications appropriate, a wide variety of data acquisition and analysis approaches exist. Conceptually, however, all designs of successful remote sensing efforts involve, at a minimum, (1) clear definition of the problem at hand, (2) evaluation of the potential for addressing the problem with remote sensing techniques, (3) identification of the remote sensing data acquisition procedures appropriate to the task, (4) determination of the data interpretation procedures to be employed and the reference data needed, and (5) identification of the criteria by which the quality of information collected can be judged.

All too often, one (or more) of the above components of a remote sensing application is overlooked. The result may be disastrous. Many resource management programs exist with little or no means of evaluating the performance of remote sensing systems in terms of information quality. Many people have acquired burgeoning quantities of remote sensing data with inadequate capability to interpret them. Many occasions have occurred when remote sensing has *or* has not been used because the problem was not clearly defined. A clear articulation of the information requirements of a particular problem and the extent to which remote sensing might meet these requirements is paramount to any successful application.

The success of many applications of remote sensing is improved considerably by taking a *multiple view* approach to data collection. This may involve *multistage* sensing wherein data about a site are collected from multiple altitudes. It may involve *multispectral* sensing whereby data are acquired simultaneously in several spectral bands. Or, it may entail *multitemporal* sensing, where data about a site are collected on more than one occasion.

In the multistage approach, satellite data may be analyzed in conjunction with high altitude data, low altitude data, and ground observations (Figure 1.15). Each successive data source might provide more detailed information over smaller geographic areas. Information extracted at any lower level of observation may then be extrapolated to higher levels of observation.

A commonplace example of the application of multistage sensing techniques is the

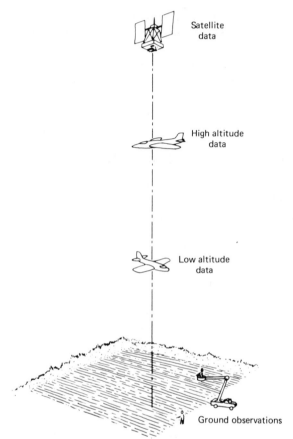

FIGURE 1.15   Multistage remote sensing concept.

detection, identification, and analysis of forest disease and insect problems. From space images, the image analyst could obtain an overall view of the major vegetation categories involved in a study area. Using this information, the areal extent and position of a particular species of interest could be determined and representative subareas could be studied more closely at a more refined stage of imaging. Areas exhibiting stress on the second-stage imagery could be delineated. Representative samples of these areas could then be field-checked to document the presence and particular cause of the stress.

After analyzing the problem in detail by ground observation, the analyst would use the remote sensor data to extrapolate his or her assessments beyond the small study areas. By analyzing the large area remote sensor data, the analyst can determine the severity and geographic extent of the disease problem. Thus, while the question on specifically *what* the problem is can generally be evaluated only by detailed ground observation, the equally important questions of *where, how much,* and *how severe* can often be best handled by remote sensing analysis.

In short, more information is obtained by analyzing multiple views of the terrain than by analysis of any single view. In a similar vein, multispectral imagery provides more information than data collected in any single spectral band. The multispectral scanner is a sensor that acquires data from multiple spectral bands simultaneously. When the signals recorded in the multiple bands are analyzed in conjunction with each other, more information becomes available than if only a single band were used or if the multiple bands were analyzed independently. The multispectral approach forms the heart of numerous remote sensing applications involving discrimination of earth resource types and conditions.

Again, multitemporal sensing involves sensing the same area at multiple times and using changes occurring with time as discriminants of ground conditions. This approach is frequently taken to monitor land use change, such as suburban development in urban fringe areas. In fact, regional land use surveys might call for the acquisition of multisensor, multispectral, multistage, multitemporal data to be used for multiple purposes!

In any approach to applying remote sensing, not only must the right mix of data acquisition and data interpretation techniques be chosen, but the right mix of remote sensing and "conventional" techniques must also be identified. The student must recognize that remote sensing is a tool best applied in concert with others; it is not an end in itself. In this regard, remote sensing data are currently being used extensively in computer-based geographic information systems (GISs). As we later describe (Sections 3.15 and 10.15) these systems permit the synthesis and display of virtually unlimited sources and types of physical and socioeconomic data—as long as they can be computer coded with reference to a common geographic base. Remote sensing data are but one of many forms of data typically incorporated in such systems.

Remote sensing affords us the capability to literally see the invisible. From remote sensing's aerial or space vantage point we can obtain a synoptic (even global) view of earth resources. We can begin to see components of the environment on an "ecosystem basis," in that remote sensing data can transcend the cultural boundaries within which much of our current resource data are collected. Remote sensing also transcends disciplinary boundaries. It is so broad in its application that nobody "owns" the field. Important contributions are made to—and benefits derived from—remote sensing by both the "hard" scientist interested in basic research and the "soft" scientist interested in its operational application.

There is little question that remote sensing will continue to play an increasingly broad and important role in natural resource management. The technical capabilities of sensors, space platforms, data communication systems, and digital image processing systems are improving on almost a daily basis. At the same time, we are witnessing an evolution of various remote sensing procedures from being purely research activities to becoming commercially available services. Most importantly, we are becoming increasingly aware of how interrelated and fragile the elements of our global resource base really are and of the role remote sensing can play in inventorying and monitoring these resources.

1.10   ORGANIZATION OF THIS BOOK

Because of the breadth of the discussion of remote sensing systems and analysis techniques presented in this book, it is important for the student to have a mental road map of the relationships among the various chapters. Chapters 2 to 6 deal with photographic remote sensing. Chapter 2 describes the basic tools used in acquiring aerial photographs: films, filters, and aerial cameras. Chapter 3 presents the basics of visual interpretation of airphotos in a broad range of applications. Chapter 4 focuses on one application area of airphoto interpretation: the analysis of various bedrock and soil types in support of land use suitability investigations. Chapter 5 describes the photogrammetric procedures by which precise spatial measurements and maps are made from airphotos. Chapter 6 covers techniques by which the darkness, or optical density, at points on a photograph may be measured and used to study the reflectance properties of objects. (Depending upon your particular discipline and course setting, you may not need to study the detailed discussion in Chapters 4 to 6.)

Discussion of nonphotographic systems begins in Chapter 7, which describes the acquisition of airborne thermal and multispectral scanner data. Chapter 8 is concerned with the collection and analysis of radar data. In essence, the discussion in Chapters 2 through 8 progresses from the simplest sensing systems to the most complex. In a sense, there is also progression from short to long wavelengths along the electromagnetic spectrum (see Figure 1.3). That is, discussion centers on photography in the UV, visible, and near-IR regions, then thermal scanning in the "heat" region, multispectral scanning, which combines the two, and radar sensing in the microwave region.

In Chapter 9 we describe the principal satellite systems used to collect remote sensing data on a global basis. These include the Landsat and SPOT satellites as well as certain meteorological satellites. Chapter 10 treats the subject of digital image processing and describes the most commonly employed procedures through which computer assisted image interpretation is accomplished.

Throughout this book, the International System of Units (SI) is used. Tables are included in the back of the book to assist the student in converting between SI units and units of other measurement systems.

SELECTED BIBLIOGRAPHY

1. American Society of Photogrammetry, *Manual of Remote Sensing*, 2nd ed., Falls Church, Va., 1983.

2. American Society of Photogrammetry, *Multilingual Dictionary of Remote Sensing and Photogrammetry*, Falls Church, Va., 1984.

3. Avery, T.E., and G.L. Berlin, *Interpretation of Aerial Photographs*, 4th ed., Burgess, Minneapolis, Minn., 1985.

4. Barrett, E.C., and L.F. Curtis, *Introduction to Environmental Remote Sensing*, 2nd ed., Halsted Press, Wiley, New York, 1982.

5. Barzegar, F., "Earth Resources Remote Sensing Platforms," *Photogrammetric Engineering and Remote Sensing*, vol. 49, no. 12, December 1983, p. 1669.

6. Bauer, M.E., et al., "Field Spectroscopy of Agricultural Crops," *IEEE Transactions on Geoscience and Remote Sensing*, vol. GE-24, no. 1, January 1986, pp. 65–75.

7. Bowker, D.E., et al., *Spectral Reflectances of Natural Targets for Use in Remote Sensing Studies*, NASA Ref. Publ. 1139, National Technical Information Service, Springfield, Va., 1985.

8. Colwell, R.N., et al., "Basic Matter and Energy Relationships Involved in Remote Reconnaissance," *Photogrammetric Engineering*, vol. 29, no. 5, 1963, pp. 761–799.

9. Curran, P.J., *Principles of Remote Sensing*, Longman, London, 1985.

10. Duggin, M.J., and T. Cunia, "Ground Reflectance Measurement Techniques: A Comparison," *Applied Optics*, vol. 22, no. 23, December 1983, pp. 3771–3777.

11. Egan, W.G., *Photometry and Polarization in Remote Sensing*, Elsevier, New York, 1985.

12. Estes, J.E., and L.W. Senger (eds.), *Remote Sensing: Techniques for Environmental Analysis*, Hamilton, Santa Barbara, Calif., 1974.

13. Harper, D., *Eye in the Sky: Introduction to Remote Sensing*, 2nd ed., Multiscience, Montreal, 1983.

14. Holz, R.K., *The Surveillant Science: Remote Sensing of the Environment*, 2nd ed., Wiley, New York, 1985.

15. Jackson, R.D., and P.N. Slater, "Absolute Calibration of Field Reflectance Radiometers," *Photogrammetric Engineering and Remote Sensing*, vol. 52, no. 2, February 1986, pp. 189–196.

16. Jackson, R.D., et al., *Hand-Held Radiometry*, USDA/SEA Agricultural Reviews and Manuals, ARM-W-19, Oakland, Calif., 1980.

17. Kalensky, Z., and D.A. Wilson, "Spectral Signatures of Forest Trees," *Proceedings: Third Canadian Symposium on Remote Sensing*, 1975, pp. 155–171.

18. Kennie, T.J.M., and M.C. Matthews, *Remote Sensing in Civil Engineering*, Wiley, New York, 1985.

19. Lintz, J., and D.S. Simonett (eds.), *Remote Sensing of Environment*, Addison–Wesley, Reading, Mass., 1976.

20. Merideth, R.W., Jr., and A.B. Sacks, "Education in Environmental Remote Sensing: A Bibliography and Characterization of Doctoral Dissertations," *Photogrammetric Engineering and Remote Sensing*, vol. 52, no. 3, March 1986, pp. 349–365.

21. National Research Council Committee on Remote Sensing for Agricultural Purposes, *Remote Sensing; with Special Reference to Agriculture and Forestry*, National Academy of Science, Washington, D.C., 1970.

22. Sabins, F.F., Jr., *Remote Sensing: Principles and Interpretation*, 2nd ed., Freeman, New York, 1986.

23. Schanda, E., *Physical Fundamentals of Remote Sensing*, Springer-Verlag, New York, 1986.

24. Siegal, B.S., and A.R. Gillespie (eds.), *Remote Sensing in Geology*, Wiley, New York, 1980.

25. Slater, P.N., *Remote Sensing: Optics and Optical Systems*, Addison–Wesley, Reading, Mass., 1980.

26. Smith, W.L. (ed.), *Remote Sensing Applications for Mineral Exploration*, Dowden, Hutchinson & Ross, Stroudsburg, Pa., 1977.

27. Swain, P.H., and S.M. Davis (eds.), *Remote Sensing: The Quantitative Approach*, McGraw–Hill, New York, 1978.

ELEMENTS OF PHOTOGRAPHIC SYSTEMS

2.1 INTRODUCTION

One of the most common, versatile, and economical forms of remote sensing is aerial photography. The basic advantages aerial photography affords over on-the-ground observation include:

1. *Improved vantage point.* Aerial photography gives a bird's-eye view of large areas, enabling us to see earth surface features in their spatial context. In short, aerial photography permits us to look at the "big picture" in which objects of interest reside. It is often difficult, if not impossible, to obtain this view of the environment through on-the-ground observation. With aerial photography, we also see the "whole picture" in that *all* observable earth surface features are recorded simultaneously. Completely different information might be extracted by different people looking at a photograph. The hydrologist might concentrate on surface water bodies, the geologist on bedrock structure, the agriculturalist on soil or crop type, and so on.

2. *Capability to stop action.* Unlike the human eye, photographs can give us a "stop action" view of dynamic conditions. For example, aerial photographs are very useful in studying dynamic phenomena such as floods, moving wildlife populations, traffic, oil spills, and forest fires.

3. *Permanent recording.* Aerial photographs are virtually permanent records of existing conditions. As such, these records can be studied at leisure, under office rather than field conditions. A single image can be studied by a large number of users. Airphotos can also be conveniently compared against similar data acquired at previous times, so that changes over time can be monitored easily.

4. *Broadened spectral sensitivity.* Film can "see" and record over a wavelength range about twice as broad as that of the human eye (0.3 to 0.9 μm versus 0.4 to 0.7 μm). With photography, invisible UV and near-IR energy can be detected and subsequently recorded in the form of a visible image; hence we can see certain phenomena the eye cannot.

5. *Increased spatial resolution and geometric fidelity.* With the proper selection of camera, film, and flight parameters, we are able to record more spatial detail on a photograph than we can see with the unaided eye. This detail becomes available to us by viewing photographs under magnification. With proper ground reference data, we can also obtain accurate measurements of positions, distances, directions, areas, heights, volumes, and slopes from airphotos. In fact, most planimetric and topographic maps are currently produced using measurements extracted from airphotos.

This and the next four chapters detail and illustrate the above characteristics of aerial photography. In this chapter, we describe the various materials and methods used to *acquire* aerial photography. The topic of *interpreting* aerial photographs is treated in Chapters 3 and 4. In Chapter 5 we examine the aspects of *measuring* and *mapping* with airphotos. In Chapter 6 we deal with the process of *obtaining radio-metric measurements* from airphotos.

2.2 EARLY HISTORY OF AERIAL PHOTOGRAPHY

Photography was born in 1839 with the public disclosure of the pioneering photographic processes of Nicephore Niepce, William Henry Fox Talbot, and Louis Jacques Mande Daguerre. As early as 1840, Argo, Director of the Paris Observatory, advocated the use of photography for topographic surveying. The first known aerial photograph was taken in 1858 by a Parisian photographer named Gaspard Felix Tournachon. Known as "Nadar," he used a balloon to ascend to a height of 80 m to obtain the photograph over Bievre, France. Balloon photography flourished after that. The earliest *existing* aerial photograph was taken from a balloon over Boston in 1860, by James Wallace Black (Figure 2.1). This photograph was immortalized by Oliver Wendell Holmes who described it in the *Atlantic Monthly*, July 1863: "Boston, as the eagle and the wild goose see it, is a very different object from the same place as the solid citizen looks up at its eaves and chimneys" [27].

As an outgrowth of their use in obtaining meteorological data, kites were used to obtain aerial photography beginning in about 1882. The first aerial photograph taken from a kite is credited to an English meteorologist, E. D. Archibald. By 1890, A. Batut of Paris had published a textbook on the latest state of the art. In the early 1900s the kite photography of an American, G. R. Lawrence, brought him worldwide attention. On April 18, 1906, he photographed San Francisco in the aftermath of the great earthquake and fire (Figure 2.2). He hoisted his camera some 600 m to obtain the picture. The camera he used was gigantic, yielding 1.4×2.4 m negatives—it reportedly weighed more than the Wright brothers' airplane with its pilot!

The airplane, which had been invented in 1903, was not used as a camera platform until 1909 when a "biosphere" motion picture photographer accompanied Wilbur Wright and took the first aerial motion pictures (Figure 2.3). They were taken

FIGURE 2.1 Balloon view of Boston photographed by James Wallace Black, October 13, 1860. This was one of the first aerial photographs taken in the United States. It was taken from a captive balloon, Professor Sam King's "Queen of the Air," at an altitude of approximately 365 m. The photograph shows a portion of the Boston business district and the masts of square-rigged ships in the adjacent harbor. (Courtesy J. Robert Quick, Wright Patterson AFB.)

FIGURE 2.2 "San Francisco in Ruins," taken by George R. Lawrence, April 18, 1906. Lawrence's mammoth camera was suspended from a battery of 17 kites flown from 610 m above a ship in San Francisco Bay. (Courtesy J. Robert Quick, Wright Patterson AFB.)

FIGURE 2.3 Centocelli, Italy—the first aerial photograph taken from an airplane, April 24, 1909. Photograph was shot through wing struts of airplane and is an oblique view of walls of Centocelli. (Courtesy J. Robert Quick, Wright Patterson AFB.)

over Centocelli, Italy, during one of Wright's training flights made for Italian Naval Officers.

Obtaining aerial photography became a much more practical matter with the airplane than it had been with kites and balloons. Photography from aircraft received heightened attention in the interest of military reconnaisance during World War I. As discussed in Chapter 3, the greatest stimulation to photointerpretation occurred during World War II. Much of the technology used to acquire and interpret aerial photography (and the other types of images we examine) is an outgrowth of early military development.

2.3 THE SIMPLE CAMERA

The cameras used in the early days of photography were often no more than a lighttight box with a pinhole at one end and the light sensitive material to be exposed positioned against the opposite end (Figure 2.4a). The amount of exposure of the film was controlled by varying the time the pinhole was allowed to pass light. Often, exposure times were in hours because of the low sensitivity of the photographic materials available and the limited light-gathering capability of the pinhole design. In time, the

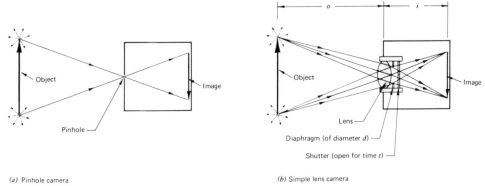

(a) Pinhole camera   (b) Simple lens camera

FIGURE 2.4   Comparison between pinhole (a) and simple lens (b) cameras.

pinhole camera was replaced by the simple lens camera, shown in Figure 2.4b. By replacing the pinhole with a lens, it became possible to enlarge the hole through which light rays from an object were collected to form an image. In addition to the lens, an adjustable *diaphragm* and an adjustable *shutter* were introduced. The diaphragm controls the diameter of the lens opening during film exposure, and the shutter controls the duration of exposure.

The design and function of modern adjustable cameras is conceptually identical to that of the early simple lens camera. To obtain sharp, properly exposed photographs with such systems, they must be focused and the proper exposure settings must be made. We shall describe each of these operations separately.

Focus

Three parameters are involved in focusing a camera: the focal length of the camera lens, f, the distance between the lens and the object to be photographed, o, and the distance between the lens and the image plane, i. The focal length of a lens is the distance from the lens at which parallel light rays are focused to a point. Object distance o and image distance i are shown in Figure 2.4b. When a camera is properly focused, the relationship among the focal length, object distance, and image distance is

$$\frac{1}{f} = \frac{1}{o} + \frac{1}{i} \qquad (2.1)$$

Since f is a constant for any given lens, as object distance o for a scene changes, image distance i must change. This is done by moving the camera lens with respect to the film plane. When focused on an object at a discrete distance, a camera can image over a range just beyond and in front of this distance with acceptable focus. This range is commonly referred to as the *depth of field*.

In aerial photography the object distances involved are normally infinite. Hence the

$1/o$ term in Eq. 2.1 goes to zero and i must equal f. Thus, most aerial cameras are manufactured with their film plane precisely located at a *fixed* distance f from their lens.

Exposure

The exposure[1] at any point in the film focal plane of a camera is determined by the irradiance at that point multiplied by the exposure time, expressed by

$$E = \frac{sd^2t}{4f^2} \tag{2.2}$$

where

E = film exposure, J mm^{-2}
s = scene brightness, J mm^{-2} sec^{-1}
d = diameter of lens opening, mm
t = exposure time, sec
f = lens focal length, mm

It can be seen from Eq. 2.2 that for a given camera and scene, the exposure reaching a film can be varied by changing the camera shutter speed t and/or the diameter of the lens opening d. Various combinations of d and t will yield equivalent exposures.

EXAMPLE 2.1

A film in a camera with a 40 mm focal length lens is properly exposed with a lens opening diameter of 5 mm and an exposure time of 1/125 sec (Condition 1). If the lens opening is increased to 10 mm, what exposure time should be used to maintain proper exposure (Condition 2)?

Solution

We wish to maintain the same exposure for Condition 1 and Condition 2. Hence,

$$E_1 = \frac{s_1(d_1)^2t_1}{4(f_1)^2} = \frac{s_2(d_2)^2t_2}{4(f_2)^2} = E_2$$

Canceling constants we obtain

$$(d_1)^2t_1 = (d_2)^2t_2$$

or

$$t_2 = \frac{(d_1)^2t_1}{(d_2)^2} = \frac{5^2}{10^2}\cdot\frac{1}{125} = \frac{1}{500}\ \text{sec}$$

---

[1]*Note.* The internationally accepted symbol for exposure is H. To avoid confusion with the use of this symbol for flying height, we use E to represent "exposure" in our discussions of photographic systems (Chapters 2 and 6). Elsewhere, E is used as the internationally accepted symbol for "irradiance."

The diameter of the lens opening of a camera is determined by adjusting the diaphragm to a particular *aperture setting*, or *F/STOP*. This is defined by

$$\text{F/STOP} = \frac{\text{lens focal length}}{\text{lens opening diameter}} = \frac{f}{d} \tag{2.3}$$

As can be seen in Eq. 2.3, as the F/STOP increases, the diameter of the lens opening decreases and, accordingly, the film exposure decreases. Because the *area* of the lens opening varies as the square of the diameter, the change in exposure with F/STOP is proportional to the square root of the F/STOP. Shutter speeds are normally established in sequential multiples of two (1/125 sec, 1/250 sec, 1/500 sec, 1/1000 sec). Thus F/STOPS vary as the square root of two (F/1.4, F/2, F/2.8, F/4. . .).

The interplay between F/STOPs and shutter speeds is well known to amateur photographers. For constant exposure, an incremental change in shutter speed setting must be accompanied by an incremental change in F/STOP setting. For example, the exposure obtained at 1/500 sec and F/1.4 could also be obtained at 1/250 sec at F/2. Short exposure times allow one to "stop action" and prevent blurring when photographing moving objects. Large lens opening diameters (small F/STOP numbers) allow more light to reach the film and are useful under low light conditions. Small lens opening diameters (large F/STOP numbers) yield greater depth of field. The F/STOP corresponding to the largest lens opening diameter is called the "lens speed." The larger the lens opening diameter (smaller F/STOP number), the "faster" the lens is.

Using F/STOPs, Eq. 2.2 can be simplified to

$$E = \frac{st}{4F^2} \tag{2.4}$$

where F = F/STOP setting = f/d.

Equation 2.4 is a convenient means of summarizing the interrelationship among film exposure, scene brightness, exposure time, and F/STOP. This relationship may be used in lieu of Eq. 2.2 to determine various F/STOP and shutter speed settings that result in identical film exposures.

EXAMPLE 2.2

A film is properly exposed when the lens aperture setting is F/8 and the exposure time is 1/125 sec (Condition 1). If the camera aperture setting is changed to F/4, what exposure time should be used to yield a proper film exposure (Condition 2)? (Note that this is simply a restatement of the condition of Example 2.1.)

Solution

We wish to maintain the *same exposure* for Condition 1 and Condition 2. With the scene brightness the same in each case,

$$E_1 = \frac{s_1 t_1}{4(F_1)^2} = \frac{s_2 t_2}{4(F_2)^2} = E_2$$

Canceling constants

$$\frac{t_1}{(F_1)^2} = \frac{t_2}{(F_2)^2}$$

and

$$t_2 = \frac{t_1(F_2)^2}{(F_1)^2} = \frac{1}{125} \cdot \frac{4^2}{8^2} = \frac{1}{500} \text{ sec}$$

2.4   BASIC NEGATIVE-TO-POSITIVE PHOTOGRAPHIC SEQUENCE

Many photographic procedures, particularly black and white techniques, employ a two-phase negative-to-positive sequence. In this process, the "negative" and "positive" materials are typically film and paper prints. Each of these materials consists of a light sensitive photographic *emulsion* coated onto a *base*, or *support*. The generalized cross sections of black and white film and print paper are shown in Figures 2.5a and b. In both cases, the emulsion consists of a thin layer of light sensitive silver halide crystals, or grains, held in place by a solidified gelatin. Paper is the base material for paper prints. Various plastics are used for film bases. When exposed to light, the silver halide crystals within an emulsion undergo a photochemical reaction forming an invisible *latent image*. Upon treatment with suitable agents in the *development process*, these exposed silver salts are reduced to silver grains that appear black, forming a visible image.

The negative-to-positive sequence of black and white photography is depicted in Figure 2.6. In Figure 2.6a, the letter *F* is shown to represent a scene that is imaged through a lens system and recorded as a latent image on a film. When processed, the film crystals exposed to light are reduced to silver. The number of crystals reduced at any point on the film is proportional to the exposure at that point. Those areas on the negative that were not exposed are clear after processing because crystals in these areas are dissolved as part of the development process. Those areas of the film that were exposed become various shades of gray, depending on the amount of exposure. Hence a "negative" image of reversed tonal rendition is produced. In Figure 2.6b the negative is illuminated and reprojected through an enlarger lens so that it is focused on print paper, again forming a latent image. When processed, the paper print produces dark areas where light was transmitted through the negative and light areas where the illuminating light was decreased by the negative. The final result is a realistic rendering of the original scene whose size is fixed by the enlarger setup. In the two-phase process of creating the final image, the negative provides an image of reversed geometry (left for right and top for bottom) and reversed brightness (light for dark and dark for light). The positive image gives a second reversal and thus true relative scene geometry and brightness.

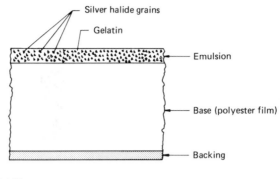

(a) Film

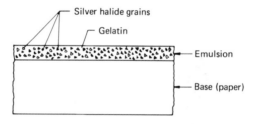

(b) Print paper

FIGURE 2.5   Generalized cross section of black and white photographic materials. (Adapted from [11].)

Most aerial photographic paper prints are produced using the negative-to-positive sequence and a *contact printing procedure* (Figure 2.6c). Here, the film is exposed and processed as usual, resulting in a negative of reversed scene geometry and brightness. The negative is then placed in emulsion-to-emulsion contact with print paper. Light is passed through the negative, thereby exposing the print paper. When processed, the image on the print is a positive representation of the original ground scene at the size of the negative.

Positive images need not be printed on print paper. For example, transparent positives are often made on plastic-based or glass-based emulsions. These types of images are referred to as *diapositives* or *transparencies*.

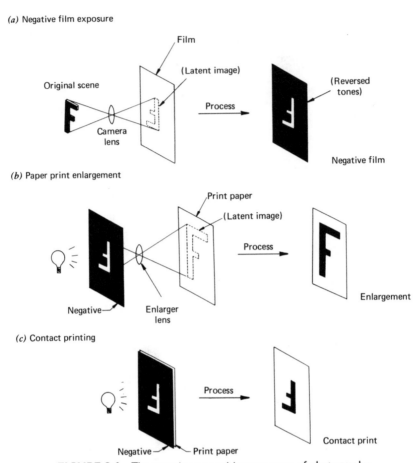

FIGURE 2.6   The negative-to-positive sequence of photography.

2.5   PROCESSING BLACK AND WHITE FILMS

Photographic processing chemically converts the latent image in an emulsion layer to a visible, stable image. It is a truly intriguing process and at the detailed level it is chemically complex [19]. Our attempt here is to treat only the salient nature of black and white film processing. (Paper print processing is identical conceptually.) The procedure entails the following steps.

1.   *Developing*.   The exposed film is first immersed in a *developer* solution. Developers are selective, *alkaline* reducing agents. They are selective in the sense that they reduce the silver of the exposed halide grains in an emulsion from a molecular ionic state to a pure atomic state. Because silver in the atomic state is black, there is proportionate correspondence of image *darkness* on the negative with object

brightness in the scene photographed. This correspondence manifests itself in the form of the shades of gray comprising the developed image.

2. *Stop bath*.   After images have been developed to the desired degree, the developing action is stopped by immersing the film in an *acidic* solution called a *stop bath*. The stop bath neutralizes the alkaline developer solution, thereby stopping the development process.

3. *Fixing*.   In the third step of the process, the film is placed in a *fixer* solution. The function of the fixing bath is to remove the unexposed silver halide grains from the emulsion, to harden the emulsion and render it chemically stable. (If the unused grains were not removed, they would be activated upon reexposure to light and eventually degrade the quality of the image.) Depending on the film and process involved, steps 2 and 3 are often combined into one operation.

4. *Washing*.   In this step, clean running water is used to wash the film to render it free of any chemical residues that would degrade the image. Chemical agents are often added to the wash to speed up the washing process.

5. *Drying*.   The final step in the process is that of drying. Either through air drying in a dust-free environment or through drying in a heated dryer, water is removed from the processed material.

2.6 SPECTRAL SENSITIVITY OF BLACK AND WHITE FILMS

Black and white aerial photographs are normally made with either *panchromatic* film or *infrared sensitive* film. The generalized spectral sensitivities for each of these film types are shown in Figure 2.7. Panchromatic film has long been the "standard" film type for aerial photography. As can be seen from Figure 2.7, the spectral sensitivity of panchromatic film extends over the UV and the visible portions of the spectrum. Infrared sensitive film is sensitive not only to UV and visible energy but also to near-infrared energy.

The use of black and white infrared photography to distinguish between deciduous and coniferous trees was illustrated in Figure 1.9. Many other applications of both panchromatic and black and white infrared aerial photography are described in Chapters 3 and 4. Here, we simply want the student to become familiar with the spectral sensitivities of these materials.

It is of interest to note what determines the "boundaries" of the spectral sensitivity of black and white film materials. As indicated in Section 2.1, we can photograph over a range of about 0.3 to 0.9 μm. The 0.9 μm limit stems from the photochemical instability of emulsion materials that are sensitive beyond this wavelength. (Certain films used for scientific experimentation are sensitive out to about 1.2 μm and form the only exception to this rule. These films are not commonly available.)

As might be suspected from Figure 2.7, the 0.3 μm limit to photography is determined by something other than film sensitivity. In fact, virtually all photographic emulsions are sensitive in this ultraviolet portion of the spectrum. The problem with

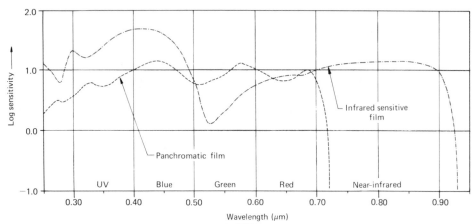

FIGURE 2.7   Generalized spectral sensitivities for black and white panchromatic and infrared sensitive films. (Adapted from [11].)

photographing at wavelengths shorter than about 0.4 μm is twofold: (1) the atmosphere absorbs or scatters this energy, and (2) glass camera lenses absorb such energy. But photography can be acquired in the 0.3 to 0.4 μm range if extremes of altitude and unfavorable atmospheric conditions are avoided. Furthermore, some improvement in image quality is realized if quartz camera lenses are used.

Figure 2.8 illustrates an interesting application of UV photography in zoological research and management. Shown are panchromatic and UV aerial photographs taken simultaneously of harp seals (*Pagophilus groelandicus*) on the snow and ice surface of the Gulf of St. Lawrence. Adult harp seals are dark in color and appear in both the panchromatic image (*a*) and the UV image (*b*). In contrast to the adults, infant harp seals have coats that appear white to the eye. Hence, they are not visible on a snow and ice background in panchromatic imagery (*a*). In the UV portion of the spectrum, the snow and ice background is still highly reflective but the "white" seal coats, which are very strong absorbers of UV energy, photograph black. Thus, both the adults and their young offspring can be detected on the UV image (*b*). This characteristic enables reliable monitoring of the change in population of this animal, which cannot be done practically over large areas using any other means. The same technique can be used to inventory other "white" objects, such as polar bears, arctic foxes, and hares on snow covered surfaces [22].

To date, the applications of aerial UV photography have been limited in number, due primarily to strong atmospheric scattering of UV energy. A notable exception is the use of UV photography in monitoring oil films on water [33]. Minute traces of floating oil, often invisible on other types of photography, can be detected in UV photography. (The use of aerial photography to study oil spills is illustrated in Chapter 3.)

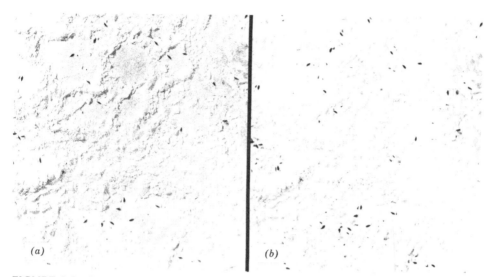

FIGURE 2.8 Panchromatic *(a)* and UV *(b)* aerial photographs of harp seals in the Gulf of St. Lawrence, March 1974; 300 m flying height. Dark-coated adult seals are visible in both images but white-coated seal pups are visible only in the UV photograph *(b)*. The UV photograph was taken with a camera equipped with a quartz lens, using panchromatic film and a camera filter that transmits UV energy (0.3 to 0.4 μm) but absorbs visible energy. (Courtesy David M. Lavigne, University of Guelph.)

2.7 COLOR FILM

Although black and white panchromatic film has long been the standard film type for aerial photography, many remote sensing applications currently involve the use of color film. The major advantage to the use of color is the fact that the human eye can discriminate many more shades of color than it can tones of gray. As we illustrate in subsequent chapters, this capability is essential in many applications of airphoto interpretation. In the remainder of this section we present the basics of how color film works. To do this we must first consider the way in which human color vision works.

Color Mixing Processes

The detailed psychophysical mechanisms by which we see color are still not fully understood, yet it is generally held that the human brain receives color impulses from the eye via three separate light receptors in the retina. These receptors respond to blue, green, and red light, respectively. What color we associate with a particular object depends on the particular amounts of blue, green, and red it reflects. That is, we physiologically mix impulses from the retina's blue receptor with those from the green and red receptors. Added together, these three impulses result in the perception of a single color for any given object.

A change in the relative quantity of blue, green, or red light coming from the object changes the color we associate with it. In short, we perceive all colors by synthesizing relative amounts of just three.

Blue, green, and red are termed *additive primaries*. Plate 1a shows the effect of projecting blue, green, and red light in partial superimposition. Where all three beams overlap, the visual effect is white because all three of the eyes' receptor systems are stimulated equally. Hence, white light can be thought of as the mixture of blue, green, and red light. Various combinations of the three additive primaries can be used to produce other colors. As illustrated, when red light and green light are mixed, yellow light is produced. Mixture of blue and red light results in the production of magenta light (bluish-red). Mixing blue and green results in cyan light (bluish-green).

Yellow, magenta, and cyan are known as the *complementary colors*, or *comple-ments*, of blue, green, and red light. Note that the complementary color for any given primary color results from mixing the remaining two primaries.

Like the eye, color television operates on the principle of additive color mixing through use of blue, green, and red dots (or vertical lines) on the picture screen. When viewed at a distance, the light from the closely spaced screen elements forms a continuous color image.

Whereas color television simulates different colors through *additive* mixture of blue, green, and red *lights*, color photography is based on the principle of *subtractive* color mixture using superimposed yellow, magenta, and cyan *dyes*. These three dye colors are termed the *subtractive primaries* and each results from subtracting one of the additive primaries from white light. That is, yellow dye absorbs the blue compo-nent of white light. Magenta dye absorbs the green component of white light. Cyan dye absorbs the red component of white light.

The subtractive color mixing process is illustrated in Plate 1b. This plate shows three circular filters being held in front of a source of white light. The filters contain yellow, magenta, and cyan dye. The yellow dye absorbs blue light from the white background and transmits green and red. The magenta dye absorbs green light and transmits blue and red. The cyan dye absorbs red light and transmits blue and green. The superimposition of magenta and cyan dyes results in the passage of only blue light from the background. This comes about since the magenta dye absorbs the green component of the white background, and the cyan dye absorbs the red component. Superimposition of the yellow and cyan dyes results in the perception of green. Likewise, superimposition of yellow and magenta dyes results in the perception of red. Where all three dyes overlap, all light from the white background is absorbed and black results.

In color photography, various proportions of yellow, magenta, and cyan dye are superimposed to control the proportionate amount of blue, green, and red light that reaches the eye. Hence, the subtractive mixture of yellow, magenta, and cyan dyes on a photograph is used to control the additive mixture of blue, green, and red light reaching the eye of the observer. To accomplish this, color film is manufactured with three emulsion layers that are sensitive to blue, green, and red light but which contain yellow, magenta, and cyan dye after processing.

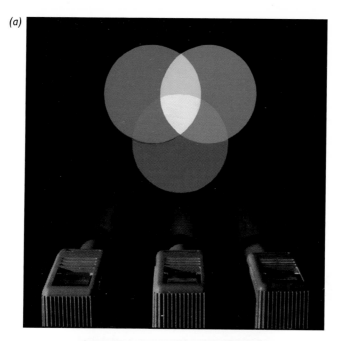

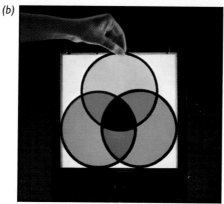

PLATE I   Color mixing processes. *(a)* Color *additive* process — operative when *lights* of different colors are superimposed. *(b)* Color *subtractive* process — operative when *dyes* of different colors are superimposed. (Courtesy Eastman Kodak Co.) (For major discussion, see Section 2.7.)

(a)

(b)

PLATE 2   Oblique normal color (a) and color infrared (b) aerial photographs showing a portion of the University of Wisconsin — Madison campus, June 27, 1968, 11:00 A.M. The football field has artificial turf with low near-infrared reflectance. (For major discussion, see Section 2.9.)

PLATE 3 Oblique normal color *(a)* and color infrared *(b)* aerial photographs showing flowing lava on the face of Kilauea Volcano, January 22, 1971, 12:15 P.M. The orange tones on the color infrared photograph represent infrared energy *emitted* from the flowing lava. The pink tones represent sunlight *reflected* from the living vegetation. (For major discussion, see Section 2.9.)

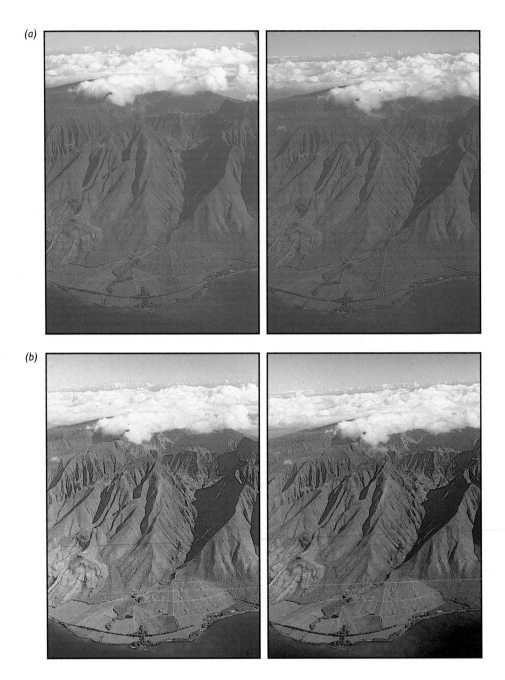

PLATE 4   Oblique aerial photographs, Island of Maui, Hawaii, November 3, 1970, 9:30 A.M. *(a)* Stereopair taken with normal color film using an ultraviolet (haze) filter. *(b)* Stereopair taken with color infrared film using a yellow filter. (For major discussion, see Section 2.10.)

(a)

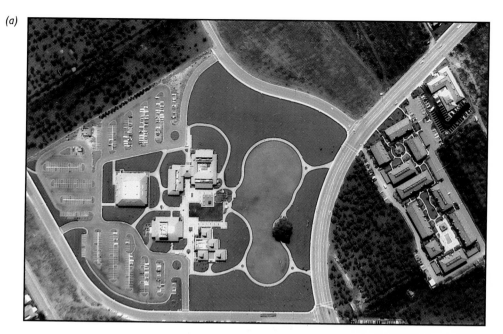

(b)

PLATE 5 Color composites produced in a color additive viewer *using the black and white photographs shown in Figure 2.30. (a)* Simulated normal color photograph. *(b)* Simulated color infrared photograph. (Courtesy International Imaging Systems.) (For major discussion, see Section 2.11.)

PLATE 6 Color infrared panoramic photograph illustrating gypsy moth defoliation of hardwood trees, central Pennsylvania, June 18, 1981. (NASA photograph courtesy USDA Forest Service.) (For major discussion, see Sections 2.11 and 3.7.)

(a) *(b)*

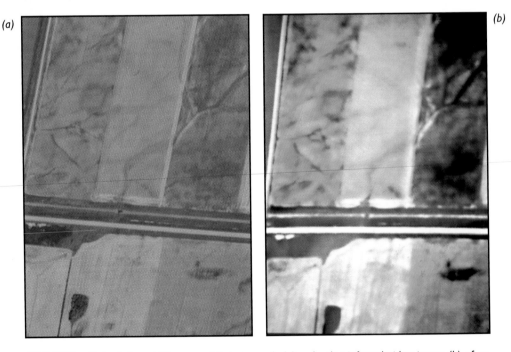

PLATE 7 Color infrared 35 mm aerial photograph *(a)* and color infrared video image *(b)* of an agricultural area in northwestern Minnesota, August 8, 1983. (Courtesy University of Minnesota Remote Sensing Laboratory.) (For major discussion, see Section 2.17.)

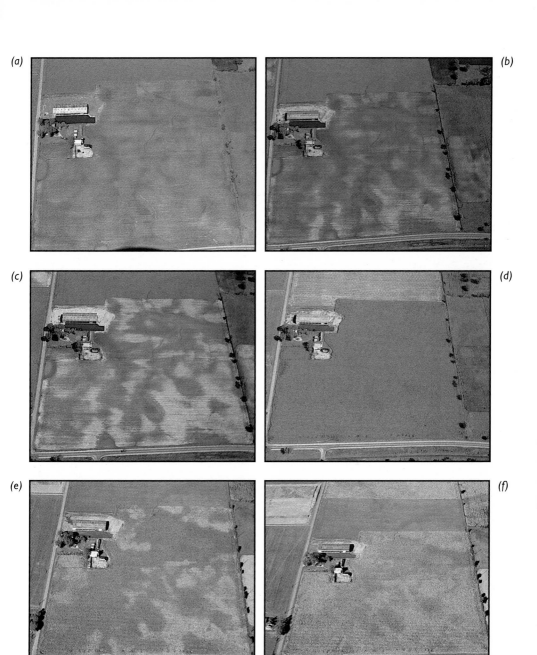

PLATE 8 Oblique color infrared aerial photographs illustrating the effects of date of photography: (a) June 30, 1969; (b) July 1, 1969; (c) July 2, 1969; (d) August 11, 1969; (e) September 17, 1969; (f) October 8, 1969. Dane County, Wisconsin. Approximate horizontal scale at photo center is 1:7600. (For major discussion, see Section 3.4.)

PLATE 9 High altitude color infrared aerial photograph. Salt Lake City, Utah, June 11, 1975. 1:140,000. (NASA photograph.) (For major discussion, see Section 3.5.)

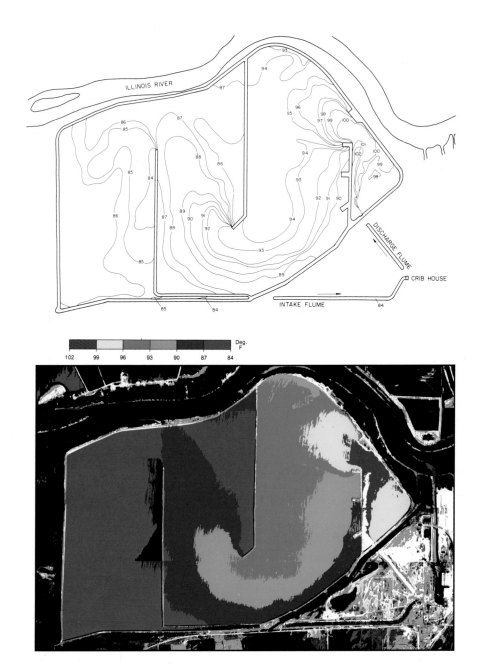

PLATE 10 Surface isotherm map and DIGICOLOR™ thermal image mosaic, Powerton Cooling Pond, Illinois, 460 m flying height, 1.5 mr IFOV. (Courtesy Daedalus Enterprises, Inc., Sargent & Lundy Engineers, and Commonwealth Edison of Illinois.) (For major discussion, see Section 7.13.)

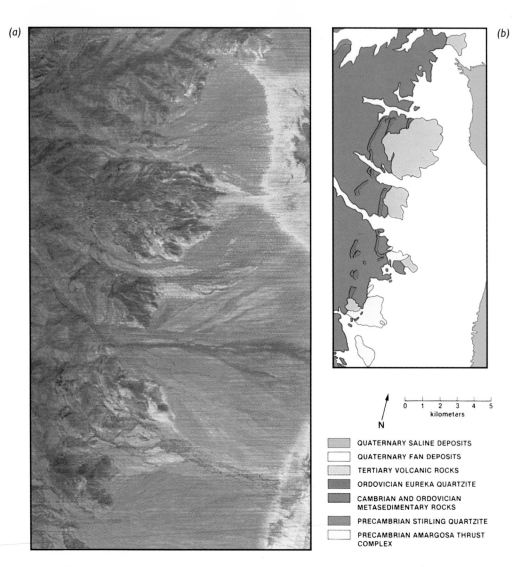

(a)

(b)

0 1 2 3 4 5
kilometers

N

QUATERNARY SALINE DEPOSITS

QUATERNARY FAN DEPOSITS

TERTIARY VOLCANIC ROCKS

ORDOVICIAN EUREKA QUARTZITE

CAMBRIAN AND ORDOVICIAN
METASEDIMENTARY ROCKS

PRECAMBRIAN STIRLING QUARTZITE

PRECAMBRIAN AMARGOSA THRUST
COMPLEX

PLATE 11 (a) Thermal Infrared Multispectral Scanner (TIMS) image, Panamint Mountains and Death Valley, California. Blue display = 8.2 to 8.6 μm, green display = 9.0 to 9.4 μm, red display = 10.2 to 11.2 μm. August 1982. (b) Generalized lithologic map of the same area. (Courtesy NASA Jet Propulsion Laboratory.) (For major discussion, see Section 7.15.)

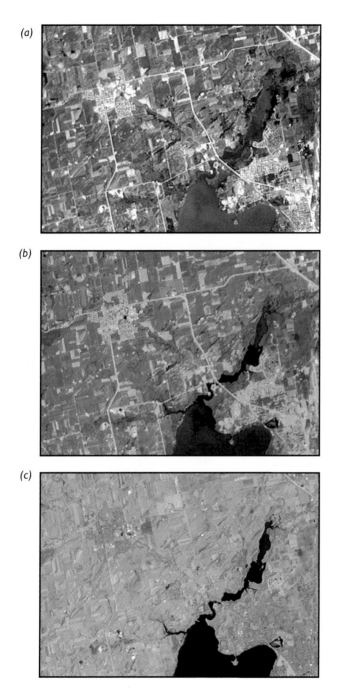

PLATE 12 Color composite Thematic Mapper images illustrating six band-color combinations, suburban Madison, Wisconsin, August 26, 1984. 1:180,000. (See Section 9.9, Table 9.5, for the specific band-color combinations shown here.)

(d)

(e)

(f)

PLATE 12 *(continued)*

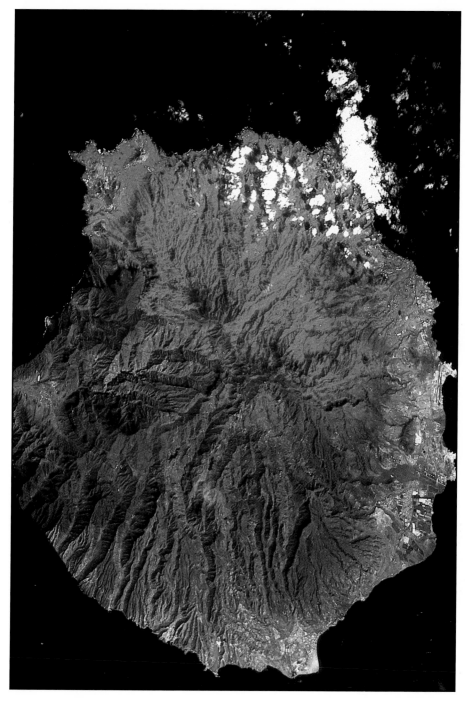

PLATE 13 SPOT-1 color composite image, multispectral mode, 20 m ground resolution, Gran Canaria, Canary Islands, February 24, 1986. 1:320,000. (Copyright © CNES, Courtesy SPOT Image Corp.) (For major discussion, see Section 9.14)

(a)

(b)

(c)

PLATE 14   Simulated SPOT images, Sherbrooke, Quebec, June 1982. *(a)* Multispectral image with 20 m resolution. *(b)* Panchromatic image with 10 m resolution. *(c)* Merged multispectral-panchromatic image. 1:44,000.   (Courtesy Départment de géographie, Université de Sherbrooke, Sherbrooke, Québec.) (For major discussion, see Section 9.14.)

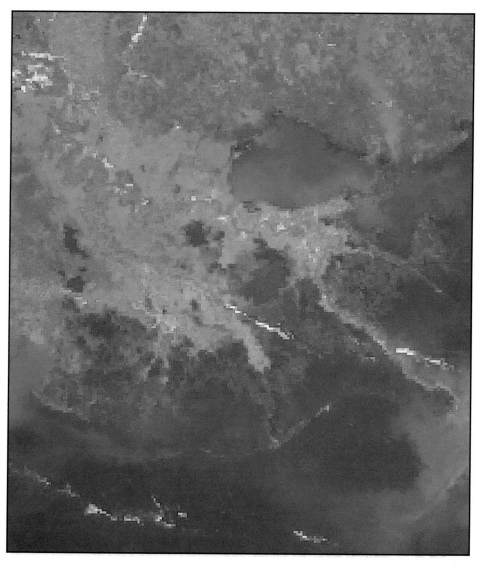

PLATE 15 NOAA-8 AVHRR color composite image, Mississippi River delta and vicinity, May 24, 1983. 1:2,200,000. (Courtesy USGS EROS Data Center.) (For major discussion, see Section 9.16.)

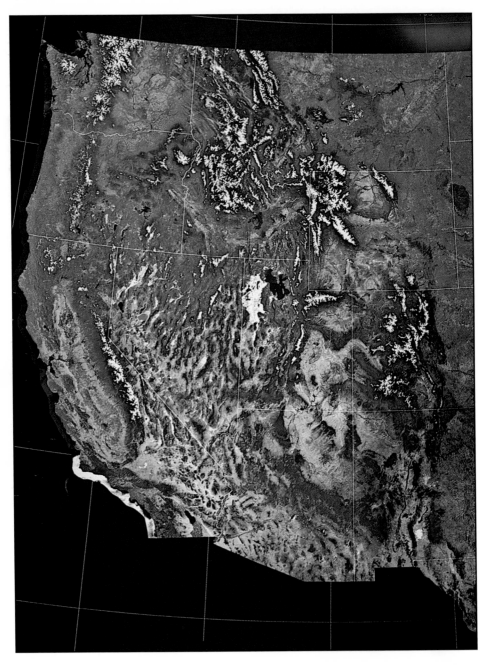

PLATE 16   NOAA-8 AVHRR color composite mosaic of the western United States, May 27-31, 1984. (Courtesy USGS EROS Data Center.) (For major discussion, see Section 9.16.)

(a)

(b)

PLATE 17 Landsat MSS images showing Boston, Cape Cod, and vicinity, July 6, 1976. 1:1,300,000. *(a)* Original color composite. *(b)* Color composite resulting from contrast stretch and edge enhancement operations. (Courtesy NASA and USGS.) (For major discussion, see Section 10.5.)

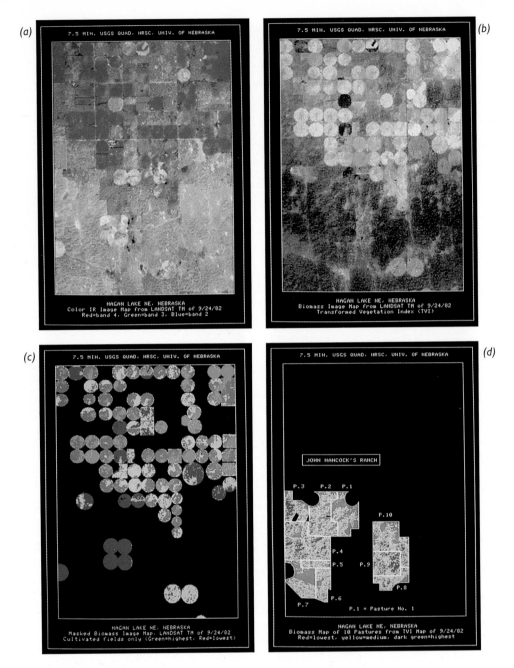

PLATE 18 Transformed Vegetation Index (TVI) images. *(a)* Raw false color composite of TM2, TM3, and TM4. *(b)* Uncalibrated TVI image. *(c)* Calibrated TVI image of selected corn fields. *(d)* Calibrated TVI image of selected pastures. (Courtesy Institute of Agricultural and Natural Resources, University of Nebraska.) (For major discussion, see Section 10.6.)

(b)

(a)

PLATE 19 IHS ratio enhancement, Gulf of Suez. *(a)* Contrast stretched and edge enhanced Landsat MSS color composite (bands 4, 5, and 7). *(b)* IHS ratio enhancement of *(a)* showing increased separability of surface features. (From [34], Chapter 10.) (For major discussion, see Section 10.6.)

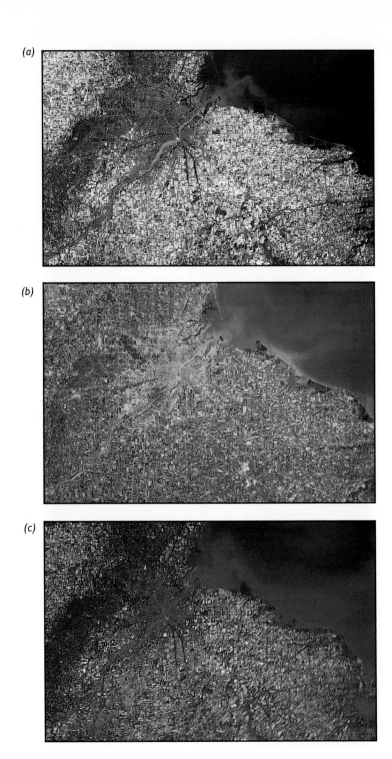

PLATE 20　Landsat MSS false color composite of Toledo, Ohio region. *(a)* Spring image (May 1975). *(b)* Summer image (August 1975). *(c)* Composite image. (Courtesy Environmental Research Institute of Michigan.) (For major discussion, see Section 10.15.)

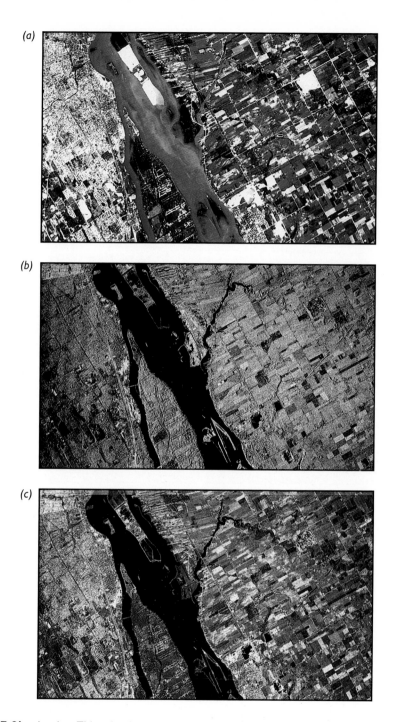

PLATE 21 Landsat TM and airborne side-looking radar images, Detroit-Windsor area (United States and Canada). 1:200,000. *(a)* Landsat TM color composite image, July 25, 1982. *(b)* Radar image, *X* band, synthetic aperture, *HH* polarization, October 4, 1984. *(c)* Radar/Landsat color composite image. (Courtesy Environmental Research Institute of Michigan.) (For major discussion, see Section 10.15.)

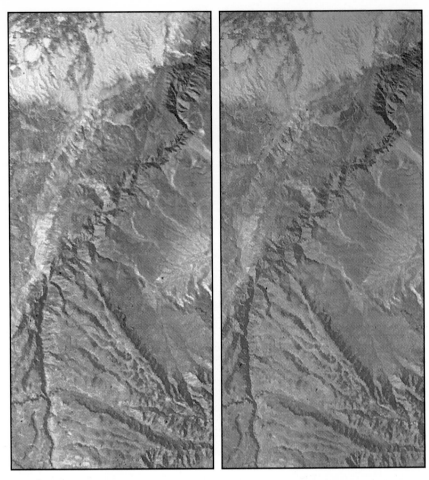

PLATE 22 False color, synthetic stereopair generated from a single Landsat MSS image and a digital elevation model. Black Canyon of the Gunnison, Colorado, September 3, 1973. 1:410,000. Maximum canyon depth is 850 m. (Courtesy USGS.) (For major discussion, see Section 10.15.)

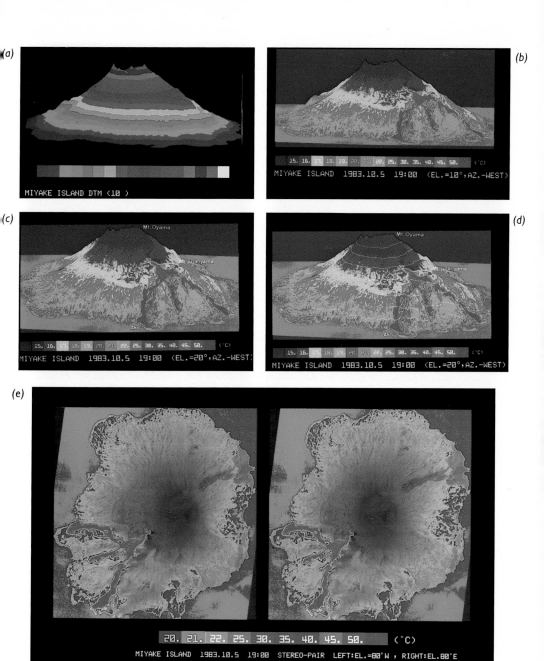

PLATE 23 Merger of elevation data and thermal scanner data, Miyake Island, Japan, October 5, 1983. (a) Perspective view of digital elevation model. (b-d) Perspective views of island created from elevation and thermal scanner data. (e) Stereopair created from elevation and thermal scanner data. (Courtesy Asia Air Survey Co., Ltd., Tokyo, Japan.) (For major discussion, see Section 10.15.)

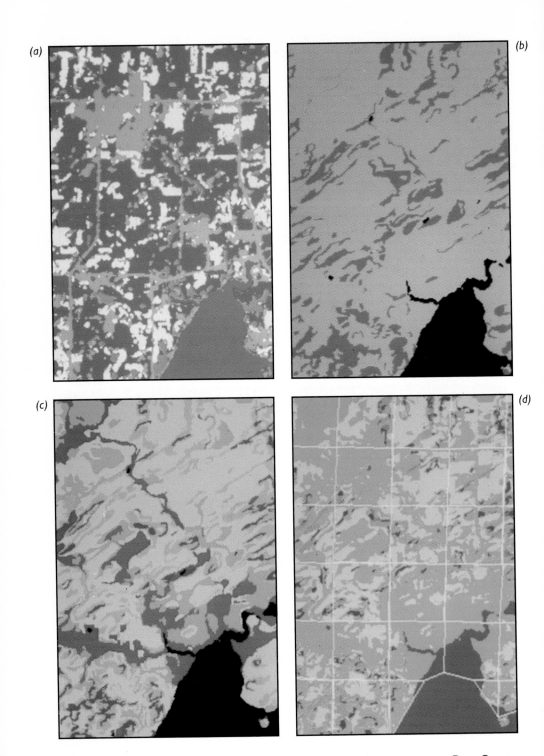

PLATE 24 Integration of remote sensing data in geographic information system, Dane County, Wisconsin, August 26, 1984. *(a)* Land cover. *(b)* Soil erodibility. *(c)* Slope. *(d)* Soil erosion potential (with Public Land Survey System section overlay). (For major discussion, see Section 10.15.)

Structure and Spectral Sensitivity of Color Film

The basic cross-sectional structure and spectral sensitivity of color film are shown in Figure 2.9. As shown in Figure 2.9a the top film layer is sensitive to blue light, the second layer to green and blue light, and the third to red and blue light. Because these bottom two layers have blue sensitivity as well as the desired green and red sensitivities, a blue absorbing filter layer is introduced between the first and second photosen-

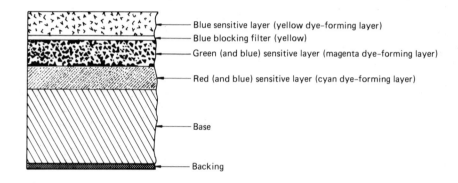

Blue sensitive layer (yellow dye-forming layer)
Blue blocking filter (yellow)
Green (and blue) sensitive layer (magenta dye-forming layer)
Red (and blue) sensitive layer (cyan dye-forming layer)

Base

Backing

(a) Generalized cross section

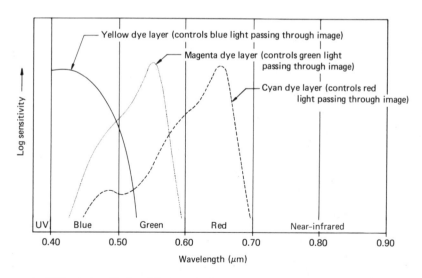

(b) Spectral sensitivities of the three dye layers

FIGURE 2.9   Structure and sensitivity of color film. (Adapted from [11, 31].)

sitive layers. This filter layer blocks the passage of blue light beyond the blue sensitive layer. This effectively results in selective sensitization of each of the film layers to the blue, green, and red primary colors. The yellow filter layer has no permanent effect on the appearance of the film because it is dissolved during processing.

From the standpoint of spectral sensitivity, the three layers of color film can be thought of as three black and white silver halide emulsions (Figure 2.9*b*). Again, the colors physically present in each of these layers after the film is processed are *not* blue, green, and red. Rather, after processing, the blue sensitive layer contains yellow dye, the green sensitive layer contains magenta dye, and the red sensitive layer contains cyan dye (see Figure 2.9*a*). The amount of dye introduced in each layer is inversely related to the intensity of the corresponding primary light present in the scene photographed. When viewed in composite, the dye layers produce the visual sensation of the original scene.

The manner in which the three dye layers of color film operate is shown in Figure 2.10. For purposes of illustration, the original scene is represented schematically in (*a*) by a row of boxes that correspond to scene reflectance in four spectral bands: blue, green, red, and IR. After exposure (*b*), the blue sensitive layer is activated by the blue

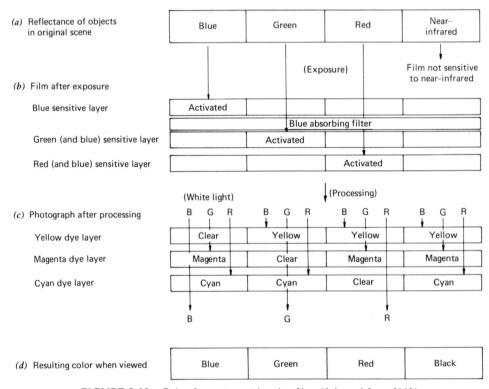

FIGURE 2.10 Color formation with color film. (Adapted from [11].)

light, the green sensitive layer is activated by the green light, and the red sensitive layer is activated by the red light. No layer is activated by the IR energy since the film is not sensitive to IR energy. During processing, dyes are introduced into each sensitivity layer in *inverse* proportion to the intensity of light recorded in each layer. Hence the more intense the exposure of the blue layer to blue light, the less yellow dye introduced in the image and the more magenta and cyan dye introduced. This is shown in (c) where, for blue light, the yellow dye layer is clear and the other two layers contain magenta and cyan dye. Likewise, green exposure results in the introduction of yellow and cyan dye, and red exposure results in the introduction of yellow and magenta dyes. When the developed image is viewed with a white light source (d), we perceive the colors in the original scene through the subtractive process. Where a blue object was present in the scene, the magenta dye subtracts the green component of the white light, the cyan dye subtracts the red component, and the image appears blue. Green and red are produced in an analogous fashion. Other colors are produced in accordance with the proportions of blue, green, and red present in the original scene.

2.8 PROCESSING COLOR FILMS

Most aerial films are manufactured to be processed to either a negative or a positive. (Some may be processed either way.) *Color negative films* produce negative images that are used in a negative-to-positive sequence in much the same manner as black and white negative films. That is, a film negative is exposed and processed and subsequently used to produce a positive (normally on color print paper). Color negatives, like black and white negatives, manifest a reversal of scene geometry and brightness. Containing yellow, magenta, and cyan dye, they also manifest a color regime that is the complement of the original scene. Positives prepared from such negatives correctly reproduce the geometry, brightness, and color of the original scene.

Color reversal films are films that can be processed to produce a positive image directly on the original film exposed in the camera. Color slides are familiar reversal film products. Their counterparts in aerial photography are referred to as color diapositives or *color positive transparencies.*

Figure 2.11 illustrates the sequence employed in processing a color positive transparency. To keep matters simple, we have assumed that the film shown in this figure has been exposed to blue light only. The exposure/processing sequence for the film is as follows.

1. The blue light reflected from the scene photographed activates the blue sensitive film layer. This results in a developable latent image being formed in the blue sensitive layer, but none in the other two layers.
2. The film is immersed in a black and white *first developer* that produces a developed image composed of pure silver in the blue sensitive layer. At this point, the green and red sensitive layers of the film still contain unexposed silver halide grains.
3. The film is reexposed by a source of white light, thus making the silver halide

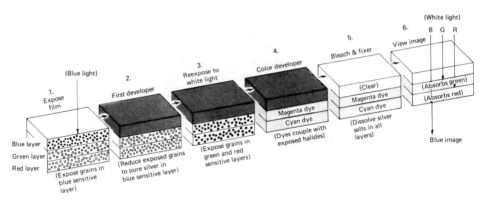

FIGURE 2.11 Color reversal process.

grains in the green and red sensitive layers developable. This step is called "flashing." In many processes flashing is accomplished chemically.

4. The film is immersed in a *color developer*, where the silver halide grains in the green and red sensitive layers are reduced to silver and at the same time magenta and cyan dyes are formed in proportion to the amounts of silver in each layer. This is called *coupler development*. After coupler development, the blue sensitive layer still contains the developed image (silver) resulting from the first developer, and thus yellow dye is not formed in the image.

5. The film is immersed in a *bleach* which, without affecting the dyes, converts the silver in all layers to soluble salts. These salts are then dissolved from all three layers in a *fixer*, leaving only the magenta and cyan dyes in the green and red sensitive layers. The film is washed to remove any remaining chemicals, then dried.

6. When white light is passed through the film during viewing, the magenta dye absorbs the green component of the light source and the cyan dye absorbs the red component. The blue component is transmitted by the clear, yellow-forming layer, resulting in perception of a blue image. Other colors are produced in an analogous fashion, through various combinations of exposure and dye introduction in the three film layers.

At this point, the student may wish to review the entire discussion of the color additive and subtractive processes and how color film dyes are used to replicate the colors in a scene. We believe that a thorough understanding of these processes is helpful in the interpretation of color photographs—it is *essential* in the interpretation of color infrared photographs.

Additional general discussion about processing color films is given in manufacturers' literature on the subject. Detailed discussion is presented in photographic handbooks [19, 31].

2.9   COLOR INFRARED FILM

The assignment of a given dye color to a given spectral sensitivity range is a film manufacturing parameter that can be varied arbitrarily. The color of the dye developed in any given emulsion layer need not bear any relationship to the color of light to which the layer is sensitive. Any desired portions of the photographic spectrum, including the near-infrared, can be recorded on color film with any color assignment.

In contrast to "normal" color film, *color infrared* film is manufactured to record green, red, and the photographic portion (0.7 to 0.9 μm) of the near-infrared scene energy in its three emulsion layers. The dyes developed in each of these layers are again yellow, magenta, and cyan. The result is a "false color" film in which blue images result from objects reflecting primarily green energy, green images result from objects reflecting primarily red energy, and red images result from objects reflecting primarily in the near-infrared portion of the spectrum.

The basic structure and spectral sensitivity of color infrared film are shown in Figure 2.12. (Note that there are some overlaps in the sensitivities of the layers.) The process by which the three primary colors are reproduced with such films is shown in Figure 2.13. Various combinations of the primary colors and complementary colors, as well as black and white, can also be reproduced on the film, depending on scene reflectance. For example, an object with a high reflectance in both green and infrared would produce a magenta image (blue + red). It should be noted that most color infrared films are designed to be used with a yellow (blue absorbing) filter over the camera lens. Some specialty films have a built-in yellow filter. As further described in Section 2.10, the filter blocks the passage of any light having a wavelength below about 0.5 μm. This means that the blue (and ultraviolet) scene energy is not permitted to reach the film, a fact that aids in the interpretation of color infrared imagery. If a minus blue filter were not used, it would be very difficult to ascribe any given image color to a particular ground reflectance because of the nearly equal sensitivity of all layers of the film to blue energy. The use of a blue absorbing filter has the further advantage of improving haze penetration because the effect of Rayleigh scatter is reduced when the blue light is filtered out.

Color infrared film was developed during World War II to detect painted targets that were camouflaged to look like vegetation. Because healthy vegetation reflects infrared energy much more strongly than it does green energy, it generally appears in various tones of red on color infrared film. However, objects painted green generally have low infrared reflectance. Thus, they appear blue on the film (Figure 2.12b) and can be readily discriminated from healthy green vegetation. Because of its genesis, color infrared film has often been referred to as "camouflage detection (CD) film." With its vivid color portrayal of near-infrared energy, color infrared film has become an extremely useful film for resource analyses.

Plate 2 illustrates normal color (*a*) and color infrared (*b*) aerial photographs of a portion of the University of Wisconsin—Madison campus. The grass, tree leaves, and football field reflect more strongly in the green than in the blue or red and thus appear green in the natural color photograph. The healthy grass and tree leaves reflect much more strongly in the infrared than in the green or red and thus appear red in the color

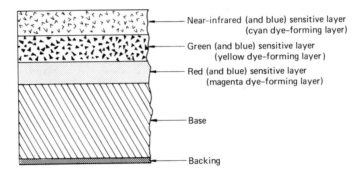

Near-infrared (and blue) sensitive layer
(cyan dye-forming layer)

Green (and blue) sensitive layer
(yellow dye-forming layer)

Red (and blue) sensitive layer
(magenta dye-forming layer)

Base

Backing

(a) Generalized cross section

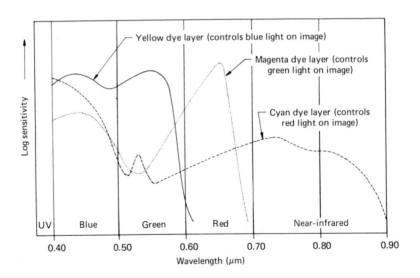

(b) Spectral sensitivities of the three dye layers

FIGURE 2.12   Structure and sensitivity of color infrared film. (Adapted from
[10, 11].)

infrared photograph. The football field has artificial turf that does not reflect well in the
infrared and thus does not appear red. The large rectangular gravel parking area
adjacent to the natural grass practice fields appears a light brown in the normal color
photograph and nearly white in the color infrared photograph. This means it has a high
reflectance in green, red, and infrared. The red-roofed buildings appear a greenish-
yellow on the color infrared film, which means that they reflect highly in the red and
also have some infrared reflectance.

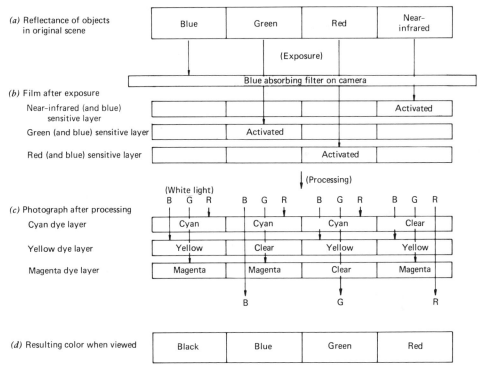

FIGURE 2.13 Color formation on color infrared film. [Adapted from [10].)

Almost every aerial application of color infrared photography deals with photographing *reflected sunlight*. The amount of energy *emitted* from the earth at ambient temperature (around 300°K) is insignificant in the range of 0.4 to 0.9 μm and hence cannot be photographed. This means that color infrared film cannot, for example, be used to detect the temperature difference between two water bodies or between wet and dry soils. As explained in Chapter 7, electronic sensors (such as radiometers or thermal scanners) operating in the wavelength range 3 to 5 or 8 to 14 μm can be used to distinguish between temperatures of such objects.

The energy *emitted* from extremely hot objects such as flames from burning wood (forest fires or burning buildings) or flowing lava *can* be photographed on color and color infrared film. Figure 2.14 shows blackbody radiation curves for earth features at an ambient temperature of 27°C (300°K) and flowing lava at 1100°C (1373°K). As calculated from Wien's Displacement Law (Eq. 1.5), the peak wavelength of the emitted energy is 9.7 μm for the earth features at 27°C and 2.1 μm for lava at 1100°C. When the spectral distribution of emitted energy is calculated, it is found that the energy emitted from the features at 27°C is essentially zero over the range of photographic wavelengths. In the case of flowing lava at 1100°C, the emitted energy in the

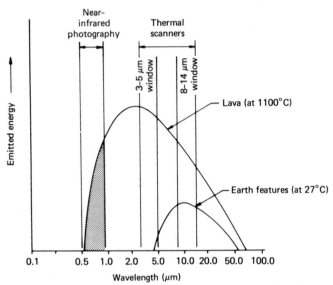

FIGURE 2.14   Blackbody radiation curves for earth surface features (at 27°C) and flowing lava (at 1100°C).

range of IR photography (0.5 to 0.9μm) is sufficient to be recorded on photographic films.

Plate 3 shows normal color (*a*) and color infrared (*b*) aerial photographs of flowing lava on the flank of Kilauea Volcano on the Island of Hawaii. Although the emitted energy can be seen as a faint orange glow on the normal color photograph, it is more clearly evident on the color infrared film. The orange tones on the color infrared photograph represent infrared energy *emitted* from the flowing lava. The pink tones represent sunlight *reflected* from the living vegetation (principally tree ferns). Keep in mind that it is *only* when the temperature of a feature is extremely high that infrared film will record energy emitted by an object. At all other times, the film is responding to *reflected* IR energy which is not directly related to the temperature of the feature.

We further examine the interpretation of color infrared photography in Chapter 3. Information about the optimum methods for exposing, storing and processing color infrared films is given in [10, 17].

2.10   FILTERS

Film type is only one variable that determines what information is recorded by a photographic remote sensing system. Equally important is the spectral makeup of the energy exposing the film. Through the use of filters, we can be selective about which wavelengths of energy reflected from a scene we allow to reach the film. Filters are transparent (glass or gelatin) materials that, by absorption or reflection, eliminate or reduce the energy reaching a film in selected portions of the photographic spectrum. They are placed in the optical path of a camera in front of the lens.

Aerial camera filters consist mainly of organic dyes suspended in glass or in a dried gelatin film. Filters are most commonly designated by *Kodak Wratten*™ filter numbers. They come in a variety of forms having a variety of spectral transmittance properties. The most commonly used spectral filters are *absorption filters*. As their name indicates, these filters absorb and transmit energy of selected wavelengths. A "yellow" filter for example, absorbs blue energy incident upon it and transmits green and red energy. The green and red energy combine to form yellow—the color we would see when looking through the filter if it is illuminated by white light (see Plate 1*b*).

Absorption filters are often used in film–filter combinations that permit differentiation of objects with nearly identical spectral response patterns in major portions of the photographic spectrum. For example, two objects may appear to reflect the same color when viewed only in the visible portion of the spectrum, but may have different reflection characteristics in the UV or near-infrared region. This was illustrated in Figure 2.8*b* with the discrimination of harp seal pups from snow using panchromatic film and a UV (Wratten™ 18A) filter. This filter passes energy in the UV (0.3 to 0.4 μm) range but absorbs all visible wavelengths. Hence, differences in UV reflectance alone are used to differentiate between objects of interest. Let us now consider the same approach for limiting photography to near-IR wavelengths.

Figure 2.15 illustrates generalized spectral reflectance curves for natural grass and

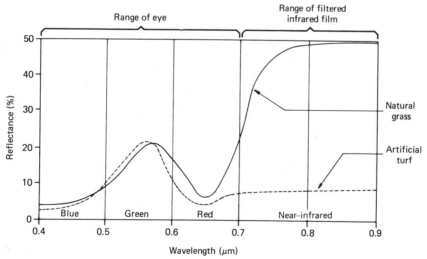

FIGURE 2.15 Generalized spectral reflectance curves for natural grass and artificial turf.

artificial turf, such as those shown in Plate 2. Because the artificial turf is manufactured with a green color to visually resemble natural grass, the reflectance in blue, green, and red is similar for both surfaces. However, the natural grass reflects very highly in the near-infrared whereas the artificial turf does not. If we wish to distinguish between natural grass and artificial turf using black and white photography, we can photograph the scene using black and white infrared sensitive film with an absorption filter over the camera lens that blocks all wavelengths shorter than 0.7 μm. Figure 2.16 illustrates the result of such photography. Figure 2.16a shows the scene as photographed on panchromatic film in which the natural grass and artificial turf have a similar photographic tone. Film 2.16b shows the scene photographed on black and white infrared film using a filter transmitting only wavelengths longer than 0.7 μm. In this case, the natural grass has a very light photographic tone (high infrared reflectance) and the artificial turf a very dark photographic tone (low infrared reflectance). The filter used in such photography, which selectively absorbs energy below a certain wavelength, is referred to as a *short wavelength blocking* filter, or a *high-pass* filter.

When one is interested in sensing the energy in only an isolated narrow portion of the spectrum, a *bandpass* filter may be used. Wavelengths above and below a specific range are blocked by such a filter. The spectral transmittance curves for a typical blocking filter and a bandpass filter are illustrated in Figure 2.17. Several blocking and bandpass filters may be used simultaneously to selectively photograph various wavelength bands on separate film images. This results in *multiband photography*, which we describe in Section 2.11.

There is a large selection of filters from which to choose for any given application. Manufacturers' literature describes the spectral transmittance properties of each available type [12]. It should be noted that *low-pass* absorption filters are not available. *Interference* filters must be used when short wavelength transmittance is desired. These filters reflect rather than absorb unwanted energy. They are used when extremely narrow bandpass characteristics are desired.

Panchromatic aerial film is usually exposed through a yellow (blue absorbing) filter to reduce the effects of atmospheric haze. Black and white infrared sensitive aerial film can be exposed through any of several filters. Typically, a yellow filter (which also transmits infrared wavelengths) is used for forestry purposes and a red (which also transmits infrared energy) or infrared-only filter is used when delineation of water bodies is desired. Normal color film is usually exposed through an ultraviolet (haze) filter and color infrared film through a yellow filter, as shown in Figure 2.18.

As described in Section 1.3, Rayleigh scattering in the atmosphere introduces a decreased sharpness and contrast in aerial photographs. This effect is most pronounced in the ultraviolet and blue wavelengths. Plate 4 illustrates the effect of filtering out blue wavelengths on sharpness and contrast. The top stereopair was photographed using normal color film with an ultraviolet (haze) filter. The bottom stereopair was photographed using color infrared film with a yellow (blue absorbing) filter. The increase in haze "penetration" using a yellow filter and color infrared film is readily apparent as is the increase in image sharpness and contrast. Some of the additional contrast seen in the lower stereopair results from the fact that color infrared film characteristically has more contrast than normal color film.

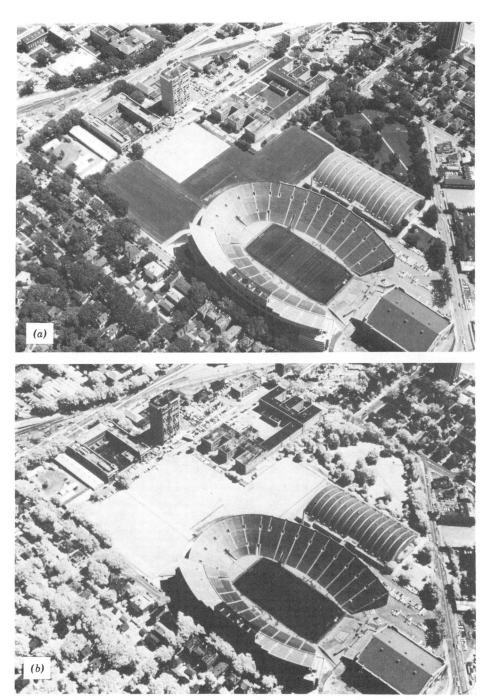

FIGURE 2.16 Simultaneous oblique aerial photographs showing the effect of filtration on discrimination of ground objects. On panchromatic film *(a)* natural grass and artificial turf have a similar tone. When scene energy is filtered such that only wavelengths longer than 0.7 μm are incident on black and white infrared film *(b)*, the natural grass has a very light tone and the artificial turf a very dark tone.

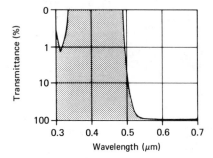

(a) Typical high-pass filter

(b) Typical bandpass filter

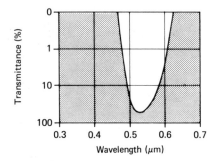

FIGURE 2.17 Typical transmission curves for filter types commonly used in aerial photography. (a) Typical high-pass filter (Kodak Wratten™ No. 12). (b) Typical bandpass filter (Kodak Wratten™ No. 58). (Adapted from [12].)

Antivignetting filters are often used to improve the uniformity of exposure throughout an image. There is a geometrically based decrease in illumination with increasing distance from the center of a photograph (to be discussed in Section 6.7). To negate the effect of this illumination *falloff*, antivignetting filters are designed to be strongly absorbing in their central area and progressively transparent in their circumferential area. To reduce the number of filters used, and thereby the number of between-filter reflections possible, antivignetting features are often built into haze and other absorption filters. (Various filters having this feature are shown in the foreground of Figure 2.22.)

A final note on filtering techniques in aerial photography is that color films (particularly infrared sensitive films) are somewhat sensitive to aging. This causes their color layers to often "go out of balance." For example, the sensitivity of the infrared sensitive

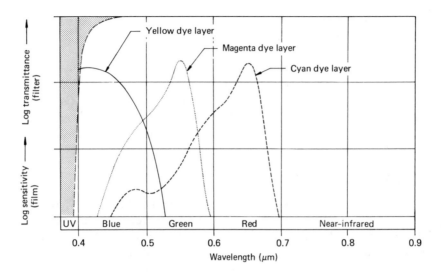

(a) Color film with ultraviolet (haze) filter

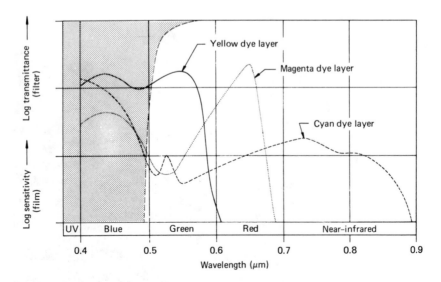

(b) Color infrared film with Wratten™ No. 12 (yellow) filter

FIGURE 2.18 Spectral sensitivities for typical color and color infrared film–filter combinations. (Adapted from [11, 12].)

layer of a film might decrease with age relative to the other two layers. Such a film might still be exposed with satisfactory results if a *color compensating* filter is used [18].

When using filters, it is often necessary to increase exposure to compensate for radiation absorption by the filter. Hence, filter manufacturers publish *filter factors*, or multiplying factors, to express the number of times by which an exposure must be increased for a given filter. Published filter factors are intended only as approximate guidelines, as actual factors vary for different exposure conditions [12].

2.11   AERIAL CAMERAS

Aerial photographs can be made with virtually any type of camera. Many successful applications have employed aerial photographs made from light aircraft with hand-held 35 mm cameras. For example, the photographs in Plates 2−4 and 8 were made in this manner. The simplicity and low cost of purchase and operation of 35 mm cameras make them ideal sensors for small area analysis. (The true size of images taken with a 35 mm system is 24 × 36 mm; the width of the film is 35 mm.) For large area coverage with 35 mm cameras, various camera mounts have been fabricated for image acquisition from light aircraft. Figure 2.19 shows such a mount that can be clamped to the left door without aircraft modification. As discussed later in this section, 70 mm cameras

FIGURE 2.19   Camera mount for attaching 35-mm camera to a light aircraft for vertical aerial photography. Camera can be slid on mount to permit film and filter changes. (Courtesy University of Minnesota Remote Sensing Laboratory.)

are also used in certain applications. (The true size of images made with these systems is 55 × 55 mm.) Most aerial photographic remote sensing endeavors, however, entail the use of aerial photography made with precision-built aerial cameras. These cameras are specifically designed to expose a large number of photographs in rapid succession with the ultimate in geometric fidelity.

There are over 100 different models of aerial cameras currently in use. They can be classified as one of four basic types: (1) *single-lens frame* cameras, (2) *multilens frame* cameras, (3) *strip* cameras, and (4) *panoramic* cameras.

Single-Lens Frame Cameras

Single-lens frame cameras are by far the most common cameras in use today. They are used almost exclusively in obtaining aerial photographs for remote sensing in general and photogrammetric mapping purposes in particular. *Mapping* cameras (often referred to as *metric* or *cartographic* cameras) are single lens frame cameras designed to provide extremely high geometric image quality. They employ a low distortion lens system held in a fixed position relative to the plane of the film. The film format size (the nominal size of each image) is commonly a square 230 mm on a side. The total width of the film used is 240 mm and the film magazine capacity ranges up to film lengths of 120 m. A frame of imagery is acquired with each opening of the camera shutter, which is generally tripped automatically at a set frequency by an electronic device called an *intervalometer*. Figure 2.20 illustrates a typical aerial mapping camera.

Recall that for an aerial camera the distance between the center of the lens system and the film plane is equal to the focal length of the lens. It is at this fixed distance that light rays coming from an effectively infinite distance away from the camera come to focus on the film. (Most mapping cameras cannot be focused for use at close range.) For mapping purposes, 152 mm focal length lenses are most widely used. Lenses with 90 and 210 mm focal lengths are also used for mapping. Longer focal lengths, such as 300 mm, are used for very high altitude applications. Frame camera lenses are somewhat loosely termed as being either (1) *normal angle* (when the angular field of

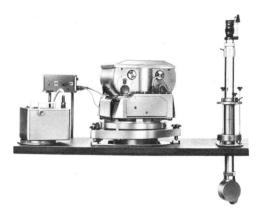

FIGURE 2.20 Aerial mapping camera, Zeiss Model RMK-A-15/23, with aircraft mount, intervalometer, and navigation telescope. (Courtesy Carl Zeiss, Inc.)

view of the lens system is up to 75°), (2) *wide angle* (when the field of view is 75° to 100°), and (3) *super wide angle* (when the field of view is greater than 100°), (angle measured along image diagonal).

Figure 2.21 illustrates the principal components of a single lens frame mapping camera. The *lens cone assembly* includes the *lens, filter, shutter,* and *diaphragm.* The lens is generally composed of multiple lens elements that gather the light rays from a scene and bring them to focus in the *focal plane.* The filter serves any of the various functions enumerated in the previous section. The shutter and diaphragm (typically located between lens elements) control film exposure. The shutter controls the duration of exposure (from 1/100 to 1/1000 sec) while the diaphragm forms an aperture that can be varied in size. The camera *body* typically houses an electrical film drive mechanism for advancing the film, flattening the film during exposure, cocking the shutter, and tripping the shutter. The *camera magazine* holds the film supply and takeup reels, the film advancing mechanism, and the film flattening mechanism. Film flattening during exposure is often accomplished by drawing the film against a vacuum plate lying behind the focal plane. The focal plane is the plane in which the film is

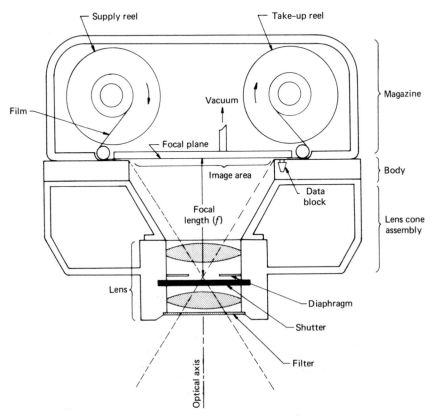

FIGURE 2.21 Principal components of a single-lens frame mapping camera.

exposed. The *optical axis* of the camera is perpendicular to the film plane and extends through the center of the lens system.

During the time a frame camera shutter is opened for exposure of a photograph, aircraft motion causes the image to blur. To negate this effect, many frame cameras have built-in *image motion compensation*. This works by moving the film across the focal plane at a rate just equal to the rate of image movement.

Figure 2.22 illustrates the modular nature of modern aerial mapping camera systems. The same camera body may be used in multiple configurations of various lens cones, filters, magazines, intervalometers, and viewing devices. Shown in Figure 2.23 is a *vertical photograph* made with a mapping camera whose optical axis was directed as nearly vertical as possible at the instant of exposure. Note the appearance of the four *fiducial marks* at the middle of the image sides. (As illustrated in Figure 5.7, some mapping cameras incorporate corner fiducials.) These marks define the frame of reference for spatial measurements made from such aerial photos (explained in Chapter 5). Lines connecting opposite fiducial marks intersect approximately at a photograph's *principal point*. As part of the manufacturer's calibration of a mapping camera, the camera focal length, the distances between fiducial marks, and the exact location of the principal point are precisely determined.

Figure 2.24 illustrates the *Large Format Camera* (LFC), a special purpose mapping camera built for NASA to meet the demands of performance at orbital altitudes. In its primary mode of operation, the LFC is carried into orbit, operated, and returned to earth while mounted in the Space Shuttle's cargo bay. It could also be mounted in a free-flying spacecraft (with film to be changed by Shuttle astronauts) or mounted in an aircraft. The LFC is a precision cartographic camera with high geometric fidelity and has an advanced image motion compensation mechanism (Shuttle ground velocity is approximately 27,000 km/hr). It has a 305 mm focal length lens and a 230 × 460 mm image format with the long dimension oriented in the direction of flight. The camera

FIGURE 2.22 Array of interchangeable system components of Wild RC-10 aerial mapping camera. (Courtesy Wild Heerbrugg, Inc.)

FIGURE 2.23   Vertical aerial photograph taken with a 230 × 230 mm precision mapping camera showing Langenburg, Germany. Note the camera fiducial marks on each side of the image. Data blocks (on left of image) record image identification, clock, level bubble, and altimeter. (Frame number is recorded in lower left corner of image. 1:13,200. (Courtesy Carl Zeiss, Inc.)

has been "space-hardened," which means that it has the pressure, temperature, and motion control systems to allow it to operate in a space environment and to withstand numerous Shuttle launches. A disassembled lens for this camera is shown in Figure 2.25. This lens has a resolution more than three times higher than that of conventional mapping lenses and geometric distortions of less than 15 μm over the full image area.

The LFC was first flown on Shuttle Mission 41-G, in October 1984. On this mission, the ground coverage of this oversized film format was approximately 180 × 360 km when the spacecraft was at a flying height of 235 km, and 285 × 570 km when at a flying height of 375 km. Stereoscopic coverage, with variable overlaps (20, 40, 60, and 80 percent), was also obtained by the system (Section 2.13).[2]

---

[2]LFC photography is available commercially from Chicago Aerial Survey, Inc., 2140 Wolf Road, Des Plaines, Ill. 60018.

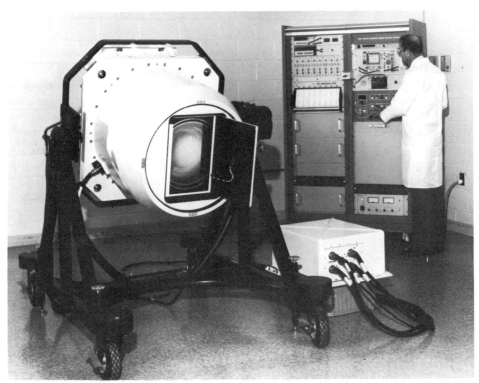

FIGURE 2.24 Large Format Camera (LFC). (Courtesy ITEK Optical Systems.)

FIGURE 2.25 Large Format Camera lens (disassembled). (Courtesy ITEK Optical Systems.)

Figure 2.26 is a full frame LFC photograph covering a 180 × 360 km area from the Italian Alps at top to the Adriatic Sea at bottom. (North is to the upper right of this figure.) The top part of this image is cloud covered, but appearing just below that area are the snow covered peaks of the Italian Alps. Lake de Garda appears at the base of the mountains. The Po River flows from upper left (west) to lower right (east) and discharges into the Adriatic Sea at lower right. The Po River flood plain is frequently flooded, and the express purpose for LFC coverage of this area was to study and map drainage patterns in the hills and mountains within the Po River basin. Figure 2.27 is an enlargement of a portion of Figure 2.26 and shows the silt-laden Po River discharging its sediments into the Adriatic Sea. Figure 2.28 is a stereopair that shows the area around Lake de Garda and illustrates the stereoscopic capability of the LFC camera system.

Also flown onboard the Space Shuttle, as part of the Spacelab program, has been the European Space Agency's *Metric Camera.* This camera is a precision 230 mm format mapping camera having a 305 mm focal length lens. It is the first of a series of space camera deployments being coordinated by the Federal Republic of Germany. Together with the Large Format Camera, this system has clearly established the feasibility and utility of photographic interpretation and mapmaking from space [4, 8].

It should be noted that there are many single-lens frame cameras that are strictly *reconnaissance* cameras, as opposed to mapping cameras. These cameras come in a wide variety of configurations and are not described in any detail here. Most are designed to faithfully record image detail without necessarily providing the geometric fidelity of mapping cameras. However, to acquire high quality color photographs these cameras must have color-corrected lenses that focus all colors at the same image plane. Many reconnaissance cameras have been designed for optimum focusing when black and white photography is taken through a minus blue filter. Such cameras are generally not acceptable for color work because blue image light that they record will be out of focus and degrade image quality.

Finally, single-lens frame cameras are normally used to produce photographs over a broad wavelength region, or band, of the electromagnetic spectrum. For example, color photography is produced over a range of about 0.4 to 0.7 μm. Terrain features having substantially different spectral response patterns over this range can normally be discriminated on color film. However, many terrain features have only slight differences in spectral reflectance and their differentiation on conventional broadband photography is often impossible. As described below, *multiband photography* can often be used to circumvent this problem.

Multilens Frame Cameras

Multiband photographs are photographs taken simultaneously from the same geometric vantage point, but with different film–filter combinations. Figure 2.29 illustrates a multilens frame camera designed to acquire multiband photography in four spectral bands. An example of the photographs acquired with a multilens camera system is shown in Figure 2.30. These photographs depict the identical scene imaged on black and white infrared film filtered for discrete wavelength bands in the blue, green, red, and near-infrared portions of the spectrum. Note that the "best" image or combi-

FIGURE 2.26 Full-frame Large Format Camera photograph, northern Italy, October 9, 1984. 1:2,000,000 (2.6 times reduction from original image size). (Courtesy NASA and ITEK Optical Systems.)

FIGURE 2.27 Enlargement of a portion of Large Format Camera photograph shown in Figure 2.26. 1:390,000 (2.0 times enlargement from original image scale). (Courtesy NASA and ITEK Optical Systems.)

nation of images for discriminating a given scene object varies with the spectral response pattern for that object. The "taking apart" of object reflectances through multiband photography normally yields enhanced contrast between different terrain feature types and between different conditions of the same feature type. To optimize this contrast, film–filter combinations are chosen for the specific features of

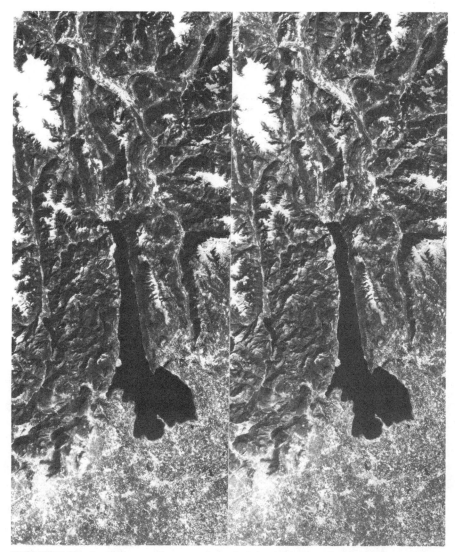

FIGURE 2.28   Large Format Camera stereopair, Lake de Garda and vicinity, Italy, October 9, 1984. 1:780,000 (same scale as original image). (Courtesy NASA and ITEK Optical Systems.)

interest in spectral regions where the maximum spectral reflectance differences are known, or are anticipated, to exist.

One basic problem in using multiband photography is the fact that simultaneous analysis of multiple images of a single ground scene is inherently difficult. *Color additive viewers* are designed to assist in the interpretation of multiband photography.

FIGURE 2.29   Multilens frame camera. (Courtesy Spectral Data Corp.)

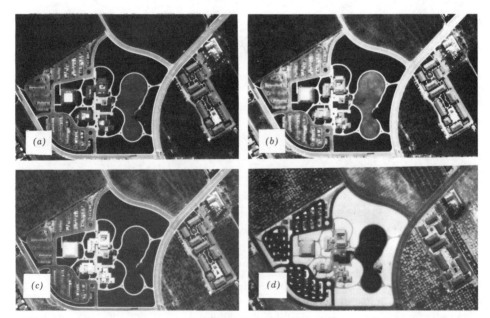

FIGURE 2.30   Multiband aerial photographs imaged on black and white infrared film through four different filters. (a) Blue filter (Wratten™ 47B). (b) Green filter (Wratten™ 57A). (c) Red filter (Wratten™ 25). (d) Infrared filter (Wratten™ 88A). (Courtesy International Imaging Systems.)

As shown in Figures 2.31 and 2.32, these devices normally incorporate four projectors that are aimed at a single viewing screen. Each projector has a variable brightness and color filter control. In the operation of the viewer, the image analyst uses up to four black and white multiband images that are in a positive transparency format. The transparency for a particular spectral band is placed in a projector and projected through the color filter (blue, green, or red) assigned to that band by the analyst. Optical superimposition of multiple bands in this fashion results in the production of *color composite images* on the viewer screen in accordance with color additive principles. Normally, three projectors are used simultaneously. Optical combination of spectral positives from the blue, green, and red portions of the spectrum results in a "true" color display. Projection of positives taken in the green, red, and the near-

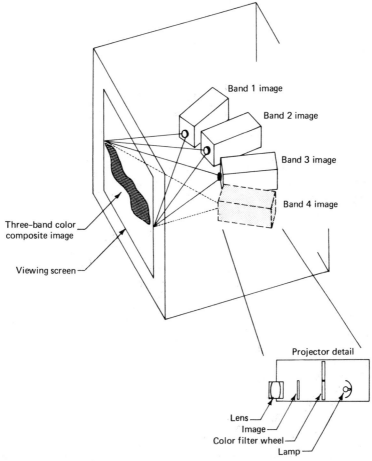

FIGURE 2.31 Color additive viewer schematic. The image analyst selects the two or three images to be optically combined. Each projector has separate brightness, filter color, and image registration controls.

FIGURE 2.32   Color additive viewer. (Courtesy Spectral Data Corp.)

infrared results in a "false" color display similar to color infrared photography. Through arbitrary assignment of positives and color filters, "exotic" color displays can be created that often enhance discrimination of features of interest. For example, the viewer might be adjusted to display a particular crop type in a unique, readily discriminated color.

Plate 5 shows color composites produced in a color additive viewer. Plate 5a shows multiband images combined to resemble a normal color photograph and Plate 5b shows images combined to resemble a color infrared photograph. For each color composite, three of the black and white positive transparencies shown in Figure 2.30 were used, as follows:

Plate 5a: normal color		Plate 5b: false color	
Camera filter	Viewer filter	Camera filter	Viewer filter
Blue (0.4–0.5 μm)	Blue	Green (0.5–0.6 μm)	Blue
Green (0.5–0.6 μm)	Green	Red (0.6–0.7 μm)	Green
Red (0.6–0.7 μm)	Red	Near-IR (0.7–0.9 μm)	Red

The camera filter colors used correspond to the spectral sensitivity of the three layers of color and color infrared film. The viewer filter colors are the three primary colors of the additive color process. Other false color combinations could be produced from the positive transparencies shown in Figure 2.30 by using different positive transparency–viewer filter combinations.

FIGURE 2.33 Array of 70 mm Hasselblad cameras used to obtain multiband photography.

As an alternative to using multilens cameras, it should be noted that multiband photography can be acquired using arrays of several single-lens frame cameras. Typical of such camera banks is the four-camera, 70 mm format Hasselblad system shown in Figure 2.33. Each camera has its own internal power supply and film advance mechanism. The images from these cameras are 55 mm square. All the cameras can be triggered simultaneously, providing multispectral capability when a different film–filter combination is used in each camera.

Strip Cameras

Strip cameras (Figure 2.34) record images by moving film past a fixed slit in the focal plane as the camera is moved forward. The shutter for a strip camera remains open continually while the picture is made. Image blur is eliminated by passing the film over the open slit at a rate equal to the speed of the moving image (*proportional* to aircraft speed). Thus, the strip camera has inherent image motion compensation. The width of the adjustable camera slit determines exposure.

Strip cameras were designed primarily for low altitude, high speed military reconnaissance. Under these flight conditions, the inherent continuous image motion compensation of the strip camera permits obtainment of very detailed photography, which could not be achieved with a frame camera. Also, for a given width of ground coverage, a smaller field of view is needed for a strip camera. For example, the same area could be covered with a 74° (side-to-side) strip camera lens as with a 90° (corner-to-corner) frame camera lens. Hence, lens distortions are less.

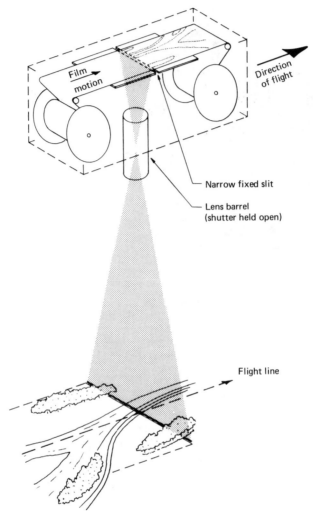

FIGURE 2.34 Operating principle of a continuous strip camera.

Strip cameras were once popular for civilian applications where detail along linear study areas is needed, as, for example, in highway or transmission line route selection. However, when a strip camera is operated at high altitude and moderate speed, the resulting imagery is distorted by any change in aircraft orientation, speed, or altitude. This factor—coupled with improvements in the lens and image motion compensation characteristics of frame cameras—makes current application of strip photography very limited.

Panoramic Cameras

The last major type of camera we consider is the panoramic camera. Like the strip camera, a panoramic camera views only a comparatively narrow angular field at any given instant through a narrow slit. Ground areas are covered by either rotating the camera lens or rotating a prism in front of the lens. Figure 2.35 illustrates the design using lens rotation.

In Figure 2.35, the terrain is scanned from side to side, transverse to the direction of flight. The film is exposed along a curved surface located at the focal distance from the rotating lens assembly, and the angular coverage of the camera can extend from horizon to horizon. The exposure slit moves along the film as the lens rotates, and the

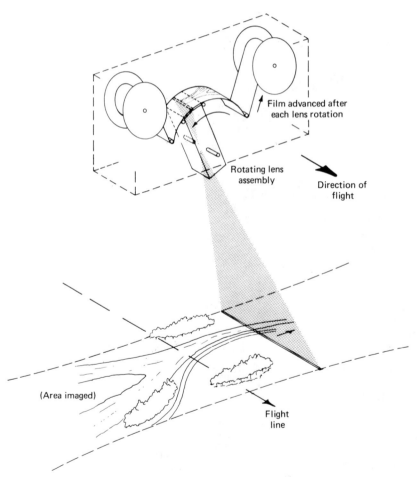

Film advanced after
each lens rotation

Rotating lens
assembly

Direction of
flight

(Area imaged)

Flight
line

FIGURE 2.35 Operating principle of a panoramic camera.

film is held fixed during a given exposure. After one scan is completed, the film is advanced for the next exposure.

Panoramic cameras incorporating the rotating prism design contain a fixed lens and a flat film plane. Scanning is accomplished by rotating the prism in front of the lens, yielding imagery geometrically equivalent to that of the rotating lens camera.

Figure 2.36 illustrates the pictorial detail and large area of coverage characteristic of panoramic photography. The distortions inherent in panoramic imaging are also apparent in the figure. Areas near the two ends of the photograph are compressed. This scale variation, called *panoramic distortion*, is a result of the cylindrical shape of the

FIGURE 2.36 Panoramic photograph with 180° scan angle. Note image detail, large area of coverage, and geometric distortion. (Courtesy USAF Rome Air Development Center.)

focal plane and the nature of scanning. Also, *scan positional distortion* is introduced in panoramic imaging due to forward motion of the aircraft during the time a scan is made.

Figure 2.37 shows an optical bar panoramic camera being loaded into a NASA U-2 reconnaissance aircraft. This camera incorporates a 610 mm focal length lens, has a total field of view of 120° (60° to each side of the flight line), and has a film capacity of 2000 m. When operated from NASA research aircraft, the camera is typically flown at an altitude of 19,800 m. This yields extremely broad ground coverage, extending 34.3 km to each side of the flight path. As shown in Figure 2.38, the camera can also be used to obtain stereoscopic coverage over the same area. Such cameras have been used extensively for high altitude aerial reconnaissance, and were used to photograph more than half the area of the moon during NASA's Apollo missions.

Compared to frame cameras, panoramic cameras cover a much larger ground area. With their narrower lens fields of view, panoramic cameras produce images with greater detail than frame images. Hence, panoramic images yield a broad, yet detailed, view of the ground. These factors make panoramic cameras ideal sensors in large area photographic analyses; *however*, panoramic photographs have the disadvantage that they lack the geometric fidelity of frame camera images.

Panoramic photography has been used extensively by the U.S. Forest Service (USFS) and the U.S. Environmental Protection Agency (EPA).

The USFS has used panoramic cameras for photographic interpretation purposes such as forest pest damage detection and planning the associated timber salvage operations (see Plate 6). The principal advantages of the panoramic camera in such

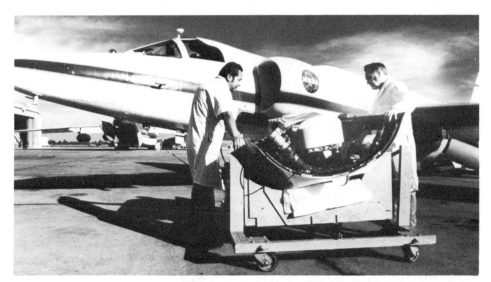

FIGURE 2.37 Optical bar panoramic camera being loaded into NASA U-2 reconnaissance aircraft. (Courtesy ITEK Optical Systems.)

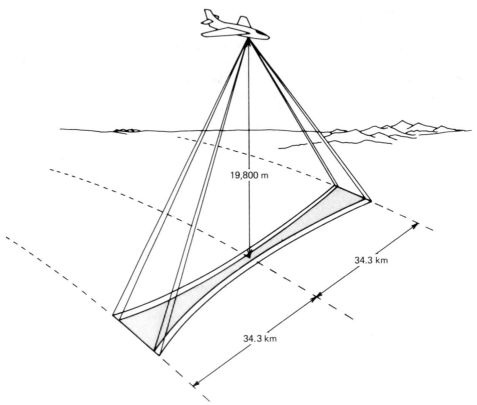

19,800 m

34.3 km

34.3 km

FIGURE 2.38 Typical ground coverage pattern using the optical bar panoramic camera (shaded area represents area of image overlap). (Adapted from ITEK Optical Systems drawing.)

applications are its high image resolution and large area of coverage. The principal disadvantages are its unusual image format of 115×1500 mm and the continuously changing photo scale [2, 6].

The EPA has operated panoramic cameras from a device called the "Enviro-Pod." The device is strapped underneath an aircraft and typically contains two panoramic cameras that record on 70 mm film. One camera is aimed vertically and the other is mounted in a forward-looking orientation. The forward-looking orientation permits the photographing of some objects that are obscured in the vertical photographs (for example, barrels under a shed roof). The Enviro-Pod is frequently used to obtain high-resolution images of industrial pollutants, hazardous waste sites, emergency episodes, and other activities of environmental consequence [14].

All photographs in the remainder of this book were taken with frame cameras.

2.12 TYPES OF AERIAL PHOTOGRAPHS

Aerial photographs are generally classified as either vertical or oblique. *Vertical photographs* are those made with the camera axis directed as vertically as possible (Figure 2.23). Vertical photography made with a single-lens frame camera is by far the most common type of aerial photography used in remote sensing applications. However, a "truly" vertical aerial photograph is rarely obtainable because of unavoidable angular rotations, or tilts, caused by the angular attitude of the aircraft at the instant of exposure. These unavoidable tilts cause slight (1 to 3°) unintentional inclination of the camera optical axis, resulting in the acquisition of *tilted photographs*.

Virtually all photographs are tilted. When tilted unintentionally and slightly, tilted photographs are usually referred to as being "vertical." For most elementary measurement applications, these photographs are treated as being vertical without introduction of serious error (see Chapter 5).

When aerial photographs are taken with an intentional inclination of the camera axis, *oblique photographs* result. *High oblique photographs* include an image of the horizon (Plate 4), and *low oblique photographs* do not (Plate 2).

2.13 TAKING VERTICAL AERIAL PHOTOGRAPHS

Most vertical aerial photographs are taken with frame cameras along *flight lines*, or *flight strips*. The line traced on the ground directly beneath the aircraft during acquisition of photography is called the *nadir line*. This line connects the image centers of the vertical photographs. Figure 2.39 illustrates the typical character of the photographic coverage along a flight line. Successive photographs are generally taken with some degree of *endlap*. Not only does this lapping ensure total coverage along a flight line, but an endlap of least 50 percent is essential for total *stereoscopic coverage* of a project area. Stereoscopic coverage consists of adjacent pairs of overlapping vertical photographs called *stereopairs*. Stereopairs provide two different perspectives of the ground area in their region of endlap. When images forming a stereopair are viewed through a stereoscope, each eye psychologically occupies the vantage point from which the respective image of the stereopair was taken in flight. The result is the perception of a three-dimensional *stereomodel*. As pointed out in subsequent chapters, most applications of aerial photographic interpretation entail the use of stereoscopic coverage and stereoviewing.

Successive photographs along a flight strip are taken at intervals that are controlled by the camera intervalometer. The area included in the overlap of successive photographs is called the *stereoscopic overlap area*. Typically, successive photographs contain 55 to 65 percent overlap to ensure at least 50 percent endlap over varying terrain, in spite of unintentional tilt. Figure 2.40 illustrates the ground coverage relationship of successive photographs forming a stereopair having approximately a 60 percent stereoscopic overlap area.

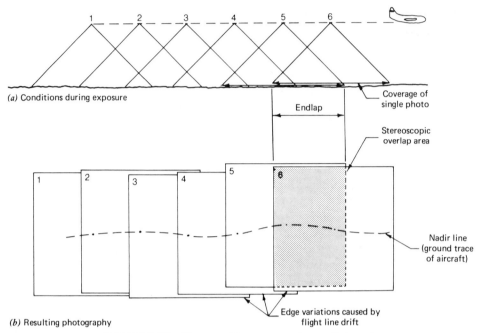

(a) Conditions during exposure

Coverage of single photo

Endlap

Stereoscopic overlap area

Nadir line (ground trace of aircraft)

Edge variations caused by flight line drift

(b) Resulting photography

FIGURE 2.39   Photographic coverage along a flight strip.

FIGURE 2.40   Acquisition of successive photographs yielding a stereopair. (Courtesy Wild Heerbrugg, Inc.)

Figure 2.41 shows LFC images of Mt. Washington and vicinity, New Hampshire. These stereopairs illustrate the effect of varying the percentage of photo overlap, and thus the base–height ratio (Section 4.4), of the photographs. These photographs were taken from a flying height of 364 km. The stereopair in *(a)* has a base–height ratio of 0.30. The stereopair in *(b)* has a base–height ratio of 1.2 and shows much greater apparent relief (greater vertical exaggeration) than *(a)*.

Most project sites are large enough for multiple flight line passes to be made over the area to obtain complete stereoscopic coverage. Figure 2.42 illustrates how adjacent strips are photographed. On successive flights over the area, adjacent strips have *sidelap* of approximately 30 percent. Multiple strips comprise what is called a *block* of

FIGURE 2.41 Large Format Camera stereopairs, Mt. Washington and vicinity, New Hampshire, April 4, 1985. 1:800,000 (1.5 times enlargement from original image scale). *(a)* 0.30 base–height ratio. *(b)* 1.2 base–height ratio. (Courtesy NASA and ITEK Optical Systems.)

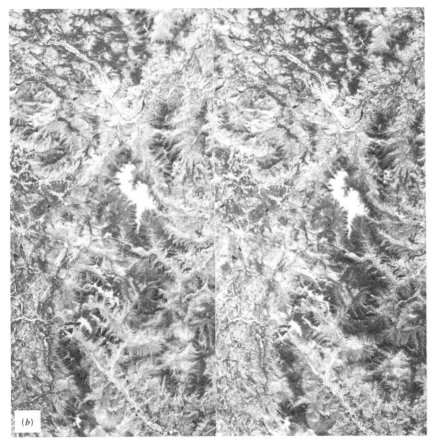

(b)

FIGURE 2.41   (continued)

photographs. Modern high altitude aerial surveys frequently employ data from the aircraft's precise inertial navigation system to control flight line direction, flight line spacing, and photo exposure intervals.

A given photographic mission can entail the acquisition of literally hundreds of exposures. Quite often, a flight *index mosaic* is assembled by piecing together the individual photographs into a single continuous picture. This enables convenient visual reference to the area included in each image. Figure 2.43 illustrates such a mosaic.

2.14   SCALE OF AERIAL PHOTOGRAPHS

The amount of detail shown in an aerial photograph is dependent, among other things, on the scale of the photograph. A photograph "scale," like a map scale, is an expression

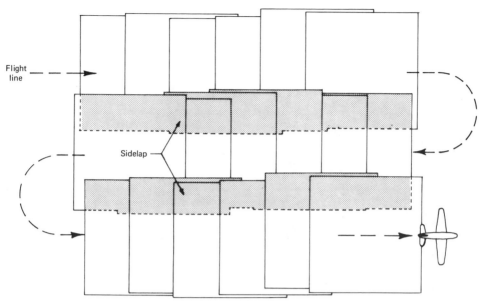

FIGURE 2.42   Adjacent flight lines over a project area.

that states that one unit (any unit) of distance on a photograph represents a specific number of units of actual ground distance. Scales may be expressed as *unit equivalents*, *representative fractions*, or *ratios*. For example, if 1 mm on a photograph represents 25 m on the ground, the scale of the photograph can be expressed as 1 mm = 25 m (unit equivalents), or 1/25,000 (representative fraction), or 1:25,000 (ratio).

Quite often the terms "large scale" and "small scale" are confused by those not working with expressions of scale on a routine basis. For example, which photograph would have the "larger" scale—a 1:10,000 scale photo covering several city blocks or a 1:50,000 photo that covers an entire city? The intuitive answer is often that the photo covering the larger "area" (the entire city) is the larger scale product. This is not the case. The larger scale product is the 1:10,000 image because it shows ground features at a larger, more detailed, size. The 1:50,000 scale photo of the entire city would render ground features at a much smaller, less detailed size. Hence, in spite of its larger ground coverage, the 1:50,000 photo would be termed the smaller scale product. A convenient way to make scale comparisons is to remember that the same objects are smaller on a "smaller" scale photograph than on a "larger" scale photo. Scale comparisons can also be made by comparing the magnitudes of the representative fractions involved. (That is, 1/50,000 is smaller than 1/10,000.)

The most straightforward method for determining photo scale is to measure the corresponding photo and ground distances between any two points. This requires that

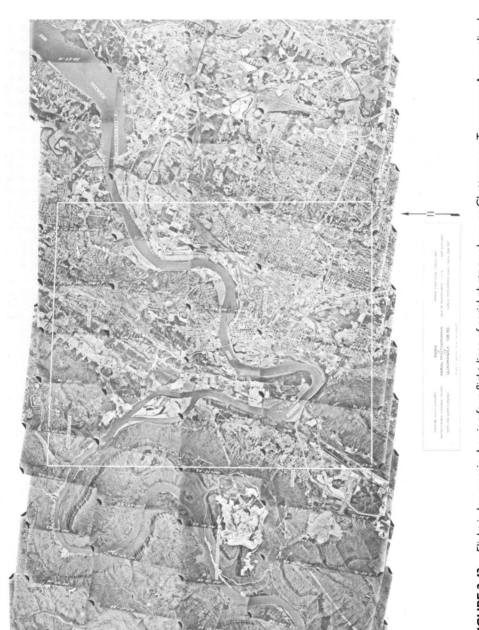

FIGURE 2.43   Flight index mosaic showing four flight lines of aerial photography over Chattanooga, Tennessee. Area outlined in white indicates coverage area of a single 1:24,000 quadrangle map. (Courtesy Mapping Services Branch, Tennessee Valley Authority.)

the points be mutually identifiable on both the photo and a map. The scale, S, is then computed as the ratio of the photo distance, d, to the ground distance, D,

$$S = \text{photo scale} = \frac{\text{photo distance}}{\text{ground distance}} = \frac{d}{D} \qquad (2.5)$$

EXAMPLE 2.3

Assume that two road intersections shown on a photograph can be located on a 1:25,000 scale topographic map. If the measured distance between the intersections is 47.2 mm on the map and 94.3 mm on the photograph, (a) What is the scale of the photograph? (b) At that scale, what is the length of a fence line which measures 42.9 mm on the photograph?

Solution

(a) The ground distance between the intersections is determined from the map scale as

$$0.0472 \text{ m} \times \frac{25{,}000}{1} = 1180 \text{ m}$$

By direct ratio, the photo scale is

$$S = \frac{0.0943 \text{ m}}{1180 \text{ m}} = \frac{1}{12{,}513} \text{ or } 1{:}12{,}500$$

(Note that because only three significant, or meaningful, figures were present in the original measurements, only three significant figures are indicated in the final result.)

(b) The ground length of the 42.9 mm fence line is

$$D = \frac{d}{S} = 0.0429 \text{ m} \div \frac{1}{12{,}500} = 536.25 \text{ m or } 536 \text{ m}$$

For a vertical photograph taken over flat terrain, scale is a function of the focal length, f, of the camera used to acquire the image and the flying height above the ground, H', from which the image was taken. In general,

$$\text{scale} = \frac{\text{camera focal length}}{\text{flying height above terrain}} = \frac{f}{H'} \qquad (2.6)$$

  Figure 2.44 illustrates how we arrive at Eq. 2.6. Shown in this figure is the side view of a vertical photograph taken over flat terrain. The center of the camera lens is located at the *exposure station*, L, at the instant of exposure. Exposure station L is at an aircraft *flying height*, H, above some *datum*, or arbitrary base elevation. The datum most frequently used is mean sea level. If flying height H and the elevation of the terrain h are known, we can determine H' by subtraction ($H' = H - h$). If we now consider terrain points A, O, and B, they are imaged at points a', o', and b' on the negative film and at a, o, and b on the positive print. Note that both the negative and the positive are schematically shown at a distance f from the camera lens. This assumes that the sizes

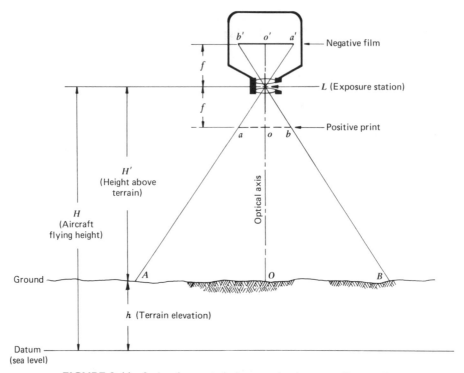

FIGURE 2.44   Scale of a vertical photograph taken over flat terrain.

of the negative and positive are equal. This is appropriate in that most positives are produced through contact printing, resulting in the depicted geometry. Finally, we can derive an expression for photo scale by observing similar triangles Lao and LAO, which are corresponding photo and ground distances. That is,

$$S = \frac{ao}{AO} = \frac{f}{H'} \tag{2.7}$$

Equation 2.7 is identical to our scale expression of Eq.2.6. Yet another way of expressing these equations is

$$S = \frac{f}{H - h} \tag{2.8}$$

Equation 2.8 is the most commonly used form of the scale equation.

EXAMPLE 2.4

A camera equipped with a 152 mm focal length lens is used to take a vertical photograph from a flying height of 2780 m above mean sea level. If the terrain is flat and located at an elevation of 500 m, what is the scale of the photograph?

Solution

$$\text{Scale} = \frac{f}{H - h} = \frac{0.152 \text{ m}}{2780 \text{ m} - 500 \text{ m}} = \frac{1}{15,000} \text{ or } 1{:}15{,}000$$

The most important principle expressed by Eq. 2.8 is that photo scale is a function of terrain elevation, h. Because of the level terrain, the photograph depicted in Figure 2.44 has a constant scale. However, *photographs taken over terrain of varying elevation will exhibit a continuous range of scales associated with the variations in terrain elevation.* Likewise, tilted and oblique photographs have nonuniform scales.

EXAMPLE 2.5

Assume a vertical photograph was taken at a flying height of 5000 m above sea level using a camera with a 152 mm focal length lens. Determine the photo scale at points A and B, which lie at elevations of 1200 and 1960 m.

Solution

By Eq. 2.8,

$$S_A = \frac{f}{H - h_A} = \frac{0.152 \text{ m}}{5000 \text{ m} - 1200 \text{ m}} = \frac{1}{25,000} \text{ or } 1{:}25{,}000$$

$$S_B = \frac{f}{H - h_B} = \frac{0.152 \text{ m}}{5000 \text{ m} - 1960 \text{ m}} = \frac{1}{20,000} \text{ or } 1{:}20{,}000$$

Often it is convenient to compute an *average scale* for an entire photograph. This scale is calculated using the average terrain elevation for the area imaged. Consequently, it is exact for distances occurring at the average elevation and is approximate at all other elevations. Average scale may be expressed as

$$S_{avg} = \frac{f}{H - h_{avg}} \tag{2.9}$$

where h_{avg} = the average elevation of the terrain shown in the photograph.

The result of photo scale variation is geometric distortion. All points on a *map* are depicted in their true relative horizontal (planimetric) positions, but points on a *photo* taken over varying terrain are displaced from their true "map positions." This difference results because a map is a scaled *orthographic* projection of the ground surface. The differing nature of these two forms of projection is illustrated in Figure 2.45. As shown, a map results from projecting vertical rays from ground points to the map sheet (at a particular scale). A photograph results from projecting converging rays through a

Top View

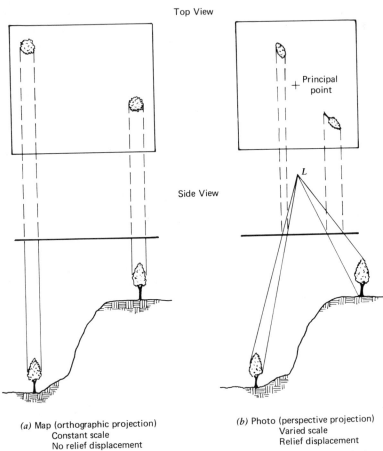

(a) Map (orthographic projection)
Constant scale
No relief displacement

(b) Photo (perspective projection)
Varied scale
Relief displacement

FIGURE 2.45 Comparative geometry of a map (a) and a vertical aerial photograph (b). Note differences in size, shape, and location of the two trees.

common point within the camera lens. Because of the nature of this projection, any variations in terrain elevation will result in scale variation *and* displaced image positions.

On a map we see a top view of objects in their true relative horizontal positions. On a photograph, areas of terrain at the higher elevations lie closer to the camera at the time of exposure and therefore appear larger than corresponding areas lying at lower elevations. Furthermore, the tops of objects are always displaced from their bases (Figure 2.45). This distortion is called *relief displacement* and causes any object standing above the terrain to "lean" away from the principal point of a photograph radially. Relief displacement is directly proportional to the height of the object imaged, inversely proportional to flying height above ground, H', and directly proportional to radial distance to the object from the principal point. Hence, extremes in relief displacement are encountered when tall objects appear at the edges of a photograph taken from a low flying height above the terrain.

By now the student should see that the inherent geometry of aerial photographs precludes their use as maps directly. However, reliable ground measurements and maps can be obtained from vertical photographs if precise photo measurements are analyzed with due regard for scale variations and relief displacement. In Chapter 5 we discuss how aerial photographs are used individually, and in stereopairs, to obtain reliable ground measurements and maps.

2.15 GROUND COVERAGE OF AERIAL PHOTOGRAPHS

The ground coverage of a photograph is, among other things, a function of camera format size. For example, an image taken with a camera having a 230 × 230 mm format (on 240 mm film) has about 17.5 times the ground area coverage of an image of equal scale taken with a camera having a 55 × 55 mm format (on 70 mm film), and about 61 times the ground area coverage of an image of equal scale taken with a camera having a 24 × 36 mm format (on 35 mm film). As with photo scale, the ground coverage of photography obtained with any given format is a function of focal length and flying height above ground, H'. Figure 2.46 illustrates the principle that for a constant flying height, the width of the ground area covered by a photo varies inversely with focal length. Consequently, photos taken with shorter focal length lenses have larger areas of coverage (and smaller scales) than do those taken with longer focal length lenses. In Figure 2.46, if $f_1 = \frac{1}{2} f_2$, $D_1 = 2D_2$, and $A_1 = 4A_2$.

For any given focal length lens, the width of the ground area covered by a photo varies directly with flying height above terrain. This is illustrated in Figure 2.47 where f = constant, but $H'_2 = 2H'_1$. In this case, $D_2 = 2D_1$ and $A_2 = 4A_1$. Again, image scale would vary inversely with flying height.

The effect flying height has on ground coverage and image scale is illustrated in Figures 2.48a, b, and c. These images were all taken over Chattanooga, Tennessee, with the same camera type, equipped with the same focal length lens, but from three different altitudes. Figure 2.48a is a high altitude, small scale image showing virtually the entire Chattanooga metropolitan area. Figure 2.48b is a lower altitude, larger scale image showing the ground area outlined in Figure 2.48a. Figure 2.48c is a yet lower altitude, larger scale image of the area outlined in Figure 2.48b. Note the trade-offs between the ground area covered by an image and the object detail available in each of the photographs. In general, the larger the scale of the photograph, the greater its ability to record detail. But, as described in the next section, photographs can possess equal scales and still not have the same spatial resolution.

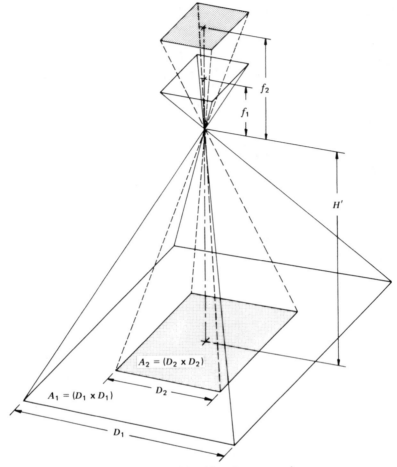

FIGURE 2.46   Effect of focal length on ground coverage.

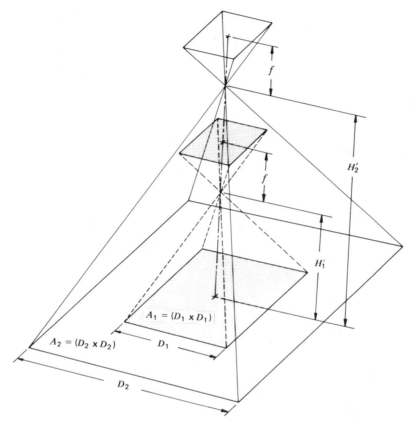

FIGURE 2.47   Effect of flying height on ground coverage.

FIGURE 2.48 *(a)* 1:240,000 vertical aerial photograph showing Chattanooga, Tennessee, May 21, 1971. This figure is a 2× reduction of an original photograph taken with $f = 152.4$ mm from 18,300 m flying height. (NASA photograph. Courtesy Mapping Services Branch, Tennessee Valley Authority.)

(b)

FIGURE 2.48 (b) 1:40,000 vertical aerial photograph providing coverage of area outlined in Figure 2.48a, February 25, 1976. This figure is a 2× reduction of an original photograph taken with $f = 152.4$ mm from 3050 m flying height. (Courtesy Mapping Services Branch, Tennessee Valley Authority.)

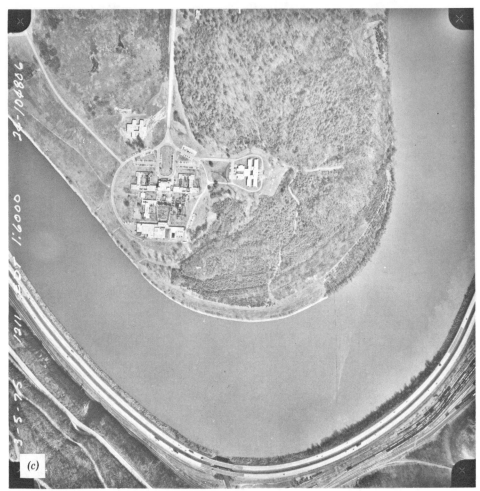

FIGURE 2.48 *(c)*. 1:12,000 vertical aerial photograph providing coverage of area outlined in Figure 2.48*b*, March 5, 1975. This figure is a 2× reduction of an original photograph taken with *f* = 152.4 mm from 915 m flying height. (Courtesy Mapping Services Branch, Tennessee Valley Authority.)

2.16 PHOTOGRAPHIC RESOLUTION

Spatial resolution is an expression of the optical quality of an image produced by a particular camera system. Resolution is influenced by a host of parameters, such as the resolving power of the film and camera lens used to obtain an image, any uncompensated image motion during exposure, the atmospheric conditions present at the time of image exposure, the conditions of film processing, and so on. Some of these elements are quantifiable. For example, we can measure the resolving power of a film by photographing a standard test chart. Such a chart is shown in Figure 2.49. It consists of

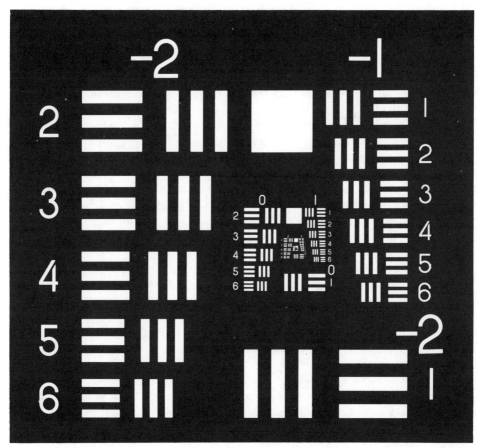

FIGURE 2.49 Resolving power test chart. (Courtesy Teledyne–Gurley Co.)

groups of three parallel lines separated by spaces equal to the width of the lines. Successive groups systematically decrease in size within the chart. The resolving power of a film is the reciprocal of the center-to-center distance (in mm) of the lines that are just "distinguishable" in the test chart image when viewed under a microscope. Hence, film resolving power is expressed in units of lines per millimeter. It is specified at a particular contrast ratio between the lines and their background. This is done because resolution is very strongly influenced by contrast. At a contrast ratio of 1.6:1, a given panchromatic film might have a resolving power of 50 lines/mm. At a contrast ratio of 1000:1 the same film might have a resolving power of 100 lines/mm.

An alternative method of determining film resolution that eliminates the subjectivity of deciding when lines are just "distinguishable" is the construction of a film's *modulation transfer function*. In this method, a microdensitometer (Section 6.5) is used to scan across images of a series of "square wave" test patterns similar to the one shown in Figure 2.50a. An ideal film would exactly record not only the brightness variation (modulation) of the test pattern, but also the distinct edges in the pattern. For actual films, the fidelity of the film recording process depends upon the spatial frequency of the pattern. For test patterns with a small number of lines per millimeter, the maximum and minimum brightness values as measured from the film image (Figure 2.50b) might correspond exactly with those of the test pattern. At the spatial frequency of this test pattern, the film's modulation transfer is said to be 100 percent. However, note that the test pattern edges are somewhat rounded on the film image. As the line width and spacing of the test pattern are reduced, density scans across the film image of the test pattern will produce both reduced modulations and increased edge rounding. This is illustrated in Figures 2.50c and d (showing 75 and 30 percent modulation transfer, respectively). By measuring film densities across many such patterns of progressively higher spatial frequency, a complete curve for the modulation transfer function can be constructed (Figure 2.51). Again, this curve expresses the fidelity with which images of features over a range of different sizes or spatial frequencies can be recorded by a given film [30].

The resolution, or modulation transfer, of any given film is primarily a function of the size distribution of the silver halide grains in the emulsion. In general, the higher the granularity of a film, the lower its resolving power. However, films of higher granularity are generally more sensitive to light, or *faster*, than those having lower granularity. Hence, there is often a trade-off between film "speed" and resolution.

The resolving power of any particular camera/film *system* can be measured by flying over and photographing a large bar target array located on the ground. The imagery thus obtained incorporates the image degradation realized in flight resulting from such factors as atmospheric effects and residual image motion during exposure (including that due to camera vibrations). The advantage to this is that we can begin to judge the *dynamic* spatial resolution of the total photographic system instead of the *static* resolution of any one of its components.

We might use the results of such a dynamic resolution test to compare various systems, but the numbers involved are difficult to interpret in a practical sense. Our interest in measuring a system's resolution goes beyond determining the ability of a system to record distinct images of small, nearly contiguous objects of a given shape on a test chart. We are interested not only in object *detection*, but also object *recognition* and *identification*. Hence, "spatial resolution" defies precise definition. At the detection level, the objective is to discern separate objects discretely. At the recognition level, we attempt to determine what objects are—for example, trees versus row crops. At the identification level, we more specifically identify objects—for example, oak trees versus corn.

The effects of scale and resolution can be combined to express image quality in terms of a *ground resolution distance* (GRD). This distance extrapolates the dynamic system resolution on a film to a ground distance. We can express this as

$$\text{GRD (m)} = \frac{\text{reciprocal of image scale}}{\text{system resolution (lines/mm)} \times 1000 \text{ mm/m}} \qquad (2.10)$$

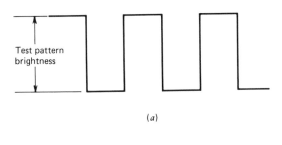

(a)

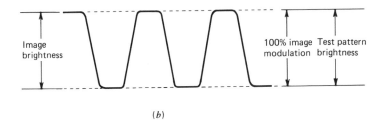

(b)

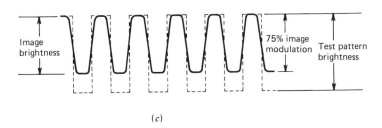

(c)

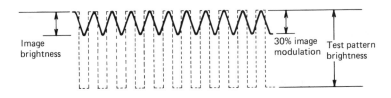

(d)

FIGURE 2.50 *(a)* Square wave test pattern. *(b)* Modulation transfer of image of test pattern shown in a. *(c, d)* Modulation transfer of images of test patterns having higher spatial frequency. (Note in *(b)* that 100 percent modulation occurs, but the image shows a reduction in edge sharpness as compared with the test pattern.) In *(c)*, edge sharpness is further reduced, and in addition, modulation transfer is reduced to 75 percent of that of the test pattern. In *(d)*, further sharpness is lost and modulation transfer is reduced to 30 percent. (Adapted from [36].)

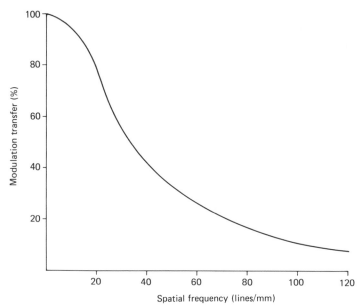

FIGURE 2.51   Curve of modulation transfer function (MTF). (Adapted from [36].)

where the 1000 is a unit conversion factor to yield the GRD in meters. For example, a 1:50,000 photograph taken with a system having a dynamic resolution of 40 lines/mm would have a ground resolution distance of

$$\text{GRD} = \frac{50,000}{(40)1000} = 1.25 \text{ m}$$

This result assumes that we are dealing with an original film, at the scale at which it was exposed. Enlargements would show some loss of image definition in the printing and enlarging process.

In summary, the ground resolution distance provides a convenient rule of thumb to compare the expected capabilities of various images to record spatial detail. However, this and any other measure of spatial resolution must be used with caution because many unpredictable variables enter into what can and cannot be detected, recognized, or identified on an aerial photograph.

2.17 NONPHOTOGRAPHIC CAMERAS

The process of photography, by definition, implies the use of a camera to record image data directly onto photographic film. Nonphotographic cameras use a camera body and lens, but record image data with light sensitive detectors that generate electrical signals that are then stored on a medium other than photographic film, such as magnetic tape or computer disks, or are fed directly into a digital computer.

Solid-State Array Cameras

Solid-State Array Cameras use one- or two-dimensional detector arrays of *charge coupled devices (CCDs)* for image data acquisition. A CCD is a microelectronic silicon chip, a solid-state sensor that detects light. When light strikes the CCD's silicon surface, electronic charges are produced, with the magnitude of the charge being proportional to the light intensity and exposure time. CCDs are capable of recording a wider range of light intensities than either photographic film or vidicon (television) cameras.

Figure 2.52, which shows a linear (one-dimensional) CCD 10,240 elements in length, illustrates the small size of CCD sensors. Because of their small size and weight, their durability, and their light sensitivity, CCDs are being employed in a number of different types of remote sensing systems. For example, the SPOT satellite (Section 9.10) uses linear arrays of 6000 elements in its panchromatic mode and 3000

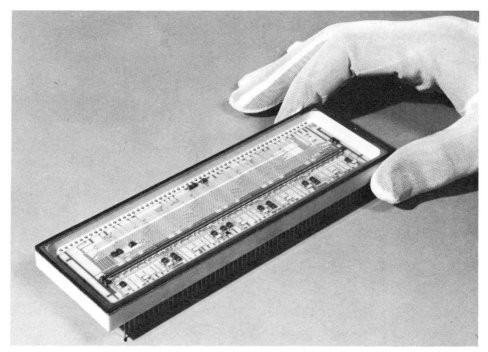

FIGURE 2.52 Linear array charge coupled device (CCD), 10,240 pixels in length, for use in a solid-state linear array camera. (Courtesy ITEK Optical Systems.)

elements in its multispectral mode. The MEIS II multispectral scanner (Section 7.15) uses a linear array of 1728 elements.

The use of a linear array to produce a two-dimensional image dictates the use of some type of scanning motion. Using a fixed camera location, this can be accomplished by rotating the camera optical system. Scanning can also be accomplished by moving the linear array relative to the scene. As shown in Figure 2.53, the linear array is normally oriented perpendicular to the direction of sensor motion. Image data in one dimension can be obtained by instantaneous sampling of the response of the detectors along the array. Successive lines forming the two-dimensional coverage are obtained by repeated sampling along the array as the sensor moves over the earth. This type of linear array scanning is referred to as *push-broom scanning.*

The use of two-dimensional arrays provides for data collection without sensor or image movement, with each detector in the array responsible for sensing one pixel in the image field. Two-dimensional array sizes typically range from 256 × 256 pixels to 2048 × 2048 pixels or more. Two-dimensional array cameras may be laboratory instru-

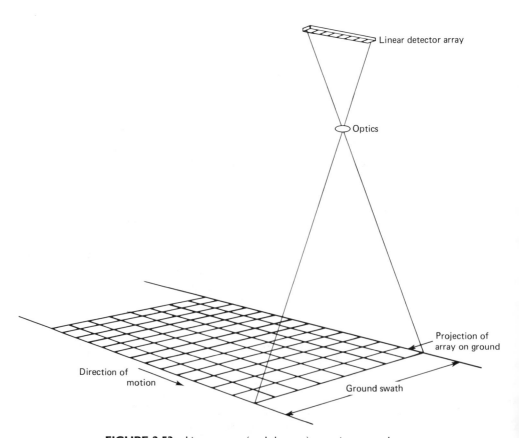

FIGURE 2.53   Linear array (push-broom) scanning procedure.

ments attached to digital computers, or may be portable cameras attached to video recorders for aerial video sensing.

Video Cameras

Video cameras are electronic sensors that generate standard television signal output, using either two-dimensional solid-state array cameras or vidicon cameras. When video cameras are used for aerial sensing, either a black and white camera, a multiband camera (color or color infrared), or multiple single-band cameras can be used. Figure 2.54 shows a typical multiband video camera that is sensitive in the green, red, and near-infrared wavelengths, simulating the spectral response of color infrared photography. Video cameras that follow the NSTC standard (U.S. and Japan) generate signals conforming to an industry standard specifying 485 lines per image frame. The odd-numbered lines are scanned in 1/60 sec and the even-numbered lines are scanned in the next 1/60 sec. If there is significant image motion, only 242 or 243 lines per frame can be utilized. If image motion is minimal, the video frame can contain the full 485 lines of good quality data. Along-line resolution varies with the equipment used but is typically on the order of 300 to 600 pixels per line. As with solid-state array cameras, video cameras can be utilized in a laboratory or for aerial video sensing.

Video Recording

Video recording involves the use of videotape recorders to record the image data from either solid-state array cameras or video cameras. Image recording can use any of a number of formats, with VHS and Beta formats being the most generally available.

The use of aerial video recorders has a number of advantages when compared with small format (35 and 70 mm) aerial photography. The image being acquired can be

FIGURE 2.54 Multiband video camera with 10 to 100 mm focal length power zoom lens. (Courtesy E. Coyote Enterprises, Inc.)

viewed in the aircraft at the time of data acquisition. Also, the resulting videotape cassettes are available for detailed analysis immediately after a flight. Hence, there are no delays for processing or special handling requirements. The resulting imagery is also inexpensive—material costs are typically lower than for 35 mm photography for the same area of coverage. Another advantage is that video cassettes have an audio track, which means that verbal comments about specific features or locations can be recorded in synchronization with the imagery.

The principal disadvantages of video recording are lower resolution, slower "shutter speeds" (1/30 or 1/60 sec for video recording versus a typical shutter speed of 1/500 sec for aerial photography), and higher initial cost, as compared with small format cameras. Also, video imagery is not inherently suited to applications where high quality "hard copy" prints of the data are required in the field. Videotapes can also be cumbersome to index and handle when subsequent viewing of discrete image segments is desired.

In addition to the portable equipment used during image acquisition and field previewing, additional hardware can be useful when interpreting videotapes in the laboratory. Video-compatible image interpretation systems (Section 3.3) are well suited to the analysis of video data. With such systems, individual video frames can be analyzed digitally using a "frame grabber" to numerically code the data. Interpreted data can also be directly transferred to a map base using a modified Zoom Transfer Scope™ (Figure 3.12).

The nature of video imagery places rather strict limitations on its applicability. Appropriate applications are those that have particular need of the advantages of video and can tolerate the relatively low image resolution. In cases where the advantages are particularly important, such as when timeliness is required in crop inventorying or disease detection, users may be more than willing to work with low-resolution data. Applications to date in which airborne video camera systems have been successfully operated are numerous and include such things as generalized agricultural land use mapping, wild rice mapping, trout stream monitoring, water quality studies, crop condition assessment, irrigation mapping, and detection of frost damage in citrus groves [24].

Figure 2.55 shows video images obtained with a system of four solid-state array cameras that employ an array of 512×403 CCD elements in each camera [21]. These cameras can be equipped with a variety of narrow bandpass filters. The bands used in this example and the cover types present in the scene are shown in the figure legend.

Plate 7 shows a 35 mm color infrared photograph (a) and a simultaneously acquired color infrared video image (b) of an agricultural area in northwestern Minnesota. Dry wheat that has been windrowed for some time is shown at lower left and lower center. Windrows of wheat cut more recently are shown at upper center and lower right. Bare soil is shown at upper left. Fallow land containing weedy areas is shown at upper right. Note that the 35 mm photograph has considerable more spatial detail than the video image (windrows can be clearly seen in the photograph, but not in the video image). However, the spectral resolution of the video image is excellent and each of the cover types described above has a significantly different color on the video image.

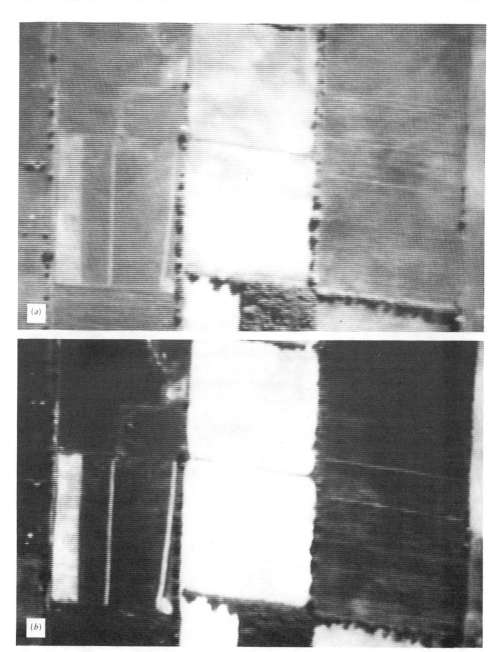

FIGURE 2.55 Aerial video images, agricultural area in Ontario, Canada, May 29, 1985: *(a)* 0.53–0.57 μm; *(b)* 0.63–0.67 μm; *(c)* 0.78–0.82 μm; *(d)* 0.88–0.92 μm. Land cover types (overlay to *(d)*): 1—bare soil (<10% short grass cover); 2—pasture; 3—bare soil (<5% newly planted corn cover); 4—mixed deciduous forest; 5—wild grass, weeds, and clover (30–50 cm high); 6—grass (>50 cm high).

(c)

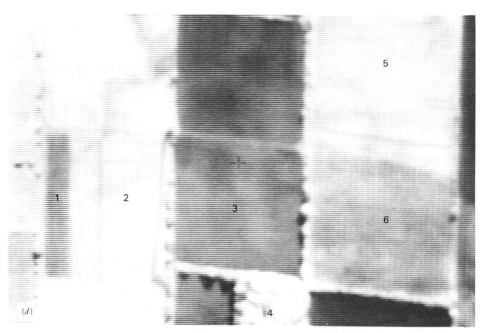

(d)

FIGURE 2.55   *(continued)*

2.18 CONCLUSION

As we indicated earlier in this chapter, aerial photography has been the historical backbone of remote sensing due to its general availability, geometric integrity, versatility, and economy. However, as with any other sensing system, aerial photography has certain limitations and requirements. Airphotos are often difficult to obtain, handle, store, calibrate, and interpret. At the same time, current technological trends seem to indicate that in the not too distant future, inherently digital recording systems will be used in many applications where aerial photographs are now employed. In any case, students of remote sensing are well advised to obtain a thorough understanding of the interpretive, geometric, and radiometric properties of airphotos. These are the subjects of the next four chapters.

SELECTED BIBLIOGRAPHY

1. American Society of Photogrammetry, *Manual of Color Aerial Photography*, Falls Church, Va., 1968.

2. American Society of Photogrammetry, *Manual of Photogrammetry*, 4th ed., Falls Church, Va., 1980.

3. American Society of Photogrammetry, Special Issue on Panoramic Photography and Forest Remote Sensing, *Photogrammetric Engineering and Remote Sensing*, vol. 48, no. 5, May 1982.

4. American Society of Photogrammetry, *Manual of Remote Sensing*, 2nd ed., Falls Church, Va., 1983.

5. Brock, G.C., *The Physical Aspects of Aerial Photography*, Dover, New York, 1967.

6. Ciesla, W.M., R.A. Allison, and F.P. Weber, "Panoramic Aerial Photography in Forest Pest Management," *Photogrammetric Engineering and Remote Sensing*, vol. 48, no.5, May 1982, pp. 719–723.

7. Doyle, F.J., "A Large Format Camera for Shuttle," *Photogrammetric Engineering and Remote Sensing*, vol. 45, no. 1, January 1979, pp. 73–78.

8. Doyle, F.J., "The Large Format Camera on Shuttle Mission 41-G," *Photogrammetric Engineering and Remote Sensing*, vol. 51, no.2, February 1985, pp. 200–203.

9. Eagan, W.G., *Photometry and Polarization in Remote Sensing*, Elsevier, Amsterdam/New York, 1985.

10. Eastman Kodak Company, *Applied Infrared Photography*, Rochester, N.Y., 1981.

11. Eastman Kodak Company, *Kodak Data for Aerial Photography*, 5th ed., Rochester, N.Y., 1982.

12. Eastman Kodak Company, *Kodak Filters for Scientific and Technical Uses*, Rochester, N.Y., 1985.

13. Eastman Kodak Company, *Photography from Lightplanes and Helicopters*, Rochester, N.Y., 1985.

14. Environmental Protection Agency, *Seeing is Believing*, U.S. Environmental Protection Agency, Office of Monitoring Systems and Quality Assurance, Publ. EPA-600/4-82-056, July 1982.

15. Everitt, J.H., and P.R. Nixon, "False Color Video Imagery: A Potential Remote Sensing Tool for Range Management," *Photogrammetric Engineering and Remote Sensing*, vol. 51, no.6, June 1985, pp.675−679.

16. Fleming, J., and R.G. Dixon, *Basic Guide to Small-Format Hand-Held Oblique Aerial Photography*, User's Manual 81-2, Canada Centre for Remote Sensing, Ottawa, Ontario, 1981.

17. Fritz, N.L., "Optimum Methods for Using Infrared-Sensitive Color Films," *Photogrammetric Engineering*, vol. 33, no. 10, October 1967, pp. 1128−1138.

18. Fritz, N.L., "Filters: An Aid in Color-Infrared Photography," *Photogrammetric Engineering and Remote Sensing*, vol. 43, no.1, January 1977, pp.61−72.

19. James, T.H., *The Theory of the Photographic Process*, 4th ed., Macmillan, New York, 1977.

20. Jensen, N., *Optical and Photographic Reconnaissance Systems*, Wiley, New York, 1968.

21. King, D., J. Vlcek, and S. Shemilt, "A Video Camera System for Multispectral Sensing," *Technical Papers of the American Society of Photogrammetry*, ASP−ACSM Annual Meeting, March 1985, pp.661−665.

22. Lavigne, D.M., "Counting Harp Seals with Ultra-violet Photography," *Polar Record*, vol. 18, no. 114, 1976, pp. 269−277.

23. Meisner, D.E., "Color Infrared Aerial Video: Applications in Natural Resource Management," *Proceedings of the 10th William T. Pecora Memorial Remote Sensing Symposium*, American Society for Photogrammetry and Remote Sensing, Ft. Collins, Colo., 1985.

24. Meisner, D.E., "Fundamentals of Airborne Video Remote Sensing," *Remote Sensing of Environment*, vol. 19, no. 1, 1986, pp.63−80.

25. Meisner, D.E., and O.M. Lindstrom, "Design and Operation of a Color Infrared Aerial Video System," *Photogrammetric Engineering and Remote Sensing*, vol. 51, no.5, May 1985, pp. 555−560.

26. Meyer, M.P., and P.D. Grumstrup, *Operating Manual for the Montana 35 mm Aerial Photography System—2nd Revision*, Research Report 78-1, University of Minnesota Remote Sensing Laboratory, St. Paul, 1978.

27. Newhall, B., *Airborne Camera*, Hastings House, New York, 1969.

28. Ondrejka, R., and G. Wood, "Snapshots from a Window on the World," *Optical Spectra*, vol. 14, no.12, December 1980, pp.53−56.

29. Richardson, A.J., R.M. Menges, and P.R. Nixon, "Distinguishing Weed from Crop Plants Using Video Remote Sensing," *Photogrammetric Engineering and Remote Sensing*, vol. 51, no.11, November 1985, pp. 1785−1790.

30. Slater, P.N., *Remote Sensing and Optical Systems*, Addison−Wesley, Reading, Mass., 1980.

31. Society of Photographic Scientists and Engineers, *Color: Theory and Imaging Systems*, Washington, D.C., 1973.

32. Thompson, L.L., "Remote Sensing Using Solid-State Array Technology," *Photogrammetric Engineering and Remote Sensing*, vol. 45, no.1, January 1979, pp. 47−55.

33. Vizy, K.N., "Detecting and Monitoring Oil Slicks with Aerial Photos," *Photogrammetric Engineering*, vol. 40, no.6, June 1974, pp. 697–708.

34. Welch, R., "Modulation Transfer Functions," *Photogrammetric Engineering and Remote Sensing*, vol. 37, no.3, March 1971, pp. 247–259.

35. Williamson, S.J., and H.Z. Cummins, *Light and Color in Nature and Art*, Wiley, New York, 1983.

36. Wolf, P.R., *Elements of Photogrammetry*, 2nd ed., McGraw-Hill, New York, 1983.

INTRODUCTION TO AIRPHOTO INTERPRETATION

3.1 INTRODUCTION

When we look at aerial photographs, we see various objects of different sizes and shapes. Some of these objects may be readily identifiable while others may not, depending on our own individual perceptions and experience. When we can identify what we see on the photographs and communicate this information to others, we are practicing *airphoto interpretation*. Aerial photographs contain raw photographic *data*. These data, when processed by a human interpreter's brain, become usable *information*.

As previously mentioned, aerial photography dates to the year 1858 and the balloon photographs of Nadar. Aerial photography did not receive much emphasis during the ensuing decades because the process was cumbersome and risky and the results uncertain. However, some scientists and inventors did recognize the potential value of aerial photographs in presenting a new view of the earth's surface. Military strategists also understood the potential of this medium for the remote acquisition of military information. During World War I, aerial photography was established as an operational military reconnaissance tool.

In the two decades between World War I and World War II, many nonmilitary applications appeared. The experience gained by World War I pilots in taking pictures from the air convinced quite a number of them that they could put their newly acquired skills to work on such civilian applications as timber surveys and mineral exploration. The U.S. Department of Agriculture's Agricultural Stabilization and Conservation Service (USDA−ASCS) began photographing selected counties of the United States on a repetitive basis in 1937. This coverage continues today. More than half of the photographic illustrations in Chapter 4 are USDA−ASCS photographs.

Military photo interpretation surged during the period of World War II and more sophisticated techniques were developed. The first widespread use of color infrared film was as "camouflage detection film" during this war.

As military applications waned after World War II, civilian interest in photo interpretation again increased and civilian uses of airphoto interpretation have now become widespread in dozens of fields from agriculture to zoology.

In this chapter, we explore the applications of airphoto interpretation to the solution of a variety of problems in different fields. Because photo interpretation is best learned through the experience of viewing hundreds of airphoto stereopairs according to the requirements of specific fields of application, we cannot hope to train our readers in photo interpretation. Here, we will simply present many potential applications of airphoto interpretation and illustrate a few with photographic examples. Chapter 4 introduces detailed training in one specific field of application—*terrain evaluation.* A complete chapter similar to Chapter 4 could be written for each of the fields of application mentioned here.

In Sections 3.2 and 3.3, we present the fundamentals of airphoto interpretation and describe basic photo interpretation equipment. This is followed by a description of geologic and soil mapping and land use/land cover mapping using airphoto interpretation. Next, we treat applications in the areas of agriculture, forestry, rangeland, water resources, urban and regional planning, wetland mapping, wildlife ecology, and archaeology. This chapter concludes with a discussion of environmental assessment and geographic information systems.

3.2 FUNDAMENTALS OF AIRPHOTO INTERPRETATION

Aerial photographs contain a detailed record of features on the ground at the time of exposure. A photo interpreter systematically examines the photos and, frequently, other supporting materials such as maps and reports of field observations. Based on this study, an interpretation is made as to the physical nature of objects and phenomena appearing in the photographs. Interpretations may take place at a number of levels of complexity, from the simple recognition of objects on the earth's surface to the derivation of detailed information regarding the complex interactions among earth surface and subsurface features. Success in photo interpretation varies with the training and experience of the interpreter, the nature of the objects or phenomena being interpreted, and the quality of the photographs being utilized. Generally, the most capable photo interpreters have keen powers of observation coupled with imagination and a great deal of patience. In addition, it is important that the interpreter have a thorough understanding of the phenomenon being studied.

A systematic study of aerial photographs usually involves several basic characteristics of features shown on a photograph. The exact characteristics useful for any specific task, and the manner in which they are considered, depend on the field of application. However, most applications consider the following basic characteristics, or variations of them: shape, size, pattern, tone (or hue), texture, shadows, site, and association.

Shape refers to the general form, configuration, or outline of individual objects. In the case of stereoscopic photographs, the object's *height* also defines its shape. The shape of some objects is so distinctive that their images may be identified solely from this criterion. The Pentagon Building near Washington, D.C., is a classic example. All shapes are obviously not this diagnostic, but every shape is of some significance to the photo interpreter.

Size of objects on photographs must be considered in the context of the photo scale. A small storage shed, for example, might be misinterpreted as a barn if size were not considered. Relative sizes among objects on photographs of the same scale must also be considered.

Pattern relates to the spatial arrangement of objects. The repetition of certain general forms or relationships is characteristic of many objects, both natural and constructed, and gives objects a pattern that aids the photo interpreter in recognizing them. An outdoor drive-in theater, for example, has a particular layout and pattern of parking spaces that aid in its identification. Drive-in theaters have been misidentified as housing subdivisions by novice photo interpreters who did not carefully consider size, shape, and pattern. Likewise, the ordered spatial arrangement of trees in an orchard is in distinct contrast to that of forest tree stands.

Tone (or *hue*) refers to the relative brightness or color of objects on photographs. Figure 1.9 showed how relative photo tones could be used to distinguish between deciduous and coniferous trees on black and white infrared photographs. Figure 4.6 shows a striking pattern of light-toned and dark-toned soils where the tonal patterns vary according to the drainage conditions of the soil (the lighter-toned areas are topographically higher and drier; the darker-toned areas are lower and wetter). Without tonal differences, the shapes, patterns, and textures of objects could not be discerned.

Texture is the frequency of tonal change on the photographic image. Texture is produced by an aggregation of unit features that may be too small to be discerned individually on the photograph, such as tree leaves and leaf shadows. It is a product of their individual shape, size, pattern, shadow, and tone. It determines the overall visual "smoothness" or "coarseness" of image features. As the scale of the photograph is reduced, the texture of any given object or area becomes progressively finer and ultimately disappears. An interpreter can often distinguish between features with similar reflectances based on their texture differences. An example would be the smooth texture of green grass as contrasted with the rough texture of green tree crowns on medium scale airphotos.

Shadows are important to interpreters in two opposing respects: (1) the shape or outline of a shadow affords an impression of the profile view of objects (which aids interpretation), and (2) objects within shadows reflect little light and are difficult to discern on photographs (which hinders interpretation). For example, the shadows cast by various tree species or cultural features (bridges, silos, towers, etc.) can definitely aid in their identification on airphotos. Also, the shadows resulting from even subtle variations in terrain elevations, especially in the case of low-sun-angle photographs, can aid in assessing natural topographic variations that may be diagnostic of various geologic landforms.

Site refers to topographic or geographic location, and is a particularly important aid in the identification of vegetation types. For example, certain tree species would be expected to occur on well-drained upland sites, whereas other tree species would be expected to occur on poorly drained lowland sites. Also, various tree species occur only in certain geographic areas (e.g., redwoods occur in California, but not Indiana).

Association refers to the occurrence of certain features in relation to others. For example, a ferris wheel might be difficult to identify if standing in a field near a barn, but would be easy to identify if in an area recognized as an amusement park.

As suggested above, the photo interpretation process is greatly aided by viewing photographs stereoscopically. This is normally accomplished through the use of *stereoscopes*, as described in Section 3.3.

The airphoto interpretation process can often be facilitated through the use of *airphoto interpretation keys*. Keys can be valuable training aids for novice interpreters and provide useful reference or refresher materials for more experienced interpreters. An airphoto interpretation key helps the interpreter evaluate the information presented on aerial photographs in an organized and consistent manner. It provides guidance about the correct identification of features or conditions on the photographic images. Ideally, a key consists of two basic parts: (1) a collection of annotated or captioned stereograms illustrative of the features or conditions to be identified, and (2) a graphic or word description that sets forth in some systematic fashion the image-recognition characteristics of those features or conditions. Two general types of airphoto interpretation keys exist, differentiated by the method of presentation of diagnostic features. A *selective key* contains numerous photographic examples with supporting text. The interpreter selects the example that most nearly resembles the feature or condition found on the photograph under study.

An *elimination key* is arranged so that the interpretation proceeds step-by-step from the general to the specific and leads to the elimination of all features or conditions except the one being identified. Elimination keys often take the form of *dichotomous keys* where the interpreter makes a series of choices between two alternatives and progressively eliminates all but one possible answer. Figure 3.1 shows a dichotomous key prepared for the identification of fruit and nut crops in the Sacramento Valley, California. The use of elimination keys can lead to more positive answers than selective keys, but may result in erroneous answers if the interpreter is forced to make an uncertain choice between two unfamiliar image characteristics.

As a generalization, keys are more easily constructed and more reliably utilized for cultural feature identification (houses, bridges, roads, water towers) than for vegetation or landform identification. However, a number of keys have been successfully employed for agricultural crop identification and tree species identification. *Such keys are normally developed and used on a region-by-region and season-by-season basis in that the appearance of vegetation can vary widely with location.*

The film—filter combination selected for aerial photography affects the amount of information that can be interpreted from the images. Numerous examples of this are scattered throughout this book, especially in the first three chapters.

The temporal aspects of natural phenomena are important for airphoto interpretation because such factors as vegetative growth and soil moisture vary during the year. For crop identification, more positive results can be achieved by obtaining aerial photographs at several times during the annual growing cycle. Observations of local vegetation emergence and recession can aid in the timing of aerial photography for natural vegetation mapping. In addition to seasonal variations, weather can cause

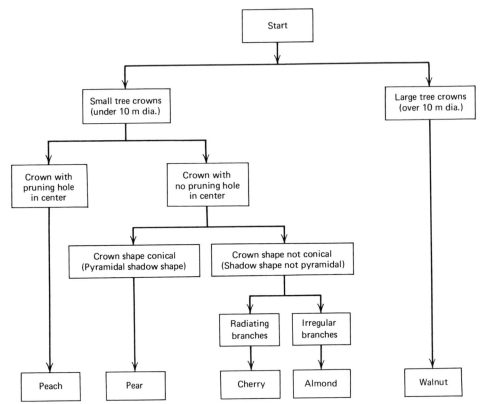

FIGURE 3.1 Dichotomous airphoto interpretation key to fruit and nut crops in the Sacramento Valley, California, designed for use with 1:6000 scale panchromatic aerial photographs. (Adapted from [7], 1st ed. Copyright © 1975, American Society of Photogrammetry, reproduced with permission.)

significant short-term changes. Because soil moisture conditions may change dramatically during the day or two immediately following a rainstorm, the timing of photography for soil studies is very critical.

As illustrated in Chapter 2, scale affects the level of useful information that can be extracted from aerial photographs. Typical scales and areas of coverage are shown in Table 3.1 for some of the more commonly available sources of airphotos. Although terminology with regard to airphoto scale has not been standardized, we can consider that *small scale* airphotos have a scale of 1:50,000 or smaller, *medium scale* airphotos have a scale between 1:12,000 and 1:50,000, and *large scale* airphotos have a scale of 1:12,000 or larger.

In the figure captions of this book, we have stated the scale of nearly every image—whether photographic, thermal, multispectral, or radar—so that the reader can develop a feel for the degree of detail that can be extracted from images of varying scales.

TABLE 3.1 Typical Aerial Photograph Scales and Areas of Coverage for 240 mm Format Film (230 × 230 mm Image)

Photo scale	Area per frame (km)	Comments
1:130,000 or 1:120,000	29.9 × 29.9 or 27.6 × 27.6	NASA high altitude photography, 152 mm focal length lens
1:80,000	18.4 × 18.4	National High Altitude Photography (NHAP) Program, 152 mm focal length lens, panchromatic film
1:65,000 or 1:60,000	14.9 × 14.9 or 13.8 × 13.8	NASA high altitude photography, 305 mm focal length lens
1:58,000	13.3 × 13.3	National High Altitude Photography (NHAP) Program, 210 mm focal length lens, color infrared film
1:40,000	9.2 × 9.2	USGS and USDA current mapping photography programs
1:24,000	5.5 × 5.5	Photography flown to match scale of USGS $7\frac{1}{2}'$ quadrangle maps
1:20,000	4.6 × 4.6	Typical scale of older (archival) USGS and USDA mapping photography
1:15,840	3.6 × 3.6	Traditional USFS photography (4 in. per mile)
1:6000	1.4 × 1.4	Typical EPA photography for emergency response and intensive analysis of hazardous waste sites

As generalizations, the following statements can be made about the appropriateness of various photographic image scales for resource studies. Small scale airphotos, such as those from the National High Altitude Photography (NHAP) program and the NASA high altitude research photography program, are used for reconnaissance mapping, large area resource assessment, and general resource management planning. Medium scale airphotos, such as the mapping program photographs of the U.S. Geological Survey (USGS), the U.S. Department of Agriculture (USDA), and the U.S. Forest Service (USFS), are used for the identification, classification, and mapping of such features as tree species, agricultural crop type, vegetation community, and soil type. Large scale airphotos are used for the intensive monitoring of specific items such as surveys of the damage caused by plant disease, insects, or tree blowdown. Large scale airphotos are also used by the U.S. Environmental Protection Agency (EPA) for emergency response to hazardous waste spills and for the intensive site analysis of hazardous waste sites.

The NHAP program, a federal multiagency activity coordinated by the USGS, has provided nationwide photographic coverage at a scale of 1:58,000 using color infrared film and of 1:80,000 using panchromatic film exposed simultaneously. Stereoscopic photographs are typically taken from an aircraft altitude of 12,200 m above mean terrain, with a sun angle of at least 30° to minimize shadows, and on days with no cloud cover and minimal haze. NHAP I began in 1980 and provided nationwide coverage under the "leaf-off" conditions of spring and fall. NHAP II began in 1985 with photography under "leaf-on" conditions. The leaf-off conditions are preferable for land cover mapping when it is important to be able to see as much detail as possible underneath trees. Leaf-on conditions are preferred for vegetation mapping. Information on the availability of NHAP photographs can be obtained from the National Cartographic Information Center (see Appendix).

3.3   BASIC PHOTO INTERPRETATION EQUIPMENT

Photo interpretation equipment generally serves one of three fundamental purposes: viewing photographs, making measurements on photographs, and transferring interpreted information to base maps or digital data bases. Basic equipment for performing each of these functions is described here. More sophisticated equipment involved in performing precise measuring and mapping tasks with aerial photographs is described in Chapter 5.

The airphoto interpretation process typically involves the utilization of stereoscopic viewing to provide a three-dimensional view of the terrain. This effect is possible because we have binocular vision. That is, since we have two eyes that are slightly separated, we continually view the world from two slightly different perspectives. Whenever objects lie at different distances in a scene, each eye sees a slightly different view of the objects. The differences between the two views are synthesized by the mind to provide depth perception. Thus, the two views provided by our separated eyes enable us to see in three dimensions.

When aerial photographs overlap, they also provide two views taken from separated positions. By viewing the left photograph of a pair with the left eye and the right photo with the right eye, we obtain a three-dimensional view of the terrain surface. A *stereoscope* facilitates the stereoviewing process. This book contains more than 50 *stereopairs*, or *stereograms*, which can be viewed in three dimensions using a lens stereoscope such as shown in Figure 3.3. An average separation of about 58 mm between common points has been used in the stereograms in this book. The exact spacing varies somewhat because of the different elevations of the points. The original vertical aerial photographs with about 60 percent endlap have been cropped and are mounted here with 100 percent overlap.

Figure 3.2 can be used to test stereoscopic vision. When this diagram is viewed through a stereoscope, the rings and other objects should appear to be at varying distances from the observer. Your stereovision ability can be evaluated by filling in Table 3.2 (answers are on second page of table). People whose eyesight is very weak in one eye may not have the ability to see in stereo. This will preclude three-dimensional viewing of the stereograms in this book. However, many people with essentially monocular vision have become very proficient photointerpreters.

FIGURE 3.2   Stereoscopic vision test. (Courtesy Carl Zeiss, Inc.)

TABLE 3.2   Stereovision Test for Use with Figure 3.2

PART I

Within the rings marked 1 through 8 are designs that appear to be at different elevations. Using "1" to designate the highest elevation, write down the depth order of the designs. It is possible that two or more designs may be at the same elevation. In this case, use the same number for all designs at the same elevation.

Ring 1		**Ring 6**	
square	(2)	lower left circle	( )
marginal ring	(1)	lower right circle	· ( )
triangle	(3)	upper right circle	( )
point	(4)	upper left circle	( )
		marginal ring	( )

Ring 7		**Ring 3**	
black flag with ball	( )	square	( )
marginal ring	( )	marginal ring	( )
black circle	( )	cross	( )
arrow	( )	lower left circle	( )
tower with cross	( )	upper center circle	( )
double cross	( )		
black triangle	( )		
black rectangle	( )		

PART II

Indicate the relative elevations of the rings 1 through 8.

( ) ( ) ( ) ( ) ( ) ( ) ( ) ( )
highest   lowest *Table continued on next page*

TABLE 3.2 *Continued*

PART III

Draw profiles to indicate the relative elevations of the letters in the words "prufungstafel" and "stereoskopisches sehen."

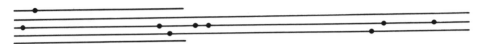

(Answers to Stereovision Test)

PART I

Ring 1

square	(2)
marginal ring	(1)
triangle	(3)
point	(4)

Ring 6

lower left circle	(4)
lower right circle	(5)
upper right circle	(1)
upper left circle	(3)
marginal ring	(2)

Ring 7

black flag with ball	(5)
marginal ring	(1)
black circle	(4)
arrow	(2)
tower with cross	(7)
double cross	(2)
black triangle	(3)
black rectangle	(6)

Ring 3

square	(4)
marginal ring	(2)
cross	(3)
lower left circle	(1)
upper center circle	(5)

PART II

(7) (6) (5) (1) (4) (2)[a] (3)[a] (8)
highest   lowest

PART III

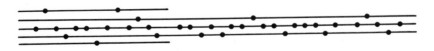

[a]Rings 2 and 3 are at the same elevation.

120

Some people will be able to view the stereograms in this book without a stereo-scope. This can be accomplished by holding the book about 20 cm from your eyes and allowing the view of each eye to drift into a straight-ahead viewing position (as when looking at objects at an infinite distance) while still maintaining focus on the stereo-gram. When the two images have fused into one, the stereogram will be seen in three dimensions. Most persons will find stereoviewing without proper stereoscopes to be a tiring procedure, producing "eyestrain." It is, however, a useful technique to employ when stereoscopes are not available.

Several types of stereoscopes are available, utilizing lenses or a combination of lenses, mirrors, and prisms.

Lens stereoscopes, such as those shown in Figures 3.3 and 3.4, are portable and comparatively inexpensive. Most are small instruments with folding legs. The lens spacing can usually be adapted from about 45 to 75 mm to accommodate individual eye spacings. Lens magnification is typically 2 power ((Figure 3.3) but may be adjustable. The stereoscope shown in Figure 3.4 may be used with either 2 or 4 power eyepieces. The principal disadvantage of small lens stereoscopes is that the photographs must be quite close together to be positioned properly underneath the lenses. Because of this, the interpreter cannot view the entire stereoscopic area of 240 mm aerial photographs without raising the edge of one of the photographs.

Mirror stereoscopes use a combination of prisms and mirrors to separate the lines of sight from each of the viewer's eyes. The mirror stereoscope shown in Figure 3.5 has a distance between the wing mirrors much greater than the eyepiece spacing so that a

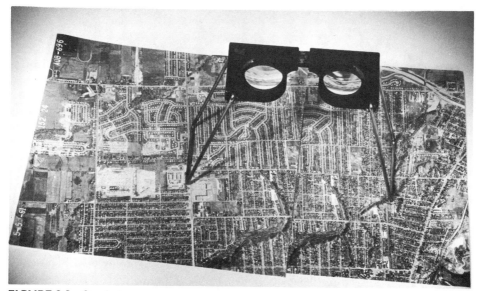

FIGURE 3.3 Simple lens stereoscope.

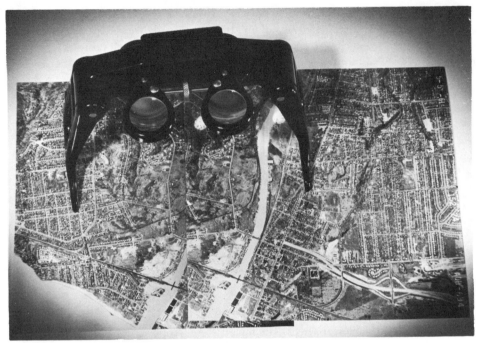

FIGURE 3.4   Abrams Model CB-1 dual power lens stereoscope.

FIGURE 3.5 Mirror stereoscope, Zeiss Model N-2, with stereomicrometer measuring equipment. (Courtesy Carl Zeiss, Inc.)

pair of 240 mm airphotos can be placed side-by-side without overlapping. Such stereoscopes typically have little or no magnification in their normal viewing mode. Binoculars can be fitted to the eyepieces to provide a magnification of 2 to 4 power, with a resulting decrease in field of view. With a mirror stereoscope using little or no magnification, the interpreter can view all or most of the stereoscopic portion of a 240 mm stereopair without moving either the photographs or the stereoscope. Also, measuring instruments can be conveniently used under the stereoscope. Figure 3.5 shows a parallax measuring device mounted over the photographs. This device is explained in Chapter 5. This type of stereoscope has the disadvantage that it is too large for easy portability and is much more costly than simple lens stereoscopes.

The *scanning mirror stereoscope* shown in Figure 3.6 can be used with 1.5 or 4.5 power magnification and has a built-in provision for moving the field of view across the entire stereo overlap area of the photographs without moving either the photographs or the stereoscope.

Figure 3.7 shows a *zoom stereoscope* that has a continuously variable magnification of 2.5 to 10 power (or 5 to 20 power with an alternative eyepiece). The image in each eyepiece can be optically rotated through 360° to accommodate uncut rolls of film taken under conditions of aircraft crab. Zoom stereoscopes such as those shown here are expensive precision instruments, typically with a very high lens resolution.

FIGURE 3.6 Scanning mirror stereoscope. Old Delft scanning stereoscope.

FIGURE 3.7 Zoom stereoscope. Bausch and Lomb Model SIS-95. (Courtesy Bausch and Lomb, Scientific Optical Products Division.)

Either paper prints or film transparencies can be viewed using a stereoscope. Paper prints are more convenient to handle, more easily annotated, and better suited to field use; transparencies have better spatial resolution and color fidelity. An interpreter would generally use a simple lens or mirror stereoscope with paper prints, and a more elaborate viewer such as the zoom stereoscope with color and color infrared film transparencies. Transparencies are placed on a *light table* (Figure 3.8) for viewing because the light source must come from behind the transparency. The spectral characteristics of the film and light table lamps should be balanced for optimum viewing conditions. Light tables typically have bulbs with a "color temperature" around 3500°K, which means that the spectral distribution of their light output is similar to that of a blackbody heated to 3500°K. The color temperature of "noon daylight" is about 5500°K; tungsten bulbs used for indoor lighting have a color temperature of about 3200°K.

The task of obtaining distance measurements from aerial photographs can be performed using any one of many measurement devices. These devices vary in their accuracy, cost, and availability. Where low orders of accuracy are acceptable, a triangular *engineer's scale* or *metric scale* is often adequate for determining photo distances. Measurement accuracy with these devices is generally improved by taking the average of several repeated measurements. Measurements are also generally more accurate when made with the aid of a magnifying lens.

In addition to measuring distances, areas are often measured on a photograph. Extremely accurate area measurements can be made from *maps* generated from airphotos in stereoplotters or orthophotoscopes (described in Sections 5.15 and 5.16). Here our attention is on measuring area directly on photographs. The accuracy of direct measurement is not only a function of the measuring device used, but also of the degree of image scale variation due to relief in the terrain and tilt in the photography. Although large errors in direct area determinations can result even with vertical photographs in regions of moderate and high relief, very accurate direct measure-

FIGURE 3.8 Light table and zoom stereoscope. Richards MIM 4 table with motorized film advance and Bausch and Lomb Model 240 stereoscope. (Courtesy The Richards Corp.)

ments may be made on vertical photos of areas of low relief. In such cases, the process involves measuring the area on the photograph, followed by a conversion to ground area using the average photo scale.

Simple scales may be used to measure the area of a simply shaped feature, such as an agricultural field. When measuring the area of an irregularly shaped region, however, other measurement methods must be used. One of the simplest techniques employs a transparent grid overlay consisting of lines forming rectangles or squares of known area. The grid is placed over the photograph and the area of a ground unit is estimated by counting grid units that fall within the unit to be measured. Perhaps the most widely used grid overlay is a *dot grid* (Figure 3.9). This grid, composed of uniformly spaced dots, is superimposed over the photo and the dots falling within the region to be measured are counted. From knowledge of the dot density of the grid, the photo area

FIGURE 3.9 Transparent dot grid overlay.

of the region can be computed. The photo area is then converted to a ground area from the average scale as follows:

$$\text{ground area} = \text{photo area} \times \frac{1}{(S_{avg})^2} \tag{3.1}$$

An alternative method of using the dot grid is possible if a ground object of known size appears in the photograph. In this case, a direct proportion between dots and equivalent ground area may be made. For example, consider the use of a dot grid to measure areas of agricultural fields appearing on a photograph. If a field of known area of 350 ha is covered by 26 dots on the photograph, the ground area of a field covered by 74 dots is

$$\text{ground area} = \frac{74 \text{ dots}}{26 \text{ dots}} \times 350 \text{ ha} = 996 \text{ ha}$$

The dot grid is an inexpensive tool and requires little training. When numerous regions are to be measured, however, the counting procedure becomes quite tedious. An alternative device is a *polar planimeter*, shown in Figure 3.10. This instrument mechanically computes areas as the interpreter traces around the boundary of an area in clockwise direction. When the boundary has been fully traced, a graduated scale expresses a number proportional to the area measured on the photograph. The boundary trace is generally repeated several times to ensure the precision of the photo area measurement. The photo area is then converted to a ground area using Eq. 3.1.

Areas may be determined most rapidly and accurately using an *electronic coordinate digitizer* (Figure 3.11). As with the planimeter, area determination involves tracing around the boundary of the region of interest. By continuously feeding the xy coordinate values of the tracing cursor into a microprocessor, the photographic area is computed and read out directly. Alternatively, the microprocessor can perform the scale conversion for direct readout of ground area in any desired units. Areas can also be determined using a *digitizing tablet* interfaced with a microcomputer. Figure 3.47 shows a large digitizing tablet; tablets as small as 254×254 mm are available for use with photographic prints or transparencies.

Once information has been interpreted from aerial photographs, it is frequently transferred to a base map. When the base map is not at the same scale as the photograph, special optical devices may be used in the transfer process. Some of these devices use high precision opaque projectors to enlarge or reduce the photographic data to the scale of the map. Other devices employ viewing systems that optically superimpose a view of the photograph and the map. By adjusting the magnification of the two views, the photo can be matched to the scale of the map.

An example of the latter device is the Bausch and Lomb *Zoom Transfer Scope*™ (ZTS) shown in Figure 3.12. This device allows the operator to simultaneously view both a map and a pair of stereo photographs. Through a combination of zoom magnification and accessory lenses, this device can accommodate a wide disparity of photo and map scales. The ZTS can optically perform a 360° image rotation, which simplifies the

FIGURE 3.10 Polar planimeter. Stationary weight is to the upper right, measurement wheel to the left, and tracing stylus to the lower right.

FIGURE 3.11 Electronic coordinate digitizer system. Magnifying stylus is shown in the center of the photo, keyboard to the left, microprocessor and display unit to the right. (Courtesy Numonics Corp.)

127

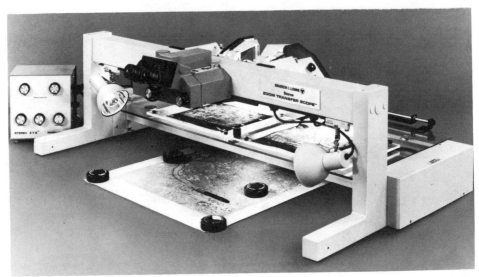

FIGURE 3.12   Stereo Zoom Transfer Scope™. (Courtesy Bausch and Lomb, Scientific Optical Products Division.)

task of orienting the photographs and the map. In addition, it has a special (anamorphic) lens system that "stretches" the image up to two times in one direction only. This stretch enables the instrument to compensate somewhat for geometric anomalies such as lens distortion and film shrinkage. It can also be used to match computer printout to photographs or maps when the printout does not have a common scale in both the vertical and the horizontal directions (most line printer output has a horizontal scale only 60 to 80 percent of the vertical scale).

The *color additive viewer* is also an item of photo interpretation equipment. As described in the previous chapter (Figure 2.33), this device color codes and superimposes three multispectral photographs to generate a more interpretable color composite. Most color additive viewers are monoscopic, but a few have been equipped for stereoscopic viewing. A color additive viewer and a ZTS can be used in combination so that interpretations made on the color additive viewer screen can be immediately transferred to a map base of differing scale.

A microcomputer-based *video image/graphics system* combines some of the functions of an electronic coordinate digitizer system and a ZTS with an array of digital image processing functions. Figure 3.13 illustrates a system that uses two video cameras with zoom lenses for data input, a microcomputer for data processing, a color display monitor, and a color ink jet printer for "hard copy" output. A variety of source materials, such as 35, 70, or 240 mm airphotos (or other images), topographic maps, and other line maps, can be "entered" into the microcomputer through the video cameras. Video signals from a video recorder can also be entered. Images or maps of different scales can be overlain in a visual manner similar to the ZTS, with the operator

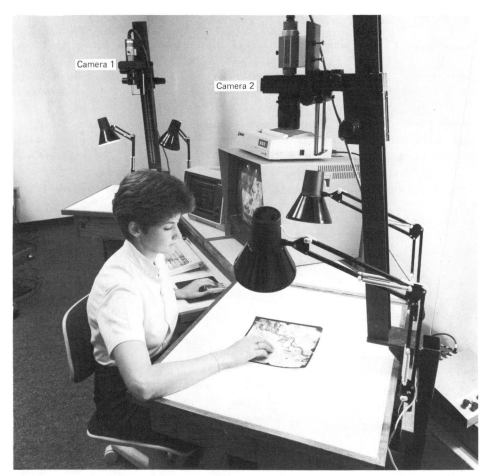

FIGURE 3.13 Microcomputer-based video image/graphics system, Aeronca Electronics Model VGS-300 Plus. (Courtesy Aeronca Electronics, Inc.)

matching scales by adjusting the video camera zoom lenses while viewing the color monitor. Alternatively, maps and images can be overlain by computer processing after they are stored in computer memory. Distances and areas can be readily calculated by the microcomputer. Also, several digital image processing functions (Chapter 10) can be accomplished and the system can "talk" to other computer-based systems through a digital communications port.

Applications for video image/graphics systems include such activities as map updating from recent aerial photographs, digitization of various features or map units, change detection analysis, and geographic information system overlays and computations (Section 3.15).

3.4 GEOLOGIC AND SOIL MAPPING

The earth has a highly complex and variable surface whose topographic relief and material composition reflect the bedrock and unconsolidated materials that underlie each part of the surface as well as the agents of change that have acted on them. Each type of rock, each fracture or other effect of internal movement, and each erosional and depositional feature bear the imprint of the processes that produced them. Persons who seek to describe and explain earth materials and structures must understand geomorphological principles and be able to recognize the surface expressions of the various materials and structures. Through the processes of airphoto interpretation and geologic and soil mapping, these materials and structures can be identified and evaluated. Geologic and soil mapping will always require a considerable amount of field exploration, but the mapping process can be greatly facilitated through the use of airphoto interpretation.

Here, we briefly describe the application of airphoto interpretation to geologic and soil mapping. Chapter 4 provides a more detailed coverage of this application and contains more than 50 aerial and space images illustrating airphoto interpretation for geologic and soil mapping.

Geologic Mapping

The first aerial photographs taken from an airplane for geologic mapping purposes were used to construct a mosaic covering Bengasi, Libya, in 1913. In general, the earliest uses of airphotos were simply as base maps for geologic data compilation, especially as applied to petroleum exploration. Some interpretive use of aerial photographs began in the 1920s. Since the 1940s, the interpretive use of airphotos for geologic mapping and evaluation has been widespread.

Geologic mapping involves the identification of landforms, rock types, and rock structure (folds, faults, fractures) and the portrayal of geologic units and structure on a map or other display in their correct spatial relationship with one another. Mineral resource exploration is an important type of geologic mapping activity. Because most of the surface and near-surface mineral deposits in accessible regions of the earth have been found, current emphasis is on the location of deposits far below the earth's surface or in inaccessible regions. Geophysical methods that provide deep penetration into the earth are generally needed to locate potential deposits and drill holes are required to confirm their existence. However, much information about potential areas for mineral exploration can be provided by interpretation of surface features on aerial photographs and satellite images.

Multistage image interpretation is often utilized in geologic studies. The interpreter may begin by making interpretations of satellite images (Chapter 9) at scales of 1:250,000 to 1:1,000,000, then examining high altitude stereoscopic aerial photographs at scales from 1:58,000 to 1:130,000. For detailed mapping, stereoscopic aerial photographs at scales as large as 1:20,000 may be utilized.

Small scale mapping typically involves the mapping of *lineaments*, regional linear features that are caused by the linear alignment of regional morphological features, such as streams, escarpments, and mountain ranges, and tonal features that in many areas are the surface expressions of fractures or fault zones. Major lineaments can range from a few to hundreds of kilometers in length. The mapping of lineaments is important in mineral resource studies because many ore deposits are located along fracture zones.

Several factors influence the detection of lineaments. One of the most important is the angular relationship between the linear feature and the illumination source. In general, features that trend parallel to the illumination source are not detected as readily as those that are oriented perpendicularly. Moderately low illumination angles are preferred for the detection of subtle topographic linear features. An example of low-sun-angle photography, taken under wintertime conditions with snow covered ground, is shown in Figure 3.14. This figure shows a Skylab photograph of northwestern Wyoming and eastern Idaho. The light-toned area at upper left is the Snake River Plain of Idaho, an extensive area of volcanic flood basalt. The dark, tree covered area at upper right is Yellowstone National Park. Below and to the left of Yellowstone Park are the Grand Teton mountains and "Jackson Hole." The tilted sedimentary rocks of the Wyoming Range and Salt River Range can be seen in the lower left quadrant, and the glaciated Wind River Range at lower right.

Many interpreters use a *Ronchi grid* for lineament mapping. The Ronchi grid is a diffraction grating commonly ruled with 78 lines/cm that enhances or suppresses linear features on an image. When an image is viewed through the grid, with the grid held

FIGURE 3.14 Low oblique Skylab 4 photograph, eastern Idaho and northwestern Wyoming (including Yellowstone and Grand Teton National Parks), 4:00 PM, January 1, 1974. Approximately 1:5,000,000 at photo center. Black and white reproduction of color original. (NASA image.)

near the eye, linear features parallel to the grid appear diffused and suppressed, and linear features perpendicular to the grid are enhanced.

Although monoscopic viewing is often suitable for lineament mapping, *lithologic mapping*, the mapping of rock units, is greatly enhanced by the use of stereoscopic viewing. As outlined in Chapter 4, the process of rock unit identification and mapping involves the stereoscopic examination of images to determine the topographic form (including drainage pattern and texture), image tone, and natural vegetative cover of the area under study. In unvegetated areas, most lithologic units are distinguishable on the basis of their topographic form and spectral properties, especially as expressed on color or color infrared film. In vegetated areas, identification is more difficult because the rock surface is obscured, and some of the more subtle aspects of changes in vegetative cover must be considered.

Because some 70 percent of the earth's land surface is covered with vegetation, a geobotanical approach to geologic unit discrimination is important. The basis of *geobotany* is the relationship between a plant's nutrient requirements and two interrelated factors—the availability of nutrients in the soil and the physical properties of the soil, including the availability of soil moisture. The distribution of vegetation can often be used as an indirect indicator of the composition of the underlying soil and rock materials. A geobotanical approach to geologic mapping using remotely sensed images suggests a cooperative effort among geologists, soil scientists, and field-oriented botanists, each of whom should be familiar with remote sensing. An especially important aspect of this approach is the identification of vegetation anomalies related to mineralized areas. Geobotanical anomalies may be expressed in a number of ways: (1) anomalous distribution of species and/or plant communities, (2) stunted growth and/or decreased ground cover, (3) alteration of leaf pigment and/or physiographic processes that produce leaf color changes, and (4) anomalous changes in the phenologic cycle, such as early foliage change or senescence in the fall, alteration of flowering periods, and/or late leaf flush in the spring. Such vegetation anomalies are best identified by analyzing photographs taken at several times during the year, with emphasis placed on the growing period, from leaf flush in the spring to fall senescence. Using this approach, "normal" vegetation conditions can be established, and anomalous conditions can be more readily identified.

Many geologists believe that reflection in spectral bands around 1.6 and 2.2 μm is particularly important for mineral exploration and lithologic mapping. These bands cannot be photographed, but they can be sensed with sensors such as the Landsat Thematic Mapper (Section 9.8) and the Airborne Imaging Spectrometer (Section 7.17). Also, the examination of multiple narrow bands in the thermal infrared spectral region shows great promise in discriminating rock and mineral types (Section 7.15).

Soil Mapping

Detailed soil surveys form a primary source of resource information about an area. Hence, they are used heavily in such activities as comprehensive land use planning. Understanding soil suitability for various land use activities is essential to preventing environmental deterioration associated with misuse of land. In short, if planning is to be an effective tool for guiding land use, it must be premised on a thorough inventory of the natural resource base. As we more fully describe in Chapter 4, soil data are an essential facet of such inventories.

Detailed soil surveys are the product of an intensive study of soil resources by trained scientists. The delineation of soil units utilizes airphoto interpretation coupled with extensive field work. Soil scientists traverse the landscape on foot, identify soils, and delineate soil boundaries. This process involves the field examination of numerous soil profiles (cross sections) and the identification and classification of soil units. The soil scientist's experience and training are relied on to evaluate the relationship of soils to vegetation, geologic parent material, landform, and landscape position. Airphoto interpretation has been utilized since the early 1930s to facilitate the soil mapping process. Typically, panchromatic aerial photographs at scales ranging from 1:15,840 to 1:40,000 have been used as mapping bases.

Agricultural soil survey maps have been prepared for portions of the United States by the USDA since about the year 1900. Most of the soil surveys published since 1957 contain soil maps printed on a photomosaic base at a scale of 1:24,000, 1:20,000, or 1:15,840. Beginning in the mid-1980s, soil survey map information for many counties has been made available both as line maps and as digital files that can be incorporated into geographic information systems (Section 3.15). The original purpose of these surveys was to provide technical assistance to farmers and ranchers for cropland and grazing operations. Soil surveys published since 1957 contain information about the suitability of each mapped soil unit for a variety of uses. They contain information for such purposes as estimating yields of common agricultural crops; evaluating rangeland suitability; determining woodland productivity; assessing wildlife habitat conditions; judging suitability for various recreational uses; and determining suitability for various developmental uses, such as highways, local streets and roads, building foundations, and septic tank absorption fields.

A portion of a 1:15,840 scale USDA soil map printed on a photo mosaic base is shown as Figure 3.15. Table 3.3 shows a sampling of the kind of soil information and interpretations contained in USDA soil survey reports (see Section 4.2 for a further description of soil characteristics and terminology). This map and table show that the nature of soil conditions and, therefore, the appropriateness of land areas for various uses can vary greatly over short distances. As with soil map data, much of the interpretive soil information (such as shown in Table 3.3) is available as computer-based files.

As described in Section 1.4, the reflection of sunlight from bare (unvegetated) soil surfaces depends on many interrelated factors, including soil moisture content, soil texture, surface roughness, the presence of iron oxide, and the organic matter content. A unit of bare soil may manifest significantly different photo tones on different days, depending especially on its moisture content. Also, as the area of vegetated surfaces (leaves, etc.) increases during the growing season, the reflectance from the scene is more the result of vegetative characteristics than the soil type.

Plate 8 illustrates the dramatically different appearance of one agricultural field, approximately 15 ha in size, during one growing season. Except for a small area at the upper right, the entire field is mapped as one soil type by the USDA (map unit BbB as

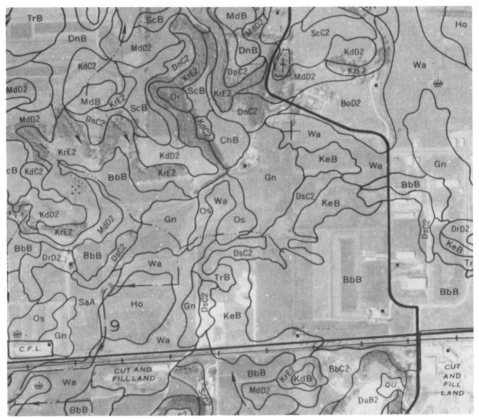

FIGURE 3.15 Portion of a USDA–SCS soil map, Dane County, Wisconsin. 1:15,840 (4 in. = 1 mile). (From [99].)

shown in Figure 3.15 and described in Table 3.3). The soil parent materials in this field consist of glacial meltwater deposits of stratified sand and gravel overlain by 45 to 150 cm of loess (wind-deposited silt). Maximum relief is about 2 m and slope ranges from 0 to 6 percent. This field was planted to corn (*Zea mays* L.) in May and harvested in November.

Plates 8*a*, *b*, and *c* illustrate the change in surface moisture patterns visible on the cultivated soil over a span of 48 hr in early summer. During this period, the corn plants were only about 10 cm tall and consequently most of the field surface was bare soil. The area received about 2.5 cm of rain on June 29. On June 30, when the photo in Plate 8*a* was exposed, the moist soil had a nearly uniform surface tone. By July 2 (8*c*), distinct patterns of dry soil surface (light photo tone) could be differentiated from areas of wet soil surface (darker photo tones). The dry areas have relatively high infiltration capacity and are slight mounds of 1 to 2 m relief. These topographic highs have very gentle slopes. Rainfall that does not infiltrate into the soil on these areas runs off onto lower portions of the landscape. These lower areas remain wet longer because they have relatively low infiltration capacity and receive runoff from the higher areas in addition to their original increment of rainfall.

TABLE 3.3 Soil Information and Interpretations for Five Soils Shown in Figure 3.15

Map unit (Figure 3.15)	Soil name	Soil description	Depth to ground-water table	Predicted corn yield (kg/ha)	Predicted degree of limitations for use as		
					Septic tank absorption fields	Sites for dwellings with basements	Golf course fairways
BbB	Batavia silt loam, gravelly substratum, 2–6% slope	100–200 cm silt over stratified sand and gravel	> 150 cm	8700	Moderate	Slight	Slight
Ho	Houghton muck, 0–2% slope	Muck at least 150 cm deep	0–30 cm	8100 (when drained)	Very severe	Very severe	Severe
KrE2	Kidder soils, 20–35% slope	About 60 cm silt over sandy loam glacial till	> 150 cm	not suited	Severe	Severe	Severe
MdB	McHenry silty loam 2–6% slope	25–40 cm silt over sandy loam glacial till	> 150 cm	7000	Slight	Slight	Slight
Wa	Wacousta silty clay loam, 0–2% slope	Silty clay loam and silt loam glacial lakebed materials	0–30 cm	7000	Very severe	Very severe	Severe

From USDA Dane County, Wisconsin, Soil Survey Report [99].

Plates 8*d*, *e*, and *f* illustrate changes in the appearance of the corn crop during the growing season. By August 11 (8*d*), the corn had grown to a height of 2 m. Vegetation completely covered the soil surface and the field had a very uniform appearance. However, by September 17 (8*e*), distinct tonal patterns were again evident. Very little rain fell on this field during July, August, and September, and growth of the corn during this period was dependent on moisture stored in the soil. In the dry areas, shown in light tan-yellow, the leaves and stalks of the corn were drying out and turning brown. In the wetter areas of pink and red photo colors, the corn plants were still green and continuing to grow.

Based on these photographs, a soil scientist was able to divide the soil moisture conditions in this field into four classes, as shown in Figure 3.16. Field inspection of selected sites in each of the four units produced the information in Table 3.4. Note that the corn yield is more than 50% greater in Unit 2 than in Unit 4.

This sequence of photographs taken during one growing season illustrates that certain times of the year are better suited to aerial photography for soil mapping purposes than others. In any given region and season, the most appropriate dates will vary widely, depending on many factors including temperature, rainfall, elevation, vegetative cover, and soil infiltration characteristics.

Works listed in the Selected Bibliography at the end of this chapter contain additional information on airphoto interpretation for geologic mapping [4, 6, 7, 43, 44,

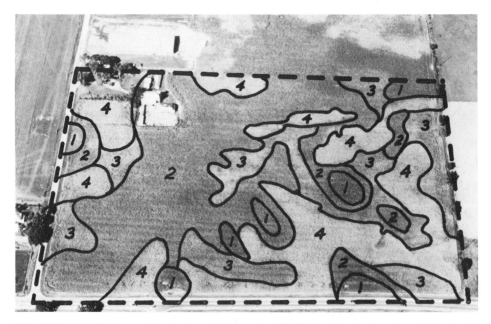

FIGURE 3.16   Oblique aerial photograph, September 17, 1969, with overlay showing four levels of soil moisture (see also Plate 8e), Dane County, Wisconsin. Approximately 1:3700 at photo center.

TABLE 3.4 Selected Characteristics of the Four Soil Units Shown in Figure 3.16

Characteristic	Unit 1	Unit 2	Unit 3	Unit 4
Thickness of silt over sand and gravel	At least 150 cm	105−135 cm	90−120 cm	45−105 cm
Soil drainage class (see Section 4.2)	Somewhat poorly drained	Moderately well drained	Moderately well to well drained	Well drained
Average corn yield (kg/ha)	Not sampled	9100	8250	5850

59, 69, 82, 84, 88] and airphoto interpretation for soil mapping [6, 7, 51, 92, 97, 98]. Chapter 4 contains a Selected Bibliography with additional works relating to geologic and soil mapping.

3.5 LAND USE/LAND COVER MAPPING

A knowledge of land use and land cover is important for many planning and management activities concerned with the surface of the earth. The use of panchromatic, medium scale aerial photographs to map land use has been an accepted practice since the 1940s. More recently, small scale aerial photographs and satellite images have been utilized for land use/land cover mapping of large areas.

The term *land cover* relates to the type of feature present on the surface of the earth. Urban buildings, lakes, maple trees, and glacial ice are all examples of land cover types. The term *land use* relates to the human activity associated with a specific piece of land. As an example, a tract of land on the fringe of an urban area may be used for single-family housing. Depending on the level of mapping detail, its *land use* could be described as urban use, residential use, or single-family residential use. The same tract of land would have a *land cover* consisting of roofs, pavement, grass, and trees. For a study of the socioeconomic aspects of land use planning (school requirements, municipal services, tax income, etc.), it would be important to know that the use of this land is for single-family dwellings. For a hydrologic study of rainfall-runoff characteristics, it would be important to know the amount and distribution of roofs, pavement, grass, and trees in this tract. Thus, a knowledge of both land use and land cover can be important for land planning and land management activities.

The USGS has devised a land use and land cover classification system for use with remote sensor data [9]. The concepts discussed in the remainder of this section are based principally on this publication.

Ideally, land use and land cover information should be presented on separate maps and not intermixed as in the USGS classification system. From a practical standpoint, however, it is most efficient to mix the two systems when remote sensing data form the principal data source for such mapping activities. While land cover information can be directly interpreted from appropriate remote sensing images, information about human activity on the land (land use) cannot always be inferred directly from land cover. As an example, extensive recreational activities covering large tracts of land are not particularly amenable to interpretation from aerial photographs or satellite images. For instance, hunting is a common and pervasive recreational use occurring on land that would be classified as some type of forest, range, wetland, or agricultural land during either a ground survey or image interpretation. Thus, additional information sources are needed to supplement the land cover data. Supplemental information is also necessary for determining the use of such lands as parks, game refuges, or water-conservation districts that may have land uses coincident with administrative boundaries not usually identifiable on remote sensor images. Recognizing that some information cannot be derived from remote sensing data, the USGS system is based on categories that can be reasonably interpreted from imagery.

The USGS land use and land cover classification system was designed according to the following criteria: (1) the minimum level of interpretation accuracy using remotely sensed data should be at least 85 percent, (2) the accuracy of interpretation for the several categories should be about equal, (3) repeatable or repetitive results should be obtainable from one interpreter to another and from one time of sensing to another, (4) the classification system should be applicable over extensive areas, (5) the categorization should permit land use to be inferred from the land cover types, (6) the classification system should be suitable for use with remote sensor data obtained at different times of the year, (7) categories should be divisible into more detailed subcategories that can be obtained from large scale imagery or ground surveys, (8) aggregation of categories must be possible, (9) comparison with future land use and land cover data should be possible, and (10) multiple uses of land should be recognized when possible.

The resulting USGS land use and land cover classification system for use with remote sensor data is shown in Table 3.5. The system is designed to use four "levels" of information, two of which are detailed in Table 3.5. A multilevel system has been devised because different degrees of detail can be obtained from different remote sensing products, depending on the sensor system and image resolution.

The USGS classification system also provides for the inclusion of more detailed land use/land cover categories in Levels III and IV. Levels I and II, with classifications specified by the USGS (Table 3.5), are principally of interest to users who desire information on a nationwide, interstate, or statewide basis. Levels III and IV can be utilized to provide information at a resolution appropriate for regional (multicounty), county, or local planning and management activities. Again, as shown in Table 3.5, Level I and II categories are specified by USGS. It is intended that Levels III and IV be designed by the local users of the USGS system, keeping in mind that the categories in each level must aggregate into the categories in the next higher level. Figure 3.17 illustrates a sample aggregation of classifications for Levels III, II, and I.

Table 3.6 lists representative image interpretation formats for the four land use and land cover classification levels. Level I was designed for use with very small scale imagery such as the Landsat Multispectral Scanner (MSS) images illustrated in Section 9.6. Level II was designed for use with small scale aerial photographs. The most widely used image type for Level II mapping has been high altitude color infrared photo-

TABLE 3.5 USGS Land Use/Land Cover Classification System for Use with Remote Sensor Data

Level I	Level II
1 Urban or built-up land	11 Residential
	12 Commercial and service
	13 Industrial
	14 Transportation, communications, and utilities
	15 Industrial and commercial complexes
	16 Mixed urban or built-up land
	17 Other urban or built-up land
2 Agricultural land	21 Cropland and pasture
	22 Orchards, groves, vineyards, nurseries, and ornamental horticultural areas
	23 Confined feeding operations
	24 Other agricultural land
3 Rangeland	31 Herbaceous rangeland
	32 Shrub and brush rangeland
	33 Mixed rangeland
4 Forest land	41 Deciduous forest land
	42 Evergreen forest land
	43 Mixed forest land
5 Water	51 Streams and canals
	52 Lakes
	53 Reservoirs
	54 Bays and estuaries
6 Wetland	61 Forested wetland
	62 Nonforested wetland
7 Barren land	71 Dry salt flats
	72 Beaches
	73 Sandy areas other than beaches
	74 Bare exposed rock
	75 Strip mines, quarries, and gravel pits
	76 Transitional areas
	77 Mixed barren land
8 Tundra	81 Shrub and brush tundra
	82 Herbaceous tundra
	83 Bare ground tundra
	84 Wet tundra
	85 Mixed tundra
9 Perennial snow or ice	91 Perennial snowfields
	92 Glaciers

graphs such as shown in Plate 9. However, small scale panchromatic aerial photographs (Figure 3.18), Landsat Thematic Mapper images (Section 9.9), and SPOT satellite images (Section 9.14) are also appropriate data sources for many Level II mapping categories. The general relationships shown in Table 3.6 are not intended to

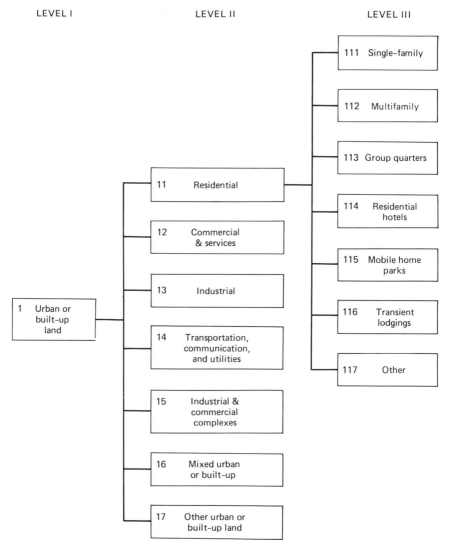

FIGURE 3.17   An example of aggregation of land use/land cover types.

TABLE 3.6   Representative Image Interpretation Formats for Various Land Use/Land Cover Classification Levels

Land use/land cover classification level	Representative format for image interpretation
I	Landsat MSS
II	Small scale aerial photography, Landsat TM and SPOT images
III	Medium scale aerial photography
IV	Large scale aerial photography

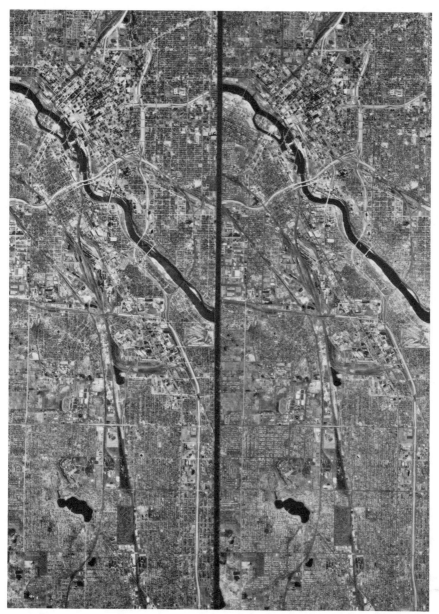

FIGURE 3.18 Small scale panchromatic aerial photographs, Minneapolis—St. Paul, Minnesota, April 1977. 1:94,000 (north to right). Stereogram. (Courtesy Mark Hurd Aerial Surveys, Inc.)

restrict users to particular scales, either in the original imagery or in the final map products. For example, Level I land use/land cover information, while efficiently and economically gathered over large areas by the Landsat satellites, could also be interpreted from conventional medium scale photography or compiled from a ground survey. Conversely, some of the Level II categories have been accurately interpreted from Landsat MSS data.

For mapping at Level III, substantial amounts of supplemental information, in addition to that obtained from medium scale images, may have to be acquired. Similarly, mapping at Level IV would also require substantial amounts of supplemental information, in addition to that obtained from large scale images.

The size of the minimum area that can be mapped as any particular land use/land cover class depends on the scale and resolution of the aerial photographs or satellite images. It also depends on the scale of data compilation and the final scale of the land use/land cover map. When land use/land cover data are to be presented in the form of maps, it is difficult to represent any unit area smaller than 2.5 mm on a side. In addition, smaller areas cause legibility problems for the map reader. Table 3.7 lists the minimum size ground areas that can be mapped at the various classification levels.

The USGS definitions for Level I classes are set forth in the following paragraphs. Since this system should be able to account for 100 percent of the earth's land surface (including inland water bodies), each square meter of the earth's land surface should fit into one of the nine Level I categories. Each Level II subcategory is explained in [9], but is not detailed here.

Urban or *built-up land* is composed of areas of intensive use with much of the land covered by structures. Included in this category are cities, towns, villages, strip developments along highways, transportation, power, and communication facilities, and areas such as those occupied by mills, shopping centers, industrial and commercial complexes, and institutions that may, in some instances, be isolated from urban areas. This category takes precedence over others when the criteria for more than one category are met. For example, residential areas that have sufficient tree cover to meet *forest land* criteria should be placed in the urban or built-up land category.

Agricultural land may be broadly defined as land used primarily for production of food and fiber. The category includes the following uses: cropland and pasture, orchards, groves and vineyards, nurseries and ornamental horticultural areas, and confined feeding operations. Where farming activities are limited by soil wetness, the

TABLE 3.7   Minimum Size of Land Use/Land Cover Units Mapped at Various Classification Levels

Land use/land cover classification level	Representative map compilation scale	Approximate minimum size area mapped[a] (ha)
I	1:500,000	150
II	1:62,500	2.5
III	1:24,000	0.35

[a]Based on minimum map unit size of 2.5 × 2.5 mm.

exact boundary may be difficult to locate and *agricultural land* may grade into *wetland*. When wetlands are drained for agricultural purposes, they are included in the *agricultural land* category. When such drainage enterprises fall into disuse and if wetland vegetation is reestablished, the land reverts to the *wetland* category.

Rangeland historically has been defined as land where the potential natural vegetation is predominantly grasses, grasslike plants, forbs, or shrubs and where natural grazing was an important influence in its precivilization state. Under this traditional definition, most of the rangelands in the United States are in the western range, the area to the west of an irregular north–south line that cuts through the Dakotas, Nebraska, Kansas, Oklahoma, and Texas. Rangelands also are found in additional regions, such as the Flint Hills (eastern Kansas), the southeastern states, and Alaska. The historical connotation of rangeland is expanded in the USGS classification to include those areas in the eastern states called brushlands.

Forest land represents areas that have a tree-crown areal density (crown closure percentage) of 10 percent or more, are stocked with trees capable of producing timber or other wood products, and exert an influence on the climate or water regime. Lands from which trees have been removed to less than 10 percent crown closure but which have not been developed for other uses are also included. For example, lands on which there are rotation cycles of clearcutting and blockplanting are part of the forest land category. Forest land that is extensively grazed, as in the southeastern United States, would also be included in this category because the dominant cover is forest and the dominant activities are forest related. Areas that meet the criteria for forest land and also urban and built-up land are placed in the latter category. Forested areas that have wetland characteristics are placed in the *wetland* class.

The *water* category includes streams, canals, lakes, reservoirs, bays, and estuaries.

The *wetland* category designates those areas where the water table is at, near, or above the land surface for a significant part of most years. The hydrologic regime is such that aquatic or hydrophytic vegetation is usually established, although alluvial and tidal flats may be nonvegetated. Examples of wetlands include marshes, mudflats, and swamps situated on the shallow margins of bays, lakes, ponds, streams, and artificial impoundments such as reservoirs. Included are wet meadows or perched bogs in high mountain valleys and seasonally wet or flooded basins, playas, or potholes with no surface water outflow. Shallow water areas where aquatic vegetation is submerged are classified as *water* and are not included in the *wetland* category. Areas in which soil wetness or flooding is so short-lived that no typical wetland vegetation is developed belong in other categories. Cultivated wetlands such as the flooded fields associated with rice production and developed cranberry bogs are classified as *agricultural land*. Uncultivated wetlands from which wild rice, cattails, and so forth are harvested are retained in the *wetland* category, as are wetlands grazed by livestock. Wetland areas drained for any purpose belong to the other land use/land cover categories such as urban or built-up land, agricultural land, rangeland, or forest land. If the drainage is discontinued and wetland conditions resume, the classification will revert to *wetland*. Wetlands managed for wildlife purposes are properly classified as *wetland*.

Barren land is land of limited ability to support life and in which less than one-third of the area has vegetation or other cover. This category includes such areas as dry salt flats, beaches, bare exposed rock, strip mines, quarries, and gravel pits. Wet, non-vegetated barren lands are included in the wetland category. Agricultural land temporarily without vegetative cover because of cropping season or tillage practices is considered *agricultural land*. Areas of intensively managed forest land that have clear-cut blocks evident are classified as *forest land*.

Tundra is the term applied to the treeless regions beyond the geographic limit of the boreal forest and above the altitudinal limit of trees in high mountain ranges. In North America, tundra occurs primarily in Alaska and northern Canada, and in isolated areas of the high mountain ranges.

Perennial snow or *ice* areas occur because of a combination of environmental factors that cause these features to survive the summer melting season. In so doing, they persist as relatively permanent features on the landscape.

As noted above, some parcels of land could be placed into more than one category and specific definitions are necessary to explain the classification priorities. This comes about because the USGS land use/land cover classification system contains a mixture of land activity, land cover, and land condition attributes.

This land use/land cover classification system is being utilized by the USGS in its land use/land cover mapping program. As a part of this program, Level I and II land use/land cover maps are being compiled for the United States to be used with the USGS 1:250,000 and 1:100,000 scale base maps. For most categories, a minimum mapping unit of 16 ha is being used. For greater detail, a minimum mapping unit of 4 ha is employed for the following Level I and II categories: urban or built-up land; water; confined feeding operations; other agricultural land; and strip mines, quarries, and gravel pits. In addition to maps, digital files are being generated. These products provide the data user with the flexibility to produce area measurements of various cover types and graphic plots of selected subsets of the original data. In a digital form, the land cover data may also be combined with other types of digital data in a geographic information system (Section 3.15).

3.6　AGRICULTURAL APPLICATIONS

When one considers the components involved in studying the worldwide supply and demand for agricultural products, the applications of remote sensing in general are indeed many and varied. The scope of the physical, biological, and technological problems facing modern agriculture is an extremely broad one that is intimately related with worldwide problems of population, energy, environmental quality, climate, and weather. These factors are in turn influenced by human values and traditions, and economic, political, and social systems. We make no attempt here to look at the "big picture" of how remote sensing is used in agriculture. Instead, we take a rather narrow view of the direct application of airphoto interpretation in three selected areas: crop type classification, crop condition assessment, and crop yield estimation.

Crop type classification (and area inventory) through airphoto interpretation is based on the premise that specific crop types can be identified by their spectral response patterns and photo texture. Successful identification of crops requires a knowledge of the developmental stages of each crop in the area to be inventoried. This information is typically summarized in the form of a *crop calendar* that lists the expected developmental status and appearance of each crop in an area throughout the year. Because of changes in crop characteristics during the growing season, photography from several dates during the growing cycle can by very useful in the interpretation process. In fact, multidate photography may be necessary for discrimination of similar crop types. The use of color and color infrared films provides advantages over the use of panchromatic film because of the increased spectral information of the color materials. Also, stereoscopic coverage provides the advantage of being able to use plant height in the discrimination process.

When only broad classes of crops are to be inventoried, single-date panchromatic photography may be sufficient. Table 3.8 shows a dichotomous airphoto interpretation key developed for the identification of major crop and land cover types in agricultural areas of California using medium scale panchromatic aerial photographs. This tabular style of dichotomous key is an alternative format to the style shown in Figure 3.1. This generalized classification scheme does not attempt to distinguish among various types of vine and bush crops, row crops, or continuous cover crops. When specific crop types are to be inventoried, a more detailed interpretation key employing multidate aerial photography using color and/or color infrared film may be required.

Figure 3.19 illustrates some of the factors important to airphoto interpretation for crop identification. The photographs shown in this figure are black and white reproductions of color infrared originals covering the same area on two different dates during the same growing season. The area shown is part of an experimental farm located in southern Minnesota. The crops present are alfalfa, corn, sunflowers, soybeans, and wheat. The photograph shown in (*a*) was taken during the early summer (June 25); the stereopair shown in (*b*) was taken in the late summer (August 17). Collectively, these images demonstrate the importance of date of photography, photo tone and texture, and stereoscopic coverage in the crop discrimination process.

Crop condition assessment can be aided by airphoto interpretation in various ways. For example, large scale airphotos have proven useful for documenting deleterious conditions due to crop disease, insect damage, plant stress from other causes, and disaster damage. The most successful applications have utilized large scale color infrared aerial photographs taken on various dates. In addition to "stress detection," such photographs can provide many other forms of information important to crop management. Table 3.9 lists the kinds of information potentially available from photo coverage obtained at different times in the growing season. In certain situations, detailed within-field interpretations of soil and crop conditions have been used as the basis for programming microprocessor controlled equipment such as fertilizer spreaders and irrigators. In this manner, crop management activities (such as fertilizer application rates) can be varied as a function of the exact geographic location within a field. (Section 10.6 discusses the use of satellite imaging for this same purpose.)

Some of the plant diseases that have been detected using airphoto interpretation are southern corn leaf blight, bacterial blight of field beans, potato wilt, sugar beet leaf spot, stem rust of wheat and oats, late blight fungus of potatoes, vineyard *Armillaria*

TABLE 3.8 Dichotomous Airphoto Interpretation Key for the Identification of Major Crop and Land Cover Types in Agricultural Areas of California for Use with Summertime Panchromatic Aerial Photographs at a Scale of 1:15,000

1. Vegetation or soil clearly discernible on photographs	See 2
1. Vegetation and soil either absent or largely obscured by artificial structures, bare rock, or water	Nonproductive lands
2. Cultivation pattern absent; field boundaries irregularly shaped	See 3
2. Cultivation pattern present; field boundaries regularly shaped	See 5
3. Trees present, covering most of ground surface	Timberland
3. Trees absent or widely scattered; ground surface covered by low-lying vegetation	See 4
4. Crowns of individual plants discernible; texture coarse and mottled	Brushland
4. Crowns of individual plants not discernible; texture fine	Grassland
5. Crop vegetation absent	Fallow
5. Crop vegetation present	See 6
6. Crowns of individual plants clearly discernible	See 7
6. Crowns of individual plants not clearly discernible	See 8
7. Alignment and spacing of individual trees at intervals of 6 m or more	Orchards
7. Alignment and spacing of individual plants at intervals of 3 m or more	Vine and bush crops
8. Rows of vegetation clearly discernible, usually at intervals of 0.5 to 1.5 m	Row crops
8. Rows of vegetation not clearly discernible; crops forming a continuous cover before reaching maturity	See 9
9. Evidence of use by livestock present; evidence of irrigation from sprinklers or ditches usually conspicuous	Irrigated pasture crops
9. Evidence of use by livestock absent; evidence of irrigation from sprinklers or ditches usually inconspicuous or absent; bundles of straw or hay and harvesting marks frequently discernible	Continuous cover crops (small grains, hay, etc.)

From [77].

mellea soil fungus, pecan root rot, and coconut wilt. Some types of insect damage that have been detected are aphid infestation in corn fields, phylloxera root feeding damage to vineyards, red mite damage to peach tree foliage, and plant damage due to fire ants, harvester ants, leaf cutting ants, army worms, and grasshoppers. Other types of plant damage that have been detected include those from moisture stress, iron deficiency, nitrogen deficiency, excessive soil salinity, wind and water erosion, rodent activity, road salts, air pollution, and cultivator damage.

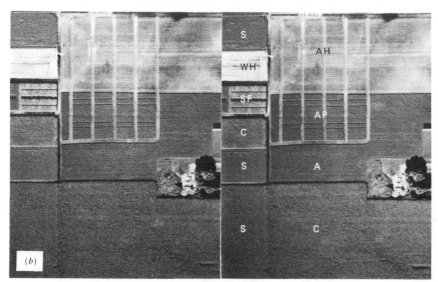

FIGURE 3.19 Black and white reproductions of large scale multidate color infrared photographs of various agricultural crops in southern Minnesota. 1:3600. *(a)* June 25, 1981. *(b)* August 17, 1981. Crops shown in *(b)* are alfalfa (A), alfalfa plots (AP), harvested alfalfa (AH), corn (C), soybeans (S), sunflowers (SF), and harvested wheat (WH). (Courtesy University of Minnesota Remote Sensing Laboratory.)

TABLE 3.9 Typical Crop Management Information Potentially Obtainable from Large Scale Color Infrared Aerial Photographs

---

Preplanting

Study variations in soil surface moisture, texture, and organic content in bare fields. Monitor residue and check conditions of terraces, grass waterways, and other surface features.

Plowing/Planting

Determine plowing and planting progress, poorly or excessively drained areas, runoff and erosion problems, and tile line locations.

Emergence

Detect delayed emergence and low plant density, looking for insect, disease, or weather problems, planting failure due to malfunctioning equipment, human error in planting, and effectiveness of preemergent herbicides. Determine necessary remedial measures (such as replanting).

Mid-growing season

Check on stand growth and development through the growing season, looking for evidence of plant loss or damage due to adverse moisture conditions, misapplication of chemicals, insects, diseases, eroded topsoil, nitrogen deficiencies, and problems in irrigation distribution. Monitor effectiveness of herbicide treatment and drainage.

Preharvest

Check stand condition and acreage to be harvested, looking for lodging, significant weed infestations, or other potential problems for harvesting operations. Check for uniformity of ripening.

Postharvest

Determine total area harvested. Check field cover in harvested areas for weed and volunteer regrowth, erosion, and soil moisture problems.

As Required

Document special situations such as flooding, drought, frost, fire, hail storms, tornados, hurricanes, or other problems.

Adapted from [11].

Airphoto interpretation for crop condition assessment is a much more difficult task than airphoto interpretation for crop type and area inventory. Ground reference data are essential and in most studies to date, comparisons have been made between healthy and stressed vegetation growing in adjacent fields or plots [7]. Under these conditions, interpreters might discriminate between finer differences in spectral response than would be possible in a noncomparative analysis—that is, the level of success would be lower if they did not know a stress existed in an area. It would also be more difficult to differentiate among the effects of disease, insect damage, nutrient deficiencies, or drought, from variations caused by plant variety, plant maturity, planting rate, or background soil color differences. Because many stress effects are most apparent during dry spells, photographs should not be taken soon after rainy weather.

In addition to crop damage due to disease, insects, and various other stresses, crop damage resulting from such disasters as flooding, drought, frost, fire, hailstorms, tornados, and hurricanes can be assessed by airphoto interpretation.

Crop yield estimation based on airphoto interpretation has met with varying degrees of success. In principle, the process is simple and straightforward. In a given study area, the interpreter needs to determine the area of each crop type and estimate the yield per unit area of each crop. The total crop production is then a simple product of the area times the yield per unit area. In practice, the process is complex. Crop yield depends, among other things, on soil moisture, soil fertility, and air and soil temperature. In addition, yield can be selectively reduced by disease, insect infestation, and other stress-producing agents. Crop yields can vary considerably within a single field, depending on soil patterns, as illustrated in Figure 3.16 and Table 3.4.

Beyond yield estimation, *crop yield prediction* can also be assisted through the interpretation process. Successful crop yield prediction must consider climatic and meteorologic conditions. Valuable input to the determination of these conditions can be obtained from meteorological satellite data (Section 9.16).

The traditional approach to crop yield estimation has been to use airphoto interpretation to identify and measure the total area of each crop type. Field inspection of small sample plots is then used to determine crop yield per unit area. A more direct approach is to acquire historical information on crop yield for individual fields and then use airphoto interpretation to determine how a specific year's yield appears to be deviating from the normal. This process requires the development of a correlation between leaf reflectance and crop yield and has met with only partial success. More than one date of photography during a growing season is normally required for successful implementation of this technique.

As mentioned earlier, many additional agricultural applications of airphoto interpretation exist. At the local level these include (1) detailed studies to determine areas that need erosion control, weed control, fertilizing, replanting, fencing, or other remedial measures; (2) farmland appraisals for taxation studies and other real estate purposes; (3) determination of the adequacy of existing irrigation systems for uniformly wetting an entire field; and (4) farm livestock surveys.

Works listed in the Selected Bibliography at the end of this chapter contain additional information on the agricultural applications of airphoto interpretation [7, 10, 11, 13, 18, 19, 33, 58, 61, 77, 79, 80, 87, 91, 103].

3.7 FORESTRY APPLICATIONS

Forestry is concerned with the management of forests for wood, forage, water, wildlife, and recreation. Because the principal raw product from forests is wood, forestry is especially concerned with timber management, maintenance and improvement of existing forest stands, and fire control. Forests of one type or another cover nearly a third of the world's land area. They are distributed unevenly and their resource value varies widely.

Airphoto interpretation provides a feasible means of monitoring many of the world's forest conditions. We will be concerned principally with the application of airphoto interpretation to tree species identification, timber cruising, and the assessment of disease and insect infestations.

The airphoto interpretation process for *tree species identification* is generally more complex than for agricultural crop identification. A given area of forest land is often occupied by a complex mixture of many tree species, as contrasted with agricultural land where large, relatively uniform fields are encountered. Also, foresters may be interested in the species composition of the "forest understory," which is often blocked from view on airphotos by the crowns of the large trees in the area.

Tree species can be identified on aerial photographs through the process of elimination. The first step is to eliminate those species whose presence in an area is impossible or improbable because of location, physiography, or climate. The second step is to establish which groups of species do occur in the area, based on a knowledge of the common species associations and their requirements. The final stage is the identification of individual tree species using basic photo interpretation principles.

The photographic characteristics of shape, size, pattern, shadow, tone, and texture, as described in Section 3.2, are used by interpreters in tree species identification. Individual tree species have their own characteristic crown *shape* and *size*. As illustrated in Figures 3.20 and 3.21, some species have rounded crowns, some have cone-shaped crowns, and some have star-shaped crowns. Variations of these basic crown shapes also occur. In dense stands, the arrangement of tree crowns produces a *pattern* that is distinct for many species. When trees are isolated, *shadows* often provide a profile image of trees that is useful in species identification. Toward the edges of the photo, relief displacement also affords somewhat of a profile view of trees. *Tone* in aerial photographs depends on many factors and it is not generally possible to correlate absolute tonal values with individual tree species. Relative tones on a single photograph, or a strip of photographs, may be of great value in delineating adjacent stands of different species. Variations in crown *texture* are important in species identification. Some species have a tufted appearance, others appear smooth, and still others look billowy.

Figures 3.22 and 3.23 illustrate how the above-described photographic characteristics can be used to identify tree species. A pure stand of black spruce (outlined area) surrounded by aspen is shown in Figure 3.22. Black spruce are coniferous trees with very slender crowns and pointed tops (Figures 3.20 and 3.21). In pure stands, the canopy is regular in pattern and the tree height is even or changes gradually with the quality of the site. The crown texture of dense black spruce stands is carpetlike in appearance. In contrast, aspen are deciduous trees with rounded crowns (Figures 3.20 and 3.21) that are more widely spaced than the spruce trees. The striking difference in photo texture between black spruce and aspen is apparent in Figure 3.22.

Stands of balsam fir and black spruce are shown in Figure 3.23. Balsam fir are symmetrical coniferous trees with sharply pointed tops (Figures 3.20 and 3.21). Since

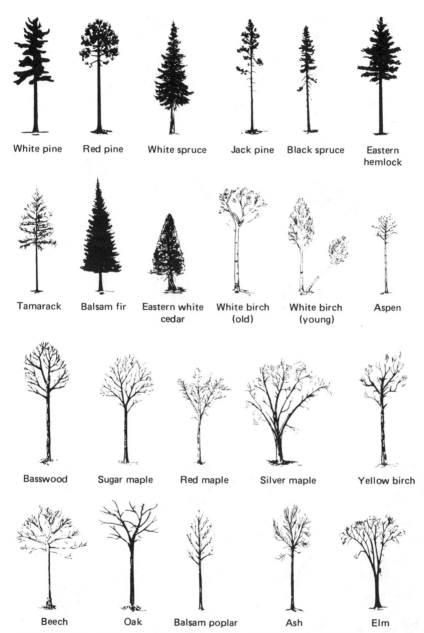

FIGURE 3.20 Silhouettes of forest trees. (From [85]. Copyright © 1961, American Society of Photogrammetry, reproduced with permission.)

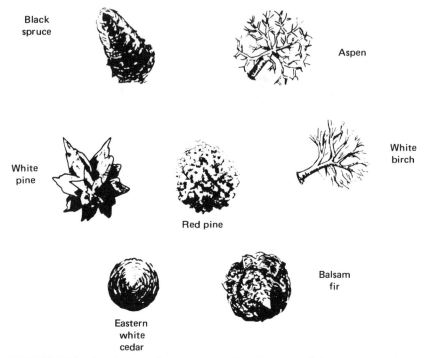

Black spruce

Aspen

White pine

White birch

Red pine

Eastern white cedar

Balsam fir

FIGURE 3.21   Aerial views of tree crowns. Note that most of these trees are shown with radial displacement (Chapter 5). (From [85]. Copyright © 1961, American Society of Photogrammetry, reproduced with permission.)

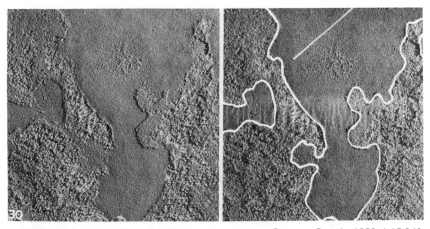

FIGURE 3.22   Black spruce (outlined area) and aspen, Ontario, Canada, 1959. 1:15,840. Stereogram. (From [108]. Courtesy Victor G. Zsilinszky, Ontario Centre for Remote Sensing.)

the crown widens rapidly toward the base with dense branching, balsam fir appears as a thicker tree than the slender black spruce. Area 2 is a pure stand of black spruce. Area 1 is a mixed stand containing 60 percent balsam fir and 40 percent black spruce. Balsam fir stands often have erratic changes in size, forming an uneven stand profile and an irregular stand pattern. Note the contrast in Figure 3.23 between the smooth, fine-textured pattern of the black spruce and the coarser-textured, more erratic pattern of the balsam fir. The process of tree species identification using airphoto interpretation is not as simple as might be implied by the straightforward examples shown in these figures. Naturally, the process is easiest to accomplish when dealing with pure, even-aged stands. Under other conditions, species identification can be an art more than a science. Identification of tree species has, however, been very successful when practiced by skilled, experienced interpreters. Field visitation is virtually always used to aid the interpreter in the type map compilation process.

The extent to which tree species can be recognized on aerial photographs is largely determined by the scale and quality of the photographs. The characteristics of tree form, such as crown shape and branching habit, are heavily used for identification on large scale photographs. The interpretability of these characteristics becomes progressively less as the scale is decreased. Eventually, the characteristics of individual trees become so indistinct that they are replaced by overall stand characteristics in terms of photographic tone, texture, and shadow pattern. On photographs at extremely large scales (such as 1:600), most species can be recognized almost entirely by their morphological characteristics. At this scale, twig structure, leaf arrangement and crown shape are important clues to species recognition. At scales of 1:2400 to 1:3000, small and medium branches are still visible and individual crowns can be clearly distinguished. At 1:8000, individual trees can still be separated, except when growing in dense stands, but it is not always possible to describe crown shape. At 1:15,840 (Figures 3.22

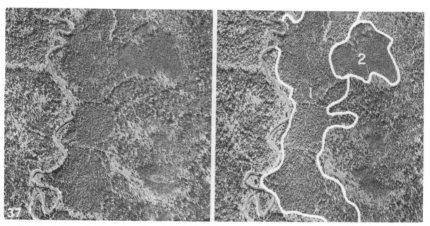

FIGURE 3.23 Balsam fir (1) and black spruce (2), Ontario, Canada, 1959. 1:15,840. Stereogram. (From [108]. Courtesy Victor G. Zsilinszky, Ontario Centre for Remote Sensing.)

and 3.23), crown shape can still be determined from tree shadows for large trees growing in the open. At scales smaller than 1:20,000, individual trees generally cannot be recognized when growing in stands, and stand tone and texture become the important identifying criteria [85].

The format most widely used for tree species identification has been panchromatic paper prints at a scale of 1:15,840 to 1:24,000. Black and white infrared paper prints are valuable in separating evergreen from deciduous types. However, color and color infrared films are being used with increasing frequency, particularly at small scales.

It is difficult to develop airphoto interpretation keys for tree species identification because individual stands vary considerably in appearance depending on age, site conditions, geographic location, geomorphic setting, and other factors. However, a number of elimination keys have been developed that have proven to be valuable interpretive tools when utilized by experienced photo interpreters. Tables 3.10, 3.11, and 3.12 are examples of such keys.

TABLE 3.10   Airphoto Interpretation Key for the Identification of Hardwoods in Summer

1. Crowns compact, dense, large	
2. Crowns very symmetrical and very smooth, oblong or oval; trees form small portion of stand	Basswood
2. Crowns irregularly rounded (sometimes symmetrical), billowy, or tufted	
3. Surface of crown not smooth, but billowy	Oak
3. Crowns rounded, sometimes symmetrical, smooth surfaced	Sugar maple,[a] beech[a]
3. Crowns irregularly rounded or tufted	Yellow birch[a]
1. Crowns small, or if large, open or multiple	
6. Crowns small or, if large, open and irregular, revealing light-colored trunk	
7. Trunk chalk white, often forked; trees tend to grow in clumps	White birch
7. Trunk light, but not white, undivided trunk reaching high into crown, generally not in clumps	Aspen
6. Crown medium sized or large; trunk dark	
8. Crown tufted, or narrow and pointed	
9. Trunk often divide, crown tufted	Red maple
9. Undivided trunk, crown narrow	Balsam poplar
8. Crowns flat topped or rounded	
10. Crowns medium sized, rounded; undivided trunk; branches ascending	Ash
10. Crowns large, wide; trunk divided into big spreading branches	
11. Top of crown appears pitted	Elm
11. Top of crown closed	Silver maple

From [85]. Copyright © 1961, American Society of Photogrammetry, reproduced with permission.
[a]A local tone-key showing levels 4 and 5 is usually necessary to distinguish these species.

Phenological correlations are useful in tree species identification. Changes in the appearance of trees in the different seasons of the year sometimes enable discrimination of species that are indistinguishable on single dates. The most obvious example is the separation of deciduous and evergreen trees that is easily made on photographs taken when the deciduous foliage has fallen. This distinction can also be discerned on spring photos taken shortly after the flushing of leaves or on fall photos taken after the trees have turned color. In the summer, panchromatic and color photographs show little difference in tone between deciduous and evergreen trees (Figure 1.9*a*). Differences in tones are generally quite striking, however, on summer color infrared and black and white infrared photographs (Figure 1.9*b*).

In spring photography, differences in the time at which species leaf out can provide valuable clues for species recognition. For example, trembling aspen and white birch consistently are among the first trees to leaf out, while the oaks, ashes, and large-tooth aspen are among the last. These two groups could be distinguished on photographs taken shortly after trembling aspen and white birch have leafed out. Tone differences between hardwoods, which are small during the summer, become definite during the fall, when some species turn yellow, and others red or brown. The best species distinctions in the fall are obtained on airphotos taken when fall coloring is at its peak, rather than when some trees have lost their levels [85].

Airphoto interpretation is used extensively for "timber cruising." The primary objective of such operations is to determine the volume of timber that might be

TABLE 3.11 Airphoto Interpretation Key for the Identification of Conifers

1. Crowns small or, if large, then definitely cone-shaped	
Crowns broadly conical usually rounded tip; branches not prominent	Cedar
Crowns narrow, often cylindrical; trees frequently grow in swamps	Swamp type black spruce
Crowns conical, deciduous, very light toned in fall, usually associated with black spruce	Tamarack
Crowns narrowly conical, very symmetrical, top pointed; branches less prominent than in white spruce	Balsam fir
Crowns narrowly conical; top often appears obtuse on photograph (except northern white spruce); branches more prominent than in balsam fir	White spruce, black spruce (except swamp type)
Crowns irregular, sometimes with pointed top; have thinner foliage and smoother texture than spruce and balsam fir	Jack pine
1. Crowns large and spreading, not narrowly conical; top often not well defined	
2. Crowns very dense, irregular or broadly conical	
Individual branches very prominent; crown usually irregular	White pine
Individual branches rarely very prominent; crown usually conical	Eastern hemlock
2. Crowns open, oval (circular in plan view)	Red pine

From [85]. Copyright © 1961, American Society of Photogrammetry, reproduced with permission.

TABLE 3.12   Dichotomous Airphoto Interpretation Key for the Identification of Several Forest Tree Species in Eastern Tennessee Using Normal Color Film Transparencies

1. Branching layered, radially triangular; crown margin serrate; crown foliage light green to moderate green	White pine
1. Branching not radially triangular; crown margin not serrate	Go to 2
2. Leaves mostly inconspicuous; tree branches virtually bare	Go to 3
2. Leaves present in crown	Go to 5
3. No foliage present; dark-colored bole and branches completely bare	White basswood
3. Very little foliage remaining (<5%)	Go to 4
4. Branching gives crown fine-textured appearance	White ash or black walnut
4. Branching appears medium textured	Yellow buckeye
5. Crown foliage thinning; trees losing a significant portion (40%) of leaves in early fall	Go to 6
5. Crown foliage dense or full; leaves abundant on branches	Go to 8
6. Branching appears finely divided or dissected; crown margin circular or oval and usually large; branches silver gray; crown foliage finely textured; crown color moderate orange yellow to dark orange yellow	American beech
6. Branching appears more massive and is moderately divided; crown shape and size variable	Go to 7
7. Crown apex domed or tufted; crown margin moderately sinuate; crown foliage colors moderate red and/or moderate reddish orange	Blackgum
7. Crown apex rounded; crown size small; crown color dark pink to grayish red	Sweetgum
8. Crown margin shape circular or oval and generally entire	Go to 9
8. Crown margin shape generally irregular with medium to large sinuations; crown apex domed, tufted, or billowy	Go to 10
9. Crown texture fine and feathery; crown small with random lineation; predominant crown colors moderate olive green to yellow green	Shortleaf pine or Virginia pine
9. Crown texture very fine; crown apex rounded to broadly oval; small-sized crowns with tufted or parted appearance; crown color light yellowish green	Black locust
10. Large masses of foliage divided and part crown; crown foliage moderate yellow green to moderate yellowish green	White oak
10. Predominant crown colors light grayish red, grayish red, or dark yellowish pink	Scarlet oak

From [7], 1st ed. Copyright © 1975, American Society of Photogrammetry, reproduced with permission.

harvested from an individual tree or (more commonly) stand of trees. To be successful, aerial photo timber cruising requires a highly skilled interpreter working with both aerial and ground data. Photo measurements on individual trees or stands are statistically related to ground measurements of tree volume in selected plots. The results are then extrapolated to large areas. The photo measurements most often used are (1) tree height or stand height, (2) tree-crown diameter, (3) density of stocking, and (4) stand area.

The height of an individual tree, or the mean height of a stand of trees, is normally determined by measuring relief displacement or image parallax (Chapter 5). The task of measuring tree-crown diameters is no different from obtaining other distance measurements on photos. Ground distances are obtained from photo distances via the scale relationship. The process is expedited by the use of special purpose overlays similar to dot grids. Overlays are also used to measure the density of stocking in an area in terms of the crown closure or percentage of the ground area covered by tree crowns. Alternatively, some measure of the number of individual crowns per unit area may be made. The accuracy of these measurements is influenced by such factors as the film−filter combination used to obtain the photography, the season of the photography, and the amount of shadow in the imagery.

Once data on individual trees or stands are extracted from photography, they are statistically related (using multiple regression) with ground data on timber volume to prepare *photo volume tables*. The volume of *individual* trees is normally determined as a function of species, crown diameter, and height, as illustrated in Table 3.13. This method of timber volume estimation is practical only on large scale photographs and is normally used to measure the volume of scattered trees in open areas. More frequently, *stand volumes* are of interest. Stand volume tables are normally based on combinations of species, height, crown diameter, and crown closure (Table 3.14).

Airphoto interpretation has been used in many instances to survey forest and urban shade tree damage from disease and insect infestations, as well as other causes. A

TABLE 3.13 Estimated Volume (m^3) of Individual Second-Growth Southern Pine Trees

Crown diameter (m)	Total tree height (m)				
	15	20	25	30	35
3	0.27	0.34	0.43	0.55	—
4	0.39	0.49	0.61	0.74	0.88
5	0.50	0.64	0.79	0.95	1.12
6	—	0.88	1.05	1.25	1.48
7	—	1.08	1.30	1.55	1.83
8	—	1.28	1.56	1.87	2.21
9	—	—	1.98	2.37	2.79

Adapted from [100].

TABLE 3.14   Estimated Volume (m³/ha) of Kentucky Hardwood Stands

Average stand height (m)	Average crown diameter (m)	Crown closure (%)								
		15	25	35	45	55	65	75	85	95
9	3−4	21	26	30	33	36	40	44	49	54
12	3−4	25	30	35	39	42	46	49	53	56
15	3−4	28	33	39	44	49	54	58	63	68
18	3−4	39	47	55	61	67	72	78	84	90
21	3−4	63	75	85	93	98	103	107	112	117
9	5−6	24	28	31	35	38	43	48	52	57
12	5−6	28	31	35	40	45	50	55	59	64
15	5−6	31	37	42	47	52	58	64	70	76
18	5−6	42	51	59	66	73	77	80	84	87
21	5−6	70	80	91	98	105	108	112	115	119
24	5−6	105	114	122	128	133	138	142	147	152
12	7−8	35	44	52	59	66	72	78	84	90
15	7−8	42	52	63	70	77	83	89	94	100
18	7−8	63	73	84	89	94	99	104	108	113
21	7−8	94	103	112	117	122	127	132	136	141
24	7−8	122	133	143	149	154	159	163	168	173
27	7−8	155	165	175	180	185	190	195	199	204
30	7−8	190	200	210	215	220	224	227	231	234
12	9+	59	72	84	89	94	99	104	108	113
15	9+	73	84	94	100	105	110	114	119	124
18	9+	91	101	110	115	120	125	130	135	140
21	9+	119	129	138	145	150	155	160	165	170
24	9+	150	159	168	175	182	186	190	195	200
27	9+	182	190	200	205	210	215	220	225	230
30	9+	213	222	231	236	241	245	248	252	255
33	9+	252	259	266	271	276	281	286	290	295

Adapted from [100].

variety of film types and scales have been utilized for damage surveys. Although panchromatic photographs have often been used, the most successful surveys have typically used medium or large scale color and color infrared photographs. Some types of tree disease damage due to bacteria, fungus, virus, and other agents that have been detected using airphoto interpretation are ash dieback, beech bark disease, Douglas fir root rot, Dutch elm disease, maple dieback, oak wilt, and white pine blister rust. Some types of insect damage that have been detected are those caused by the balsam wooly aphid, black-headed budworm, Black Hills bark beetle, Douglas fir beetle, gypsy moth larva, pine butterfly, mountain pine beetle, southern pine beetle, spruce bud-worm, western hemlock looper, western pine beetle, and white pine weevil. Other types of forest damage that have been detected include those resulting from air pollution (e.g., ozone, sulfur dioxide, "smog"), animals (e.g., beaver, deer, porcu-pine), fire, frost, moisture stress, soil salinity, nutrient imbalance, and storms.

Representative examples of airphotos depicting forest damage (due to gypsy moth defoliation) are included in Plate 6 and Figure 6.14. Plate 6 shows a small center portion (the black circle is the exact center of the frame) of a color infrared optical bar camera photograph (Section 2.11). This photograph was taken as part of a USFS program aimed at assessing gypsy moth defoliation in hardwood forests in the north-east and determining the effectiveness of direct control of the gypsy moth with microbial and chemical insecticides. Color infrared film was selected because inter-preters found that there is a greater contrast between the gray color of defoliated areas and the bright red of undamaged trees on this film type than can be seen on black and white or normal color film.

The site shown in Plate 6 is a ridge in the Appalachian Mountains of central Pennsylvania. The thin, light-toned line that runs from upper right (northeast) to lower left (southwest) is a ridge-top road. The trees on the slopes are almost exclusively hardwoods that consist of several species of oak, hickory, maple, and yellow poplar. Some evergreen stands (mostly red pine and white pine) can be seen at lower right; their dark reddish color is in sharp contrast to the bright red color of the hardwoods. Agricultural fields can be seen at the upper left. Heavy and widespread defoliation (greater than 60 percent) is present on much of the southeast-facing slope, and moderate and widespread defoliation (30−60 percent) is present on much of the northwest-facing slope.

In this discussion we have highlighted the application of airphoto interpretation to tree species identification, timber cruising, and forest damage assessment. However, the forest management applications of airphoto interpretation extend far beyond the scope of these three activities. Additional applications include such tasks as forest land appraisal, timber harvest planning, monitoring logging and reforestation, planning and assessing applications of herbicides and fertilizer in forest stands, assessing plant vigor and health in forest nurseries, mapping "forest fuels" to assess fire potential, planning fire suppression activities, assessing potential slope failures and soil erosion, planning forest roads, inventorying forest recreation resources, censusing wildlife and assessing wildlife habitat, and monitoring vegetation regrowth in fire lanes and power line rights-of-way.

Again, the success of virtually all of the above applications is premised on the existence of high quality reference data to aid in the interpretation. The use of airphotos and "conventional" ground methods of observation and measurement are typically closely intertwined. For example, timber volume inventories are basically premised on extensive ground measurement in sample plots (of tree volumes), but airphotos are used to stratify the area to be inventoried and establish the location of these plots (typically based on interpreted tree type, stand area, and stocking density information). Thus, the interpretation process complements, rather than replaces, the field activities.

Works listed in the Selected Bibliography contain additional information on the forestry applications of airphoto interpretation [6, 7, 10, 15, 24, 25, 39, 42, 47, 67, 72–77, 85, 91, 100, 108].

3.8 RANGELAND APPLICATIONS

As previously mentioned (Section 3.5), rangeland has historically been defined as land where the potential natural vegetation is predominately grasses, grasslike plants, forbs, or shrubs and where natural grazing was an important influence in its precivilization state. Rangelands not only provide forage for domestic and wild animals, they represent areas potentially supporting land uses as varied as intensive agriculture, recreation, and housing. Rangelands frequently also represent sources for minerals, oils, and water.

Given the expanse and remoteness of rangelands, and the diversity and intensity of pressures upon them, airphoto interpretation has been shown to be a valuable range management tool. Fundamentally, airphoto interpretation has received extensive use in inventorying and monitoring each of the major components of rangeland ecosystems—vegetation, soils, and animals. In that we treat the principles of applying airphoto interpretation to each of these areas elsewhere, we only wish to emphasize their relevance to range management here. Works listed in the Selected Bibliography contain additional information on the range management applications of airphoto interpretation [5, 7, 36, 81]. Also, we briefly illustrate the application of digitally processed satellite data to rangeland biomass estimation in Section 10.6.

3.9 WATER RESOURCE APPLICATIONS

Whether for irrigation, power generation, drinking, manufacturing, or recreation, water is one of our most critical resources. Airphoto interpretation can be used in a variety of ways to help monitor the quality, quantity, and geographic distribution of this resource. In this section, we are concerned principally with the use of airphoto interpretation in water pollution detection, lake eutrophication assessment, and flood damage estimation. Before describing each of these applications, let us review some of the basic properties of the interaction of sunlight with clear water.

In general, most of the sunlight that enters a clear water body is absorbed within about 2 m of the surface. The degree of absorption is highly dependent on wavelength. Near-infrared wavelengths are absorbed in only a few tenths of a meter of water, resulting in very dark image tones of even shallow water bodies on infrared photos. Absorption in the visible portion of the spectrum varies quite dramatically with the characteristics of the water body under study. From the standpoint of photography of bottom details through clear water, the best light penetration is achieved between the wavelengths of 0.48 and 0.60 μm. Although blue wavelengths penetrate well, they are extensively scattered and an "underwater haze" results. Red wavelengths penetrate only a few meters.

The analysis of underwater features is often permitted by using films sensitive to at least the wavelengths of 0.48 to 0.60 μm. Excellent photographs of bottom details in clear ocean water can be achieved using both normal color and color infrared photography. White sand bottoms under clear ocean water will appear blue-green using normal color film and blue using color infrared film (with a yellow filter). Bottom details are somewhat sharper using color infrared film because the blue wavelengths are filtered out and, thus, the effects of "underwater haze" are minimized. With such photography, the color infrared film becomes essentially a two-layer film because there is almost no infrared reflection from the water and, therefore, virtually no image on the infrared sensitive film layer.

Figure 3.24 illustrates the penetration of different wavelengths of sunlight into clear ocean water. The upper part of the photographs shows an exposed coral reef (varying amounts are exposed in the different frames due to wave action). The high infrared reflectance from the exposed coral results from the presence of algae that live in a symbiotic relationship with the coral. Most of the underwater reef consists of coral whose uppermost surfaces come to within about 0.3 m of the water surface. The keyhole-shaped area in the photo center has water depths ranging from very shallow near the dry white sand beach at lower right to a maximum of about 2 m near the center of the round part of the keyhole (upper left part of the photos).

Water Pollution Detection

All naturally occurring water contains some impurities. Water is considered polluted when the presence of impurities is sufficient to limit its use for a given domestic and/or industrial purpose. Not all pollutants are the result of human activity. Natural sources of pollution include such things as minerals leached from soil and decaying vegetation. When dealing with water pollution, it is appropriate to consider two types of sources: point and nonpoint. *Point sources* are highly localized, such as industrial outfalls. *Nonpoint sources*, such as fertilizer and sediment runoff from agricultural fields, have large and dispersed source areas.

Each of the following categories of materials, when present in excessive amounts, can result in water pollution [101]: (1) organic wastes contributed by domestic sewage and industrial wastes of plant and animal origin that remove oxygen from the water through decomposition; (2) infectious agents contributed by domestic sewage and by certain kinds of industrial wastes that may transmit disease; (3) plant nutrients that promote nuisance growths of aquatic plant life such as algae and water weeds; (4) synthetic-organic chemicals such as detergents and pesticides resulting from chemical technology that are toxic to aquatic life and potentially to humans; (5) inorganic chemical and mineral substances resulting from mining, manufacturing processes, oil plant operations, and agricultural practices that interfere with natural stream purification, destroy fish and aquatic life, cause excessive hardness of water supplies, produce corrosive effects, and in general add to the cost of water treatment; (6) sediments that fill streams, channels, harbors, and reservoirs, cause abrasion of hydroelectric power and pumping equipment, affect the fish and shellfish population by blanketing fish

FIGURE 3.24 Black and white copies of color and color infrared photographs, Hanauma Bay, Island of Oahu, Hawaii, June 1972. *(a)* Normal color film (0.40 to 0.70 μm). *(b)* Color infrared film

with a Wratten No. 15 filter (0.50 to 0.90 μm). *(c)* Color infrared film with a Wratten No. 29 filter (0.60 to 0.90 μm). *(d)* Color infrared film with a Wratten No. 87 filter (0.74 to 0.90 μm).

nests, spawn, and food supplies, and increase the cost of water treatment; (7) radioactive pollution resulting from the mining and processing of radioactive ores, from the use of refined radioactive materials, and from fallout following nuclear testing; (8) temperature increases that result from the use of water for cooling purposes by steam electric power plants and industries, and from impoundment of water in reservoirs, and which have harmful effects on fish and aquatic life, and reduce the capacity of the receiving water to assimilate wastes.

It is rarely possible to make a positive identification of the type and concentration of a pollutant by airphoto interpretation alone. However, it is possible to use airphoto interpretation to identify the point at which a discharge reaches a body of water and to determine the general dispersion characteristics of its plume. In some instances, such as the case of sediment suspended in water, it is possible to make valid observations about sediment concentrations using quantitative photographic radiometry (Chapter 6) coupled with the laboratory analysis of selective water samples.

Sediment pollution is often clearly depicted on aerial photographs. Figure 3.25 shows the dispersal plume of water containing suspended solids flowing into a lake. During the 48 hr prior to the date of the photograph, more than 75 mm of rain fell on the 6136 ha Pheasant Branch Watershed (Section 3.15). The erosion of soil from agricultural fields and home construction sites in the watershed, coupled with a heavy steam flow, resulted in the transportation of a large volume of tan-colored suspended solids (silt and clay) that entered the lake and circulated (driven by the wind) to the

FIGURE 3.25 Black and white copy of a low altitude (flying height = 900 m) color infrared oblique 35 mm aerial photograph showing the dispersal plume of silt-laden water flowing into a lake. Pheasant Branch Creek and Lake Mendota, Wisconsin, June 27, 1969.

right along the lakefront properties. The lake water has a low reflectance of sunlight, similar to that for "Water (Clear)" shown in Figure 1.10. The spectral response pattern of the suspended solids resembles that of "Dry Bare Soil (Gray-Brown)" shown in Figure 1.10. Because the spectral response pattern of the suspended materials is distinct from that of the natural lake water, these two materials can be readily distinguished on the photograph.

Additional examples of water containing suspended solids flowing into water bodies are shown in Figure 2.27 (LFC photograph showing the Po River flowing into the Adriatic Sea) and Figure 4.60a (Landsat MSS image showing the Mississippi River flowing into the Gulf of Mexico).

When point-source pollutants—such as domestic and industrial wastes—enter natural water bodies, there is typically a dispersal plume similar to that shown in Figure 3.25. If pollutants have reflectance characteristics different from the water bodies, their mixing and dispersal can be traced on aerial photographs. Aerial photographs have been successfully used in the enforcement of antipollution laws. In such cases, it is normally mandatory that reference water samples be collected from within the plume and outside the plume coincident with the time of aerial photography. The aerial photographs can be used as evidence in court cases to establish the source of the pollutant samples collected. However, extreme care must be taken to follow the legal rules of evidence pertaining to photographic exhibits.

Materials that form films on the water surface, such as oil films, can also be detected through the use of aerial photography. Oil enters the world's water bodies from a variety of sources, including natural seeps, municipal and industrial waste discharges, urban runoff, and refinery and shipping losses and accidents. Thick *oil slicks* have a distinct brown or black color. Thinner *oil sheens* and *oil rainbows* have a characteristic silvery sheen or iridescent color banding but do not have a distinct brown or black color. The principal reflectance differences between water bodies and oil films in the photographic part of the spectrum occur between 0.30 and 0.45 μm. Therefore, the best results are obtained when normal color or ultraviolet aerial photography is employed. An example of an oil film on a water surface is shown in Figure 3.26. This photograph shows a small portion of the St. Lawrence River downstream from a point where a barge transporting No. 6 bunker oil ran aground on a shoal in the river. Currents, combined with winds, quickly dispersed the spilled oil over a 129 km stretch of the river. Aerial photography was used to deploy oil cleanup resources at the time of the spill and to assess damage to the natural and artificial components of the river environment after the fact.

Lake Eutrophication Assessment

Water quality in inland lakes is often described in terms of *trophic state* (nutritional state). A lake choked with aquatic weeds or a lake with extreme-nuisance algal blooms is called a *eutrophic* (nutrient-rich) lake. A lake with very clear water is called an *oligotrophic* (low nutrient, high oxygen) lake. The general process by which lakes age is referred to as *eutrophication*. Eutrophication is a natural process expressed in terms of geologic time. However, when influenced by human activity the process is greatly

FIGURE 3.26 Black and white copy of a color aerial photograph showing an oil film on a water surface. St. Lawrence River at International Bridge between Ontario and New York, northeast of Kingston, Ontario, June 24, 1976. (Courtesy Environmental Protection Agency.)

accelerated and may result in "polluted" water conditions. Such processes are termed *cultural eutrophication* and are intimately related to land use/land cover.

What constitutes an unacceptable degree of eutrophication is a function of who is making the judgment. Most recreational users of water bodies prefer clear water free of excessive *macrophytes* (large aquatic plants) and *algae*. Swimmers, boaters, and water skiers prefer lakes relatively free of submersed macrophytes, while persons fishing for bass and similar fish generally prefer some macrophytes. Large concentrations of blue-green algae have an unpleasant odor that is offensive to most people, especially during "blooms," or periods following active algal growth. Green algae tend to be less bothersome, unless present in large quantities.

The use of airphoto interpretation coupled with selective field observations is an effective technique for mapping aquatic macrophytes. Macrophyte community mapping can be accomplished through the use of airphoto interpretation keys, as shown in Table 3.15. More detailed information regarding total plant biomass or plant density can be achieved by utilizing photographic radiometry (Chapter 6) techniques. Airphoto interpretation has been used to economically plan and monitor operations such as mechanical harvesting or chemical treatment of weeds.

Concentrations of free-floating algae are a good indicator of a lake's trophic status. Excessive concentrations of blue-green algae are especially prevalent under eutrophic conditions. Seasonally, blooms of blue-green algae occur during warm water conditions in late summer, whereas diatoms are more common in the cold water of spring

TABLE 3.15 Airphoto Interpretation Key for the Identification of Aquatic Vegetation Community Types, for Use with Medium Scale Late-Summer Color Infrared Aerial Photographs of Lake Wingra, Wisconsin

Map Unit	Tone	Texture	Location	Shape
Milfoil community	Deep orange	Mottled	0.7−2.7 m water depth	Variable (distinct boundaries)
Water lily beds	Bright pink	Fine	0.35−0.80 m water depth (protected areas)	Round to elongate
Green algae mat	Very light tan	Very smooth	Overgrowth on milfoil (near storm sewer outfalls)	Amorphous (indistinct boundaries)
Coontail bed	Deep red	Uniform to rough	Edges of milfoil beds	Variable
Potamogeton−milfoil complex	Dark green	Uniform	Near shore	Variable
Floating-leaved *potamogeton*	Medium pink	Coarse	1.0−2.0 m water depth	Round
Shallow-water marl	Light turquoise	Uniform	0.35−0.80 m water depth	Elongate (sharp boundaries)
Deep water	Deep blue	Uniform	More than 3.0 m water depth	—

Adapted from [1].

and fall. Green algae are typically present at any point in the seasonal cycle of lakes. Because the different broad classes of algae have somewhat different spectral response patterns, they can be distinguished by aerial photography. However, the wavelengths corresponding to peak reflectance of blue-green and green algae are often close together and the most positive results can be obtained using narrow-band multiband photography with filters selected to maximize the differences between spectral response. Multiband photography has also been used to study the chlorophyll concentration of water bodies. With increases in concentration, green band reflectance increases significantly and blue band reflectance decreases. As illustrated in Chapter 6 (Figure 6.28), such differences can be quantified from aerial photographs.

Flood Damage Estimation

The use of aerial photography for *flood damage estimation* is illustrated in Figures 3.27 and 3.28. Such photographs help document the need for federal disaster relief funds, when appropriate, and can be utilized by insurance agencies to assist in assessing the monetary value of property loss.

Figure 3.27 is a multidate sequence of photographs showing river flooding and its aftereffects. Figure 3.27a is a late-summer USDA−ASCS airphoto showing the normal appearance of the Pecatonica River as it meanders through cropland in southern Wisconsin. Figure 3.27b shows the same area near the peak of a flood whose severity is expected only once each 100 years. The flood water is about 3 m deep in the area at the center of this photograph. On the day before this photograph was taken, more than 150 mm of rain fell in a 2.5 hr period on the Pecatonica River watershed, which contains roughly 1800 km² above this area. Figure 3.27c shows the same area 3 weeks after flooding. The soils in the flooded area are moderately well drained to poorly drained silt loam alluvial soils that are high in fertility and in moisture supplying capacity. The darkest soil tones in Figure 3.27c correspond to the poorly drained areas that are still quite wet 3 weeks after flooding. The widespread crop damage can be clearly seen on this photograph. Figure 3.27d was taken 6 weeks after the flooding. Although the soil conditions have returned to normal, the widespread crop damage is still very evident on this photograph. The streaked pattern of light-toned lines in the right-hand part clearly shows the direction of river flow at the time of flooding. Note that each light-toned streak is just downstream from a tree or group of trees and aligned with the direction of flow.

Figure 3.28 shows panchromatic and infrared photographs taken by the Tennesee Valley Authority (TVA) for flood damage assessment purposes. Note that the limits of the stream water and the presence of water and wet soils in the fields can be seen more distinctly in the black and white infrared photograph (b). As further described in Chapter 4, aerial photographs are used extensively in delineating flood prone areas for land use planning and flood insurance programs.

Flood damage assessment across large areas can be facilitated by the use of satellite images. Figure 9.12b is a Landsat MSS image showing flooding of the Wisconsin River.

Other Selected Applications

A knowledge of *groundwater location* is important for both water supply and pollution control analysis. The identification of topographic and vegetation indicators of groundwater and the determination of the location of *groundwater discharge areas* (springs and seeps) can assist in the location of potential well sites. Also, it is important to be able to identify *groundwater recharge zones* in order to protect these areas (via zoning restrictions) from activities that would pollute the groundwater supply. Presently available airphoto interpretation techniques cannot be used directly to map the depth to water in a groundwater system. However, vegetation types have been successfully used as indicators of approximate depth to groundwater. Estimates of *groundwater use* have also been made based on the interpretation of crop type, area, and irrigation method.

Additional water resource applications of airphoto interpretation include hydro-

FIGURE 3.27   Black and white copies of panchromatic and color infrared aerial photographs showing flooding and its aftereffects, Pecatonica River near Gratiot, Wisconsin. *(a)* USDA–ASCS panchromatic photograph, August 27, 1962. 1:10,000. *(b)* Oblique color infrared photograph, June 30, 1969. *(c)* Oblique color infrared photograph, July 22, 1969. *(d)* Oblique color infrared photograph, August 11, 1969. The flying height for photos *(b)* to *(d)* was 1100 m.

FIGURE 3.27   *(continued)*

FIGURE 3.28 Flooding of Bear Creek, northwest Alabama, April 3, 1969. 1:9000. *(a)* Panchromatic film with a Wratten No. 12 (yellow) filter, 9:43 A.M. *(b)* Black and white infrared film with a Wratten No. 12 filter, 12:51 P.M. (Courtesy Mapping Services Branch, Tennessee Valley Authority.)

logic watershed assessment, reservoir site selection, shoreline erosion studies, snow cover mapping, and survey of recreational use of lakes and rivers. Works listed in the Selected Bibliography contain additional information on the water resources applications of airphoto interpretation [6, 7, 84, 94].

3.10   URBAN AND REGIONAL PLANNING APPLICATIONS

Urban and regional planners require nearly continuous acquisition of data to formulate governmental policies and programs. These policies and programs might range from the social, economic, and cultural domain to the context of environmental and natural resource planning. The role of planning agencies is becoming increasingly more complex and is extending to a wider range of activities. Consequently, there is an increased need for these agencies to have timely, accurate, and cost-effective sources of data of various forms. Several of these data needs are well served by airphoto interpretation. A key example is land use/land cover mapping, discussed in Section 3.5. Another example is the use of airphoto interpretation to contribute data for land use suitability evaluation purposes, as outlined in Section 4.3. Here we discuss the utility of airphoto interpretation in population estimation, housing quality studies, traffic and parking studies, site selection processes, and urban change detection.

Population estimates can be indirectly obtained through airphoto interpretation. The procedure is to use medium to large scale aerial photographs to estimate the number of dwelling units of each housing type in an area (single-family, two-family, multiple-family) and then multiply the number of dwelling units by the average family size per dwelling unit for each housing type. The identification of housing types is based on such criteria as size and shape of buildings, yards, courts, and driveways.

Airphoto interpretation can also assist in *housing quality studies*. Many environmental factors affecting housing quality can be readily interpreted from aerial photographs, whereas others (such as the interior condition of buildings) cannot be directly interpreted. A reasonable estimate of housing quality can usually be obtained through statistical analysis of a limited, carefully selected set of environmental quality factors. Environmental factors that are interpretable from aerial photographs and that have been found to be useful in housing quality studies include house size, lot size, building density, building setback, street width and condition, curb and sidewalk condition, driveway presence/absence, garage presence/absence, vegetation quality, yard and open space maintenance, proximity to parkland, and proximity to industrial land use. Large scale panchromatic photography has typically been used for housing quality studies. However, large to medium scale color infrared film has been shown to be superior in evaluating vegetation condition (lawns, shrubs, and trees).

Airphoto interpretation can assist in *traffic and parking studies*. Traditional on-the-ground vehicle counts show the number of vehicles passing a few selected points over a period of time. An aerial photograph shows the distribution of vehicles over space at an instant of time. Vehicle spacings—and thus areas of congestion—can be evaluated by viewing such photographs. Average vehicle speeds can be determined when the photographic scale and time interval between exposures of overlapping photographs are known. The number and spatial distribution of vehicles parked in open-air lots and streets can be inventoried from aerial photographs. Not all vehicles in urban areas are visible on aerial photographs, however. Vehicles in tunnels and enclosed parking will obviously not be visible. In an area of tall buildings, streets near the edges of the photographs may be hidden from view because of the radial relief displacement of the buildings. In addition, it may be difficult to discern vehicles in shadow areas on films of high contrast.

Airphoto interpretation can assist in various location and siting problems, such as *transportation route location, sanitary landfill site selection, power plant siting location*, and *transmission line location*. The same general decision-making process is followed in each of these selection processes. First the factors to be assessed in the route/site selection process are determined. Natural and cultural features plus various economic, social, and political factors are considered. Then data files containing information on these factors are assembled and alternative routes/sites are then analyzed and the final route/site is selected. Airphoto interpretation and photogrammetry are useful in collecting much of the natural and cultural data dealing with topography, geology, soils, potential construction materials, vegetation, land use, wetland location, historical/archaeological sites, and natural hazards (earthquakes, landslides, floods, volcanoes, and tsunami). Various methods for obtaining such natural and cultural data through photo interpretation are described elsewhere in this chapter. The task of analyzing the data is greatly facilitated by the use of a geographic information system. This topic is covered in Section 3.15.

Urban change detection mapping and analysis can be facilitated through the interpretation of multidate aerial photographs. Figure 3.29 illustrates the changes in an urban fringe area (Madison, Wisconsin) over a period of 43 years. The 1937 photograph (*a*) shows the area to be entirely agricultural land. The 1955 photograph (*b*) shows that a "beltline" highway has been constructed across the top of the area and that a gravel pit has begun operation in a glacial outwash plain at lower left. The 1968 photograph (*c*) shows that commercial development has begun at upper left and that single-family housing development has begun at lower right. A school has been constructed at lower center and the gravel pit continues operation. The 1980 photograph (*d*) shows that the commercial and single-family development has continued. Multiple-family housing units have been constructed at left. The gravel pit site is now a sanitary landfill site.

Airphoto interpretation for urban change detection and analysis can be facilitated through the use of a Zoom Transfer Scope™ or a video image/graphics system (Section 3.3) as an aid in comparing photographs of two different dates, or comparing a photograph with a map.

Several works listed in the Selected Bibliography contain additional information on the applications of airphoto interpretation to urban and regional planning activities [2, 3, 6, 7, 10, 20, 33, 60].

FIGURE 3.29 Multidate aerial photographs illustrating urban change, southwest Madison, Wisconsin. 1:20,000. (a) July 6, 1937. (b) September 5, 1955. (c) June 4, 1968.

(d) April 22, 1980. ((a), (b), and (c) are USDA–ASCS photos. (d) is courtesy Dane County Regional Planning Commission.)

3.11 WETLAND MAPPING

The value of the world's wetland systems has gained increased recognition. Wetlands contribute to a healthy environment in many ways. They act to retain water during dry periods, thus keeping the water table high and relatively stable. During periods of flooding, they act to reduce flood levels and to trap suspended solids and attached nutrients. Thus, streams flowing into lakes by way of wetland areas will transport fewer suspended solids and nutrients to the lakes than if they flow directly into the lakes. The removal of such wetland systems because of urbanization or other causes typically causes lake water quality to worsen. In addition, wetlands are important feeding, breeding, and drinking areas for wildlife, and provide a stopping place and refuge for waterfowl. As with any natural habitat, wetlands are important in supporting species diversity, and have a complex and important food web. Scientific values of wetlands include a record of biological and botanical events of the past, a place to study biological relationships, and a place for teaching. It is especially easy to obtain a feel for the biological world by studying a wetland. Other human uses include low-intensity recreation and esthetic enjoyment [14].

Accompanying the increased interest in wetlands has been an increased emphasis on inventorying. The design of any particular wetland inventory is dependent on the objectives to be met by that inventory. Thus, a clearly defined purpose must be established before the inventory is even contemplated [53]. Wetland inventories may be designed to meet the general needs of a broad range of users, or to fulfill a very specific purpose for a particular application. Multipurpose and single-purpose inventories are both valid ways of obtaining wetland information, but the former minimizes duplication of effort. To perform a wetlands inventory, a classification system must be devised that will provide the information necessary to the inventory users. The system should be based primarily on enduring wetland characteristics so that the inventory does not become outdated too quickly, but the classification should also accommodate user information requirements for ephemeral wetland characteristics. In addition, the inventory system must provide a detailed description of specifically what is considered to be a wetland. If the wetland definition used for various "wetland maps" is not clearly stated, then it is not possible to tell if apparent wetland changes noted between maps of different ages result from actual wetland changes or are due to differences in concepts of what is considered a wetland.

In 1954, the U.S. Fish and Wildlife Service (USFWS) conducted an inventory of wetlands in the United States. It was a single-purpose inventory to assess the amount and types of waterfowl habitat. In 1975, the USFWS initiated a *National Wetlands Inventory* program to prepare multipurpose wetland maps of the United States that provide data to a wide variety of potential users including wildlife managers, hydrologists, landscape planners, economists, engineers, and other public and private users. The purpose of this inventory is to provide data that will facilitate the management of wetland areas on a sound, multiple-use basis. The USFWS wetland classification system has been designed to meet three long-range objectives: (1) to group ecologically similar habitats, so that comparative value judgments can be made; (2) to furnish units for inventory and mapping; and (3) to provide uniformity in concepts and terminology throughout the United States.

A *wetland* is defined by the USFWS [22] as land where the water table is at, near, or above the land surface long enough to promote the formation of hydric (wet) soils or to support the growth of hydrophytes (plants that grow in water or very wet soil). Permanently flooded areas lying below the deep-water boundary of wetland are defined as *deep-water habitats*. In freshwater wetlands, this boundary is generally considered to be 2 m below the seasonal low water level. In saline-water wetlands, this boundary is generally considered to coincide with the elevation of the extreme low water of spring tide.

The National Wetlands Inventory is producing a series of wetland inventory maps and reports concerning the current status of wetlands of the United States [96]. Two series of wetland maps are being prepared: (1) small scale (typically 1:100,000) and (2) large scale (1:24,000). The primary map product is the large scale map, which shows the location, shape, and characteristics of wetlands and deepwater habitats on a USGS base map. Map data can also be supplied to users on magnetic tape in a polygon format in most of the common map projections. The large scale maps are useful for site-specific project evaluation and more than half of the continental United States has been mapped on this basis by the USFWS. The small scale maps are being produced only in limited areas on a user-funded basis and are being used chiefly for watershed and regional planning. Airphoto interpretation techniques are being utilized to assist in the wetland mapping process, with NHAP 1:58,000 color infrared photographs being the most widely used data source. With photographs of this scale, wetlands as small as $\frac{1}{2}$ to 1 ha in size are being mapped by the USFWS. Satellite data from the Landsat TM and SPOT sensors will also be utilized in monitoring mesoscale wetland losses and gains and updating existing wetland maps.

Many individual states and local units of government are also concerned with wetland mapping. Mapping scales used by states and local units of government generally fall in the range of 1:2400 to 1:62,500, with 1:24,000 the most widely used scale. In many cases, very large scale wetland mapping is required when land use restrictions are to be based on the inventory data.

An example of wetland mapping is shown in Figures 3.30 and 3.31. Figure 3.30 is a 5.7× enlargement of a color infrared airphoto that was used for wetland vegetation mapping at an original scale of 1:60,000. The vegetation classification system and airphoto interpretation key are shown in Table 3.16. The wetland vegetation map (Figure 3.31) shows the vegetation in this scene grouped into nine classes. The smallest units mapped at the original scale of 1:60,000 are a few distinctive stands of reed canary grass and cattails about $\frac{1}{3}$ ha in size. Most of the units mapped are much larger than this size.

Several works listed in the Selected Bibliography contain additional information on wetland classification and airphoto interpretation for wetland mapping [22, 23, 27, 53, 66, 96].

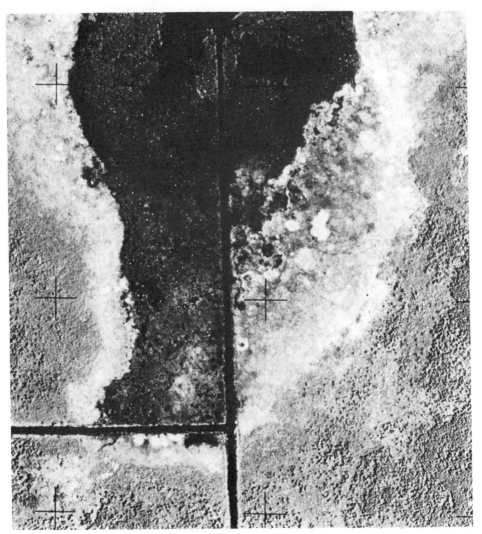

FIGURE 3.30 Black and white copy of a color infrared aerial photograph of Sheboygan Marsh, Wisconsin, June 4, 1972. 1:10,500 (enlarged 5.7 times from 1:60,000). Grid ticks appearing in image are from a reseau grid included in camera focal plane (Section 9.5). (NASA image.)

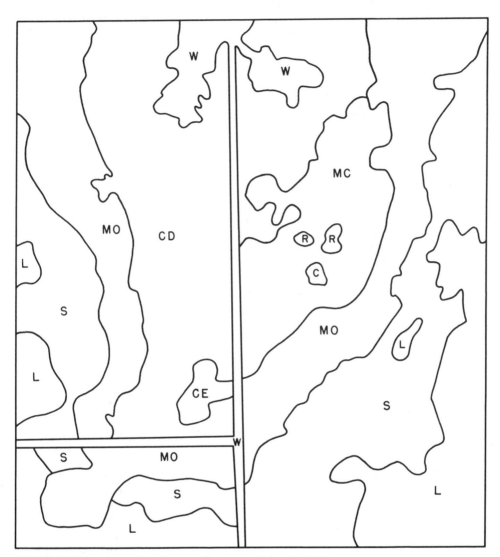

FIGURE 3.31 Vegetation classes in Sheboygan Marsh. 1:10,500.

W = Open water
D = Deep water emergents
E = Shallow water emergents
C = Cattail (solid stand)
O = Sedges and grasses

R = Reed canary grass (solid stand)
M = Mixed wetland vegetation
S = Shrubs
L = Lowland conifer forest

TABLE 3.16 Airphoto Interpretation Key to Vegetation Classes in Sheboygan Marsh For Use with Late-Spring 1:60,000 Color Infrared Film

Map symbol (Figure 3.31)	Class definition and airphoto interpretation key
W	*Open water:* Areas of open water produce a dark blue image. The dark color and uniform smooth texture of the open water is in distinct contrast with the lighter tones of the surrounding vegetation.
D	*Deep water emergents:* These exist in water depths of 0.15–0.45 m or more and consist predominantly of cattail (*Typha latifolia, T. angustifolia*), burreed (*Sparganium eurycarpum*), and sometimes reedgrass (*Phragmites communis*). These species, when interspersed with water, form an image made up of a dull bluish color with soft texture, a tone produced by background reflectance of water blending with the vegetation reflectance. This subcommunity is sometimes interspersed with shallow water emergents.
E	*Shallow water emergents:* These consist of a mixture of such wetland species as cattail (*Typha latifolia, T. angustifolia*), arrowhead (*Saggitaria latifolia*), water plantain (*Alisma plantago-aquatica*), burreed (*Sparganium eurycarpum*), and several sedge species (*Carex lacustris, C. rostrata, C. stricta, C. aquatilis*) in water depths of 0.15 m or less. A medium bluish tone is produced which is lighter than the deep water areas.
C	*Cattail-solid stand:* This consists of solid stands of cattail (*Typha latifolia, T. angustifolia*) which appear as mottled white patches in water ranging in depth from 0.10 to 0.75 m.
O	*Sedges and grasses:* The main components of a sedge meadow, sedges (*Carex lacustris, C. rostrata, C. stricta, C. aquatilis*) and grasses (*Spartina* sp, *Phragmites* sp, *Calamagrostis* sp), are generally interspersed with small depressions of shallow water which together produce a continuous pattern of bluish water color intermixed with small white blotches.
R	*Reed canary grass-solid stand:* Reed canary grass appears as a uniform vegetation type that produces a bright white tone on the image. Reed canary grass occurs in small irregular patches and as linear features along stream banks. It is often difficult to differentiate from sedges and grasses because of the almost identical tones produced. Large areas of the species that were planted for marsh hay often retain their unnatural rectangular boundaries.
M	*Mixed wetland vegetation:* This consists primarily of sedges (*Carex rostrata, C. stricta, C. lacustris*), forbs (march dock, *Rumex brittanica*; marsh bellflower, *Campanula aparinoides*; and marsh bedstraw, *Galium trifidum*), grasses (bluejoint, *Calamagrostis canadensis*), and cord grass (*Sparganium* sp). This community produces an interlacing pattern of magenta tones, light blues, and white colors, indicating the mixture of the component species.
S	*Shrubs:* This consists of buttonbush (*Cephalanthus occidentalis* L.), alder (*Alnus rugosa*), willow (*Salix interior, S. petiolaris, S. bebbiana*) and red osier dogwood (*Cornus stolonifera*). Shrubby areas have an intense magenta tone with coarse texture.
L	*Lowland conifer forest:* This consists, at this site, primarily of tamarack (*Larix laricina*) and white cedar (*Thuja occidentalis*) that display a deep mauve tone with considerable texture.

3.12   **WILDLIFE ECOLOGY APPLICATIONS**

The term *wildlife* refers to animals that live in a wild, undomesticated state. *Wildlife ecology* is concerned with the interactions between wildlife and their environment. Related activities are *wildlife conservation* and *wildlife management*. Two aspects of wildlife ecology for which airphoto interpretation can most readily provide useful information are wildlife habitat mapping and wildlife censusing.

A *wildlife habitat* provides the necessary combination of climate, substrate, and vegetation that each animal species requires. Within a habitat, the functional area that an animal occupies is referred to as its *niche*. Throughout evolution, various species of animals have adapted to various combinations of physical factors and vegetation. The adaptations of each species suit it to a particular habitat and rule out its use of other places. The number and type of animals that can be supported in a habitat are determined by the amount and distribution of food, shelter, and water in relation to the mobility of the animal. By determining the food, shelter, and water characteristics of a particular area, general inferences can be drawn about the ability of that area to meet the habitat requirements of different wildlife species. Because these requirements involve many natural factors, the interpretation techniques described elsewhere in this chapter for mapping land cover, soil, forests, wetlands, and water resources are applicable to wildlife habitat analysis.

Figure 3.32 illustrates wildlife habitat mapping. This figure shows the Sheboygan Marsh, which was also shown in Figure 3.30 for the purpose of illustrating wetland vegetation mapping. In Figure 3.32, the nine vegetation classes shown in Figure 3.31 have been grouped into five wildlife habitat types, as follows: (1) *open water*; (2) *aquatic vegetation* (cattail, burreed, and reed grass); (3) *sedge meadow* (sedges and grasses); (4) *shrubs* (alder, willow, and dogwood); and (5) *lowland conifer forest* (tamarack and white cedar). Each of these five habitat types supports a significantly different population of mammals, birds, and fish. For example, a careful examination of the "aquatic vegetation" habitat area of Figure 3.32 on the original color infrared transparency (1:60,000) reveals that there are more than 100 white spots on the photograph, each surrounded by a dark area. Each of these white spots is a muskrat hut. Within the area of this photograph, muskrat huts can be found only in the area identified as aquatic vegetation habitat.

Wildlife censusing can be accomplished by ground surveys, aerial visual observations, or aerial photography. Ground surveys rely on statistical sampling techniques and are often tedious, time consuming, and inaccurate. Many of the wildlife areas to be sampled are often nearly inaccessible on the ground. Aerial visual observations involve attempting to count the number of individuals of a species while flying over a survey area. Although this can be a low cost and relatively rapid type of survey, there are many problems involved. Aerial visual observations require quick decisions on the part of the observer regarding numbers, species composition, and percentages of various age and sex classes. Aggregations of mammals or birds may be too large for accurate counting in the brief time period available. In addition, low-flying aircraft almost invariably disturb wildlife, with much of the population taking cover before being counted.

Vertical aerial photography is the best method of accurately censusing many wildlife

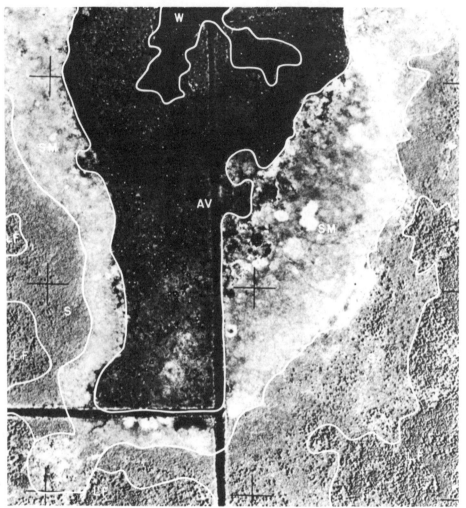

FIGURE 3.32   Wildlife habitat types in Sheboygan Marsh. 1:10,500.

W = Open water   S = Shrubs
AV = Aquatic vegetation   LF = Lowland conifer forest
SM = Sedge meadow

populations [48]. If the mammals or birds are not disturbed by the aircraft, the airphotos will permit very accurate counts to be undertaken. In addition, normal patterns of spatial distribution of individuals within groups will be apparent. Aerial photographs provide a permanent record that can be examined any number of times. Prolonged study of the photographs may reveal information that could not have been otherwise understood.

A variety of mammals and birds have been successfully censused using vertical aerial photography, including moose, elephants, whales, elk, sheep, deer, antelope, sea lions, caribou, beavers, seals, geese, ducks, flamingos, gulls, oyster catchers, and penguins. Vertical aerial photography obviously cannot be used to census all wildlife populations. Only those that frequent relatively open areas during daylight hours can be counted.

Wildlife censusing also requires that individual animals be large enough to be resolved on the photographs. A scale not smaller than 1:8000 is recommended for large mammals such as elk, whereas scales as large as 1:3000 should be used for smaller mammals such as sheep, deer, and antelope [7]. A critical factor is the tonal contrast between the animal and its surroundings. For example, flocks of snow geese, which are large white birds, can be identified at a scale of 1:12,000 against a dark background. Individual birds are identifiable at scales of 1:4000 to 1:6000 [48]. Dark-colored wildlife species often can be discerned better in the winter against a snow or ice background than in the summer with a soil, vegetation, or water background. This is also the time of year when many species tend to band together, and the leaves have fallen from deciduous trees, making censusing possible even in certain kinds of forests. Special film—filter combinations can be selected to maximize the contrast. For example, the use of ultraviolet aerial photography for censusing harp seals was described in Chapter 2 (Figure 2.8).

The counting of individual animals on photographs may present a problem when large numbers are present. Transparent grid overlays are often used as an aid in estimating numbers. Photographs can also be used to stratify population densities (individuals per unit area) for use in stratified sampling techniques. Alternatively photographs can be digitized (Chapter 6) and digital computers used to automatically "count" individuals.

Figure 3.33 shows a prairie dog colony on a plateau in South Dakota. Prairie dogs feed upon grasses and broad-leaved plants and construct burrows with mounded entrances. They disturb the ground in the vicinity of the colony, making the area susceptible to invasion by plants that exist in disturbed areas. The lighter-toned area on the plateau in the center of the photograph is covered by such vegetation (mostly forbs) and the surrounding darker-toned area is covered by native prairie grass. Each white spot in this lighter-toned area is the bare soil associated with one prairie dog mound.

Figure 3.34 shows a large group of beluga whales (small white whales) that have congregated in an arctic estuarine environment principally for the purpose of calving. At the image scales shown here, it is possible to determine the number and characteristics of individual whales and to measure their lengths. On the full 240 × 240 mm frame from which Figure 3.34 was rephotographed, a total of about 1600 individual whales were counted. At the original film scale of 1:2000, the average adult length was measured as 4 m and the average calf length was measured as 2 m. Numerous adults with calves can be seen, especially in the enlargement (Figure 3.34b). "Bachelor groups" of eight and six males can be seen at the lower left and lower right of Figure 3.34b.

Several works listed in the Selected Bibliography contain additional information on the wildlife ecology applications of airphoto interpretation [6, 7, 37, 38, 48].

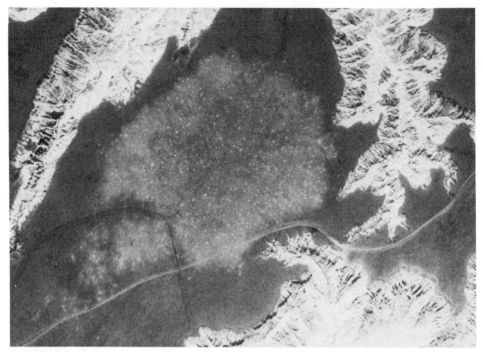

FIGURE 3.33   Prairie dog colony, Cuny Table, South Dakota, July 7, 1981. 1:10,400. Panchromatic film with a red filter. (Courtesy Remote Sensing Institute, South Dakota State University.)

3.13   ARCHAEOLOGICAL APPLICATIONS

Archaeology is concerned with the scientific study of historic or prehistoric peoples by analysis of the remains of their existence, especially those remains that have been discovered through earth excavation.

The earliest archaeological investigations dealt with obvious monuments of earlier societies. The existence of these sites was often known from historical accounts. Airphoto interpretation has proven particularly useful in locating sites whose existence has been lost to history. Both surface and subsurface features of interest to archaeologists have been detected using airphoto interpretation.

Surface features include visible ruins, mounds, rock piles, and various other surface markings. Examples of visible ruins are rock structures such as Stonehenge (England), castles (throughout Europe), and Indian dwellings in the southwestern United States. Examples of mounds are the bird-shaped and serpent-shaped Indian mounds of the midwestern United States. Examples of rock structures are the various medicine wheels such as the Bighorn Medicine Wheel in Wyoming and the Moose Mountain Medicine Wheel in Saskatchewan. Other surface markings include Indian pictographs and the ancient Nazca Lines in Peru.

Figure 3.35 shows the Nazca Lines. They are estimated to have been made at least

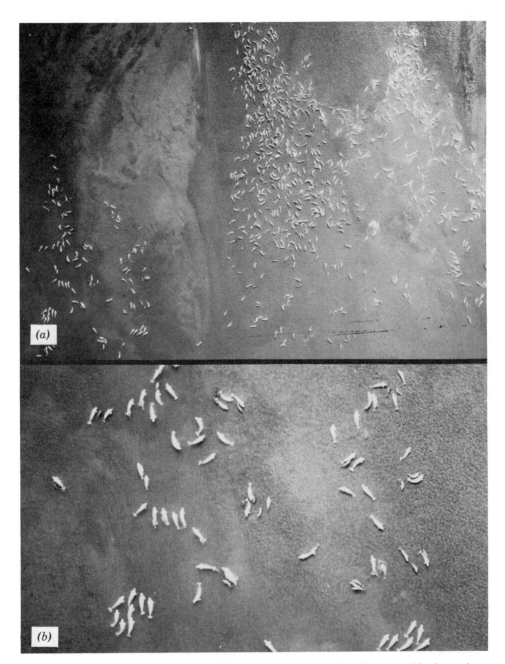

FIGURE 3.34 Large group of beluga whales, Cunningham Inlet, Somerset Island, northern Canada, July 30, 1973. (Black and white copy of photograph taken with Kodak Water Penetration Color Film, SO-224.) *(a)* 1:2400 *(b)* 1:800; a 3× enlargement of the lower left portion of *(a)* (Courtesy J.D. Heyland, Metcalfe, Ontario.)

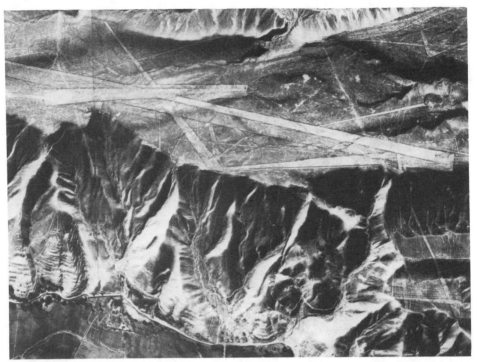

FIGURE 3.35   Vertical photomosaic showing Nazca Lines, Peru. (From [56]. Courtesy Long Island University Press.)

1500 years ago and cover an area of about 500 km². Many geometric shapes have been found, as well as narrow straight lines that extend for as long as 8 km. They were made by clearing away literally millions of rocks to expose the lighter-toned ground beneath. The cleared rocks were piled around the outer boundaries of the "lines." These markings were first noticed from the air during the 1920s. At that time, it was hypothesized that they formed a gigantic astronomical calendar, a belief still held by some scientists. The definite reason for their construction remains unknown.

Subsurface archaeological features include buried ruins of buildings, ditches, canals, and roads. When such features are covered by agricultural fields or native vegetation, they may be revealed on aerial photographs by tonal anomalies resulting from subtle differences in soil moisture or crop growth. On occasion, such features have been revealed by ephemeral differences in frost patterns.

Figure 3.36 shows the site of the ancient city of Spina on the Po River delta in Italy. Spina flourished during the fifth century B.C. and later became a "lost" city whose very existence was doubted by many. An extensive search for Spina ended in 1956 when it was identified on aerial photographs by an Italian archaeologist. Ancient Spina was a city of canals and waterways. The dark-toned linear features in Figure 3.36 are areas of dense vegetation growing in wet soils at the former location of the canals. The lighter-toned rectangular areas are sparse vegetation over sand and the rubble of brick

FIGURE 3.36 Oblique aerial photograph showing site of the ancient city of Spina, Italy. (Courtesy Fotoaerea Valvassori, Ravenna, Italy.)

foundations. The light-toned linear features that run diagonally across this photograph are present-day drainage ditches.

The sites of more than a thousand Roman villas have been discovered in northern France through the use of 35 mm aerial photography. The buildings were destroyed in the third century A.D., but their foundation materials remain in the soil. Figures 3.37 and 3.38 illustrate sites that are in areas of fertile loess soils over the white chalk bedrock that was used as foundation material by the Romans. In Figure 3.37, deep winter plowing has scraped the foundations and brought up fragments of white chalk that stand out against the darker background of loess soils. The villa foundation revealed in this manner is 320 m long. In Figure 3.38, we see the villa foundation because of differences in crop vigor. The area shown in this figure has recently been converted from pasture to cropland. In the early years following such conversion, farmers apply little or no fertilizer to the fields. The cereal crops over the foundation materials are light-toned owing to both the lack of fertilizer and a period of drought

FIGURE 3.37   Oblique 35 mm airphoto of recently plowed field that reveals the foundation of a 320 m long Roman villa in northern France. (Photograph by R. Agache. From [105]. Courtesy The Council for British Archaeology, London.)

prior to the date of photography. The crops are darker-toned over the remainder of the field. The main building (in the foreground) was 95 × 60 m.

Works listed in the Selected Bibliography contain additional information on the archaeological applications of airphoto interpretation [6, 7, 10, 30, 51, 56, 63, 64, 105, 106].

3.14   ENVIRONMENTAL ASSESSMENT

Many human activities produce potentially adverse environmental effects. Examples include the construction and operation of highways, railroads, pipelines, airports, industrial sites, power plants, and transmission lines; subdivision and commercial developments; sanitary landfill and hazardous waste disposal operations; and timber harvesting and strip mining operations.

With concern for the environmental effects of such activities in mind, the U.S. Congress passed the *National Environmental Policy Act* (NEPA) of 1969. This established as national policy the creation and maintenance of conditions that encourage harmony between people and their environment and minimize environmental degradation. This act requires that *environmental impact statements* be prepared for any federal action having significant impact on the environment. The key items to be evaluated in an environmental impact statement are (1) the environmental impact of

FIGURE 3.38 Oblique 35 mm airphoto of a cereal crop field in northern France. Differences in crop vigor reveal the foundation of a Roman villa. (Photograph by R. Agache. From [105]. Courtesy The Council for British Archaeology, London.)

the proposed action; (2) any adverse environmental effects that cannot be avoided should the action be implemented; (3) alternatives to the proposed action; (4) the relationship between local short-term uses of the environment and the maintenance and enhancement of long-term productivity; and (5) any irreversible and irretrievable commitments of resources that would be involved in the proposed action should it be implemented. Since the passage of NEPA, many states have also passed environmental impact assessment legislation. These cover other-than-federal actions at the local level.

The principal biophysical effects of human activity on the environment include (1) interruptions and other changes in natural drainage conditions causing ponding, fluctuations of the groundwater table, alterations to stream flow characteristics, soil erosion, and siltation; (2) changes in water turbidity, suspended load, and temperature; (3) increases in chemical pollutants such as salt, heavy metals, and insecticides; (4) changes in vegetation caused by site clearing and alterations to site conditions; and (5) changes in wildlife population and distribution caused by opening up new habitat, destroying existing habitat, altering migratory habits, and disrupting breeding and spawning [17].

Environmental impact statements are usually required to contain specific information on the magnitude and characteristics of environmental impact. An assessment of physical site characteristics involves an inventory of physiographic, geologic, soil, vegetative, wildlife, watershed, and airshed conditions [102]. The assessment will typically draw on expertise of persons from many areas such as civil engineering, forestry, landscape architecture, geography, geology, seismology, soils engineering, pedology, botany, biology, zoology, hydrology, water quality chemistry, water quality biology, sanitary engineering, meteorology, air quality chemistry, and air pollution engineering. Many of the remote sensing and image interpretation techniques set forth in this book can be utilized to assist in the preparation of environmental impact statements.

Concern for the hazards connected with the disposal of various deleterious materials led to the passage of the federal *Resource Conservation Recovery Act (RCRA)* in 1976 (several amendments have added to its original regulations). Among the provisions of the RCRA is a requirement for states to inventory open dumps and landfills associated with both municipal and industrial activities. These inventories help the states determine and control the potential impact of seepage, drainage, and fumes from surface impoundments and from landfills and open dumps.

The EPA is involved with aerial remote sensing for hazardous waste site investigations and assessments in support of EPA's permitting and enforcement activities. Aerial photography is one of the EPA's principal remote sensing tools and both frame cameras and panoramic cameras are used. One type of EPA aerial photography is its "emergency response photography" to the spillage of hazardous materials. Such airphotos are used to determine the extent and location of visible spillage, vegetation damage, and threats to natural drainage and human welfare. The EPA also conducts intensive site analyses of waste sites by examining existing (historical) photographs and augmenting these with current photographic coverage when necessary. These analyses may include characterizing changes in surface drainage conditions through time; identifying the location of landfills, waste treatment ponds, and lagoons and their subsequent burial and abandonment; and detecting and identifying drums containing waste materials. Also, photo interpretation may be used to help locate potential sites for drilling and sampling of hazardous wastes.

Another application of large scale airphotos has been their use in the identification of failing septic systems. The principal manifestations of septic system failure are typically the upward or lateral movement of partially treated or untreated wastewater toward the soil surface. As the effluent moves upward and approaches the ground surface, the large amount of nutrients in the effluent causes enhanced growth in the vegetation directly above it. When the effluent reaches the surface, the overabundance of nutrients, coupled with an imbalance in the soil's air/water ratio, causes the vegetation to become stressed and eventually die. Finally, the effluent surfaces and either stands on the ground surface or flows downslope, often manifesting the same growth–stress–death pattern as it moves. Both normal color and color infrared photographs at a scale of around 1:8000 have been used for the detection of such situations [34, 89]. Open areas can be photographed throughout much of the year. Areas with sparse tree cover should be photographed during early spring (after grasses have emerged, but before tree leaves have appeared) or late fall (after tree leaves have dropped). Areas of dense tree cover may be impossible to analyze using airphoto interpretation at any time.

An analysis of the photo characteristics of color, texture, site, and association, along with collateral soil information, is important for the identification of failing septic systems. Stereoscopic viewing is also important because it allows for the identification of slope, relief, and direction of surface drainage.

For additional information regarding airphoto interpretation for environmental assessment, works listed in the Selected Bibliography can be consulted [32, 34, 57, 89, 101, 102].

3.15 GEOGRAPHIC INFORMATION SYSTEMS

Information extracted through the process of airphoto interpretation is almost always "mapped" in some sense. That is, the resource manager normally wishes to display and analyze the interpreted information in a spatial context. This may involve nothing more than manually transferring interpreted information to topographic maps with the aid of rulers or other simple devices. The map thus provides a geographic frame of reference for the interpreted data.

In addition to mapping one set of data, it is often desirable to interrelate several resource features on a common base. To illustrate this, consider the information needs of a hydrologist who wishes to study erosion and sedimentation in a watershed. In such an application, it is critical to be able to identify the likely sources of sediment. At a minimum, this identification process would involve the study of topographic slope, soil erodibility, and surface runoff characteristics on a watershedwide basis. If topographic maps, detailed soil survey maps, and land cover maps exist for the watershed, the analyst would have the raw data needed for the study. However, more often than not the maps will be at incompatible scales. Beside this scale problem, the analyst in this case needs information derived from each of the existing map sources, instead of the original mapped data. That is, *slope* information must be derived from *contour* information, *soil erodibility* from *soil type*, and surface *runoff potential* from *land cover* (including land management practices). Hence, to develop an information base for the analysis, the hydrologist might perform the following tasks:

I. For each data source, the map sheets covering the watershed would be carefully joined together to form one large sheet for each type of data (contours, soils, land cover). The boundary of the watershed would then be delineated on each data map and the maps would be converted to a common scale, either by redrafting or through photographic reproduction.

2. Next, the necessary information would be derived from the source maps. Slope would be determined from the contours shown on the topographic map. Soil erodibility would be derived from the soil map and a table listing erodibility for each soil type (similar to Table 3.3). Runoff potential would be derived from the land cover map using a table that lists runoff for each cover type.

3. The analyst would then have to *merge* the three sets of derived information. This involves interrelating the information sets throughout the watershed to locate the areas where combinations of site characteristics indicate high soil erosion potential (i.e., steep slopes and highly erodible soil/cover combinations).

The information merging procedure was historically performed by a *map overlay method.* First, each derived data set was prepared on a transparent map sheet. These maps were coded in gray tones according to the degree or severity of the condition being depicted. For example, the steeper the slope in an area, the darker it was depicted on the "slope" overlay. The three factors would then be merged by overlaying the transparent sheets. The darkest areas on the composite map would indicate a combination of factors representing high potential sediment source areas.

The principal advantage of the map overlay method is that it requires little special-ized equipment. However, certain difficulties are inherent in this approach. The tasks of bringing the data to a common scale and format and deriving the applicable characteristics are time consuming and expensive. Because they are tailored to a specific analysis, the overlay sheets may not be applicable to other studies. Also, the overlay technique provides little potential for differential weighting of individual factors in a *modeling* context. Finally, it is difficult to quantify the results of the overlay analysis, since manual computation of areas on the composite map can be extremely time consuming.

By computer coding land information, the difficulties of the manual overlay tech-nique are greatly reduced. Data that relate to the land and are recorded according to location are called *georeferenced* or *geocoded* data. The location specification of such data may be as simple as a street address or as complex as geodetic survey reference. A spatially ordered collection of such data is called a *geobased file.* A system designed to store, manipulate, and display these data is called a *geographic information system (GIS).* Normally, these systems are computer based. Table 3.17 lists some of the many types of data that may be included in a geographic information system. Note that to support various modeling functions, GISs must be capable of handling both *locational data* and *attribute* or *descriptive* data about features.

Figure 3.39 conceptually illustrates one way in which georeferenced data can be computer analyzed in our example study of soil erosion potential. In this illustration, the data maps (*a*) are computer coded with respect to a grid (*b*). The data maps are encoded by recording the information category most dominant in each cell in the grid. That is, each cell is assigned a single soil type in the soil data file, a single cover type in the land cover file, and an average elevation in the topographic file. The task of geocoding the data can be tedious and costly. Yet, once this task is accomplished, the analysis of geocoded data can be performed quickly and accurately. With the pre-viously mentioned steps, the activity of making the data types compatible is inherently

TABLE 3.17   Examples of Data Types
Applicable to Geographic Information Systems
(with Examples of Derivable Information Shown
in Parentheses)

Area Features

Terrain elevation (slope, aspect)

Soil types (permeability, texture, depth,
   agricultural potential)

Land cover (runoff potential, wildlife habitat)

Bedrock geology (mineral resources, stability)

Land ownership parcels (land use, land value)

Surface hydrology (open water, wetlands, flood
   plains)

Subsurface hydrology (aquifer recharge area,
   water source potential)

General climate (temperature, precipitation)

Microclimate (frost pockets, fog prone areas)

Zoning districts (land use restrictions, land use
   plans)

Water and sewer districts (service capacities)

Census tracts (socioeconomic data)

Linear Features

Transportation system (service capacity, travel
   proximity)

Utility system (service capacity)

Waterways (proximity)

Shoreline (recreational resources)

Point Features

Historic sites

Unique natural areas

Mine operations

accomplished by encoding the maps on a common grid. The job of interpreting applicable characteristics (slope, erodibility, and runoff) from the original data is a simple one for the computer. The *overlay* or *composite* analysis consists of evaluating the data values within each cell in the combined grid matrix. Complex weighting schemes may be applied to increase the importance of the more critical variables. The resulting output grid can be displayed as a matrix of printed characters whose density (darkness) relates to the output values. In our case, dark character patterns could be chosen to represent high potential soil erosion areas. Output can also be generated on a line plotter, a color monitor, or a precision film recorder. (Plate 24 illustrates color

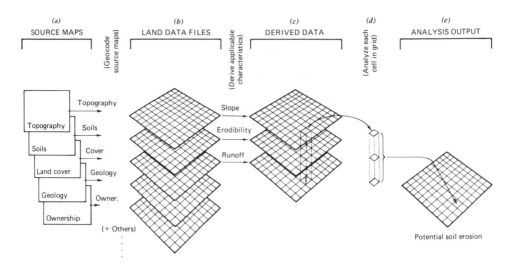

FIGURE 3.39 Analysis procedure using geocoded data.

monitor displays of data manipulated in a geographic information system.) In addition to graphic output, the results of the analysis can easily be quantified, since the computer can calculate areas by simply counting grid cells and multiplying by the area of each cell. Locations of areas of particular interest are obtainable through their grid cell "addresses."

Figures 3.40 to 3.43 are computer printouts illustrating the analysis procedure shown in Figure 3.39 applied to the Pheasant Branch Watershed in Wisconsin. This watershed is 6136 ha in size and contains about 75 percent agricultural land, 20 percent nonagricultural open land (forest, wetland, and other open land), and 5 percent developed land. During periods of heavy rainfall, a great deal of soil erosion takes place in this watershed and vast quantities of silt and clay are removed from the land, transported by the streams, and flow into Lake Mendota as suspended solids (see Figure 3.25). Figures 3.40 to 3.42 are examples of *derived data* from which the *analysis output* Figure 3.43) was obtained.

Figure 3.40 shows the topographic slope in each 1-ha cell, Figure 3.41 gives the soil erodibility in each cell, and Figure 3.42 shows the runoff potential. Each data type is coded into the computer as one of ten classes (coded as 0 to 9). The computer printout displays the data using a series of symbols of differing densities. Figure 3.40, for example, shows the percentage of slope in each cell using the symbol "." to represent a 0 percent slope, "," to represent a 1 to 2 percent slope, "+" to represent a 3 to 4 percent slope, and so on, for a total of ten levels. For each of these three data types (Figures 3.40 to 3.42), the frequency of occurrence of each level of data is shown opposite the heading "FREQUENCY" at the bottom of the printout. For example, we can see that the watershed contains 195 ha of land with a 0 percent slope, 1508 ha with a 1 to 2 percent slope, 1281 ha with a 3 to 4 percent slope, and so on. Figure 3.43 was obtained

FIGURE 3.40 Computer printout showing topographic slope in the Pheasant Branch Watershed. Darker symbols represent steeper slopes.

FIGURE 3.41 Computer printout showing soil erodibility in the Pheasant Branch Watershed. Darker symbols represent more erodible soils.

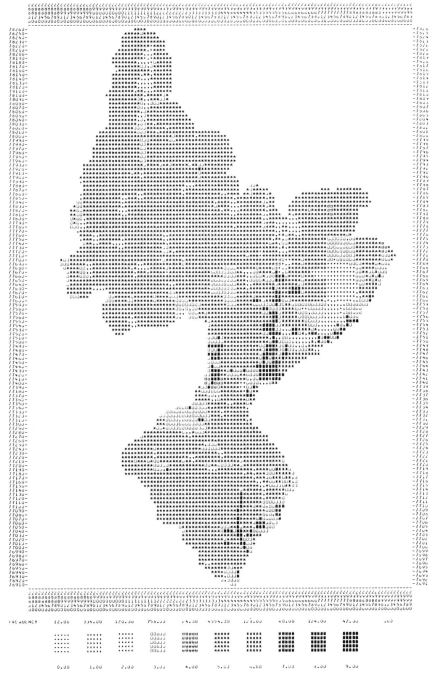

FIGURE 3.42 Computer printout showing runoff potential in the Pheasant Branch Watershed. Darker symbols represent higher runoff potential.

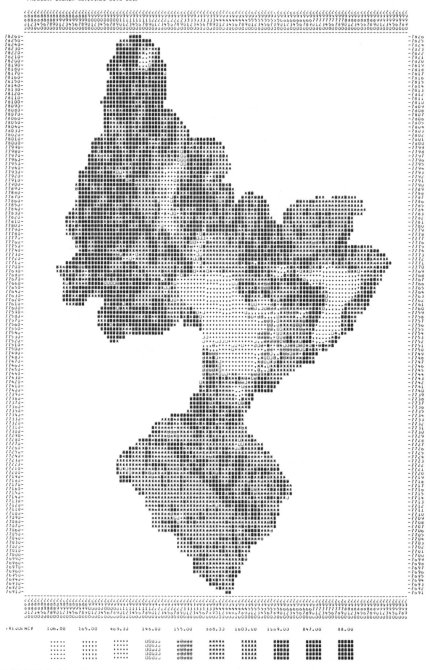

FIGURE 3.43 Computer printout showing potential soil erosion in the Pheasant Branch Watershed. This analysis output was obtained by combining the three previous figures digitally. Darker symbols represent higher potential soil erosion.

by combining the values of the three data types (topographic slope, soil erodibility, and runoff potential) on a cell-by-cell basis and displaying the total in ten-level computer line printer output. In Figure 3.43, the lighter symbols represent areas with low potential for soil erosion and the darker symbols represent areas with high potential for soil erosion. In this example, each of the three data items is given equal weight. However, different weights could be attached to each data type.

By studying Figure 3.43, persons concerned with soil erosion in the watershed and siltation in the lake can ascertain where the areas having the greatest soil erosion problems are located. Each cell in the data bank has a specific geographic location based on its coordinates in the Universal Transverse Mercator geographic coordinate system (coordinates are specified by the five-digit numbers that frame the printout). If the data base also contained information on land ownership, the land owners in the greatest problem areas could be identified.

A host of other forms of analysis may also be performed on geocoded data. For example, a computer can derive simulated perspective views of the landscape from the topographic data file. Figure 5.26b illustrates this type of product. In addition, land cover or remote sensing data from another data file can be added to the perspective view (Plate 23). Proposed changes in vegetative cover or topography can be analyzed in this manner to evaluate the visual impact of the changes. Similarly, the *viewshed*, or region visible from a given point (or along a given route), can be computed from topographic data. Viewshed maps are useful for evaluating the visual impact of proposed features such as power lines or strip mines.

The number, form, and complexity of data analyses possible with georeferenced data are virtually limitless. Generally, these activities can be categorized as either *surface analysis* or *overlay analysis*. Surface analysis involves the study of the interrelationships among data elements in one data layer. For example, the grouping and labeling of the raw soil data into soil erodibility categories is one form of surface analysis. The synthesizing of slope, soil erodibility, and runoff potential data is one simple form of overlay analysis. Students can probably think of many other surface or overlay analyses related to their particular field of study. In all cases, we can call on the computer to perform comparisons and calculations with the multiple-input data set that might be quite laborious using any other means of analysis. Furthermore, all results of the computer analyses are easily quantified and spatially referenced. They are also amenable to revision as new data become available.

Because of their flexibility and accuracy, computer-based geographic information systems are being implemented in numerous resource management applications. These systems are ideal for such applications as land capability/suitability analysis, environmental impact assessment, industrial site selection, transportation route location, transmission line routing, subdivision site analysis, open space planning, wildlife habitat analysis, mineral resource planning, and forest land management. Because of the initial expense for the geocoding process, the information system approach is appropriate only where the analysis is complex and extensive. Yet with the ever-increasing number of constraints on the use and management of resources and the ready availability of computer resources, a geographic information system is quickly becoming a necessity in many applications.

Figure 3.44 schematically illustrates some of the equipment used in assembling a geographic information system. The equipment shown includes input devices used to encode tabular data and maps, digital data storage devices, and graphic output devices.

Several *data encoding formats* may be used to geocode land data. The basic consideration is whether the data type is composed of point, linear, or areal features. Some examples of point features are historical sites and unique natural areas. While such sites may not actually be "points," these features are characterized by highly discrete locations. Linear features, such as transportation lines or waterways may be encoded as a series of straight-line segments called *links*.

Many forms of resource data are areal in nature. Figure 3.45 illustrates two formats commonly used to encode areal data *(a)*. The *grid cell* or *raster format* that was described in our example is illustrated in Figure 3.45*b*. To reiterate, the dominant information class is recorded for each cell in the data matrix. Note that the finer the grid used, the more geographic specificity there will be in the data file. A coarse grid requires less data storage space, but will provide a less accurate geographic description of the original data. Also, when using a very coarse grid, several data types may occur in each cell. It may therefore be necessary to list the percentages of several important data types occurring in each of the grid cells. This requirement complicates the encoding and analysis procedures. In general, the cell size used in a grid format imposes a limit on the scale of the analysis that can be performed with the stored data.

The *polygon* or *vector* format of data encoding is illustrated in Figure 3.45*c*. Using this format, feature boundaries are converted to straight-sided polygons that approximate the original regions. In *topological coding*, these polygons are encoded by determining the coordinates of their vertices, called *nodes*, which can be connected to form *arcs*. Polygons are recovered by connecting arcs. This format provides a more accurate description of feature boundaries, and requires less data storage space than does the grid format. However, polygon encoded data are less amenable to the overlay analysis procedure and, so, many systems use a polygon format for inputting the maps and convert the data to a grid format for the overlay procedure.

Regardless of the format used, there are several ways in which land data can be geographically referenced. The identification can be *nominal*, or "named," in which case the reference is only indirectly related to a ground coordinate system. Examples of nominal references are street addresses, census tract numbers, and ZIP codes. Resource data are generally referenced to ground coordinates, using either a *relative* or *absolute* coordinate system. A *relative coordinate system* is based on a grid that is arbitrarily defined for the study area. Because such data cannot be easily related to other data sets, this approach has many shortcomings. An *absolute coordinate system* references the data to a specific geographic coordinate system. This generally involves a planar map projection, such as the Universal Transverse Mercator (UTM) system. The UTM coordinate system is based on a series of 60 zones worldwide, each covering 6° of longitude in a north–south strip. Also frequently used in the United States is the *State Plane Coordinate System*. This system consists of 120 zones designed to optimally represent sections of the individual states. Either Lambert Conformal Conic or

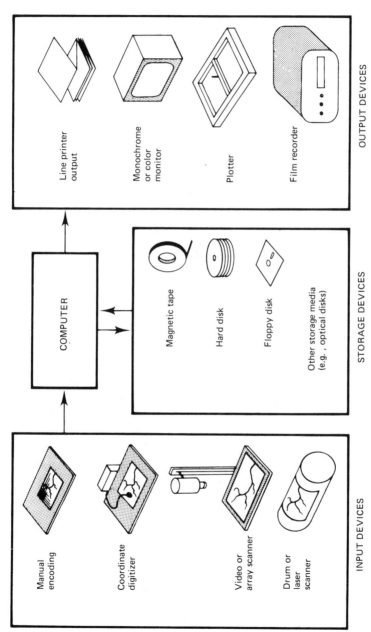

FIGURE 3.44 Typical equipment used in geographic information systems.

INPUT DEVICES

Manual encoding

Coordinate digitizer

Video or array scanner

Drum or laser scanner

COMPUTER

STORAGE DEVICES

Magnetic tape

Hard disk

Floppy disk

Other storage media (e.g., optical disks)

OUTPUT DEVICES

Line printer output

Monochrome or color monitor

Plotter

Film recorder

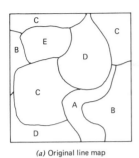 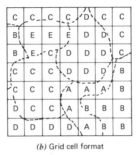 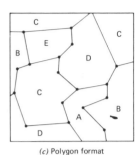

(a) Original line map   (b) Grid cell format   (c) Polygon format

FIGURE 3.45 Grid versus polygon encoding formats.

Transverse Mercator projections (or both) are used, depending on the shape of each state.

The comparative nature of these two map projections is illustrated in Figure 3.46. In the Lambert Conformal Conic projection, points on the earth are projected onto a cone that intersects the earth's surface at two parallels of latitude. Along these two circles the scale will be exact. If the parallels are close in a north–south direction, the map scale will be reasonably accurate no matter how far the map is extended in an east–west direction. Thus, the Lambert projection is useful for mapping states that are relatively wide in an east–west direction. This projection is said to be *conformal* because the scales in all directions are equivalent.

The Transverse Mercator projection uses a cylindrical surface that intersects the earth along two lines parallel to a meridian of longitude, called the central meridian. In this case, the scale will be exact along the two north–south lines of intersection. This projection is reasonably accurate within a narrow east–west zone, and may be extended indefinitely in a north–south direction. It is therefore useful for states that are narrow in the east–west direction.

Planar projections are convenient in that map presentation and area computation are simplified. However, difficulties are encountered when study regions cover more than one planar zone. An alternative that circumvents this problem is *geodetic referencing*, in which the coordinates are directly referenced to latitude and longitude. In any case, data referenced to one coordinate system can be converted into other coordinate systems by using mathematical transformation formulas.

There are several means by which geographic data may be computer coded, or *digitized*. One method is *manual digitization*, in which a transparent coordinate grid is placed over each data map prior to encoding. If a point, linear feature, or polygonal feature is to be encoded, the coordinates that define the feature are measured on the overlay. Grid format data can be encoded by listing the dominant class in each cell on the overlay. The recorded category information and coordinate values are then input to the computer. The advantage of the manual method is that no specialized input equipment is required. The disadvantage is that it is relatively time consuming, particularly if detailed data are to be encoded.

A more efficient method for encoding land data is provided by *semiautomated digitization*. This technique uses a precision coordinate digitizer (Figure 3.47) that

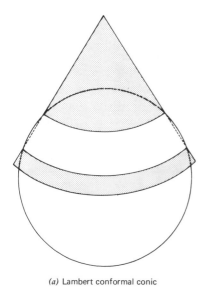

(a) Lambert conformal conic

(b) Transverse mercator

FIGURE 3.46 Commonly used map projections.

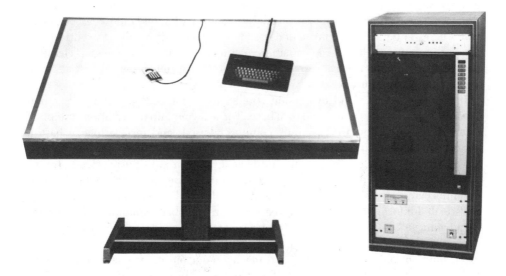

FIGURE 3.47 Precision coordinate digitizer. (Courtesy Altek Corp.)

continuously records the (x, y) location of a movable cursor (center left on table in figure). A data map is mounted on the digitizing table and the features are manually traced by an operator. A microprocessor transforms the input values into map coordinates and records them on magnetic tape (right side in Figure 3.47). The system shown in the figure also has a keyboard for entering annotation data. Semiautomated digitization is clearly less time consuming than the manual technique. Further automation can be provided by automatic digitizing systems. Here, the digitizing can be performed by any of a number of devices (e.g., video camera, array scanner, drum, or laser beam scanner). These systems normally are connected to a display that enables an operator to edit the data. In each of these methods, there is a trade-off between the initial expense and maintenance cost of the specialized equipment and the operational efficiency in the geocoding process.

Frequently, land information may be obtained directly in computer-compatible form. For example, digitized elevation data are available for the entire United States from the National Cartographic Information Center of USGS. These data consist of elevations encoded in a grid cell format at various spatial resolutions (e.g., 30 m cells over 7.5×7.5 min quadrangle blocks). As we see in later chapters, several forms of remote sensing data are available in a digital, grid cell format (for example, the land cover data shown in Plate 24). If necessary, these data can be reformatted using a process called *resampling* (Section 10.2) to match the geometry of the other information contained in a GIS. Also, software exists to convert such raster data to a vector format (and vice versa) if required.

Information on land *ownership* is often the most important data type in a land information system. Ownership information is useful as a primary data source, since several types of data such as land use and land value can be keyed to individual ownership parcels of land. Ownership information is also very useful *after* the data analysis, since it provides a means to take action based on the results of a study. For example, in our potential soil erosion analysis, information on land parcel ownership would be essential when taking action based on the analysis results. In short, ownership data permit us to link the information relating to physical and biological characteristics of the land (the natural resource data) to the proprietary interests that control the use of those resources.

In many countries, land ownership is officially registered with the government, providing a continuously updated data base. These ownership information systems are called *cadastres*. They are generally computer based, and form a logical base for comprehensive land information systems.

The United States currently does not have a uniform multipurpose cadastral system. Hence it lacks a detailed, land-parcel-level data base on which a comprehensive land information system can be conveniently established. Increasingly, many users of land-related information (from resource managers to urban economists) are realizing the advantages that would be afforded by a cadastre-based comprehensive land information system. With such a system, it would be possible to merge information concerning not only land planning and management but environmental protection, real estate assessment, and land transfer. This would provide maximum accessibility and benefit to all users of land-related information, public and private, collective and individual.

In closing this chapter, we must point out that we have only treated the basic concepts of geographic information systems. The detailed study of these systems is the subject of entire books and courses. While space limits further detailed description of these systems here, we illustrate the important relationship between remote sensing and geographic information systems in several other locations in this book (principally in Chapter 10).

SELECTED BIBLIOGRAPHY

1. Adams, M.S., et al., *Assessment of Aquatic Environment by Remote Sensing*, IES Report 84, Institute for Environmental Studies, University of Wisconsin–Madison, 1977.

2. Adeniyi, P.O., "Land Use Change Analysis Using Sequential Aerial Photography and Computer Techniques," *Photogrammetric Engineering and Remote Sensing*, vol. 46, no. 11, 1980, pp. 1447–1464.

3. Adeniyi, P.O., "An Aerial Photographic Method for Estimating Urban Population," *Photogrammetric Engineering and Remote Sensing*, vol. 49, no. 4, April 1983, pp. 545–560.

4. Allum, J.A.E., *Photogeology and Regional Mapping*, Pergamon, Elmsford, N.Y., 1966.

5. American Society for Photogrammetry and Remote Sensing, *Proceedings: 10th William T. Pecora Memorial Remote Sensing Symposium*, Ft. Collins, Colo., 1985.

6. American Society of Photogrammetry, *Manual of Photographic Interpretation*, Falls Church, Va., 1960.

7. American Society of Photogrammetry, *Manual of Remote Sensing*, 2nd ed., Falls Church, Va., 1983.

8. American Society of Photogrammetry, *Renewable Resources Management—Applications of Remote Sensing* (Proceedings: RNRF Symposium on the Application of Remote Sensing to Resource Management), Falls Church, Va., 1983.

9. Anderson, J.R., et al., *A Land Use and Land Cover Classification System for Use with Remote Sensor Data*, USGS Professional Paper 964, U.S. Gov. Printing Office, Washington, D.C., 1976.

10. Avery, T.E., and G.L. Berlin, *Interpretation of Aerial Photographs*, 4th ed., Burgess, Minneapolis, Minn., 1985.

11. Baber, J.J., Jr., and A.D. Flowerday, "Use of Low Altitude Aerial Biosensing with Color Infrared Photography as a Crop Management Service," *Technical Papers of the American Society of Photogrammetry*, ASP–ACSM Fall Technical Meeting, 1979, pp. 252–259.

12. Baker, R.D. et al., "Land Use/Land Cover Mapping from Aerial Photographs," *Photogrammetric Engineering and Remote Sensing*, vol. 45, no. 5, 1979, pp. 661–668.

13. Bauer, M.E., "The Role of Remote Sensing in Determining the Distribution and Yield of Crops," *Advances in Agronomy*, vol. 27, 1975, pp. 271–304.

14. Bedford, B.L., E.H. Zimmerman, and J.H. Zimmerman, *The Wetlands of Dane County, Wisconsin*, Dane County Regional Planning Commission, Madison, Wisc., 1974.

15. Befort, W., "Large-Scale Sampling Photography for Forest Habitat-Type Identification,"

Photogrammetric Engineering and Remote Sensing, vol. 52, no. 1, January 1986, pp. 101–108.

16. Benson, M.L., et al., "A Practical Field Stereo Viewer for 230-mm Color Transparencies," *Photogrammetric Engineering and Remote Sensing*, vol. 51, no. 11, November 1985, pp. 1723–1724.

17. Bird and Hale Ltd., *Surveillance of the Environmental Effects of a Highway Facility by Remote Sensing: A State of the Art*, Ontario Ministry of Transportation and Communications, Downsville, January 1977.

18. Blazquez, C.H., and F.W. Horn, Jr., *Aerial Color Infrared Photography: Applications in Citriculture*, NASA Ref. Publ. 1067, U.S. Gov. Printing Office, Washington, D.C., 1980.

19. Blazquez, C.H., R.A. Elliott, and G.J. Edwards, "Vegetable Crop Management with Remote Sensing," *Photogrammetric Engineering and Remote Sensing*, vol. 47, no. 4, April 1981, pp. 543–547.

20. Branch, M.C., *City Planning and Aerial Information*, Harvard Univ. Press, Cambridge, Mass., 1971.

21. Brown, D.E., and A.M. Winer, "Estimating Urban Vegetation Cover in Los Angeles," *Photogrammetric Engineering and Remote Sensing*, vol. 52, no. 1, January 1986, pp. 117–123.

22. Carter, V., "Coastal Wetlands: The Present and Future Role of Remote Sensing," *Proceedings: Eleventh International Symposium on Remote Sensing of Environment*, April 1977, pp. 301–323.

23. Carter, V., D.L. Malone, and J.H. Burbank, "Wetland Classification and Mapping in Western Tennessee," *Photogrammetric Engineering and Remote Sensing*, vol. 45, no. 3, March 1979, pp. 273–284.

24. Ciesla, W.M., "Mission: Track the Gypsy from 65,000 Feet," *American Forests*, vol. 90, no. 7, July 1984, pp. 30–33 and 54–56.

25. Ciesla, W.M., D.D. Bennett, and J.A. Caylor, "Mapping Effectiveness of Insecticide Treatments against Pandora Moth with Color-IR Photos," *Photogrammetric Engineering and Remote Sensing*, vol. 50, no. 1, January 1984, pp. 73–79.

26. Collins, S.H., "Stereoscopic Depth Perception," *Photogrammetric Engineering and Remote Sensing*, vol. 47, no. 1, January 1981, pp. 45–52.

27. Cowardin, L.M., et al., *Classification of Wetlands and Deepwater Habitats of the United States*, U.S. Fish and Wildlife Service Publ. FWS/OBS-79/31, Washington, D.C., 1979.

28. Cravat, H.R., and R. Glaser, *Color Aerial Stereograms of Selected Coastal Areas of the United States*, U.S. Department of Commerce, Washington, D.C., 1971.

29. Dalsted, K.J., B.K. Worcester, and L.J. Brun, "Detection of Saline Seeps by Remote Sensing Techniques," *Photogrammetric Engineering and Remote Sensing*, vol. 45, no. 3, March 1979, pp. 285–291.

30. Deuel, L., *Flights into Yesterday—The Story of Aerial Archaeology*, St. Martin's Press, New York, 1969.

31. Deuell, R.L. and T.M. Lillesand, "An Aerial Photographic Procedure for Estimating Recreational Boating Use on Inland Lakes," *Photogrammetric Engineering and Remote Sensing*, vol. 48, no. 11, November 1982, pp. 1713–1717.

32. Erb, T.L., et al., "Analysis of Landfills with Historic Airphotos," *Photogrammetric Engineering and Remote Sensing*, vol. 47, no. 9, September 1981, pp. 1363–1369.

33. Estes, J.E., and L.W. Senger, *Remote Sensing—Techniques for Environmental Analysis*, Hamilton, Santa Barbara, Calif., 1974.

34. Evans, B.M., "Aerial Photographic Analysis of Septic System Performance," *Photogrammetric Engineering and Remote Sensing*, vol. 48, no. 11, November 1982, pp. 1709–1712.

35. Everitt, J.H., and P.R. Nixon, "Using Color Aerial Photography to Detect Camphorweed Infestations on South Texas Rangelands," *Photogrammetric Engineering and Remote Sensing*, vol. 51, no. 11, November 1985, pp. 1793–1797.

36. Everitt, J.H., and P.R. Nixon, "False Color Video Imagery: A Potential Remote Sensing Tool for Range Management," *Photogrammetric Engineering and Remote Sensing*, vol. 51, no. 6, June 1985, pp. 675–679.

37. Ferguson, E.L., and D.S. Gilmer, "Small-Format Cameras and Fine-Grain Film Used for Waterfowl Population Studies," *Journal of Wildlife Management*, vol. 44, no. 3, 1980, pp. 691–694.

38. Ferguson, E.L., D.G. Jorde, and J.J. Sease, "Use of 35-mm Color Aerial Photography to Acquire Mallard Sex Ratio Data," *Photogrammetric Engineering and Remote Sensing*, vol. 47, no. 6, June 1981, pp. 823–827.

39. Forestry Applications Project, *Photointerpretation Guide for Forest Resource Inventories*, Doc. No. LEC-4302, U.S. Gov. Printing Office, Washington, D.C., 1975.

40. Gammon, P.T., and V. Carter, "Vegetation Mapping with Seasonal Color Infrared Photographs," *Photogrammetric Engineering and Remote Sensing*, vol. 45, no. 1, January 1979, pp. 87–97.

41. Gerster, G., *Flights of Discovery—The Earth from Above*, Paddington Press, New York, 1978.

42. Gimbarzevsky, P., *Remote Sensing in Forest Damage Detection and Appraisal: Selected Annotated Bibliography*, Report BC-X-253, Pacific Forest Research Centre, Victoria, British Columbia, 1984.

43. Goetz, A.F., and L.C. Rowan, "Geologic Remote Sensing," *Science*, vol. 211, no. 4484, 20 February 1981, pp. 781–791.

44. Goetz, A.F., B.N. Rock, and L.C. Rowan, "Remote Sensing for Exploration: An Overview," *Economic Geology*, vol. 78, no. 4, June–July 1983, pp. 573–590.

45. Greenlee, D.D., *Application of Spatial Analysis Techniques to Remotely Sensed Images and Ancillary Geocoded Data*, USGS, Sioux Falls, S. Dak., 1980.

46. Grumstrup, P.D., et al., "Aerial Photographic Assessment of Transmission Line Structure Impact on Agricultural Crop Production," *Photogrammetric Engineering and Remote Sensing*, vol. 48, no. 8, August 1982, pp. 1313–1317.

47. Heller, R.W., "Remote Sensing: Its State-of-the-Art in Forestry," *Proceedings: 10th William T. Pecora Memorial Remote Sensing Symposium*, American Society for Photogrammetry and Remote Sensing, Ft. Collins, Colo., 1985, pp. 18–29.

48. Heyland, J.D., "Vertical Aerial Photography as an Aid in Wildlife Population Studies," *First Canadian Symposium on Remote Sensing*, 1972, pp. 121–136.

49. Holz, R.K., *The Surveillant Science—Remote Sensing of the Environment*, 2nd ed., Wiley, New York, 1985.

50. Howard, J.A., *Aerial Photo-Ecology*, American Elsevier, New York, 1970.

51. International Society of Photogrammetry, Commission VII, "Transactions of the Symposium on Photo Interpretation," *International Archives of Photogrammetry*, vol. 14, Uitgeverij Waltman, Delft, 1962.

52. Johnson, P.L. (ed.), *Remote Sensing in Ecology*, Univ. of Georgia Press, Athens, 1969.

53. Johnston, C.A., *Considerations for Wetland Inventories in Wisconsin*, M.S. thesis (Soil Science and Land Resources), University of Wisconsin–Madison, 1977.

54. Kennie, T.J.M., and M.C. Matthews (eds.), *Remote Sensing in Civil Engineering*, Halsted Press, Wiley, New York, 1985.

55. Kiefer, R.W. (ed.), *Civil Engineering Applications of Remote Sensing*, Proceedings: Specialty Conference of the Aerospace Division of the ASCE, Madison, Wis., August 13–14, 1980.

56. Kosok, P., *Life, Land and Water in Ancient Peru*, Long Island Univ. Press, New York, 1965.

57. Kroeck, R.M., and G.A. Shelton, *Overhead Remote Sensing for Assessment of Hazardous Waste Sites*, Report 600/X-82-019, Environmental Protection Agency, Environmental Monitoring Systems Laboratory, Las Vegas, November 1982.

58. Ladouceur, G., R. Allard, and S. Ghosh, "Semi-automatic Survey of Crop Damage Using Color Infrared Photography," *Photogrammetric Engineering and Remote Sensing*, vol. 52, no. 1, January 1986, pp. 111–115.

59. Lattman, L.H., and R.G. Ray, *Aerial Photographs in Field Geology*, Holt, Rinehart & Winston, New York, 1965.

60. Lindgren, D.T., *Land Use Planning and Remote Sensing*, Nijhoff, Dordrecht, 1985.

61. Lintz, J., and D.S. Simonett (eds.), *Remote Sensing of Environment*, Addison–Wesley, Reading, Mass., 1976.

62. Lyon, J.G., J.F McCarthy, and J.T. Heinen, "Video Digitization of Aerial Photographs for Measurement of Wind Erosion Damage on Converted Rangeland," *Photogrammetric Engineering and Remote Sensing*, vol. 52, no. 3, March 1986, pp. 373–377.

63. Lyons, T.R., and T.E. Avery, *Remote Sensing: A Handbook for Archeologists and Cultural Resource Managers*, National Park Service, Washington, D.C., 1977.

64. Lyons, T.R., and F.J. Mathien (eds.), *Cultural Resources Remote Sensing*, Cultural Resources Management Division, National Park Service, Washington, D.C., 1980.

65. Martin, F.C., "Using a Geographic Information System for Forest Land Mapping and Management," *Photogrammetric Engineering and Remote Sensing*, vol. 51, no. 11, November 1985, pp. 1753–1759.

66. Mead, R.A., and P.T. Gammon, "Mapping Wetlands Using Orthophotoquads and 35-mm Aerial Photographs," *Photogrammetric Engineering and Remote Sensing*, vol. 47, no. 5, May 1981, pp. 649–652.

67. Meyer, M.P., "Place of Small-Format Aerial Photography in Resource Surveys," *Journal of Forestry*, vol. 80, no. 1, 1982, pp. 15–17.

68. Milfred, C.J., and R.W. Kiefer, "Analysis of Soil Variability with Repetitive Aerial Photography," *Soil Science Society of America Journal*, vol. 40, no. 4, July–August 1976, pp. 553–557.

69. Miller, V.C., *Photogeology*, McGraw–Hill, New York, 1961.

70. Morgan, K.M., et al., "Airphoto Analysis of Erosion Control Practices," *Photogrammetric Engineering and Remote Sensing*, vol. 46, no. 5, May 1980, pp. 637–640.

71. Muehrcke, P.C., *Map Use—Reading, Analysis, and Interpretation*, 2nd ed., J.P. Publ. Madison, Wis., 1986.

72. Murtha, P.A., *A Guide to Air Photo Interpretation of Forest Damage in Canada*, Publ. No. 1292, Canadian Forestry Service, Ottawa, Ontario, 1977.

73. Murtha, P.A., "Some Air-Photo Scale Effects on Douglas-Fir Damage Type Interpretation," *Photogrammetric Engineering and Remote Sensing*, vol. 49, no. 3, March 1983, pp. 327–335.

74. Murtha, P.A., and J.A. McLean, "Extravisual Damage Detection? Defining the Standard Normal Tree," *Photogrammetric Engineering and Remote Sensing*, vol. 47, no. 4, April 1981, pp. 515–522.

75. Myers, B.J., and M.L. Benson, "Rainforest Species on Large-Scale Color Photos," *Photogrammetric Engineering and Remote Sensing*, vol. 47, no. 4, April 1981, pp. 505–513.

76. Myers, B.J., et al., "Shadowless or Sunlit Photos for Forest Disease Detection?" *Photogrammetric Engineering and Remote Sensing*, vol. 50, no. 1, January 1984, pp. 63–72.

77. National Research Council, *Remote Sensing with Special Reference to Agriculture and Forestry*, NRC/NAS, Washington, D.C., 1970.

78. Paine, D.P., *Aerial Photography and Image Interpretation for Resource Management*, Wiley, New York, 1981.

79. Payne, J.A., et al., "Detection of Peach and Pecan Pests and Diseases with Color Infrared Aerial Photography," *Proceedings: 3rd Biennial Workshop on Color Aerial Photography in the Plant Sciences*, American Society of Photogrammetry, Falls Church, Va., 1971.

80. Philipson, W.R., and T. Liang, "An Airphoto Key for Major Tropical Crops," *Photogrammetric Engineering and Remote Sensing*, vol. 48, no. 2, February 1982, pp. 223–233.

81. Poulton, C.E., "Evolution of Remote Sensing in Range Management, Speculations on Its Future," *Proceedings: 10th William T. Pecora Memorial Remote Sensing Symposium*, American Society for Photogrammetry and Remote Sensing, Ft. Collins, Colo., 1985, pp. 2–17.

82. Ray, R.G., *Aerial Photographs in Geologic Interpretation and Mapping*, USGS Professional Paper 373, U.S. Gov. Printing Office, 1960.

83. Robinson, A., et al., *Elements of Cartography*, 5th ed., Wiley, New York, 1984.

84. Sabins, F.F., Jr., *Remote Sensing—Principles and Interpretation*, 2nd ed., Freeman, New York, 1986.

85. Sayn-Wittgenstein, L., "Recognition of Tree Species on Air Photographs by Crown Characteristics," *Photogrammetric Engineering*, vol. 27, no. 5, December 1961, pp. 792–809.

86. Sayn-Wittgenstein, L., *Recognition of Tree Species on Aerial Photographs*, Report FMR-X-118, Forest Management Institute, Ottawa, Ontario, 1978.

87. Seevers, P.M., "Practial Application and Physiological Relationships of Color Infrared Photography Relative to Monitoring Agricultural Crops," *Proceedings: 7th Biennial Workshop on Color Aerial Photography in the Plant Sciences and Related Fields*, American Society of Photogrammetry, Falls Church, Va., 1979, pp. 201–208.

88. Siegal, B.S., and A.R. Gillespie (eds), *Remote Sensing in Geology*, Wiley, New York, 1980.

89. Slonecker, E.T., "Septic Field Failure Analysis via Color/Color Infrared Aerial Photography," *Proceedings: Eighth Biennial Workshop on Color Aerial Photography in the Plant Sciences and Related Fields*, American Society of Photogrammetry, Falls Church, Va., April 1981, pp. 11–18.

90. Smith, B.D., "Determining Definitive Disease Losses from Cotton Root Rot Employing Remote Sensing," *Proceedings: 6th Biennial Workshop on Color Aerial Photography in the Plant Sciences and Related Fields*, American Society of Photogrammetry, Falls Church, Va., 1977, pp. 1–5.

91. Smith, J.L., "Evaluation of the Effects of Photo Measurement Errors on Predictions of Stand Volume from Aerial Photography," *Photogrammetric Engineering and Remote Sensing*, vol. 52, no. 3, March 1986, pp. 401–410.

92. Soil Conservation Society of America, *Remote Sensing for Resources Management*, Ankeny, Iowa, 1982.

93. Spurr, S.H., *Photogrammetry and Photo-interpretation*, Ronald Press, New York, 1960.

94. Strandberg, C.H., *Aerial Discovery Manual*, Wiley, New York, 1967.

95. Thompson, M.M., *Maps for America*, 2nd ed., USGS, Washington, D.C., 1981.

96. Tiner, R.W., Jr., *Wetlands of the United States: Current Status and Recent Trends*, National Wetlands Inventory, Fish and Wildlife Service, Washington, D.C., 1984.

97. UNESCO, *Aerial Surveys and Integrated Studies—Proceedings of The Toulouse Conference*, UNESCO Publications Center, Paris 1968.

98. U.S. Department of Agriculture, *Aerial-Photo Interpretation in Classifying and Mapping Soils*, Agriculture Handbook 294, U.S. Gov. Printing Office, Washington, D.C., 1969.

99. U.S. Department of Agriculture, *Soil Survey of Dane County, Wisconsin*, U.S. Gov. Printing Office, Washington, D.C., 1977.

100. U.S. Department of Agriculture, *Forester's Guide to Aerial-Photo Interpretation*, Agriculture Handbook 308, U.S. Gov. Printing Office, Washington, D.C., 1978.

101. U.S. Senate, 88th Congress, *A Study of Pollution—Water*, Committee on Public Works, Washington, D.C., 1963.

102. Warden, R.E., and W.T. Dagodag, *A Guide to the Preparation and Review of Environmental Impact Reports*, Security World Pub. Co., Los Angeles, 1976.

103. Wildman, W.E., "Color Infrared: A Valuable Tool in Vineyard Management," *Proceedings: 7th Biennial Workshop on Color Aerial Photography in the Plant Sciences and Related Fields*, American Society of Photogrammetry, Falls Church, Va., 1979, pp. 229–238.

104. Williams, T.H.L., "Implementing LESA on a Geographic Information System—A Case Study," *Photogrammetric Engineering and Remote Sensing*, vol. 51, no. 12, December 1985, pp. 1923–1932.

105. Wilson, D.R. (ed.), *Aerial Reconnaissance for Archaeology*, Research Report no. 12, Council for British Archaeology, London, 1975.

106. Wilson, D.R., *Air Photo Interpretation for Archaeologists*, St. Martin's Press, New York, 1982.

107. Witmer, R.E., "U.S. Geological Survey Land Use and Land Cover Classification System," *Journal of Forestry*, vol. 76, 1978, pp. 661–666.

108. Zsilinszky, V.G., *Photographic Interpretation of Tree Species in Ontario*, Ontario Department of Lands and Forests, Downsview, 1966.

AIRPHOTO INTERPRETATION FOR TERRAIN EVALUATION

4.1 INTRODUCTION

Various terrain characteristics are important to soil scientists, geologists, geographers, civil engineers, urban and regional planners, landscape architects, real estate developers, and others who wish to evaluate the suitability of the terrain for various land uses. Because terrain conditions strongly influence the capability of the land to support various species of vegetation, an understanding of airphoto interpretation for terrain evaluation is also important for botanists, foresters, wildlife ecologists, and others concerned with vegetation mapping and evaluation.

The principal terrain characteristics that can be estimated by means of airphoto interpretation are bedrock type, landform, soil texture, site drainage conditions, susceptibility to flooding, and depth of unconsolidated materials over bedrock. In addition, the slope of the land surface can be estimated by airphoto interpretation and measured by photogrammetric methods (Chapter 5).

In this chapter, we consider the terrain characteristics and airphoto identification of most of the common bedrock types and associated residual soils, followed by a consideration of transported soils and organic soils. The airphoto interpretation process described herein emphasizes terrain characteristics that are visible on stereoscopic aerial photographs. The geological terminology employed follows that set forth in the American Geological Institute *Dictionary of Geological Terms* [1].

4.2 SOIL CHARACTERISTICS

The term "soil" has specific scientific connotations to different groups involved with soil surveying and mapping. For example, engineers and agricultural soil scientists each have a different concept of soils and use a different terminology in describing soils. Most engineers consider all unconsolidated earth material lying above bedrock to be "soil." Agricultural soil scientists regard "soil" as a material that develops from a geologic parent material through the natural process of weathering and contains a certain amount of organic material and other constituents that support plant life. For example, a 10 m thick deposit of glacial till over bedrock might be extensively

211

weathered and altered to a depth of 1 m. The remaining 9 m would be relatively unaltered. An engineer would consider this a soil deposit 10 m thick lying over bedrock. A soil scientist would consider this a soil layer 1 m thick lying over glacial till parent material. We use the soil science (pedalogical) concept of soil in this chapter.

Through the processes of weathering, including the effects of climate and plant and animal activity, unconsolidated earth materials develop distinct layers that soil scientists call *soil horizons*. The top layer is designated the *A horizon* and called the *surface soil*, or *topsoil*. It can range from about 0 to 60 cm in thickness and is typically 15 to 30 cm. The A horizon is the most extensively weathered horizon. It contains the most organic matter of any horizon and has had some of its fine-textured particles washed down into lower horizons. The second layer is designated the *B horizon* and called the *subsoil*. It can range from 0 to 250 cm in thickness and usually is 45 to 60 cm. The B horizon contains some organic matter and is the layer of accumulation for the fine-textured particles washed down from the A horizon. The portion of the soil profile occupied by the A and B horizons is called the *soil* (or *solum*) by soil scientists. The *C horizon* is the underlying geologic material from which the A and B horizons have developed and is called the *parent material* (or *initial material*). The concept of soil profile development into distinct horizons is vitally important for agricultural soils mapping and productivity estimation, as well as for many developmental uses of the landscape.

There are three principal origins of soil materials. *Residual soils* are formed in place from bedrock by the natural process of weathering. *Transported soils* are formed from parent materials that have been transported to their present location by wind, water, and/or glacial ice. *Organic soils* (muck and peat) are formed from decomposed plant materials in a very wet environment, typically in shallow lakes or areas with a very high ground water table.

Soils consist of combinations of solid particles, water, and air. Particles are given size names, such as gravel, sand, silt, and clay, based on particle size. Particle size terminology is not standardized for all disciplines and several classification systems exist. Typical particle size definitions for engineers and agricultural soil scientists are shown in Table 4.1. For our purposes, the differences in particle size definitions between engineers and soil scientists for gravel, sand, silt, and clay are relatively unimportant. We use the soil science definition because it has a convenient system for naming combinations of particle sizes.

Figure 4.1 shows the system used by soil scientists to give textural names to specific combinations of sand, silt and clay. When a soil contains a significant amount of gravel, the term "gravelly" (20 to 50 percent gravel) or "very gravelly" (more than 50 percent gravel) is used in addition to the basic textural name. For example, a soil containing 60 percent sand, 30 percent silt, and 10 percent clay would be called "sandy loam." A soil containing 60 percent gravel, 24 percent sand, 12 percent silt, and 4 percent clay would be called "very gravelly sandy loam." Note that the proportions of sand, silt, and clay are the same for both examples.

We consider materials containing more than 50 percent silt and clay to be *fine-textured* and materials containing more than 50 percent sand and gravel to be *coarse-textured*.

The descriptions of many of the stereopair illustrations contained in this chapter

TABLE 4.1 Soil Particle Size Designations

	Soil particle size (mm)	
Soil particle size name	Engineering definition	Agricultural soil science definition
Gravel	2.0−76.2	2.0−76.2
Sand	0.074−2.0	0.05−2.0
Silt	0.005−0.074	0.002−0.05
Clay	Below 0.005	Below 0.002

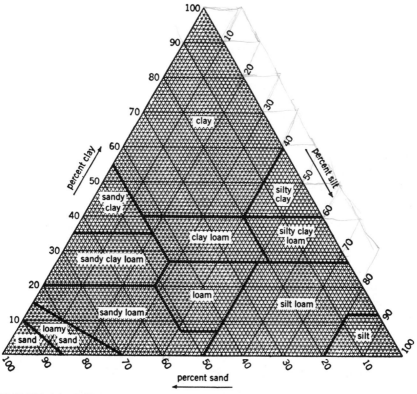

FIGURE 4.1 USDA textural triangle chart showing the percentages of sand, silt, and clay in the basic USDA soil textural classes. (After USDA [27].)

include reference to the soil texture, soil drainage condition, and depth to bedrock of the terrain shown in the illustrations. In the case of residual soils, where the depth to bedrock is commonly only 1 to 2 m, the textures specified are generally representative of the B and C horizon textures. In the case of transported soils, where the weathered soil profile is commonly only a small fraction of the total thickness of the unconsolidated transported material (e.g., a 30 m high river terrace might have a weathered profile only 1 m thick), emphasis is on describing the texture of the parent material. Not all the information given in figure descriptions was obtained solely by airphoto interpretation. In cases where specific soil information is given, USDA-SCS soil survey reports were consulted for information regarding soil texture, drainage class, and depth to bedrock.

Soils have characteristic drainage conditions that depend on surface runoff, soil permeability, and internal soil drainage. We use the USDA [27] soil drainage classification system for soils in their natural condition, with the following seven soil drainage classes:

Very poorly drained.   Natural removal of water from the soil is so slow that the water table remains at or near the surface most of the time. Soils of this drainage class usually occupy level or depressed sites and are frequently ponded.

Poorly drained.   Natural removal of water from the soil is so slow that it remains wet for a large part of the time. The water table is commonly at or near the ground surface during a considerable part of the year.

Somewhat poorly drained.   Natural removal of water from the soil is slow enough to keep it wet for significant periods but not all the time.

Moderately well drained.   Natural removal of water from the soil is somewhat slow so that the soil is wet for a small but significant part of the time.

Well drained.   Natural removal of water from the soil is at a moderate rate without notable impedance.

Somewhat excessively drained.   Natural removal of water from the soil is rapid. Many soils of this drainage class are sandy and very porous.

Excessively drained.   Natural removal of water from the soil is very rapid. Excessively drained soils may be on steep slopes, may be very porous, or both.

The above descriptions refer to natural soil drainage. We use the term *artificial drainage* to refer to the enhancement of natural soil drainage by various human activities including ditching and the installation of underground tile drains.

4.3   LAND USE SUITABILITY EVALUATION

Terrain information can be used to evaluate the suitability of land areas for a variety of land uses. Our emphasis is on suitability for developmental purposes, principally urban and suburban land uses.

The topographic characteristics of an area are one of the most important determinants of the suitability of an area for development. For subdivision development, slopes in the 2 to 6 percent range are steep enough to provide for good surface drainage and interesting siting, and yet flat enough so that no significant site development problems will be encountered provided the soil is well drained. Some drainage problems may be encountered in the 0 to 2 percent range, but these can be readily overcome unless there is a large expanse of absolutely flat land with insufficient internal drainage. The site plan in the 6 to 12 percent range may be more interesting than in the 2 to 6 percent range, but will be more costly to develop. Slopes over 12 percent present problems in street development and lot design and also pose serious problems when septic tanks are used for domestic sewage disposal. Severe limitations to subdivision development occur on slopes over 20 percent. For industrial park and commercial sites, slopes of not more than 5 percent are preferred.

The soil texture and drainage conditions also affect land use suitability. Well-drained, coarse-textured soils present few limitations to development. Poorly drained or very poorly drained, fine-textured soils can present severe limitations. Shallow groundwater tables and poor soil drainage conditions cause problems in septic tank installation and operation, in cellar and foundation excavation, and in keeping cellars water-free after construction. In general, depths to the water table of at least 2 m are preferred. Depths of 1 to 2 m may be satisfactory where public sewage disposal is provided and buildings are constructed without basements.

Shallow depths to bedrock cause problems in septic tank installation and maintenance, in utility line construction, in cellar and foundation excavation, and in street location and construction, especially when present in combination with steep slopes. Depths to bedrock over 2 m are preferred. Sites with a depth to bedrock of 1 to 2 m are generally unsatisfactory but the development of these areas may be feasible in some cases. These sites are generally unsatisfactory where septic tank sewage disposal is to be provided. Also, additional excavation costs are involved where basements and public sewage disposal facilities are to be constructed. A depth to bedrock of less than 1 m presents serious limitations to development and is an unsatisfactory condition in almost all cases of land development.

Slope stability problems occur with certain soil–slope conditions. Although we will not discuss techniques for slope stability analysis using airphoto interpretation, it should be mentioned that numerous areas of incipient landslide failure have been detected by airphoto interpretation.

Despite the emphasis here on land development, it must be recognized that certain land areas may be worthy of preservation in their natural state because of outstanding topographic or geologic characteristics or because rare or endangered plant or animal species occupy those areas. In addition, the maintenance of prime agricultural land for agricultural rather than developmental use must be an important consideration in all land use planning decisions. Similar concerns also apply to the preservation of wetland systems. Various airphoto interpretation techniques discussed in Chapter 3 and this chapter are applicable to the assessment of land for these purposes.

4.4 ELEMENTS OF AIRPHOTO INTERPRETATION FOR TERRAIN EVALUATION

Airphoto interpretation for terrain evaluation is based on a systematic observation and evaluation of key elements that are studied stereoscopically. These are topography, drainage pattern and texture, erosion, photo tone, and vegetation and land use.

Topography

Each landform and bedrock type described has its own characteristic topographic form, including a typical size and shape. In fact, there is often a distinct topographic change at the boundary between two different landforms.

With vertical photographs having a normal 60 percent overlap, most individuals see the terrain exaggerated in height about three or four times. Consequently, slopes appear steeper than they actually are. The specific amount of vertical exaggeration observed in any given stereopair is a function of the geometric conditions under which the photographs are viewed and taken. The ground distance between the photo centers at the times of exposure is called the *air base*. The ratio between the air base and the flying height above ground determines the vertical exaggeration. The larger the *base–height ratio*, the greater the vertical exaggeration. Table 4.2 lists various actual and apparent slopes based on the rule-of-thumb that

$$\tan(\text{apparent slope angle}) = \tan(\text{true slope angle}) \times 3$$

Drainage Pattern and Texture

The drainage pattern and texture seen on aerial photographs are indicators of landform and bedrock type and also suggest soil characteristics and site drainage conditions.

Six of the most common drainage patterns are illustrated in Figure 4.2. The *dendritic drainage pattern* is a well-integrated pattern formed by a main stream with its tributaries branching and rebranching freely in all directions and occurs on relatively homogeneous materials such as horizontally bedded sedimentary rock and granite. The *rectangular drainage pattern* is basically a dendritic pattern modified by structural bedrock control such that the tributaries meet at right angles and is typical of

TABLE 4.2   Slope Exaggeration on Stereo Airphotos

Actual terrain slope	Approximate apparent slope on stereo airphotos
0°	0°
2°	6°
5°	15°
10°	28°
15°	39°
30°	60°
45°	72°
60°	79°
90°	90°

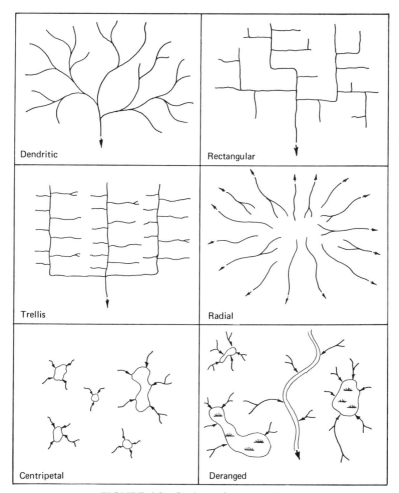

FIGURE 4.2   Six basic drainage patterns.

flat-lying massive sandstone formations with a well-developed joint system. The *trellis drainage pattern* consists of streams having one dominant direction, with subsidiary directions of drainage at right angles, and occurs in areas of folded sedimentary rocks. The *radial drainage pattern* is formed by streams that radiate outward from a central area as is typical of volcanoes and domes. The *centripetal drainage pattern* is the reverse of the radial drainage pattern (drainage is directed toward a central point) and occurs in areas of limestone sinkholes, glacial kettle holes, volcanic craters, and other depressions. The *deranged drainage pattern* is a disordered pattern of aimlessly directed short streams, ponds, and wetland areas typical of ablation glacial till areas.

The previously described drainage patterns are all "destructional" drainage patterns resulting from the erosion of the land surface; they should not be confused with "constructional" drainage features that are remnants of the mode of origin of landforms such as alluvial fans and glacial outwash plains.

Coupled with drainage pattern is drainage texture. Figure 4.3 shows *coarse-textured* and *fine-textured* drainage patterns. Coarse-textured patterns develop where the soils and rocks have good internal drainage with little surface runoff. Fine-textured patterns develop where the soils and rocks have poor internal drainage and high surface runoff. Also, fine-textured drainage patterns develop on soft, easily eroded rocks, such as shale, whereas coarse-textured patterns develop on hard, massive rocks, such as granite.

Erosion

Gullies are the smallest drainage features that can be seen on aerial photographs and may be as small as a meter wide and a hundred meters long. Gullies result from the erosion of unconsolidated material by runoff and develop where rainfall cannot adequately percolate into the ground, but instead collects and flows across the surface in small rivulets. These initial rivulets enlarge and take on a particular shape characteristic of the material in which they are formed. As illustrated in Figures 4.4 and 4.5, short

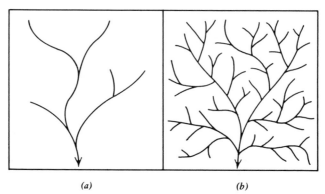

(a)   (b)

FIGURE 4.3   Illustrative drainage patterns. *(a)* Coarse-textured dendritic pattern. *(b)* Fine-textured dendritic pattern.

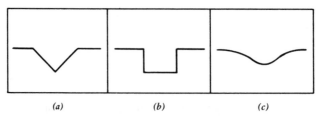

(a)   (b)   (c)

FIGURE 4.4   Illustrative gully cross sections. *(a)* Sand and gravel. *(b)* Silt. *(c)* Silty clay or clay.

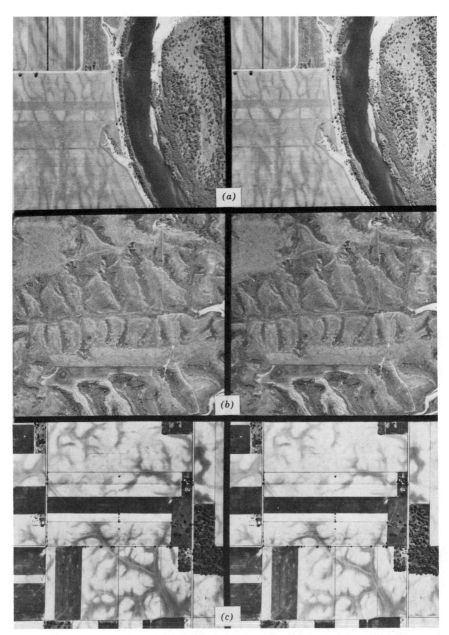

FIGURE 4.5 Stereograms illustrating basic gully shapes. *(a)* Sand and gravel terrace, Dunn County, Wisconsin. *(b)* Loess (wind-deposited silt), Buffalo County, Nebraska. *(c)* Silty clay loam glacial till, Madison County, Indiana. 1:20,000. (USDA—ASCS photos.)

gullies with V-shaped cross sections tend to develop in sand and gravel; gullies with U-shaped cross sections tend to develop in silty soils; and long gullies with gently rounded cross sections tend to develop in silty clay and clay soils.

Photo Tone

The term *photo tone* refers to the "brightness" at any point on a panchromatic photograph. The absolute value of the photo tone depends not only on certain terrain characteristics but also on photographic factors such as film–filter combination, exposure, and photographic processing. Photo tone also depends on meteorological and climatological factors such as atmospheric haze, sun angle, and cloud shadows. Because of the effect of these non-terrain-related factors, photo interpretation for terrain evaluation must rely on an analysis of *relative* tone values, rather than absolute tone values. Relative tone values are important because they often form distinct photographic patterns that may be of great significance in airphoto interpretation.

The effect of terrain conditions on relative photo tone is illustrated in Figure 4.6. In the case of bare soils (nonvegetated soils), the lighter-toned areas tend to have a

FIGURE 4.6 Airphoto illustrating effect of terrain conditions on relative photo tones, Madison County, Indiana. 1:16,000. (USDA–ASCS photo.)

topographically higher position, a coarser soil texture, a lower soil moisture content, and a lower organic content. Figure 4.6 shows the striking mottled tonal pattern typical of fine-textured glacial till soils. The tonal differences are caused by differences in sunlight reflection due principally to the varying moisture content of the soil. The lighter-toned areas are somewhat poorly drained silt loam soils on rises $\frac{1}{3}$ to 1 m above the surrounding darker-toned areas of very poorly drained silty clay loam soils. The degree of contrast between lighter- and darker-toned bare soils varies depending on the overall moisture conditions of the soil, as illustrated in Plate 8.

The sharpness of the boundary between lighter and darker-toned areas is often related to the soil texture. Coarser-textured soils will generally have sharper gradations between light and dark tones while finer-textured soils will generally have more gradual gradations. These variations in tonal gradients result from differences in capillary action occurring in soils of different textures.

Our discussion of airphoto interpretation for terrain evaluation relates primarily to panchromatic film because this film type has historically received the most use for this purpose. Subtle differences in soil and rock colors can be more readily detected using color film as compared with panchromatic film and subtle differences in soil moisture and vegetation vigor can be more readily detected using color infrared film. Because there is a wide variety of soil and vegetation colors possible on color and color infrared films, it is not possible to consider them all here. Therefore, our discussion of *photo tone* will describe tone as the shades of gray seen on panchromatic photographs. Persons working with color or color infrared photographs of specific geographic regions at specific times of the year can work out their own criteria for *tone and color* evaluation following the principles in this chapter.

Vegetation and Land Use

Differences in natural or cultivated vegetation often indicate differences in terrain conditions. For example, orchards and vineyards are generally located on well-drained soils, whereas truck farming activities often take place on highly organic soils such as muck and peat deposits. In many cases, however, vegetation and land use obscure differences in terrain conditions and the interpreter must be careful to draw inferences only from meaningful differences in vegetation and land use.

Figure 4.7a shows a very poorly drained area of organic soils (darker-toned area running across center of photo) surrounded by a moderately well drained area of glacial till soils. The distinct differences in vegetation and land use on these soils reflect the variations in terrain conditions associated with these soil materials.

The vegetation cover in agricultural areas changes during the year and, during the summer growing season, dense cultivated vegetation commonly obscures tonal patterns due to soil differences. Figure 4.7b shows an area of fine-textured glacial till similar to that shown in Figure 4.6. The soil patterns are similar across the entire area of the photograph but the variations in crop types and stages cause a very different appearance in different fields. The mottled tone pattern typical of glacial till is clearly seen in the bare soil fields, but is obscured in the fields with significant crop cover.

FIGURE 4.7 Airphotos illustrating vegetation and land use patterns. *(a)* Waukesha County, Wisconsin. *(b)* Madison County, Indiana. 1:23,000. (USDA—ASCS photos.)

4.5 THE AIRPHOTO INTERPRETATION PROCESS

Through an analysis of the elements of photo interpretation (topography, drainage pattern and texture, erosion, photo tone, vegetation, and land use), the photo interpreter can identify different terrain conditions and can determine the boundaries between them. Initially, photo interpreters will need to consider carefully each of the above elements individually and in combination in order to estimate terrain conditions. After some experience, these elements are often applied subconsciously as the interpreter develops the facility to recognize certain recurring airphoto patterns almost instantaneously. In complex areas, the interpreter should not make snap decisions about terrain conditions, but should carefully consider the topography, drainage pattern and texture, erosion, photo tone, vegetation, and land use characteristics exhibited on the aerial photographs.

In the remainder of this chapter, we examine each of the principal bedrock and transported soil types common on the earth's surface, as well as organic deposits. For each of these, we consider geologic origin and formation, soil and/or bedrock characteristics, implications for land use planning, and airphoto identification using the elements of airphoto interpretation for terrain evaluation. Our illustrations are limited to occurrences in the United States. We emphasize the recognition of clear-cut examples of various bedrock and transported soil types. In nature, there are many variations to each type. Interpreters working in specific localities can use the principles set forth here to develop their own photo interpretation keys.

In cases where distinctions in airphoto appearance must be made for different climatic situations, we will speak of "humid" and "arid" climates. We will consider *humid climates* to occur in areas that receive 50 cm or more rainfall per year and *arid climates* to occur in areas that receive less than 50 cm per year rainfall. In the United States, farming without irrigation is feasible in areas with a rainfall of about 50 cm per year or more. Areas receiving less than 50 cm per year rainfall generally require irrigation for farming.

Even the most searching and capable airphoto analysis can benefit from field verification as the airphoto interpretation process is seldom expected to stand alone. The photo interpreter should consult existing topographic, geologic, and soil maps and should conduct a selective field check. The principal benefits of airphoto interpretation for terrain evaluation should be a savings in time, money, and effort. The use of airphoto interpretation techniques can allow for terrain mapping during periods of unsuitable weather for field mapping and can provide for more efficient field operations.

4.6 SEDIMENTARY ROCKS

The principal sedimentary rock types to be considered are sandstone, shale, and limestone. Sedimentary rocks are by far the most common rock type exposed at the earth's surface and extend over approximately 75 percent of the earth's land surface (igneous rocks extend over approximately 20 percent and metamorphic rocks over about 5 percent).

Sedimentary rocks are formed by the consolidation of layers of sediments that have settled out of water or air. Sediments are converted into coherent rock masses by lithification, a process that involves cementation and compaction by the weight of overlying sediments.

Clastic sedimentary rocks are rocks containing discrete particles derived from the erosion, transportation, and deposition of preexisting rocks and soils. The nature of the constituent particles and the way in which they are bound together determine the texture, permeability, and strength of the rocks. Clastic sedimentary rocks containing primarily gravel-sized particles are called *conglomerate*, those containing primarily sand-sized particles are called *sandstone*, those containing primarily silt-sized particles are called *siltstone*, and those containing primarily clay-sized particles are called *shale*.

Limestone has a high calcium carbonate content and is formed from chemical or biochemical action. Chemically formed limestone results from the precipitation of calcium carbonate from water. Biochemically formed limestone results from chemical processes acting on shells, shell fragments, and plant materials.

The principal sedimentary rock characteristics that affect the airphoto appearance of the terrain are *bedding*, *jointing*, and *resistance to erosion*.

Sedimentary rocks are typically stratified or layered as the result of variations in the depositional process. The individual strata or layers are called *beds*. The top and bottom of each bed have more or less distinct surfaces, called bedding planes, that delineate the termination of one bed and the beginning of another with somewhat different characteristics. Individual beds may range in thickness from a few millimeters to many meters. Beds in their initial condition usually are nearly horizontal but may be tilted to any angle by subsequent movements of the earth's crust.

Joints are cracks through solid bodies of rock with little or no movement parallel to joint surfaces. Joints in sedimentary rocks are primarily perpendicular to bedding planes and form plane surfaces that may intersect other joint planes. Several systematic joints constitute a joint set and when two or more sets are recognized in an area, the overall pattern is called a joint system. Because joints are planes of weakness in rocks, they often form surfaces clearly visible on aerial photographs, especially in the case of sandstone. Streams often follow joint lines and may zig-zag from one joint line to another.

The *resistance to erosion* of sedimentary rocks depends on rock strength, permeability, and solubility. Rock strength depends principally on the strength of the bonding agent holding the individual sediment particles together and on the thickness of the beds. Thick beds of sandstone cemented by quartz are very strong and may be used as building materials. Thin beds of shale are often so weak that they can be shattered by hand into flakes and plates. Rock permeability refers to the ability of the rock mass to transmit water and depends on the size of the pore spaces between sediment particles and on the continuity of their connections. Sandstone is generally a very permeable rock. Shale is usually quite impermeable and water moves principally along joint planes rather than in sediment void spaces. Limestones high in calcium carbonate are soluble in water and may dissolve under the action of rainfall and ground water movement.

We first consider the characteristics of sandstone, shale, and limestone, and then examine the characteristics of interbedded sedimentary rocks, both horizontally bedded and tilted.

Sandstone

Sandstone deposits commonly occur in beds a few meters thick interbedded with shale and/or limestone. We discuss such occurrences later in this section. Here we are concerned primarily with sandstone formations about 10 m or more in thickness.

Sandstone *bedding* is often prominent on airphotos, especially when the sandstone beds occur over softer, more easily eroded formations such as shale. *Jointing* is prominent, with a joint system consisting of two or three dominant directions. The *resistance to erosion* varies, depending on the strength of the cementing agent. Sandstone cemented with iron compounds and silica is typically very strong, whereas sandstone cemented with carbonates is generally quite weak. Since sandstone is very permeable, most rainfall percolates downward through the rock rather than becoming erosion-producing surface runoff. Sandstone cemented with carbonates may weaken as percolating water dissolves the cementing agent.

In arid areas, there is seldom a residual soil cover over sandstone because any weathered sand particles are removed by wind erosion. In humid areas, the depth of residual soil cover depends on the strength of the cementing agent, but is commonly less than 1 m and seldom more than 2 m. The residual soil texture in humid areas depends on the particle size of the sandstone and on the strength of the cementing agent. Weakly cemented sandstone weathers to sand while residual soils formed from strongly cemented sandstone may contain some silt and clay. Residual soils are typically well drained to excessively drained sand, loamy sand and sandy loam.

Areas of massive sandstone beds with a residual soil cover are commonly undeveloped because of a combination of their typically rugged topography and shallow depths to bedrock. Buried sandstone strata are often an excellent source of groundwater for both individual homeowners and municipalities. Well-cemented sandstone rock is often used as building stone for residential construction.

Airphoto Identification of Horizontally Bedded Sandstone

Topography: Bold, massive, relatively flat-topped hills with nearly vertical or very steep hillsides. *Drainage:* Coarse-textured, joint-controlled, modified dendritic pattern; often a rectangular pattern caused by perpendicular directions of joint sets. *Erosion:* Few gullies; V-shaped if present in residual soil. *Photo tone:* Generally light-toned due to light rock color and excellent internal drainage of both residual soil and sandstone rock. Reddish sandstone in arid areas may photograph with a somewhat dark tone on panchromatic film. A dense tree cover over sandstone in humid areas generally appears dark, but in this case the interpreter is looking at the tree canopy rather than the soil or rock surface. *Vegetation and land use:* Sparse vegetation in arid areas. Commonly forested in humid areas as residual soil is too well drained to support crops. In a humid climate, flat-topped sandstone ridges with a loess cover (Section 4.9) are often farmed. *Other:* Sandstone is sometimes mistakenly identified as granite (Section 4.7).

Figure 4.8 shows horizontally bedded sandstone in an arid climate interbedded with a few thin shale beds. The bedding can best be seen by inspecting the valley walls where the deeply incised stream cuts across the terrain. The direction of the major joint set is nearly vertical on the page; a secondary direction is perpendicular to the major joint set. These joint sets only partially control the direction of flow of the major stream, but strongly influence the direction of secondary drainage.

Figure 4.9 shows horizontally bedded sandstone in an arid climate. There is virtually no interbedded shale and the photo tone is very light. As in the previous figure, the joint sets are prominent. Photo interpreters must be careful to distinguish between bedding and jointing in order to properly identify the attitude of the beds (horizontally bedded or tilted). In Figure 4.9, the two principal directions of jointing are clearly expressed, while the bedding is more subtle.

Figure 4.10 shows horizontally bedded sandstone in a humid climate. Note the massive hills and the nearly continuous tree cover. The residual soils here are well-drained sandy loam with many sandstone rock fragments at least 50 cm deep over sandstone bedrock.

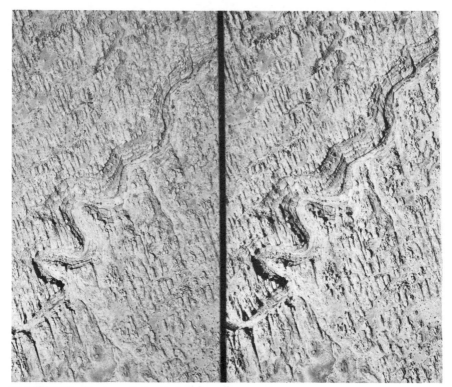

FIGURE 4.8 Horizontally bedded sandstone in an arid climate, Southern Utah, September 1952. 1:20,000. Stereogram. (USGS photos.)

Shale

Deposits of shale are common throughout the world, as both thick deposits and thin deposits interbedded with sandstone and limestone. Shale *bedding* is very extensive with beds typically 1 to 20 cm in thickness. Bedding is not always visible on aerial photographs. However, if beds with a distinct difference in color or resistance to erosion are present, or if shale is interbedded with sandstone or limestone, bedding may be seen. The effect of *jointing* is not always strong enough to alter the surface drainage system into a significantly joint-controlled pattern. The *resistance to erosion* is low, compared with other sedimentary rock types. Since shale is relatively impermeable, most rainfall runs off the ground surface causing extensive erosion.

The depth of residual soil cover is generally less than 1 m and seldom more than 2 m. The residual soil is high in silt and clay, with textures typically silty loam, silty clay loam, silty clay, and clay. Internal soil drainage is typically moderately well drained or poorer, depending on soil texture and on soil and rock structure.

Although the topography in shale areas is generally favorable to urban develop-

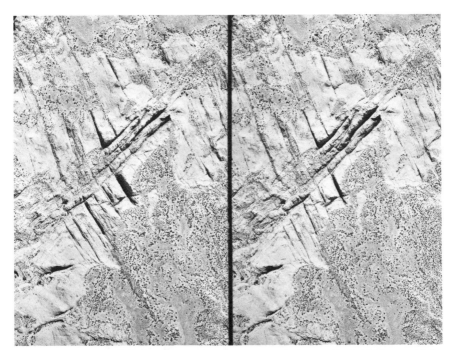

FIGURE 4.9 Horizontally bedded sandstone in an arid climate, Garfield County, Utah, July 1960. 1:30,800. Stereogram. (USDA–ASCS photos.)

ment, the soil drainage and depth to bedrock conditions may limit residential development by causing problems in basement excavation and in septic tank installation and maintenance. The groundwater supply is extremely variable in shale bedrock. If the shale is strongly jointed, groundwater may be available. In many cases, however, it will be necessary to drill through the shale into an underlying water-bearing stratum.

Airphoto Identification of Horizontally Bedded Shale

Topography: In an arid climate, minutely dissected terrain with steep stream/ gully side slopes resulting from rapid surface runoff associated with short-duration heavy rainfall. In a humid climate, gently to moderately sloping, softly rounded hills. *Drainage:* A dendritic pattern with gently curving streams; fine-textured in arid climates and medium- to fine-textured in humid climates. *Erosion:* Gullies in residual soil have gently rounded cross sections. *Photo tone:*

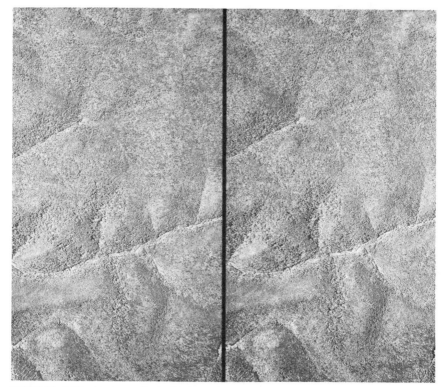

FIGURE 4.10 Horizontally bedded sandstone in a humid climate, McKean County, Pennsylvania, October 1958. 1:33,300. Stereogram. (USDA—ASCS photos.)

Varies widely, generally dark-toned compared with sandstone and limestone. Differences in photo tone may outline bedding. *Vegetation and land use:* Arid areas usually barren, except for desert vegetation. Humid areas intensively cultivated or heavily forested. *Other:* Shale is sometimes mistakenly identified as loess (Section 4.9).

Figure 4.11 shows horizontally bedded shale in an arid climate. A comparison with Figure 4.8 illustrates the contrast in bedding, jointing, and resistance to erosion between shale and sandstone.

Figure 4.12 shows horizontally bedded shale in a humid climate. Note the well-developed medium-textured dendritic drainage pattern. The banding seen in various portions of the photograph is caused by differences in the residual soil texture and moisture conditions resulting from variations in the composition of the individual shale beds. The residual soils here are moderately well-drained shaly silt loam 50 to 100 cm deep over shale bedrock.

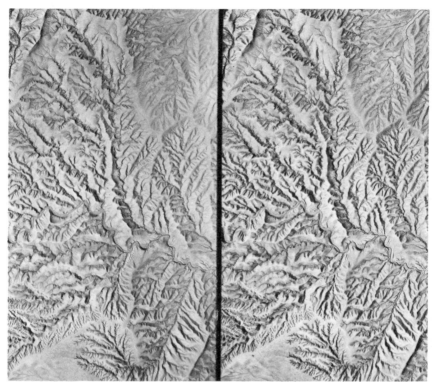

FIGURE 4.11 Horizontally bedded shale in an arid climate, Utah, November 1952. 1:26,700. Stereogram. (USGS photos.)

Limestone

Limestone consists mainly of calcium carbonate, which is soluble in water. Limestone that contains a significant amount of calcium carbonate and magnesium carbonate (or calcium magnesium carbonate) is called dolomitic limestone, or dolomite, and is less soluble in water. Limestone occurs throughout the world. An area of very soluble limestone occurs in the United States in a region spanning portions of Indiana, Kentucky, and Tennessee.

Limestone *bedding* is generally not prominent on airphotos unless the limestone is interbedded with sandstone or shale. *Jointing* is strong and determines the location of many of the pathways for subsurface drainage. However, jointing is generally not prominent on airphotos of limestone in a humid climate. The *resistance to erosion* varies, depending on the solubility and jointing of the rock. Since calcium carbonate is soluble in water, many limestone areas have been severely eroded by rainfall and groundwater action.

FIGURE 4.12   Horizontally bedded shale in a humid climate, Hunterdon County, New Jersey, June 1963. 1:36,400. Stereogram. (USDA–ASCS photos.)

The ground surface in areas of soluble limestone in humid climates is typically dotted with literally thousands of roughly circular depressions called *sinkholes*. They form when surface runoff drains vertically through the rock along joint planes and the intersections of joint planes, gradually enlarging the underground drainageways by solution and causing the ground surface to collapse and form sinkholes.

There is generally only a shallow residual soil cover over limestone in arid areas where limestone often caps ridges and plateaus. In humid areas, the depth of residual soil cover is extremely variable and depends on the amount of solution weathering. Generally, residual soil depth ranges from 2 to 4 m for soluble limestone (which typically occurs as valleys or plains) and is somewhat less for dolomite (which may cap ridges and plateaus). The residual soil in humid areas contains a great deal of clay. Soil textures of clay, silty clay, clay loam, and silty clay loam are common. Soils are often well drained, except in sinkhole bottoms, due to soil structure and solution openings in the underlying rock. If these soils are extensively disturbed by human activity—such as subdivision development—soil drainage can become very poor.

Although limestone areas may be generally satisfactory for urban development, there are limiting characteristics that must be carefully considered. Because the residual soils contain a great deal of clay, they are relatively poor foundation soils. Often, it will be necessary to locate foundations directly on bedrock for proper building support. Although the soils are well drained in a natural condition, there may be problems with septic tank operation because of a low percolation rate in the disturbed soil. Groundwater may be difficult to locate and may be very "hard." In addition, effluent from septic tanks can often contaminate the groundwater. There is usually considerable variation in topography, depth to bedrock, and soil drainage conditions, requiring careful soils exploration and mapping before development proceeds. Sinkhole collapse under heavy loads such as construction equipment, highways, and airport runways is a serious problem in some limestone areas.

Airphoto Identification of Horizontally Bedded Limestone

This discussion refers to soluble limestone in humid climates. *Topography:* A gently rolling surface broken by numerous roughly circular sinkholes that are typically 3 to 15 m in depth and 5 to 50 m in diameter. *Drainage:* Centripetal drainage into individual sinkholes. Very few surface streams. Surface streams from adjacent landforms or rock types may disappear underground via sinkholes when streams reach the limestone. *Erosion:* Gullies with gently rounded cross sections develop in the fine-textured residual soil. *Tone:* Mottled tone due to extensive sinkhole development. *Vegetation and land use:* Typically farmed, except for sinkhole bottoms that are often wet or contain standing water a portion of the year. *Other:* Limestone with extensive sinkhole development might be mistakenly identified as ablation till (Section 4.10). Dolomitic limestone is more difficult to identify than soluble limestone. It is generally well drained and has subtle sinkholes.

Figure 4.13 shows horizontally bedded soluble limestone in a humid climate. Note the extensive sinkhole development (up to 40 sinkholes per square kilometer are present) and the complete lack of surface streams. The residual soils here are well-drained silty clay loam and silty clay 1.5 to 3 m deep over limestone bedrock.

Interbedded Sedimentary Rocks

Rock formations with alternating layers of different sedimentary rock types are called *interbedded sedimentary rocks*. The appearance of the resulting terrain depends on the thickness of the beds and their attitude (horizontal or tilted). As illustrated in Figure 4.14, horizontal strata of differing resistance to erosion result in a stair-stepped terrain, often with steeply incised streams, and folded strata result in a series of linear, often curving, ridges and valleys. The resistant strata that form plateaus and ridges are typically sandstone in humid climates and sandstone or limestone in arid climates.

FIGURE 4.13   Horizontally bedded soluble limestone in a humid climate, Harrison County, Indiana, May 1960. 1:20,000. Stereogram. (USDA—ASCS photos.)

Airphoto Identification of Horizontally Bedded Interbedded Sedimentary Rocks

Topography: When resistant strata are on the order of 10 m or more in thickness, a distinct stair-stepped terrain is evident on the photographs. When the thickness of resistant strata is only a few meters, the terrain will be stair-stepped, but slope changes may be difficult to observe on airphotos at commonly utilized scales (1:20,000 and smaller). In humid climates, topographic differences between the terrain on different rock types are typically more subdued than in arid climates. *Drainage:* Typically dendritic, with density determined by relative amounts of sandstone, shale, and limestone. *Erosion:* Varies with residual soil type. *Photo tone, vegetation, and land use:* Differences in photo tone that appear as contours on hillsides often help accentuate the presence of different sedimentary beds. These tonal differences may be caused by differences in vegetation type and vigor over different rock types, or by differences in rock and residual soil cover in nonvegetated areas. Figure 4.12 illustrated banding due to differences in crop growth over shale beds of

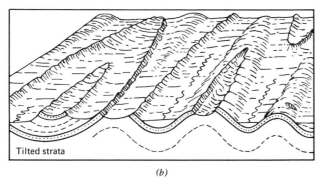

(a)

(b)

FIGURE 4.14 Schematic diagram showing the physiographic expression of horizontal and tilted sedimentary rock strata. (Original drawn by A. N. Strahler [23].)

varying residual soil texture and moisture conditions. In a similar fashion, sandstone and shale interbedded in a humid climate might have a forest cover over the sandstone and agricultural land use over the shale. In addition, in agricultural areas, strip farming and contour plowing can help accentuate the appearance of horizontally bedded sedimentary rocks, although it must be recognized that changes in strip crops do not necessarily occur at the changes between rock types. *Other:* Horizontally bedded sandstone over shale is sometimes mistakenly identified as flood basalt over shale (Section 4.7).

Figure 4.15 shows horizontally bedded sandstone over shale in an arid climate. This stereogram shows a small portion of an extensive sandstone-capped plateau cut by more than 20 fingerlike valleys arranged in a dendritic pattern. Two distinct light-toned beds of resistant sandstone with a thin shale bed between them form the cap rock and are underlain by less resistant darker-toned beds of shale. The forest cover is

FIGURE 4.15 Horizontally bedded sandstone over shale in an arid climate, Chapin Mesa, Mesa Verde National Park, Colorado, September 1965. 1:49,200. Stereogram. (USGS photos.)

greater than would normally be expected on sandstone in an arid climate (the area shown receives 45 cm per year rainfall) because the plateau is covered with loess, a fertile wind-deposited silt (Section 4.9).

Figure 4.16 shows horizontally bedded sandstone over shale in an arid climate (near Figure 4.15). Note the numerous alternations of layers of sandstone and shale in the cap rock that is underlain by soft shale.

Figure 4.17 shows horizontally bedded sandstone and shale in a humid climate. Here, the alternating beds of sandstone and shale are relatively thin and slope changes on hillsides can be seen by careful inspection of the stereogram. The relief is more rugged than would be expected for shale and less rugged than for sandstone. The drainage texture is coarser than for shale and finer than for sandstone. There are more forested areas than would be expected for shale and more agricultural land than for sandstone. These observations lead the interpreter to conclude that sandstone and shale are present in roughly equal amounts. Numerous tonal differences can be seen as hillside contours, indicating the horizontal nature of the bedding.

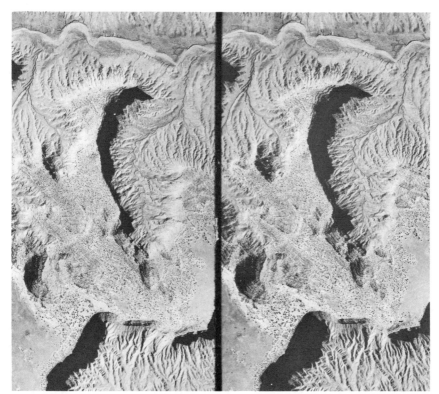

FIGURE 4.16 Horizontally bedded sandstone over shale in an arid climate, Montezuma County, Colorado, September 1965. 1:32,000. Stereogram. (USGS photos.)

We refer to sedimentary rocks that have been folded or warped from their original horizontal bedding planes as *tilted sedimentary rocks*. Figure 4.18 illustrates how tilted sedimentary rocks can form linear ridges and valleys with occurrences of folded bedding convex upward referred to as *anticlines* and those of folded bedding convex downward as *synclines*. When the longitudinal axes of anticlines and synclines are horizontal, ridges of resistant sedimentary rock can run parallel for many kilometers (Figure 4.18a). When the axes are plunging, ridges curve in a zig-zag fashion, as illustrated in Figure 4.18b.

The terms *strike* and *dip* are used to indicate the direction and amount of inclination of tilted sedimentary beds. As illustrated in Figure 4.18c, a horizontal line along the beds gives the *direction of strike* (conventionally expressed as a compass direction). The *direction of dip* is perpendicular to the direction of strike and points downslope. The *amount of dip* is the inclination of the beds from the horizontal, measured along the direction of dip. If we assume that the ridges in Figure 4.18c run northwest– southeast, we would say that the direction of strike of the beds is northwest–southeast

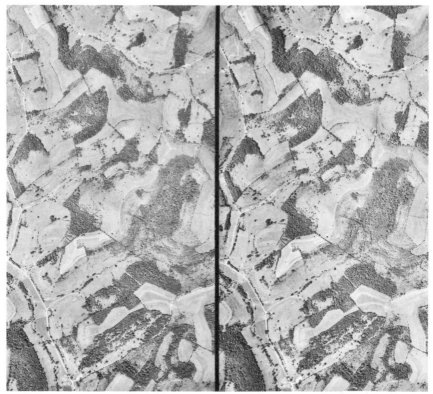

FIGURE 4.17   Horizontally bedded sandstone and shale in a humid climate, Green County, Pennsylvania, August 1958. 1:30,800. Stereogram. (USDA–ASCS photos.)

and the direction of dip of the beds is northeast. The amount of dip of the beds is about 10°. Since the directions of strike and dip are perpendicular, we could fully describe the attitude of these beds as dipping to the northeast at 10°.

Airphoto Identification of Tilted Interbedded Sedimentary Rocks

Topography: A series of straight or curving ridges. *Drainage:* A trellis drainage pattern with major streams running along valley bottoms and secondary streams flowing down dip and scarp slopes and joining the major streams at right angles, as shown in Figure 4.18c. *Erosion:* Varies with residual soil type. *Photo tone:* Varies with rock type. *Vegetation and land use:* Varies with rock type; a typical occurrence for tilted sedimentary rocks in a humid area would be forested sandstone ridges and farmed shale valleys.

Figure 4.19 is a radar image (Chapter 8) illustrating a plunging anticline and

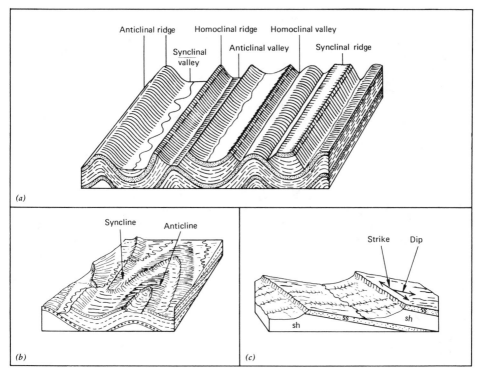

FIGURE 4.18 Schematic diagram showing topographic forms associated with tilted sedimentary rock strata. *(a)* From Thornbury [25]; *(b)* original drawn by E. Raisz [23]; *(c)* original drawn by A. N. Strahler [23].)

syncline in a humid climate. The linear forested bands are sandstone ridges that form an anticline at the top portion of the image and a syncline at the bottom portion. Note that in a plunging anticline, the beds dip away from the axis of the fold, whereas in a plunging syncline, the beds dip toward the axis of the fold. Another radar image of folded sedimentary rocks (in the Appalachian Mountains) is shown as Figure 8.26.

Figure 4.20 shows a tightly folded anticline in an arid climate. The anticline is composed of alternating beds of sandstone (ridges) and shale (valleys) that dip outward from the center of the anticline.

Figure 4.21 is a stereotriplet showing an anticline in a humid climate. The anticline is a wooded ridge consisting of sandstone with some interbedded shale. In the right-hand stereopair, the beds are dipping to the right; in the left-hand pair, to the left. The soils on the wooded anticline are well-drained stony silt loam 1.0 to 1.5 m deep over sandstone and shale bedrock. Soils in the farmed portion of the central valley and the farmed area to the right of the anticline are moderately well drained silt loam and silty clay loam 1.0 to 2.5 m deep over shale bedrock. Soils on the wooded hills near the bottom center of the figure are well-drained sandy loam 30 to 50 cm deep over sandstone.

FIGURE 4.19   Radar image illustrating folded sedimentary rocks in a humid climate, Ouchita Mountains, Le Flore County, Oklahoma. 1:170,000 (NASA image.)

4.7 IGNEOUS ROCKS

Igneous rocks are formed by the cooling and consequent solidification of magma, a molten mass of rock material. Igneous rocks are divided into two groups: intrusive and extrusive. *Intrusive igneous rocks* are formed when magma does not reach the earth's surface but solidifies in cavities or cracks it has made by pushing the surrounding rock apart, or by melting or dissolving it. *Extrusive igneous rocks* are formed when magma reaches the ground surface.

Intrusive igneous rocks commonly occur in large masses in which the molten magma has cooled very slowly and solidified into large crystals. The crystal grains interlock closely to produce a dense, strong rock that is free of cavities. Erosion of overlying materials exposes intrusive igneous rocks.

Extrusive igneous rocks occur as various volcanic forms, including lava flows, lava cones, cinder and spatter cones, tuff cones, and volcanic ash deposits. These rocks have cooled more rapidly than intrusive rocks and consequently have smaller crystals.

Intrusive Igneous Rocks

Intrusive igneous rocks range from granite, a light-colored, coarse-grained rock consisting principally of quartz and feldspar, to gabbro, a dark-colored, coarse-grained

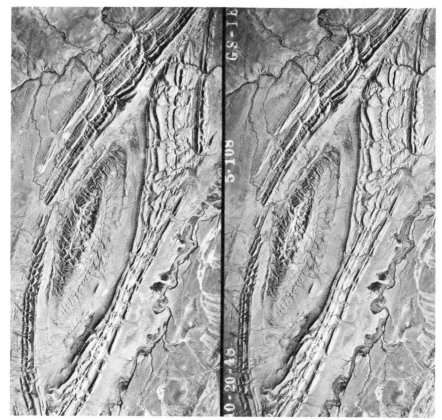

FIGURE 4.20 Tilted interbedded sandstone and shale (anticline) in an arid climate, Fremont County, Wyoming, October 1948. 1:47,200. Stereogram. (USGS photos.)

rock consisting principally of ferromagnesian minerals and feldspar. There are many intrusive igneous rocks intermediate between granite and gabbro in composition, such as granodiorite and diorite. We consider only the broad class of intrusive igneous rocks called *granitic rocks*, a term used to describe any coarse-grained, light-colored, intrusive igneous rock.

Granitic rocks typically occur as large masses such as the Sierra Nevada Mountains and the Black Hills of South Dakota. Figure 4.22 illustrates the occurrence of granite in the Black Hills. The intrusive mass has warped the overlying sedimentary rocks upward and subsequent erosion has left a central area of crystalline rocks surrounded by tilted sedimentary rocks. The intense heat and pressure of the magma altered some of the sedimentary rocks into a metamorphic rock known as schist. The central core contains granitic rocks.

Granitic rocks occur as massive, *unbedded* formations. They are often strongly

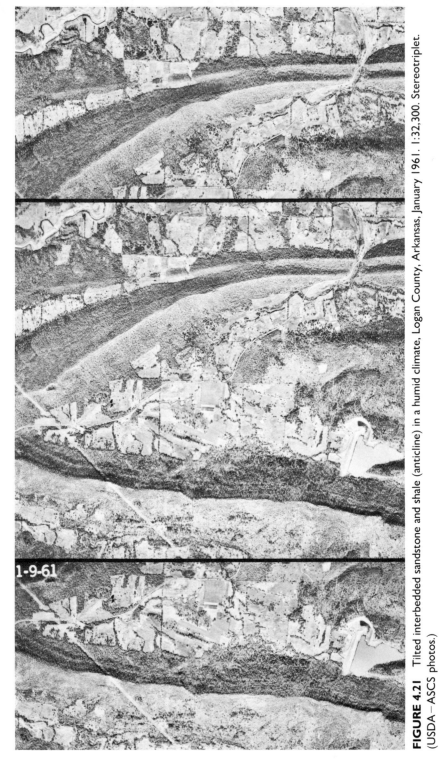

FIGURE 4.21 Tilted interbedded sandstone and shale (anticline) in a humid climate, Logan County, Arkansas, January 1961. 1:32,300. Stereotriplet. (USDA–ASCS photos.)

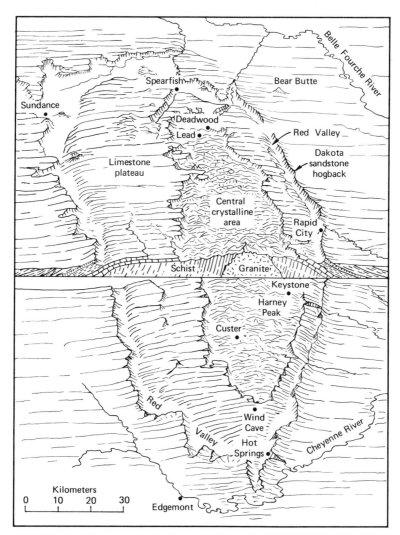

FIGURE 4.22 Schematic diagram illustrating granitic core and upwarped sedimentary rocks, Black Hills, South Dakota. (Original drawn by A. N. Strahler [23].)

fractured into a series of irregularly oriented *joints* as a result of cooling from a molten state and/or pressure relief as overburden is eroded. Granitic rocks have a high *resistance to erosion*. As they weather, they tend to break or peel in concentric sheets through a process called exfoliation.

In arid areas, the depth of residual soil cover over granitic bedrock is typically very thin (less than $\frac{1}{2}$ m), except in fracture zones where it may be thicker. In humid areas, the depth to bedrock is typically 1 to 2 meters. The residual soil texture in humid areas is typically loamy sand, sandy loam, or sandy clay loam. Granitic rocks yield essentially no water, except in fracture zones. Limited water may be available from the sandy soil above the solid rock.

Areas of massive granitic rocks with residual soil cover are typically not well suited to urban development because of a combination of rugged topography, shallow depth to bedrock, and poor groundwater supply.

Airphoto Identification of Granitic Rocks

Topography: Massive, rounded, unbedded, domelike hills with variable summit elevations and steep side slopes. Often strongly jointed with an irregular and sometimes gently curving pattern. Joints may form topographic depressions in which soil and vegetation accumulate and along which water tends to flow. *Drainage and erosion:* Coarse-textured dendritic pattern with a tendency for streams to curve around the bases of domelike hills. Secondary drainage channels form along joints. Few gullies, except in areas of deeper residual soil. *Photo tone:* Light-toned due to light rock color. Darker-toned in depressions which form along joints. *Vegetation and land use:* Sparse vegetation in an arid climate. Often forested with some bare rock outcrops in a humid climate. Vegetation may be concentrated in depressions that form along some joints. *Other:* Granitic rocks are sometimes mistakenly identified as horizontally bedded sandstone (Section 4.6). The principal differences in airphoto identification of granitic rocks versus sandstone can be summarized as follows. (1) *Evidences of bedding:* Granitic rocks are unbedded; sandstone is bedded. (2) *Topography:* Granitic outcrops have variable summit elevations, sandstone caprocks form plateaus; granitic rocks have rounded cliffs, sandstone has vertical cliffs; granitic microfeatures are rounded, sandstone microfeatures are blocky. (3) *Joint pattern:* Granitic rocks have an irregular joint pattern with some distinct linear depressions; sandstone has a joint system consisting of two or three principal directions.

Figure 4.23 shows granitic rocks in an arid climate with very little soil or vegetative cover. Note the massive, unbedded formation with rounded cliffs. Note also that a number of joints are enlarged and form depressions with some soil and vegetative cover.

Figure 4.24 shows granitic rocks in an area with 50 cm per year rainfall. There is some soil cover and considerable forest cover. Note that the bare rock outcrops have variable elevations, rounded forms, and a somewhat irregular joint system.

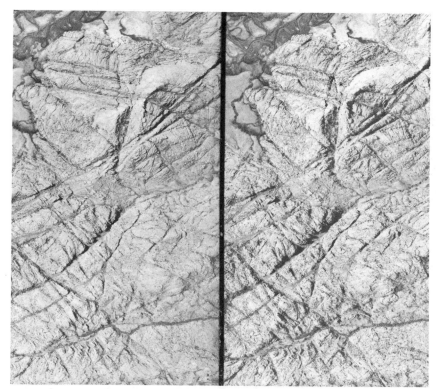

FIGURE 4.23 Granitic rocks in an arid climate, Wyoming, July 1947. 1:37,300. Stereogram. (USGS photos.)

Extrusive Igneous Rocks

Extrusive igneous rocks consist principally of lava flows and pyroclastic materials. Lava flows are the rock bodies formed from the solidification of molten rock that issued from volcanic cones or fissures with little or no explosive activity. In contrast, pyroclastic materials, such as cinders and ash, were ejected from volcanic vents.

The form of lava flows depends principally on the viscosity of the flowing lava. The viscosity of lava increases with the proportion of silica (SiO_2) and alumina (Al_2O_3) in the lava. The least viscous (most fluid) lavas are the basaltic lavas, which contain about 65 percent silica and alumina. Andesitic lavas are intermediate in viscosity and contain about 75 percent silica and alumina. Rhyolitic lavas are very viscous and contain about 85 percent silica and alumina.

Several basic volcanic forms are recognized.

Strato volcanoes (also called composite volcanoes) are steep-sided, cone-shaped, volcanoes composed of alternating layers of lava and pyroclastic materials. The lava is

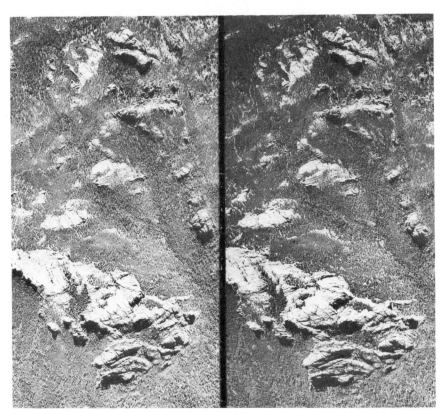

FIGURE 4.24   Granitic rocks, Black Hills, Pennington County, South Dakota, August 1962. 1:20,000. Stereogram. (USDA–ASCS photos.)

typically andesitic or rhyolitic and side slopes can be 30° or more. Many strato volcanoes are graceful cones of striking beauty and grandeur. Each of the following mountains is a strato volcano: Shasta (California), Hood (Oregon), Ranier (Washington), St. Helens (Washington), Fujiyama (Japan), Vesuvius (Italy), and Kilimanjaro (Tanzania).

Shield volcanoes (also called Hawaiian-type volcanoes) are broad, gently sloping volcanic cones of flat domical shape built chiefly of overlapping basaltic lava flows. Side slopes generally range from about 4 to 10°. The Hawaiian vocanoes Haleakala, Mauna Kea, Mauna Loa, and Kilauea are shield volcanoes.

Flood basalt (also called plateau basalt) consists of large scale eruptions of very fluid basalt that build broad, nearly level plains, some of which are at high elevation. Extensive flood basalt flows form the Columbia River and Snake River plains of the northwest United States.

Airphoto Identification of Lava Flows (Excluding Flood Basalt)

Topography: A series of tonguelike flows that may overlap and interbed, often with associated cinder and spatter cones. Viscous lavas (andesite and rhyolite) form thick flows with prominent, steep edges. Fluid lavas (basalt) form thin flows, seldom exceeding 15 m in thickness. *Drainage and erosion:* Lava is well drained internally and there is seldom a well-developed drainage pattern. *Photo tone and vegetation:* The color of unweathered, unvegetated, lava is dark-toned in the case of basalt, medium-toned for andesite, and light-toned for rhyolite. In general, recent unvegetated flows are darker-toned than weathered, vegetated flows. *Land use:* Recent flows are seldom farmed or developed.

Figure 4.25 shows a viscous lava flow that emanated from Mt. Shasta, California. This flow is 60 m thick and has a 30° slope on its front face. This lava flow is also seen in Figure 8.31.

Figure 4.26 shows basaltic lava flows with a 6° slope on the southwest flank of Mauna Loa, a 4200 m high (above sea level) active shield volcano on the island of Hawaii. The darker-toned, unvegetated areas are lava flows dating to 1907 (center of figure) and

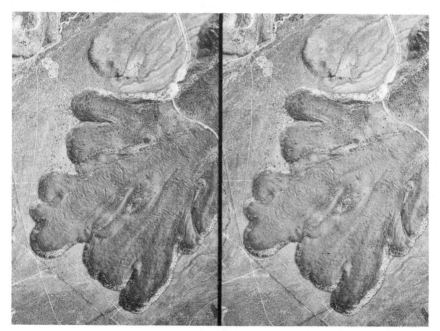

FIGURE 4.25 Viscous lava flow in an arid climate, Siskiyou County, California, August 1955. 1:33,000. Stereogram. (USDA—ASCS photos.)

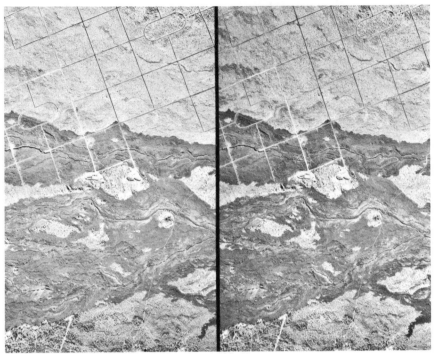

FIGURE 4.26   Basaltic lava flow, Mauna Loa Volcano, Island of Hawaii, March 1965. 1:36,400. Stereogram. (USDA–ASCS photos.)

1887 (lower portion of figure). The surrounding lighter-toned, sparsely vegetated areas are older flows. The recent flows have a rough surface, excessive internal drainage, and essentially no soil cover or vegetation. This area receives an annual rainfall of 125 cm, but the terrain is dry because of the excessive drainage and strong winds. Note the extensive subdivision being carved into these lava flows in a grid pattern with no apparent sensitivity to terrain conditions and no apparent consideration of the future volcanic activity that will some day cover the area of this subdivision.

Pyroclastic materials include cinders, spatter, and ash which form cinder cones, spatter cones, and tuff cones.

Cinders are irregular, spongy fragments of lava, approximately 4 to 32 mm in size, ejected by volcanic explosions. Cinders are usually solid (cooled) when they strike the ground and form *cinder cones* (steep-sided, cone-shaped hills of cinders that have piled up around volcanic vents). Cinder cones are usually less than 300 m high and typically have a bowl- or funnel-shaped depression (crater) at the summit. Side slopes are typically very smooth, unless eroded, and stand at the natural angle of repose of loose cinders. Lava flows often issue from near the base of cinder cones.

Spatter is volcanic ejecta thrown out in a very fluid condition with fragments that remain partly fluid when they strike the ground, so that they flatten out and often stick together. Spatter forms *spatter cones* (steep-sided cones built by the accumulation of spatter). Spatter cones are smaller and steeper sided than cinder cones, typically less than 15 m high, and are often found along volcanic *rift zones* (highly fractured linear belts on the flanks of volcanoes). Lava flows often issue from near the base of spatter cones.

Volcanic *ash* consists of fine-grained volcanic ejecta, 4 mm or smaller. Consolidated volcanic ash is called *tuff*, which forms *tuff cones* around volcanic vents. Tuff cones are relatively uncommon. In Hawaii, they form as the result of moderately explosive eruptions near the ocean when molten magma encounters either seawater or ground-water, causing the explosive eruption. Tuff cones are much broader in proportion to their height than cinder or spatter cones and their craters are broad and saucer-shaped.

Figure 4.27 shows cinder cones in the summit crater of Haleakala Volcano. Note their smooth side slopes and the lava flow that emanated from the base of the cinder cone near the top of the figure. There is very little vegetation on the cinder cones. The rainfall is about 50 cm per year but the cinder cones are excessively drained and have virtually no residual soil.

Figure 4.28 shows several volcanic forms in Craters of the Moon National Monu-

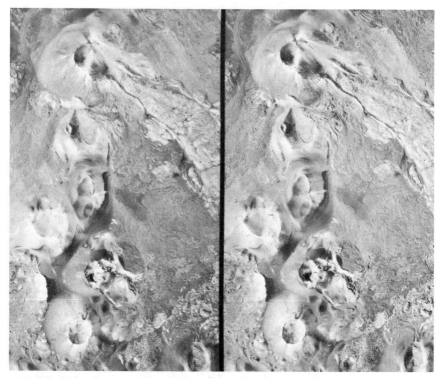

FIGURE 4.27 Cinder cones and lava flows, Haleakala National Park, Island of Maui, Hawaii, January 1965. 1:28,600. Stereogram. (USDA−ASCS photos.)

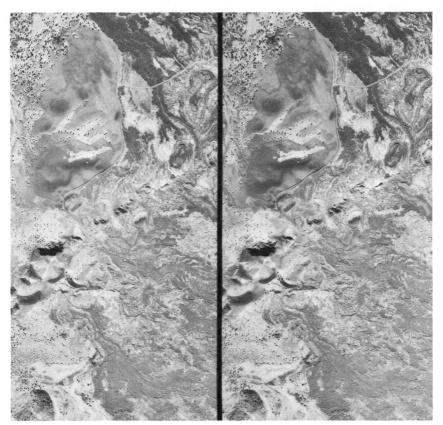

FIGURE 4.28   Cinder cones, spatter cones, and lava flows in an arid climate. Craters of the Moon National Monument, Idaho, July 1959. 1:26,700. Stereogram. (USDA—ASCS photos.)

ment. It is estimated that lava erupted here for many thousands of years and ceased about 1600 years ago. A large, smooth-sided cinder cone 150 m high is at the upper left. A series of spatter cones along a rift zone runs diagonally from lower left to upper right through the center of the figure. A series of basaltic lava flows is at the lower right.

Figure 4.29 shows a tuff cone, the world-famous Diamond Head in Honolulu. This tuff cone was formed an estimated 100,000 years ago. This crater is much larger and flatter than a cinder cone crater. The average height of the uneven rim is 125 m, but it rises to 225 m at the lower right because the prevailing wind at the time of formation was from upper left to lower right. The annual rainfall here is just under 50 cm per year.

Flood basalt deposits result from horizontal and overlapping flows of very fluid lava that issue from fissures. Commonly, the lava flows over an older eroded land surface and gradually buries hills and valleys, transforming the terrain into a relatively featureless plain. Individual flows are typically 15 to 30 m thick, sometimes much thicker. At times, flood basalt flows are interbedded with fluvial and lacustrine soils or

FIGURE 4.29 Tuff cone, Honolulu, Hawaii, February 1965. 1:25,000. Stereogram. (USDA—ASCS photos.)

with residual soils, indicating that, in places, considerable time elapsed between successive flows. Flood basalts are also called *plateau basalts* because they build broad, nearly level plains, some of which are at high elevation.

Flood basalt deposits are extensive in the northwest United States. The flood basalts of the Columbia River Plain are about 60 million years old and cover an area of about 400,000 km² in Washington, Oregon, and Idaho with an average thickness of 625 m and a maximum thickness greater than 3000 m. The Snake River Plain in Idaho is a similar mass of younger flood basalt. The nature of these plateaus is best seen along the side walls of the deep valleys cut into the flood basalt by the Columbia and Snake Rivers.

Flood basalt deposits typically exhibit columnar jointing, as illustrated in Figure 4.30. These joints form when the basalt, which solidified at several hundred degrees Celsius, cools to ambient air temperature and further contracts and cracks. The columns are typically six-sided and $\frac{1}{2}$ to 1 m wide. Flood basalt deposits are well drained internally because of the strong columnar jointing. In fact, several major streams flowing from the mountains just north of the Snake River Plain disappear underground when they reach the flood basalt and emerge nearly 200 km away as springs in the side of the basalt-walled Snake River Canyon.

FIGURE 4.30 Exceptionally well-developed columnar jointing, Devil's Postpile National Monument, California, June 1971.

Airphoto Identification of Flood Basalt

Topography: A nearly level surface, often cut by major streams that form deep valleys. Sometimes found as high plateaus. Columnar jointing (just barely visible at a photo scale of 1:20,000) can be seen on valley and escarpment walls. *Drainage:* Very few surface streams because of the excellent internal drainage. *Erosion:* Gullies generally not prominent, except in areas of deeper residual soil. *Photo tone:* Basalt rock has a dark tone. This dark tone is usually best seen along valley walls and escarpment faces as the ground surface often has some vegetation, especially when a soil cover is present. *Land use:* In arid areas, flood basalt with a soil cover is often farmed in areas near streams where the land can be irrigated. In nonirrigated arid areas, flood basalt plains are used for very low density grazing or left idle. *Other features:* Landslides are often found along flood basalt cliffs, especially where streams undercut the base of the slopes. *Other:* Flood basalt plateaus are sometimes mistakenly identified as sandstone-capped plateaus (Section 4.6). The principal differences in airphoto identification of flood basalt plateaus versus sandstone-capped plateaus can be summarized as follows. (1) *Tone of bare rock:* Basalt is dark-toned; sandstone is light-toned. (2) *Rock jointing:* Flood basalt exhibits columnar jointing; sandstone has extensive joint systems with two or three principal directions. As a result, flood basalt canyon and cliff edges have a serrated appearance, while sandstone canyon and cliff edges have a blocky appearance. (3) *Drainage:* Flood basalt has principally internal drainage; sandstone has a low-density modified dendritic pattern (rectangular or angular)

Figure 4.31 shows an irrigated area of flood basalt on the Snake River Plain. Note the sinuous dark-toned irrigation canal at the upper left. The rock can be identified as flood basalt because of the characteristics exhibited along the sides of the canyon, which cuts through several individual flows. The serrated edges of the canyon walls are caused by columnar jointing. The rock on the sunlit portions of the canyon walls is dark-toned. (Be careful not to confuse shadows with dark-toned materials!)

Figure 4.32 shows columnar jointing in flood basalt a few kilometers west of the area shown in Figure 4.31. Figure 4.32*b* is a closeup showing individual columns approximately $\frac{1}{3}$ m across. Clusters of columns 1 to 2 m across break off as a unit and fall to the base of the cliffs, leaving serrated canyon edges such as those in Figure 4.31.

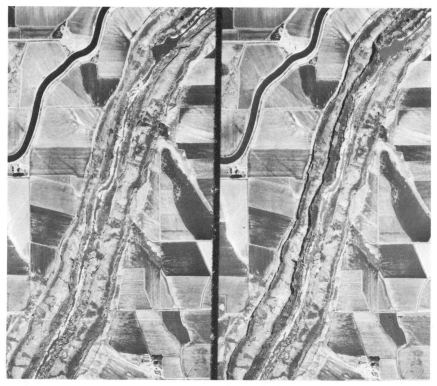

FIGURE 4.31 Flood basalt, irrigated plateau in an arid climate, Jerome and Twin Falls Counties, Idaho, July 1957. 1:20,000. Stereogram. (USDA−ASCS photos.)

FIGURE 4.32   Flood basalt, Snake River Canyon near Twin Falls, Idaho, August 1977. ((b) is a stereogram.)

Figure 4.33 shows a flood basalt plateau in an arid climate. The basalt flow originally covered a larger area than presently shown, but erosion of the plateau is steadily reducing its size. Weathering of the softer underlying rock has resulted in landslide failures along the basalt cap. The edges of the basalt cliffs have a dark tone and exhibit columnar jointing.

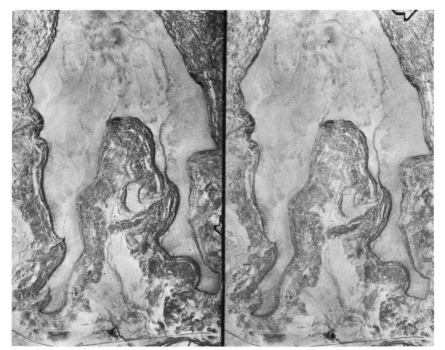

FIGURE 4.33 Flood basalt plateau in an arid area, New Mexico, May 1955. 1:68,000. Stereogram. (USGS photos.)

4.8 METAMORPHIC ROCKS

Common metamorphic rocks are quartzite, slate, marble, gneiss, and schist. They are formed from preexisting sedimentary or igneous rocks due principally to the action of heat and pressure. Occasionally, chemical action or shearing stresses are also involved. The minerals in any rock are generally stable under a limited range of temperature and pressure. When high temperatures and pressures are imposed, the preexisting rocks undergo a metamorphosis and a new mineral composition, texture, and/or structure results. Minimum conditions for metamorphic change are estimated at temperatures in excess of 100°C along with a pressure equal to that found 3 km below the earth's surface. Maximum conditions are estimated to be a temperature of 800°C and a pressure equal to that found 35 km below the earth's surface. Above these conditions, magma is formed, resulting in igneous rocks.

Most metamorphic rocks have a distinct banding that can be seen via field observations and which sets them apart from sedimentary and igneous rocks.

Metamorphic rocks can be found throughout the world. However, since their extent is limited, the airphoto identification of metamorphic rocks is not covered here.

In addition, the airphoto identification of metamorphic rocks is more difficult than for sedimentary and igneous rocks and interpretive techniques for metamorphic rocks are not well established.

4.9   AEOLIAN DEPOSITS

Aeolian deposits are created by the erosion, transportation, and deposition of unconsolidated materials by the wind. The principal aeolian deposits are sand dunes and loess.

Sand Dunes

Sand dunes are mounds, hills, or ridges of windblown sand. They are found where there is a source of sand, a wind strong enough to erode and transport sand-sized particles, and a land surface on which to deposit the sand. These conditions are commonly found inland from sandy beaches with onshore winds, close to streams with sandy bottoms exposed during the dry season, and in desert areas where the disintegration of sandstone and other rocks provides the sand. In addition, glacial outwash deposits and sandy glacial lakebed areas often provide a source of sand.

Because wind velocities are seldom strong enough to lift sand-sized particles more than 1 to 2 m from the ground surface, sand grains are transported by "saltation," a process whereby the grains travel by bouncing and rolling generally within about $\frac{1}{2}$ to 1 m above the ground surface.

Sand dunes tend to form with an asymmetrical cross section, with a slope of 5 to 10° on the windward slope and 30 to 34° on the leeward slope. Unless stabilized by vegetation, sand dunes tend to migrate downwind because sand particles are blown from the windward to the leeward side of the dunes. Sand dune movement is generally less than 30 m per year.

Sand dunes vary in shape depending on such factors as the quantity and particle size of the sand, the strength and direction of the wind, and the vegetation conditions. The basic sand dune shapes to be discussed are transverse, barchan, parabolic, and longitudinal, as illustrated in Figure 4.34.

Transverse dunes tend to form in areas where there is a large supply of sand and little vegetation. These dunes often cover large areas and develop a wavelike form with sinuous ridges and troughs perpendicular to the direction of prevailing wind. Transverse sand dunes have an asymmetrical cross section with a width about seven times their height. They have a typical height of 5 to 15 m, with a maximum of about 100 m. Transverse dunes may grade into barchan dunes as the sand supply lessens.

Crescent-shaped *barchan dunes* tend to form in areas where there is a limited amount of sand and little vegetation. The tips, or horns, of the barchan dunes point downwind and sand grains are swept around the barchan as well as up and over the crest. The dune cross section is asymmetrical at the crest, but may become nearly symmetrical on the horns. Barchan dunes have a typical height of 5 to 15 m, up to a maximum of about 30 m. Barchan dunes migrate readily, with smaller dunes moving faster than larger dunes. Near the sand source, there is often a dune complex of

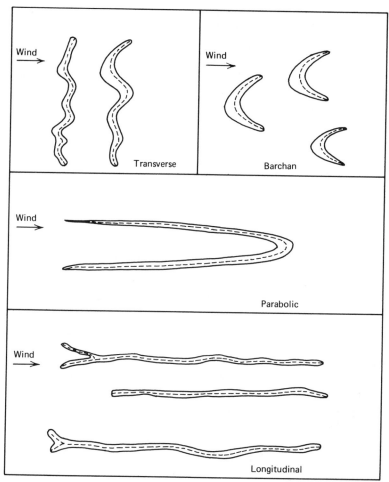

FIGURE 4.34 Basic sand dune shapes. Dune crests shown by dashed lines.

transverse and barchan dunes. Individual, often extremely well-developed barchan dunes tend to develop some distance downwind from the source.

Parabolic dunes have a crescent shape with long horns pointed into the wind. They typically form where vegetation anchors portions of the horns, allowing the center of the dune to migrate, resulting in a hairpin-shaped dune. Once the basic parabolic shape has formed, most parabolic dunes are fixed in place and do not migrate. The dune cross section is asymmetrical at the crest and nearly symmetrical on the horns. Parabolic dunes typically have a height of up 15 m.

Longitudinal dunes are long, nearly straight ridges of sand that form parallel to the direction of the wind. They are found where strong prevailing winds converge and blow in a constant direction. The dune cross section is symmetrical, with a width several times the height. Longitudinal dunes are typically less than 15 m high and several kilometers long. However, in large desert areas, they may be as high as 200 m and as long as 300 km. Such massive longitudinal dunes are often called seif dunes.

Nearly 100 percent of the particles found in sand dunes fall within the very narrow range of 0.05 to 0.5 mm, attesting to the excellent sorting power of the wind. When soils develop on stabilized sand dunes, they tend to be thin, sandy, and excessively well drained.

Sand dunes are generally unfavorable locations for urban development due to the possibility of blowing sand and migrating dunes. However, at times sand dune areas are developed, as in the case of many lakeshore sites. Many sand dune areas, such as those along the shorelines of the Great Lakes and the Atlantic Ocean, are unique natural areas with very fragile plant communities. Development is discouraged in these areas for this reason.

Airphoto Identification of Sand Dunes

Topography: Previously described. *Drainage:* Excellent internal drainage. *Erosion:* Frequent wind erosion when dunes are not stabilized by vegetation and wind velocities are sufficient to erode and transport sand grains. Some water erosion of steeper slopes. *Photo tone:* Sand without a vegetative cover photographs very light on panchromatic film. There is often a sharp contrast between sand dunes and surrounding materials due to a combination of soil moisture and vegetation type and vigor. *Vegetation and land use:* Active (migrating) dunes have essentially no vegetative cover. Stabilized dunes often have a grass or shrub cover. Agricultural crops are rare. Orchards and vineyards may be present. Stabilized dunes in humid areas may be used for grazing. *Other:* Stabilized sand dunes in a humid glaciated area are sometimes mistakenly identified as eskers (Section 4.10).

Figure 4.35 shows transverse sand dunes in an arid climate. The direction of the wind that formed these dunes was from upper left to lower right. The dunes are located in a valley between sandstone ridges.

Figure 4.36 shows barchan sand dunes in an arid climate formed by wind blowing from top to bottom (of the figure) across a smooth, gently sloping plain that descends to the Salton Sea. These dunes range in height from 3 to 10 m, with a horn-to-horn width of 50 to 250 m.

Figure 4.37 shows parabolic sand dunes in an arid climate formed by wind blowing from upper left to lower right.

Figure 4.38 shows longitudinal sand dunes in an arid climate formed by wind blowing from upper left to lower right. Note that when two longitudinal dunes merge into one, they join together downwind of the location of the two separate dunes (see also Figure 4.34).

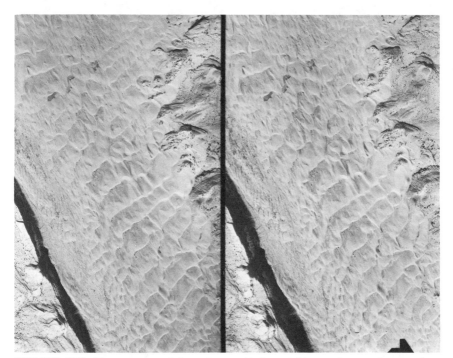

FIGURE 4.35 Transverse sand dunes in an arid climate, Navajo County, Arizona, September 1951. 1:26,700. Stereogram. (USGS photos.)

Figures 4.39 and 4.40 show exceptionally large transverse sand dunes in the Sand Hills area of west-central Nebraska. The Sand Hills cover an area of more than 50,000 km², the largest continuous dune field in the Western Hemisphere. These dunes were formed by winds blowing from the upper left (northwest). In portions of west-central Nebraska, aeolian deposits change from transverse dunes to longitudinal dunes to loess as one proceeds downwind from the source. Figure 4.39 is a Landsat image (Chapter 9) covering an area 127 × 152 km. Here, the dunes can be seen as roughly parallel transverse ridges, often with wet soils or lakes between the dunes. Figure 4.40 is an airphoto stereopair covering an area 2.0 × 3.1 km. The dunes in the area of this illustration are typically 50 to 100 m high and 1500 m wide. The vegetative cover on the dunes is principally grass and the dunes are used for grazing of beef cattle.

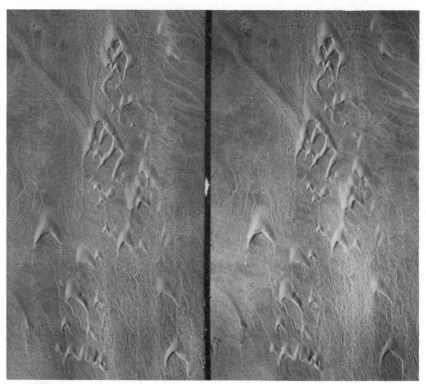

FIGURE 4.36

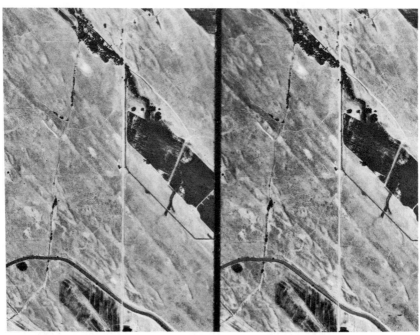

FIGURE 4.37

258

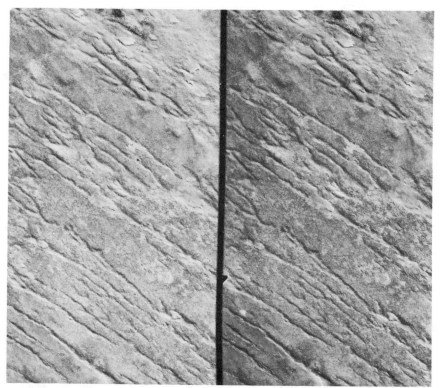

FIGURE 4.38 Longitudinal sand dunes in an arid climate, Great Sand Dunes National Monument, Colorado, September 1955. 1:20,000. Stereogram. (USDA−ASCS photos.)

FIGURE 4.36 Barchan sand dunes in an arid climate, Imperial County, California, November 1959. 1:20,000. Stereogram. (USDA−ASCS photos.)

FIGURE 4.37 Parabolic sand dunes in an arid climate, Bingham County, Idaho, June 1960. 1:20,000. Stereogram. (USDA−ASCS photos.)

FIGURE 4.39 Exceptionally large transverse sand dunes, west central Nebraska, May 1973. 1:1,000,000. Landsat Multispectral Scanner band 7 (near-infrared). (NASA image.)

Loess

Loess consists of unconsolidated, generally unstratified, silt-sized windborne deposits that may contain minor amounts of fine sand and clay. Loess and loesslike materials cover about one-tenth of the world's land area. Extensive loess deposits occur in the

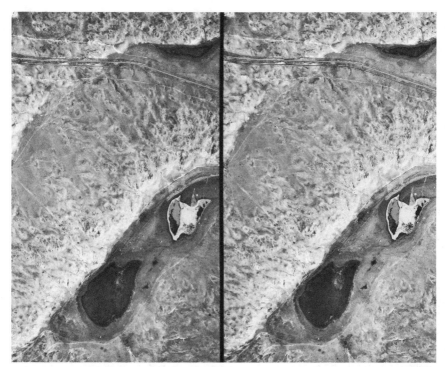

FIGURE 4.40 Exceptionally large transverse sand dunes. Southeast corner of Sheridan County, Nebraska, August 1954. 1:33,300. Stereogram. (USDA—ASCS photos.) *Note:* The location of the center of Figure 4.40 is 5.0 cm right and 6.5 cm down from the upper left corner of Figure 4.39.

midwestern United States and in Washington and Idaho. Many of the best agricultural areas occur on loess soils. Corn is extensively cultivated on the loess plains of Illinois and Iowa with a rainfall of 75 to 100 cm/year. Wheat is grown where the rainfall is less, as on the loess plains of Kansas and Nebraska and in the Palouse region of eastern Washington.

Loess generally consists of silt removed from desert areas by wind erosion or silt removed from sediments deposited by meltwater streams flowing from glaciers. In China, loess deposits thicker than 150 m occur to the lee of deserts. In Illinois, loess deposits thicker than 30 m are present to the lee of the Mississippi River Valley. Both loess thickness and loess particle size decrease with increasing distance from the source of the materials.

Loess typically has a yellow to buff color, contains at least 60 to 70 percent silt-sized particles and has a silt loam or silty clay loam texture. Loess has a tendency to cleave along vertical planes whenever exposed by water erosion or human activity. As a result, many stable vertical faces, up to 6 m in height, can be found in loess areas along gully sides and in highway cuts. The reason why loess remains stable in vertical cuts is not clearly understood but may be due to calcification of vertical root casts and other vertical cracks in the soil. Loess soils are typically well drained in their natural state, with a vertical permeability as much as 20 times greater than permeability in a horizontal direction. When loess is disturbed by human activity such as urban development or rural highway construction, the vertical drainage is impeded and poorly drained soils result. Loess is easily eroded by moving water and special care must be taken in the construction of drainage facilities, especially open ditches. Loess soils have a relatively low density (high air void space) compared with other soils. Loess has been called a "collapsible" material that may undergo excessive loss of strength or excessive settlement when subjected to an increase in moisture content, a heavy vertical load, vibrations, or a combination of these factors.

Great care must be taken in the development of loess areas. Potential problems can include septic tank failure, excessive foundation settlement, severe water erosion, and frost damage. In addition, special consideration must be given to the unusual slope stability characteristics of loess.

Airphoto Identification of Loess

Topography: Thick undissected loess deposits typically have a gently undulating surface, with roughly parallel crests some 500 to 1000 m apart aligned transversely to the wind direction. Thin loess deposits form a mantle over the underlying rock and unconsolidated materials and the resulting ground surface tends to follow the contours of the underlying materials. However, there is a tendency for loess to smooth out the terrain, with thinner deposits found on ridges and thicker deposits in valleys. Very often, loess deposits are minutely dissected by stream and gully erosion. *Drainage and erosion:* In dissected loess areas, there is an intricately carved landscape formed by many streams and gullies. The overall drainage pattern is typically a modified dendritic pattern known as a pinnate (featherlike) drainage pattern, as illustrated in Figure 4.41. Gullies are U-shaped, with broad, flat bottoms and steep sides, often marked with small soil slips called "catsteps." *Photo tone:* Characteristically light because of good internal soil drainage. Often have tonal contrasts between gully bottoms, gully sides, and upland areas due to different vegetation types (e.g., trees versus grass). *Vegetation and land use:* Typically farmed, except on steeper slopes or in low rainfall areas.

Figure 4.5*b* illustrates a gully system in loess more than 5 m thick in central Nebraska, an area with about 60 cm/year rainfall used for grazing. The soil is a well-drained silt loam. Note the pinnate gully pattern and the broad-bottomed, steep-sided gullies with active erosion at their heads.

Figure 4.42 illustrates loess approximately 20 m thick just east of the Missouri River in Iowa. The loess is so strongly dissected that sharp-edged hills remain. This landscape is typical of thick dissected loess along the Mississippi and Missouri Rivers in the midwest United States. Distinct U-shaped gullies can be seen several places, especially in the central and lower portions of the stereogram.

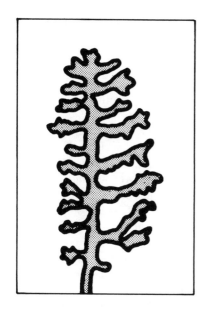

FIGURE 4.41 Outline of pinnate gully system typical of erosion of loess deposits (sketched from Figure 4.5b).

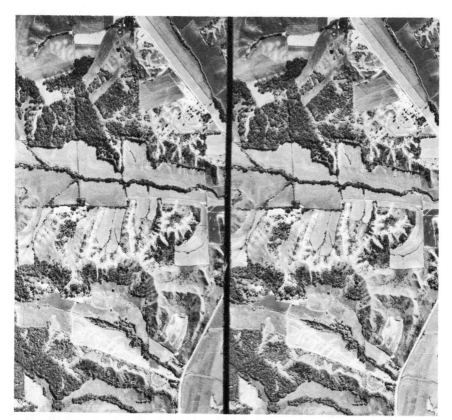

FIGURE 4.42 Loess in a humid climate, Pottawattamie County, Iowa, September 1966. 1:22,200. Stereogram. (USDA—ASCS photos.)

4.10   GLACIAL LANDFORMS

Today, most of the water on the surface of the earth is in liquid form, in lakes and oceans. About 2 percent is in solid form, as glacial ice, at high latitudes and high elevations. About 10 percent of the earth's land surface is presently covered with glacial ice. During the past one million or more years, there have been repeated advances of glacial ice over about 30 percent of the earth's land surface. The major advances occurred during periods when the earth's climate was colder than at present. Glaciation occurred both in the form of *valley glaciation*, in which tongues of ice occupied mountain valleys, and as *continental glaciation*, huge lobes of ice covering portions of several continents with an ice thickness up to 3 km. This size staggers the imagination and helps to explain the capability of a glacial advance to sculpt the terrain in its path. We discuss principally depositional landforms resulting from continental glaciation. Four distinct advances (or stages) have been identified in the United States. The most recent ice advance was during the Wisconsinan Stage of glaciation that occurred during the period more than 70,000 to about 10,000 years ago.

As ice moves over the earth's surface, it abrades and plucks materials from the surface over which it moves. Some materials are carried within the ice and some are carried on the surface. Some materials are ground to a fine powder, whereas some are scarcely modified by glacial erosion and transportation. Some materials are sorted and rounded by flowing water.

Materials deposited by glaciation are called *glacial drift*. There are four principal kinds of glacial drift: (1) *till*, unsorted, unstratified material deposited directly from glacial ice with relatively little water-sorting action; (2) *ice-contact stratified drift*, material partly water-sorted and crudely stratified, deposited adjacent to melting ice; (3) *outwash*, sediment deposited away from melting ice by meltwater streams; and (4) *glaciolacustrine deposits*, sediments deposited in ephemeral glacial lakes. These *materials* are found in a variety of *landforms*, as categorized in Table 4.3.

Figure 4.43 depicts the formation and resulting physiographic relationships of the landforms listed in Table 4.3. The formation of these landforms is explained as each is discussed.

Till Landforms

Two forms of till have been recognized: basal till and ablation till. *Basal till* (also known as lodgement till) was deposited from the base of the glacier. Pressure melting of the flowing ice freed drift particles and allowed them to be plastered, under pressure, under the glacial ice. Very little particle size sorting was involved and crushing and abrasion of particles were often intense. *Ablation till* was deposited when materials that had been transported on or near the surface of the ice accumulated on the ground as the ice melted. Many of the finer particles (silt and clay) carried on the ice were washed away during the process of melting.

Till textures can vary greatly, depending on the nature of the rock and/or soil material eroded by the glacial ice. In southeastern Wisconsin, for example, till of the portion of the Green Bay Lobe that eroded sandstone and dolomite typically has a

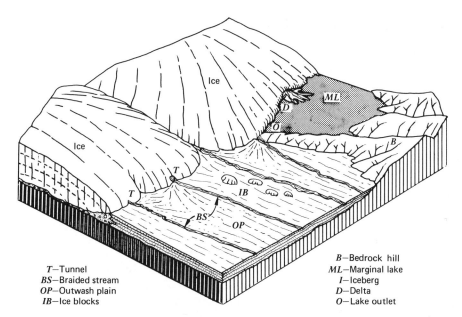

T—Tunnel
BS—Braided stream
OP—Outwash plain
IB—Ice blocks

B—Bedrock hill
ML—Marginal lake
I—Iceberg
D—Delta
O—Lake outlet

(a) With the ice front stabilized and the ice in a wasting, stagnant condition, various depositional features are built by meltwaters.

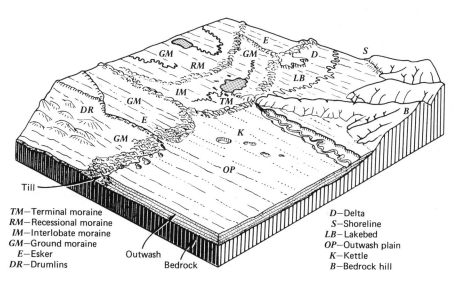

TM—Terminal moraine
RM—Recessional moraine
IM—Interlobate moraine
GM—Ground moraine
E—Esker
DR—Drumlins

Till

Outwash

Bedrock

D—Delta
S—Shoreline
LB—Lakebed
OP—Outwash plain
K—Kettle
B—Bedrock hill

(b) After the ice has wasted completely away, a variety of new landforms made under the ice is exposed to view.

FIGURE 4.43 Schematic diagram showing glacial landforms resulting from continental glaciation. (Original drawn by A.N. Strahler [23].)

TABLE 4.3   Landforms Resulting from Continental Glaciation

Till Landforms	Outwash Landforms
End moraine	Outwash plain
Terminal moraine	Valley train
Recessional moraine	Outwash terrace
Interlobate moraine	Glaciolacustrine Landforms
Ground moraine	Lakebed
Ablation ground moraine	Beach ridge
Basal ground moraine	Delta
Drumlin	
Ice-Contact Stratified Drift Landforms	
Esker	
Kame	

texture of sandy loam or gravelly loam, whereas till of the portion of the Lake Michigan Lobe that eroded shale and lake clays has a texture of silty clay loam and clay loam. With till derived from the same rock and/or soil material, ablation till would tend to have a coarser texture than basal till because of the mode of formation.

End moraines are ridgelike deposits of till, with varying proportions of ice-contact stratified drift inclusions, that have accumulated along the margins of glacial ice. As illustrated in Figure 4.43, end moraines associated with the farthest extent of an advance of a lobe of glacial ice are called *terminal moraines*, those associated with temporary periods of a stationary ice front behind the terminal moraine are called *recessional moraines*, and those formed between two lobes of glacial ice are called *interlobate moraines*.

At the time of end moraine formation, there is an equilibrium between the rate of advance of the glacial ice and the rate of melting of the ice, causing a period when the ice front is stationary. At this time, materials carried within or on the ice are deposited by ablation at the ice front. When the rate of melting exceeds the rate of ice flow toward the margins, the ice front retreats and a thinner deposit of till is spread across the terrain, forming ground moraine areas. A few small end moraines may be formed by the bulldozing action of the advancing ice. Glacial ice tends to override such moraines when their height exceeds 10 m. Thus, most end moraines have been formed principally by ablation. Interlobate moraines typically contain more ice-contact stratified drift than terminal or recessional moraines.

Numerous irregularly shaped depressions called *kettles* are found in end moraines. They were formed by the melting of buried blocks of ice after sedimentation had ceased at the site of the kettles. Kettles are also found in association with eskers, kames, and outwash.

End moraines can be found throughout the glaciated portions of the world. A small moraine may have a length of only a few kilometers, a width of less than $\frac{1}{2}$ km, and a height of less than 15 m. A large moraine may have a length over 150 km, a width of 10 km or more, and a height up to about 150 m.

End moraines often have a wide variation in soil and drainage conditions. Sand and gravel are found in localized stratified drift deposits, often as lenses surrounded by till. Very poorly drained fine-textured and organic soils are often found in kettle holes.

End moraine areas are typically better suited to low-density residential development than to intensive urban development because of the variable terrain and soil conditions. The characteristics of end moraine areas are often well suited to the development of golf courses, campgrounds, and other recreational uses.

Airphoto Identification of End Moraines

Topography: Hummocky and variable, a disordered arrangement of hillocks and depressions. Lack of continuity among hillock-top elevations and a lack of continuity among depression-bottom elevations. Viewed over a large area, end moraines form gently curving or lobe-shaped belts of hummocky ablation till (Figure 4.43). *Drainage and erosion:* A deranged drainage pattern; aimlessly directed short streams, ponds, and marshes at widely differing elevations. When present, gullies can indicate soil texture. *Photo tone:* A striking mottled pattern, with light and dark areas being related to topography and surface soil texture and moisture content. This mottled pattern is especially evident when photographs are taken in the spring (little or no crop cover) 1 to 2 days after a rainfall. The mottled pattern may be difficult to discern in midsummer photographs when crops are mature. *Vegetation and land use:* Variable, depending on slope, soil, and moisture conditions. Typically farmed on slopes less than 12 percent. End moraine crests and other portions with slopes over 12 percent usually wooded. Excessively well-drained pockets of stratified drift typically wooded.

Figure 4.44 shows an end moraine in a humid climate. Note the hummocky topography, variable hilltop and pond elevation, lack of an integrated surface drainage pattern, and mottled photo tone. The soil parent material is well drained to somewhat excessively drained sandy loam till with pockets of stratified drift. The weathered soil profile is thin on hilltops and steep slopes. Very poorly drained mineral and organic soils are found in many depressions (kettle holes). The depth of till over bedrock is approximately 60 to 100 m.

Ablation ground moraine areas consist of ablation till that was deposited under conditions of a retreating ice front, as previously described. The physical characteristics—as well as the appearance on aerial photographs—of ablation ground moraine areas are similar to end moraine areas, except that (1) the ablation till of ablation ground moraine areas forms a general ground cover instead of occurring as ridgelike lobes; (2) the topographic relief is generally less in ablation ground moraine areas; (3) the thickness of ablation till over basal till or bedrock is generally less in ablation ground moraine areas; and (4) the ablation till cover of ablation ground moraine areas may be discontinuous.

Basal ground moraine areas consist of basal till that was deposited at the base of glacial ice, as previously described. Great thicknesses of basal till can be built up as the ice continues to ride over the already deposited basal till, plastering on more and more

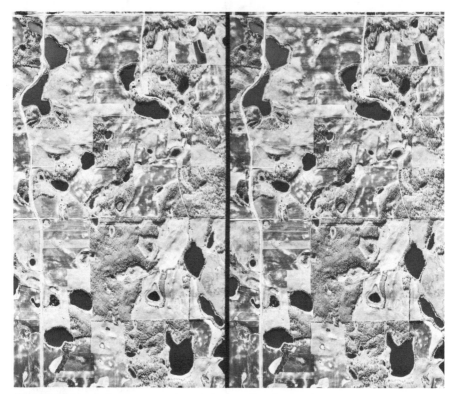

FIGURE 4.44   End moraine in a humid climate, Clay County, Minnesota, November 1959. 1:30,000. Stereogram. (USDA–ASCS photos.)

material. Large areas of northern Indiana have a basal till cover 15 to 100 m thick built up from several ice advances. In the case of ablation till, only the materials existing in or on the ice at the time of melting can be deposited. Thus, the thickness of ablation till in ablation ground moraine areas is likely to be less than that of basal till in basal ground moraine areas. However, deposits of ablation till as thick as 40 m have been reported in ablation ground moraine areas.

Large basal ground moraine areas that consist of thick basal till are typically rather flat plains with local relief of only a few meters. Sometimes the terrain may have a series of elongated rises whose crests are aligned with the direction of ice movement, forming a grooved terrain of *minidrumlins*. Although the topography is favorable, basal ground moraine areas may or may not be well suited to urban development, depending on the soil and drainage conditions.

Airphoto Identification of Basal Ground Moraine Areas

This discussion refers principally to basal ground moraine areas of Wisconsinan age. Older basal ground moraine areas characteristically have greater relief and a more completely formed surface drainage system than described here. *Topography:* Broad, gently rolling plains with a swell-and-swale terrain that contain many shallow depressions with no natural drainage outlet. *Drainage and erosion:* The surface drainage pattern is not well developed because of the flat terrain and young age of the landform. A discontinuous and disordered network of broad, gently curving (fine-textured type) gullies roughly connects into an incipient dendritic pattern. Most of the surface precipitation drains into the ground rather than running off through surface drainage channels, unless farmers have constructed artificial drainage channels. *Photo tone:* A striking mottled pattern of light and dark tones, especially well seen in spring airphotos taken 1 to 2 days after a rainfall. *Vegetation and land use:* In most cases, the land has been cleared of native growth and is cultivated.

Figure 4.45 shows a typical basal ground moraine area in central Indiana. The striking mottled pattern results from different soil moisture conditions on the rises and depressions. The typical elevation difference between adjacent rises and depressions

FIGURE 4.45 Basal ground moraine in a humid climate, Madison County, Indiana, May 1961. 1:20,000. Stereogram. (USDA–ASCS photos.)

is $\frac{1}{2}$ to 1 m. The total elevation difference in the area shown in this figure is about 3 m. The soils on the rises are somewhat poorly drained and have a silt loam surface soil texture. The soils in the depressions are very poorly drained and have a silty clay loam surface soil texture. The weathered soil profile is about 1 m in thickness. The underlying till parent material is a loam to clay loam till under both the rises and depressions. The soils in the depressions are so poorly drained that tile drains or surface ditches are required to remove excess water so that the area can be farmed. The depth of till over bedrock in this area is at least 30 m.

Drumlins are composed of compact till molded into smooth, oval-shaped hills resembling an inverted spoon. They are shaped by the weight of the overriding glacial ice and have their long axes parallel to the direction of glacial ice movement. Drumlins are excellent examples of natural streamlining. Most well-formed drumlins have a length at least several times their width. The drumlin end facing the direction from which the ice came is decidedly steeper than the down-ice end. The high point on a drumlin is typically two-fifths of the length back from the nose. From this high point, the drumlin tapers gently toward the tail where it blends smoothly into the surrounding terrain. Drumlin sides are typically steeper than the nose, locally attaining slopes up to about 35 percent. Drumlins typically have a height of 10 to 50 m, a width of 200 to 600 m, and a length of 1 to 3 km. However, proportions ranging from nearly circular to a length/width ratio of 50:1 can be found. Single isolated drumlins are rare. Usually drumlins occur in large groups in areas of thick till in a belt 15 to 30 km wide located at least several kilometers up-ice from the end moraine of the stage of glaciation during which they were formed. They may be surrounded by and altered by recessional moraines.

Large groups of drumlins occur in New York (about 10,000) and Wisconsin (about 5000). Both Bunker Hill and Breed's Hill, which played historic roles in the Revolutionary War, are drumlins.

Drumlins can be found with a variety of till textures. Because of topographic limitations, high-density urban development is not desirable in drumlin areas.

Airphoto Identification of Drumlins

Topography: Streamlined, ice-molded shape, with typical dimensions as previously described. In drumlin belts, adjacent drumlins may be separated from each other only indistinctly and shapes may vary widely. *Drainage:* Essentially no drainage pattern develops on drumlins because of their small size. Very poorly drained, marshy areas may occur in the depressions between drumlins. *Erosion:* Because of the steep side slopes, erosion may be sheet erosion rather than rill and gully erosion. *Photo tone, vegetation, and land use:* The photo tone on drumlins often contrasts with the tone on the adjacent lowland because of differences in vegetation (e.g., trees on drumlin versus crops on lowland; different crops on drumlin versus lowland; crops on drumlin versus marsh vegetation on lowland) or soil moisture (e.g., well-drained soils on drumlin versus poorly drained soils on lowland). The long dimensions of cultivated fields tend to be aligned with the drumlin axes.

Figure 4.46 shows drumlins in a humid climate. These drumlins are 25 to 30 m high, 300 to 500 m wide, and about 1.5 km long. The direction of ice movement was from right to left. The broad depressions between drumlins that have a faintly mottled, drab gray tone on the photos are occupied by very poorly drained silty clay loam soils.

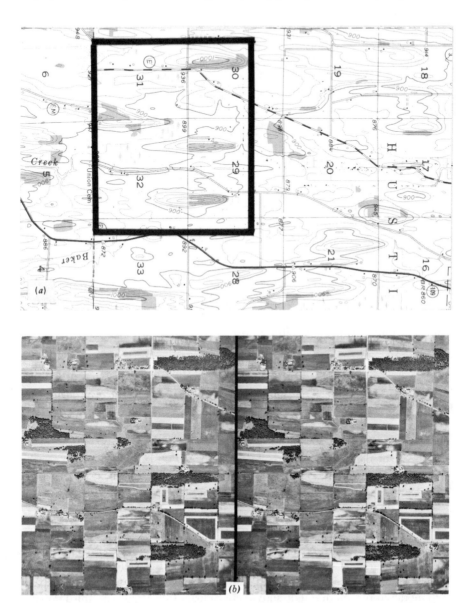

FIGURE 4.46 Drumlins in a humid climate, Dodge County, Wisconsin. (a) Topographic map, 20-ft (6.1-m) contour interval, 1955. 1:62,500. (USGS.) (b) Aerial photographs, June 1956. 1:43,500. Stereogram. (USDA—ASCS photos.) The outlined portion of the topographic map shows the area covered by the stereogram.

Ice-Contact Stratified Drift Landforms

Ice-contact stratified drift consists of materials partly water-sorted and crudely strati-fied, deposited adjacent to melting ice. Deposition can take place upon, against, or underneath the wasting terminal zone of the glacier and is likely to be sporadic and irregular. Ice is likely to melt from beneath accumulating ice-contact sediments, or from a supporting position beside them, causing sagging, collapse, or slump. The principal landforms resulting from this process are eskers and kames.

Eskers are long, sinuous ridges of ice-contact stratified drift deposited from streams flowing on, within, or under the glacial ice. Eskers are typically 5 to 20 m high (maximum over 50 m), 50 to 100 m wide (maximum over 250 m), and 100 m to several kilometers long (maximum over 250 km with short gaps). Side slopes are typically 30 to 45 percent (60 percent maximum). Eskers are often aligned with their length along the direction of ice movement. Some eskers are relatively straight while others have wide curves resembling stream meanders. At times they may branch, forming a series of esker ridges in a dendritic pattern. Eskers may connect "downstream" with fans or deltas. They may form a braided pattern or grade into kames. Eskers can have a wide range in crest elevation and may cross drumlins or bedrock hills.

Eskers are composed principally of stratified sand and gravel with parent material textures of gravelly sand and very gravelly sand. Soils developed on eskers are usually excessively well drained because of the elevated topographic position and coarse-textured parent material.

Eskers are excellent sources of sand and gravel for construction projects. In fact, many eskers near urban areas have been almost entirely removed for construction materials. On the other hand, eskers can provide excellent locations for hiking trails due to their linear nature and often-forested vegetation.

Airphoto Identification of Eskers

Topography: Size and shape previously described. *Drainage and erosion:* Little surface drainage or gullying due to small size and coarse-textured materials. *Photo tone, vegetation, and land use:* The photo tone on eskers typically contrasts with the tone on the adjacent landform (usually ground moraine) because of differences in vegetation (e.g., trees on esker versus crops on ground moraine; grass on esker versus row crops on ground moraine). Sand and gravel pits common (portions of esker may have been removed), especially near roads that cut eskers.

Figure 4.47 shows a portion of an esker in a ground moraine area in a humid climate. This esker is 10 m high, 100 m wide, and 27 km long (with small gaps). The esker soils are excessively well drained stratified sand and gravel. The ground moraine soils are well to moderately well drained sandy loam to loam till. About one-third down from the top of the figure, there is an area of very poorly drained mineral and organic soils on both sides of the esker.

FIGURE 4.47   Esker in a humid climate, Oconto County, Wisconsin, May 1958. 1:20,000. Stereogram. (USDA—ASCS photos.)

Kames are moundlike hills or ridges of ice-contact stratified drift that may occur individually or in groups. Some kames are formed by deposition in crevasses and other openings within or on the surface of stagnant or nearly stagnant glacial ice that later melted away, leaving isolated or semi-isolated mounds of ice-contact stratified drift that we call *individual kames.* Another type of kame results from deposition of fanlike deposits built outward from the ice, or inward against the ice, or between two lobes of ice, which later melted and collapsed, forming large irregular mounds of ice-contact stratified drift called *kame complexes.* Kame complexes grade into kame terraces, ablation till, and eskers, and also form integral parts of some end moraines.

Individual kames are typically 15 to 25 m high and up to 150 m wide. Kame complexes cover a much larger area and often blend into eskers or end moraines. The characteristics of interlobate moraines are closer to our description of kame complexes than end moraines because they contain so much ice-contact stratified drift.

Kames are composed principally of stratified sand and gravel and tend to be somewhat finer-textured than eskers. Typical kame parent material textures are sand, gravelly sand, and very gravelly sand. Soil drainage is excessive due to the elevated topographic position and coarse-textured parent material.

Kames are very good sources of sand and gravel for construction projects. They can also provide excellent locations for recreational development such as hiking trails and picnic areas because of their varied topography.

Airphoto Identification of Kames

Topography: Individual kames are isolated, conical to irregularly shaped mounds with steep side slopes. Kame complexes have a hummocky topography, with variable hilltop and depression-bottom elevations, that has been described as resembling crumpled aluminum foil. *Drainage and erosion:* Drainage is mostly internal with few gullies. Most depressions in kame complexes are dry rather than containing ponds or marshes. When gullies are present, they are the V-shaped (sand and gravel) type. *Photo tone:* Generally light-toned. *Vegetation and land use:* Typically grass or tree covered. May be used for grazing but seldom planted in row crops. Vegetation often contrasts with that on adjacent landform (e.g., grass or trees on kames versus row crops on end moraine). Sand and gravel pits often seen in kame areas. *Other:* Since kame complexes intergrade with end moraines, especially interlobate moraines, airphoto identification of kame complexes versus end moraines can become difficult. The following criteria can be used to differentiate between kame complexes and end moraines: (1) Kame complexes have steeper side slopes and sharper ridges than end moraines. (2) Kame complexes have dry depressions while end moraines often have ponds and marshes in depressions. (3) Kame complexes tend to have a uniform light tone while end moraines have a mottled tone pattern. (4) Kame complexes usually have a grass or tree cover while end moraines usually have a row crop cover (except that end moraines are often tree covered at their crests where they may contain significant amounts of stratified drift).

Figure 4.48 shows a large kame complex located on a portion of an interlobate moraine that extends for more than 200 km in eastern Wisconsin. This kame complex is 45 m high and has side slopes of 25 to 40 percent. Note the dry depressions and the even light tone on this excessively well drained kame complex. The kame complex is composed of stratified sand and gravel with some cobblestones. It is too steep and dry for cultivation and is used for perennial pasture. An esker runs from left to right across the bottom of the figure. At the top of the figure is a very poorly drained area of mineral and organic soils that appears as a mottled, darker-toned area with a stream meandering from right to left. This area is subject to ponding after heavy rains and can be farmed only if tile drains or ditches are used to drain excessive water.

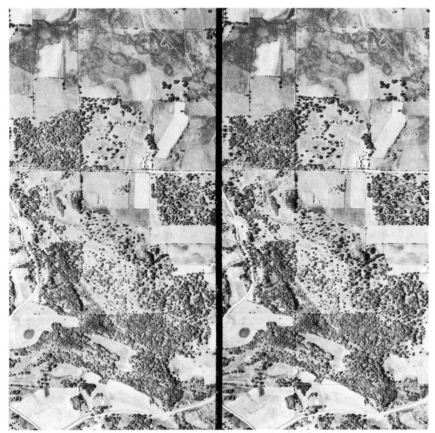

FIGURE 4.48   Kame complex and esker in a humid climate, Walworth County, Wisconsin, October 1956. 1:20,000. Stereogram. (USDA—ASCS photos.)

Outwash Landforms

Outwash sediments are stratified drift deposited by streams flowing away from glacial ice. Outwash consists mainly of layers of sand and gravel that have come to rest on the beds of meltwater streams as they flow away from the glacier. The silt and clay particles are carried in suspension downstream from the outwash plain and are eventually deposited in glacial lakes, on stream flood plains, or in the ocean. Outwash sediments typically form a series of fans that spread out downstream from the ice and often coalesce. The individual apexes of the fans can often be recognized. The streams that distribute and deposit the outwash sediments take on a braided pattern as they flow down the fans and the remnants of braiding are clearly visible on present-day aerial photographs (the braided distributary channels of a present-day alluvial fan are shown in Figure 4.56). Numerous chunks of ice may be carried in the streams and form kettle holes upon melting.

Outwash sediments which form broad, nearly level plains are called *outwash plains*. Those confined to a valley are called *valley trains*. Outwash sediments with numerous kettle holes are called *pitted outwash*. Outwash plains and valley trains are often eroded by streams leaving *outwash terraces*.

Outwash deposits are almost ideally suited to urban development, except for excessively pitted areas. The nearly level terrain poses no limitations to development. The granular materials provide excellent foundation supporting strength and drainage conditions are favorable to development. In some valley train areas, the water table may be near the ground surface causing foundation problems. Where septic tanks are employed for the disposal of domestic sewage, there is a potential danger of drinking water contamination due to the porous nature of the outwash materials. The nearly level terrain allows for intensive subdivision development. Lower density subdivisions can be placed on nearby end moraines, along with low-density recreational development.

Airphoto Identification of Outwash Sediments

Topography: Nearly level surface sloping away from the source of the materials. Former distributary channels remain as a braided series of small depressions (less than $\frac{1}{2}$ m deep). Numerous kettles in the case of pitted outwash. Outwash plains appear as a series of coalescing fans on a photo mosaic. Valley trains are confined by valley walls. Outwash terraces form steep escarpments above streams. *Drainage and erosion:* Internal drainage is rapid and there are few surface streams or drainage ditches. The former distributary channels are a relic, not a present-day drainage pattern. *Photo tone:* Overall light photo tone with former distributary channels appearing darker and giving a distinct "braided" or "wormlike" mottled tone. *Vegetation and land use:* Typically farmed in areas with sufficient rainfall, unless excessively pitted.

Figure 4.49 shows a portion of a large outwash plain just beyond the terminal moraine of Wisconsinan age glaciation in southern Wisconsin. The area generally to the left of the road that runs vertically in the figure is an outwash plain with a 0.25 percent slope from bottom to top in this figure. The area generally to the right of the road is the outermost extent of the terminal moraine. The glacial meltwater that formed this outwash plain flowed from bottom to top in this figure (note the braided pattern of the former distributary channels). The outwash material is 20 m thick over bedrock and contains 60 to 70 percent gravel, 25 to 35 percent sand, and 1 to 5 percent silt and clay. There is a 1 to 1.5 m loess cover over the outwash so that the soil is classified well drained rather than excessively drained, as might be expected with stratified sand and gravel. As a result, this loess covered outwash plain is one of the finest agricultural areas in the state.

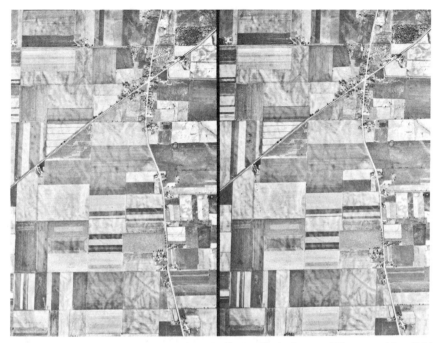

FIGURE 4.49 Outwash plain in a humid climate, Rock County, Wisconsin, May 1956.
1:40,000. Stereogram. (USDA−ASCS photos.)

Figure 4.50 shows an outwash terrace about 30 m above the Chippewa River in Wisconsin. Note the well-developed braided pattern of former distributary channels and the V-shaped (sand and gravel type) gullies along the terrace face above the river. The outwash material is stratified sand with some gravel and contains 5 to 15 percent fine gravel, 80 to 90 percent sand, and 1 to 5 percent silt and clay. These sandy soils are somewhat excessively drained and subject to wind erosion. Note that the terrace face above the river appears to have a slope of at least 60°. The natural angle of repose of this material is around 30°. Taking stereo exaggeration into account and applying Table 4.2, we find that the angle should appear to be about 60° on the stereogram to most observers.

Glaciolacustrine Landforms

As illustrated in Figure 4.43, ephemeral glacial lakes can be formed at the margin of glacial ice. Sediments deposited in the relatively quiet lake waters are called *glacial lakebed* deposits. Materials reworked into distinct linear ridges at the lake shoreline(s) are called *beach ridges*. Where streams enter the lake, *deltas* may be formed (Section

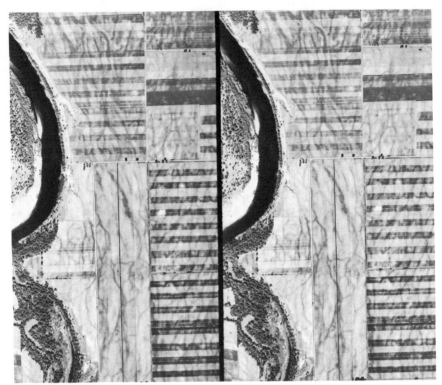

FIGURE 4.50 Outwash terrace in a humid climate, Dunn County, Wisconsin, July 1958. 1:26,700. Stereogram. (USDA—ASCS photos.)

4.11). In areas of sandy near-shore lakebed deposits, the wind may later rework the dry materials into sand dunes.

Numerous glacial lakebeds of widely varying size can be found in glaciated areas. Perhaps the largest region of glacial lakebed deposits is the area of the glacial Great Lakes where glacial lakes existed along an ice front more than 2000 km long from the upper St. Lawrence to Saskatchewan. One of the lakes, glacial Lake Agassiz, left deposits over an area of 500,000 km². In contrast, the glacial lakebed and beach ridge shown in Figure 7.15 occupied an area of only 8 km².

Glacial lakebed deposits consist principally of the finer-textured products of glacial erosion (silt and clay). Near the lake shorelines, some sandy areas can be found where waves have sorted the sediments, washing finer-textured materials out to deeper waters and spreading a veneer of sandy material in shallow water areas. Deep-water deposits are typically alternating layers (varves) of silty clay and clay. It has been hypothesized that each pair of layers represents one year's deposition, with silty clay deposited during the summer and clay deposited during the calmer winter conditions when the water surface is frozen. The thickness of these varves varies, but is rarely in excess of 5 cm. Lakebed soils typically have a seasonally high groundwater level and are somewhat poorly to poorly drained.

Although glacial lakebed topography is favorable for urban development, soil and drainage conditions pose severe limitations to building and road construction and to septic tank use. Glacial lakebed areas are commonly in agricultural use. Where outlets are available, tile drains and ditches are provided to improve drainage for agricultural purposes.

Airphoto Identification of Glacial Lakebeds

Topography: Very flat with undulations less than $\frac{1}{2}$ m high. *Drainage:* A general lack of surface drainage despite the very poor internal drainage. This is because of the flat topography, lack of a drainage outlet, and high groundwater table. Streams originating beyond the margin of the lakebed may meander across the lakebed (as in the case of the Red River of the North shown in Figure 4.51), but there is seldom much of a surface drainage network connected with these streams. Artificial drainage is common in agricultural areas; buried tile drains and a network of open ditches may be seen on airphotos. *Erosion:* Few gullies due to flat topography and lack of an integrated surface drainage network. Some fine-textured type gullies may be seen draining into large streams, especially if the streams are entrenched. *Photo tone:* Darker tone than surrounding better drained materials. Often a striking mottled tone of uneven linears, with the lighter-toned areas slightly higher and drier and the darker-toned areas slightly lower and wetter. *Vegetation and land use:* Typically farmed where climate is satisfactory.

Figure 4.51 illustrates the relationships among lakebed, shoreline, and till deposits in Walsh County, North Dakota. The initial glaciation of this area produced a continuous cover of till over sedimentary bedrock. The till cover is thinner in the ground moraine area covering the higher elevations of bedrock and thicker on the end moraine. The waters of glacial Lake Agassiz covered about 60 percent of this county (including most of the Edinburg Moraine) to depths ranging to at least 135 m. As lake waters receded, at least 10 beach ridges were formed, with at least four of them concentrated in the portion of the figure labeled "beach lines and delta deposits."

Figure 4.52 shows a glacial lakebed in the southeast corner of Walsh County. This area receives an average of 47 cm rainfall per year. The principal crop is hay. Note the striking mottled tone of uneven linears. The origin of these linears is not well understood. The following hypotheses have been given: (1) the linear ridges formed when the lakebed was shallow by the squeezing of soft lake sediment up into the cracks of thick lake ice; (2) the lineations resulted when wind-driven ice blocks moved over the lake and dragged on the soft sediments of the nearly flat lake floor; (3) the lineations are shoreline features; (4) the lineations are an unusual form of permafrost patterned ground or fracture fillings formed in lake ice; (5) the lineations result from the cracking

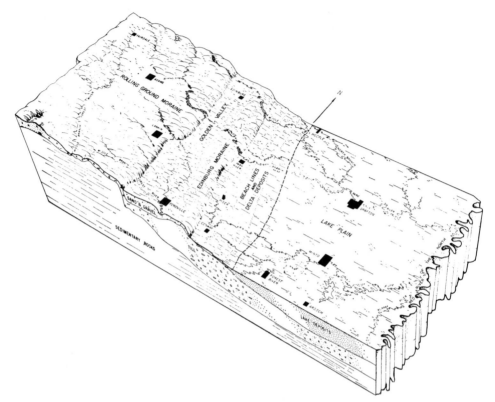

FIGURE 4.51   Schematic diagram illustrating the relationships among lakebed, shoreline, and till deposits in Walsh County, North Dakota. (From USDA–ASCS [28].)

of clay soils upon drying; and (6) lineations are reflections of bedrock jointing. The most recent (1972) USDA-SCS soil survey [28] recognizes the existence of an irregular pattern of ridges only 15 to 30 cm high that are separated by slightly concave areas, but both the lower and higher areas are included in the same soil map unit. The lakebed soils in this figure are very poorly drained, with 75 cm of silty clay over varved lacustrine clay, and have a seasonal water table within 90 to 150 cm of the ground surface.

Beach ridges are often, although not always, present at the margins of glacial lakebeds where they have been formed by wave action. Large beach ridges are likely to be associated with rising water levels and the advance of shorelines upon the land, because of continuous reworking and concentration of beach sediment. A series of small ridges is more commonly associated with receding shorelines.

Beach ridge soils are typically excessively drained sand and gravel. Beach ridges are often important sources of construction materials in glacial lakebed areas. Also, beach

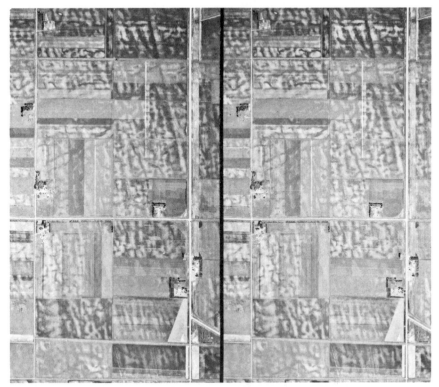

FIGURE 4.52 Glacial lakebed, Walsh County, North Dakota, July 1962. 1:36,400. Stereogram. (USDA−ASCS photos.)

ridges provide suitable foundation strength and can serve as the location for transportation routes where construction on lakebed soils would cause severe problems.

Airphoto Identification of Beach Ridges

Topography: Individual ridges can be as large as 5 to 10 m high, 200 to 1000 m wide, and many kilometers long. A series of small ridges left by receding waters is typically 1 to 2 m high, less than 100 m wide, and of variable length. Beach ridges are asymmetrical in cross section with a smooth, steep slope facing the lake and an irregular, gentle slope away from it. *Drainage and erosion:* Well drained internally due to coarse-textured soil. Few gullies. In the case of large individual ridges, the upslope area adjacent to the beach ridge may be wet as the beach ridge acts as a small dam blocking drainage. Occasional streams may cross the ridge. Some water flows through the base of the ridge and may leave a wet area immediately in front of the ridge. In the case of a series of ridges, the areas between the ridges are often very wet with a groundwater table at or near the surface. *Photo tone, vegetation, and land use:* Often contrast with less well drained soils to either side of the beach ridge.

Figure 4.53 shows an individual beach ridge in Niagara County, New York, 13 km south of the present shoreline of Lake Ontario. Most of Niagara County was once covered by a glacial lake. At one stage in the successive lowering of the lake levels to the present level of Lake Ontario, about 12,000 years ago, glacial "Lake Iroquois" had its shoreline at the location of this figure. The resulting beach ridge is 5 to 6 m high, 300 to 600 m wide, and many kilometers long. Note that a major highway and several houses are located on the beach ridge whereas there are no houses and only minor roads on either side of the ridge. The beach ridge soils are excessively drained sand and

FIGURE 4.53 Beach ridge in a humid climate, Niagara County, New York, August 1958. 1:20,000. Stereogram. (USDA—ASCS photos.)

gravel containing 20 to 45 percent gravel, 45 to 65 percent sand, and 0 to 25 percent silt and clay. These soils are warm and dry in the early spring and provide very good growing conditions for early fruit and vegetable crops. To the left of the beach ridge are poorly drained to very poorly drained lakebed soils (very fine sand, silt, and clay), deposited during a higher lake level, which are not suited to growing fruit (note the complete lack of orchards to the left of the beach ridge). The dark-toned area just at the right-hand edge of the beach ridge is a poorly drained to very poorly drained area of fine sand where groundwater seeping under the beach ridge emerges. The far right-hand portion of the figure is somewhat poorly drained, loamy-textured, shallow-water lakebed deposits over till. Some fruit is grown on these soils, but they are not as well suited for this purpose as the beach ridge soils.

Figure 4.54 shows a series of more than a dozen small beach ridges along Lake Michigan. These ridges are less than 2 m high, sandy, and mostly tree covered (pines, spruce, and fir). The interridge depressions have a groundwater table at or near the surface most of the year and have principally marsh vegetation (sedges and grasses).

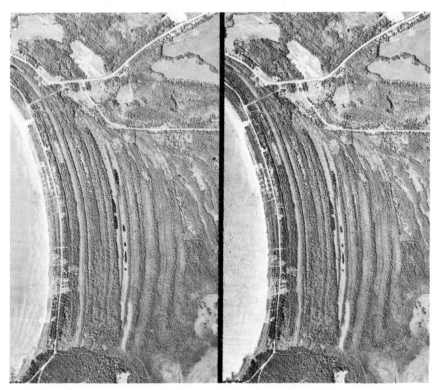

FIGURE 4.54 Beach ridges in a humid climate, Door County, Wisconsin, September 1961. 1:25,000. Stereogram. (USDA–ASCS photos.)

Soils in the interridge areas are highly organic (mostly peat). Toward the right-hand portion of the figure, where the deposits are older, many shrubs and trees (tamarack, ash, and willow) are growing on the wet organic soils. The flat-topped hill in the upper right-hand portion of the figure, which rises 20 m above the surrounding terrain, is horizontally bedded dolomite with a thin veneer (less than 1 m thick) of well-drained sandy loam till.

4.11   FLUVIAL LANDFORMS

Fluvial landforms are created by the erosion, transportation, and deposition of unconsolidated materials by the action of flowing water. The principal fluvial landforms to be described are alluvial fans, flood plains, and deltas.

The ability of flowing water to erode and transport soil and rock particles depends on water velocity and particle size, as shown in Figure 4.55. It requires a greater velocity to erode particles than it does to keep them moving (transportation). As velocities fall below a certain value, deposition takes place. The larger particles are bounced and rolled along the stream bed *(bed load)*. The smaller particles are picked up and carried forward in suspension *(suspended load)*. Certain particles, especially sand-sized particles, may travel by suspension or as a bed load at different times, depending on the stream velocity. Small particles require a considerable velocity to erode them, but, once moving, can be transported in suspension over a wide range of stream velocities. The greatest erosion and transportation of sediments takes place during floods. The increase in velocity and volume of water results in an increase in both the size and volume of materials that can be transported.

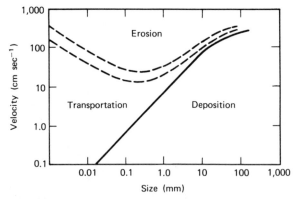

FIGURE 4.55 Relationships among erosion, transportation, and deposition as a function of stream velocity and particle size. (Modified from Twidale [26].)

The term *stream competence* refers to the maximum-size particles a stream can transport at a given velocity. *Stream capacity* refers to the maximum amount of materials the stream can transport and is related to stream volume. A small, rapid stream can move relatively large particles, and while its competence is great, the amount of material that can be moved (capacity) is small. A large, slow-moving stream may carry in suspension a great quantity of small particles and have a small competence but a large capacity.

As shown in Figure 4.55, deposition takes place selectively by particle size as the stream velocity decreases. Rapidly flowing mountain streams often deposit sand and gravel as *alluvial fans* at the base of the mountains as the stream velocities decrease and the streams are no longer competent to transport such large size particles. Streams flowing on *flood plains* will deposit much material both along their channels and by overbank flooding. As streams enter lakes or oceans, *deltas* are often formed as a result of the rapid decrease in stream velocity. The description of each of these landforms follows.

Alluvial Fans

Alluvial fans occur at the base of steep slopes where streams discharge into an area having a more subdued relief. The fans are built of coarse-textured materials eroded from the higher elevations and transported downslope. As stream velocities decrease upon flowing from the upland area, the streams are no longer competent to transport the larger sized particles and deposition occurs. Stream channels are relatively fixed at their canyon mouth but are free to wander downslope, forming a braided pattern. As this process proceeds over a long period of time, the fan builds upward and outward with the stream swinging over perhaps 90° right and left until a surprisingly symmetrical and uniform alluvial fan has been formed.

Alluvial fans are best developed in arid areas at the base of high mountain ranges. Approximately 30 percent of the land area of the southwest United States is covered by alluvial fans that can be up to 15 km long and several hundred meters thick. In humid areas alluvial fans are smaller, typically only a few hundred meters long. Slopes on alluvial fans are in the 2 to 15 percent range, with steeper slopes at the head of the fan and gentler slopes near the base.

Alluvial fan materials are principally sand and gravel, with some silt. Alluvial fans are often the only source of water in arid areas. The surface water percolates into the ground and the porous soil mass acts as an underground storage reservoir. Shallow wells are best located near the base of the fans where the depth to water is least and there may be some pressure head.

Alluvial fan soils provide good foundation conditions for highways and buildings. The sloping terrain provides good view sites for subdivision development and the location below mountain valleys may provide a cooling breeze at night. However, the shifting stream channels and frequent flooding that can occur on alluvial fans present serious limitations to development. Major sections of the Alaska Highway have been rerouted following destruction of the original road crossing alluvial fans. Subdivisions in the Denver area and several southern California locations have been severely damaged by shifting alluvial fan distributary channels.

Airphoto Identification of Alluvial Fans

Topography: Fan-shaped, with a slope of 2 to 15 percent away from apex. *Drainage and erosion:* Excellent internal drainage. Limited surface drainage system with few gullies. Numerous distributary (constructional) channels. *Photo tone:* Generally light; distributary channels may be darker. *Vegetation and land use:* General lack of vegetation along active distributary channels; may be heavier vegetation at base of fan due to groundwater seepage. Humid areas often cultivated; natural vegetation on fan may contrast with adjacent landforms.

Figure 4.56 shows coalescing alluvial fans along the western edge of Death Valley. The slope of the alluvial surface is 12 percent in the mountain valley, 10 percent at the apex of the fan, and 8 percent at the base of the fan. Numerous distributary channels are clearly visible on the photograph. Note the darker tone and presence of vegetation near the base of the fan (resulting from higher soil moisture content) and the topographic and tonal contrast between the base of the fan and the adjacent light-toned valley floor.

Flood Plains

Flood plains are depositional landforms created by the processes of stream meandering and overbank flooding. Stream meandering is the result of a stream's adjustment to its environment in order to carry its load most efficiently. Meandering streams tend to follow certain mathematical rules with regard to meander wavelength, meander amplitude, stream flow volume, stream flow velocity, channel width, channel depth, flood plain slope, and river gradient.

Because water velocities are highest there, river banks normally erode on the outside and downstream side of each curve, though during high flow periods the river tends to follow a straighter course and erode on the inside of the curves. The inside of each curve is normally a place of deposition of gravel and sand called a *point bar deposit.* As the radius of river meanders becomes larger, a point is reached where meanders are cut off and an abandoned meander called an *oxbow* remains. When oxbows are filled with standing water, they are called *oxbow lakes.* Meanders tend to migrate, both laterally and downslope, which also results in shifting channel patterns.

Streams on a flood plain often overflow their banks and, as they do, some alluvial material is deposited just outside the normal stream channel as a *natural levee.* Natural levees are too small to be noticed on many streams. However, large rivers such as the Mississippi often have prominent levees. Artificial levees are sometimes constructed atop natural levees to protect flood plains from subsequent flooding. If a river restrained by an artificial levee cannot overflow its banks and deposit its sediment load on

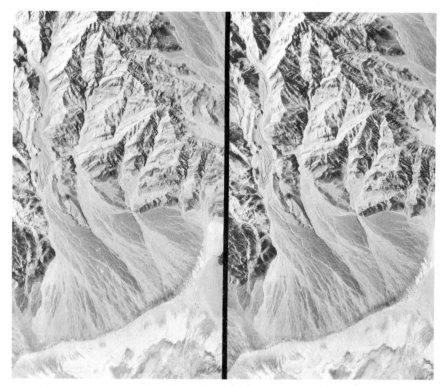

FIGURE 4.56 Alluvial fans in an arid climate, Inyo County, California (Death Valley), October 1952. 1:75,000. Stereogram. (USGS photos.)

the floodplain, it tends to deposit materials in its own channel. This new sediment tends to raise the level of the riverbed. To prevent the next flood from overflowing, the artificial levee must be constructed even higher. Artificial levee construction on one stretch of a river may lead to increased flooding on other stretches of the river. Overbank flooding results when streams overflow their levees and slow-moving waters cover much of the flood plain. Deposits from these slow-moving waters are called *slack water deposits* (also called *backswamp deposits*).

Flood plain terrain has an overall level relief with minor irregularities and a gentle downstream gradient. The texture of flood plain materials varies greatly because they have slowly accumulated over years of shifting stream courses and overbank flooding. Point bar deposits consist principally of gravel and sand. Natural levees contain principally sand and silt. Oxbows often contain standing water or very poorly drained organic soils. Slack water deposits are usually poorly drained silts and clays. The depth to bedrock is variable, depending on the nature of the buried terrain. Wider flood plains generally have greater depths to bedrock. Using airphoto interpretation, the present surface soils can be effectively estimated, but it must be realized that materials will vary with depth because a variety of flood plain features can lie buried beneath the present land surface.

Development on flood plains must proceed with extreme caution. Annual losses of life and property on flood plains are staggering. In addition to the danger of flooding, serious foundation limitations are imposed by the extremely variable soils and and high groundwater table. If development is to take place on flood plains, it must be preceded by a careful study of the soils present, the internal soil drainage and groundwater conditions, and the frequency and severity of flooding that can be expected. Flood plains are better suited to agricultural or parkland uses that can withstand periodic flooding with comparatively low losses.

Mapping of flood plains for developmental planning and flood insurance purposes has received major emphasis in the United States. In this process, the *floodway* (area covered by a flood) is delineated for floods occurring with a given probability. The determination of the limits of a given flood often incorporates flood plain terrain evaluation, topographic mapping through photogrammetric techniques, and hydrologic modeling.

Airphoto Identification of Flood Plains

Topography: Generally level with small downstream gradient. Natural levees slightly higher position. Slack water deposits in lowest position. *Drainage and erosion:* A principal stream flows on its flood plain. On wide flood plains, secondary streams may be present near the outer edges of the flood plain (yazoo streams) and flow a considerable distance before connecting with the principal stream. Because groundwater tables are high and the terrain level, and because of periodic flooding on the flood plain, there is seldom an integrated drainage pattern connected with the principal stream. *Photo tone:* A complex pattern of tones is present, reflecting the variety of soil and moisture conditions. Point bar deposits have a light tone that may alternate with darker-toned depressions between point bars. Natural levees are lighter-toned than surrounding slack water deposits. Slack water deposits are darker-toned, often with distinct artificial drainage features. Oxbows have a uniform gray tone if filled with standing water, or a darker tone if occupied by organic soils. *Vegetation and land use:* Often agricultural use, especially drained slack water deposits. Natural marsh or swamp vegetation in organic oxbow deposits. Point bar deposits that flood annually may be barren; those that flood only occasionally may be farmed.

Figure 4.57 is a photo mosaic (note photo numbers at upper right of each frame) showing a portion of the flood plain of the White River. The shifting channels of the river can be clearly seen (note numerous oxbows). Figure 4.58 shows a portion of the area covered in Figure 4.57 (photo QQ-IV-74). The present course of the stream meanders across the top of Figure 4.58. The trees immediately below the river are growing on a small natural levee. Numerous arc-shaped point bar deposits can be seen in the upper right of the figure below the river. These are small, well-drained, sandy rises with a nearly white photo tone. In the lower center of the figure are two well-developed oxbows. These contain standing water for part of the year, but are gradually becoming filled with organic material. In the lower left of the figure are poorly drained slack water deposits with a clay loam texture. Note the striped pattern caused by numerous ditches constructed to drain these soils to allow cultivation.

Deltas

Deltas form where streams discharge into bodies of quiet water (lakes and oceans). The stream velocity rapidly decreases and deposition of sediment takes place.

Most deltas have shifting multiple distributary channels (analogous to alluvial fans) and form fan shapes, as in the case of the Nile Delta. Such deltas are called *arcuate deltas*. Streams carrying a large load of silt and clay tend to flow within a few relatively stable distributary channels confined by natural levees (analogous to river flood plains) and to form branching deltas, as in the case of the Mississippi Delta. Such deltas are called *birdfoot deltas*.

Arcuate delta soils typically contain a great deal of sand with some gravel. Arcuate deltas deposited in former glacial lakes are often used as sources of sand and gravel for construction activities. Arcuate deltas protruding into present-day lakes often make excellent sites for recreational development. Topography is favorable for active sports, lake access is convenient, sloping sandy beaches may be present, and occasional flooding from distributary channels can be tolerated. Power plants often compete with recreational uses for space on arcuate deltas as site conditions are also favorable for power plant location, as long as potential flooding is taken into account in site design.

Birdfoot delta site conditions present limitations to development because soil and drainage are extremely variable, as in the case of river flood plains, and the delta is subject to overbank flooding. The use of birdfoot deltas for agriculture is important on a worldwide scale.

Airphoto Identification of Deltas

Topography: Nearly level surface bounded by upland areas and water. Overall arcuate or birdfoot shape. *Drainage and erosion:* Distributary streams present. Arcuate deltas have one or more main channels arranged in a fan-shaped radial pattern. Also, former distributary channels (typically braided) are present. Birdfoot deltas have one major channel plus several large branches extending in random directions. Birdfoot deltas may have numerous ponds and low wet areas. Gullies seldom present. *Photo tone:* Variable, depending on soil and moisture conditions. Arcuate deltas tend to be light-toned, with a braided pattern revealing former distributary channels. Birdfoot deltas resemble river flood plains, with natural levees, slack water deposits, and so on. *Vegetation and land use:* Variable, depending on climate and depth to water table. Some deltas used extensively for agriculture; others undisturbed marshland.

FIGURE 4.57 Flood plain in a humid climate, Knox and Gibson Counties, Indiana, August 1958. 1:76,000. (USDA−ASCS photomosaic.)

FIGURE 4.58 Flood plain in a humid climate, Gibson County, Indiana, August 1958. 1:22,200. (USDA – ASCS photo.)

Figure 4.59 shows a small arcuate delta formed where a stream flows into a deep lake. Note the recreational development on this delta.

Figure 4.60 contains two Landsat images (see Chapter 9) showing the extensive birdfoot delta of the Mississippi River. Figure 4.60a shows the river flowing within its banks and pouring vast quantities of silt into the Gulf of Mexico. Figure 4.60b shows the many distributary channels of the delta, each confined by a natural levee. Figure 9.39 and Plate 15 also show the Mississippi delta.

Figure 4.61 shows a small birdfoot delta formed where a stream flows into a shallow lake. Note that the natural levee of the stream carries well into the lake, forming the birdfoot delta. Numerous cottages are located on the natural levee to the left of the stream. To both sides of the levees are very poorly drained organic soils plus some standing water with aquatic vegetation. In these early July photographs, there is a great deal of sun glitter (specular reflection) on the left photograph, making stereo-viewing somewhat distracting.

The birdfoot delta of the Po River in Italy is shown in Figures 2.26 and 2.27.

FIGURE 4.59   Arcuate delta in a humid climate, Tompkins County, New York, July 1964. 1:20,000. Stereogram. (USDA–ASCS photos.)

4.12 ORGANIC SOILS

Organic deposits are widely distributed throughout the world. They form wherever production of organic matter exceeds its mineralization, usually under conditions of almost continuous water saturation that limits the circulation of oxygen through the soil, slows the decomposition of organic matter, and permits its accumulation. The principal organic soils are muck and peat. *Muck* is dark-colored organic soil material that is partially decomposed. *Peat* is organic soil material that is relatively unde-composed with recognizable plant fragments. Peat becomes muck upon further decomposition.

Muck and peat occur in wet, low areas of the landscape in association with numerous landforms, especially in glaciated areas and on flood plains (the presence of organic soils was mentioned in several figure descriptions). The conversion of living vegetation to peat and muck is a dynamic process resulting in organic deposits of variable age, size, thickness, number of layers of materials, and stage of decomposition. Airphoto interpretation can be effectively utilized to delineate the extent and general nature of organic deposits, but field soil borings are required for information about the total thickness of the deposits and their composition at depth.

Peat soils can be described as *sedimentary peat, fibrous peat,* or *woody peat,* depending on the nature of the plant fragments. Organic soil formation typically begins in shallow lakes or ponds with aquatic vegetation (water lilies, duckweed, algae). The annual addition of decaying plants results in a soft, oozy, structureless *sedimentary peat.* As organic material builds up on the pond bottom and water depths decrease, marsh vegetation (cattails, sedges, grasses) encroaches on the pond, decreasing the open water surface and the amount of aquatic vegetation. The peat resulting from the decomposition of marsh vegetation is a *fibrous peat* with a firm but porous interwoven network of stems, roots, and leaf fragments. The final stage of native vegetation that typically establishes itself upon a layer of fibrous peat is a swamp forest (tamarack, alder, willow). Decomposition of leaves, needles, bark, twigs, and cones produces *woody peat.*

Mineral soils typically have 1.5 to 2.5 grams of solid material per cubic centimeter of soil volume (g/cc). Organic soils typically have only 0.5 g/cc solid material and have been found with densities as low as 0.1 g/cc. The volume not occupied by solid particles is occupied by water plus a small amount of air if the soils are not saturated. Mineral soils usually have a ratio of water to solids of 5 to 20 percent on a weight basis. Organic soils typically have a ratio of 100 to 500 percent, which means that there is more water than solid material in muck and peat deposits.

Muck and peat present extremely poor foundations for construction activities and should be avoided in urban and suburban development. Highways crossing muck and peat are susceptible to both soil failure and excessive settlement, unless elaborate (and expensive) design and construction procedures are utilized.

Muck and peat in suitable climates are often drained and farmed for crops such as potatos, peppermint, celery, onions, and sod for lawns. In such cases, care must be taken not to overdrain the organic soils as they are susceptible to an irreversible hardening that restricts water movement and root penetration. In addition, dry muck

(a)

FIGURE 4.60 Birdfoot delta, Mississippi River, and Gulf of Mexico below New Orleans. (a) Landsat Multispectral Scanner band 5 (red). (b) Landsat Multispectral Scanner band 7 (near-infrared). January 16, 1973. 1:1,100,000. (NASA images.)

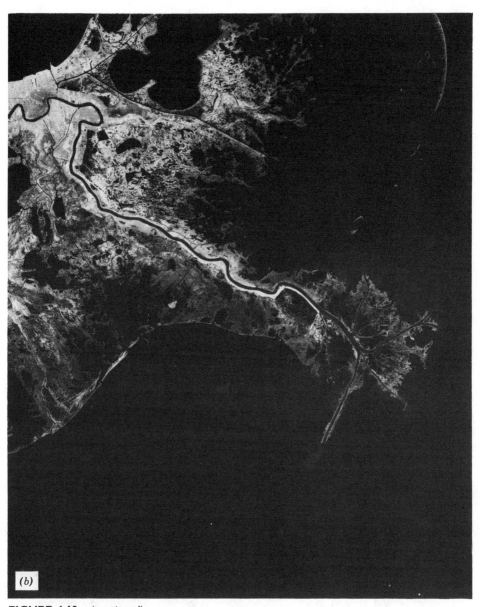

(b)

FIGURE 4.60 *(continued)*

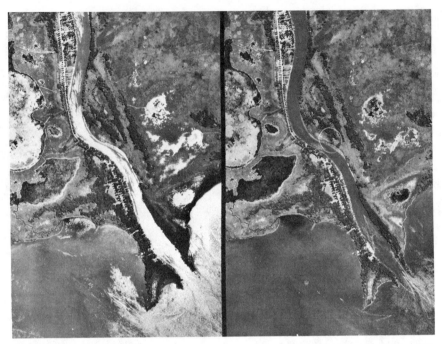

FIGURE 4.61   Birdfoot delta in a humid climate, Jefferson County, Wisconsin, July 1957. 1:28,600. Stereogram. (USDA—ASCS photos.)

and peat present a fire hazard. Fires on these materials are difficult to control and may burn for months, polluting the air and destroying the organic material. Many wetland areas with organic soils provide an important, productive wildlife habitat for both resident species and migrating birds. When such areas are drained and farmed (or dredged for other uses), important wildlife habitats are often destroyed permanently. Organic soil areas in their natural state adjacent to inland lakes often serve to trap silt and nutrients which may otherwise contribute to the eutrophication of lakes. If such areas are drained and farmed, lake water quality usually worsens.

Airphoto Identification of Organic Soils

Organic soils are found in topographic depressions in areas such as end moraine and ground moraine, flood plains (especially oxbows), depressions between sand dunes, depressions between beach ridges, limestone sinkholes, and kettle holes. *Topography:* Very flat; often sharp contrast with surrounding material. *Drainage and erosion:* Typically very poorly drained with water table at or near the ground surface for much of the year. Few gullies. Artificial drainage if drained for farming. *Photo tone; vegetation, and land use:* Bare (unvegetated) soil has a very dark tone. Native grass, sedge, and shrub vegetation has a drab gray, mottled appearance. Drained agricultural areas have a distinctive pattern (Figure 4.62) of artificial drainage ditches and intensively farmed areas.

Figure 4.62 shows organic soils in Jefferson County, Wisconsin, a county with nearly 20 percent of its land area occupied by organic soils. Organic soils occupy the left and bottom portions of the figure. The upper right portion is principally glacial till (note the well-formed drumlin at extreme upper right). A large area of organic soils has been drained and farmed, as indicated by the elaborate system of drainage ditches and intensive cultivation. The remainder of the organic soil area is in native vegetation, principally marsh grass, with some trees and shrubs. The organic soils here are fibrous peat, 2 to 5 m thick, in a former glacial lakebed. They contain 80 to 95 percent organic matter and 5 to 20 percent mineral matter.

FIGURE 4.62 Organic soils in a humid climate, Jefferson County, Wisconsin, July 1957. 1:36,400. Stereogram. (USDA–ASCS photos.)

SELECTED BIBLIOGRAPHY

1. American Geological Institute, *Dictionary of Geological Terms*, rev. ed., Anchor Press/ Doubleday, Garden City, N.Y., 1976.

2. American Society of Photogrammetry, *Manual of Photographic Interpretation*, Falls Church, Va., 1960.

3. Avery, T.E., and G.L. Berlin, *Interpretation of Aerial Photographs*, 4th ed., Burgess, Minneapolis, Minn., 1985.

4. Avery, T.E., and D.M. Richter, "An Airphoto Index to Physical and Cultural Features in Eastern U.S.," *Photogrammetric Engineering*, vol. 31, no. 5, pp. 896–914, 1965.

5. Bates, R.L., and J.A. Jackson (eds.), *Glossary of Geology*, 2nd ed., American Geological Institute, Alexandria, Va., 1980.

6. Belcher, D.J., et al., *A Photo-analysis Key for the Determination of Ground Conditions*, 6 vols., Cornell University, Ithaca, N.Y. (for U.S. Office of Naval Research), 1951.

7. Denny, C.S., et al., *A Descriptive Catalog of Selected Aerial Photographs of Geologic Features in the United States*, USGS Professional Paper 590, U.S. Govt. Printing Office, Washington, D.C., 1968.

8. Garver, J.B., and H.A. Curran, *Atlas of Landforms*, 3rd ed., Wiley, New York, 1984.

9. Hurlbut, C.S. (ed.), *The Planet We Live on—Illustrated Encyclopedia of Earth Sciences*, Harry N. Abrams, New York, 1976.

10. Kiefer, R.W., "Landform Features in the United States," *Photogrammetric Engineering*, vol. 33, no. 2, pp. 174–182, 1967.

11. Kiefer, R.W., "Terrain Analysis for Metropolitan Fringe Area Planning," *Journal of the Urban Planning and Development Division*, ASCE, vol. 93, no. UP4, Proc. Paper 5649, December 1967, pp. 119–139.

12. Leuder, D.R., *Aerial Photographic Interpretation*, McGraw–Hill, New York, 1959.

13. Macdonald, G.A., A.T. Abbott, and F.L., Peterson, *Volcanoes in the Sea—The Geology of Hawaii*, 2nd ed., Univ. of Hawaii Press, Honolulu, 1983.

14. Miller, V.C., *Photogeology*, McGraw–Hill, New York, 1961.

15. Mollard, J.D., "Techniques of Aerial-Photographic Study," *Reviews in Engineering Geology*, vol. 1, pp. 105–127, Geological Society of America, Reston, Va., 1962.

16. Mollard, J.D., and J.R. Janes, *Airphoto Interpretation and the Canadian Landscape*, Canadian Govt. Publishing Centre, Hull, Quebec, 1984.

17. Parvis, M., "Drainage Pattern Significance in Airphoto Identification of Soils and Bedrocks," *Photogrammetric Engineering*, vol. 16, 1950, pp. 387–409.

18. Ray, R.G., *Aerial Photographs in Geologic Interpretation and Mapping*, USGS Professional Paper 373, U.S. Govt. Printing Office, Washington, D.C., 1960.

19. Richter, D.M., "An Airphoto Index to Physical and Cultural Features in Western U.S.," *Photogrammetric Engineering*, vol. 33, no. 12, pp. 1402–1419, 1967.

20. Sauer, E.K., "Hydrogeology of Glacial Deposits from Aerial Photographs," *Photogrammetric Engineering and Remote Sensing*, vol. 47, no. 6, June 1981, pp. 811–822.

21. Shelton, J.S., *Geology Illustrated*, Freeman, San Francisco, 1966.

22. Siegal, B.B., and A.R. Gillespie, *Remote Sensing in Geology*, Wiley, New York, 1980.

23. Strahler, A.N., *Physical Geography*, 4th ed., Wiley, New York, 1975.

24. Sullivan, W., *Landprints*, Times Books, New York, 1984.

25. Thorbury, W.D., *Principles of Geomorphology*, 2nd ed., Wiley, New York, 1969.

26. Twidale, C.R., *Analysis of Landforms*, Wiley, New York, 1976.

27. U.S. Department of Agriculture, *Soil Survey Manual*, USDA Handbook 18, U.S. Govt. Printing Office, Washington, D.C., August 1951.

28. USDA–SCS, *Soil Survey of Walsh County, North Dakota*, USDA in cooperation with the North Dakota Agricultural Experiment Station, U.S. Govt. Printing Office, Washington, D.C., September 1972.

29. von Bandat, H.F., *Aerogeology*, Gulf Pub. Co., Houston, Tex, 1962.

30. Way, D., *Terrain Analysis, A Guide to Site Selection Using Aerial Photographic Interpretation*, 2nd ed., Dowden, Hutchinson & Ross, Stroudsburg, Pa., 1978.

CHAPTER
FIVE

PHOTOGRAMMETRY

5.1 INTRODUCTION

Photogrammetry is the science, art, and technology of obtaining reliable measurements and maps from photographs. The principles of photogrammetry are important to the photo interpreter because they are essential to *quantifying* interpreted terrain features in terms of their location and extent. This quantification process is significant because the interpreter's concern for *what* is present in imagery is almost always accompanied with a concern for *where* interpreted items are on the ground and over *what areal extent*. Photogrammetry deals primarily with these last two concerns.

Photogrammetric analysis procedures can range from obtaining approximate distances and elevations using relatively unsophisticated equipment and simple geometric concepts to obtaining extremely precise maps and measurements using sophisticated instrumentation and complex computational techniques. Although most applications of photogrammetry involve aerial photographs, terrestrial photographs (taken from earth-based cameras) may also be used. Applications of terrestrial photogrammetric techniques range from accurately recording the scene of an automobile accident to mapping the human body in medical studies.

The most common use of photogrammetry is in the preparation of topographic maps. For example, virtually all USGS quadrangle maps are prepared photogrammetrically. Likewise, photogrammetry stands as the workhorse for mapping in engineering, forestry, geography, geology, planning, soil science, and a host of other fields.

In this chapter, we introduce only the most basic aspects of the broad subject of photogrammetry. Our objective is to provide the student with a fundamental understanding of how aerial photographs can be used to measure and map earth surface features. We discuss the following photogrammetric activities.

1. *Determining horizontal ground distances and angles from measurements made on a vertical photograph.* In Section 2.14, we introduced the concept of scale variation and relief displacement for photographs taken over areas of varied relief. In this chapter, we illustrate how to compensate for these relief effects when making distance and angle measurements on photographs. This involves measuring the xy coordinates of image points on the photograph and projecting them into a ground coordinate system. This projection requires knowledge of the terrain

300

elevation at each point, from which the local photo scale is found. The conversion to ground coordinates is then performed by simply dividing the photocoordinates for any given point by the local scale at the point. Once the endpoints of a line are located in the ground coordinate plane, relief distortions are eliminated and one can mathematically derive the length and bearing (compass direction) of the line. The angle between two lines may be similarly determined.

2. *Determination of object heights from relief displacement measurement.* Relief effects are often bothersome in the interpretation process, yet they can be useful in many cases. For example, they permit the interpreter to measure the heights of vertical objects appearing on a photograph. Recall that because of the perspective view of an aerial photograph, only features lying directly beneath the photo principal point are imaged in a maplike top view. Away from the center of the photograph, relief displacement causes features to appear to lean away radially from the center of the photograph (Figure 2.45). The magnitude of relief displacement depends on the flying height, the distance from the photo principal point to the feature, and the height of the feature. Because these factors are geometrically related, we can measure an object's relief displacement and radial position on a photograph and thereby determine the height of the object. This technique provides limited accuracy, but is useful in applications where only approximate object heights are needed.

3. *Determination of object heights and terrain elevations by measurement of image parallax.* The previous operations are performed using vertical photos individually. Many photogrammetric operations involve analyzing images in the area of overlap of a stereopair. Within this area, we have two views of the same terrain, taken from different vantage points. Between these two views, the relative positions of features lying closer to the camera (at higher elevation) will change more from photo to photo than the positions of features farther from the camera (at lower elevation). This change in relative position is called *parallax*. It can be measured on overlapping photographs and used to determine object heights and terrain elevations.

4. *Use of ground control points.* The accuracy of photogrammetric measurements is premised on the use of *ground control*. These are points that can be accurately located on the photograph and for which we have information on their ground coordinates and/or elevations. This information is used as "geometric ground truth" to calibrate photo measurements. For example, we commonly use ground control to determine the true (slightly tilted) angular orientation of a photograph, the flying height of a photograph, and the airbase of a pair of overlapping photographs (the distance between successive photo centers). This information is critical in a host of photogrammetric operations.

5. *Generation of maps in stereoplotters.* A *stereoplotter* is an instrument designed for the production of topographic maps from stereopairs. With this type of instrument, the photographs are mounted in special projectors that can be mutually oriented to precisely correspond to the angular tilts present when the photographs were taken. Once oriented properly, the projectors recreate an accurate model of

the terrain that, when viewed stereoscopically, can be used to plot a planimetric map having no relief distortions. In addition, topographic contours can be plotted on the map and the height of vertical features appearing in the model can be determined.

6. *Generation of orthophotographs.*   A stereoplotter is designed to transfer *map* information, without distortions, from stereophotographs. A similar device can be used to transfer *image* information, with distortions removed. The resulting undistorted image is called an *orthophotograph*. Orthophotos combine the geometric utility of a map with the extra information provided by a photograph. Frequently, a map showing cultural features or contours is overprinted onto the orthophoto, creating a "photomap."

7. *Preparation of a flight plan to acquire aerial photography.*   Whenever new photographic coverage of an area is to be obtained, a photographic flight mission must be planned. This process begins with selecting an image scale, camera lens and format size, and desired image overlap. The flight planner can then determine such geometric factors as the appropriate flying height, the distance between image centers, the direction and spacing of flight lines, and the number of images required to cover the study area. Based on these factors, a flight map and a list of specifications are prepared for the firm providing the photographic services.

Each of these photogrammetric operations is covered in separate sections in this chapter. We first discuss some general geometric concepts that are basic to these techniques.

5.2   GEOMETRIC ELEMENTS OF A VERTICAL PHOTOGRAPH

Many basic photogrammetric procedures involve the use of *vertical* photographs. As discussed earlier (Section 2.12), vertical photographs are those taken with the camera axis directed as vertically as possible. For a truly vertical photograph, the camera axis would be in perfect alignment with the direction of gravity. Because of unavoidable angular tilts of the aircraft during the instant of exposure, virtually all aerial photographs are slightly tilted. However, unintentional tilts are normally less than 1° and rarely greater than 3°. For many photogrammetric operations such tilts are negligible and the resulting photos are treated as being truly vertical without serious error.

The basic geometric elements of a vertical aerial photograph are depicted in Figure 5.1. Light rays from terrain objects are imaged in the plane of the film negative after intersecting at the camera lens exposure station, L. The negative is located behind the lens at a distance equal to the lens focal length, f. Assuming the size of a paper print positive (or film positive) equal to that of the negative, positive image positions can be depicted diagrammatically in front of the lens in a plane located at a distance f. This rendition is appropriate in that most photo positives used for measurement purposes are contact printed, resulting in the geometric relationships shown.

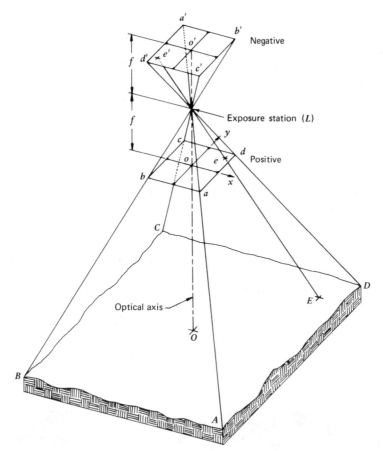

FIGURE 5.1 Basic geometric elements of a vertical photograph.

The x and y coordinate positions of image points are referenced with respect to axes formed by straight lines joining the opposite fiducial marks recorded on the positive (Figure 2.23). The x axis is arbitrarily assigned to the fiducial axis most nearly coincident with the line of flight, and is taken as positive in the forward direction of flight. The positive y axis is located 90° counterclockwise from the positive x axis. Because of the precision with which the fiducial marks and the lens are placed in a metric camera, the photocoordinate origin, o, can be assumed to coincide exactly with the *principal point*, the intersection of the lens optical axis and the film plane. The point where the prolongation of the optical axis of the camera intersects the terrain is referred to as the *ground principal point*, O. Images for terrain points A, B, C, D, and E appear geometrically reversed on the negative at a', b', c', d', and e' and in proper geometric relationship on the positive at a, b, c, d, and e. (Throughout this chapter we refer to points on the image with lowercase letters and corresponding points on the terrain with uppercase letters.)

The xy photocoordinates of a point are the perpendicular distances from the xy coordinate axes. Points to the right of the y axis have positive x coordinates and points to the left have negative x coordinates. Similarly, points above the x axis have positive y coordinates and those below have negative y coordinates.

Measurements of photocoordinates may be obtained using any one of many measurement devices. These devices vary in their accuracy, cost, and availability. For rudimentary photogrammetric problems—where low orders of measurement accuracy are acceptable—a triangular *engineer's scale* or *metric scale* may be used. When using these scales, measurement accuracy is generally improved by taking the average of several repeated measurements. Measurements are also generally more accurate when made with the aid of a magnifying lens. Movable magnifying eyepieces are built-in features of *glass scales* (Figure 5.2). Because of their dimensional stability, glass scales are generally more accurate than conventional scales. Photographic measurements may also be obtained with a *coordinate digitizer* (Figures 3.11 and 3.47). This device continuously displays the xy positions of a special reference mark as it is positioned anywhere on the photograph.

The extreme in accuracy of photocoordinate measurement is obtainable with a precision instrument called a *comparator*. Figure 5.3 illustrates a *monocomparator*, which is used to make measurements on one photograph at a time. *Stereocomparators*

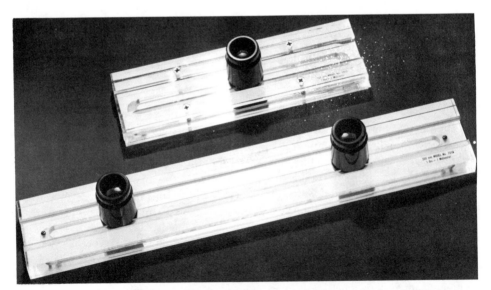

FIGURE 5.2 Glass scales for photographic measurements. Readings on scale etched in glass are taken through magnifying eyepieces that slide along the scales. (Courtesy Teledyne–Gurley Co.)

FIGURE 5.3 Kern model MK #2 monocomparator. (Courtesy Kern and Co., Inc.)

are also available for making measurements on stereo photographs. Comparators are used primarily to obtain precise (on the order of 1 to 5 μm) photocoordinate measurements necessary for analytic photogrammetry (Section 5.12).

Irrespective of what device is used to measure photocoordinates, these measurements contain errors of varying sources and magnitudes. These errors stem from sources such as camera lens distortions, atmospheric refraction, earth curvature, failure of the fiducial axes to intersect at the principal point, and shrinkage or expansion of the photographic material on which measurements are made. Sophisticated photogrammetric analyses include corrections for all these errors. For simple measurements made on paper prints, usually only a correction for shrinkage or expansion of the paper is made. This is true because errors introduced by slight tilt in the photography will outweigh the effect of the other distortions.

The shrinkage or expansion of a paper print can be determined by comparing the measured distances between opposite fiducial marks on a print with their corresponding values obtained during camera calibration. The ratio of these distances is then used as a correction factor to be applied to each x and y photocoordinate employed in any subsequent analysis.

EXAMPLE 5.1

The calibrated x and y fiducial distances for a camera are 233.48 and 233.78 mm. The corresponding x and y measured distances on a photographic print from this camera are 232.37 and 232.36 mm. The uncorrected x and y photocoordinates of a point measure 101.63 and 94.32 mm. Find the corrected photocoordinates of the point.

Solution

$$\text{Correction factor for } x = \frac{\text{calibrated distance}}{\text{measured distance}} = \frac{233.48}{232.37} = 1.0048$$

$$\text{Correction factor for } y = \frac{\text{calibrated distance}}{\text{measured distance}} = \frac{233.78}{232.36} = 1.0061$$

$$\text{Corrected } x \text{ coordinate} = 1.0048 \times 101.63 = 102.12 \text{ mm}$$

$$\text{Corrected } y \text{ coordinate} = 1.0061 \times 94.32 = 94.90 \text{ mm}$$

5.3 DETERMINING HORIZONTAL GROUND LENGTHS, DIRECTIONS, AND ANGLES FROM PHOTOCOORDINATES

In Figure 5.1, we illustrated the geometry of a vertical photograph taken over flat terrain. In such a case, the photograph will accurately represent the geometry of the imaged terrain. Like a map, the photograph will be characterized by a constant scale. Distances measured on the photograph may therefore be converted to ground lengths by simply dividing by the photo scale. Similarly, angles may be directly measured on the photograph.

Figure 5.4 illustrates the geometry of a photograph taken over terrain of varied relief. In this figure, the datum plane has been set at the average terrain elevation (not at mean sea level). If all terrain points were to lie at this common elevation, terrain points A and B would be located at A' and B', and would be imaged at points a' and b' on the photograph. Due to the varied relief, however, the position of point A is shifted radially outward on the photograph (to a), and the position of point B is shifted radially inward (to b). These changes in image position are the relief displacements of points A and B. Figure 5.4b illustrates the effect they have on the geometry of the photo. Because A' and B' lie at the same terrain elevation, the image line $a'b'$ accurately represents the scaled horizontal length and orientation of the ground line AB. When the relief displacements are introduced, the resulting line ab has a considerably altered length and orientation.

Angles are also distorted by relief displacements. In Figure 5.4b, the horizontal ground angle ACB is accurately expressed by $a'cb'$ on the photo. Due to the displacements, the distorted angle acb will appear on the photograph. Note that, because of the radial nature of relief displacements, angles about the origin of the photo (such as aob) will not be distorted.

When points lie at different elevations, lengths and angles can be computed indirectly by the following method. First, the photocoordinates of points on the

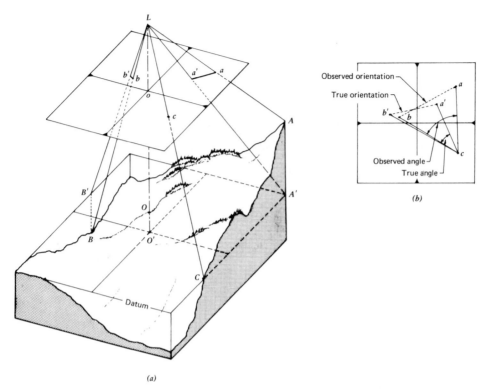

FIGURE 5.4 Relief displacement on a photograph taken over varied terrain. *(a)* Displacement of terrain points. *(b)* Distortion of horizontal angles measured on photograph.

photograph are converted to a datum-level ground coordinate system. This involves multiplying the photocoordinates of each point by the inverse of the image scale *at that point*. (Note that this requires knowledge of the terrain elevation at each point.) Once the points are located in the ground coordinate system, the relief effects are eliminated. Lengths, directions, and angles may therefore be mathematically computed from the ground coordinates.

Figure 5.5 illustrates the geometry associated with determining the ground coordinates from measured photocoordinates. The exposure station is at flying height H above datum, and terrain points A and B lie at elevations h_A and h_B above datum. As shown in the figure, arbitrary X and Y ground coordinates are defined directly beneath the photographic x and y axes at the datum elevation. The ground coordinates (X_A, Y_A) and (X_B, Y_B) can be calculated based on measurement of photocoordinates (x_a, y_a) and (x_b, y_b) as described below.

From similar triangles LO_AA' and Loa',

$$\frac{x_a}{X_A} = \frac{f}{H - h_A}$$

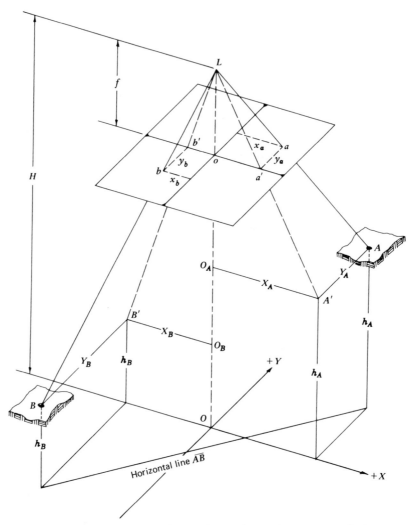

FIGURE 5.5 Determination of ground coordinates from measured photocoordinates.

from which we obtain

$$X_A = \frac{(H - h_A)}{f} x_a \qquad (5.1)$$

From similar triangles $LA'A$ and $La'a$,

$$\frac{y_a}{Y_A} = \frac{f}{H - h_A}$$

from which we obtain

$$Y_A = \frac{(H - h_A)}{f} y_a \tag{5.2}$$

Note that $(H - h_A)/f$ is the reciprocal of the scale at point A. Thus, as mentioned previously, the conversion to ground coordinates simply involves multiplying by the inverse of the photo scale at the point under consideration. Consequently, the ground coordinates for point B can be expressed as

$$X_B = \frac{(H - h_B)}{f} x_b \tag{5.3}$$

and

$$Y_B = \frac{(H - h_B)}{f} y_b \tag{5.4}$$

Given the ground coordinates of points A and B, the horizontal length of the line AB may be mathematically determined using the Pythagorean theorem. As shown in Figure 5.6, the line AB represents the hypotenuse of a right triangle whose legs are equal to $(X_A - X_B)$ and $(Y_A - Y_B)$. By the Pythagorean theorem,

$$AB = [(X_A - X_B)^2 + (Y_A - Y_B)^2]^{1/2} \tag{5.5}$$

EXAMPLE 5.2

With reference to Figure 5.5, assume that the vertical photograph depicted was taken from an altitude of 964 m above datum with a 152.4 mm focal length camera. The photographic coordinates for ground points A and B measure as $x_a = +46.82$ mm, $y_a = +53.64$ mm, $x_b = -35.51$ mm, and $y_b = -43.17$ mm. The elevations of points A and B are known to be 213 m and 152 m above datum. Find the horizontal length of ground line AB.

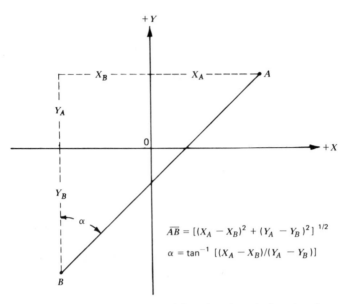

FIGURE 5.6 Determination of line length and direction from ground coordinates.

Solution

Using Eqs. 5.1 through 5.4,

$$X_A = \frac{(H - h_A)}{f} x_a = \frac{(964 - 213)}{152.4} 46.82 = 230.72 \text{ m}$$

$$Y_A = \frac{(H - h_A)}{f} y_a = \frac{(964 - 213)}{152.4} 53.64 = 264.33 \text{ m}$$

$$X_B = \frac{(H - h_B)}{f} x_b = -\frac{(964 - 152)}{152.4} 35.51 = -189.20 \text{ m}$$

$$Y_B = \frac{(H - h_B)}{f} y_b = -\frac{(964 - 152)}{152.4} 43.17 = -230.01 \text{ m}$$

From Eq. 5.5,

$$AB = [(230.72 + 189.20)^2 + (264.33 + 230.01)^2]^{1/2} = 649 \text{ m}$$

The direction of ground line AB with respect to the ground coordinate axis system can also be found from the ground coordinates. Considering the direction to be a clockwise angular departure of a line from the direction of the $+Y$ axis, the direction of

AB is labeled as the angle α in Figure 5.6. This angle may be found trigonometrically from the ground coordinates as

$$\text{direction } B \text{ to } A = \alpha = \tan^{-1}\left(\frac{X_A - X_B}{Y_A - Y_B}\right) \tag{5.6}$$

EXAMPLE 5.3

For the previous example, determine the direction of the line from point B to A with respect to the $+Y$ ground axis.

Solution

Using the coordinates computed in Example 5.2

$$\alpha = \tan^{-1}\left(\frac{230.7 + 189.2}{264.3 + 230.0}\right) = 40°21'$$

5.4 RELIEF DISPLACEMENT OF VERTICAL FEATURES

In Figure 5.4, we illustrated the effect of relief displacement on a photograph taken over varied terrain. In essence, an increase in the elevation of a feature causes its position on the photograph to be displaced radially outward from the principal point. Hence, when a vertical feature is photographed, relief displacement causes the top of the feature to lie farther from the photo center than its base. As a result, vertical features appear to lean away from the center of the photograph.

The pictorial effect of relief displacement is illustrated by the aerial photographs shown in Figure 5.7. These photographs depict the construction site of the Watts Bar Nuclear Plant adjacent to the Tennessee River. An operating coal-fired steam plant with its fan-shaped coal stockyard is shown in the upper right of Figure 5.7a; the nuclear plant is shown in the center. Note particularly the two large cooling towers adjacent to the plant. In (a) these towers appear nearly in top view because they are located very close to the principal point of this photograph. However, the towers manifest some relief displacement as the top tower appears to lean somewhat toward the upper right and the bottom tower toward the lower right. In (b) the towers are shown at a greater distance from the principal point. Note the increased relief displacement of the towers. We now see more of a "side view" of the objects since the images of their tops are displaced farther than the images of their bases. These photographs illustrate the radial nature of relief displacement and the increase in relief displacement with an increase in the radial distance from the principal point of a photograph.

The geometric components of relief displacement are illustrated in Figure 5.8, which shows a vertical photograph imaging a tower. The photograph is taken from flying height H above datum. When considering the relief displacement of a vertical feature, it is convenient to arbitrarily assume a datum plane placed at the base of the feature. If this is done, the flying height, H, must be correctly referenced to this same

(a)

FIGURE 5.7 Vertical photographs of the Watts Bar Nuclear Power Plant Site, near Kingston, Tennessee, January 31, 1977. In *(a)* the two plant cooling towers appear near the principal point and

datum, *not* mean sea level. Thus, in Figure 5.8 the height of the tower (whose base is at datum) is h. Note that the top of the tower, A, is imaged at a in the photograph whereas the base of the tower, A', is imaged at a'. That is, the image of the top of the tower is radially displaced the distance d from that of the bottom. The distance d is the relief displacement of the tower. The equivalent distance projected to datum is D. The distance from the photo principal point to the top of the tower is r. The equivalent distance projected to datum is R.

(b)

exhibit only slight relief displacement. The towers manifest severe relief displacement in (b). (Courtesy Mapping Services Branch, Tennessee Valley Authority.)

We can express d as a function of the dimensions shown in Figure 5.8. From similar triangles $AA'A''$ and LOA''

$$\frac{D}{h} = \frac{R}{H}$$

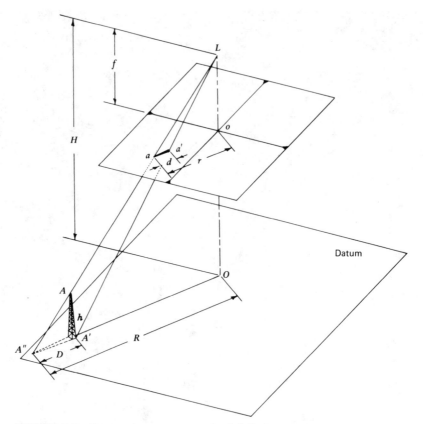

FIGURE 5.8   Geometric components of relief displacement.

Expressing distances D and R at the scale of the photograph we obtain

$$\frac{d}{h} = \frac{r}{H}$$

Rearranging the above equation

$$d = \frac{rh}{H} \tag{5.7}$$

where
   d = relief displacement
   r = radial distance on the photograph from the principal point to the displaced
       image point
   h = height above datum of the object point
   H = flying height above the same datum chosen to reference h

An analysis of Eq. 5.7 indicates mathematically the nature of relief displacement seen pictorially. That is, relief displacement of any given point increases as distance from the principal point increases (this can be seen in Figure 5.7), and it increases as the elevation of the point increases. Other things being equal, it decreases with an increase in flying height. Hence, under similar conditions high altitude photography of an area manifests less relief displacement than low altitude photography. Also, there is no relief displacement at the principal point (since $r = 0$).

Equation 5.7 also indicates that relief displacement increases with the feature height, h. This relationship makes it possible to indirectly measure heights of objects appearing on aerial photographs. By rearranging Eq. 5.7, we obtain

$$h = \frac{dH}{r} \tag{5.8}$$

To use eq. 5.8, both the top and base of the object to be measured must be clearly identifiable on the photograph and the flying height H must be known. If this is the case, d and r can be measured on the photograph and used to calculate the object height, h. (When using Eq. 5.8, it is important to remember that H must be referenced to the elevation of the base of the feature, not to mean sea level.)

EXAMPLE 5.4

For the photo shown in Figure 5.8, assume that the relief displacement for the tower at A is 2.01 mm, and the radial distance from the center of the photo to the top of the tower is 56.43 mm. If the flying height is 1220 m above the base of the tower, find the height of the tower.

Solution

By Eq. 5.8,

$$h = \frac{dH}{r} = \frac{2.01 \text{ mm } (1220 \text{ m})}{56.43 \text{ mm}} = 43.4 \text{ m}$$

While measuring relief displacement is a very convenient means of calculating heights of objects from aerial photographs, the reader is reminded of the assumptions implicit in the use of the method. We have assumed use of truly vertical photography, accurate knowledge of the flying height, clearly visible objects, precise location of the principal point, and a measurement technique whose accuracy is consistent with the degree of relief displacement involved. If these assumptions are reasonably met, quite reliable height determinations may be made using single prints and relatively unsophisticated measuring equipment.

In addition to calculating object heights, quantification of relief displacement can be used to correct the image positions of terrain points appearing in a photograph. Keep in mind that terrain points in areas of varied relief exhibit relief displacements as do vertical objects. This was illustrated in Figure 5.4. The image positions of terrain points A and B were radially displaced from the positions they would have occupied had they been at datum elevation. Using Equation 5.7, we can compute the magnitude of these displacements (with h and H expressed relative to an arbitrary datum elevation). By laying off the computed displacement distances radially on the photograph, the datum-level image positions of the points will be located. This adjustment removes the relief distortions at these points, resulting in planimetrically correct image positions at datum scale. The scale can be determined from the flying height above datum $(S = f/H)$. Ground lengths, directions, angles, and areas may then be directly determined from these corrected image positions. This procedure represents an alternative approach to the measurement techniques presented in Section 5.3.

EXAMPLE 5.5

Referring to the vertical photograph depicted in Figure 5.4, assume that the radial distance r_a to point A is 63.84 mm and the radial distance r_b to point B is 62.65 mm. Flying height H is 1220 m above datum, point A is 152 m above datum, and point B is 168 m below datum. Find the radial distance and direction one must lay off from points a and b to plot a' and b'.

Solution

By Eq. 5.7

$$d_a = \frac{r_a h_a}{H} = \frac{63.84 \text{ mm} \times 152 \text{ m}}{1220 \text{ m}} = 7.95 \text{ mm (plot inward)}$$

$$d_b = \frac{r_b h_b}{H} = \frac{62.65 \text{ mm} \times (-168 \text{ m})}{1220 \text{ m}} = -8.63 \text{ mm (plot outward)}$$

5.5 IMAGE PARALLAX

In previous sections, we have seen that an object can be located in a ground coordinate system from measurements on a single photograph only if the object's elevation is known. This restriction can be overcome by making measurements on stereopairs and using the principle of *parallax*. The term parallax refers to the apparent change in relative positions of stationary objects caused by a change in viewing position. This phenomenon is observable when one looks at objects through a side window of a moving vehicle. With the moving window as a frame of reference, objects such as mountains at a relatively great distance from the window appear to move very little within the frame of reference. In contrast, objects close to the window, such as roadside trees, appear to move through a much greater distance.

In the same way that the close trees move relative to the distant mountains, terrain features close to an aircraft (that is, at higher elevation) will appear to move relative to the lower elevation features when the point of view changes between successive exposures. These relative displacements form the basis for three-dimensional viewing of overlapping photography. In addition, they can be measured and used to compute the elevations of terrain points.

Figure 5.9 illustrates the nature of parallax on overlapping vertical photographs taken over varied terrain. Note that the relative positions of points A and B change with the change in viewing position (in this case, the exposure station). Note also that the *parallax displacements occur only parallel to the line of flight*. In theory, the direction

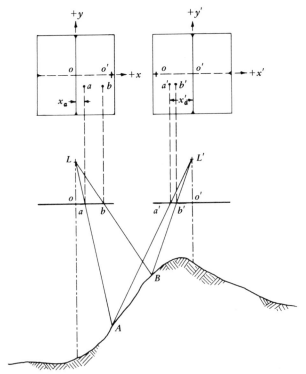

FIGURE 5.9 Parallax displacements on overlapping vertical photographs.

of flight should correspond precisely to the fiducial x axis. In reality, however, unavoidable changes in the aircraft orientation will usually slightly offset the fiducial axis from the flight axis. The true flight line axis may be found by first locating on a photograph the points that correspond to the image centers of the preceding and succeeding photographs. These points are called the *conjugate principal points*. A line drawn through the principal points and the conjugate principal points defines the flight axis. As shown in Figure 5.10, all photographs except those on the ends of a flight strip normally have two sets of flight axes. This happens because the aircraft's path between exposures is normally curved. In Figure 5.10, the flight axis for the stereopair formed by photos 1 and 2 is flight axis 12. The flight axis for the stereopair formed by photos 2 and 3 is flight axis 23.

The line of flight for any given stereopair defines a photocoordinate x axis for use in parallax measurement. Lines drawn perpendicular to the flight line and passing through the principal point of each photo form the photographic y axes for parallax

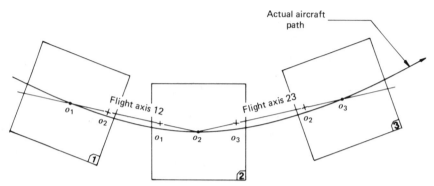

FIGURE 5.10   Flight line axes for successive stereopairs along a flight strip.

measurement. The parallax of any point, such as A in Figure 5.9, is expressed in terms of the flight line coordinate system as

$$p_a = x_a - x_a'$$ (5.9)

where p_a is the parallax of point A, x_a is the measured x coordinate of image a on the left photograph of the stereopair, and x_a' is the x coordinate of image a' on the right photograph. The x axis for each photo is considered positive to the right of each photo principal point. This makes x_a' a negative quantity in Figure 5.9.

Figure 5.11 shows overlapping vertical photographs of a terrain point, A. Using parallax measurements, we may determine the elevation at A and its ground coordinate location. Referring to Figure 5.11a, the horizontal distance between exposure stations L and L' is called B, the *air base*. The triangle in Figure 5.11b results from superimposition of the triangles at L and L' in order to graphically depict the nature of parallax p_a as computed from Eq. 5.9 algebraically. From similar triangles $La_x'a_x$ (Figure 5.11b) and LA_xL' (Figure 5.11a)

$$\frac{p_a}{f} = \frac{B}{H - h_A}$$

from which

$$H - h_A = \frac{Bf}{p_a}$$ (5.10)

Rearranging

$$h_A = H - \frac{Bf}{p_a}$$ (5.11)

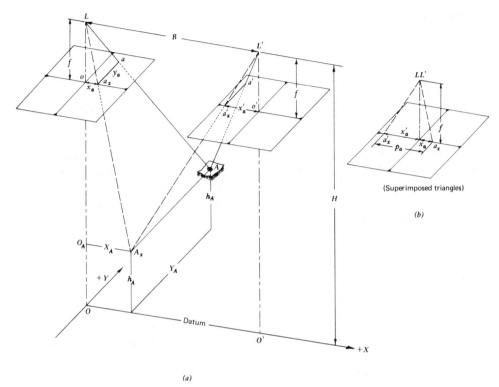

(a)

FIGURE 5.11   Parallax relationships on overlapping vertical photographs. (a) Adjacent photographs forming a stereopair. (b) Superimposition of right photograph onto left.

Also, from similar triangles $LO_A A_x$ and Loa_x,

$$\frac{X_A}{H - h_A} = \frac{x_a}{f}$$

from which

$$X_A = \frac{x_a(H - h_A)}{f}$$

and substituting Eq. 5.10 into the above equation yields

$$X_A = B\frac{x_a}{p_a} \qquad (5.12)$$

A similar derivation using y coordinates yields

$$Y_A = B\frac{y_a}{p_a} \qquad\qquad (5.13)$$

Equations 5.11 to 5.13 are commonly known as the *parallax equations*. In these equations, X and Y are ground coordinates of a point with respect to an arbitrary coordinate system whose origin is vertically below the left exposure station and with positive X in the direction of flight; p is the parallax of the point in question; and x and y are the photo coordinates of the point on the left-hand photo. The major assumptions made in the derivation of these equations are that the photos are truly vertical and that they are taken from the same flying height. If these assumptions are sufficiently met, a complete survey of the ground region contained in the photo overlap area of a stereopair can be made.

EXAMPLE 5.6

The length of line AB and the elevation of its endpoints, A and B, are to be determined from a stereopair containing images a and b. The camera used to take the photography has a 152.4 mm lens. The flying height was 1200 m (average for the two photos) and the air base was 600 m. The measured photographic coordinates of points A and B in the "flight line" coordinate system are $x_a = 54.61$ mm, $x_b = 98.67$ mm, $y_a = 50.80$ mm, $y_b = -25.40$ mm, $x'_a = -59.45$ mm, and $x'_b = -27.39$ mm. Find the length of line AB and the elevations of A and B.

Solution

From Eq. 5.9,

$$p_a = x_a - x'_a = 54.61 - (-59.45) = 114.06 \text{ mm}$$
$$p_b = x_b - x'_b = 98.67 - (-27.39) = 126.06 \text{ mm}$$

From Eqs. 5.12 and 5.13

$$X_A = B\frac{x_a}{p_a} = \frac{600 \times 54.61}{114.06} = 287.27 \text{ m}$$

$$X_B = B\frac{x_b}{p_b} = \frac{600 \times 98.67}{126.06} = 469.63 \text{ m}$$

$$Y_A = B\frac{y_a}{p_a} = \frac{600 \times 50.80}{114.06} = 267.23 \text{ m}$$

$$Y_B = B\frac{y_b}{p_b} = \frac{600 \times (-25.40)}{126.06} = -120.89 \text{ m}$$

Applying the Pythagorean Theorem

$$AB = [(469.63 - 287.27)^2 + (-120.89 - 267.23)^2]^{1/2} = 428.8 \text{ m}$$

From Eq. 5.11, the elevations of A and B are

$$h_A = H - \frac{Bf}{p_a} = 1200 - \frac{600 \times 152.4}{114.06} = 398 \text{ m}$$

$$h_B = H - \frac{Bf}{p_b} = 1200 - \frac{600 \times 152.4}{126.06} = 475 \text{ m}$$

In many circumstances, an image interpreter is interested only in calculating approximate elevations, tree heights, building heights, slopes, and so on. If both ground principal points of a stereopair are at nearly the same elevation, and the bases of the objects to be analyzed are at essentially the same elevation, an approximate relationship for computing changes in elevation can often be applied. This equation is

$$\Delta h = \frac{\Delta p H'}{b + \Delta p} \tag{5.14}$$

where Δh is the difference in elevation between two points whose parallax *difference* is Δp, H' is the flying height *above ground*, and b is the average photo air base. The average air base is found by measuring the distance between the principal point and conjugate principal point on both the left and right photos and averaging the measurements.

EXAMPLE 5.7

A tower manifests a parallax difference of 1.69 mm between its top and its base on photographs taken from an altitude above ground of 1200 m. If the average photo base is 76.14 mm, how tall is the tower?

Solution

From Eq. 5.14

$$\Delta h = \frac{1.69 \times 1200}{76.14 + 1.69} = 26 \text{ m}$$

5.6 PARALLAX MEASUREMENT

To this point in our discussion, we have said little about how parallax measurements are made. In Example 5.6 we assumed that x and x' for points of interest were measured directly on the left and right photos, respectively. Parallaxes were then calculated from the algebraic differences of x and x', in accordance with Eq. 5.9. This procedure becomes cumbersome when many points are analyzed, since two measurements are required for each point.

Figure 5.12 illustrates the principle behind methods of parallax measurement that

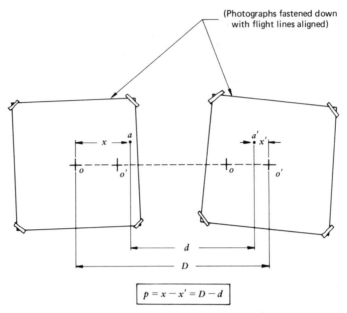

FIGURE 5.12   Alignment of a stereopair for parallax measurement.

require only a single measurement for each point of interest. If the two photographs constituting a stereopair are fastened to a base with their flight lines aligned, the distance D remains constant for the setup and the parallax of a point can be derived from measurement of the single distance d. That is, $p = D - d$. Distance d can be measured with a simple scale, *assuming a and a' are identifiable.* In areas of uniform photo tone, individual features may not be identifiable, making the measurement of d very difficult.

Employing the principle illustrated in Figure 5.12, a number of devices have been developed to increase the speed and accuracy of parallax measurement. These devices also permit parallax to be easily measured in areas of uniform photo tone. All employ stereoscopic viewing and the principle of the *floating mark*. This principle is illustrated in Figure 5.13. While viewing through a stereoscope, the image analyst uses a device that places small identical marks over each photograph. These marks are normally dots or crosses etched on transparent material. The marks—called *half marks*—are positioned over similar areas on the left-hand photo and the right-hand photo. The left mark is seen only by the left eye of the analyst and the right mark is seen only by the right eye. The relative positions of the half marks can be shifted along the direction of flight until they visually fuse together, forming a single mark that appears to "float" at a specific level in the stereomodel. The apparent elevation of the floating mark varies with the spacing between the half marks. Figure 5.13 illustrates how the fused marks can be made to float and can actually be set on the terrain at particular points in the stereomodel. Half mark positions (a,b), (a,c), and (a,d) result in floating mark positions in the model at B, C, and D.

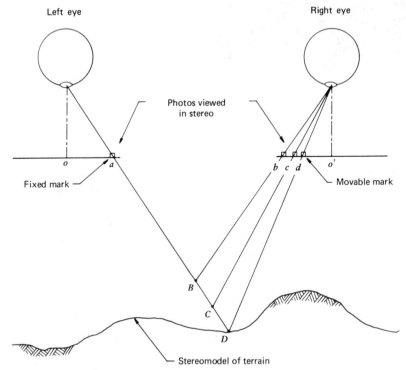

FIGURE 5.13 Floating mark principle. (Note that only the right half mark is moved to change the apparent height of the floating mark in the stereomodel.)

One of the most common devices employing the floating mark principle for parallax measurement is the *parallax bar*. Figure 5.14 shows a parallax bar oriented under a mirror stereoscope. The parallax bar consists of two half marks positioned on a bar. The distance between the marks can be varied and is precisely measured with the microm-eter screw shown at the right end of the bar. Here the left half mark is fixed in position while the right half mark is moved by turning the micrometer. The micrometer is turned in order to set the floating mark at various apparent elevations within the stereomodel.

Measurements read from the micrometer of a parallax bar are converted to parallax values using the equation

$$p = r + C \tag{5.15}$$

where
  r = the parallax bar reading
  C = a constant that relates r and p

FIGURE 5.14 Parallax bar oriented under a mirror stereoscope. (Courtesy Wild Heer-brugg, Inc.)

The constant C is called the *parallax bar constant*. Its value depends on the distance between the stereophotos (D in Figure 5.12) and therefore will be different for each stereophoto setup. The algebraic sign of C can be plus or minus, depending on the design of the parallax bar. The numerical value of the constant is determined by directly measuring the parallax at a given point using a scale and comparing the measured parallax, p, to the bar reading, r, at the point. Then C is computed from

$$C = p - r \tag{5.16}$$

Once C is determined, it can be used in Eq. 5.15 to convert bar readings at any points in the stereomodel to parallax values. These may then be used in the parallax equations.

To minimize measurement errors and the effects of tilt, unequal flying heights, and print shrinkage, two values of C are normally determined and their mean is used. This involves measuring the parallax and taking parallax bar readings at two reference points. The two principal points are often used for this purpose. As can be seen in Figure 5.15, the parallax of the left photo ground principal point O_1 is $p_{0_1} = x_{0_1} -$

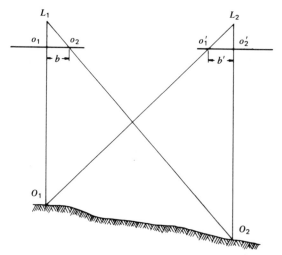

FIGURE 5.15 Parallax of the principal points.

$(-x'_{0_1}) = 0 - (-b') = b'$. The parallax of O_2 is $p_{0_2} = x_{0_2} - x'_{0_2} = b - 0 = b$. In short, the parallax of the left ground principal point is photo base b' measured on the right photo, and the parallax of the right ground principal point is photo base b measured on the left photo. Parallax bar readings for these two points are used to find an average setup constant.

EXAMPLE 5.8

A stereopair was taken with a 152 mm camera from a flying height of 1200 m above mean sea level. The air base at the time of exposure was 400 m. Photo base b on the left photo was measured as 94.38 mm and b' on the right photo was measured as 94.02 mm. With the photos properly oriented, parallax bar readings were taken on the left and right photo principal points o_1 and o_2 and the results were 10.27 and 10.75 mm. Parallax bar readings of 9.86 and 14.16 mm were also taken on two unknown points A and B. The photocoordinates of A and B were measured in the flight axis system of the left photo as $x_a = 49.48$ mm, $y_a = 46.65$ mm, $x_b = 82.29$ mm, and $y_b = -42.63$ mm. Determine the elevations of points A and B and the horizontal length of line AB.

Solution

From Eq. 5.16

$$C_1 = b' - r_{0_1} = 94.02 - 10.27 = 83.75 \text{ mm}$$
$$C_2 = b - r_{0_2} = 94.38 - 10.75 = 83.63 \text{ mm}$$
$$C_{\text{avg}} = \frac{83.75 + 83.63}{2} = 83.69 \text{ mm}$$

By Eq. 5.15

$$p_a = r_a + C = 9.86 + 83.69 = 93.55 \text{ mm}$$
$$p_b = r_b + C = 14.16 + 83.69 = 97.85 \text{ mm}$$

By Eq. 5.11

$$h_a = H - \frac{Bf}{p_a} = 1200 - \frac{400(152)}{93.55} = 550 \text{ m}$$

$$h_b = H - \frac{Bf}{p_b} = 1200 - \frac{400(152)}{97.85} = 579 \text{ m}$$

By Equations 5.12 and 5.13

$$X_A = B\left(\frac{x_a}{p_a}\right) = 400\left(\frac{49.48}{93.55}\right) = 212 \text{ m}$$

$$X_B = B\left(\frac{x_b}{p_b}\right) = 400\left(\frac{82.29}{97.85}\right) = 336 \text{ m}$$

$$Y_A = B\left(\frac{y_a}{p_a}\right) = 400\left(\frac{46.65}{93.55}\right) = 199 \text{ m}$$

$$Y_B = B\left(\frac{y_b}{p_b}\right) = 400\left(\frac{-42.63}{97.85}\right) = -174 \text{ m}$$

The horizontal length of line AB is

$$AB = [(X_A - X_B)^2 + (Y_A - Y_B)^2]^{1/2}$$

$$AB = [(212 - 336)^2 + (199 + 174)^2]^{1/2} = 393 \text{ m}$$

A very simple device for measuring parallax is the *parallax wedge*. It consists of a transparent sheet of plastic on which are printed two converging lines or rows of dots (or graduated lines). Next to one of the converging lines is a scale that shows the horizontal distance between the two lines at each point. Consequently, these graduations can be thought of as a series of parallax bar readings.

Figure 5.16 shows a parallax wedge set up for use. The wedge is positioned so that one of the converging lines lies over the left photo in a stereopair and one over the right photo. When viewed in stereo, the two lines fuse together over a portion of their length, forming a single line that appears to float in the stereomodel. Because the lines on the wedge converge, the floating line appears to slope through the stereoscopic image.

Figure 5.17 illustrates how a parallax wedge might be used to determine the height of a tree. In Figure 5.17a, the position of the wedge has been adjusted until the sloping line appears to intersect the top of the tree. A reading is taken from the scale at this point (58.55 mm). The wedge is then positioned such that the line intersects the base of

FIGURE 5.16 Parallax wedge oriented under lens stereoscope.

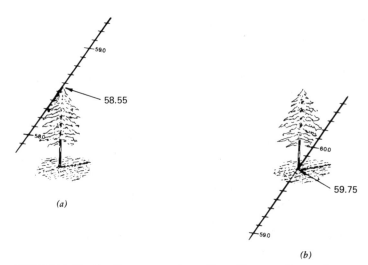

FIGURE 5.17 Parallax wedge oriented for taking a reading on the top (a) and base (b) of a tree.

the tree, and a reading is taken (59.75 mm). The difference between the readings (1.20 mm) is used to determine the tree height.

EXAMPLE 5.9

The flying height for an overlapping pair of photos is 1600 m above the ground and the photo air base is 75.60 mm. Find the height of the tree illustrated in Figure 5.17.

Solution

From Eq. 5.14

$$\Delta h = \frac{\Delta p H'}{b + \Delta p}$$

$$\Delta h = \frac{1.20 \times 1600}{75.60 + 1.20} = 25 \text{ m}$$

Parallax wedges can also be used to measure absolute parallax. As with the parallax bar, a constant for each measurement setup is obtained by shifting the wedge under the stereoscope until the fused line intersects at the image of a point whose parallax was measured with a scale. A parallax wedge constant is then determined as before (Eq. 5.16) and the parallax at any point is obtained by piercing the image with the floating line, reading the wedge, and applying the wedge constant.

The parallax wedge is a very simple, inexpensive, and rapid (with practice) device for parallax measurement. Although we later discuss much more complex, expensive, and accurate means of measuring stereoscopic parallax, the student should not lose sight of the principle and utility of less sophisticated equipment. Only then can trade-offs between measurement cost and accuracy be evaluated.

5.7   GROUND CONTROL FOR AERIAL PHOTOGRAPHY

As we have indicated throughout, most remote sensing analyses involve some form of ground reference data. Photogrammetric operations are no exception. In fact, for most photogrammetric activities one form of ground reference data is essential—ground control. *Ground control* refers to physical points on the ground whose ground positions are known with respect to some horizontal coordinate system and/or vertical datum. When mutually identifiable on the ground and on a photograph, ground control points can be used to establish the exact spatial position and orientation of a photograph relative to the ground at the instant of exposure.

Ground control points may be *horizontal control points, vertical control points,* or both. Horizontal control point-positions are known planimetrically in some *XY* coordinate systems (for example, a State Plane Coordinate System). Vertical control points have known elevations with respect to a level datum (for example, mean sea level). A single point with known planimetric position and known elevation can serve as both a horizontal and vertical control point.

Historically, ground control has been established through ground surveying techniques in the form of triangulation, trilateration, traversing, and leveling. Currently, the establishment of ground control is aided by the use of inertial surveying procedures and satellite global positioning systems. The details of these and other more sophisticated surveying techniques used for establishing ground control are not important for the student to understand. It does warrant reiteration, however, that *accurate ground control is essential to virtually all photogrammetric operations* because photogrammetric measurements can only be as reliable as the ground control on which they are based. Measurements on the photo can be accurately extrapolated to the ground only when we know the location and orientation of the photograph relative to the ground at the instant of exposure. Ground control is required to determine these factors.

As we mentioned, ground control points must be clearly identifiable both on the ground and on the photography being used. Often, control points are selected and surveyed after photography has been taken, thereby ensuring that the points are identifiable on the image. Cultural features, such as road intersections, are often used as control points in such cases. If a ground survey is made prior to a photo mission, control points may be premarked with artificial targets to aid in their identification on the photography. Crosses that contrast with the background land cover make ideal control point markers. Their size is selected in accordance with the scale of the photography to be flown and their material form can be quite variable. In many cases, markers are made by simply painting white crosses on roadways. Alternatively, markers can be painted on contrasting sheets of masonite, plywood, or heavy cloth.

5.8   USE OF GROUND CONTROL IN DETERMINING THE FLYING HEIGHT AND AIR BASE OF AERIAL PHOTOGRAPHS

Flying Height Determination

As indicated throughout this chapter, knowledge of the flying height from which a photograph was taken, H, is essential in numerous photogrammetric computations.

Depending on the information available and the accuracy requirements of the task at hand, H can be found in many ways. As mentioned earlier, some mapping cameras record an altimeter reading on each photograph, from which an approximate H can be determined. Alternatively, if a level ground line of known length and elevation appears on a photograph, the length of the line as imaged on the photograph and the camera focal length can be used to find H.

EXAMPLE 5.10

A level fenceline 200 m long is recorded on a vertical photograph taken with a camera having a 152 mm lens. A topographic map indicates that the fenceline is at an elevation of 1120 m above sea level. If the fenceline is 20.00 mm long on the photograph, determine the flying height above sea level.

Solution

The basic equation for photo scale S is

$$S = \frac{f}{H - h}$$

Solving for H,

$$H = \frac{f}{S} + h = \frac{152 \text{ mm}}{20.00 \text{ mm}/200 \text{ m}} + 1120 \text{ m} = 2640 \text{ m}$$

If ground control is available on an image, it can be used to obtain a more accurate measurement of H. For example, if the images of two horizontal/vertical ground control points, A and B, are contained on a vertical photograph, H can be determined by measuring the photocoordinates of the control points and determining the horizontal ground length of the line between A and B. This length is expressed through the Pythagorean theorem as

$$(AB)^2 = (X_A - X_B)^2 + (Y_A - Y_B)^2$$

Substitution of Eqs. 5.1 to 5.4 into the above results in

$$(AB)^2 = \left[\frac{(H - h_A)}{f} x_a - \frac{(H - h_B)}{f} x_b \right]^2 + \left[\frac{(H - h_A)}{f} y_a - \frac{(H - h_B)}{f} y_b \right]^2 \quad (5.17)$$

where ground length AB, elevations h_A and h_B, and focal length f are known, and where photocoordinates (x_a, y_a) and (x_b, y_b) have been measured. This expression takes on the form of a quadratic equation $aH^2 + bH + c = 0$, where a, b, and c represent numbers obtained by substituting the known values in the expression for $(AB)^2$. The solution for the quadratic form of the equation is

$$H = \frac{-b \pm \sqrt{b^2 - 4ac}}{2a}$$

While the above expression provides a direct solution for H, formation and solution of the quadratic are rather tedious and a trial-and-error approach to finding H is often quicker and easier to employ. In this approach, an initial approximation of H, called H_1, is made from the altimeter reading, or from a computation similar to that in Example 5.10. Next, Eq. 5.17 is solved for an approximate AB, called AB_1, based on H_1. Then AB_1 is compared to the true length AB, and if they do not agree, a refined estimate of H (called H_2) is made from

$$H_2 = \frac{AB}{AB_1} (H_1 - h_{AB}) + h_{AB} \tag{5.18}$$

where h_{AB} is the average elevation of the two endpoints of line AB. The new value for H found in Eq. 5.18, H_2, is then used to solve for another value of AB, AB_2. The computed AB_2 value is compared to the true AB value and the process is repeated until the computed and true values agree. Normally, agreement is reached after two iterations.

EXAMPLE 5.11

Control points A and B appear on a vertical photograph taken with a camera having a 152.4 mm lens. The horizontal ground distance between A and B is 650 m and the elevations of A and B are 213 and 152 m above sea level. The photocoordinates of the points are $x_a = +46.82$ mm, $y_a = +53.64$ mm, $x_b = -35.51$ mm, and $y_b = -43.17$ mm. Calculate the flying height of the photograph using the trial-and-error approach.

Solution

(a) Find the photo distance of line ab:

$$ab = [(x_a - x_b)^2 + (y_a - y_b)^2]^{1/2}$$
$$ab = [(46.82 + 35.51)^2 + (53.64 + 43.17)^2]^{1/2} = 127.08 \text{ mm}$$

(b) Find first approximation H_1 from the basic scale equation:

$$H_1 = \frac{f}{S} + h_{AB} = \frac{152.4}{127.08/650} + 182.5 = 962 \text{ m}$$

(c) Find AB from Eq. 5.17:

$$(AB_1)^2 = \left[\frac{(962 - 213)}{152.4} 46.82 + \frac{(962 - 152)}{152.4} 35.51 \right]^2$$
$$+ \left[\frac{(962 - 213)}{152.4} 53.64 + \frac{(962 - 152)}{152.4} 43.17 \right]^2$$

$$(AB_1)^2 = (230.11 + 188.73)^2 + (263.62 + 229.45)^2$$

$$AB_1 = 646.9 \text{ m (compared to the true length } AB \text{ of 650 m)}$$

(d) Find second approximation H_2 from Eq. 5.18:

$$H_2 = \frac{650}{646.9} (962 - 182.5) + 182.5 = 965.7 \text{ m}$$

(e) Find AB_2 from Eq. 5.17:

$$(AB_2)^2 = \left[\frac{(965.7 - 213)}{152.4} \; 46.82 + \frac{(965.7 - 152)}{152.4} \; 35.51 \right]^2$$

$$+ \left[\frac{(965.7 - 213)}{152.4} \; 53.64 + \frac{(965.7 - 152)}{152.4} \; 43.17 \right]^2$$

$$(AB_2)^2 = (231.24 + 189.60)^2 + (264.93 + 230.49)^2$$

$$AB_2 = 650.04 \text{ (compared to the true length } AB \text{ of 650 m)}$$

Therefore, $H = 965.7$ m above sea level.

Air Base Determination

As with determining the flying height of a photograph, the air base between successive photographs can be found from ground control by various methods. If flying height H is known and one vertical control point is available in the overlap area of successive photos, the airbase may be calculated from Eq. 5.10.

EXAMPLE 5.12

A stereopair was exposed from a flying height of 1620 m above sea level using a camera with a 152.4 mm lens. Vertical control point A has an elevation of 252 m above sea level and a parallax of 85.48 mm. Find the air base of the stereopair.

Solution

By rearranging Eq. 5.10

$$B = (H - h_A) \frac{p_a}{f} = (1620 - 252) \frac{85.48}{152.4} = 767.3 \text{ m}$$

If two control points appear in the overlapping area of a stereopair, the air base can be calculated by expressing the horizontal distance between the points in terms of rectangular coordinates. Again, the Pythagorean theorem is used, and the coordinates of the control points are found from the parallax equations. The line length between two points A and B is thereby expressed as

$$AB = [(X_A - X_B)^2 + (Y_A - Y_B)^2]^{1/2}$$

Substitution of Eq. 5.12 and 5.13 into the above for the coordinates of A and B gives

$$AB = \left[\left(\frac{Bx_a}{p_a} - \frac{Bx_b}{p_b} \right)^2 + \left(\frac{By_a}{p_a} - \frac{By_b}{p_b} \right)^2 \right]^{1/2}$$

Finally, solving for B,

$$B = \left[\frac{(AB)^2}{\left(\dfrac{x_a}{p_a} - \dfrac{x_b}{p_b} \right)^2 + \left(\dfrac{y_a}{p_a} - \dfrac{y_b}{p_b} \right)^2} \right]^{1/2} \tag{5.19}$$

EXAMPLE 5.13

Control points A and B appear in the overlap area of a stereopair. The horizontal ground length of the line between the points is known to be 2617 m. The measured parallax of point a is 85.14 mm, and that of point b is 89.27 mm. The "flight line" coordinates of the points on the left-hand photo are $x_a = 27.14$ mm, $y_a = 62.39$ mm, $x_b = 17.42$ mm, and $y_b = -70.10$ mm. Find the air base of the stereopair.

Solution

$$B = \left[\frac{2617^2}{\left(\dfrac{27.14}{85.14} - \dfrac{17.42}{89.27}\right)^2 + \left(\dfrac{62.39}{85.14} + \dfrac{70.10}{89.27}\right)^2} \right]^{1/2} = 1718 \text{ m}$$

5.9   STEREOSCOPIC PLOTTING INSTRUMENTS

As we mentioned in the introductory section of this chapter, the most widespread use of photogrammetry is in the preparation of topographic maps. *Stereoplotters* are precision instruments designed for this purpose. Two projectors are used that can be adjusted in their position and angular orientation to duplicate the exact relative position and orientation of the aerial camera at the instants the two photos of a stereopair were exposed. That is, if the photographs were taken when the camera was tilted, these tilts are precisely recreated in the projection process. Likewise, the base distance between exposures and differences in flying heights are simulated by adjusting the relative positions of the projectors.

Conceptually, the operating principle of a stereoplotter is quite simple. Each photograph in a stereopair is the result of rays projected from the terrain, through a lens, onto an image plane that has a particular position and attitude. In a stereoplotter, the direction of projection is simply reversed. We project rays from the photographs (in the same relative orientation in which they were taken) to form a greatly reduced scale model of the terrain in the overlap area. The model can be viewed and measured in three dimensions and can be projected orthographically to a map sheet. This process eliminates the perspective view distortions present when we attempt to map directly from a single photo. It also eliminates errors introduced by tilts and unequal flying heights when measuring parallax on stereopairs.

There are many different types of stereoplotters but all of them are made up of three basic components:

1. A projection system (to create the terrain model).
2. A viewing system (to enable the instrument operator to see the model stereo-scopically).
3. A measuring and tracing system (for measuring elevations in the model and tracing features onto a map sheet).

Figure 5.18 illustrates a *direct optical projection* plotter. Such systems directly project overlapping images onto a *tracing table* where the terrain model is viewed in

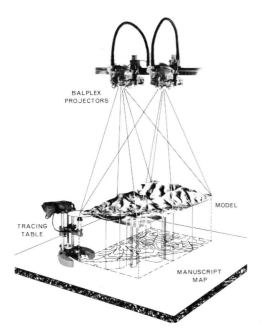

BALPLEX
PROJECTORS

MODEL

TRACING
TABLE

MANUSCRIPT
MAP

FIGURE 5.18 Stereomodel projected in a Balplex stereoplotter. (Courtesy TBR Associates, Inc.)

stereo. The projectors can be both translated along and rotated about their x, y, and z axes. This permits the instrument operator to perform a *relative orientation* to recreate the position and angular orientation of the two photographs at the time of exposure. This is done by adjusting the projectors until all conjugate image points coincide in the y direction (at this point, only the elevation-caused x parallax remains). The two projectors are then adjusted in tandem to arrive at an *absolute orientation* of the projected model. This is accomplished by scaling and leveling the pair of projectors until the images of ground control points occupy their appropriate preplotted positions on the map manuscript (Figure 5.18). Following these two orientation procedures, a geometrically correct model will be projected and a complete topographic map may be drawn.

The instrument shown in Figure 5.18 uses reduced size diapositives printed on glass plates. Figure 5.19 illustrates a stereoplotter that uses full-sized images and employs three projectors. The three projectors enable two adjacent stereopairs to be oriented at once.

In a direct projection plotter, both images in a stereopair are projected onto the same surface. In order to see stereo, the operator's eyes must view each image separately. This can be accomplished by using an *anaglyphic viewing system*, in which one photo is projected through a cyan filter and the other through a red filter. By viewing the model through eyeglasses having corresponding color filters, the operator's left eye will see only the left photo and his or her right eye will see only the right photo.

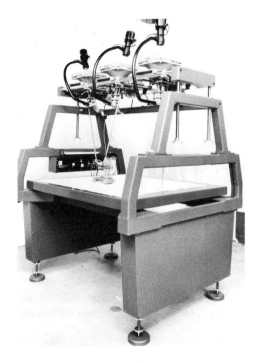

FIGURE 5.19 Kelsh Model KPP-3B stereo-plotter instrument. (Courtesy Kelsh Instrument Division, Danko Arlington, Inc.)

Anaglyphic viewing systems cannot be used with color photography. Even in the case of viewing black and white images, these sysems reduce the brightness and resolution of the projected images. An alternative projection method employs a *polarized platen viewer (PPV)* system, which uses polarizing filters and eyeglass lenses instead of colored filters. *Stereo image alternator (SIA)* systems use shutters in the projectors to rapidly alternate the projection of the two photos. The operator views the model through a synchronized shutter system, causing the left eye and right eye to see the images from the corresponding projector only.

Portions of the stereomodel are projected onto a *tracing table platen*, which has a small point of light at its center. This point forms a floating mark whose elevation can be adjusted by raising or lowering the platen. Because the stereomodel has been absolutely oriented to ground control, the platen table height can be equated to terrain elevations. These elevations may be directly read from a height meter on the tracing platen.

Features are mapped planimetrically in the model by tracing them with the floating mark, while continuously raising and lowering the mark to maintain contact with the terrain. Relief displacement of the plotted positions is eliminated by this process. A pencil attached to the platen plots the feature being traced onto the map manuscript, which is located on the plotter table.

Contours are compiled by setting the platen height meter at a desired contour elevation and moving the floating mark along the terrain so that it just maintains contact with the surface of the model. For the novice, these plotting operations seem

FIGURE 5.20 Wild A-10 Autograph stereoplotter (left) and coordinatograph (right). (Courtesy Wild Heerbrugg, Inc.)

impossible to perform. It takes considerable training and experience to become proficient at the art of accurate topographic map preparation using a stereoplotter.

To this point, we have discussed direct optical projection plotters only. Figure 5.20 illustrates a plotter in which the stereophotos are not projected to form the stereomodel. Instead, the operator directly views the photographs in stereo through a binocular system. The viewing optics are connected to the measuring and tracing system by a precise mechanical linkage. At any planimetric position and height in the model, the linkage focuses the viewing optics on the portions of the photographs that would have been projected onto the platen in a direct projection plotter. In this way, the plotter simulates the direct projection of the rays. These *mechanical or optical–mechanical projection plotters* provide increased accuracy in map production.

While viewing the stereomodel in a mechanical plotter, the operator typically translates the floating mark in *x* and *y* by adjusting two handwheels (the white disks in Figure 5.20). At the same time, the floating mark is raised and lowered using a foot disc (the black disc on the floor in Figure 5.20). As the floating mark is moved, its position is transferred to a plotting table where the map manuscript is compiled. This may be performed mechanically, using a *coordinatograph*, or electronically, using a digitizer and electronic plotter (the coordinatograph is illustrated in Figure 5.20). In either case, scale changes may be introduced in the transfer process to achieve various map-to-terrain model scales.

All of the plotters described in this section rely on an operator to position the floating mark on the surface of the stereomodel. This process involves continuously correlating conjugate images, an activity the human mind efficiently performs when viewing in stereo. However, the process can also be performed by an *electronic image correlator*, enabling the plotting process to be highly automated. This increases the speed and ease of map production. In complex terrain, however, the system may be unable to correlate the conjugate images, requiring human intervention.

Figure 5.21 illustrates an *analytical stereoplotter*. Conceptually, analytical plotters operate through the formation of a *mathematical model* of the terrain imaged by a stereopair. This is done by linking a comparator type viewing and measuring system to a digital computer. This results in a system that is extremely versatile and accurate in that it has virtually no optical or mechanical limitations. The system's computer can be programmed to handle any type of photography (for example, oblique or panoramic photos) and to correct for complex combinations of image distortions. The operator simply feeds the camera focal length and other calibration data into the computer. Then, under cursor control, the coordinates of the fiducial marks and several ground control points are measured and the computer performs the complete orientation of the stereomodel. Positions in the model can then be mathematically transformed into ground coordinates and elevations. The system shown in Figure 5.21 permits the simultaneous viewing, in color, of the stereomodel and digitized line work. The external graphics monitor is used for reviewing and editing the digitized data. A broad range of software is available for such activities as menu-driven coding of map features (e.g., roads, fencelines, drainage, etc.), digital terrain model profiling, and continuous digitizing.

FIGURE 5.21 Intergraph InterMap Analytic photogrammetric work station. (Courtesy Intergraph Corp.)

A detailed discussion of stereoplotter systems is clearly beyond the scope of this book. Our intent has been to present the basic concepts and general distinctions. Additional technical details can be found in the literature listed in the Selected Bibliography at the end of this chapter.

5.10 ORTHOPHOTOS

As implied by their name, orthophotos are orthographic photographs; in essence, they are "photomaps." Like maps, they have one scale (even in varying terrain), and like photographs, they show the terrain in actual detail (not by lines and symbols). Hence, orthophotos give the resource analyst the "best of both worlds"—a product that can be easily interpreted like a photograph, but one on which true distances, angles, and areas may be measured directly. Because features can be photo interpreted in their true, planimetric positions, orthophotos make excellent base maps for resource surveys. They also enhance the communication of the resource data, since users can often relate better to the orthophoto than to a conventional line and symbol base map.

Orthophotos are generated from overlapping conventional photos in a process called *differential rectification*. The result of this process is elimination of photo scale variation and image displacement resulting from relief and tilt. Figure 5.22 illustrates the effect of this process. Figure 5.22a is a conventional (perspective) photograph of a power line clearing traversing a hilly forested area. The excessively crooked appearance of the clearing is due to relief displacement. Figure 5.22b is a portion of an orthophoto covering the same area. In this image, relief displacement has been removed and the true path of the power line is shown.

Orthophotos are prepared in instruments called *orthophotoscopes* in much the same manner as maps are prepared in stereoplotters. However, instead of plotting *selected* features in the stereomodel onto a base map, *all* points of the stereomodel are photographed onto an *orthophoto negative*, which is then used to print the orthophotograph.

A direct optical projection orthophotoscope is shown in Figure 5.23. In operation, diapositives for a stereopair are relatively and absolutely oriented in the instrument as if normal map compilation were to commence. Unlike that of a normal stereoplotter, however, the floating mark for an orthophotoscope is a very small slit in a film holder (Figure 5.24) containing the orthophoto negative. A small area of the negative is exposed to light through the slit that is continuously scanned across the film. At the end of each scan, the slit is moved over and scans in reverse to expose an adjacent strip of film. In this way, the film is eventually exposed to the full stereomodel through the small slit. Along the way, the instrument operator controls the height of the film holder, keeping the slit just in contact with the terrain. Hence, point by point, the scale variation and relief displacement present in the original photography are removed by varying the projection distance. (All tilt distortions are previously eliminated in the process of orienting the stereomodel.)

Orthophotos alone do not convey topographic information. However, they can be used as base maps for contour line overlays prepared in a separate stereoplotting

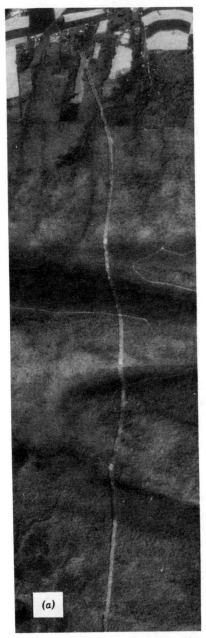
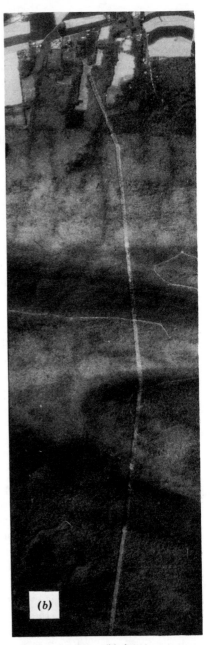

FIGURE 5.22 Portion of a perspective photograph *(a)* and an orthophoto *(b)* showing a power line clearing traversing hilly terrain. (Note the excessive crookedness of the power line clearing in the perspective photo that is eliminated in the orthophoto.) (Courtesy USGS.)

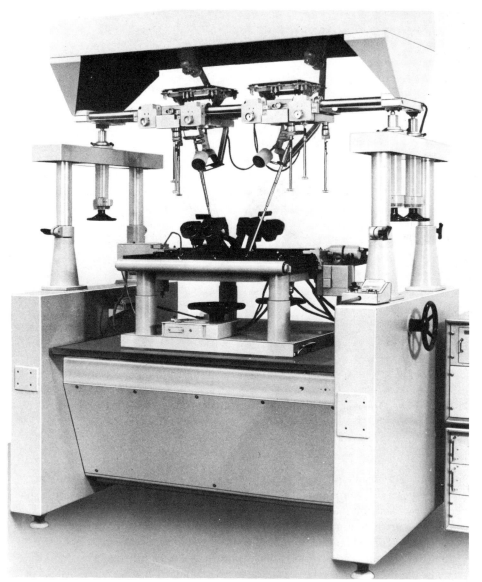

FIGURE 5.23 Engins Matra 9300 System consisting of plotter and orthophotographic table containing film holder. (Courtesy Engins Matra–Division Optique.)

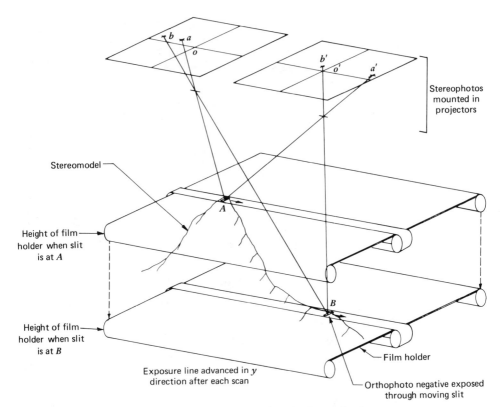

FIGURE 5.24 Operating principle of direct optical projection orthophotoscope.

operation. The result of overprinting contour information on an orthophoto is a *topographic orthophotomap*. Much time is saved in the preparation of such maps because the instrument operator need not map the planimetric data in the map compilation process. Figure 5.25 illustrates a portion of a topographic orthophotomap.

The method of orthophoto preparation illustrated in Figure 5.24 is termed "on line" in that the terrain scanning and film exposure occur simultaneously. In "off-line" systems, the stereomodel is first scanned using a standard floating mark, instead of the film holder slit. During this process, the scan line elevation profiles are stored in digital form. At a later time, the digital profiles are read by instruments that automatically raise and lower the film holder while exposing a negative. An off-line system offers the advantage that the operator can vary the terrain scanning rate, devoting more time to complex topography. Also, the profiles can be rechecked, and mistakes can be corrected. Most modern orthophoto systems are digitally based because of these advantages.

The digital terrain profiles generated in the off-line process represent a data base

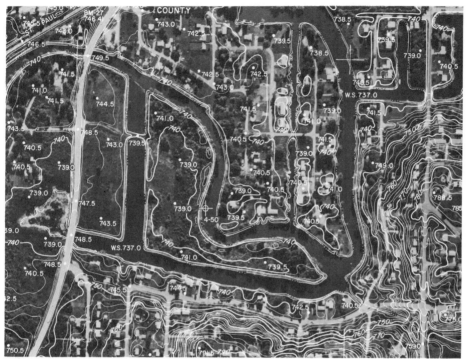

FIGURE 5.25   Portion of a 1:4800 topographic orthophotomap. Photography taken in 1975 at the Fox Chain of Lakes, Illinois. (Courtesy Alster and Associates, Inc.)

that can be used for a variety of purposes. For example, a contour line overlay for the orthophoto can be automatically drawn. Figure 5.26*a* shows a contour map generated in this manner. In Figure 5.26*b*, the digital data have been computer processed to derive a three-dimensional perspective view of the terrain. One of the most extensive uses of digital profile data is the generation of digital elevation models for use in GISs (Section 3.15) and various digital image processing operations (Chapter 10).

Orthophotographs may be viewed stereoscopically when they are paired with *stereomates*. These products are photographs made in an orthophoto instrument by *introducing* image parallax as a function of known terrain elevations obtained during the production of their corresponding orthophoto. Figure 5.27 illustrates an orthophoto and a corresponding stereomate that may be viewed stereoscopically. These products were generated as a part of a stereoscopic orthophotomapping program undertaken by the Canadian Forest Management Institute. The advantage of such products is that they combine the attributes of an orthophoto with the benefits of stereo observation.

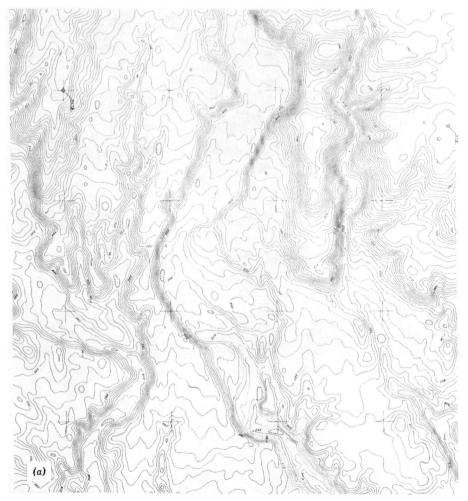

FIGURE 5.26 Typical off-line digital terrain profile products. *(a)* Contour map generated automatically from terrain profile data. *(b)* Three-dimensional perspective view generated for terrain depicted in *(a)*. (Courtesy Riverside County Flood Control and Water Conservation District, Riverside, Calif.)

5.11 FLIGHT PLANNING

Frequently, the objectives of a photographic remote sensing project can only be met through procurement of new photography of a study area. These occasions can arise for many reasons. For example, photography available for a particular area could be outdated for applications such as land use mapping. In addition, available photography may have been taken in the wrong season. For example, photography acquired for topographic mapping is usually flown in the fall or spring to minimize vegetative cover.

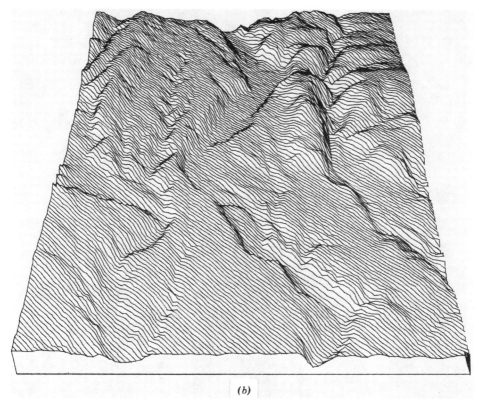

(b)

FIGURE 5.26 *(continued)*

This photography will likely be inappropriate for applications involving vegetation analysis. Furthermore, existing photos could be at an inappropriate scale for the application on hand or they could have been taken with an unsuitable film type. Frequently, analysts who require color infrared coverage of an area will find that only black and white panchromatic photography is available. Highly specialized applications may require unusual film–filter combinations or exposure settings, making it highly unlikely that existing photography will be suitable.

When new photography is required, the interpreter is frequently involved in planning the flight. He or she soon learns first hand that one of the most important parameters in an aerial mission is beyond the control of even the best planner—the weather. In most areas, only a few days of the year are ideal for aerial photography. In order to take advantage of clear weather, commercial aerial photography firms will fly many jobs in a single day, often at widely separated locations. Flights are usually scheduled between 10 A.M. and 2 P.M. for maximum illumination and minimum shadow. Overall, a great deal of time, effort, and expense go into the planning and execution of a photographic mission. In many respects, it is an art as well as a science.

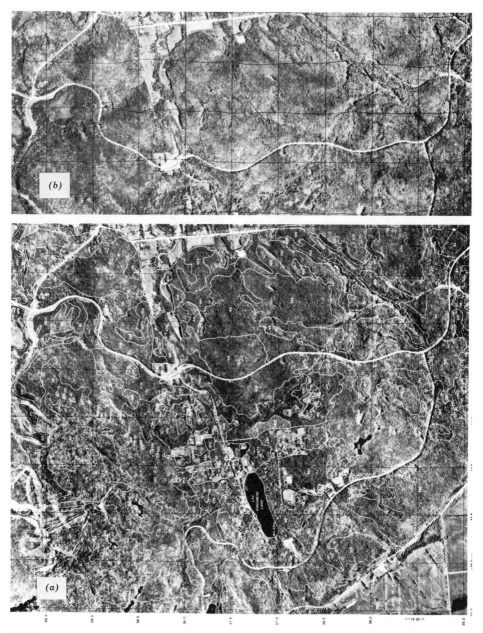

FIGURE 5.27 Stereo orthophotograph showing a portion of Gatineau Park, Canada. An ortho-photo (a) and a stereomate (b) provide for three-dimensional viewing of the terrain. Measurements made from, or plots made on, the orthophoto have map accuracy. Forest type information is overprinted on this scene along with a UTM grid. Note that the UTM grid is square on the orthophoto but is distorted by the introduction of parallax on the stereomate. 1:38,000. (Courtesy Forest Management Institute, Canadian Forestry Service.)

Below, we discuss the geometric aspects of the task of flight planning. The parameters needed for this task are (1) the focal length of the camera to be used; (2) the camera format size; (3) the photo scale desired; (4) the size of the area to be photographed; (5) the average elevation of the area to be photographed; (6) the overlap desired; (7) the sidelap desired; and (8) the ground speed of the aircraft to be used.

Based on the above parameters, the mission planner prepares computations and a flight map that indicate to the flight crew (1) the flying height above datum from which the photos are to be taken; (2) the location, direction, and number of flight lines to be made over the area to be photographed; (3) the time interval between exposures; (4) the number of exposures on each flight line; and, (5) the total number of exposures necessary for the mission.

Flight plans are normally portrayed on a map for the flight crew. However, old photography, an index mosaic, or even a satellite image may be used for this purpose. The computations prerequisite to preparing a flight plan are given in the following example.

EXAMPLE 5.14

A study area is 10 km wide in the east–west direction and 16 km long in the north–south direction (see Figure 5.28). A camera having a 152.4 mm focal length lens and a 230 mm format is to be used. The desired photo scale is 1:25,000 and the nominal endlap and sidelap are to be 60 and 30 percent. Beginning and ending flight lines are to be positioned along the boundaries of the study area. The only map available for the area is at a scale of 1:62,500. This map indicates that the average terrain elevation is 300 m above datum. Perform the computations necessary to develop a flight plan and draw a flight map.

Solution

(a) Use north–south flight lines to minimize the number of lines.

(b) Find the flying height above terrain ($H' = f/S$) and add the mean site elevation to find flying height above mean sea level:

$$H = \frac{f}{S} + h_{avg} = \frac{0.1524 \text{ m}}{1/25,000} + 300 \text{ m} = 4110 \text{ m}$$

(c) Determine ground coverage per image from film format size and photo scale:

$$\text{coverage per photo} = \frac{0.23 \text{ m}}{1/25,000} = 5750 \text{ m on a side}$$

(d) Determine ground separation between photos on a line for 40 percent advance per photo (i.e., 60 percent endlap):

$$0.40 \times 5750 \text{ m} = 2300 \text{ m between photo centers}$$

(e) Assuming an aircraft speed of 160 km/hr, the time between exposures is

$$\frac{2300 \text{ m/photo}}{160 \text{ km/hr}} \times \frac{3600 \text{ sec/hr}}{1000 \text{ m/km}} = 51.75 \text{ sec (use 51 sec)}$$

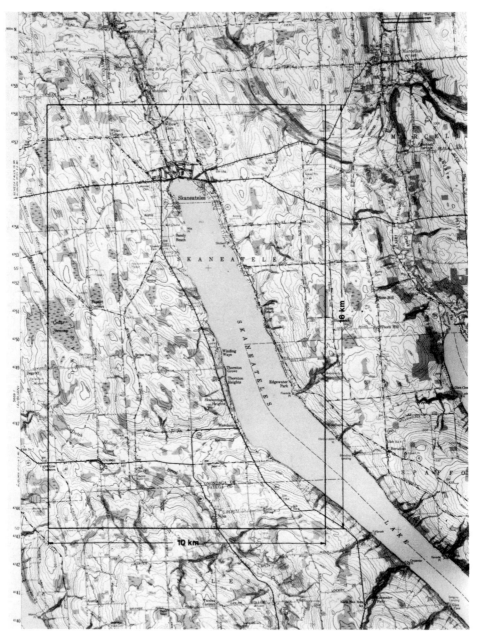

FIGURE 5.28   A 10 × 26 km study area over which photographic coverage is to be obtained.

(f) Because the intervalometer can only be set in even seconds (this varies between models), the number is rounded off. By rounding down, at least 60 percent coverage is ensured. Recalculate the distance between photo centers, using the reverse of the above equation:

$$51 \text{ sec/photo} \times 160 \text{ km/hr} \times \frac{1000 \text{ m/km}}{3600 \text{ sec/hr}} = 2267 \text{ m}$$

(g) Compute the number of photos per 16 km line by dividing this length by the photo advance. Add one photo to each end and round the number up to ensure coverage

$$\frac{16,000 \text{ m/line}}{2267 \text{ m/photo}} + 1 + 1 = 9.1 \text{ photos/line (use 10)}$$

(h) If the flight lines are to have a sidelap of 30 percent of the coverage, they must be separated by 70 percent of the coverage

$$0.70 \times 5750 \text{ m coverage} = 4025 \text{ m between flight lines}$$

(i) Find the number of flight lines required to cover the 10 km study area width by dividing this width by distance between flight lines (note: this division gives number of spaces between flight lines; add 1 to arrive at the number of lines):

$$\frac{10,000 \text{ m width}}{4025 \text{ m/fl. line}} + 1 = 3.48 \text{ (use 4)}$$

The adjusted spacing between lines for using 4 lines is

$$\frac{10,000 \text{ m}}{4-1 \text{ spaces}} = 3333 \text{ m/space}$$

(j) Find the spacing of flight lines on map (1:62,500 scale):

$$3333 \text{ m} \times \frac{1}{62,500} = 53.3 \text{ mm}$$

(k) Find total number of photos needed:

$$10 \text{ photos/line} \times 4 \text{ lines} = 40 \text{ photos}$$

(Note: The first and last flight lines in this example were positioned coincident with the boundaries of the study area. This provision ensures complete coverage of the area, under the "better safe than sorry" philosophy. Often, a savings in film, flight time, and money is realized by experienced flight crews by moving the first and last lines in toward the middle of the study area.)

The above computations would be summarized on a flight map as shown in Figure 5.29. In addition, a set of detailed specifications outlining the material, equipment, and procedures to be used for the mission would be agreed upon prior to the mission. These specifications typically spell out the requirements and tolerances for flying the

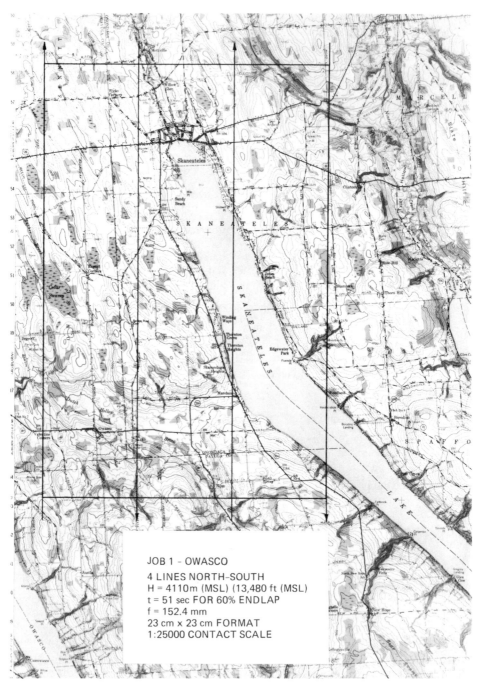

JOB 1 - OWASCO

4 LINES NORTH-SOUTH
H = 4110m (MSL) (13,480 ft (MSL)
t = 51 sec FOR 60% ENDLAP
f = 152.4 mm
23 cm x 23 cm FORMAT
1:25000 CONTACT SCALE

FIGURE 5.29 Flight map for Example 5.14. (Lines indicate centers of each flight line to be followed.)

mission, the form and quality of the products to be delivered, and the ownership rights to the original images. Among other things, mission specifications normally include such details as mission timing, ground control requirements, camera calibration characteristics, film and filter type, exposure conditions, scale tolerance, endlap, sidelap, tilt and crab, photographic quality, product indexing, and product delivery schedules.

5.12 ANALYTIC PHOTOGRAMMETRY

Historically, most photogrammetric operations have been premised on the physical projection and measurement of images with the aid of precise optical–mechanical equipment. In contrast, modern photogrammetry depends much more extensively on mathematical modeling to solve photogrammetric problems. Many of these procedures are premised on the basic *projective relationships* that exist when coordinate positions on airphotos are related to their counterparts on the ground. One of these basic relationships is the *collinearity condition*: that the exposure station, any ground point, and its photographic image all lie along the same straight line. Knowledge about any two of these three points allows mathematical description of the orientation of the line in space. Likewise, the intersection of lines specified from multiple images can be computed mathematically. *Analytic photogrammetry*, which forms the heart of analytical plotters, is primarily concerned with the application of these principles of solid analytic geometry. Analytic photogrammetry is now the basis for most modern photogrammetric procedures, including the generation of orthophotos and the compilation of digital maps. Analytic techniques embody precise photographic coordinate measurement with comparators, construction of mathematical models to describe the projective geometry of photographs (alone, in pairs, in strips, and in blocks), and the solution of these models using numerical methods instead of the analog methods emphasized in this chapter.

Analytic solutions to photogrammetric problems tend to be characterized by the highest order of accuracy. Analytic procedures effectively eliminate systematic errors such as film shrinkage, lens distortion, atmospheric refraction, earth curvature, and so on. Being premised on mathematical (instead of physical) models, analytic methods are virtually free of mechanical or optical limitations.

SELECTED BIBLIOGRAPHY

1. American Society of Photogrammetry, *Handbook of Nontopographic Photogrammetry*, Falls Church, Va., 1979.

2. American Society of Photogrammetry, *Manual of Photogrammetry*, 4th ed., Falls Church, Va., 1980.

3. American Society of Photogrammetry, Special 50th Anniversary Issue, *Photogrammetric Engineering and Remote Sensing*, vol. 50, no. 9, September 1984.

4. Burnside, C.D., *Mapping from Aerial Photographs*, Granada, London, 1979.

5. Ghosh, S.K., *Analytical Photogrammetry*, Pergamon, New York, 1979.

6. Lee, J.E., and S.D. Johnson, "Expectancy of Cloudless Photographic Days in the Contiguous United States," *Photogrammetric Engineering and Remote Sensing*, vol. 51, no. 12, December 1985, pp. 1883–1891.

7. Moffitt, F.H., and E.M. Mikhail, *Photogrammetry*, 3rd ed., Harper & Row, New York, 1980.

8. Wolf, P.R., *Elements of Photogrammetry*, 2nd ed., McGraw–Hill, New York, 1983.

CHAPTER SIX

RADIOMETRIC CHARACTERISTICS OF AERIAL PHOTOGRAPHS

6.1 INTRODUCTION

Thus far in our discussion of photographic remote sensing, we have described the basic interpretive and geometric characteristics of airphotos. This chapter deals with the *radiometric* characteristics of aerial photographs. These characteristics determine how a specific film—exposed and processed under specific conditions—responds to scene energy of varying intensity. Knowledge of these characteristics is often useful, and sometimes essential, to the process of photographic image analysis. This is particularly true when one attempts to establish a quantitative relationship between the tonal values on an image and some ground phenomenon. For example, one might wish to measure the darkness, or optical density, of a transparency at various image points in a corn field and correlate these measurements with a ground-observed parameter such as crop yield. If a correlation exists, the relationship could be used to predict crop yield based on photographic density measurements at other points in the scene. Such an effort can be successful only if the radiometric properties of the particular film under analysis are known. Even then, the analysis must be undertaken with due regard for such extraneous sensing effects as differing levels of illumination across a scene, atmospheric haze, and so on. If these factors can be sufficiently accounted for, considerable information can be extracted from the tonal levels expressed on a photograph. In short, image density measurements may sometimes be used in the process of determining the type, extent, and condition of ground objects. In this chapter, we discuss how density measurements are taken, and how the analyst can attempt to account for the factors that influence them.

Depending on the context and schedule for the course in which the student is using this book, the level of detail presented in this chapter may not be necessary. Chapters 7 to 10 have been written in anticipation of some students "skipping over" this chapter. However, command of the material in this chapter will facilitate the student's understanding of the comparative advantages and disadvantages of quantitative photographic versus nonphotographic remote sensing.

6.2   FILM EXPOSURE AND DENSITY

A photograph can be thought of as a visual record of the response of many small detectors to energy incident upon them. The energy detectors in a photographic record are the silver halide grains in the film emulsion and the energy causing the response of these detectors is referred to as a film's *exposure*. (See Section 2.3.) During the instant that one "takes" a photograph, the different reflected energy levels in the scene irradiate the film for the same length of time. A scene is visible on a processed film only because of the irradiance differences among scene elements. These in turn are caused by the reflectance differences among scene elements. Thus, *film exposure at a point in a photograph is directly related to the reflectance of the object imaged at that point. Theoretically, film exposure varies linearly with object reflectance, with both being a function of wavelength.*

There are many ways of quantifying and expressing film exposure. Most photographic literature uses units of the form *meter-candle-seconds (MCS)* or *ergs/cm²*. The student first "exposed" to this subject might feel hopelessly lost in understanding unit equivalents in photographic radiometry. This comes about since many exposure calibrations are referenced to the sensitivity response of the human eye, through definition of a "standard observer." Such observations are termed *photometric* and result in photometric, rather than radiometric, units. To avoid unnecessary confusion over how exposure is measured and expressed in absolute terms, we will deal with *relative* exposures and not be directly concerned about specifying any absolute units.

The result of exposure[1] at a point on a film, after development, is a silver deposit whose darkening, or light-stopping, qualities are systematically related to the amount of exposure at that point. One measure of the "darkness" or "lightness" at a given point on a film is *opacity*, O. Since most quantitative remote sensing image analyses involve the use of negatives or diapositives, opacity is determined through measurement of film *transmittance, T*. As shown in Figure 6.1, transmittance *T* is the ability of a film to pass light. At any given point *p*, the transmittance is

$$T_p = \frac{\text{light passing through the film at point } p}{\text{total light incident upon the film at point } p} \tag{6.1}$$

Opacity *O* at point *p* is

$$O_p = \frac{1}{T_p} \tag{6.2}$$

Although transmittance and opacity adequately describe the "darkness" of a film emulsion, it is often convenient to work with a logarithmic expression, *density*. This is an appropriate expression, since the human eye responds to light levels nearly loga-

---

[1]*Note*. The internationally accepted symbol for exposure is *H*. To avoid confusion with the use of this symbol for flying height, we use *E* to represent "exposure" in our discussions of photographic systems (Chapters 2 and 6). Elsewhere, *E* is used as the internationally accepted symbol for "irradiance."

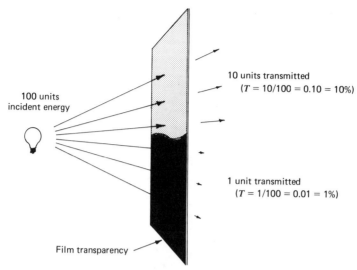

FIGURE 6.1 Film transmittance. To measure transmittance, a negative
or positive transparency is illuminated from one side and the light transmitted through the image is measured on the other. Shown is a section of an
image having a transmittance of 0.10 (or 10 percent) at one image point and
0.01 (or 1 percent) at another.

rithmically. Hence, there is a nearly linear relationship between image density and its
visual tone. Density D at a point p is defined as the common logarithm of film opacity at
that point

$$D_p = \log(O_p) = \log\left(\frac{1}{T_p}\right) \tag{6.3}$$

Instruments designed to measure density by shining light through film transparencies are called *transmission densitometers*. Density measurements may also be made
from paper prints with a *reflectance densitometer*, but more precise measurements can
be made on the original film material. When analyzing density on a transparency, the
process normally involves placing the film in a beam of light that passes through it. The
darker an image is, the smaller the amount of light that is allowed to pass, the lower the
transmittance, the higher the opacity, and the higher the density. Some sample values
of transmittance, opacity, and density are indicated in Table 6.1.

There are some basic differences between the nature of light absorptance in black
and white versus color films. Densities measured on black and white film are controlled by the amount of developed silver in the image areas of measurement. In color
photography, the processed image contains no silver and densities are caused by the
absorption characteristics of the film's three dye layers: yellow, magenta, and cyan.

TABLE 6.1 Sample Transmittance, Opacity, and Density Values

% Transmittance	T	O	D
100	1.0	1	0.00
50	0.50	2	0.30
25	0.25	4	0.60
10	0.10	10	1.00
1	0.01	100	2.00
0.1	0.001	1000	3.00

The image analyst is normally interested in investigating the image density of each of these dye layers separately. Hence, color film densities are normally measured through each of three filters chosen to isolate the spectral regions of maximum absorption of the three film dyes.

6.3 FILM CHARACTERISTIC CURVES

An essential task in quantitative film analysis is to relate image density values measured on a photograph to the exposure levels that produced them. This is done to establish the cause (exposure) and effect (density) relationship that characterizes a given photograph.

Since density is a logarithmic parameter, it is convenient to also deal with exposure E in logarithmic form (log E). If one plots density values as a function of the log E values that produced them, curves similar to those shown in Figure 6.2 will be obtained.

The curves shown in Figure 6.2 are for a typical black and white negative film (a) and a color reversal film (b). Every film has a unique $D-log E$ curve, from which many of the characteristics of the film may be determined. Because of this, these curves are known as *characteristic curves*. (Plotting D versus log E to express the nature of the photographic response was first suggested in the 1890s by Hurter and Driffield. Consequently, characteristic curves are often referred to as $H and D$ as well as $D-log E$ curves.)

Characteristic curves are different for different film types, for different manufacturing batches within a film type, and even for films of the same batch. Manufacturing, handling, storage, and processing conditions all affect the response of a film (indicated by its $D-log E$ curve). In the case of color film, characteristic curves also differ between one emulsion layer and another.

Figure 6.3 illustrates the various film response characteristics extractable from a $D-log E$ curve. The curve shown is typical of a black and white negative film (similar characteristics are found for each layer of a color film). There are three general

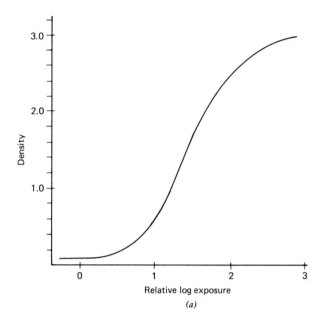

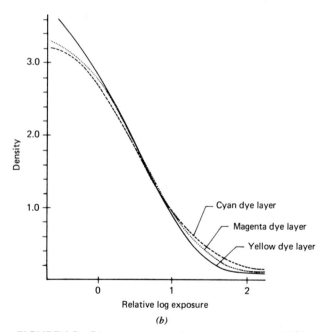

FIGURE 6.2 Film density versus log exposure curves. *(a)* Black and white negative film. *(b)* Color reversal film (positive film). (These curves are referred to as film characteristic curves, *D*−log *E* curves, or *H* and *D* curves.)

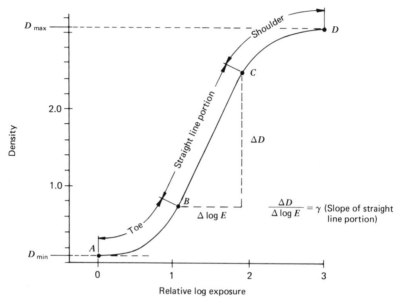

FIGURE 6.3   Components of a characteristic curve.

divisions to the curve. First, as the exposure increases from that of point A to that of point B, the density increases from a minimum, D_{min}, at an increasing rate. This portion of the curve is called the *toe*. As exposure increases from point B to point C, changes in density are nearly linearly proportional to changes in log exposure. This region is called the *straight-line portion* of the curve. Finally, as log exposure increases from point C to point D, the density increases at a decreasing rate. This portion is known as the *shoulder* of the curve. The shoulder terminates at a maximum density, D_{max}. Remember that this curve applies to a negative film. For a positive film (Figure 6.2b), the relationship is reversed. That is, density decreases with increasing exposure.

It should be noted that even in areas of a film where there is no exposure, a minimum density D_{min} results from two causes: (1) The plastic base of the film has some density D_{base}, and (2) some density develops even when an unexposed emulsion is processed. This second type of density is called *fog*, or *net fog*, D_{fog}. D_{min} is sometimes called *gross fog* and is expressed as

$$D_{min} = D_{base} + D_{fog} \qquad (6.4)$$

The range of densities a film provides is simply the difference between D_{max} and D_{min}.

Another important characteristic of the D–log E curves is the slope of the linear portion of the curve. This slope is called *gamma* (γ) and is expressed as

$$\gamma = \frac{\Delta D}{\Delta \log E} \tag{6.5}$$

Gamma is an important determinant of the *contrast* of a film. While the term contrast has no rigid definition, in general the higher the gamma, the higher the contrast of a film. With high contrast film, a given scene exposure range is distributed over a large density range; the reverse is true of low contrast film. For example, consider a photograph taken of a light gray and a dark gray object. On high contrast film, the two gray levels may lie at the extremes of the density scale, resulting in nearly white and nearly black images on the processed photograph. On low contrast film, both gray values would lie at nearly the same point on the density scale, showing the two objects in about the same shade of gray.

Gamma is a function of not only emulsion type but also film development conditions. For example, gamma can be varied by changing developer, development time, and/or temperature. For any given developer, gamma is usually increased with longer development time or higher development temperature.

An important basic characteristic of a film is its *speed*, which expresses the level of exposure to which the film will respond. This parameter is graphically represented by the horizontal position of the characteristic curve along the log E axis. A "fast" film is one that will accommodate low exposure levels (that is, it lies farther to the left on the log E axis). For a given level of scene energy, a fast film will require a shorter exposure time than will a slow film. This is advantageous in aerial photography, since it reduces image blur due to the flight motion. However, high speed films are generally characterized by larger film grains, limiting the spatial resolution of images. Thus, no single film speed will be optimum in all cases.

The speed of nonaerial films is typically stated using the ISO (ASA) system. This system is generally not used to specify the speed of aerial photographic films. Rather, for panchromatic aerial films, the American National Standard for film responsivity is the *aerial film speed (AFS)*. By definition

$$AFS = \frac{3}{2E_0} \tag{6.6}$$

where E_0 is the exposure (in meter-candle-seconds) at the point on the characteristic curve where the density is 0.3 above $D_{\min}$ under strictly specified processing conditions. For other processing conditions and for color and infrared sensitive films, *effective aerial film speeds* are used to indicate sensitivity. These values are determined empirically, often by comparison with black and white films in actual flight tests.

Knowledge of film speed is essential for proper exposure of aerial film in flight. A *Kodak Aerial Exposure Computer*, based on effective aerial film speeds, is available to assist aerial photographers in obtaining properly exposed photography. With the computer, a lens opening and shutter speed combination is suggested for a given film based on the film speed, the date of photography, the latitude of the flight area, the time of day, the flight altitude, and the haze condition.

Two other useful film characteristics can be determined from the $D-\log E$ curve. These are a film's *exposure latitude* and its *radiometric resolution*. These characteristics are best described with reference to Figure 6.4, where the $D-\log E$ curves for two different negative films are shown.

The term *exposure latitude* expresses the range of log E values that will yield an acceptable image on a given film. For most films, good results are obtained when scenes are recorded over the linear portion of the $D-\log E$ curves and a fraction of the toe of the curve (Figure 6.4). Features recorded on the extremes of the toe or shoulder of the curve will be underexposed or overexposed. In these areas, different exposure levels will be recorded at essentially the same density, making discrimination difficult. Note in Figure 6.4 that Film 2 has a much larger exposure latitude than Film 1. (Also note that Film 2 is a "slower" film than Film 1.)

The term "exposure latitude" is also used to indicate the range of variation from the optimum camera exposure setting that can be tolerated without excessively degrading the image quality. For example, an exposure latitude of $\pm\frac{1}{2}$ stop is generally specified for color infrared film. This means that the F/STOP setting can be $\frac{1}{2}$ stop above or below the optimum setting and still produce an acceptable photograph.

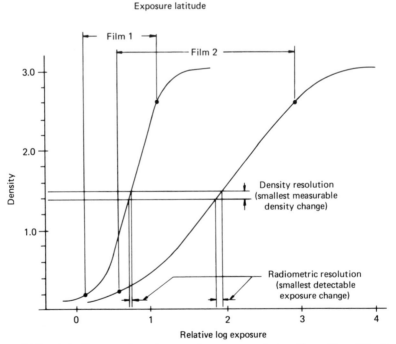

FIGURE 6.4   Exposure latitude and radiometric resolution of two films. (Film 2 has larger exposure latitude but poorer radiometric resolution than Film 1.)

Radiometric resolution is the smallest difference in exposure that can be detected in a given film analysis. It is not a characteristic of a film per se but is set by the ability of a given densitometer to discriminate between density levels. In turn, this density resolvability is used to determine the radiometric resolution using the characteristic curve, as shown in Figure 6.4. Radiometric resolution is inversely proportional to contrast, so for a given density resolvability, a higher contrast film (that is, Film 1 in Figure 6.4) is able to resolve smaller differences in exposure.

The trade-offs between contrast, exposure latitude, and radiometric resolution can now be seen. Although exceptions to the rule exist, low contrast films offer greater radiometric range (exposure latitude) at the expense of radiometric resolution. High contrast films offer a smaller exposure range but improved radiometric resolution.

6.4 PREPARING CHARACTERISTIC CURVES

To this point, we have not dealt with the manner in which characteristic curves are actually prepared. This is a three-step process. First, a series of known, controlled exposures is impressed on the unexposed film in the laboratory. After processing, the film densities are measured with a densitometer at each of the known exposure levels. The density measurements are then plotted against the log of the known exposure values.

One method of placing known exposures onto a film would be to take a series of photographs of a constant light source using varying camera shutter speeds. In this way, the film would be exposed to a series of different, known exposures. In practice, film exposure is normally controlled by exposing the film by a light source through a series of filters of varying, known transmittances. These filters modulate the intensity of the source light, resulting again in a series of known exposures.

Controlled film exposures are made in a device called a *sensitometer*, the basic components of which are illustrated in Figure 6.5. This device consists of a light source, a shutter mechanism, and a system for modulating the intensity of the light reaching the film. The function of each of these components is outlined below.

Sensitometer light sources are selected to be spectrally equivalent to the illumination used to expose the film under field conditions. For aerial films, the light source is generally chosen to approximate daylight spectral quality. This is normally accomplished through use of a tungsten lamp and appropriate spectral correction filters.

Sensitometer shutters are designed to provide a range of possible shutter times for proper exposure of various film types. In lieu of an adjustable shutter, neutral density filters may be used to control exposure.

Film exposure is modulated by introducing either a continuous or stepped density wedge between the color corrected source light and the film. The *step wedge* (Figure 6.6a) is the more common means of exposure control. It usually consists of 21 "steps" of known density that attenuate the source light into nominal steps of 0.15 log E. This provides for a uniformly stepped log E range of 0 to 3 (that is, a relative E range of 1 to 1000). The sensitometer exposes a "picture" of this wedge (Figure 6.6c) onto the film. After processing, the image density of each of the steps in the picture is measured with

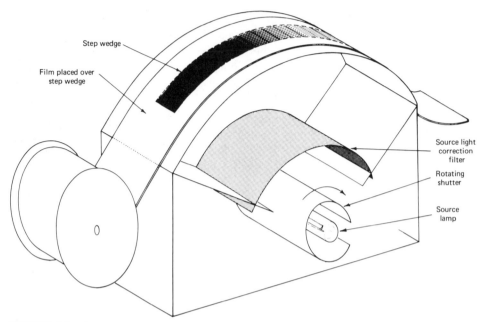

Step wedge

Film placed over
step wedge

Source light
correction
filter

Rotating
shutter

Source
lamp

FIGURE 6.5 Schematic of a sensitometer.

a densitometer (Figure 6.7). The measured step densities are then plotted against the step number or the scale of relative log exposure (Figure 6.8). (If the sensitometer illumination intensity is known absolutely, a plot of D versus log *absolute* exposure would result. As long as each roll of film is calibrated with the same sensitometer, the relative exposure reference system is adequate.)

Normally, the step wedge image used to prepare a characteristic curve is physically exposed on the beginning and/or end of the roll of film exposed in flight. This helps ensure identical handling and processing conditions for the calibration wedge and the mission imagery to which it applies.

$D-\log E$ curves are the primary mechanism for monitoring the quality and repeatability of photographic processing. Even more important to us, these curves are the only frame of reference by which density measurements from mission imagery can be associated with scene exposures. *Consequently, sensitometric control is a necessity for virtually all quantitative radiometric film analyses.*

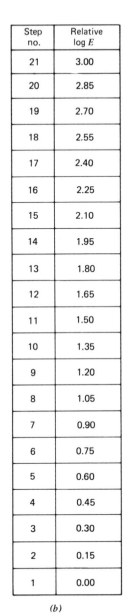

Step no.	Relative log E
21	3.00
20	2.85
19	2.70
18	2.55
17	2.40
16	2.25
15	2.10
14	1.95
13	1.80
12	1.65
11	1.50
10	1.35
9	1.20
8	1.05
7	0.90
6	0.75
5	0.60
4	0.45
3	0.30
2	0.15
1	0.00

(a)

(b)

(c)

FIGURE 6.6 Step wedge used in D–log E curve preparation. A calibrated wedge having steps of known transmittance *(a)* is introduced between the sensitometer light source and the film to be calibrated (see Figure 6.5). This results in exposure of the film to a series of known relative log E values *(b)*. The exposed picture of the step wedge is processed *(c)* and the density of each step is measured.

FIGURE 6.7 Densitometer being used to measure step wedge densities. A density reading is taken on each step of the step wedge picture.

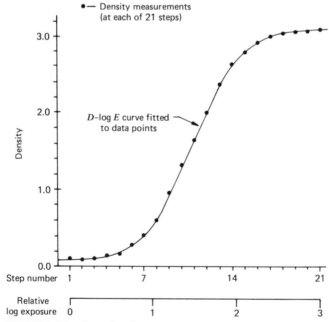

FIGURE 6.8 Plot of a characteristic curve from density measurements obtained from picture of the step wedge.

6.5 DENSITOMETERS

As previously stated, density is measured with an instrument called a *densitometer* (or *microdensitometer* when small film areas are measured). While many varieties of densitometers exist, most have the same six basic components, shown in Figure 6.9:

1. *Light source.* Supplies energy to illuminate the image with a beam of incident radiation.
2. *Aperture assembly.* Provides for selectable spot sizes over which density measurements can be made.
3. *Filter assembly.* Allows selection of spectral bands when making density measurements on color film.
4. *Receiver.* A photoelectric device, normally a photomultiplier tube (PMT), that responds electronically to the component of the illuminating beam transmitted through the image.
5. *Electronics.* Amplify the output of the receiver, convert it logarithmically to a density value, and express it in a digital representation. Calibration controls enable the density readings to be standardized to a calibration step wedge.
6. *Readout/recorder.* Indicates the density value. Some densitometers have a provision for recording density value on computer-compatible tape.

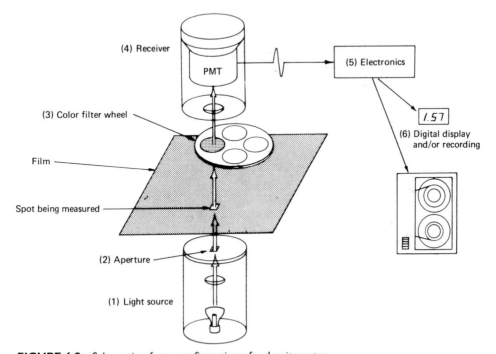

FIGURE 6.9 Schematic of one configuration of a densitometer.

With *spot* densitometers, different reading positions on the image are located by manually translating the image under analysis with respect to the measurement optics. These devices are convenient in applications where conventional visual interpretation is supported by taking a small number of density readings at discrete points of interest in an image. Applications calling for density measurements throughout an entire image dictate the use of *scanning* densitometers.

There are basically two types of scanning densitometers: *flatbed* systems and *rotating drum* systems. Figure 6.10 illustrates the comparative nature of scanning in each of these system types. In a flatbed system (Figure 6.10*a*), the image under study is translated with respect to the source/receiver optics in a flat plane. Readings are taken at discrete intervals along scan lines in the *x* direction. At the end of each scan line, the instrument "steps" in the *y* direction to scan along a line contiguous to the previous one. The process is repeated until a complete set of data is collected over the image area of interest.

Rotating drum scanners (Figure 6.10*b*) accomplish the scanning task in a different fashion. With these systems, the film is mounted over a square opening in a rotating drum such that it forms a portion of the drum's circumference. The *x* coordinate scanning motion is provided by the rotation of the drum. The *y* coordinate motion comes from incremental translation of the source/receiver optics after each drum rotation. A flatbed and a rotating drum densitometer are shown in Figures 6.11 and 6.12. Note that the drum scanner shown in Figure 6.12 has the capability to both "read" and "write" film images. Hence it can be used to measure film densities from a given image *or* generate an image from given density values.

The output from a scanning densitometer is essentially a fine matrix of measurements covering an image. This matrix is composed of spatially ordered picture elements (pixels) whose size is determined by the aperture of the source/receiving optics used during the scanning process. As the apertured measuring spot is scanned across the image, the continuous output from the photomultiplier tube is converted to a

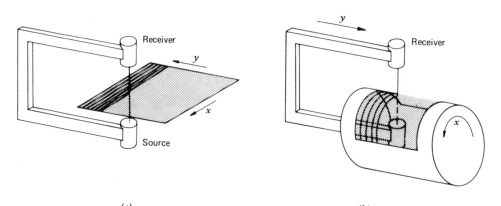

(a)   (b)

FIGURE 6.10   Flatbed *(a)* and rotating drum *(b)* scanning densitometer operation.

FIGURE 6.11 Perkin–Elmer PDS Model 1010A flatbed scanning densitometer. (Courtesy Perkin– Elmer Corp.)

series of discrete numerical values on a pixel-by-pixel basis. This analog-to-digital (A-to-D) conversion process normally results in recording the density data on magnetic tape in binary form as integer values. For example, the density measurement range of 0 to 3 might be expressed in 256 integer gray levels.

The result of the scanning densitometric measuring process is illustrated in Figure 6.13. Shown in (*a*) is a portion of a positive transparency whose numerical representation stemming from the scanning process is shown in (*b*). Such *xy* matrices of contiguous pixel values are termed *rasters*. The raster shown in (*b*) is for representation purposes only, in that a *very* large measurement aperture is shown. In actuality, pixels as small as 50 to 100 μm are common. Note that the data volumes in such rasters can "overwhelm" the image analyst. For example, assuming a scanning aperture and scan line spacing of 100 μm were used, 10 density observations per lineal millimeter in both *x* and *y* would result, yielding 100 observations for a 1 mm square film area! Triple this data quantity is involved when color photography is scanned sequentially through blue, green, and red filters, to analyze the response of each film dye layer. Obviously, such data loads can be handled only by computer. However, the inherent advantage of scanning systems is the fact that their data can be recorded directly in a computer-compatible form. This characteristic also typifies certain *video* and *array digitizers*. These devices are designed to very rapidly encode images numerically for subsequent computer analysis. Although such systems sometimes lack the spatial and radiometric resolution of densitometers, their data outputs have essentially the same form—spatially ordered, digital image representations.

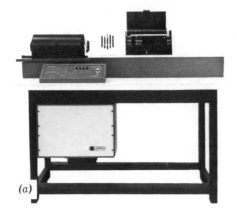

(a)

FIGURE 6.12 Rotating drum scanning densitometer. (Courtesy Optronics International, Inc.) (a) Optronics Model P-1700 system, including densitometer (upper right), electronics (lower left), and film recorder (upper left). (b) Closeup of densitometer, showing drum, light source (center), and receiver (bottom center).

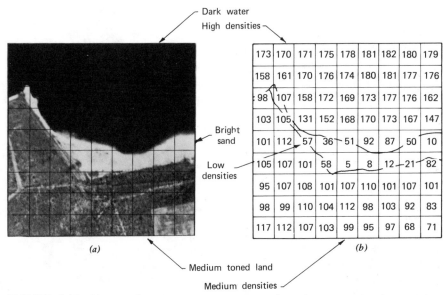

Dark water
High densities

Bright sand

Low densities

Medium toned land
Medium densities

FIGURE 6.13 Numerical image representation resulting from scanning densitometer measurements. *(a)* Original photograph (print shown here but transparency used in actual scanning operation). *(b)* Numerical representation of image in *(a)*.

6.6 SELECTED EXAMPLES OF DENSITOMETRIC ANALYSIS

As mentioned previously, a primary advantage of measuring image densities is the ability to quantify the radiometric dimension of photography as an aid in the interpretation process. This process normally takes on the following form. First, we collect ground reference data at points of known ground condition and measure the density on the image at these points. Next, we establish a relationship between the ground condition and image density. To reliably do this, we convert the density D values to exposure E values via the $D-\log E$ curve, and compare the exposure values to our ground reference data. After determining the relationship between exposure and ground conditions at the ground reference points, we may apply it to other points on the image to determine ground conditions from corresponding densities. We consider two selected examples to illustrate this ability. The first deals with the analysis of a black and white image using a spot densitometer, and the second treats the analysis of a color infrared image using a scanning densitometer.

Shown in Figure 6.14 is a panchromatic photograph of a portion of a hardwood forest that has been severely defoliated by a gypsy moth infestation. In dealing with such problems, the forest manager can plan suppression measures only if he or she has knowledge of the extent, severity, and spread pattern of the defoliating agent. This

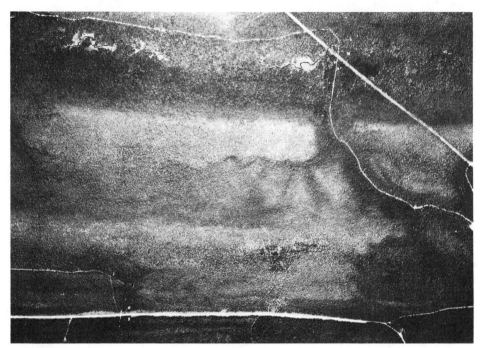

FIGURE 6.14 Panchromatic aerial photograph showing a portion of the Bald Eagle State Forest, Pennsylvania, July 1, 1975. (Note excessive defoliation of the hardwood forest, except along the roadway where spraying has been used to combat the gypsy moth.) (Courtesy U.S. Forest Service.)

information is routinely gathered through ground surveys and aerial sketch-mapping procedures. (The latter involves visual observation of the area from an aircraft and in-flight sketching of problem locations.) Ground surveys for large areas are very time consuming and require a large work force of trained personnel. Aerial sketch-mapping also requires a great deal of time, highly skilled observers, and extended periods of good weather. Both of these methods are very expensive and their results are highly qualitative and subjective. A more objective approach to performing such a defoliation survey might be to employ aerial photography and image density measurements to assist in estimating the extent and severity of the defoliation present.

Suppose we wish to categorize the defoliation areas shown in Figure 6.14 into three levels of severity: high, medium, and low. We could do this by first measuring the image densities at ground reference areas known to characterize each of these categories. Then, working through the $D-\log E$ curve for the film under analysis, we could determine the $\log E$ (and by taking the antilog, exposure E) occurring within each ground reference area. Since exposure E is known to vary with object reflectance R, we could use density as an indirect measure of tree reflectance. We will assume that we have determined (on the basis of reference data) that the reflectance of any tree shown in the scene is a direct function of its remaining foliage. Hence, we can use the densities measured on the image at the ground reference areas, along with the $D-\log E$ curve for the film, to categorize all the trees in the image into defoliation levels. For example, assume that the average density values measured over many ground truth plots representative of each defoliation class are as shown below.

Defoliation class	Average density reading
High	0.50
Medium	1.10
Low	2.00

The $D-\log E$ curve for the film under study is shown in Figure 6.15. From this curve, we determine the relative $\log E$ values associated with the average density measurements for the reference data plots. Having relative $\log E$ values, taking antilogs yields the relative exposure E values associated with each defoliation class.

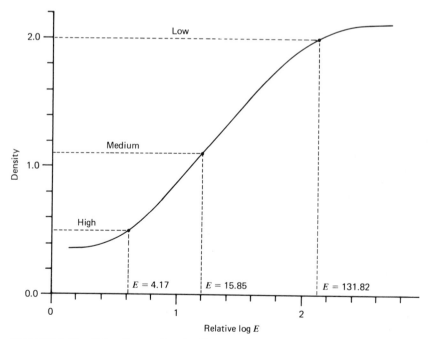

FIGURE 6.15   *D*-log *E* curve for the film imaging the defoliation site.

The results of this process are summarized below.

Defoliation class	Density	Relative log E	Relative E
High	0.50	0.62	4.17
Medium	1.10	1.20	15.85
Low	2.00	2.12	131.82

In order to establish class boundaries, we will assume that *high* defoliation is related to exposure values within the range bounded by relative $E = 0$ and the exposure midway between 4.17 and 15.85. This value is $E = 10.01$. Similarly, we will assume that the lower bound of the exposure for *low* defoliation areas is halfway between relative E values 15.85 and 131.82. This value is 73.84. Note again that this rationale assumes that the extent of defoliation varies linearly with reflectance and, therefore, exposure. In this manner, the class boundaries are established midway between E values *not* log E values. (A more statistical approach to establishing these boundaries would be to gather several sample values for each class, to calculate means and standard deviations, and to derive class boundaries on this basis. These techniques are described in Chapter 10.)

Again using the $D-\log E$ curve for the film, the boundaries between defoliation classes can be expressed in terms of density. This amounts to finding the relative log E values for the class boundaries and determining the associated density D values. The results of this effort are summarized below.

	Defoliation class		
	High	Medium	Low
Relative E	< 10.01	10.01–73.84	> 73.84
Relative log E	< 1.00	1.00– 1.87	> 1.87
Density	< 0.90	0.90– 1.90	> 1.90

Now that our exposure boundaries have been converted to density values, we could analyze the extent of defoliation at any arbitrary point in the scene simply by measuring the image density at the point. We could also level-slice (Section 10.4) the original image into defoliation classes by setting the limits of each slice at the computed density boundary between classes. Figure 6.16 illustrates the results of such an approach. Figure 6.16a shows the level-sliced image as displayed on a CRT screen. This display quantitatively expresses the three brightness regimes in the original scene. Note that

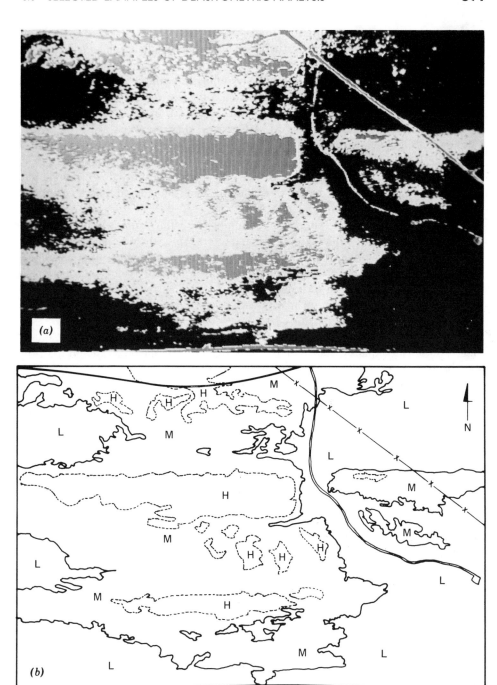

FIGURE 6.16 Defoliation map obtained by level-slicing the photograph shown in Figure 6.14. (a) Level-sliced display. (b) Resulting map. Three classes of defoliation severity are shown: high (H), medium (M), and low (L).

some subjective judgments must be made to discount extraneous features such as roadways and powerlines in order to arrive at a finished defoliation map, as shown in Figure 6.16b.

Our second example of densitometric analysis illustrates the basic form and utility of scanning microdensitometer data obtained from color infrared imagery. Figure 6.17a is a black and white copy (to show the details) of a small portion of a color infrared aerial photograph taken by NASA on July 31, 1974, over Madison, Wisconsin. The flying height was 18,300 m and the lens focal length was 152.5 mm, yielding a photo scale of 1:120,000. Figure 6.17a has been enlarged 9.2 times from the original, giving a scale here of about 1:13,000. This photograph shows a portion of an urban area containing streets, buildings, grass, and trees, as well as part of a lake crossed by railroad tracks and a causeway.

The original positive transparency was scanned in a drum-scanning microdensitometer sequentially through blue, green, and red filters. Since the original film was color infrared, scanning through a blue filter primarily yields information on green reflectance from the scene, scanning through a green filter primarily yields information on red reflectance, and scanning through a red filter primarily yields information on infrared reflectance. (We say "primarily" because of the slight overlaps in film layer sensitivities and color dye densities.)

The spot size used for scanning was 100 μm. The original film scale was 1:120,000. Since photo scale equals distance on the film divided by distance on the ground, the spot size on the ground can be calculated as

$$\text{ground spot size} = \frac{\text{distance on film (spot size)}}{\text{photo scale}}$$

or

$$\text{spot size} = \frac{100 \ \mu\text{m}}{1/120,000} = 100 \ \mu\text{m} \times 120,000 = 12 \times 10^6 \ \mu\text{m} = 12 \ \text{m}$$

The scene shown here contains 5106 pixels, each 12×12 m in size.

The scanning microdensitometer records film density as one of 256 levels for each pixel. Ignoring Figures 6.17b and c for the moment, note that d to f are "level slices" of the original film image as scanned through each of the blue, green, and red filters. These computer printouts show "scene brightness values" (the inverse of film density levels) in a range from 0 to 255. High scene brightness values mean high reflectance from the ground, low values mean low reflectance. In these figures, the original film density information stored in the computer has been "sliced," or divided, into nine levels for display purposes and printed out in symbols of varying darkness. The least dark symbol (•) represents the lowest scene brightness (highest film density). The darkest symbol (■) represents the highest scene brightness (lowest film density). In effect, the computer printouts are "negative" images. The level slices are accomplished by taking equal increments of scene brightness values. In Figure 6.17d, each

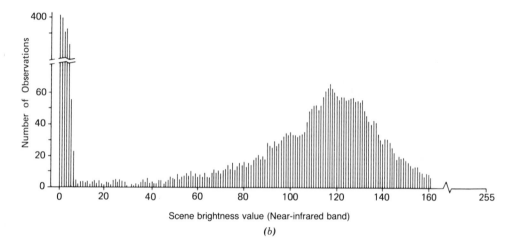

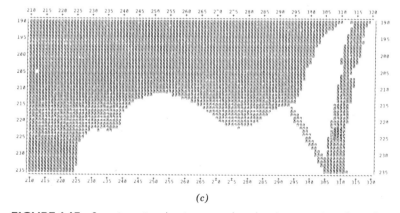

FIGURE 6.17 Scanning microdensitometer data showing a portion of an urban area and a lake. (a) Airphoto of scene. 1:13,000. (b) Histogram of infrared band scene brightness values. (c) "Classification" of scene into "land" (0) and "water" (blank). (d) Level slice of green sensitive film layer. (e) Level slice of red sensitive film layer. (f) Level slice of infrared sensitive film layer.

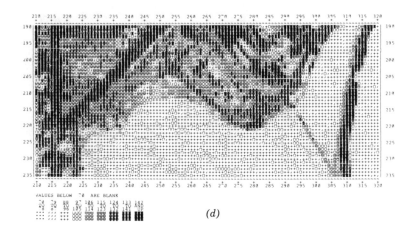

(d)

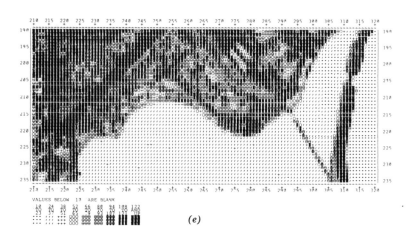

(e)

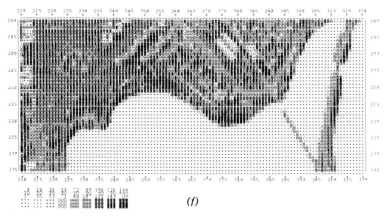

(f)

FIGURE 6.17 *(continued)*

symbol represents nine levels of scene brightness information stored in the computer (70–78, 79–87, 88–96, etc.); in Figure 6.17e, each symbol represents 14 levels; in Figure 6.17f, each symbol represents 18 levels.

Returning to Figure 6.17b, the distribution of scene brightness values in the infrared sensitive layer of the film is shown by a histogram of the brightness values obtained through the red filter. A great many values lie in the low data range of 0 to 5 because there is very little reflection from the lake water in the infrared portion of the spectrum. The remainder of the scene brightness values (6 to 161) represent various amounts of reflectance from the land portion of the scene. By comparing the patterns of Figures 6.17a with 6.17f, we can see that the highest infrared reflectance comes from the various areas of grass and trees (note the dark tones in 6.17f along the lakefront park) and the lowest land infrared reflectance comes from two rooftops near row 197, column 277.

Because there is a distinct difference between the infrared reflectance of land and water, a "classification" of this scene into the categories "land" and "water" can be made by means of a level slice. Figure 6.17c illustrates such a classification, where the land areas are shown by the symbol ∅ (scene brightness values 6 to 161) and the water areas remain blank (scene brightness values 0 to 5). This is a very accurate classification with virtually no misclassified pixels. The single apparent exception is the pixel at row 205, column 212, a land area that has been classified as water. This 12×12 m area has a very low scene reflectance in all three bands and appears to be a very dark building shadow.

A comparison of Figures 6.17d, e, and f shows variations in scene brightness values of various objects in the green, red, and infrared bands. Water in the lake (which contains a great deal of algae at the time of this late July image) has the highest reflectance in green and the lowest in the infrared. The greatest distinction between concrete streets and the surrounding grass and trees is in the green band, the least in the infrared band (note the street running vertically along columns 215 and 217 and the street running diagonally from row 200, column 218 to row 190, column 250).

Note that the example classification we have presented here is an extremely simple one. Further classification of the urban area into different land cover types (roofs, pavement, grass, trees, etc.) cannot be accurately accomplished using a level slice of a single band, but would require looking simultaneously at reflectance in two, three, or more bands. Furthermore, some of these bands might have to be located outside the spectral limits of photography. As we see in Chapter 7, multispectral scanners provide just such data. Although these systems lack the spatial resolution of photographic systems, their data are inherently amenable to computer processing in that they may be provided in digital form directly. Array cameras (see Section 2.17) provide the same general advantage to the image acquisition process, that is, direct gathering of digital remote sensor data without intervening densitometric analysis of photographs.

6.7   GEOMETRIC FACTORS INFLUENCING FILM EXPOSURE

Up to this point in our discussion, we have assumed that film exposure (and hence density) variations are related solely to variations in ground object type and/or condition. This assumption is a great oversimplification since many factors that have nothing to do with the type or condition of a ground feature can and do influence film exposure measurements. Because these factors influence exposure measurements but have nothing to do with true changes in ground cover type or condition, we term them *extraneous effects*. Extraneous effects are of two general types: geometric and atmospheric. We treat the atmospheric effects in the next section; here we discuss the major geometric effects that influence film exposure.

Probably the most important geometric effect influencing film exposure is *exposure falloff*. This extraneous effect is a variation in focal plane exposure purely associated with the distance an image point is from the image center. Because of falloff, *a ground scene of spatially uniform reflectance does not produce spatially uniform exposure in the focal plane*. Instead, for a uniform ground scene, exposure in the focal plane is at a maximum at the center of the film format and decreases with radial distance from the center.

The factors causing falloff are depicted in Figure 6.18, which shows a film being exposed to a ground area assumed to be of uniform brightness. For a beam of light coming from a point directly on the optical axis, exposure E_o is directly proportional to the area, A, of the lens aperture and inversely proportional to the square of the focal length of the lens, f^2. However, for a beam exposing a point at an angle θ off the optical axis, exposure E_θ is reduced from E_0 for three reasons:

1. The effective light collecting area of the lens aperture, A, decreases in proportion to cos θ when imaging off-axis areas ($A_\theta = A \cos \theta$).

2. The distance from the camera lens to the focal plane, f_θ, increases as $1/\cos \theta$ for off-axis points, $f_\theta = f/\cos \theta$. Since exposure varies inversely as the square of this distance, there is an exposure reduction of $\cos^2\theta$.

3. The effective size of a film area element, dA, projected perpendicular to the beam decreases in proportion to cos θ when the element is located off-axis, $dA_\theta = dA \cos \theta$.

Combining the above effects, the overall theoretical reduction in film exposure for an off-axis point is

$$E_\theta = E_0 \cos^4\theta \tag{6.7}$$

where
θ = the angle between the optical axis and the ray to the off-axis point
E_θ = the film exposure at the off-axis point
E_0 = the exposure that would have resulted if the point had been located at the optical axis

The systematic effect expressed by the above equation is compounded by differential transmittance of the lens and by *vignetting effects* in the camera optics. Vignetting refers to internal shadowing resulting from the lens mounts and other aperture

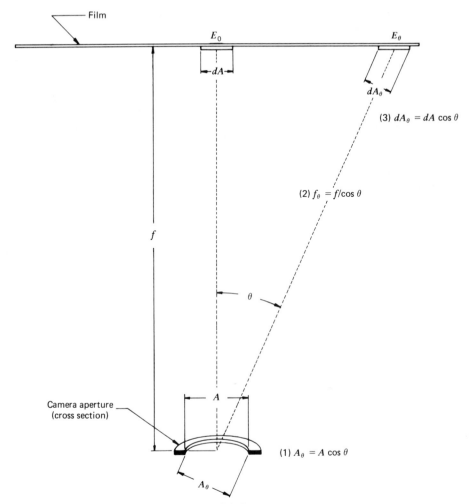

FIGURE 6.18 Factors causing exposure falloff.

surfaces within the camera. The effect of vignetting varies from camera to camera and varies with aperture setting for any given camera.

Falloff and vignetting are normally mitigated at the time of exposure by using antivignetting filters (see Section 2.10). When such filters are not used, or when they fail to negate the exposure variations completely, it is appropriate to correct off-axis exposure values by normalizing them to the value they would possess had they been at the center of the photograph. This is done through the application of a correction model that is determined (for a given F/STOP) by a radiometric calibration of the camera. This calibration essentially involves photographing a scene of uniform brightness, measuring exposure at various θ locations, and identifying the relationship that best describes the falloff. For most cameras this relationship takes on the form

$$E_\theta = E_0 \cos^n\theta \tag{6.8}$$

Because modern cameras are normally constructed in such a way that their actual falloff characteristics are much less severe than the theoretical $\cos^4$ falloff, n in the above equation is normally in the range 1.5 to 4. All exposure values measured off-axis are then corrected in accordance with the falloff characteristics of the particular camera in use.

To illustrate the application of the falloff correction, assume that a relative exposure value of 100 units is measured at a point located 80 mm from the principal point of a given film positive. Let us also assume that the photograph was made with a camera having a 152.4 mm focal length lens (Figure 6.19) and the radiometric calibration of the

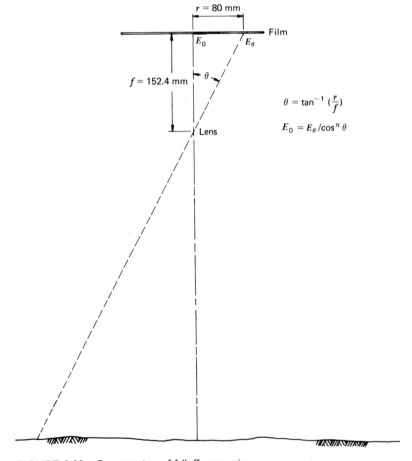

FIGURE 6.19 Computation of falloff correction.

camera indicates a falloff relationship of $E_\theta = E_0 \cos^3\theta$. To normalize the off-axis exposure measurement to its equivalent value at the principal point,

$$\theta = \tan^{-1}\left(\frac{80}{152.4}\right) = 27.7°$$

From Eq. 6.8

$$E_0 = \frac{E_\theta}{\cos^n\theta} = \frac{100}{\cos^3(27.7°)} = 144$$

It should be noted that exposure falloff is a systematic camera system effect that must always be dealt with in exposure measurements. If one does not correct for falloff by using the above procedure, the effect should at least be minimized by confining density measurements to the near-center portions of images.

Another geometric factor influencing film exposure is illustrated in Figure 6.20, which shows a pair of oblique photographs of the same area taken from different vantage points. The photographs were obtained within a 5-min time span by flying a circle around the building complex in the scene. The camera settings were identical for the photographs and the photographs were processed and printed under identical conditions. The variations in exposure in the scene are caused solely by variations in object reflectance with viewing angle. Note, for example, the change in appearance of the fields (A, B, and C) from image to image. These changes illustrate the point that natural materials are not truly diffuse reflectors. That is, their reflectance depends on the angle from which they are illuminated and viewed. The magnitude of this reflectance variation is a function of the material involved and the range of variation of the angular sun−object−image relationship in a scene. This relationship is shown in Figure 6.21. It is defined in terms of three angles: the *solar elevation*, the *azimuth angle*, and the *viewing angle*. A change in any of these angles may change the apparent reflectance of objects.

Figure 6.22 illustrates other geometric effects that might influence the apparent reflectance and exposure produced by various terrain features. In (*a*) the effect of *differential shading* is illustrated in profile view. Recall that the relief displacement of an aerial photograph causes vertical features to be imaged slightly in side view as well as in top view. Since the sides of the features may be either sunlit or shaded, varied exposures can result from identical ground objects. In (*a*), the photograph receives more energy from the sunlit side of the tree at B than from the shaded side of the tree at A. Differential shading is clearly a function of solar elevation and object height, with a stronger effect at low solar angles. The effect is also compounded by differences in slope and aspect (slope orientation) over terrain of varied relief.

Photographs may also show the effects of *differential atmospheric scattering*. As shown in Figure 6.23, scatter is a directional phenomenon. That is, the quantity of light scattered from a molecule in the atmosphere will vary from a minimum at 90° from the direction of solar rays to maximum values at angles of 0 and 180°. What we are

(a)

(b)

FIGURE 6.20 Oblique photographs taken within a 5 min time span from an aircraft circling around a building complex in an agricultural area. Note the change in apparent reflectance for fields A, B, and C with the change in sun−object−image angular orientation between exposures. (Courtesy Calspan Corp.)

concerned with here is the component of scattered light that enters the camera lens directly, adding to the light reflected from ground features. In some analyses, the variation in this "airlight" component is small and can be ignored. However, under hazy conditions, differential quantities of airlight often result in varied total exposure across a photograph.

Figure 6.22*b* illustrates the problem of differential scattering. The film receives little backscatter in the ray from point *C*, which is viewed at an angle near 90° from the sunlight ray. More backscatter is found in the ray from *D*, which is viewed nearly at 180° from its original direction.

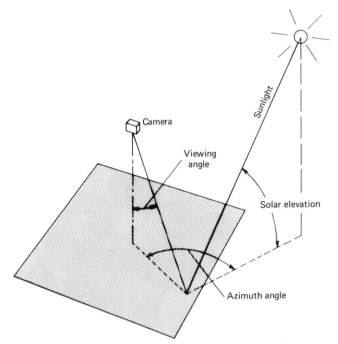

FIGURE 6.21   Sun–object–image angular relationship.

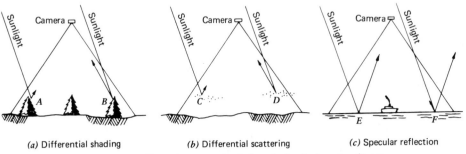

(a) Differential shading   (b) Differential scattering   (c) Specular reflection

FIGURE 6.22   Geometric effects that cause variations in focal plane irradiance.

Yet another problem in many analyses is the presence of *specular* reflections in a scene. Photographs taken over water bodies often show areas of specular reflections. They represent the extreme in directional reflectance. Figure 6.22c illustrates the geometric nature of this problem. Immediately surrounding point E on the image, a considerable increase in exposure would result from specular reflection. This is illustrated in Figure 6.24, which shows areas of specular reflection from the right

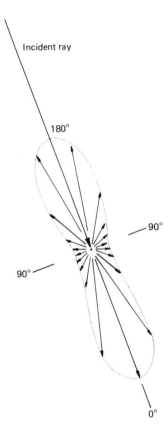

FIGURE 6.23   Directional nature of atmospheric scatter.

half of the lake shown in the image. These mirrorlike reflections normally contribute little information about the true character of the objects involved. For example, the small water bodies just below the larger lake take on a tone similar to that of some of the fields in the area. Because of the low information content of specular reflections, they are avoided in most radiometric analyses.

Before closing our discussion of geometric factors influencing exposure determinations, we must point out the impact that image scale and densitometer measurement spot size have on density readings. To illustrate the importance of these factors, consider the problem of obtaining interpretable densitometric measurements in an agricultural inventory (as illustrated in Figure 6.25). Depending on the problem at

FIGURE 6.24 Aerial photograph containing areas of specular reflection from water bodies. This image is a portion of a photograph taken over Green Lake, Green County, Wisconsin, July 31, 1974. 1:105,000. Cloud shadows indicate direction of sunlight at time of exposure. Reproduced from color infrared original. (NASA image.)

hand, an image scale and spot size combination may be chosen such that each pixel covers a single plant, an entire field, or a group of fields. Note that the density reading at each measurement spot is an aggregate of all density values contained within the spot. Hence, an inappropriate reading may result if the feature of interest does not completely fill the viewing spot of the densitometer. For example, bare soil might affect the readings taken over an individual plant. To negate this, a small spot size may be employed. While spot sizes as small as 5 μm and below are available, at these measurement sizes the grains of the film may tend to dominate the density measurement rather than the exposure character of the image itself. Such measurements would tell the image analyst nothing about ground conditions.

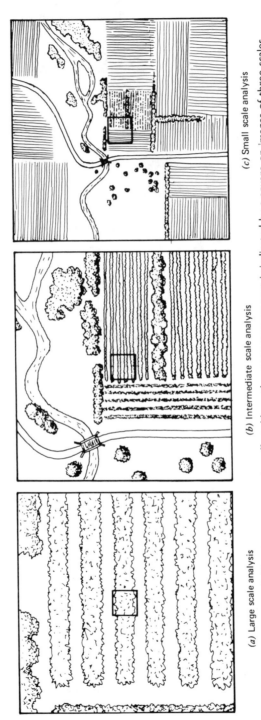

(a) Large scale analysis

(b) Intermediate scale analysis

(c) Small scale analysis

FIGURE 6.25 Image scale/densitometer spot size effect. Here, the measurement spot is indicated by a square on images of three scales.

6.8 ATMOSPHERIC EFFECTS

The atmosphere is an ever-present extraneous influence on exposure. The form and magnitude of atmospheric effects can vary somewhat during the course of a given flight mission and will usually vary radically between missions. Atmospheric effects must be accounted for if object reflectance comparisons between missions are to be made on the basis of exposure measurements.

The atmosphere affects photographic exposure measurements in many ways. As noted in Chapter 1, the atmosphere modifies the intensity and spectral composition of the illuminating energy used in photography. This energy is composed of *sunlight* and *skylight*. Here we use the term "sunlight" to refer to the direct solar component of object irradiation, and "skylight" to refer to the indirect component of object irradiation. (Skylight is diffuse light that has been scattered at least once within the earth's atmosphere.) Sunlight and skylight sources of energy differ in their relative intensity, spectral composition, and geometric distribution. The relative dominance of sunlight versus skylight in any given scene is strongly dependent on weather conditions. A rough comparison of the relative irradiance due to sunlight versus skylight under varying weather conditions is given in Table 6.2. Naturally, the intensity of sunlight and skylight is a function not only of weather but also of latitude, season of year, time of day, and local topography.

The relative spectral constituency of sunlight versus skylight on a clear day is shown in Figure 6.26. Under clear conditions skylight is generally characterized by a high proportion of "blue" energy due to the dominance of Rayleigh scattering of short wavelength energy by the gas molecules in the atmosphere. In contrast, the sunlight energy curve peaks toward the longer visible wavelengths.

Rayleigh scatter is always accompanied by some degree of Mie scatter owing to the presence of such atmospheric constituents as smoke, dust, or water droplets. As indicated in Section 1.3, Mie scattering generally influences energy of longer wavelengths than does Rayleigh scatter. Hence, depending on the particular conditions at hand, the atmosphere can range from being very "blue" to nearly "white." In short, the intensity and spectral composition of photographic source energy vary with atmospheric condition, time, and location. Since many densitometric image analysis proce-

TABLE 6.2 Relative Irradiance Ratios of Sunlight to Skylight for Different Weather Conditions

Weather condition	Solar/sky irradiance
Sunny, clear sky	7/1
Sunny, hazy sky	3/1
Sun through thin clouds	1/1

Adapted from [13].

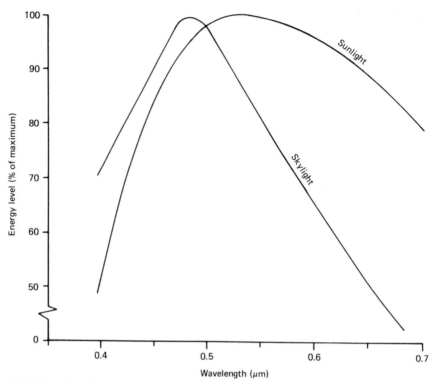

FIGURE 6.26 Relative spectral distribution of sunlight and skylight on a clear day. (Adapted from [13].)

dures attempt to measure the relative return of energy at various wavelengths (spectral reflectance), it is necessary to account for the variations in source intensity at these wavelengths. Put more simply, spectral reflectance is a measure of the *proportion of the incident energy* at various wavelengths that is reflected from a scene. Hence, to determine this proportion we must have knowledge of the magnitude of the *incident* energy on a scene at the time of measurement, on a wavelength band-by-wavelength band basis.

The atmosphere affects exposure in two almost contradictory ways. First, it attenuates (reduces) the energy illuminating a ground object (or being reflected from a ground object). Second, it acts as a reflector itself, adding scattered "hazelight" or "airlight" to the exposure. These two effects are illustrated in Figure 6.27. By expressing the atmospheric factors mathematically, exposure may be related to ground reflectance using the equation

$$E = A \rho + B \tag{6.9}$$

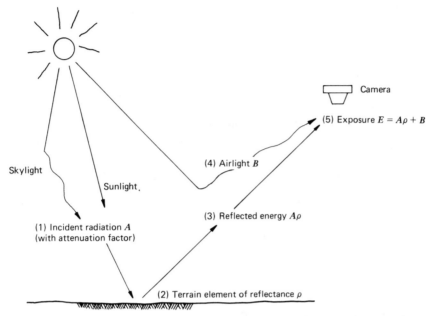

FIGURE 6.27 Factors relating film exposure to ground reflectance. Attenuated sunlight and skylight *(A)*, is reflected from a terrain element having reflectance (ρ). The energy reflected from the terrain element *(Aρ)* combines with airlight *(B)* to cause exposure *(E)* at the corresponding point on the film. Exposure $E = A\rho + B$. (Adapted from [13].)

where

E = total energy (exposure) incident on the film at a given point

A = factor proportional to the sunlight and skylight on the ground feature, reduced to include the effect of atmospheric attenuation

ρ = reflectance of a given ground feature

$A\rho$ = energy received by camera *from the feature*

B = "airlight," additional energy received by camera, *from the atmosphere and not from the object*

Equation 6.9 is of particular importance because it permits quantification, in terms of A and B, of all source/atmosphere parameters contributing to film exposure. These factors always change on a mission-by-mission basis and can change even within a single mission (depending on the extent and location of the coverage). It is worthy to note that the airlight (B) component of exposure is essentially "noise" in that it contains no ground reflectance information.

The visual manifestation of airlight in photography is an overall increase in scene brightness and a decrease in image contrast. This comes about since B adds a constant amount of exposure to both image highlights and shadows, but the effect on the logarithmic density values is proportionately greater at lower exposure levels than at higher ones. Consequently, the total range of log exposure values (and, accordingly, density values) recorded for a given scene is reduced. If, for example, the highest exposure in a haze-free scene is 991 exposure units and the lowest exposure level is 1 unit, $\log E$ varies from 0 to 2.996. Now consider the addition of 9 units of exposure B to all scene elements. The scene exposure would vary from 10 to 1000, and the $\log E$ range would vary from 1 to 3—a loss of 33 percent of the log exposure range. Thus, the range of exposure incident on the film would be much smaller, and therefore the range of densities recorded on the film would be much smaller.

Airlight manifests itself particularly in high altitude photographs. Because of high haze reflectance levels, such imagery generally has less contrast than comparable low altitude photographs. Also, because of preferential scattering of blue energy, high altitude color images generally have a bluer overall tone than do their low altitude counterparts.

6.9 DETERMINING COMPARATIVE REFLECTANCES OF OBJECTS FROM EXPOSURE MEASUREMENTS

Whenever comparisons are to be made between images taken under different illumination or atmospheric conditions, A and B must be accounted for in order to relate exposure to ground reflectance. If A and B can be determined for any given image, density measurements made on the image can be used to compute the absolute reflectances of ground objects. This involves reformulating Eq. 6.9 as

$$\rho = \frac{E - B}{A} \tag{6.10}$$

To apply Eq. 6.10 in the determination of the reflectance of a given object, we first measure the density of the object's image. Working through the $D - \log E$ curve for the film, we determine the exposure, E, associated with the density value. If A, B, and E were known we could solve Eq. 6.10 for ρ. The problem is, how can we determine A and B?

One means of determining A and B is by placing objects of known reflectance in a scene prior to a photographic mission. *Calibrated reflectance panels* can be used for this purpose. Such panels are generally fabricated as large sheets of material finished in varying shades of neutral gray. The surfaces of these panels are textured so that they reflect as diffusely as possible. The reflectance of each panel is measured via a spectrometer at the time of manufacture. Periodic checks on the reflectance of a panel are made to detect any changes due to handling, weathering, and so on.

Theoretically, by placing just two reflectance panels in a scene, we can determine A and B. Consider two panels of known reflectances ρ_1 and ρ_2. From Eq. 6.9, we can express the exposures resulting at the film plane from each of these objects as

$$E_1 = A \rho_1 + B \tag{6.11}$$

and

$$E_2 = A \rho_2 + B \tag{6.12}$$

By measuring the density of the image at each of the panel points (and working through the $D-\log E$ curve) we can determine E_1 and E_2. So the only unknowns remaining in Eqs. 6.11 and 6.12 are A and B. They are determined by solving the equations simultaneously. (If more than two panels are used for a calibration a least-squares solution for A and B can be obtained.)

Other approaches to determining A and B are employed when calibration reflectance panels cannot be placed in a scene. For example, when high altitude imagery is acquired it is impractical in terms of field logistics to use panels that are large enough to be resolved on the image. A solution to this problem is to simply identify various objects in the scene whose reflectance has been either measured or estimated. Large continuous surfaces, such as pavements or flat roofs, are used for this purpose. They are used as "reflectance panels" in an analysis identical to that just described.

There are two other basic approaches to estimating A and B. In the first approach, B is approximated by the minimum exposure measurement value found in a scene. The rationale for this approach is that the minimum exposure will occur at an image point with little to no reflectance and/or direct solar illumination and, therefore, exposure at that point will be due solely to B. In the second approach, exposure measurements are made just inside and outside of shadows covering areas of uniform reflectance. For example, measurements might be made inside and outside of a building shadow cast onto a parking lot. A different exposure would result from the measurement position just in sunlight than from that just in shadow, where the only illumination is due to skylight. A minimum of two such sunlight/skylight observations can be used to find B. In practice, more than two observations are made and a least-squares solution for B is attained. Once B is computed, an object of known (or estimated) reflectance ρ is located in the scene, its exposure E is measured, and A is determined from solution of Eq. 6.9 [13].

No matter how A and B are determined in any analysis, they must be found for each wavelength band of image density measurement. Accordingly, in calibrating color imagery, one determines three A's and B's for the blue, green, and red sensitive film layers, respectively. These parameters can then be used to estimate object reflectances in each of the film response bands. Thus we can obtain *spectral* reflectance estimates for objects appearing in the photograph. Naturally these reflectance determinations will be limited in their spectral range and specificity to the limits set by the particular film used. For example, color film could be used to estimate spectral reflectance in the three broad spectral ranges defined by the blue, green, and red response ranges of the film's three sensitivity layers. Color infrared film could be used in the same manner to obtain reflectance data over the broad spectral ranges of green, red, and reflected infrared energy. Multiband photography could also be used in order to overcome the fixed spectral range and bandwidths of color and color infrared film.

6.10   SPECTRAL RATIOING

Spectral reflectance data generated from color or multiband photography can be analyzed independently on a band-by-band basis or in combinations of two or more bands. One means of conveniently analyzing two or more bands is by taking between-band ratios of reflectance. Normally, the *ratios* of reflectances in a scene tell the image analyst more about the objects photographed than do the reflectances measured in any single band.

Spectral ratioing of reflectance data can be performed in many different ways. Photographically, we can ratio the film response in two separate film layers by making duplicate transparencies of an original image on a band-by-band basis. For example, an original color image could be rephotographed on black and white film through blue, green, and red color separation filters. The result would be three *separation images*, each representing essentially the response of an individual color layer of the original image. When a positive separation image of one color band is placed (in registration) over a negative separation image of another, the composite *ratio mask* displays densities proportional (logarithmically) to the ratio of the reflectances in the two spectral bands.

Figure 6.28 illustrates the results of level-slicing a ratio mask (*b*) prepared from the original color photograph shown in (*a*). While reproduced in black and white here, the original photograph used in this example was a normal color photograph. It was made on September 9, 1973, over the western end of Lake Ontario from the Skylab space station, orbiting at 435 km. The large urban complex on the north shore of the lake is Toronto. The light-toned discharge along the south shore is the Welland Canal. Shown in (*b*) is a level-sliced image of the blue-to-green reflectance ratio recorded in the original photograph (*a*). The ratio mask prepared for this purpose was composed of separation images processed to compensate for the contrast-diminishing effects of *B* in each analysis band. The resulting ratios were compared to reference data and were found to correlate with the chlorophyll concentration in the lake and various optical water quality parameters. Such information is proving to be valuable in such applications as statewide monitoring of the status of eutrophication of inland waters.

Although the spectral ratioing process illustrated in Figure 6.28 was performed photographically, it could also have been done numerically. Numerical spectral ratioing involves the use of scanning microdensitometer data. These data are in a form that makes them inherently amenable to mathematical comparison. Reflectance ratios between bands can be easily obtained through software that transforms "raw" density readings in separate bands into reflectance values that can be manipulated in any mathematical form. The computer deals with a numerical approximation of the $D-\log$

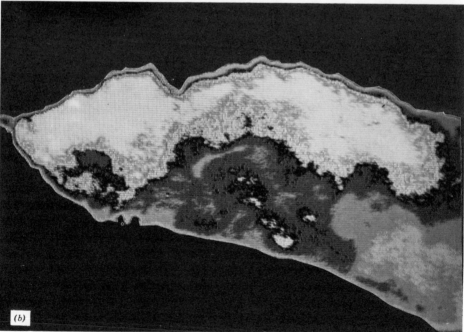

FIGURE 6.28 Blue-to-green reflectance ratio distribution extracted from Skylab photograph of Lake Ontario, September 9, 1973. *(a)* Black and white reproduction of original Skylab color photograph. *(b)* Level-sliced image of blue-to-green ratio mask. Ratio distribution correlates with surface data on chlorophyll concentration and optical water quality parameters. (Courtesy Calspan Corp.)

391

E curve for each film layer to transform raw density readings into exposure values. The A and B calibration parameters are applied to these values to yield object reflectances. Then spectral ratios (or other mathematical comparisons) are computed and output in any one of many formats. As we see in the following chapters, computer output products can range from line printer listings to color-coded film products.

Digital spectral ratios are often a convenient means of "classifying" land cover in a scene. These and other classification procedures are discussed in Chapter 10 when we discuss digital image processing. A point we wish to indicate here is the value of ratio techniques in helping to negate the various extraneous factors that influence not only photographic radiometry data, but sensor data in general. Spectral ratios negate the effect of any extraneous factors in sensor data that act equally in all wavelengths of analysis. This concept is best illustrated by a simplified example.

Consider two objects (1 and 2) located at different positions within a scene sensed in three bands (blue, green, red). Let $\rho_{1,B}$ represent the reflectance of object 1 in the blue band, and so on. Using this notation, the reflectances for the objects in each band are

$$\rho_{1,B} \; ; \; \rho_{2,B}$$
$$\rho_{1,G} \; ; \; \rho_{2,G}$$
$$\rho_{1,R} \; ; \; \rho_{2,R}$$

Let us assume that there exists a set of image position-related extraneous factors (such as viewing geometry effects) that act to reduce the apparent reflectance in all bands at point 1 by a factor of 0.6 and increase the apparent reflectance at point 2 by 1.3. The resulting *apparent* reflectance values would be

$$0.6 \, \rho_{1,B} \; ; \; 1.3 \, \rho_{2,B}$$
$$0.6 \, \rho_{1,G} \; ; \; 1.3 \, \rho_{2,G}$$
$$0.6 \, \rho_{1,R} \; ; \; 1.3 \, \rho_{2,R}$$

With the extraneous factors acting equally in all bands, the reflectance in any two bands can be ratioed and the effect of the extraneous factors is self-compensated. For example, ratioing the apparent values in the blue and green bands for points 1 and 2, we obtain

$$\frac{0.6 \, \rho_{1,B}}{0.6 \, \rho_{1,G}} = \frac{\rho_{1,B}}{\rho_{1,G}}$$

and

$$\frac{1.3 \, \rho_{2,B}}{1.3 \, \rho_{2,G}} = \frac{\rho_{2,B}}{\rho_{2,G}}$$

Although the single-band reflectance values are influenced by the extraneous factors, the ratios of the apparent reflectances are not.

Note that simple between-band ratios only negate multiplicative extraneous effects. When additive effects are present, we must ratio between-band differences. For example, consider point 1 in our example. Let us assume that, in addition to the 0.6 multiplicative factor, we have a 10 unit additive factor operative on the reflectance at this point. The consequent apparent reflectances would be

$$0.6 \, \rho_{1,B} + 10$$
$$0.6 \, \rho_{1,G} + 10$$
$$0.6 \, \rho_{1,R} + 10$$

By ratioing two between-band differences, such as $(B - G)/(R - G)$, we obtain

$$\frac{(0.6 \, \rho_{1,B} + 10) - (0.6 \, \rho_{1,G} + 10)}{(0.6 \, \rho_{1,R} + 10) - (0.6 \, \rho_{1,G} + 10)} = \frac{0.6 \, (\rho_{1,B} - \rho_{1,G})}{0.6 \, (\rho_{1,R} - \rho_{1,G})} = \frac{\rho_{1,B} - \rho_{1,G}}{\rho_{1,R} - \rho_{1,G}}$$

It can be seen that our ratio of between-band differences has eliminated the influence of extraneous effects. These ratios would be compared with reference data to determine if meaningful correlations exist between the ratio values and the information sought in the analysis.

A point to be emphasized is that the ratio techniques described here compensate only for those factors that *act equally on the various bands* under analysis. As such, they are only an approximation of a full correction—although generally a very useful approximation.

6.11   CONCLUSION

In this chapter we have discussed the basic radiometric characteristics of aerial photographs. From this discussion it should be remembered that in order to obtain quantitative spectral response data about ground objects from aerial photographs the following prerequisites must be met:

1.   The photography must be sensitometrically calibrated to obtain its density/log exposure characteristics.
2.   Numerical representations of the photography must be obtained through the process of spot or scanning densitometry.
3.   Extraneous geometric effects, such as exposure falloff, must be eliminated in the data analysis.
4.   Illumination and atmospheric effects must be accounted for to compare data acquired at two different locations or times.

When properly acquired, calibrated, and analyzed, aerial photographs can be used to measure the spectral reflectance characteristics of ground features. These data may assist in the process of identifying and judging the condition of objects "automatically." In subsequent chapters, we see how multispectral scanner data may also be used in these procedures. The primary advantages of using the multispectral scanner data for "automated" interpretation are (1) they are originally collected in digital form, (2) they can be obtained over a larger range of intensities and wavelengths, yet in more discrete wavelength bands, and (3) they are more readily calibrated than photographic data. In contrast, photographic data offer advantages of increased spatial detail and greater availability. Hence, the choice of using photographic versus multispectral scanner data varies with application. For small area analysis, where spatially detailed information is required and broadband reflectances suffice, photographs may be the only cost-effective source of radiometric data. For most large area analyses, digital multispectral scanner data are generally preferred.

SELECTED BIBLIOGRAPHY

 1. American Society of Photogrammetry, *Manual of Color Aerial Photography*, Falls Church, Va., 1968.

 2. American Society of Photogrammetry, *Manual of Remote Sensing*, 2nd ed., Falls Church, Va., 1983.

 3. Brock, G.C., *The Physical Aspects of Aerial Photography*, Dover, New York, 1967.

 4. Everitt, J.H., and P.R. Nixon, "Using Color Aerial Photography to Detect Camphorweed Infestations on South Texas Rangelands," *Photogrammetric Engineering and Remote Sensing*, vol. 51, no. 11, November 1985, pp. 1793–1797.

 5. Everitt, J.H., A.H. Gerbermann, and M.A. Alaniz, "Microdensitometry to Identify Saline Rangelands on 70-mm Color-Infrared Aerial Film," *Photogrammetric Engineering and Remote Sensing*, vol. 47, no. 9, September 1981, pp. 1357–1362.

 6. Everitt, J.H., A.J. Richardson, and A.H. Gerbermann, "Identification of Rangeland Sites on Small Scale (1:120,000) Color-Infrared Aerial Photos," *Photogrammetric Engineering and Remote Sensing*, vol. 51, no. 1, January 1985, pp. 89–93.

 7. Everitt, J.H., et al., "Leaf Reflectance–Nitrogen–Chlorophyll Relations in Buffelgrass," *Photogrammetric Engineering and Remote Sensing*, vol. 51, no. 4, April 1985, pp. 463–466.

 8. Frank, T.D., and S.A. Isard, "Alpine Vegetation Classification Using High Resolution Aerial Imagery and Topoclimatic Index Values," *Photogrammetric Engineering and Remote Sensing*, vol. 52, no. 3, March 1986, pp. 381–388.

 9. James, T.H., *The Theory of the Photographic Process*, 4th ed., Macmillan, New York, 1977.

 10. Jensen, N., *Optical and Photographic Reconnaissance Systems*, Wiley, New York, 1968.

 11. Lee, Y.J., and R.W. McKelvey, "Digitized Small Format Aerial Photography as a Tool for Measuring Food Consumption by Trumpeter Swans," *Photogrammetric Engineering and Remote Sensing*, vol. 50, no. 2, February 1984, pp. 215–219.

12. Murtha, P.A., and J.A. McLean, "Extravisual Damage Detection? Defining the Standard Normal Tree," *Photogrammetric Engineering and Remote Sensing*, vol. 47, no. 4, April 1981, pp. 515–522.

13. Piech, K.R., and J.E. Walker, "Aerial Color Analyses of Water Quality," *Journal of Surveying and Mapping Division, American Society of Civil Engineers*, vol. 97, no. SU2, 1971, pp. 185–197.

14. Scarpace, F.L., et al., "Wetland Mapping from Digitized Aerial Photography," *Photogrammetric Engineering and Remote Sensing*, vol. 47, no. 6, June 1981, pp. 829–838.

15. Slater, P.N., *Remote Sensing Optics and Optical Systems*, Addison–Wesley, Reading, Mass., 1980.

16. Society of Photographic Scientists and Engineers, *Color: Theory and Imaging Systems*, Washington, D.C., 1973.

17. Society of Photographic Scientists and Engineers, *Handbook of Photographic Science and Engineering*, Wiley, New York, 1973.

18. Stimson, A., *Photometry and Radiometry for Engineers*, Wiley, New York, 1974.

19. Todd, H.N., and R.D. Zakia, *Photographic Sensitometry*, 2nd ed., Morgan & Morgan, Dobbs Ferry, N.Y., 1974.

20. Turner, B.J., and D.N. Thompson, "Barrier Island Vegetation Mapping Using Digitized Aerial Photography," *Photogrammetric Engineering and Remote Sensing*, vol. 48, no. 8, August 1982, pp. 1327–1335.

THERMAL AND MULTISPECTRAL SCANNING

7.1 INTRODUCTION

So far in our discussions, we have been concerned principally with sensing energy in the photographic portion of the electromagnetic energy spectrum (wavelength range about 0.3 to 0.9 μm). Through the use of thermal and multispectral scanning, this range can be extended to wavelengths of about 14 μm. Thermal scanning *(thermography)* gives us the opportunity to measure the radiant temperature of earth surface features from a distance by sensing in the wavelength range 3 to 14 μm. Multispectral scanning gives us the opportunity to sense in a wider range of wavelength bands, from the photographic through the thermal, including bands that lie between the photographic and thermal wavelength bands.

In this chapter, we begin with a discussion of the general principles of thermography. We then describe thermal scanning equipment and image geometry, as well as the interpretation and calibration of thermal imagery. The chapter concludes with a discussion of multispectral scanner equipment and the images produced by such systems.

7.2 SENSING RADIANT TEMPERATURES

Considerable interest in temperature measurement has been generated from its application in energy conservation studies. By now the student is probably familiar with "heat pictures" taken to detect building heat loss. However, the primary utility of aerial thermography to date has been in a host of other applications. This is because temperature is one of the principal controls on virtually all physical, chemical, and biological processes in the environment. Consequently, temperature data take on importance in a wide range of earth resource management activities.

One normally thinks of temperature measurement as involving some measuring instrument being placed in contact with, or being immersed in, the body whose temperature is to be measured. When this is done, *kinetic temperature* is measured.

Kinetic temperature is an "internal" manifestation of the average translational energy of the molecules constituting a body. In addition to this internal manifestation, objects radiate energy as a function of their temperature. This emitted energy is an "external" manifestation of an object's energy state that may be remotely sensed and used to determine the *radiant temperature* of the object.

Earth surface features emit radiation primarily in the thermal infrared wavelengths. As we have seen previously, photographic film cannot be made sensitive to this long wavelength portion of the spectrum. Regrettably, much confusion exists between the terms thermal imagery and infrared photography. As shown in Figure 7.1, the two processes involve completely different detection mechanisms. Infrared photography results from the *photochemical* detection of near-IR energy. This near-IR energy is not directly related to temperature, except in the case of very hot objects (Section 2.9).

In order to sense the longer wavelength thermal infrared energy, *electronic* detectors must be used. The output from an electronic detector may be recorded in a number of ways, such as on magnetic tape. For visual analysis, the output may be displayed as an image on film. The resulting product is a thermal image, or *thermogram*. In this case, the film is used merely as a recording medium, not as the original detection device. As such, the product is *not* referred to as a photograph.

Implicit in the understanding of thermal sensing techniques is an understanding of the physics of thermal radiation. This includes consideration of the basic nature of thermal radiation, how such radiation interacts with the atmosphere, and how it interacts with ground targets. These topics are discussed in the first portion of this chapter. This discussion is followed by treatment of the processes of collecting, processing, and interpreting thermal sensor data. Much of this material relates not only to thermal scanning, but also to the multispectral scanning techniques described later in this chapter.

7.3 BLACKBODY RADIATION

We have previously described the physics of electromagnetic radiation in accordance with the concepts of blackbody radiation (see Section 1.2). Recall that any object having a temperature greater than absolute zero ($0°K$, or $-273°C$) emits radiation whose intensity and spectral composition are a function of the material type involved and the temperature of the object under consideration. Figure 7.2 shows the spectral distribution of the energy radiated from the surface of a blackbody at various temperatures. All such blackbody curves have similar form and, in accordance with *Wien's Displacement Law* (Section 1.2), their energy peaks shift toward shorter wavelengths with increases in temperature.

The *total* radiant exitance coming from the surface of a blackbody at any given temperature is given by the area under its spectral radiant exitance curve. That is, if a sensor were able to measure the radiant exitance from a blackbody at all wavelengths, the signal recorded would be proportional to the area under the blackbody radia-

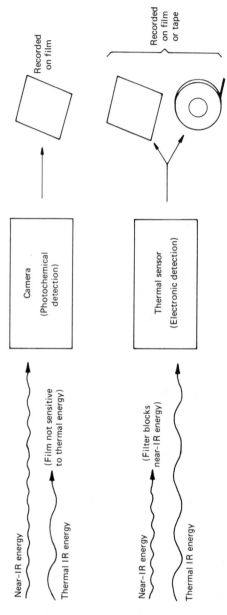

FIGURE 7.1 Energy detection and recording in thermography versus photography.

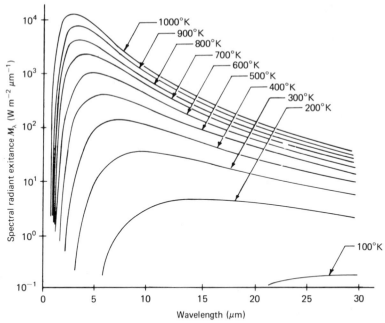

FIGURE 7.2 Spectral distribution of energy radiated from blackbodies of various temperatures.

tion curve for the given temperature. This area is described mathematically by the *Stefan–Boltzmann Law*

$$M = \int_0^\infty M(\lambda)d\lambda = \sigma T^4 \tag{7.1}$$

where

$$W = C_\varepsilon T^4$$
ε emmisivity of an object

M = total radiant exitance, W m^{-2}
σ = Stefan–Boltzmann constant, 5.6697×10^{-8} W m^{-2} °K^{-4}
T = the temperature of the blackbody (°K)

Equation 7.1 indicates that the total radiant exitance from the surface of a blackbody varies as the fourth power of absolute temperature. The remote measurement of radiant exitance M from a surface can therefore be used to infer the temperature T of the surface. In essence, it is this indirect approach to temperature measurement that is used in thermal sensing. Radiant exitance M is measured over a discrete wavelength range and used to find the radiant temperature of the radiating surface.

7.4   RADIATION FROM REAL MATERIALS

While the concept of a blackbody is a convenient theoretical vehicle to describe radiation principles, real materials do not behave as blackbodies. Instead, all real materials emit only a fraction of the energy emitted from a blackbody at the equivalent temperature. The "emitting ability" of a real material, compared to that of a blackbody, is referred to as a material's *emissivity*, ϵ.

Emissivity ϵ is a factor that describes how efficiently an object radiates energy compared to a blackbody. By definition,

$$\epsilon(\lambda) = \frac{\text{radiant exitance from an object at a given temperature}}{\text{radiant exitance from a blackbody at the same temperature}} \tag{7.2}$$

Note that ϵ can have values between 0 and 1. Like reflectance, emissivity can vary with wavelength and viewing angle. Depending on the material, emissivity can also vary somewhat with temperature.

A *graybody* has an emissivity less than 1 but constant at all wavelengths. At any given wavelength the radiant exitance from a graybody is a constant fraction of that of a blackbody. If the emissivity of an object varies with wavelength, the object is said to be a *selective radiator*. Figure 7.3 illustrates the comparative emissivities and spectral radiant exitances for a blackbody, a graybody (having an emissivity of 0.5), and a selective radiator.

Many materials radiate like blackbodies over certain wavelength intervals. Figure 7.4a illustrates the spectral radiant exitance associated with a blackbody and quartz. Note that quartz radiates like a blackbody at wavelengths less than 6 μm but as a selective radiator beyond this wavelength. Many minerals can be distinguished from each other by sensing in very narrow wavelength bands in the region 8–14 μm. As shown in Figure 7.4b, water is very close (ϵ = 0.96 to 1.00) to behaving as a blackbody radiator.

The 8 to 14 μm region of spectral radiant exitance curves is of particular interest since it not only includes an atmospheric window, but also contains the peak energy emissions for most surface features. That is, the ambient temperature of earth surface features is normally in the neighborhood of 300°K, at which temperature the peak emissions will occur at approximately 9.7 μm. For these reasons, most thermal sensing is performed in the 8 to 14 μm region of the spectrum. The emissivities of different objects vary greatly with material type in this range. However, for any given material type, the emissivity can often be considered constant in the 8 to 14 μm range when broadband (8–14μm) sensors are being used. In short, within this spectral region most materials can be treated as graybodies. Table 7.1 indicates some typical values of emissivity for various common materials. (Additional discussion of emissivity is given in [14].)

It should be noted that, as objects are heated above ambient temperature, their emissive radiation peaks shift to shorter wavelengths. In special purpose applications, such as forest fire mapping, systems operating in the 3 to 5 μm atmospheric window

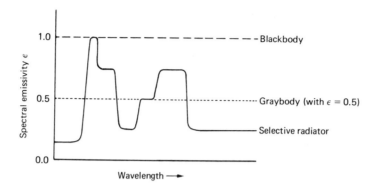

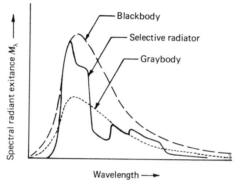

FIGURE 7.3 Spectral emissivities and radiant exitances for a blackbody, a graybody, and a selective radiator. (Adapted from [14].)

may be used. These systems offer improved definition of hot objects at the expense of the surrounding terrain at ambient temperature [13].

7.5 ATMOSPHERIC EFFECTS

As is the case with aerial photography, the atmosphere has a significant effect on the intensity and spectral composition of the energy recorded by a thermal system. As mentioned, atmospheric windows (Figure 7.5) influence the selection of the optimum spectral bands within which to measure thermal energy signals. Within a given window, the atmosphere intervening between a thermal sensor and the ground can increase or decrease the apparent level of radiation coming from the ground. The effect that the atmosphere has on a ground signal will depend on the degree of atmospheric absorption, scatter, and emission at the time and place of sensing.

Gases and suspended particles in the atmosphere may absorb radiation emitted

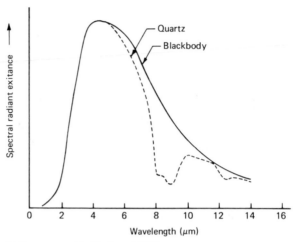

(a) Quartz versus blackbody at 600°K

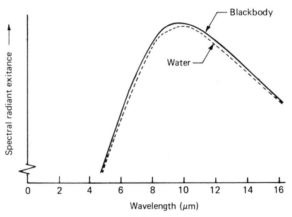

(b) Water versus blackbody at 300°K

FIGURE 7.4 Comparison of spectral radiant exitances for quartz and water versus blackbodies. ((a) Adapted from [30].)

FIGURE 7.5 Atmospheric absorption of the wavelength range 0 to 15 μm. Note the presence of atmospheric windows in the thermal wavelength regions 3 to 5 μm and 8 to 14 μm. (Adapted from [14].)

TABLE 7.1 Typical Emissivities of Various Common Materials

Material	Typical emissivity ε
Human skin	0.98
Seawater	0.98
Distilled water	0.96
Ice	0.96
Tree leaves	0.96
Wet soil	0.95
Glass	0.94
Paint (average of 16 colors)	0.94
Brick	0.93
Dry soil	0.92
Concrete	0.92
Sand	0.91
Wood	0.90
Granitic rock	0.89
Snow	0.85
Sheet iron (rusted)	0.70
Cast iron	
(Tarnished)	0.63
(Polished)	0.21
Buffed stainless steel	0.16
Highly polished gold	0.02

Adapted from [3, 14].

Atmospheric molecules responsible for absorption

from ground objects, resulting in a decrease in the energy reaching a thermal sensor. Ground signals can also be attenuated by scattering in the presence of suspended particles. On the other hand, gases and suspended particles in the atmosphere may emit radiation of their own, adding to the radiation sensed. Hence, atmospheric absorption and scattering tend to make the signals from ground objects appear colder than they are, and atmospheric emission tends to make ground objects appear warmer than they are. Depending on atmospheric conditions during imaging, one of these effects will outweigh the other. This will result in a biased sensor output. Both effects are directly related to the atmospheric path length, or distance, through which the radiation is sensed.

Thermal sensor measurements of temperature can be biased by as much as 2°C or more when acquired at altitudes as low as 300 m. Of course, meteorological conditions have a strong influence on the form and magnitude of the thermal atmospheric effects. Fog and clouds are essentially opaque to thermal radiation. Even on a clear day, aerosols can cause major modifications of signals sensed. Dust, carbon particles, smoke, and water droplets can all modify thermal measurements. These atmospheric constituents vary with site, altitude, time, and local weather conditions.

Atmospheric effects on radiant temperature measurements usually may not be ignored. The various strategies commonly employed to compensate for atmospheric effects are described later in this chapter. We now consider how thermal radiation interacts with ground objects.

7.6 INTERACTION OF THERMAL RADIATION WITH TERRAIN ELEMENTS

In thermography we are interested in the radiation emitted from terrain features. However, the energy radiated *from* an object usually is the result of energy incident *on* the feature. In Section 1.4 we introduced the basic notion that energy incident on the surface of a terrain element can be absorbed, reflected, or transmitted. In accordance with the principle of conservation of energy, we can state the relationship between incident energy and its disposition upon interaction with a terrain element as

$$E_I = E_A + E_R + E_T \tag{7.3}$$

where
E_I = energy incident on the surface of the terrain element
E_A = component of the incident energy absorbed by the terrain element
E_R = component of the incident energy reflected by the terrain element
E_T = component of the incident energy transmitted by the terrain element.

If Eq. 7.3 is divided by the quantity E_I, we obtain the relationship

$$\frac{E_I}{E_I} = \frac{E_A}{E_I} + \frac{E_R}{E_I} + \frac{E_T}{E_I} \tag{7.4}$$

The terms on the right side of Eq. 7.4 comprise ratios that are convenient in further describing the nature of thermal energy interactions. We define

$$\alpha(\lambda) = \frac{E_A}{E_I}$$

$$\rho(\lambda) = \frac{E_R}{E_I} \tag{7.5}$$

$$\tau(\lambda) = \frac{E_T}{E_I}$$

where
$\alpha(\lambda)$ = *absorptance* of the terrain element
$\rho(\lambda)$ = *reflectance* of the terrain element
$\tau(\lambda)$ = *transmittance* of the terrain element

We can now restate Eq. 7.3 in the form

$$\alpha(\lambda) + \rho(\lambda) + \tau(\lambda) = 1 \tag{7.6}$$

which defines the interrelationship between a terrain element's absorbing, reflecting, and transmitting properties.

Another ingredient necessary is the *Kirchhoff Radiation Law*. It states that the spectral emissivity of an object equals its spectral absorptance, $\epsilon(\lambda) = \alpha(\lambda)$. Paraphrased, "good absorbers are good emitters." While Kirchhoff's Law is based on conditions of thermal equilibrium, the relationship holds true for most sensing conditions. Hence, if we apply it in Eq. 7.6 we may replace $\alpha(\lambda)$ with $\epsilon(\lambda)$, resulting in

$$\epsilon(\lambda) + \rho(\lambda) + \tau(\lambda) = 1 \tag{7.7}$$

Finally, in most remote sensing applications the objects we deal with are assumed to be opaque to thermal radiation. That is, $\tau(\lambda) = 0$ and it is therefore dropped from Eq. 7.7 such that

$$\epsilon(\lambda) + \rho(\lambda) = 1 \tag{7.8}$$

Equation 7.8 demonstrates the direct relationship between an object's emissivity and its reflectance in the thermal region of the spectrum. The lower an object's reflectance, the higher its emissivity. The higher an object's reflectance, the lower its emissivity. For example, water has nearly negligible reflectance in the thermal spectrum. Therefore its emissivity is essentially 1. In contrast, a material such as sheet metal is highly reflective of thermal energy, so it has an emissivity much less than 1.

The emissivity of an object has an important implication when measuring radiant temperatures. Recall that the *Stefan–Boltzmann Law*, as stated in Eq. 7.1 ($M =$

σT^4), applied to blackbody radiators. We can extend the blackbody radiation principles to real materials by reducing the radiant exitance M, by the emissivity factor ϵ, such that

$$M = \epsilon \sigma T^4 \qquad (7.9)$$

Equation 7.9 describes the interrelationship between the measured signal a thermal sensor "sees," M, and the parameters of temperature and emissivity. Note that because of emissivity differences, earth surface features can have the same temperature and yet have completely different radiant exitances.

The output from a thermal sensor is a measurement of the radiant temperature of an object, T_{rad}. Often, the user is interested in relating the radiant temperature of an object to its kinetic temperature, T_{kin}. If a sensor were to view a blackbody, T_{rad} would equal T_{kin}. For all real objects, however, we must account for the emissivity factor. Hence, the kinetic temperature of an object is related to its radiant temperature by

$$T_{rad} = \epsilon^{1/4} T_{kin} \qquad (7.10)$$

Equation 7.10 expresses the fact that for any given object the radiant temperature recorded by a remote sensor will also be less than the kinetic temperature of the object. This effect is illustrated in Table 7.2, which shows the kinetic versus the radiant temperatures for four objects having the same kinetic temperature, but different emissivities. Note how kinetic temperatures are always underestimated if emissivity effects are not accounted for in analyzing thermal sensing data.

A final point to be made here is that *thermal sensors detect radiation from the surface (approximately the first 50 μm) of ground objects.* This radiation may or may not be indicative of the internal bulk temperature of an object. For example, on a day of low humidity, a water body having a high temperature will manifest evaporative cooling effects at its surface. Although the bulk temperature of the water body could be substantially warmer than that of its surface temperature, a thermal sensor would record only the surface temperature.

TABLE 7.2   Kinetic versus Radiant Temperature for Four Typical Material Types

Object	Emissivity ϵ	Kinetic temperature T_{kin} [°K (°C)]	Radiant temperature $T_{rad} = \epsilon^{1/4} T_{kin}$ [°K (°C)]
Blackbody	1.00	300 (27)	300.0 (27.0)
Vegetation	0.98	300 (27)	298.5 (25.5)
Wet soil	0.96	300 (27)	297.0 (24.0)
Dry soil	0.92	300 (27)	293.8 (20.8)

7.7 THERMAL ENERGY DETECTORS

At the heart of both imaging and nonimaging thermal sensing systems is some form of radiation detector. Detectors serve to transform incident radiation levels into electrical signals that can be recorded in various fashions. Two broad categories of detectors are commonly in use: *thermal* detectors (bolometers) and *quantum* or *photon* detectors. Each of these types of detectors is described below.

Thermal detectors are devices that change their temperature in response to absorption of incident radiation. This change in temperature is then monitored electrically. Typically, thermal detectors contain materials whose electrical resistance depends on temperature. Thus, as the levels of incident radiation change, the temperature of the detector material changes, the resistance of the material changes, and the change in resistance is monitored through appropriate electrical circuitry. Such detector systems have the advantage of being extremely accurate and their response is not a function of the wavelength of the impinging radiation. A major disadvantage of thermal detectors is their comparatively long response time (the elapsed time between a change in incoming energy level and a resulting change in the monitored electrical signal).

In comparison to thermal detectors, quantum detectors are capable of very rapid (less than 1 μsec) response. Basically, quantum detectors operate on the principle of direct interaction between photons of radiation incident on them and the energy levels of electrical charge carriers within the detector material. With their rapid response characteristics, photon detectors are in widespread use in remote sensing systems. Major drawbacks of photon detectors are their narrow-band spectral response characteristics and the necessity to cool them to temperatures approaching absolute zero for optimum performance. Normally the detector is surrounded by a *dewar* containing liquid helium or nitrogen. A dewar is a double-walled insulated vessel that acts like a thermos bottle to prevent the liquid coolant from boiling away at a rapid rate.

The spectral sensitivity range and the operating temperatures of three photon detectors in common use today are included in Table 7.3.

TABLE 7.3 Characteristics of Photo Detectors in Common Use

Type	Abbreviation	Useful spectral Range (μm)	Operating temperature [°K (°C)]
Mercury-doped germanium	Ge:Hg	3–14	30 (−243)
Indium antimonide	InSb	3–5	77 (−196)
Mercury cadmium telluride	HgCdTe, MCT, or "trimetal"	8–14	77 (−196)

Adapted from [14].

7.8 THERMAL RADIOMETERS

The most basic form of radiant temperature sensor is the thermal *radiometer*. This nonimaging device quantitatively measures and records the radiant temperatures of objects within its field of view. A radiometer contains the following components:

1. *Collecting optics.* To concentrate radiated energy from the area over which a measurement is taken.
2. *Filter.* To limit the spectral operating range of the instrument.
3. *Detector.* To convert the radiation passing through the optical and filter systems into an electrical signal.
4. *Electronics.* To amplify the signal from the detector.
5. *Readout.* To record and display the detector signals. The detector output is normally recorded on magnetic tape, or in the form of a "strip chart."

Figure 7.6 is a schematic of a radiometer. In operation, the instrument's collecting optics focus energy radiated from a ground element onto the detector. Reflecting optics (mirrors) are normally used since glass lenses absorb thermal infrared radiation. A rotating "chopper" mirror is introduced in the optical path to permit the detector to alternately view the ground and a calibrated internal temperature reference. The energy seen—both from the ground and the electrically heated internal reference source—is filtered in the desired spectral measurement band (normally 8 to 14 μm). The signal from the detector is processed electronically so that its amplitude is related to the response difference between the ground element and the reference. Finally, the signal is displayed and/or recorded on some device.

The basic operating configuration of an airborne radiometer is shown in Figure 7.7. In Figure 7.7a, the radiometer is positioned vertically to view ground elements directly below the aircraft (that is, at the nadir) along the direction of flight. Note that the radiometer records the radiant temperature measured along a narrow-width path on the ground. Figure 7.7b illustrates the "thermal profile" format of the output recorded on a strip chart over the sensing path.

At any instant in time, a radiometer senses the thermal radiation within its *instantaneous field of view (IFOV)*. The IFOV, β, of a radiometer is determined by the instrument's optical system and the size of its detector element. The IFOV is normally expressed as the cone angle within which incident energy is focused on the detector. (See β in Figure 7.7a). All radiation propagating toward the instrument within the IFOV contributes to the detector response at any instant. As shown in Figure 7.8, the segment of the ground surface measured within the IFOV of a radiometer is normally a circle of diameter D given by

$$D = H'\beta \qquad (7.11)$$

where
D = diameter of the circular ground area viewed
H' = flying height above the terrain
β = IFOV of the system (expressed in radians)

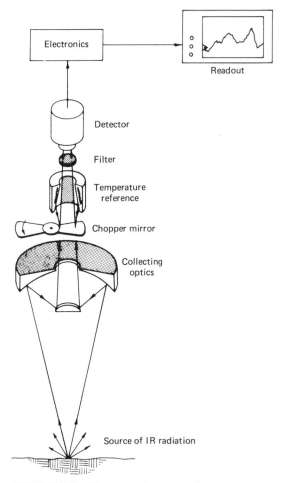

FIGURE 7.6 Thermal radiometer schematic.

The diameter D of the ground area sensed by a radiometer at any instant in time is loosely referred to as the system's *spatial resolution*. The ground segment sensed at any instant is called the ground *resolution element* or *resolution cell*. For example, the spatial resolution of a radiometer having a 2.5 milliradian (mr) IFOV and being operated from 1000 m above terrain can be found from Eq. 7.11 as $D = 1000$ m $\times$ $(2.5 \times 10^{-3}$ rad$) = 2.5$ m. That is, the ground resolution element, or cell, would be 2.5 m in diameter under the indicated operating conditions. Because the sensor integrates its measurement over the full IFOV, objects having different temperatures will not be differentiated when they occur within a single resolution cell. Accordingly, a small IFOV is desirable for high spatial detail.

On the other hand, a large IFOV means a greater quantity of total energy is focused onto the radiometer detector. This permits more sensitive temperature measurements

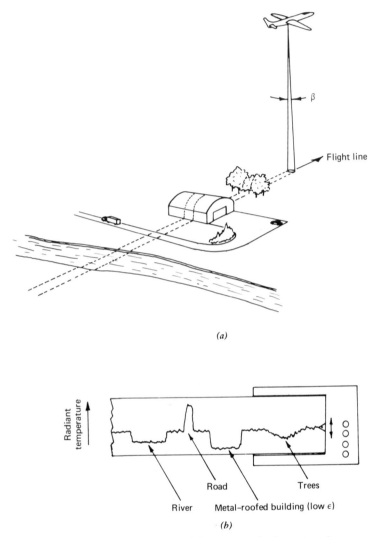

(a)

(b)

FIGURE 7.7 Basic operating configuration of thermal radiometers. *(a)* Flight configuration. *(b)* Resulting instrument output.

to be made. The result is an improvement in the *radiometric resolution,* or the ability to discriminate very slight energy differences. Thus, the selection of the radiometer resolution involves two complementary concerns, spatial and thermal detail.

Figure 7.9 shows a typical thermal radiometer, Barnes Model PRT-5, which operates in the wavelength band 8 to 14 μm. At right is the 1.6 kg optical head that can be hand-held for field work or rigidly mounted over a "belly hole" in an aircraft. At left is the electronic control unit, which also contains the battery power supply. The unit is normally supplied with a 35 mr (2°) IFOV for terrestrial field work, but can also be

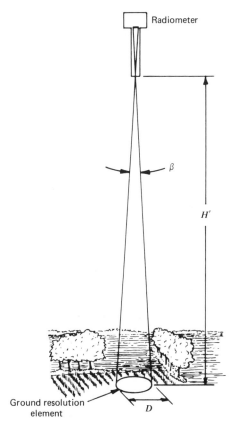

Radiometer

β

H'

Ground resolution
element

D

FIGURE 7.8 Instantaneous field of view and resulting ground area sensed by a radiometer.

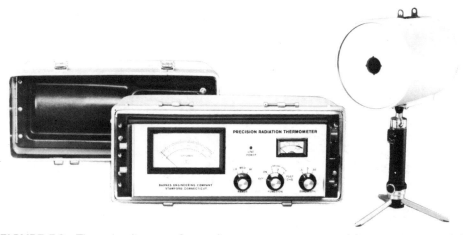

PRECISION RADIATION THERMOMETER

BARNES ENGINEERING COMPANY
STAMFORD CONNECTICUT

FIGURE 7.9 Thermal radiometer. Spot radiant temperatures are read from meter on control unit. (Courtesy Barnes Engineering Co.)

supplied with a 2.5 mr IFOV for aircraft use. It has a temperature range of -50 to $+150°C$ and responds to temperature changes as small as $0.1°C$. Its readings can be calibrated absolutely to about $0.5°C$.

7.9   THERMAL SCANNERS

Whereas thermal radiometers are nonimaging sensors, thermal scanners produce images. Instead of generating a one-dimensional profile of radiant temperature along the flight line, a thermal scanner builds up a two-dimensional record of radiant temperature data for a swath beneath the aircraft (Figure 7.10a). The scanner contains a rotating mirror assembly (Figure 7.10b) that moves the IFOV of a photon detector along *scan lines* that run perpendicular to the direction of flight. This allows the scanner to repeatedly measure the emitted energy from one side of the aircraft to the other along successive scan lines. Data are collected within an arc below the aircraft typically of some 90 to 120°. Over the remaining portion of the mirror rotation (270 to 240°) the detector views its own housing.

As shown in Figure 7.10c, the detector signal along each scan line is related to the radiant energy emitted from ground objects along the scan line. The plane's forward motion causes a new strip of the ground surface to be covered by successive scan lines. Contiguous scan lines result in a series of detector signal outputs covering a swath below the aircraft. The signal for each line may be used to modulate the intensity of a

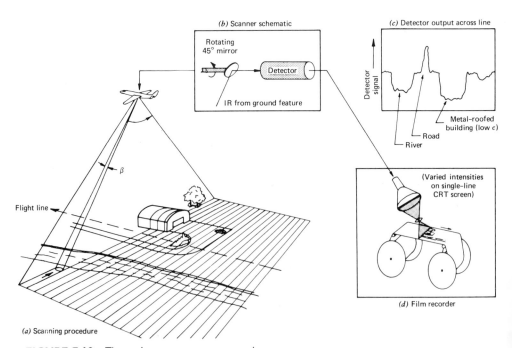

FIGURE 7.10   Thermal scanner system operation.

single-line cathode ray tube, exposing an image line on black and white film (Figure 7.10d). The film is advanced at a rate proportional to the angular flight velocity of the plane. This is determined by the ratio of the aircraft ground speed, V, to its flying height above the terrain H'. With the film advance rate synchronized with the V/H' ratio, underlap or overlap between adjacent scan lines on the film is prevented.

Thermal scanner data are normally recorded in flight on a digital tape recorder. Tape records the data much more faithfully than does film because film has a limited recording range (fixed by its latitude of underexposure and overexposure). Additionally, tape data are in a form that may be computer processed. As we describe later in this chapter, the ability to computer process thermal scanner data makes the data amenable to a host of analysis capabilities that are cumbersome when dealing with film-recorded data. In addition to being recorded on tape or film, scan line output signals are generally monitored in flight on an oscilloscope, or some other real-time monitor. This assures the scanner operator that the system is operating properly and that the various scanner controls are set properly.

Figure 7.11 illustrates schematically the basic operation of a thermal scanner system incorporating in-flight oscilloscopic signal monitoring and both tape and film recording. A *glow tube* type film recorder is depicted in this case (as opposed to the CRT

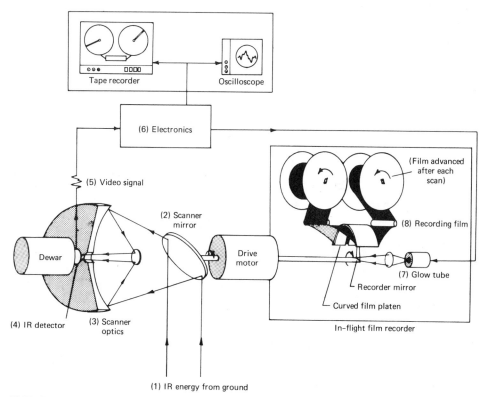

FIGURE 7.11 Thermal scanner schematic.

recorder shown in Figure 7.10). The entire system works as follows. Radiation from the ground (1) is received at the rotating scanner mirror (2). Additional optics (3) focus the incoming energy on the detector (4) which is encased by a dewar filled with a liquid helium or nitrogen coolant. The detector converts the incoming radiation level into an electrical (video) signal (5) which is amplified by the system electronics (6). The signal is displayed on the oscilloscope and recorded on tape on a line-by-line basis. In glow tube film recording, the amplified detector signal is used to modulate the variable intensity of the tube (7). The light from the tube is scanned across the recording film (8) via a rotating mirror synchronized with the scanning mirror. In such systems the film is pressed against a circular focal plane called a *platen*. Again, the film is advanced in proportion to the flight V/H' ratio.

When processed, a thermal scanner film record is a graphical representation of the detector response on a scan line-by-scan line basis. On the original negative, ground surfaces having high radiant temperatures result in image areas having high film densities. Accordingly, prints made from negatives show high radiant temperature areas as lighter-toned image areas.

Figure 7.12 shows the components of a typical scanner system employing magnetic tape recording. The scanning mirror, detector, and two internal temperature references (T_1 and T_2) are located in the scan head, which is gyroscopically stabilized in flight. The scanner mirror views one temperature reference at the beginning and one at the end of each scan line. The control console is used to monitor and adjust the operation of the scanner.

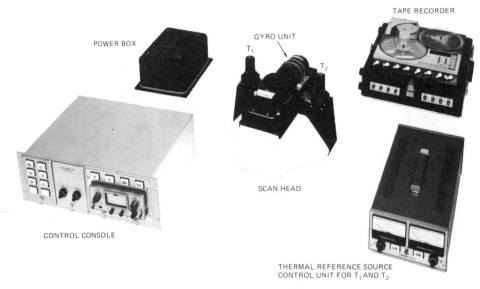

FIGURE 7.12   Thermal scanner system. (Courtesy Daedalus Enterprises, Inc.)

7.10 INTERPRETING THERMAL SCANNER IMAGERY

Successful interpretations of thermal imagery have been made in many fields of application. These include such diverse tasks as determining rock type and structure, locating geologic faults, mapping soil type and soil moisture, locating irrigation canal leaks, determining the thermal characteristics of volcanoes, studying evapo-transpiration from vegetation, locating cold water springs, locating hot springs and geysers, determining the extent and characteristics of thermal plumes in lakes and rivers, determining the extent of active forest fires, and locating underground coal mine fires.

Most thermal scanning operations, such as geologic and soil mapping, are qualitative in nature. In these cases, it is not usually necessary to know absolute ground temperatures and emissivities, but simply to study relative differences in the radiant temperatures within a scene. However, some thermal scanning operations require quantitative data analysis in order to determine absolute temperatures. An example would be the use of thermal scanning as an enforcement tool by a state department of natural resources to monitor surface water temperatures of the effluent from a nuclear power plant.

Various times of day can be utilized in thermal scanning studies. Many factors influence the selection of an optimum time or times for acquiring thermal data. Mission planning and image interpretation must take into consideration the effects of diurnal temperature variation. The importance of diurnal effects is shown in Figure 7.13, which illustrates the relative radiant temperatures of soils and rocks versus water during a typical 24 hr period. Note that just before dawn, a quasi-equilibrium condition is reached where the slopes of the temperature curves for these materials are very small. After dawn, this equilibrium is upset and and the materials warm up to a peak that is reached sometime after noon. Maximum scene contrast normally occurs at about this time and cooling takes place thereafter.

Temperature extremes and heating and cooling rates can often furnish significant information about the type and condition of an object. Note, for example, the temperature curve for water. It is distinctive for two reasons. First, its range of temperature is quite small compared to that of soils and rocks. Second, it reaches its maximum temperature an hour or two after the other materials. As a result, terrain temperatures are normally higher than those of water during the day and lower than water temperatures during the night. Shortly after dawn and near sunset, the curves for water and the other features intersect. These points are called thermal *crossovers* and indicate times at which no radiant temperature difference exists between two materials.

The extremes and rates of temperature variation of any earth surface material are determined, among other things, by the material's thermal conductivity, capacity, and inertia. *Thermal conductivity* is a measure of the rate at which heat passes through a material. For example, heat passes through metals much faster than through rocks. *Thermal capacity* determines how well a material stores heat. Water has a very high thermal capacity compared to other material types. *Thermal inertia* is a measure of the response of a material to temperature changes. It increases with an increase in material conductivity, capacity, and density. In general, materials with high thermal inertia

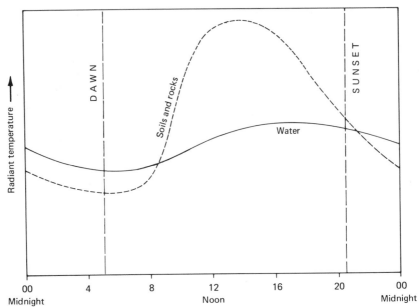

FIGURE 7.13   Generalized diurnal radiant temperature variations for soils and rocks versus water.

have more uniform surface temperatures throughout the day and night than materials of low thermal inertia.

During the daytime, direct sunlight differentially heats objects according to their thermal characteristics and their sunlight absorption, principally in the visible and near-infrared portion of the spectrum. Reflected sunlight can be significant in imagery utilizing the 3 to 5 μm band. Although reflected sunlight has virtually no direct effect on imagery utilizing the 8 to 14 μm band, daytime imagery contains thermal "shadows" in cool areas shaded from direct sunlight by objects such as trees, buildings, and some topographic features. Also, slopes receive differential heating according to their orientation. In the Northern Hemisphere, south-facing slopes receive more solar heating than north-facing slopes. Many geologists prefer "predawn" imagery for their work as this time of day provides the longest period of reasonably stable temperatures, and "shadow" effects and slope orientation effects are minimized. However, aircraft navigation over areas selected for thermal image acquisition is more difficult during periods of darkness, when ground features cannot be readily seen by the pilot. Other logistics also enter into the timing of thermal scanning missions. For example, scanning of effluents from power plant operations normally must be conducted during periods of peak power generation.

A number of thermal images are illustrated in the remainder of this chapter. In all cases, darker image tones represent cooler radiant temperatures and lighter image tones represent warmer radiant temperatures. This is the representation most commonly used in thermograms, although exceptions do exist.

Figure 7.14 illustrates the contrast between daytime (*a*) and nighttime (*b*) thermal images. The water in this scene (note the large lake at right and the small, lobed pond in lower center) appears cooler (darker) than its surroundings during the daytime and warmer (lighter) at night. The kinetic water temperature has changed little during the few hours of elapsed time between these images. However, the surrounding land areas have cooled considerably during the evening hours. Again, water normally appears cooler than its surroundings on daytime thermal images and warmer on nighttime thermal images, except for the case of open water surrounded by frozen or snow covered ground where the water would appear warmer day and night. Trees can be seen many places in these images (note the area above and to the right of the small pond). Trees generally appear cooler than their surroundings during the daytime and warmer at night. Tree shadows appear in many places in the daytime image (note the residential area at upper left) but are not noticeable in the nighttime image. Paved areas (streets and parking lots) appear relatively warm both day and night. The pavement surfaces heat up to temperatures higher than their surroundings during the daytime and lose heat relatively slowly at night, thus retaining a temperature higher than their surroundings.

Figure 7.15 is a daytime thermal image showing the former shoreline of glacial Lake Middleton, an ephemeral glacial lake that is now primarily agricultural fields. This was a small lake, about 800 ha in extent at its maximum. At its lowest level, the lake was only about 80 ha in size. The beach ridge associated with this lowest lake level is shown at *B*. The ridge is most evident at the lower right because the prevailing winds at the time of its formation were from the upper left. The ridge is a small feature, only 60 m wide and $\frac{1}{2}$ to 1 m higher than the surrounding lakebed material. The beach ridge has a fine sandy loam surface soil 0.3 to 0.45 m thick underlain by deep sandy materials. The lakebed soils (*A*) are silt loam to a depth of at least 1.5 m and are seasonally wet with a groundwater table within 0.6 m of the ground surface in the early spring. At the time of this thermal image, most of the area shown here was covered with agricultural crops. The scanner sensed the radiant temperature of the vegetation over the soils rather than the bare soils themselves. Based on field radiometric measurements, the radiant temperature of the vegetation on the dry, sandy beach ridge soil is 16°C, whereas that over the wetter, siltier lakebed soil is 13°C. Although prominent on this thermal image, the beach ridge is often overlooked on panchromatic aerial photographs and is only partially mapped on a recent USDA−SCS soil map of the area. Also seen on this thermal image are trees at *C*, bare soil at *D*, and closely mowed grass (a sod farm) at *E*.

Figure 7.16 contains two nighttime thermal images illustrating the detectability of relatively small features on large scale imagery. In Figure 7.16*a* (9:50 P.M.), a group of 28 cows can be seen as white spots near the upper left. In Figure 7.16*b* (1:45 A.M.), they have moved near the bottom of the image. (Deer located in flat areas relatively free of obstructing vegetation have also been detected, with mixed success, on thermal imagery [11]). The large, rectangular, very dark-toned object near the upper right of Figure 7.16*a* is a storage building with a sheet metal roof having a low emissivity. Although the kinetic temperature of the roof may be as warm as or warmer than the surrounding ground, its radiant temperature is low due to its low emissivity.

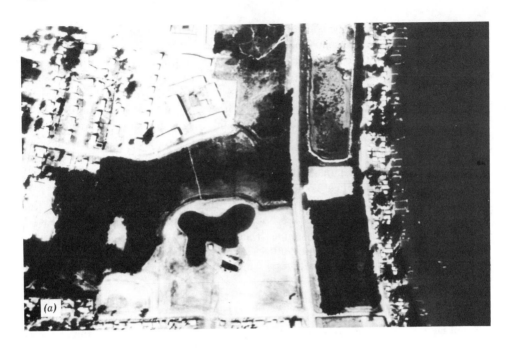

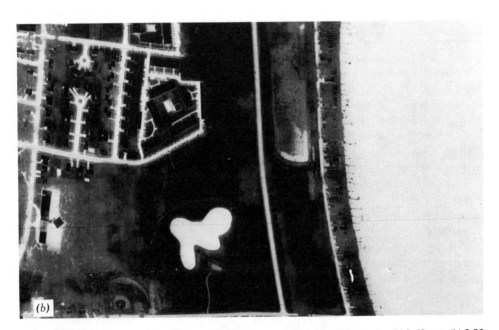

FIGURE 7.14   Daytime and nighttime thermal images, Middleton, Wisconsin. *(a)* 2:40 P.M. *(b)* 9:50 P.M. September 17, 1971; 600 m flying height, 5 mr IFOV. (Courtesy National Center for Atmospheric Research.)

FIGURE 7.15 Daytime thermal image. Middleton, Wisconsin, 9:40 A.M., September 18, 1971, 600 m flying height, 5 mr IFOV. (Courtesy National Center for Atmospheric Research.)

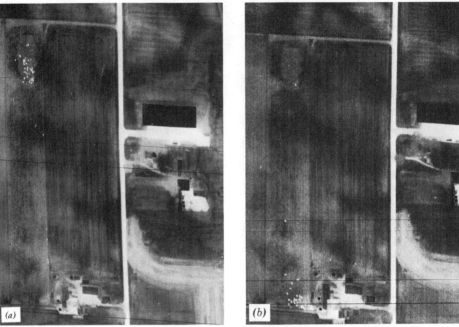

FIGURE 7.16 Nighttime thermal images, Middleton, Wisconsin. *(a)* 9:50 P.M., September 17, 1971. *(b)* 1:45 A.M., September 18, 1971. 600 m flying height, 5 mr IFOV. (Courtesy National Center for Atmospheric Research.)

Figure 7.17 illustrates the heated cooling water from a coal-fired power plant discharging into Lake Michigan. This daytime thermal image shows that the plant's cooling system is recirculating its heated discharge water. Heated water initially flows to the right. Winds from the upper right at 5 m/sec cause the plume to double back on itself, eventually flowing into the intake channel. The ambient lake temperature is about 4°C. The surface water temperatures in the plume are 11°C near the submerged discharge and 6°C in the intake channel. On a late winter day with cold lake temperatures, such as shown here, the recirculating plume does not cause problems with the power plant operation. However, such an event could cause operational problems during the summer because the intake water would be warmer than acceptable for the cooling system.

Figures 7.18, 7.19, and 7.21 show the application of thermography to heat loss studies. Figure 7.18 shows a midday winter thermal image of a portion of the University of Wisconsin—Madison campus, including the football stadium shown photographically in Plate 2. Prominent warm areas in the stadium are the press box at left (warmed by solar heating of the large, east-facing glass windows) and the heated office under the stadium seating area along the right (warmed by heat loss from heated office space). The letter "W" can be faintly seen in the stands below the press box. The stadium seats are painted red, except for certain seat areas painted white in the form of

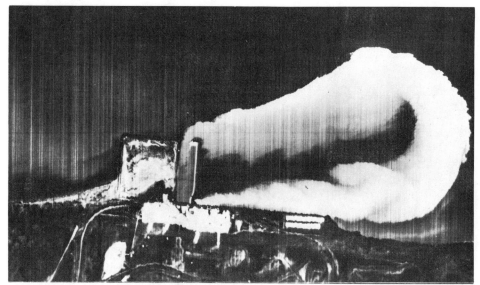

FIGURE 7.17 Daytime thermal image, Oak Creek Power Plant, Wisconsin, 1:50 P.M., March 27, 1974, 800 m flying height, 2.5 mr IFOV. (Courtesy Wisconsin Department of Natural Resources.)

a W. The white W area reflects more sunlight than the red seats and therefore is cooler and has a darker tone on this thermal image. To the right of and below the stadium are two large athletic buildings. Both are radiating a large amount of infrared energy. A residential area, with homes radiating varying amounts of infrared energy, can be seen near the left edge of the image.

The use of aerial thermography to study heat loss from buildings is being investigated in many cities. Figure 7.19 illustrates the typical form of imagery acquired in such studies. Note the striking differences among the radiant temperatures of various roofs, as well as the temperature differences between various house roofs and garage/carport roofs of the same house. Such images are often useful in assessing inadequate or damaged insulation and roofing materials. The dark-toned streaks aligned from upper right to lower left on the ground areas between houses result from the effects of wind on the snow covered ground.

Although aerial thermography can be used to estimate the amount of energy radiated from the roofs of buildings, *the emissivity of the roof surfaces must be known to determine the kinetic temperature of the roof surfaces*. With the exception of unpainted sheet metal roofs (Figure 7.16), which have a very low emissivity, roof emissivities vary from 0.88 to 0.94.

Thermal scanning of roofs to estimate heat loss is best accomplished on cold winter nights at least 6 to 8 hr after sunset, in order to minimize the effects of solar heating. Alternatively, surveys can be conducted on cold overcast winter days. In any case, roofs should be neither snow covered nor wet. Because of the side-looking characteristics of scanner images, the scanner vertically views the roof tops of buildings only

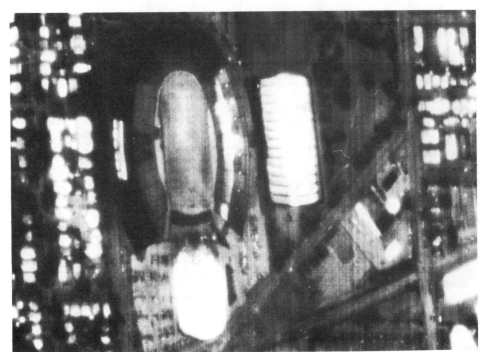

FIGURE 7.18 Daytime thermal image, Madison, Wisconsin, 12:00 noon, December 1, 1975, overcast day, 300 m flying height, 2.5 mr IFOV. (Courtesy Wisconsin Department of Natural Resources.)

directly beneath the plane. At the edge of the scan, it views the rooftops plus a portion of building sides. Roof pitch affects the temperature of roofs. A flat roof directly faces a night sky that is 20 to 30°C cooler than ambient air temperature and will therefore lose heat by radiation. Sloping roofs often receive radiation from surrounding buildings and trees, keeping their surfaces warmer than flat roofs. Attic ventilation characteristics must also be taken into account when analyzing roof heat loss.

When mapping heat loss by aerial thermography, it must also be realized that heat loss from roofs constitutes only a portion of the heat lost from buildings, as heat is also lost through walls, doors, windows, and foundations. It is estimated that a house with comparable insulation levels in all areas loses about 10 to 15 percent of its heat through the roof. Homes with well-insulated walls and poorly insulated ceilings may lose more heat through the roof.

An alternative and supplement to aerial thermography is the use of ground-based systems such as the equipment shown in Figure 7.20. The video camera and display unit weigh 6 kg and can be used to monitor the outside or inside of buildings. This equipment has an operating range of −20 to +900°C and can resolve temperature

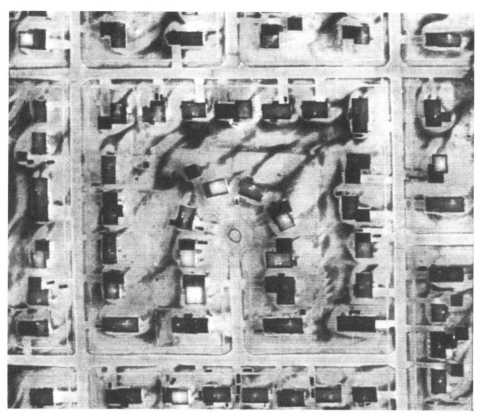

FIGURE 7.19 Nighttime thermal image depicting building heat loss in an Iowa city, approximately 2:00 A.M., January 1978; snow covered ground, air temperature approximately −4°C, 460 m flying height, I mr IFOV. (Courtesy Iowa Utility Association.)

differences of 0.2°C on surfaces whose temperatures average 30°C. A variety of ground-based scanning equipment is available from several manufacturers. The thermogram is generally displayed on a CRT screen that can be photographed for a permanent image. In addition, profile traces and isometric displays are available as options on some systems. Depending on the detector used, the systems operate in the 2 to 5 μm or 8 to 14 μm wavelength bands. When operating in the range 2 to 5 μm, care must be taken not to include reflected sunlight in the scene.

Figure 7.21 illustrates the use of aerial thermography to detect heat loss from a steam line located on an old stone arch bridge that crosses a deep gorge on the Cornell University campus. The surface of the bridge is constructed of steel-reinforced concrete that has been added to improve the structural integrity of the bridge. Maintenance personnel were aware of the steam leak before thermal scanning of the area, but

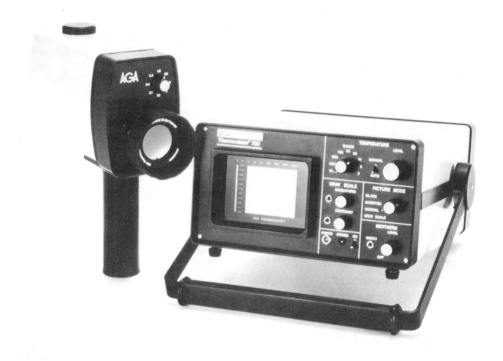

FIGURE 7.20   Thermovision™ camera and display unit. (Courtesy AGA Corp.)

one entire lane of the bridge was apparently hot and they were reluctant to cut through the reinforced concrete on a "fishing expedition" to locate the defective section of steam line. Using various enhancements of the thermogram shown as Figure 7.21a, they were able to locate the heat source, which turned out to be a 6 mm diameter hole in a 10 cm diameter steam line. The line is insulated with asbestos and encased in a 30 cm diameter clay tile located 60 cm below the road surface. The clay tile casing compounded the problem of precisely locating the steam leak using conventional means. That is, the casing ducted the steam a substantial distance from the leak. This caused the illusion of a general steam line failure, but close inspection of the thermo-grams indicated the exact site of the leak. Figure 7.21b shows the same bridge after correction of the steam leak.

FIGURE 7.21 Thermal images showing steamline heat loss, Cornell University, Ithaca, New York. *(a)* January 29, 1975. *(b)* November 16, 1976. (Courtesy Cornell University and Daedalus Enterprises, Inc.)

7.11 GEOMETRIC CHARACTERISTICS OF THERMAL SCANNER IMAGERY

Airborne thermal scanning systems are generally operated at altitudes in the range 300 to 12,000 m. Table 7.4 summarizes the spatial resolution and ground coverage that would result at various operating altitudes when using a system having a 90° total field

TABLE 7.4   Ground Resolution at Nadir and Swath Width for Various Flying Heights of a Scanner Having a 90° Total Field of View and a 2.5 mr IFOV

Altitude	Flying height above ground (m)	Ground resolution at nadir (m)	Swath width (m)
Low	300	0.75	600
Medium	6,000	15	12,000
High	12,000	30	24,000

of view and a 2.5 mr IFOV. The ground resolution at nadir is calculated from Eq. 7.11 $(D = H'\beta)$. The swath width W can be calculated from

$$W = 2H'\tan\theta \qquad (7.12)$$

where
  W = swath width
  H' = flying height above terrain
  θ = one-half the total field of view of the scanner

As with aerial photographs, scanner images contain various geometric distortions that affect the image interpretation process. Scanner image distortions are somewhat more complex than those characterizing photography and it is impossible to negate their effect completely. As a consequence, thermal imagery is rarely used as a tool for precision mapping. Instead, data extracted from thermal imagery are normally registered to some base map when positional accuracy is required in the interpretation process. This registration process must be done with due regard for distortions caused by the following:

1. Systematic variations in scale and relief displacement introduced by the geometry of scanning.
2. Random variations in aircraft flight parameters during image acquisition.

We discuss these sources of distortion under four separate headings, though they occur simultaneously.

Tangential Scale Distortion

Unless it is geometrically rectified, thermal imagery manifests severe scale distortions in a direction perpendicular to the flight direction. The problem arises because a scanner mirror rotating at constant angular velocity does not result in a constant speed of the scanner's IFOV over the terrain. As shown in Figure 7.22, for any increment of time, the mirror sweeps through a constant incremental arc, $\Delta\theta$. Because the mirror rotates at a constant angular velocity, $\Delta\theta$ is the same at any scan angle θ. However, as the distance between the nadir and the ground resolution cell increases, the linear ground velocity of the resolution cell increases. Hence, the ground element, ΔX, covered per unit time increases with increasing distance from the nadir. To record the resulting signal on film properly, the spot of light in the film recorder the resulting signal on film properly, the spot of light in the film recorder must be swept at a correspondingly varied speed across the film. While this is done in some CRT-based recorders, most systems record at a constant sweep rate (as for example, the film recorder depicted in Figure 7.11). This results in image scale compression at points away from the nadir, as the ground spot covers a greater distance at its increasing ground speed. The resulting distortion is known as *tangential scale distortion*. Note that it occurs only in the along-scan direction, perpendicular to the direction of flight. Image scale in the direction of flight is essentially constant.

Figure 7.23 schematically illustrates the effect of tangential distortion. Shown in Figure 7.23a is a hypothetical vertical aerial photograph taken over flat terrain containing patterns of various forms. An unrectified line scanner image of the same area is shown in Figure 7.23b. Note that because of the constant longitudinal scale and varying lateral scale of the thermal imagery, objects do not maintain their proper shapes. Linear features—other than those parallel or normal to the scan lines—take on an S-shaped *sigmoid curvature*. Extreme compression of ground features characterizes the image near its edges. These effects are illustrated in Figure 7.24, which shows an aerial photograph and thermogram of the same area. The flight line for the thermogram is vertical on the page. Note that the photograph and thermogram are reproduced with the same scale along the flight line, but that the scale of the thermogram is compressed in a direction perpendicular to the flight line. Two diagonal roads that are straight on the aerial photograph take on a sigmoid curvature on the thermogram. Note also the light-toned water and trees on this nighttime thermogram (compared with Figure 7.14).

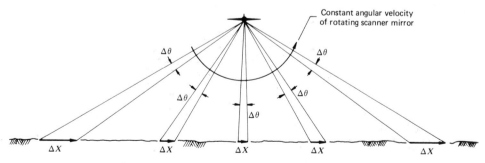

Resulting variations in linear velocity of ground resolution element

FIGURE 7.22   Source of tangential scale distortion.

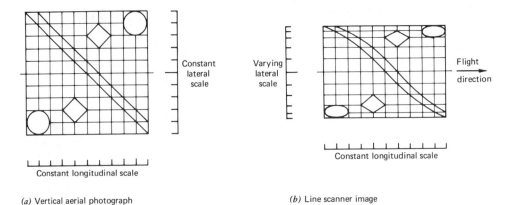

(a) Vertical aerial photograph   (b) Line scanner image

FIGURE 7.23   Tangential scale distortion in unrectified line scanner imagery.

Figure 7.25 further illustrates tangential scale distortion. This scanner image shows a group of cylindrical oil storage tanks. The flight line was from left to right. Note how the scale becomes compressed at the top and bottom of the image, distorting the circular shape of the tank tops. Note also that the scanner views the sides as well as the tops of features located away from the flight line.

Tangential scale distortion normally precludes useful interpretation near the edges of unrectified thermal imagery. Likewise, geometric measurements made on unrectified scanner imagery must be corrected for this distortion. Figure 7.26 shows the elements involved in computing true ground positions from measurements made on a distorted image. On unrectified imagery, y coordinates will relate directly to *angular* dimensions, not to lineal dimensions. This results in the geometric relationship depicted in the figure, where the film plane is shown as a curved surface below the aircraft. In order to determine the ground position Y_p corresponding to image point p, we must first compute θ_p from the relationship

$$\frac{y_p}{y_{max}} = \frac{\theta_p}{\theta_{max}}$$

Rearranging

$$\theta_p = \frac{y_p \theta_{max}}{y_{max}} \tag{7.13}$$

where
  y_p = the distance measured on the image from the nadir line to point p
  y_{max} = the distance from the nadir line to the edge of the image
  θ_{max} = one-half the total field of the view of the scanner

FIGURE 7.24 Comparison of aerial photograph and thermal image illustrating tangential distortion, Iowa County, Wisconsin. (a) Panchromatic aerial photograph, May 19, 1968, 3000 m flying height. (b) Nonrectified thermal image, 6:00 A.M., September 1971, 300 m flying height. ((a) Courtesy USDA—ASCS. (b) Thermal image courtesy National Center for Atmospheric Research.)

FIGURE 7.25 Thermal image illustrating tangential distortion, 5:00 P.M., March 1977, 100 m flying height. (Courtesy Texas Instruments Inc.)

Once θ_p has been computed, it may be trigonometrically related to ground distance Y_p by

$$Y_p = H' \tan \theta_p \tag{7.14}$$

When determining ground positions on unrectified imagery, the above process must be applied to each y coordinate measurement. Alternatively, the correction can be implemented electronically in the film recording process, resulting in *rectilinearized* images. In addition to permitting direct measurement of positions, rectilinearized imagery improves the ability to obtain useful interpretations in areas near the edge of images.

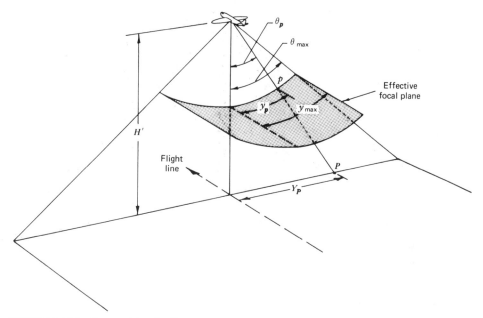

FIGURE 7.26 Tangential scale distortion correction.

Resolution Cell Size Variations

Unlike radiometers, thermal scanners sense radiated energy over ground resolution cells of continuously varying size. An increased cell size is obtained as the IFOV of a scanner moves outward from the flight nadir.

The geometric elements defining the size of the ground resolution cell are shown in Figure 7.27. At the nadirline, the ground resolution cell has a dimension of $H'\beta$. At a scan angle of θ, the distance from the aircraft to the cell becomes $H'_\theta = H'\sec\theta$. Hence the size of the resolution cell increases. The cell has dimensions of $(H'\sec\theta)\beta$ in the direction of flight and $(H'\sec^2\theta)\beta$ in the direction of scanning. These are actually the *nominal* dimensions of the measurement cell. The *true* size and shape of a ground resolution cell are a function not only of β, H', and θ, but also of the *response time* of a particular scanner's electronics. The response time is a measure of the time that a scanner takes to respond electronically to a change in ground emitted energy. With this added restriction, we see that optics control the resolution cell size in the direction of flight, while both optics and electronics influence the cell size in the direction of scan. Because of system response time limitations, the resolution cell size along a scan line can be as much as three to four times that in the direction of flight.

Although it is rarely critical to know the precise degree of resolution cell size variation, it is important to realize the effect this variation has on the interpretability of the imagery at various scan angles. The scanner output at any point represents the integrated temperature of all features within the ground resolution cell. Because the

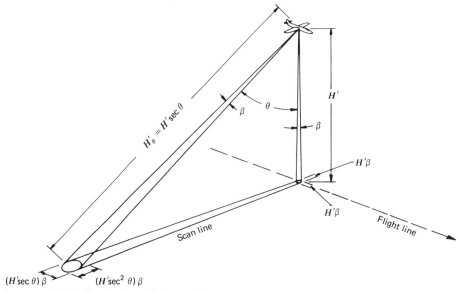

FIGURE 7.27 Resolution cell size variation.

cell increases in size near the edge of the image, only larger terrain features will completely fill the IFOV and be independently resolved on the image. When objects smaller than the area viewed by the IFOV are imaged, background features also contribute to the recorded signal. Thus, *for an object to be registered with the proper radiant temperature, its size must be larger than the ground resolution cell.* This effect may again limit the image analysis to the central portion of the thermogram, even after rectilinearization is performed. However, an advantage of the changing size of the ground resolution cell is that it compensates for off-nadir radiometric falloff. If the ground resolution cell area were constant, the irradiance received by the scanner would decrease as $1/H'^2_\theta$. But, since the ground resolution cell area increases as H'^2_θ, the irradiance falloff is precisely compensated and a consistent temperature signal is recorded over uniform surfaces.

One-Dimensional Relief Displacement

Figure 7.28 illustrates the nature of relief displacement characterizing thermograms. Since all objects are viewed by the scanner only along "side-looking" scan lines, relief displacement occurs only in this single direction. (See also Figure 7.25.) An advantage to relief displacement is that it affords an opportunity to see a side view of objects. On the other hand, it can obscure the view of objects of interest. For example, a thermal mission might be planned to detect heat losses in steam lines in an urban setting. Tall buildings proximate to the objects of interest may completely obscure their view. In

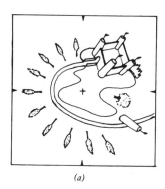 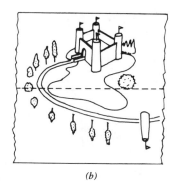

(a)   (b)

FIGURE 7.28 Relief displacement on a photograph versus a scanner image. In a vertical aerial photograph *(a)* vertical features are displaced radially from the principal point. In a line scanner image *(b)* vertical features are displaced at right angles from the nadir.

such cases it is often necessary to cover the study area twice, in perpendicular flight directions.

Figure 7.29 is a thermal image illustrating one-dimensional relief displacement. Note that the displacement of the tops of the tall buildings is greater with increasing distance from the nadir.

Figure 7.30 is a thermal image illustrating tangential distortion and one-dimensional relief displacement. Note that the straight roads and field boundaries running diagonally across the image have taken on a sigmoid curvature. Also note the "side view" of the houses in the subdivision at upper left and the water tower near the upper right center.

Flight Parameter Distortions

Because scanner imagery is collected in a continuous fashion, it lacks the consistent relative orientation of image points found on instantaneously imaged aerial photographs. That is, aerial thermography is a dynamic continuous process rather than an intermittent sampling of discrete perspective projections as in photography. Because of this, any variations in the aircraft flight trajectory during scanning affect the relative positions of image points recorded on a thermogram.

Figure 7.31 illustrates the effect of variations in the aircraft velocity to height (V/H') ratio. Note that changes in aircraft velocity and/or height during the image recording process expand or contract image scale in the direction of flight. To avoid this expansion or compression in the flight direction during imaging, the mirror scan rate and the image recording rate must be synchronized with the V/H' ratio. Any residual distor-

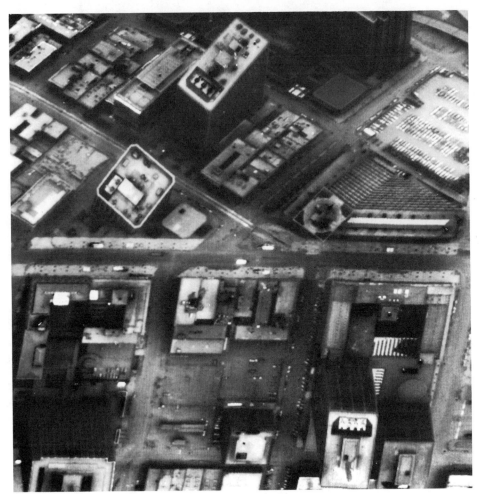

FIGURE 7.29 Thermal image illustrating one-dimensional relief displacement, San Francisco, California, predawn, 1500 m flying height, 1 mr IFOV. (Courtesy NASA.)

tions, if the synchronization is not done precisely, must be dealt with in the interpretation process through some form of optical or mathematical fit to ground control.

A variety of distortions associated with aircraft attitude (angular orientation) deviations are shown in Figure 7.32. The figure shows the effect that each type of distortion would have on the image of a square grid on the ground. This grid is shown in Figure 7.32a.

Figure 7.32b gives a sketch of a thermal image acquired under constant aircraft altitude and attitude conditions. Only the tangential scale distortion is present in this case. In Figure 7.32c the effect of aircraft *roll* about its flight axis is shown. Roll causes the ground grid lines to be imaged at varying times in the mirror rotation cycle.

FIGURE 7.30 Thermal image illustrating tangential distortion and one-dimensional relief displacement, Central Pennsylvania, early evening, August 20, 1968, 300 m flying height, 3 mr IFOV. (Courtesy HRB−Singer, Inc.)

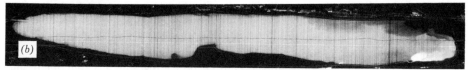

FIGURE 7.31 Effect of nonsynchronized image recording rate and V/H′ ratio. Images from two missions over Onondaga Lake, Syracuse, New York. Features shown in *(a)* are compressed and features shown in *(b)* are expanded in flight direction. (Courtesy USAF Rome Air Development Center.)

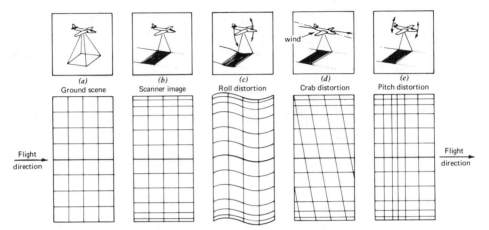

FIGURE 7.32 Scanner imagery distortions induced by aircraft attitude deviations.

Consequently, the image takes on a wavy appearance. This effect may be negated by the process of *roll compensation*. This involves using a gyroscope to monitor aircraft roll on a line-by-line basis and appropriately advancing or retarding the start time of each film recorder trace. Figure 7.33 illustrates the effect of roll compensation.

When extreme crosswind is encountered during thermal data acquisition, the axis of the aircraft must be oriented away from the flight axis slightly to counteract the wind. This condition is called *crab* and causes a skewed image (Figure 7.32d). Crab distortion can be corrected by rotating the scanner in its ring mount during flight or by computer processing the distorted data. Most often, crab distortion is avoided by not acquiring thermal data under high crosswind conditions.

Finally, as illustrated in Figure 7.32e, variations in aircraft *pitch* might distort scanner imagery. The resulting local scale changes in the flight direction due to pitch are generally slight enough that they may be ignored in most analyses.

7.12 RADIOMETRIC CALIBRATION OF THERMAL SCANNERS

As mentioned previously, the general lack of geometric integrity of thermal scanner imagery precludes its use as a precision mapping tool. Because of this, photographic imagery is normally acquired simultaneously with thermal imagery. Naturally, when nighttime thermal missions are flown, simultaneous photography is usually not feasible. In such cases, photography can be taken on the day before or after a mission. Sometimes, new photography is not needed and existing photography is used. In any case, the photography expedites object identification and study of spatial detail, and affords positional accuracy. The thermal imagery is then used solely for its radiometric information content. In order to obtain accurate radiometric information from the scanner data, the scanner must be radiometrically calibrated.

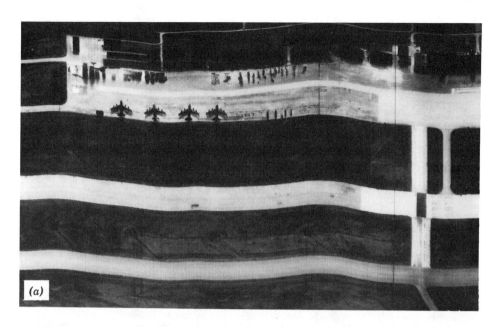

FIGURE 7.33 Effect of roll compensation on thermal image geometry. *(a)* Without roll compensation. *(b)* With roll compensation. Daytime thermal images, 300 m flying height. (Courtesy Texas Instruments Inc.)

There are numerous approaches to scanner calibration, each with its own degree of accuracy and efficiency. What form of calibration is used in any given circumstance is a function of not only the equipment available for data acquisition and processing, but also the requirements of the application at hand. We limit our discussion here to a general description of the following calibration methods:

1. Airborne radiometer referencing.
2. Internal blackbody source referencing.
3. Air-to-ground correlation.
4. Repetitive site coverage.

As will become apparent in the following discussion, a major distinction between the first two methods and the last two methods is that the former do not account for atmospheric effects but the latter do.

Airborne Radiometer Referencing

The radiometer reference approach is based on the premise that an airborne radiometer can be more precisely calibrated than a scanner system. By simultaneously operating both systems, the radiometer output can be used to calibrate the scanner imagery. The radiometer is normally mounted vertically in the aircraft to yield a continuous profile of apparent radiation temperatures along the flight path nadirline (as in Figure 7.7). Temperature values derived from the radiometer data are treated as an absolute frame of reference for calibrating the scanner output. To determine the calibration relationship, the image analyst correlates numerous scanner output values along the nadirline to their radiometer counterparts (Figure 7.34). Once the calibration relationship is defined, it is used to relate output values at other points in the scanner image to their temperature (as measured by the radiometer). The scanner output values may be obtained by densitometric analysis of a film record or tape recorded values may be used if available.

An important part of the radiometer referencing procedure is the ability to geometrically relate the radiometer output trace to the scanner data. This is normally accomplished through some form of electronic synchronization. Figure 7.35 illustrates the output from a system wherein the scanner image itself contains a trace of the flight nadirline (the wavy line in Figure 7.35a) and the radiometer output trace (Figure 7.35b). The arrows relate the trace to the image at two points where major temperature changes occur. Such imagery provides a single record from which the analyst can determine where the radiometer was sensing at any given point in time and what its output was for that point. By measuring the image density adjacent to the nadirline trace, the calibration relationship can be found.

It should be noted that the scanner calibration accuracy in the radiometer referencing approach is contingent on accurate calibration of the radiometer. Consequently, the radiometer is normally calibrated under laboratory conditions prior to each flight. Furthermore, emissivity effects must be accounted for in the data analysis and mea-

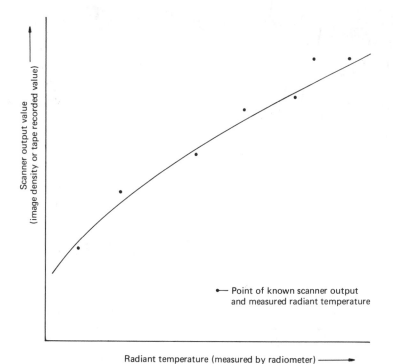

FIGURE 7.34 Sample calibration curve used to correlate scanner output with radiant temperature measured by radiometer.

surements must be made over areas of uniform temperature throughout the IFOV of each sensor. Most importantly, the accuracy of the entire process is limited because it does not account for the thermal effects of the atmosphere intervening between the aircraft and the ground.

Internal Blackbody Source Referencing

Current generations of thermal scanners normally incorporate internal temperature references (Figure 7.12). These take the form of two "blackbody" radiation sources positioned so that they are viewed by the scanner mirror during each scan. The temperatures of these sources can be precisely controlled and are generally set at the "cold" and "hot" extremes of the ground scene to be monitored. Along each scan line, the scanner optics sequentially view one of the radiation standards, scan across the ground scene below the aircraft, and then view the other radiation standard. This cycle is repeated for each scan line.

Figure 7.36 illustrates the configuration of an internally calibrated scanner. The arrangement of the reference sources, or "plates," relative to the field of view of the scanner is shown in Figure 7.36*a*. The detector signal typical of one scan line is

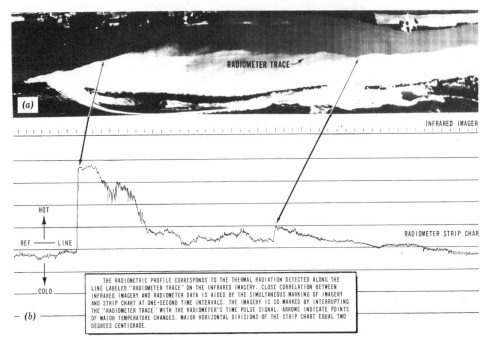

FIGURE 7.35   Airborne radiometer referencing. *(a)* Thermal scanner image containing a nadir-line trace. *(b)* Radiometer output trace. Nuclear power plant effluent, Connecticut River, near Haddam, Connecticut, 1:45 P.M., September 9, 1968, 300 m flying height, 3 mr IFOV. (Courtesy HRB–Singer, Inc.)

illustrated in Figure 7.36*b*. The scanner mirror sequentially looks at the cold temperature reference plate (T_1), then sweeps the ground, and finally looks at the hot reference plate (T_2). The scanner output at the two temperature plates is recorded along with the image data. This provides a continuously updated reference by which the other scanner output values can be related to absolute radiant temperature.

The internal source referencing approach is normally employed in systems that incorporate tape recording (although film recording can also be used). The procedure permits perfectly acceptable calibration accuracy for many applications. Actual versus predicted temperature discrepancies of less than 0.3°C are typical for missions flown at altitudes up to 600 m under clear, dry weather conditions. However, internal calibration still does not account for atmospheric effects. As indicated earlier (Section 7.5), under many prevailing mission conditions the atmosphere can bias scanner temperature measurements by as much as 2°C.

Air-to-Ground Correlation

Atmospheric effects can be accounted for in thermal scanner calibration by using empirical or theoretical atmospheric models. Theoretical atmospheric models use observations of various environmental parameters (such as temperature, pressure, and

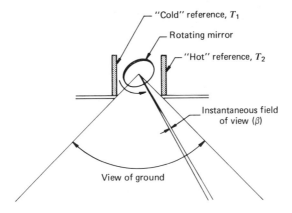

(a) Reference plate arrangement

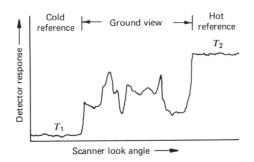

(b) Typical detector output for one scan line

FIGURE 7.36 Internal blackbody source calibration.

CO_2 concentration) in mathematical relationships that predict the effect the atmosphere will have on the signal sensed. Because of the complexity of measuring and modeling the factors that influence atmospheric effects, these effects are normally eliminated by correlating scanner data with actual surface measurements on an empirical basis.

Air-to-ground correlation is frequently employed in calibration of thermal water quality data, such as those acquired over heated water discharges. Surface temperature measurements are taken on the ground simultaneously with the passage of the aircraft. Thermometers, thermistors, or radiometers operated from boats are commonly used for this purpose. Multiple surface temperature measurements are made and, in a manner similar to the "radiometer reference" method, scanner output values are correlated with the ground-based surface temperatures. Once a calibration relationship is defined, it is used to predict temperatures at points on the scanner imagery where no ground data exist.

The reader can no doubt appreciate the expense and logistical problems involved in trying to collect surface temperature measurements throughout a study area precisely coincident with the passage of an aircraft. Also, there are often problems in geometrically relating the positions where ground measurements are taken with their counterparts on the imagery. Furthermore, in areas of rapidly changing temperature, the point value measured on the ground may not be representative of the area integrated within the scanner IFOV. Finally, in such applications as heated water discharge mapping it is difficult to measure detailed surface temperature patterns on the ground without disturbing the phenomenon one is trying to observe!

Repetitive Site Coverage

Some calibration schemes make use of repetitive data acquisition over a site to empirically determine the effect the atmosphere has on the scanner signal. The objective here is to eliminate the need for surface data collection and still account for atmospheric effects.

Many variations of the repetitive coverage approach exist. *Atmospheric profiling* is one representative approach. It has been used in such applications as monitoring power plant heated water discharges in New York State [28]. The technique involves collecting radiometer data and thermal imagery on at least four repetitive passes over a given target area. Each pass is taken at a different altitude, ranging from the altitude at which imagery is to be interpreted to the lowest altitude permitted by terrain and aircraft operating restrictions.

The profiling technique entails analyzing the change in radiometer output as a function of altitude. An area on the ground whose temperature is assumed to be constant during the course of the overflights is used as a temperature reference. The temperature recorded by the radiometer is plotted at each altitude over the reference area against altitude H', as shown in Figure 7.37. This figure illustrates the altitude−temperature curves representative of three different site conditions. The different shapes of these curves indicate the variability of atmospheric effects.

Once determined, the altitude−temperature curve is extrapolated to altitude zero, the ground. In this manner the atmospheric attenuation factor ΔT at the altitude of imaging can be found. An assumption is made that this factor is constant throughout the image, making it possible to determine any surface temperature value from

$$T_g = T_0 + \Delta T \tag{7.15}$$

where
  T_0 = observed temperature at the data collection altitude
  ΔT = temperature change caused by atmospheric effects
  T_g = actual surface temperature

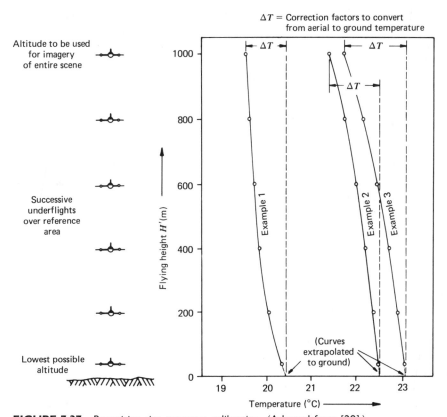

FIGURE 7.37 Repetitive site coverage calibration. (Adapted from [28].)

Other repetitive coverage schemes exist where common points are viewed from different angles rather than altitudes. In all such approaches the intent is to be able to account for atmospheric effects without requiring the acquisition of surface temperature measurements.

7.13 TEMPERATURE MAPPING WITH THERMAL SCANNER DATA

In many applications of thermal scanning techniques, it is of interest to prepare "maps" of surface temperature distributions. Techniques for generating thermal maps from scanner data can take on a host of forms, covering a wide range of complexity, cost, and accuracy. Thermal maps can range from the original distorted film record of relative radiometric temperature to a computer generated color-coded map of absolute temperatures.

In the remainder of this chapter, we describe the various approaches to temperature mapping with thermal scanner data in a very general manner. We first consider image-based procedures where the film record is the primary subject of the analysis, and then numerically based procedures where analog data are converted to a digital record that is subjected to computer analysis. We assume in each case that we are dealing with temperature mapping of water bodies. We do so to eliminate the problem of considering various object emissivities, which is required in mapping of terrestrial temperatures.

Image-Based Procedures

A thermal scanner image recorded in flight is perhaps the crudest form of thermal map. Such an image is a qualitative depiction of emitted thermal radiation and the image has low geometric and radiometric integrity. Yet, for many applications flight-recorded images suffice as final products. Often the ability to see and interpret relative temperature differences in relative positions is all that is required. For example, numerous general inventories of point sources of thermal pollution have been made through direct visual interpretation of "raw" thermal imagery. However, when *quantitative* temperature and position information are to be extracted from flight-recorded imagery, the image analyst must process the thermal data with due regard for the geometric distortions and radiometric effects involved. The most important geometric effect to account for in analyzing scanner data is tangential distortion (Section 7.11). This is done most often by using rectilinearized imagery. However, point-by-point computation of ground position may be performed with nonrectilinearized data (Figure 7.26). Radiometric information may be quantitatively interpreted from the tonal levels on the film by densitometric analysis or by using an electronic image analyzer.

Figure 7.38 illustrates common enhancements of thermal imagery generated with an electronic image analyzer. Figure 7.38a shows a black and white monitor display of a thermal scanner image of heated water being discharged into a lake. In Figure 7.38b the original display has been "level-sliced." Using calibration relationships, discrete temperature ranges can be isolated in terms of image density and color coded electronically (shown here in black and white). In this manner, the distribution of temperatures can be readily delineated in detail. Surface isotherms can be mapped in this manner.

In Figure 7.38c, a pseudo-three-dimensional display illustrates the original image in a horizontal plane in an isometric projection, with image density (manifesting temperatures) shown in vertical relief above the plane. Single profile lines making up the isometric display may also be viewed individually. In addition, numerical measurements of temperature can be made along any profile line as desired.

In summary, quantitative analysis of film recorded thermal scanner data entails measurement of image densities—with either a densitometer or an electronic image analyzer. Using density–temperature calibration relationships, surface temperatures can be determined and thermal maps can be generated, with point-by-point correction for tangential distortion or through the use of rectilinearized imagery.

Numerically Based Procedures

Because the photographic image is not the most accurate medium on which to record the scanner signals, quantitative analysis of thermal scanner data is generally performed using the tape recorded version of the data. The analog tape records detector responses over a greater range, with greater radiometric detail, and in a more linear fashion than in-flight film recording systems. For most quantitative analyses, the analog tape record is converted to digital data and processed by computer. The *analog-to-digital (A-to-D)* conversion involves transforming the continuous format of the analog signal to a series of discrete numerical representations. This entails sampling the continuous analog signal at a set time interval and numerically recording the signal level at each sample point. A familiar example of an A-to-D processor is a scanning microdensitometer (Section 6.5), which converts the continuous analog record of density on a film into a series of integers. In the case of thermal scanner data, the conversion is done by playing the analog tape signal into an electronic A-to-D conversion system. These systems consist of an analog tape recorder, a minicom-

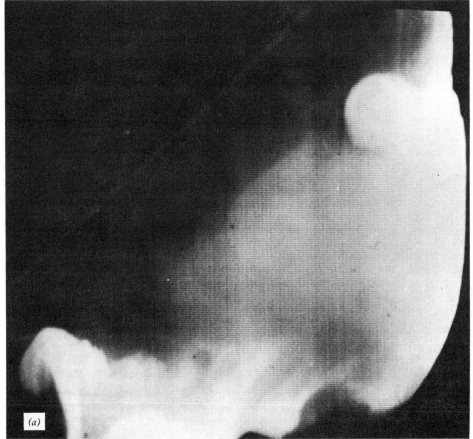

(a)

FIGURE 7.38   Thermal image enhancement through electronic image analysis. *(a)* Original image. *(b)* Level-sliced image (black and white reproduction of color-coded original). *(c)* Pseudo-three-dimensional display of temperature distribution.

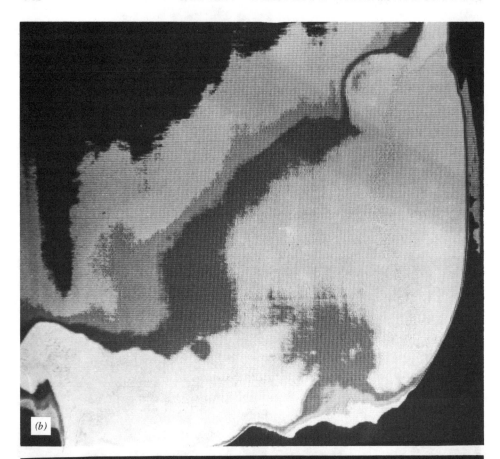

(b)

(c)

FIGURE 7.38   *(continued)*

puter, and a digital tape drive. The output of the A-to-D process is a computer-compatible tape.

Figure 7.39 is a graphical representation of the A-to-D conversion process. The analog signal recorded in flight is a continuous record of the voltage output of the thermal scanner detector, shown by the continuous line plotted in the figure. The signal level is numerically measured at a set interval of time ΔT indicated by the dashed lines. The sampling rate for a particular signal is determined by the highest frequency of change in the signal. The sampling rate must be at least twice as high as the highest frequency present in the original signal in order to adequately represent the signal. Sampling rates of 500 to 1000 points per scan line are not uncommon. This rate again depends on the system available and the application at hand.

Signal voltages are normally converted to integer values in the A-to-D sampling process. For example, a scanner signal voltage range of 0 to 2 V might correspond to an integer range of 0 to 255. Accordingly, a voltage of 0.46 recorded on the analog tape (at a in Figure 7.39) would be recorded as an integer value of 59 on the digital tape. Assignment of integers, rather than decimal numbers, improves the efficiency with which the data can be stored and manipulated in subsequent computer processing.

Because computers operate on numbers expressed in binary notation (base 2), signal voltage is normally converted to binary numbers. Most often, an eight-digit binary number is used. In base 10, an eight-digit number allows a range of $0 - 99,999,999$ (10^8 values). Similarly, in base 2, an eight-digit number would permit a range of 2^8 (256) values, or $0 - 255$. In computer science, a binary digit is called a *bit*.

The product of the A-to-D conversion is thus a two-dimensional matrix of pixels that numerically represents the scanner signal recorded over a scene. Each pixel is spatially referenced in terms of scan line in the direction of flight and column number in the sequence of sampled points along a scan line. This effectively establishes an xy reference grid for locating and addressing features on the imagery.

In computer-compatible form, scanner data may be processed, analyzed, and displayed in a variety of ways. For example, consider scanner data for which a

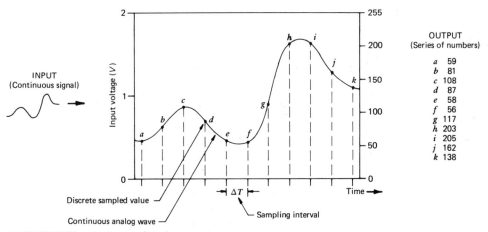

FIGURE 7.39 Analog-to-digital conversion process.

correlation has been developed to relate scanner output values to absolute ground temperatures. The computer can apply this calibration relationship to each point in the digital data set, producing a matrix of absolute temperature values.

The precise form of a calibration relationship will vary with the temperature range in question, but for the sake of the example, we assume that a linear fit of the digital data to radiant exitance is appropriate. Under this assumption, a digital number, N, recorded on the computer tape, can be expressed by

$$N = A + B\epsilon T^4 \tag{7.16}$$

where

A and B = system response parameters determined from one of the sensor calibration procedures described earlier

ϵ = emissivity at the point of measurement

T = kinetic temperature at the point of measurement

Once A and B are determined, kinetic temperature T for any observed number N is given by

$$T = \left(\frac{N - A}{B\epsilon}\right)^{1/4} \tag{7.17}$$

The parameters A and B can be obtained from internal blackbody calibration, air-to-ground correlation, or any of the other calibration procedures. Assuming the internal calibration approach, if T_1 and T_2 are the known temperatures of two internal reference plates and N_1 and N_2 are the corresponding digital numbers obtained when the scanner views these plates

$$N_1 = A + B\epsilon T_1^4$$

and

$$N_2 = A + B\epsilon T_2^4$$

Solving the above equations simultaneously, assuming $\epsilon = 1$ for the calibration plates,

$$A = N_1 - \frac{(N_1 - N_2)}{(T_1^4 - T_2^4)} T_1^4$$

and

$$B = \frac{N_1 - N_2}{T_1^4 - T_2^4}$$

With parameters A and B known, Equation 7.17 can be used to determine the kinetic temperature for any ground point for which N is observed *and* the emissivity is known.

Calibrated thermal data may be further processed and displayed in a number of different forms. Figure 7.40 illustrates two common forms of data display. An original

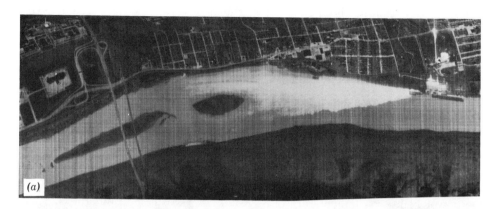

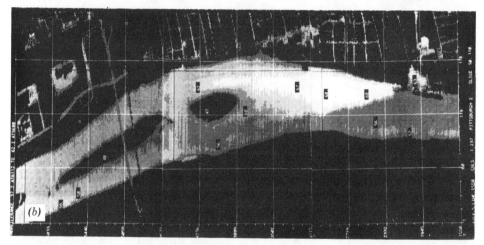

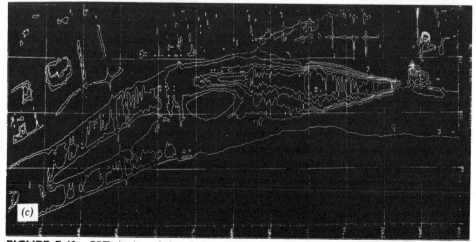

FIGURE 7.40   CRT display of digital thermal data. *(a)* Original thermal image. *(b)* Annotated CRT gray-shade map. *(c)* CRT isothermal "contour map." (Courtesy U.S. Air Force Avionics Laboratory and HRB–Singer, Inc.)

scanner image is shown in Figure 7.40*a*. An annotated, gray shaded map, generated by a computer-driven cathode ray tube (CRT), is shown in Figure 7.40*b*. An isothermal "contour map" is shown in 7.40*c*. These maps can be displayed on CRTs, film recorders, or produced on computer-driven line plotters. In the process of preparing such maps, point-by-point tangent corrections can be applied to rectilinearize the data.

Plate 10 shows a thermal image mosaic generated from digital data that have been calibrated, rectilinearized, and color coded into discrete temperature regions. This color-coded thermal image and accompanying surface isotherm map are a commercial product prepared for a client who desired the information in degrees Fahrenheit. The color-coded image shows the circulation pattern in a power plant cooling pond. At the time of this image, heated water enters the pond at 102°F (39°C) and is recirculated to the power plant at a temperature of 84°F (29°C). The surface isotherm map was prepared from subsets of the color-coded thermal image through the use of a Zoom Transfer Scope™ (Figure 3.12) to match the image scale with the base map scale.

7.14   FLIR SYSTEMS

To this point in our discussion of aerial thermography, we have emphasized scanners that view the terrain directly beneath an aircraft. *Forward-Looking Infrared (FLIR)* systems can be used to acquire oblique views of the terrain ahead of an aircraft. Figures 7.41 and 7.42 are images acquired by such a system in the daytime. Conceptually, the FLIR system used to produce these images operates on the same basic principles as a line scanning system. However, the mirror for the system points forward and optically sweeps the field of view of a linear array of thermal detectors across the scene of interest. The signals from the detectors are used to drive a similar array of light-emitting diodes (LEDs). In turn, the intensities of the LED array are converted to a standard video signal using a solid-state array camera. Hence, the data can be recorded and viewed using standard video cassette recorder (VCR) equipment. (Solid-state array cameras and video recording are described in Section 2.17.)

Modern FLIR systems are extremely portable (typically weighing less than 30 kg) and can be operated on a wide variety of fixed-wing aircraft and helicopters, as well as from ground-based mobile platforms. FLIR imagery has been used extensively in military applications. Civilian use of FLIR is increasing in applications ranging from forest fire control, to electrical transmission line maintenance, to law enforcement.

7.15   MULTISPECTRAL SCANNERS

As with thermal scanners, *multispectral scanner (MSS)* systems utilize electronic energy detectors. However, rather than collecting only thermal IR data, they are designed to sense energy in a number of narrow spectral bands simultaneously. These bands may range from ultraviolet wavelengths through the visible, near-IR, mid-IR, and thermal IR portions of the spectrum.

In Section 2.11 we described the basic principles and advantages of using multiband

FIGURE 7.41 Forward-Looking Infrared (FLIR) image of storage tanks. Note level of liquid in each tank. (Courtesy Texas Instruments Inc.)

camera systems. We saw that by analyzing a scene in several spectral bands, we can greatly improve our ability to distinguish the identity and condition of terrain features. Multispectral scanners operate on the same principle of selective sensing in multiple spectral bands, but these instruments have some inherent advantages over their photographic counterparts:

1. Photographic systems are limited to the spectral range 0.3 to 0.9 μm. Utilizing electronic detectors, multispectral scanners can extend the range of sensing from 0.3 to approximately 14 μm.

2. Multiband photographic systems use separate optical systems to collect each of the spectral images independently. This leads to problems in ensuring that data in separate bands are comparable to one another spatially and radiometrically. Multispectral scanners use the same optical system to collect data in all spectral bands simultaneously.

3. Multiband photographic data are somewhat difficult to calibrate radiometrically because they stem from the photochemical processes of photography. Multispectral scanner data are generated electronically and are therefore more amena-

FIGURE 7.42   Forward-Looking Infrared (FLIR) image of urban area. (Courtesy Texas Instruments Inc.)

ble to calibration. The electronic format of the scanner output also permits recording over a greater range of values.

4. Photographic systems require an onboard supply of film that must be physically transported to the ground for processing. MSS data may be electronically transmitted to ground receiving stations. This characteristic is particularly important when sensing from space platforms.

5. Multiband photographic systems yield pictorial images that are generally interpreted *visually* using a color additive viewer. While this is an efficient analysis approach for many applications, it has limitations. When many feature types are to be interpreted, more than three bands may need to be analyzed simultaneously. Over large study areas, visual interpretation of more than three bands becomes quite cumbersome. Multispectral scanner data, being in an electronic format, can be dealt with in a *digital* form. Hence, the data are amenable to computer assisted analysis techniques, which tend to be more quantitative and automated than visual interpretation. The computer has little trouble "looking at" and "comparing" multiple image data sets simultaneously.

The operation of an airborne MSS system is illustrated in Figure 7.43. In essence, the multispectral scanner is simply a multiple-detector extension of the thermal scanner. In fact, many organizations that acquire thermal imagery do so with one or more thermal channels of an MSS, in lieu of using a single-channel thermal scanner. As shown in Figure 7.43a, the line-scanning collection geometry of the MSS is identical to that of a thermal scanner. A rotating mirror moves the field of view of the scanner along a scan line perpendicular to the direction of flight. The forward motion of the aircraft advances the viewed strip between scans, causing a two-dimensional image data set to be recorded.

Figure 7.43 illustrates the components of a typical scanner. Here again, the scanning mirror and optics are similar to those used in a thermal scanner. The difference is that the thermal scanner filters the incoming radiation to focus just the thermal wavelengths on a single detector. In the MSS, the incoming energy is separated into several spectral components that are sensed independently. A *dichroic grating* is used to separate the non-thermal wavelengths from the thermal wavelengths in the incoming radiation. The non-thermal wavelength component is directed from the grating through a prism (or diffraction grating) that splits the energy into a continuum of UV, visible, and IR wavelengths. At the same time, the dichroic grating disperses the thermal component of the incoming signal into its constituent wavelengths. By placing an array of detectors at the proper geometric positions behind the grating and the prism, the incoming beam is essentially "pulled apart" into multiple narrow bands, or channels, each of which is measured independently. Figure 7.43 illustrates a 5-channel scanner. Scanners with as many as 128 channels have been used for research purposes.

As shown in Figure 7.43, the signals generated by each of the detectors of an MSS are amplified by the system electronics and recorded by a multichannel magnetic tape recorder. If the MSS data analysis procedure is to be pictorially oriented, the scanner output is normally recorded on an analog recorder and converted to images after the flight using a ground-based film recorder. If the analysis procedure is to be numerically oriented, it is preferable to electronically convert the analog scanner output signal to a numerical (digital) format prior to recording in flight. This operation is performed using an A-to-D process, as illustrated previously in Figure 7.39. The digitization process ensures that data collected in several spectral bands are precisely synchronized. These data are initially recorded on high-density digital tape onboard the aircraft. On the ground, the tape is converted to computer-compatible tape (CCT) for subsequent processing.

Figure 7.44 shows a multispectral scanner system that acquires digital data in 11 bands within the wavelength range 0.42 to 13.0 μm. Seven of these bands have been designed to correspond to the wavelength bands of the Landsat Thematic Mapper (Section 9.8). This scanner has an IFOV of 2.5 mr and a total scan angle of 86°.

Figure 7.45 shows images acquired with another 11-channel MSS in the vicinity of the University of Michigan—Ann Arbor Campus. Each of the images shown in Figure 7.45 represents a unique spectral view of the same scene. The first 10 channels of data were acquired in narrow bands ranging from 0.380 to 1.060 μm. Band 11 is a thermal channel (9.75 to 12.25 μm). Note the relative tonal variations of different scene

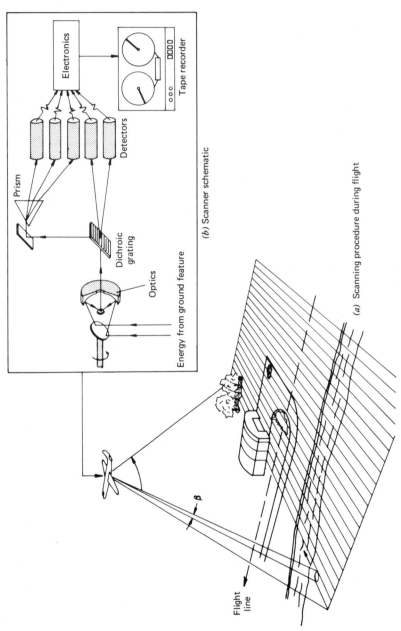

(b) Scanner schematic

(a) Scanning procedure during flight

FIGURE 7.43 Multispectral scanner system operation.

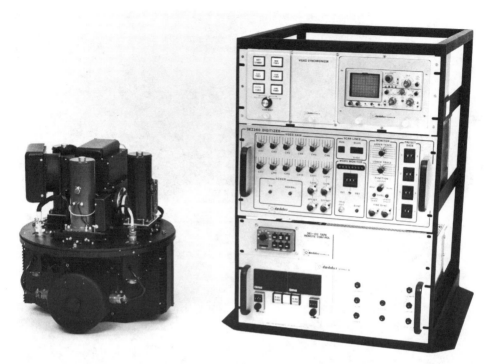

FIGURE 7.44 Eleven-band digital mirror-sweep multispectral scanner system. (Courtesy Daedalus Enterprises, Inc.)

features both within and between the various bands. Some features are easily differentiated in a single band. For example residential streets (A) can be separated from surrounding areas of grass (B) on every image. This is due to large reflectance (channels 1 to 10) and exitance (channel 11) differences for these two feature types throughout the range of sensing. Note, however, that the *relative* signals received from each cover type vary. The streets appear nearly white due to high reflectance in all seven of the visible images (0.380 to 0.700 μm). The grass has much lower visible reflectance and therefore appears much darker in tone in these bands. In the near-infrared channels (8 to 10) a *tonal reversal* occurs because of the high infrared reflectance of the grass compared to the streets. The streets also have a higher radiant temperature than the grass (channel 11).

While it is quite easy to distinguish streets from grass in all 11 channels in Figure 7.45, note how difficult it is to distinguish water (C) from grass (B) in the visible channels, due to the low visible reflectance of both features. In the near-infrared channels (8 to 10), water has even lower reflectance as a result of its absorbing qualities at these wavelengths. The reverse is true of the grass due to its very high infrared reflectance.

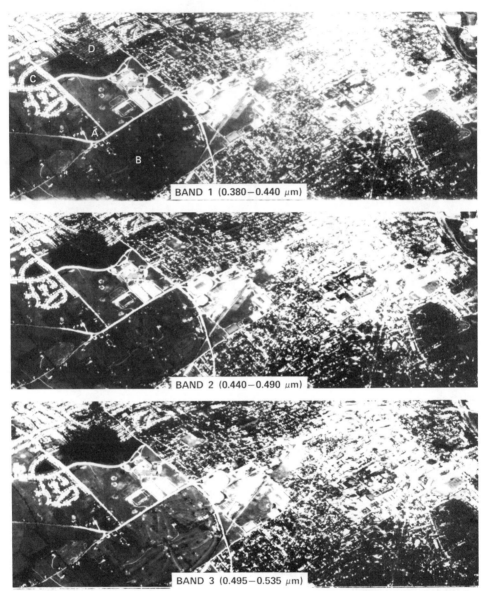

FIGURE 7.45   Eleven-band multispectral scanner images, Ann Arbor, Michigan. (Courtesy Bendix Corp.)

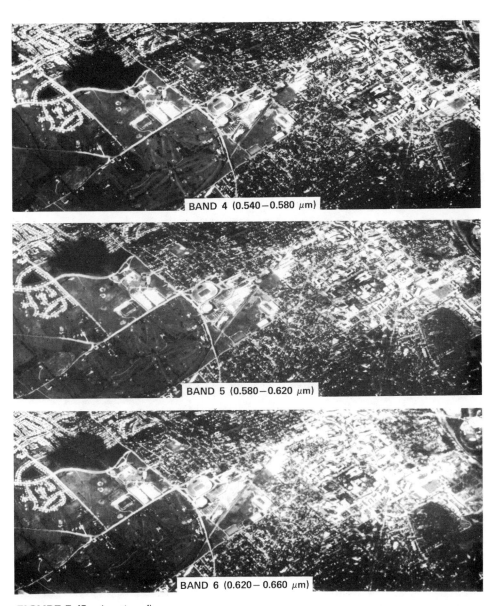

BAND 4 (0.540—0.580 μm)

BAND 5 (0.580—0.620 μm)

BAND 6 (0.620—0.660 μm)

FIGURE 7.45 *(continued)*

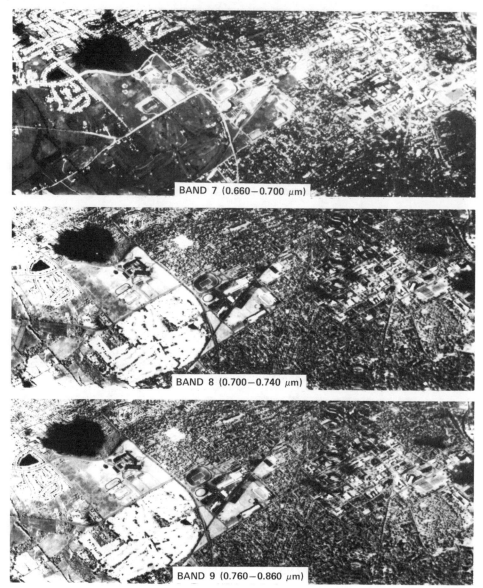

BAND 7 (0.660−0.700 μm)

BAND 8 (0.700−0.740 μm)

BAND 9 (0.760−0.860 μm)

FIGURE 7.45   *(continued)*

A cloud shadow can be seen at *D*. Some details can be seen in the shadow area in channel 1 because the shadow area is somewhat illuminated by Rayleigh scatter of sunlight and skylight. The shadow area is darkest in the near-infrared bands where Rayleigh scatter is low. No effects of the shadow area are seen in the thermal channel because the cloud is in motion and all objects in the scene have sufficient thermal

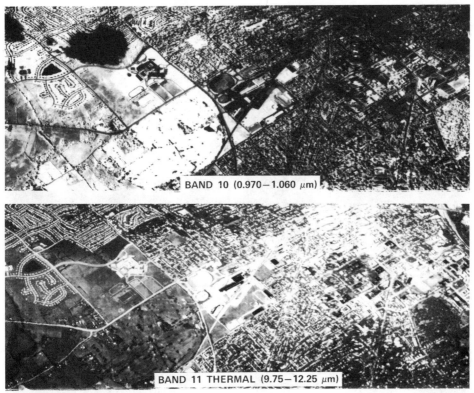

BAND 10 (0.970−1.060 μm)

BAND 11 THERMAL (9.75−12.25 μm)

FIGURE 7.45 *(continued)*

inertia to prevent significant cooling during the brief time they are in the cloud shadow.

Figure 7.46 shows images acquired with an eight-band MSS over the Potomac River just south of Washington, D.C. (this same area appears at lower center in Figure 8.23, a radar image of Washington, D.C., and vicinity). Various features are imaged differently in the individual bands. For example, the highway interchange area in the lower right shows a distinct tonal reversal between the pavement and grass in the visible bands (1 to 3) and the near-infrared bands (4 and 5); tones reverse again between the near-infrared and the mid-infrared bands (6 and 7). The plume of warm water entering the river at upper left is seen only in the thermal band (8). The dock at top center is most clearly seen in the mid-infrared and thermal infrared bands (6 to 8). The land mass above the interchange appears very differently in the various bands. Few details in this area are seen in the blue and green bands (1 and 2); the land mass nearly blends with the river water in these bands. The near- and mid-infrared bands all show this area clearly, but with distinctly different tonal values. Several other features in this scene also manifest significantly different tonal values in the various bands shown in this figure.

FIGURE 7.46   Eight-band multispectral scanner images, Potomac River south of Washington, D.C., 2100 m flying height, 2.5 mr IFOV. (Courtesy NASA.)

Figure 7.47 shows a *linear array* multispectral scanner system. This system employs push-broom scanning, as described in Section 2.17. Recall that push-broom scanning systems do not employ a scanning mirror. Rather, they employ linear arrays of CCDs oriented perpendicular to the flight path. A line of image data is obtained by

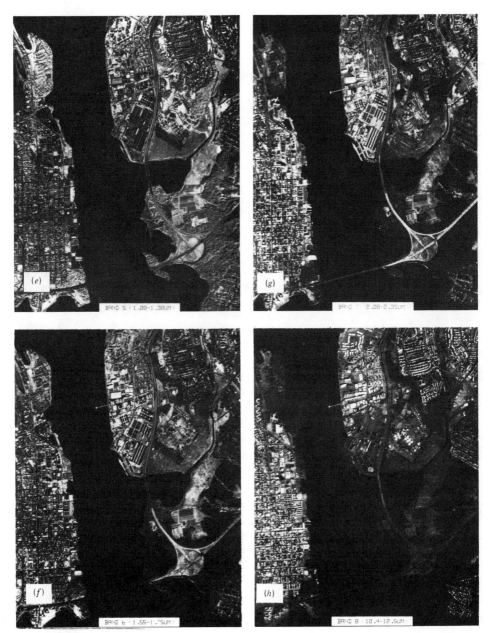

FIGURE 7.46 *(continued)*

sampling the output from the detectors along the array and successive lines of coverage are obtained by repeated sampling along the array as the aircraft (or satellite) progresses along the flight line.

Compared with conventional mirror-scanning systems, push-broom scanners offer

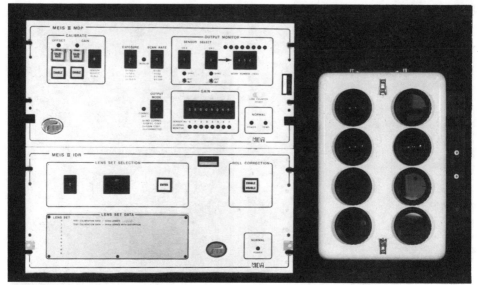

FIGURE 7.47   MEIS II linear array multispectral scanner system. (Courtesy Canada Centre for Remote Sensing.)

several advantages. They are generally smaller in size and weight, and require less power for their operation. Having no moving parts, they have higher reliability and longer life expectancy. At the same time, they have higher geometric fidelity, better spatial resolution, and increased radiometric accuracy. One disadvantage to push-broom systems is the need to calibrate many more detectors. Another current limitation of these systems is the fact that CCDs have not been developed to sense wavelengths longer than the near-IR. (Ongoing research and development will likely overcome this limitation in the future.)

The system shown in Figure 7.47 is the *Multispectral Electrooptical Imaging Scanner (MEIS II)*. It incorporates eight 1728-element linear arrays (one behind each lens) that acquire data in eight spectral bands ranging from 0.39 to 1.1 μm, with an IFOV of 0.70 mr and a total field of view of 40°. The wavelength bands are selected by filters mounted in front of the scanner lenses. Different wavelength band combinations can, therefore, be used for different applications. Data are encoded as 8-bit numbers resulting in 256 possible signal levels. Figure 7.47 shows the eight lens positions; interchannel registration is achieved digitally by the real-time processor incorporated into the system [20].

Figure 7.48 shows a stereopair of an agricultural area in Ontario, Canada, acquired by the MEIS II scanner operated in a stereo mode. These images were obtained on a single flight line by using an external mirror attachment to create a forward-looking and an aft-looking channel in addition to the normal downward-looking channels. One channel is aimed 30° from vertical ahead of the aircraft and the other is aimed 30° from vertical behind the aircraft. The resulting images were geometrically corrected using

FIGURE 7.48 Stereoscopic MEIS II multispectral scanner image of an agricultural area west of Ottawa, Canada. October 31, 1983. Green band (0.51 to 0.60 μm), 6700 m flying height, 0.70 mr IFOV. (Courtesy Data Acquisition Division, Canada Centre for Remote Sensing.)

attitude and velocity data from an inertial navigation system in order to produce stereo images of compatible geometry.

The MEIS system was developed for the Canada Centre for Remote Sensing and was the first airborne push-broom scanner to be used operationally. A similar "first" in push-broom scanning technology was the German *Modular Optoelectronic Multi-spectral Scanner (MOMS)* that was the first push-broom scanning system to be tested from space (during a 1983 Space Shuttle mission). The MOMS system acquired monochromatic images of selected areas at a resolution of 20 m.

Plate 11a shows imagery that was obtained with NASA's *Thermal Infrared Multi-spectral Scanner (TIMS)*, a multispectral scanner that operates exclusively in the thermal infrared portion of the spectrum. It utilizes six narrow bands located between 8.2 and 12.2 μm and has an IFOV of 2.5 mr and a total field of view of 80°. This instrument has great potential for geologic mapping because the spectral exitance of various minerals, especially silicates, is distinct in the wavelength region 8 to 14 μm. Three of the TIMS bands were used to produce Plate 11a. In this color composite, channel 1 (8.2 to 8.6 μm) is displayed as blue, channel 3 (9.0 to 9.4 μm) is displayed as green, and channel 5 (10.2 to 11.2 μm) is displayed as red. Image enhancement techniques were also used to maximize the differences among rock units. Plate 11 b is a generalized lithologic map of the same area that was redrawn and color coded to illustrate the specific features recognizable within the TIMS data. The silica-rich quartzite rocks stand out as red because their emissivity in channel 5 is much greater than in channels 1 and 3. The Cambrian and Ordovician metasedimentary rocks are blue-green because their emissivity is higher in channels 1 and 3 than in channel 5. The volcanic rocks have a magenta color because their emissivity is high in channels 1 and 5 and low in channel 3. Details in the hues of the fan gravels appear to be related to the source materials for the gravel, the erosional age of the surface, and the desert varnish surface conditions [16].

7.16   MSS OPERATION AND DESIGN CONSIDERATIONS

Because MSS systems are designed to sense energy over a very small IFOV (to optimize spatial resolution) and in narrow wavelength bands (to optimize spectral resolution), a very limited amount of energy is incident on each of a system's detectors. Hence, the detectors must be very sensitive to output a *signal* significantly stronger than the level of system *noise* (extraneous, unwanted responses).

Figure 7.49 illustrates the effect of noise on an MSS signal. Figure 7.49a shows the signal from one detector as it would appear in the absence of system noise. The variations in the MSS signal strength shown in (a) relate directly to the characteristics of the terrain covered by the scan line. The large changes in signal most likely correspond to changes in cover type, while the more subtle fluctuations would probably indicate cover type subclasses and different conditions within each cover type.

In Figure 7.49b, random noise has been added to the signal. The effect of the noise is to mask the signal fluctuations that are weak in comparison to the noise level. In this example, we would be unable to evaluate the subtle within-cover-type variations because of the level of noise. The dominant variations within the cover types would still be interpretable, but with reduced accuracy. At a higher level of noise, even stronger

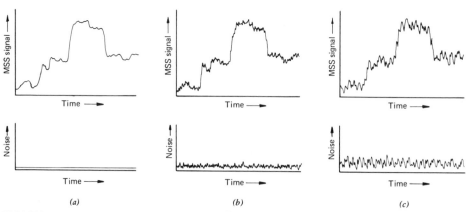

FIGURE 7.49   Effect of noise on MSS signal. *(a)* Signal along one scan line without nosie. *(b)* Signal with low noise component. *(c)* Signal with high noise component.

signal fluctuations will be masked. In Figure 7.49c, increased noise masks all but the strongest variations in the signal.

It can be seen that the critical factor is the noise level *relative* to the signal strength. Thus, the quality of the output can be specified by a *signal-to-noise (S/N) ratio.* As shown in Figure 7.49, the *S/N* ratio directly affects the radiometric resolution of the data (that is, the ability to detect slight radiance differences). In addition to radiometric resolution, *S/N* is related to spatial and spectral resolution, as well as many other factors. Several basic factors relating to the ratio can be expressed as

$$\left(\frac{S}{N}\right)_\lambda \propto D_\lambda \beta^2 \left(\frac{H'}{V}\right)^{1/2} \Delta\lambda L_\lambda \qquad (7.18)$$

where

D_λ = detectivity (measure of detector
performance quality)
β^2 = (instantaneous field of view)^2 }   (these determine
$(H'/V)^{1/2}$ = (flying height/aircraft velocity)$^{1/2}$ }   *spatial* resolution)
$\Delta\lambda$ = spectral bandwidth of the channel
(*spectral* resolution)
L_λ = spectral radiance of ground feature

(Note that the *S/N* value is partially based on wavelength-dependent parameters. Accordingly, different *S/N* values are applicable to each channel of an MSS.)

Equation 7.18 expresses some of the trade-offs implicit in the design and operation of an MSS. For example, we can note the trade-off between spectral and spatial resolution. To maintain the same *S/N* while improving spatial resolution by a factor of 4 (decreasing β by a factor of 2), we must degrade the spectral resolution by a factor of 4 (increase $\Delta\lambda$ by a factor of 4).

In addition to the basic factors listed in Eq. 7.18, numerous other factors will affect the signal-to-noise performance of any given scanner system. Some of these factors are atmospheric attenuation, the design of the system's optical components, and the noise characteristics of the system electronics. This book does not detail the design and operation of MSS systems, yet the image analyst should have some feeling for the many factors that influence the quality of the data generated by these systems.

We have already mentioned that MSS data may be output either as hard copy images or in numerical form. One advantage of the numerical format is the ability to apply quantitative *preprocessing operations* prior to analyzing the data. These operations improve the quality of the image data. They are discussed at length in Chapter 10, but it is appropriate to mention some of the basic points here.

One task frequently performed during preprocessing is *geometric correction* of the MSS data. The precise nature of the geometric correction procedure employed depends upon the particular design of the scanner. For example, the corrections applied to mirror sweeping and push-broom scanning systems will be different. However, the intent is the same—to correct for any systematic distortions due to the geometric conditions of scanning, and any random distortions caused by variations in aircraft flight parameters during image acquisition. Also, geometric preprocessing functions are commonly applied to MSS data to rescale and rotate the image data so that they will correspond to a specific map or be compatible with the file structure of a geographic information system for a given area.

Frequently, preprocessing of MSS data also involves making *radiometric corrections*. Most MSS systems use an internal reference source to radiometrically calibrate the data collected in each channel. Internal blackbody sources are used to calibrate the thermal channels. Either ambient skylight energy or an internal calibration lamp is used to calibrate the non-thermal channels. Numerous extraneous radiometric factors that influence the MSS signal can also be treated by preprocessing. These extraneous effects include variations in solar illumination, atmospheric transmittance, and viewing geometry. Techniques such as between-band ratios can be used to reduce these effects. Once again, illustration of these operations is included in Chapter 10.

7.17   IMAGING SPECTROMETRY

Imaging spectrometry refers to the acquisition of images in many, very narrow, contiguous spectral bands throughout the visible, near-IR, and mid-IR portions of the spectrum. NASA has developed several imaging spectrometers that use linear array detectors to gather data in 128 or more spectral bands. The intent of these systems is to permit discrimination among earth surface features that have diagnostic absorption and reflection characteristics over narrow wavelength intervals that are "lost" within the bandwidths of the various channels of a conventional multispectral scanner. This concept is illustrated in Figure 7.50, which shows the laboratory-measured reflectance spectra for a number of common minerals over the wavelength range 2.0 to 2.5 μm. Note the diagnostic absorption features for these various material types over this spectral range. Also shown on this figure is the bandwidth of band 7 of the Landsat Thematic Mapper (Section 9.8). Whereas this latter sensor obtains only one data point corresponding to the integrated response over a spectral band 0.27 μm wide, an imaging spectrometer is capable of obtaining many data points over this range using bands on the order of 0.01 μm wide. Therefore, the imaging spectrometer can produce data of sufficient spectral resolution for direct identification of the materials, whereas the broader band system Thematic Mapper cannot resolve these diagnostic spectral differences [10].

Extensive imaging spectrometry research has been conducted with data acquired by the *Airborne Imaging Spectrometer (AIS)*. This system collects 128 channels of data, which are approximately 9.3 nm wide (just under 0.01 μm), in contiguous bands between 1.2 and 2.4 μm. The IFOV of the AIS is 1.9 mr and the system is typically operated from an altitude of 4200 m above the terrain. This yields a narrow swath 32 pixels wide beneath the flight path with a ground pixel size of approximately 8 × 8 m.

Figure 7.51 shows an AIS image, acquired over Van Nuys, California, on the first engineering test flight of the AIS in November 1982. This image covers the area outlined in black lines on the corresponding photographic mosaic. Notable features include a field in the lower portion of the image, a condominium complex in the center,

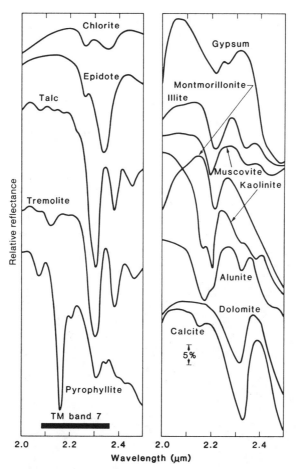

FIGURE 7.50 Selected laboratory spectra of minerals showing diagnostic absorptance and reflectance characteristics. The bandwidth of band 7 of the Landsat Thematic Mapper (Chapter 9) is also shown. (From [10]. Copyright © 1985 by the AAAS. Courtesy NASA Jet Propulsion Laboratory.)

and a school in the upper half of the image. On this test flight, images were acquired in only 32 contiguous spectral bands in the region from 1.5 to 1.2 μm. A composite of the 32 AIS images, each in a different 9.3 nm wide spectral band and each 32 pixels wide, is shown below the photographic mosaic. The most obvious feature in the AIS images is the loss of detail in the atmospheric water absorption band centered around 1.4 μm. However, there is some detail visible in the spectral images in this band. Details associated with reflectance variations are identified with arrows. For instance,

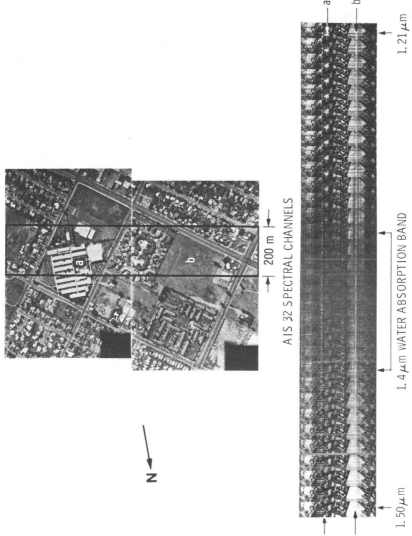

FIGURE 7.51 Airphoto mosaic and 32 spectral bands of AIS images covering portion of the same area, Van Nuys, California. A school courtyard (*a*) and an open field (*b*) are shown on the mosaic. The vertical black lines outline the coverage of the corresponding 32 pixel wide AIS images taken in 32 spectral bands between 1.50 and 1.21 µm. The individual AIS images taken in 9.3 nm wide, contiguous, spectral intervals are shown at the bottom. The spectral reflectance behavior of the well-watered courtyard and the open field are quite different and are primarily associated with differences in irrigation practices. (From [10]. Copyright © 1985 by the AAAS. Courtesy

the reflectance of a well-watered courtyard lawn inside the school grounds (location *a*) drops significantly beyond 1.4 μm in comparison with the reflectance of the unwatered field (location *b*).

The AIS was designed primarily as an engineering test bed for detector development. Several other systems are under development to extend both the spectral and spatial coverage of the AIS. For example, the *Airborne Visible–Infrared Imaging Spectrometer (AVIRIS)* is expected to collect data in 224 bands 10 nm wide, in the region 0.4 to 2.4 μm. Flown on NASA's U-2 aircraft at an altitude of 20 km, the swath width will be 11 km with a ground pixel resolution of approximately 20 m. Planned for the early 1990s is the *Shuttle Imaging Spectrometer Experiment (SISEX)*, which will acquire data on a global basis in 128 spectral bands, with a swath width of 12 km and a ground IFOV of 30 m (from a Shuttle altitude of 250 km). Proposed for the mid-1990s is the *High Resolution Imaging Spectrometer (HIRIS)*. This system is similar to SISEX, but will provide a greater swath width. It is one of the *Earth Observing System (EOS)* instruments being considered for the Space Platform as part of the Space Station.

In composite, imaging spectrometry holds the potential to provide a quantum jump in the quality of spectral data obtained about earth surface features. These sensors will also provide a quantum jump in the quantity of data acquired. Hence, research is continuing on how to optimize the analysis of the high volumes of data acquired by these systems.

7.18 CONCLUSION

In this chapter, we have treated the basic theory and operation of thermal and multispectral scanning systems. We have illustrated selected examples of thermal and multispectral data interpretation, processing, and display, with an emphasis on data gathered using airborne systems. In Chapter 9, we illustrate thermal and multispectral sensing from space platforms, with an emphasis on the Landsat sweep-scanning multispectral scanner and Thematic Mapper systems, and the SPOT linear array multispectral scanner.

SELECTED BIBLIOGRAPHY

1. Abrams, M.J., et al., "Geologic Mapping Using Thermal Images," *Remote Sensing of Environment*, vol. 16, no. 1, 1984, pp. 13–34.

2. American Society of Photogrammetry, *Thermosense II—Second National Conference on Thermal Infrared Sensing Technology for Energy Conservation Programs*, Falls Church, Va., 1979.

3. American Society of Photogrammetry, *Manual of Remote Sensing*, 2nd ed., Falls Church, Va., 1983.

4. Aronoff, S., and G.A. Ross, "Detection of Environmental Disturbance Using Color Aerial Photography and Thermal Infrared Imagery," *Photogrammetric Engineering and Remote Sensing*, vol. 48, no. 4, April 1982, pp. 587–591.

5. Barnes, W.L., "MODIS: A Moderate-Resolution Imaging System for the Space Station Polar-Orbiting Platform," *Proceedings: 10th William T. Pecora Memorial Remote Sensing Symposium*, American Society for Photogrammetry and Remote Sensing, Ft. Collins, Colo., 1985, pp. 529–542.

6. Best, R.G., et al., "Aerial Thermal Infrared Census of Canada Geese in South Dakota," *Photogrammetric Engineering and Remote Sensing*, vol. 48, no. 12, December 1982, pp. 1869–1877.

7. Brown, R.J., J. Cihlar, and P.M. Teillet, "Quantitative Residential Heat Loss Study," *Photogrammetric Engineering and Remote Sensing*, vol. 47, no. 9, September 1981, pp. 1327–1333.

8. Cihlar, J., *Thermal Infrared Remote Sensing: A Bibliography*, Research Report 76-1, Canada Center for Remote Sensing, Ottawa, March 1976.

9. Eidenshink, J.C., "Detection of Leaks in Buried Rural Water Pipelines Using Thermal Infrared Images," *Photogrammetric Engineering and Remote Sensing*, vol. 51, no. 5, May 1985, pp. 561–564.

10. Goetz, A.H., et al., "Imaging Spectrometry for Earth Remote Sensing", *Science*, vol. 228, no. 4704, 7 June 1985, pp. 1147–1153.

11. Graves, H.B., E.D. Bellis, and W.M. Knuth, "Censusing White-Tailed Deer by Airborne Thermal Infrared Imagery," *The Journal of Wildlife Management*, vol. 36, no. 3, 1972, pp. 875–884.

12. Hatfield, J.L., J.P. Millard, and R.C. Goettelman, "Variability of Surface Temperature in Agricultural Fields of Central California," *Photogrammetric Engineering and Remote Sensing*, vol. 48, no. 8, August 1982, pp. 1319–1325.

13. Hirsch, S.N., R.F. Kruckeberg, and F.H. Madden, "The Bispectral Forest Detection System," *Proceedings: 7th International Symposium on Remote Sensing of Environment*, University of Michigan, Ann Arbor, 1971, pp. 2253–2259.

14. Hudson, R.D., Jr., *Infrared System Engineering*, Wiley, New York, 1969.

15. Jensen, J.R., E.J. Christensen, and R. Sharitz, "Nontidal Wetland Mapping in South Carolina Using Airborne Multispectral Scanner Data," *Remote Sensing of Environment*, vol. 16, no. 1, 1984, pp. 1–12.

16. Kahle, A.B., and A.F.H. Goetz, "Mineralogic Information from a New Airborne Thermal Infrared Multispectral Scanner," *Science*, vol. 222, no. 4619, 7 October 1983, pp. 24–27.

17. Leckie, D.G., "An Error Analysis of Thermal Infrared Line-Scan Data for Quantitative Studies," *Photogrammetric Engineering and Remote Sensing*, vol. 48, no. 6, June 1982, pp. 945–954.

18. LeDrew, E.F., and S.E. Franklin, "The Use of Thermal Infrared Imagery in Surface Current Analysis of a Small Lake," *Photogrammetric Engineering and Remote Sensing*, vol. 51, no. 5, May 1985, pp. 565–573.

19. Marshall, S.J., *Infrared Thermography of Buildings: An Annotated Bibliography*, U.S. Army Corps of Engineers, Cold Regions Research and Engineering Laboratory, Hanover, N.H., 1977.

20. McColl, W.D., R.A. Neville, and S.M. Till, "Multi-Detector Electro-optical Imaging Scanner MEIS II," *Proceedings: Eighth Canadian Symposium on Remote Sensing, Montreal, Quebec, May 1983*, L'Association québecoise de télédétection and the Canadian Remote Sensing Society, 1984, pp. 71–79. [Available from L'Association québecoise de télédétection, Sainte-Foy, Quebec]

21. Mintzer, O.W., F.A. Kulacki, and L.E. Winget, "Measuring Heat Loss from Flat-Roof Buildings with Calibrated Thermography," *Photogrammetric Engineering and Remote Sensing*, vol. 49, no. 6, June 1983, pp. 777–788.

22. Nash, D.B., "Detection of Bedrock Topography beneath a Thin Cover of Alluvium Using Thermal Remote Sensing," *Photogrammetric Engineering and Remote Sensing*, vol. 51, no. 1, January 1985, pp. 77–88.

23. Neillis, M.D., "Interpretation of Thermal Infrared Imagery for Irrigation Water Resources Management," *Journal of Geography*, vol. 84, no. 1, 1985, pp. 11–14.

24. Philpot, W.D., and W.R. Philipson, "Thermal Sensing for Characterizing the Contents of Waste Storage Drums," *Photogrammetric Engineering and Remote Sensing*, vol. 51, no. 2, February 1985, pp. 237–243.

25. Ripple, W.J., "Asymptotic Reflectance Characteristics of Grass Vegetation," *Photogrammetric Engineering and Remote Sensing*, vol. 51, no. 12, December 1985, pp. 1915–1921.

26. Sadler, S.A., "Analysis of Effective Radiant Temperatures in a Pacific Northwest Forest Using Thermal Infrared Multispectral Scanner Data," *Remote Sensing of Environment*, vol. 19, no. 2, pp. 105–116.

27. Savastano, K.J., K.H. Faller, and R.L. Iverson, "Estimating Vegetation Coverage in St. Joseph Bay, Florida with an Airborne Multispectral Scanner," *Photogrammetric Engineering and Remote Sensing*, vol. 50, no. 8, August 1984, pp. 1159–1170.

28. Schott, J.R., and R.H. Tourin, "A Completely Airborne Calibration of Aerial Infrared Water-Temperature Measurements," *Proceedings: 10th International Symposium on Remote Sensing of Environment*, Environmental Research Institute of Michigan, Ann Arbor, 1975, pp. 477–484.

29. Schott, J.R., "Temperature Measurement of Cooling Water Discharged from Power Plants," *Photogrammetric Engineering and Remote Sensing*, vol. 45, no. 6, June 1979, pp. 753–761.

30. Simon, I., *Infrared Radiation*, Litton Educational Pub., New York, 1966.

31. Slater, P.N., "Survey of Multispectral Imaging Systems for Earth Observations," *Remote Sensing of Environment*, vol. 17, no. 1, 1985, pp. 85–102.

32. Vlcek, J., "A Field Method for Determination of Emissivity with Imaging Radiometers," *Photogrammetric Engineering and Remote Sensing*, vol. 48, no. 4, April 1982, pp. 609–614.

33. Vlcek, J., and D. King, "Detection of Subsurface Soil Moisture by Thermal Sensing: Results of Laboratory, Close-Range, and Aerial Studies," *Photogrammetric Engineering and Remote Sensing*, vol. 49, no. 11, November 1983, pp. 1593–1597.

34. Warren, C. (ed.), *Proceedings: Third Biennial Infrared Information Exchange*, AGA Corp., Secaucus, N.J., 1977.

35. Wolfe, W.L., and G.J. Zissis (eds.), *The Infrared Handbook*, U.S. Gt. Printing Office, Washington, D.C., 1978.

MICROWAVE SENSING

8.1 INTRODUCTION

An increasing amount of valuable environmental and resource information is being acquired by sensors that operate in the *microwave* portion of the electromagnetic spectrum. In the context of the sensors we have discussed thus far, microwaves are not "micro" at all. That is, the microwave portion of the spectrum includes wavelengths within the approximate range of 1 mm to 1 m. Thus, the longest microwaves are about 2,500,000 times longer than the shortest light waves!

There are two distinctive features that characterize microwave energy from a remote sensing standpoint.

1. Microwaves are capable of penetrating the atmosphere under virtually all conditions. Depending on the wavelengths involved, microwave energy can "see through" haze, light rain and snow, clouds, and smoke.

2. Microwave reflections or emissions from earth materials bear no direct relationship to their counterparts in the visible or thermal portions of the spectrum. For example, surfaces that appear "rough" in the visible portion of the spectrum may be "smooth" as seen by microwaves. In general, microwave responses afford us a markedly different "view" of the environment—one far removed from the views experienced by sensing light or heat.

In this chapter we discuss both *active* and *passive* microwave sensing systems. Recall that the term "active" refers to a sensor that supplies its own source of energy or illumination. *Radar* is an active microwave sensor and it is the major focus of attention in this chapter. To a lesser extent, we also treat the passive counterpart to radar, the *microwave radiometer*. This device responds to the extremely low levels of microwave energy that are naturally emitted and/or reflected from terrain features.

It should be recognized that practical resource management experience with radar and passive microwave systems is quite limited compared to photographic or scanning systems. We hope to illustrate here that, limited as this experience might be, the outlook for extensive application of microwave sensing is an extremely promising one.

8.2 **RADAR DEVELOPMENT**

The word *radar* is an acronym for *radio detection and ranging*. As its name implies, radar was developed as a means of using radio waves to detect the presence of objects and determine their range (position). The process entails transmitting short bursts, or pulses, of microwave energy in the direction of interest and recording the strength and origin of "echoes" or "reflections" received from objects within the system's field of view.

Radar systems may or may not produce images and they may be ground-based or mounted in aircraft or spacecraft. A common form of nonimaging radar is the type used to measure vehicle speeds. These systems are termed *Doppler radar* systems because they utilize Doppler effect frequency shifts in the transmitted and returned signals to determine an object's velocity. Doppler frequency shifts are a function of the relative velocities of a wave transmitter and a reflector. For example, we perceive Doppler shifts in sound waves as a change in pitch, as in the case of a passing car horn or a train whistle. As we see later, Doppler radar systems are not used in remote sensing per se, but the Doppler shift principle is often used in analyzing the data generated from other forms of radar.

Another common form of radar is the *plan position indicator (PPI)* radar. PPI systems have a circular display screen on which a radial sweep indicates the position of radar "echoes." PPI radar essentially images a continuously updated plan-view map of objects surrounding its rotating antenna. PPI systems are common in weather forecasting, air traffic control, and navigational applications. However, these systems are not appropriate to most remote sensing applications because they have rather poor spatial resolution.

The spatial resolution of a radar system is determined, among other things, by the size of its antenna. For any given wavelength, the larger the antenna, the better the spatial resolution. To circumvent this problem, most airborne radar remote sensing is done with systems that use an antenna fixed below the aircraft and pointed to the side. Such systems are termed *side-looking radar (SLR)* or *side-looking airborne radar (SLAR)*. SLAR systems produce continuous strips of imagery depicting very large ground areas located adjacent to the aircraft flight line. Figure 8.1 is a typical SLAR image showing an urban area.

SLAR was first developed for military reconnaissance purposes in the early 1950s. It became an ideal military reconnaissance system not only because it affords nearly an all-weather operating capability, but also because it is an active, day-or-night imaging system. The military genesis of SLAR has had two general impacts on its subsequent application to civilian remote sensing uses. First, there has been a time lag between military development, declassification, and civilian application. Less obvious, but nonetheless important, is the fact that military SLAR systems were developed to look at military targets. Terrain features that "cluttered" SLAR imagery and masked objects of military importance were naturally not of interest in original system designs. However, with military declassification and improvement in nonmilitary capabilities, SLAR has evolved into a powerful tool for acquiring natural resource data.

FIGURE 8.1   SLAR image, San Diego, California, 12,000 m flying height, X band, synthetic aperture. 1:250,000. (Courtesy Aero Service Division, Western Geophysical Company of America, and Goodyear Aerospace Corp.)

Although SLAR acquisition and analysis techniques have been developed to a high degree of sophistication, it should be pointed out that the application of radar technology to earth resource sensing is still in an active state of advancement. What determines the overall "radar reflectivity" of various earth resources under various conditions is still not know precisely. Even though much is yet to be learned about how radar signals interact with the natural environment, productive applications of existing radar technology have been many and varied.

The first large scale project for mapping terrain with SLAR was a complete survey of the Darien province of Panama [38]. This survey was undertaken in 1967 and resulted in images used to produce a mosaic of a 20,000 km^2 ground area (Figure 8.2). Prior to that time, this region had never been photographed or mapped in its entirety because of persistent (nearly perpetual) cloud cover. The success of the Panama radar mapping project lead to the application of radar remote sensing throughout the world. Since the early 1970s, extensive radar mapping programs have been conducted by several governments, as well as by mining and petroleum companies.

In 1971, a radar survey was begun in Venezuela that resulted in the mapping of nearly 500,000 km^2 of land. This project resulted in improvements of the accuracy of the location of the boundaries of Venezuela with its neighboring countries. It also

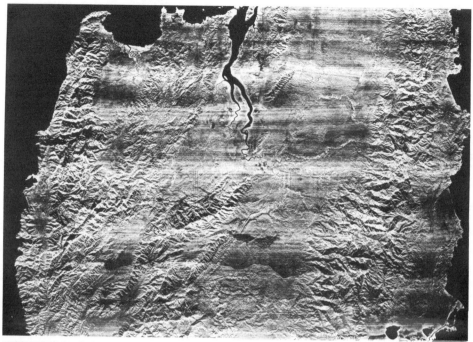

FIGURE 8.2 SLAR image mosaic, Darien Province, Panama, 8000 m flying height, *K* band, real aperture. 1:1,150,000. (Courtesy Westinghouse Electric Corp.)

permitted a systematic inventory and mapping of the country's water resources, including the discovery of the previously unknown source of several major rivers. Likewise, improved geologic maps of the country were produced. Figure 8.3 is a SLAR image mosaic of the Guyana shield area of south Venezuela illustrating the utility of SLAR images for this purpose. This mosaic shows extensive faulting and jointing in an area of granitic rocks and quartzite.

Also beginning in 1971 was Project Radam (standing for *Radar of the Amazon*), a reconnaissance survey of the Amazon and the adjacent Brazilian northeast. This survey was the largest radar mapping project ever undertaken. By the end of 1976, more than 160 radar mosaic sheets covering an area in excess of 8,500,000 km² had been completed. Scientists used these radar mosaics as base maps in a host of studies, including geologic analysis, timber inventory, transportation route location, and mineral exploration. Large deposits of important minerals were discovered after intensive analysis was made of newly discovered features shown by radar. Mapping of previously uncharted volcanic cones, and even large rivers, resulted from this project. In such remote and cloud covered areas of the world, radar imagery is a prime source of inventory information about potential mineral resources, forestry and range resources, water supplies, transportation routes, and sites suitable for agriculture.

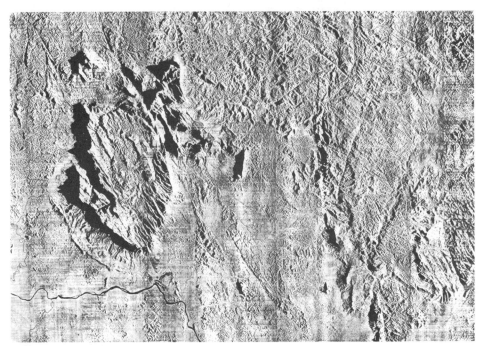

FIGURE 8.3   SLAR image mosaic, south Venezuela, 1971, X band, synthetic aperture. 1:250,000. (Courtesy International Aero Service Corp. and Goodyear Aerospace Corp.)

Radar imagery has also been used extensively to monitor the surface of the oceans to determine wind, wave, and ice conditions. As we illustrate later in this chapter, SLAR data have also been used to study ocean bottom contours under some conditions. Numerous other applications of radar have been demonstrated in the areas of geologic mapping, mineral exploration, flood inundation mapping, and small scale thematic mapping.

Radar remote sensing from space began with the launch of *Seasat* in 1978 and continued with the *Shuttle Imaging Radar (SIR)* experiments in the 1980s. Though extensive, radar imagery is currently neither as available nor as well understood as other image products. Furthermore, relatively little research has been conducted on assessing the synergistic effects of combining optical and microwave measurements, even though the scene attributes affecting optical and microwave radiation are different and complementary. Experience to date suggests, however, that radar imagery— particularly that acquired from satellite platforms—will play an increasingly important role in various earth resource management applications.

8.3   SLAR SYSTEM OPERATION

The basic operating principle of a SLAR system is shown in Figure 8.4. Microwave energy is transmitted from an antenna in very short bursts or pulses. These high energy pulses are emitted over a time period on the order of microseconds (10^{-6} sec). In Figure 8.4*a*, the propagation of one pulse is shown by indicating the wavefront locations at successive increments of time. Beginning with the solid lines (labeled 1 through 10), the transmitted pulse moves radially outward from the aircraft in a focused beam. Shortly after time 6, the pulse reaches the house, and a reflected wave (dashed line) is shown beginning at time 7. At time 12, this return signal reaches the antenna, and is registered at that time on the antenna response graph (Figure 8.4*b*). At time 9, the transmitted wavefront is reflected off the tree and this "echo" reaches the antenna at time 17. Because the tree is less reflective of radar waves than the house, a weaker response is recorded in Figure 8.4*b*.

By electronically measuring the return time of signal echoes, the range, or distance, between the transmitter and reflecting objects, may be determined. Since the energy propagates in air at approximately the velocity of light *c*, the slant range, *SR*, to any given object is given by

$$SR = \frac{ct}{2} \tag{8.1}$$

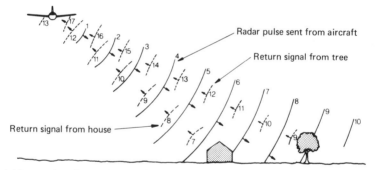

(a) Propagation of one radar pulse (indicating the wavefront location at time intervals 1–17)

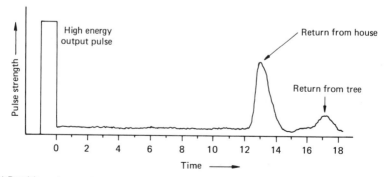

(b) Resulting antenna return

FIGURE 8.4 Operating principle of side-looking airborne radar (SLAR).

where
  SR = slant range (direct distance between transmitter and object)
  c = speed of light (3×10^8 m/sec)
  t = time between pulse transmission and echo reception

(Note that the factor 2 enters into the equation because the time is measured for the pulse to travel both the distance to and from the target, or twice the range.) This principle of determining distance by electronically measuring the transmission–echo time is central to imaging radar systems.

The manner in which SLAR images are created is illustrated in Figure 8.5. As the aircraft advances, the antenna (1) is continuously repositioned in the flight direction at the aircraft velocity V_a. The antenna is switched from a transmitter to a receiver mode by a synchronizer switch (2). Each transmitted pulse (3) returns echoes from terrain features occurring along a single antenna beamwidth. These echoes are received by the airborne antenna and processed to produce an amplitude/time video signal (4). This signal is used to generate an image product in a film recorder (5). The signal modulates the intensity of a single-line cathode ray tube, exposing an image line on the film. Thus, each line in the image product is a tonal representation of the strength of signals returned from a single radar pulse. Between lines, the film is advanced at a velocity V_f which is proportional to the aircraft velocity V_a. In this way, the combined response of many pulses will yield a two-dimensional image product. Strips may be imaged on both sides of the aircraft or only on one side. Each strip may extend to the side from a distance of approximately half the aircraft flying height out to 100 km or more.

8.4 SPATIAL RESOLUTION OF SLAR SYSTEMS

The ground resolution cell size of a SLAR system is controlled by two independent sensing system parameters: *pulse length* and *antenna beamwidth*. The pulse length of the radar signal is determined by the length of time that the antenna emits its burst of energy. As can be seen in Figure 8.5, the signal pulse length dictates the spatial resolution in the direction of energy propogation. This direction is referred to as the *range* direction. The width of the antenna beam determines the resolution cell size in the flight, or *azimuth*, direction. We consider each of these elements controlling radar spatial resolution separately.

Range Resolution

For a SLAR system to image separately two ground features that are close to each other in the range direction, it is necessary for all parts of the two objects' reflected signals to be received separately by the antenna. Any time overlap between the signals from two objects will cause their images to be blurred together. This concept is illustrated in Figure 8.6. Here a pulse of length PL (determined by the duration of the pulse transmission) has been transmitted toward buildings A and B. Note that the slant-

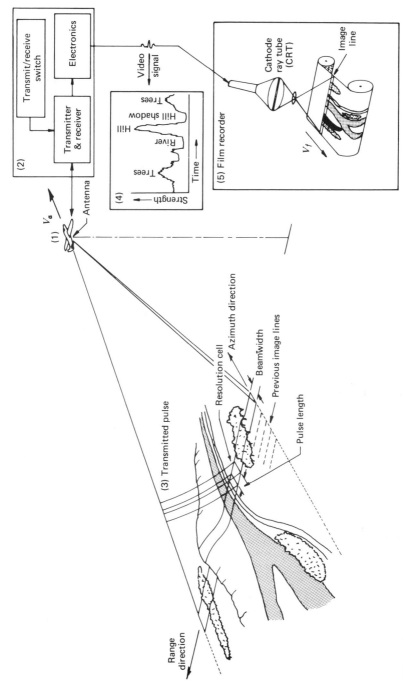

FIGURE 8.5 Side-looking airborne radar (SLAR) system operation. (Adapted from [38].)

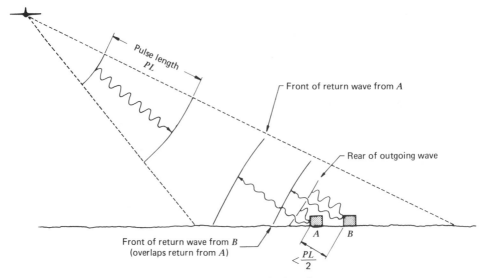

FIGURE 8.6   Dependence of range resolution on pulse length.

range distance (the direct sensor-to-target distance) between the buildings is less than *PL*/2. Because of this, the pulse has had time to travel to *B* and have its echo return to *A* while the end of the pulse at *A* continues to be reflected. Consequently, the two signals are overlapped and will be imaged as one large object extending from building *A* to building *B*. If the slant-range distance between *A* and *B* were anything greater than *PL*/2, the two signals would be received separately, resulting in two separate image responses. Thus, the slant-range resolution of a SLAR system is independent of the distance from the aircraft and is equal to half the transmitted pulse length.

Although the *slant-range* resolution of a SLAR system does not change with distance from the aircraft, the corresponding *ground* distance does. As shown in Figure 8.7, the ground resolution in the range direction varies inversely with the cosine of the angle between the horizontal ground plane and the line connecting the radar antenna and the object being sensed. This angle is called the *depression angle*, θ_d. The complement of the depression angle is called the *look angle*, θ_l.

Accounting for the depression angle effect, the ground resolution in the range direction, R_r, is found from

$$R_r = \frac{c\tau}{2 \cos \theta_d} \tag{8.2}$$

where τ = the pulse duration.

EXAMPLE 8.1

A given SLAR system transmits pulses over a duration of 0.1 μsec. Find the range resolution of the system at a depression angle of 45°.

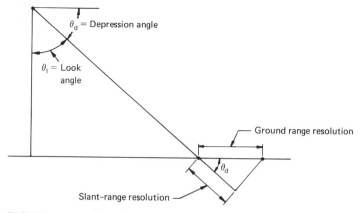

FIGURE 8.7 Relationship between slant-range resolution and ground-range resolution.

Solution

From Eq. 8.2

$$R_r = \frac{(3 \cdot 10^8 \text{ m/sec})(0.1 \cdot 10^{-6} \text{ sec})}{2 \cdot 0.707} = 21 \text{ m}$$

Azimuth Resolution

As shown in Figure 8.8, the resolution of a SLAR system in the azimuth direction, R_a, is determined by the angular *beamwidth*, β, of the antenna and the ground range, GR. As the antenna beam "fans out" with increasing distance from the aircraft, the azimuth resolution deteriorates. Objects at points A and B in Figure 8.8 would be resolved (imaged separately) at GR_1 but not at GR_2. That is, at distance GR_1, A and B result in separate return signals. At distance GR_2, A and B would be in the beam simultaneously and would not be resolved.

Azimuth resolution R_a is given by

$$R_a = GR \cdot \beta \tag{8.3}$$

EXAMPLE 8.2

A given SLAR system has a 1.8 mr antenna beamwidth. Determine the azimuth resolution of the system at ranges of 6 and 12 km.

Solution

From Eq. 8.3

$$R_{a_{6 \text{ km}}} = (6 \cdot 10^3 \text{ m})(1.8 \cdot 10^{-3}) = 10.8 \text{ m}$$

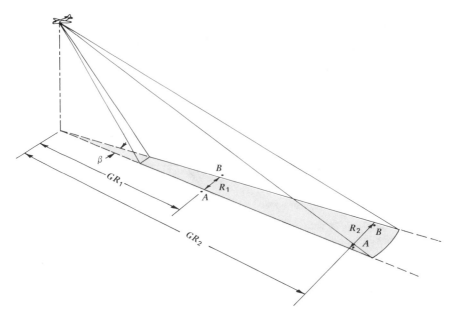

FIGURE 8.8   Dependence of azimuth resolution (R_a) on antenna beamwidth (β) and ground range *(GR)*.

and

$$R_{a_{12 \text{ km}}} = (12 \cdot 10^3 \text{ m})(1.8 \cdot 10^{-3}) = 21.6 \text{ m}$$

The beamwidth of the antenna of a SLAR system is directly proportional to the wavelength of the transmitted pulses, λ, and inversely proportional to the length of the antenna, *AL*. That is

$$\beta = \frac{\lambda}{AL} \tag{8.4}$$

For any given wavelength, antenna beamwidth can be controlled by one of two different means: (1) by controlling the *physical* length of the antenna, or (2) by synthesizing an *effective* length of the antenna. Those systems wherein beamwidth is controlled by the physical antenna length are called *brute force*, *real aperture*, or *noncoherent* radars. As expressed by Eq. 8.4, the antenna in a brute force system must be many wavelengths long for the antenna beamwidth to be narrow. For example, to achieve even a 10 mr beamwidth with a 5 cm wavelength radar, a 5 m antenna is required [$(5 \cdot 10^{-2} \text{ m})/(10 \cdot 10^{-3}) = 5$ m]. To obtain a resolution of 2 mr, we would need an antenna 25 m long! Obviously, antenna length requirements of brute force systems present considerable logistical problems when detailed resolutions are sought.

Brute force systems enjoy relative simplicity of design and data processing. Because of resolution problems, however, their operation is often restricted to relatively short-range, low altitude operation and the use of relatively short wavelengths. These restrictions are unfortunate because short-range, low altitude operation limits the area of coverage obtained by the system and short wavelengths experience more atmospheric attenuation and dispersion.

The deficiencies of brute force operation are overcome in *synthetic aperture radar (SAR)* systems. These systems employ a short physical antenna, but through modified data recording and processing techniques they synthesize the *effect* of a very long antenna. The result of this mode of operation is a very narrow effective antenna beamwidth, even at far ranges, without requiring a physically long antenna or a short operating wavelength. For example, in a synthetic aperture system, a 2 m antenna can be made effectively 600 m long.

The basic principle of synthetic aperture SLAR operation is illustrated in Figure 8.9. In essence, return signals from the center portion of the beamwidth are discriminated by detecting Doppler frequency shifts. Recall that a Doppler shift is a change in wave frequency as a function of the relative velocities of a transmitter and a reflector. Within the wide antenna beam, returns from features in the area ahead of the aircraft (Figure 8.9) will have upshifted (higher) frequencies resulting from the Doppler effect. Conversely, returns from the area behind the aircraft will have downshifted (lower) frequencies. Returns from features near the centerline of the beamwidth will experience little or no frequency shift. By processing the return signals according to their Doppler shifts, a very small effective beamwidth can be generated.

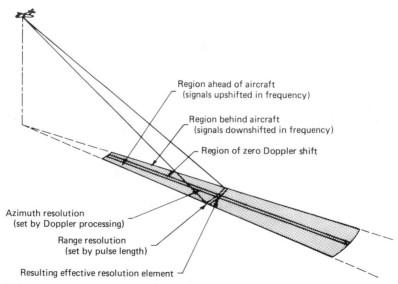

FIGURE 8.9 Determinants of resolution in synthetic aperture SLAR.

Acquiring synthetic aperture radar data typically requires a rather complex integrated array of onboard navigational and control systems. Figure 8.10 illustrates an aircraft equipped for this purpose. With this system, location accuracy is provided by both Doppler and inertial navigation equipment. In addition, a mapping camera and a multispectral camera bank provide photographic coverage to complement the radar data.

The details of synthetic aperture signal recording and processing are very complex and therefore beyond the scope of this discussion. The basic concept is to record both the amplitude *and* the frequency of signals returned from objects throughout the time period in which they are within the beam of the moving antenna. The frequency information is obtained by comparing the reflected return signals with a controlled frequency "reference signal" generated internally by the system. The comparison is made by having the ground-reflected signal interfere with the reference signal. These signals interfere in various patterns, depending on their comparative frequencies. The patterns are typically recorded on magnetic tape, but a photographic process that produces a "signal film" can also be used. Figure 8.11 shows such a film, which in effect is the radar equivalent to an optical hologram. As with optical holograms, signal films cannot be interpreted directly, but may be converted to an image form by passing laser light through them [32]. The complex apparatus used to produce radar images in this manner is shown in Figure 8.12.

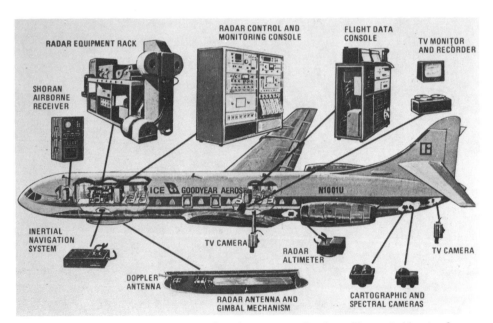

FIGURE 8.10   SLAR aerial survey aircraft and equipment. Goodyear Electronic Mapping System (GEMS), *X* band, synthetic aperture. (Courtesy Aero Service Division, Western Geophysical Company of America, and Goodyear Aerospace Corp.)

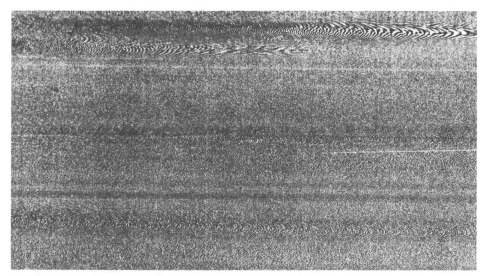

FIGURE 8.11 Synthetic aperture SLAR signal film. (Courtesy Aero Service Division, Western Geophysical Company of America, and Goodyear Aerospace Corp.)

FIGURE 8.12 Optical processor used to produce final images from synthetic aperture SLAR signal films. (Courtesy Aero Service Division, Western Geophysical Company of America, and Goodyear Aerospace Corp.)

Optical processing of synthetic aperture data has the advantage that it can be approximately one hundred times faster than digital processing (for processing to comparable resolutions). Optical processing, therefore, is typically used for preliminary review of large quantities of radar data. Detailed analyses often involve digital processing of the data. With digital processing, fewer processing artifacts (such as dust, film grain, and lens aberrations) are present to degrade the geometric and radiometric fidelity of the data. Likewise, digital processing preserves the full dynamic range of the data and the digital data can be readily manipulated and analyzed using digital image processing techniques (Chapter 10).

Because the signals received by a synthetic aperture system are recorded over a long time period, the aircraft translates the real antenna over a correspondingly long distance. This distance becomes the length of the "synthetic" antenna. The azimuth resolution with this effective antenna length is greatly improved. Of interest is that this resolution is essentially independent of range because at long range an object is in the beam longer; hence returns from it are recorded over a longer distance.

A final point about synthetic aperture radar systems is that both *unfocused* and *focused* systems exist. Again the details of these systems are beyond our immediate concern. The interesting point about these systems is that the theoretical resolution of *unfocused* systems is a function of wavelength and range, not antenna length. The theoretical resolution of a *focused* system is a function of antenna length, regardless of range or wavelength. More particularly, the resolution of a focused synthetic aperture system is one-half the actual antenna length. In theory, the resolution for a 1 m antenna would be 0.5 m, whether the system were operated from an aircraft or a spacecraft! However, since short antennas have stability problems, radar system design is replete with trade-offs among operating range, resolution, wavelength, antenna size, and overall system complexity.

8.5   GEOMETRIC CHARACTERISTICS OF SLAR IMAGERY

The geometry of SLAR imagery is fundamentally different from that of both photography and scanner imagery. This difference basically results because SLAR is a *distance* rather than an *angle* measuring system. The influences this has on image geometry are many and varied. Here we limit our discussion to treatment of the following geometric elements of SLAR image acquisition and interpretation: *scale distortion*, *relief displacement*, and *parallax*.

Slant-Range Scale Distortion

SLAR systems use one of two types of image recording systems. A *slant-range* image recording system involves a constant CRT sweep rate across each line. Consequently, the spacing between return signals on slant-range imagery is directly proportional to the time interval between echoes from adjacent terrain features. This interval is directly proportional to the *slant,* rather than *horizontal,* distance between the sensor and any given object. In a *ground-range* image recording system, the CRT sweep incorporates a hyperbolic timing correction in which the spacing between image points is approximately proportional to the horizontal ground distance between terrain features.

Figure 8.13 illustrates the characteristics of slant-range and ground-range image recording. *A*, *B*, and *C* represent objects of equal size that are equally separated in the near, middle, and far range. The respective ground ranges to the points are GR_A, GR_B, and GR_C. Based directly on the signal return time, the *slant-range* image shows unequal distances between the features as well as unequal widths for the features. The result is a varying image scale that is at a minimum in the near range and which progresses hyperbolically to a maximum at the far range. Therefore, on a slant-range presentation, object width $A_1 < B_1 < C_1$ and distance $AB < BC$. Applying a hyperbolic correction, a *ground-range* image of essentially constant scale can be formed with width $A = B = C$ and distance $AB = BC$.

Obviously, the scale distortions inherent in slant-range imagery preclude its direct use for accurate planimetric mapping. However, approximate ground range, *GR*, can be derived from slant range, *SR*, and flying height, *H'*, under the assumption of flat terrain. From Figure 8.13 it can be seen that

$$SR^2 = H'^2 + GR^2$$

so

$$GR = (SR^2 - H'^2)^{1/2} \tag{8.5}$$

Therefore, a ground-range distance can be calculated from an image slant-range distance if the flying height is known. The assumption of flat terrain should be noted, however, and it should be pointed out that flight parameters also affect both range and azimuth scales. The range scale will vary with changes in aircraft altitude, and the azimuth scale will be dependent on precise synchronization between the aircraft ground speed and the proportional film transport speed past the CRT.

Maintaining consistent scale in the collection and recording of SLAR data is a complex task. Whereas scale in the range (or across track) direction is determined by the speed of light, scale in the azimuth (or along track) direction is determined by the speed of the aircraft. To reconcile and equalize these independent scales, strict control of flight parameters is needed. In most systems, this is provided by an *inertial navigator and control system.* This device guides the aircraft at the appropriate flying height, along the proper course. Angular sensors measure aircraft roll, crab, and pitch and maintain a constant angle of the antenna beam with respect to the line of flight. Inertial systems also provide the output necessary to synchronize the film recording velocity proportionally with the aircraft ground speed.

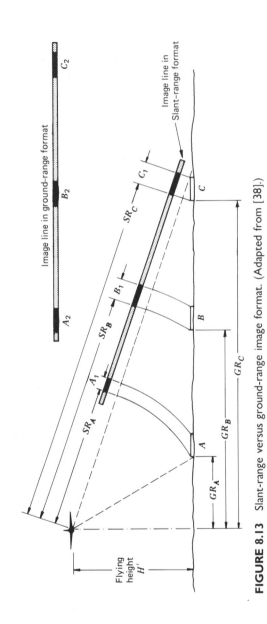

FIGURE 8.13 Slant-range versus ground-range image format. (Adapted from [38].)

Relief Displacement

As in line scanner imagery, relief displacement in SLAR images is one dimensional and perpendicular to the flight line. However, unlike scanner imagery and photography, the *direction* of relief displacement is reversed. This is because radar images display ranges, or distances, from terrain features to the antenna. When a vertical feature is encountered by a radar pulse, the top of the feature is reached before the base. Accordingly, return signals from the top of a vertical feature will reach the antenna before returns from the base of the feature. This will cause a vertical feature to "lay over" the closer features, making it appear to lean toward the nadir. This radar *layover effect*, most severe at near range, is compared to photographic relief displacement in Figure 8.14.

Terrain slopes facing the antenna at near range are often displayed with a dramatic layover effect. This occurs whenever the terrain slope is steeper than a line perpendicular to the direction of the radar pulse, expressed by its depression angle. This condition is met by the left sides of features A and B in Figure 8.15. As such, the tops of these slopes will be imaged before their bases, causing layover. It can be seen in the image representations that the amount of layover displacement is greatest at short range, where the depression angle is greater.

When the slope facing the antenna is less steep than the line perpendicular to the depression direction, as in feature D in Figure 8.15, no layover occurs. That is, the radar pulse reaches the base of the feature before the top. The slopes of the surfaces will not be presented in true size, however. As shown in feature D, the size of the sloped surface is compressed on the image. This *foreshortening effect* gets more severe as the slope's steepness approaches perpendicularity to the depression direction. In feature C, the front slope is precisely perpendicular to the depression direction, and it can be seen that the image of the front slope has been foreshortened to zero length.

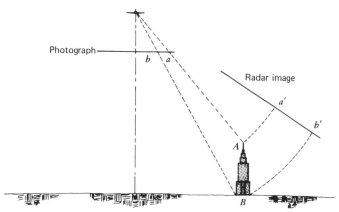

FIGURE 8.14 Relief displacement on SLAR images versus photographs.

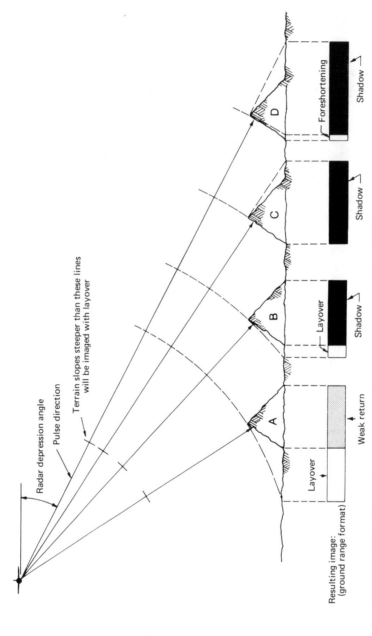

FIGURE 8.15 Effects of terrain relief on SLAR images. (Adapted from [38].)

Foreshortening and layover are obviously interrelated to the phenomenon of radar shadow. Slopes facing away from the radar antenna will return weak signals or no signal at all. In Figure 8.15, the right side of feature *A* faces away from the aircraft, but it is less steep than the depression angle and will therefore be illuminated by the radar pulse. This illumination, however, will be very slight and the resulting return signals will be weak, causing a fairly dark image area. In feature *B*, its right side is parallel to the depression angle and will therefore not be illuminated. As a result, the antenna will receive no return signals for a period of time and the image area will be totally black. When a slope faces away from the aircraft and is steeper than the depression angle, as in features *C* and *D*, the area of nonillumination will extend beyond the sloped area, masking down-range features in a radar shadow. As shown in Figure 8.15, the shadow length increases with range because of the decrease in depression angle. Thus, a feature that casts an extensive shadow at far range *(D)* can be completely illuminated at close range *(A)*.

Parallax

When an object is imaged twice from two different flight lines, differential relief displacements cause image parallax on SLAR imagery. This allows images to be viewed stereoscopically. Stereo SLAR imagery can be obtained by flying on parallel flight lines over the same area and viewing terrain features from opposite sides (Figure 8.16a). However, because the radar sidelighting effect will be reversed on the two images in

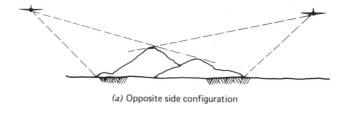

(a) Opposite side configuration

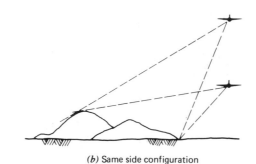

(b) Same side configuration

FIGURE 8.16 Flight orientations to produce parallax on SLAR images.

the stereopair, stereoscopic viewing is somewhat difficult using this technique. Accordingly, stereo radar imagery is often flown using the same flight line but different altitudes. The resulting effect is called *altitude parallax*. In this case, the direction of illumination and the sidelighting effects will be similar on both images (Figure 8.16*b*). (It is also possible to acquire stereo radar imagery in the same side configuration by using the same altitude on successive flight lines spaced some distance apart and varying the antenna depression angle. As we discuss in Section 8.9, this procedure was used on the Shuttle Imaging Radar-B mission.)

Figure 8.17 shows a stereo radar image produced by sensing from two different altitudes with a look direction to the left. Note that there are larger shadow areas in the right image. This means that the flying height was lower for the right image than for the left image.

In addition to providing a stereoscopic view, image parallax may be measured and used to compute approximate feature heights. As with aerial photography, parallax is determined by measuring mutual image displacements on the two images forming a stereomodel. Such measurements are part of the science of *radargrammetry* [35–37], a field beyond the scope of our interest in this text.

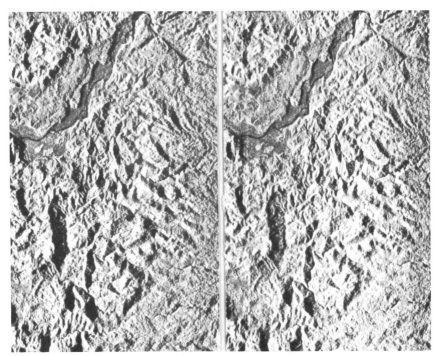

FIGURE 8.17 Stereo SLAR image, *X* band, synthetic aperture, obtained by flying same flight line at different altitudes. (Courtesy Aero Service Division, Western Geophysical Company of America, and Goodyear Aerospace Corp.)

8.6 TRANSMISSION CHARACTERISTICS OF RADAR SIGNALS

The two primary factors influencing the transmission characteristics of the signals from any given radar system are the wavelength and the polarization of the energy pulse used. Table 8.1 lists the common wavelength bands used in pulse transmission. The letter codes for the various bands (K, X, L, etc.) were originally selected arbitrarily to ensure military security during the early stages of development of radar. They have continued in use as a matter of convenience and various authorities designate the various bands in slightly different wavelength ranges.

Naturally, the wavelength of a radar signal determines the extent to which it is attenuated and/or dispersed by the atmosphere. Serious atmospheric effects on radar signals are confined to the shorter operating wavelengths (less than 3 cm). Even at these wavelengths, under most operating conditions the atmosphere only slightly attenuates the signal. As one would anticipate, attenuation generally increases as operating wavelength decreases, and the influence of clouds and rain is variable. Whereas radar signals are relatively unaffected by clouds, echoes from heavy precipitation can be considerable. Precipitation echoes are proportional, for a single drop, to the quantity D^6/λ^4, where D is the drop diameter. With the use of short wavelengths, radar reflection from water droplets is substantial enough to be used in PPI systems to distinguish regions of precipitation. For example, areas in the atmosphere containing heavy rain provide strong echoes on radars operating at 1 cm or less. At the same time, the effect of rain is negligible with wavelengths of operation greater than 3 cm. So—short of the condition of a very heavy rainstorm—radar can be used through clouds, smoke, or fog. This feature, combined with day/night operation, makes radar a particularly valuable tool when time-dependent operations are undertaken.

Irrespective of wavelength, radar signals can be transmitted and/or received in different modes of *polarization*. That is, the signal can be filtered in such a way that its

TABLE 8.1 Radar Band Designations

Band designation	Wavelength λ cm	Frequency $\nu = c\lambda^{-1}$ [MHz (10^6 cycles sec^{-1})]
K_a	0.75–1.1	40,000–26,500
K	1.1–1.67	26,500–18,000
K_u	1.67–2.4	18,000–12,500
X	2.4 –3.75	12,500–8,000
C	3.75–7.5	8,000–4,000
S	7.5 –15	4,000–2,000
L	15 –30	2,000–1,000
P	30 –100	1,000–300

Adapted from [14].

electrical wave vibrations are restricted to a single plane perpendicular to the direction of wave propagation. (Unpolarized energy vibrates in all directions perpendicular to that of propagation.) A SLAR signal can be transmitted in either a horizontal *(H)* or a vertical *(V)* plane. Likewise, it can be received in either a horizontal or vertical plane. Thus, we have the possibility of dealing with four different combinations of signal transmission and reception: *H* send, *H* receive; *H* send, *V* receive; *V* send, *H* receive; and *V* send, *V* receive. *Like-polarized* imagery results from the *HH* or *VV* combinations. *Cross-polarized* imagery is obtained from *HV* or *VH* combinations. *Circular polarization*, where the plane of wave vibrations rotates as the waves propagate, can also be utilized. Since various objects modify the polarization of the energy they reflect to varying degrees, the mode of signal polarization influences how the objects look on the resulting imagery. We illustrate this in Section 8.8.

8.7   EARTH SURFACE FEATURE CHARACTERISTICS INFLUENCING RADAR RETURNS

A host of earth surface feature characteristics work hand-in-hand with the wavelength and polarization of radar signals to determine the intensity of radar returns from various objects. These factors are many, varied, and complex. Although several theoretical models have been developed to describe how various objects reflect radar energy, most practical knowledge on the subject has been derived from empirical observation. It has been found that the primary factors influencing objects' return signal intensity are their geometric and electrical characteristics; these are described below. Radar wave interactions with soil, vegetation, water, and ice are also described.

Geometric Characteristics

One of the most readily apparent features of radar imagery is its "sidelighted" character. This arises through variations in the relative sensor/terrain geometry for differing terrain orientations, as illustrated in Figure 8.18. Local variations in terrain slope result in varying angles of signal incidence. The *local incidence angle* is the angle between the incident radar beam at the ground and the normal to the ground surface at the point of incidence. For flat terrain, the local incidence angle is the same as the look angle. Variations in local incidence angle result in relatively high returns from slopes facing the sensor, and relatively low returns, or no returns, from slopes facing away from the sensor. In Figure 8.18, the return strength versus time graph has been positioned over the terrain such that the signals can be correlated with the feature that produced them. Above the graph is the corresponding image line, in which the signal strength has been converted schematically to brightness values. The response from this radar pulse initially shows a high return from the slope facing the sensor. This is followed by a duration of no return signal from areas blocked from illumination by the radar wave. This *radar shadow* is completely black and sharply defined, unlike shadows in photography that are weakly illuminated by energy scattered by the

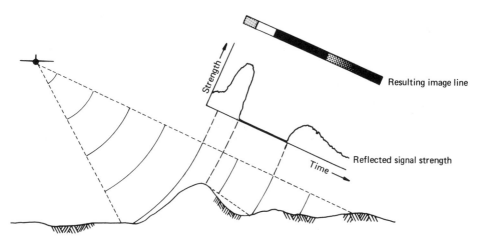

FIGURE 8.18   Effect of sensor/terrain geometry on SLAR imagery. (Adapted from [38].)

atmosphere. Following the shadow, a relatively weak response is recorded from the terrain that is not oriented toward the sensor.

In general, radar backscatter and shadow areas are affected by different surface properties over a range of local incidence angles. For local incidence angles of 0 to 30°, radar backscatter is dominated by topographic slope. For angles of 30 to 70°, surface roughness dominates. For angles greater than 70°, radar shadows dominate the image [18].

Figure 8.19 illustrates radar reflection from surfaces of varying roughness and geometry. The *Rayleigh criterion* states that surfaces can be considered "rough," and act as diffuse reflectors (Figure 8.19*a*), if the root-mean-square (rms) height of the surface variations exceeds one-eight of the wavelength of sensing ($\lambda/8$) divided by the cosine of the local incidence angle [51]. Such surfaces scatter incident energy in all directions and return a significant portion of the incident energy to the radar antenna. Surfaces are considered "smooth" by the Rayleigh criterion, and act as specular reflectors (Figure 8.19*b*), when their rms height variation is less than approximately $\lambda/8$ divided by the cosine of the local incidence angle. Such surfaces reflect most of the energy away from the sensor, resulting in a very low return signal.

The Rayleigh criterion does not consider that there can be a category of surface relief that is intermediate between definitely rough and definitely smooth surfaces. A *modified Rayleigh criterion* is used to typify such situations. This criterion considers rough surfaces to be those where the rms height is greater than $\lambda/4.4$ divided by the cosine of the local incidence angle and smooth when the rms height variation is less than $\lambda/25$ divided by the cosine of the local incidence angle [30, 51]. Intermediate values are considered to have intermediate roughnesses. Table 8.2 lists the surface height variations that can be considered "smooth," "intermediate," and "rough" for various radar bands, for local incidence angles of 20, 45, and 70°. (Values for other

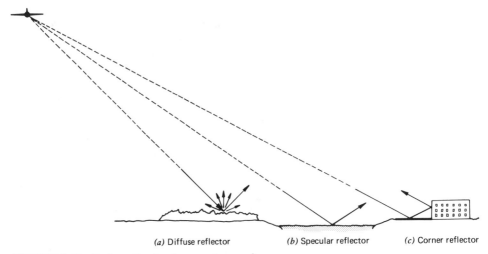

(a) Diffuse reflector   (b) Specular reflector   (c) Corner reflector

FIGURE 8.19   Radar reflection from various surfaces.

TABLE 8.2   Definition of SLAR Surface Roughness Categories for Three Local Incidence Angles[a]

Roughness category	Root-mean-square surface height variation (cm)		
	K_a Band ($\lambda = 0.86$ cm)	X Band ($\lambda = 3.2$ cm)	L Band ($\lambda = 23.5$ cm)
(a) Local Incidence Angle of 20°			
Smooth	< 0.04	< 0.14	< 1.00
Intermediate	0.04–0.21	0.14–0.77	1.00–5.68
Rough	> 0.21	> 0.77	> 5.68
(b) Local Incidence Angle of 45°			
Smooth	< 0.05	< 0.18	< 1.33
Intermediate	0.05–0.28	0.18–1.03	1.33–7.55
Rough	> 0.28	> 1.03	> 7.55
(c) Local Incidence Angle of 70°			
Smooth	< 0.10	< 0.37	< 2.75
Intermediate	0.10–0.57	0.37–2.13	2.75–15.6
Rough	> 0.57	> 2.13	> 15.6

Adapted from [51].
[a]The table is based on a modified Rayleigh criterion.

wavelength bands and/or incidence angles can be calculated from the information given above.)

The shape and orientation of objects must be considered as well as their surface roughness when evaluating radar returns. A particularly bright response results from a *corner reflector*, as illustrated in Figure 8.19c. In this case, adjacent smooth surfaces cause a double reflection that yields a very high return. Because corner reflectors generally cover only small areas of the scene, they often appear as bright "sparkles" on the image. This effect is illustrated in Section 8.8 (Figures 8.22 and 8.23). Within urban areas, there can be variations in return from the same land cover type, depending on the orientation of streets and building walls relative to the radar azimuth direction [7].

It is worthy to note that some features, such as corn fields, might appear rough when seen in both the visible and the microwave portion of the spectrum. Other surfaces, such as roadways, may be diffuse reflectors in the visible region but specular reflectors of microwave energy. In general, SLAR images manifest many more specular surfaces than do photographs.

Electrical Characteristics

The electrical characteristics of terrain features work closely with their geometric characteristics to determine the intensity of radar returns. One measure of an object's electrical character is the *complex dielectric constant*. This parameter is an indication of the reflectivity and conductivity of various materials.

In the microwave region of the spectrum, most natural materials have a dielectric constant in the range 3 to 8 when dry. On the other hand, water has a dielectric constant of approximately 80. Thus, the presence of moisture in either soil or vegetation can significantly increase radar reflectivity. In fact, changes in radar signal strength from one material to another are often linked to changes in moisture content much more closely than they are to changes in the materials themselves. Because plants have large surface areas and often have a high moisture content, they are particularly good reflectors of radar energy. Plant canopies with their varying complex dielectric constants and their microrelief often dominate the texture of SLAR image tones.

Metal objects also give high returns, and metal bridges, silos, railroad tracks, and poles usually appear as bright spots on SLAR images.

Soil Response

Because the dielectric constant for water is at least 10 times that for dry soil, the presence of water in the top few centimeters of bare (unvegetated) soil can be detected in radar imagery. Soil moisture and surface wetness conditions become particularly apparent at longer wavelengths. Soil moisture normally limits the penetration of radar waves to depths of a few centimeters. However, signal penetrations of several meters have been observed under extremely dry soil conditions with *L*-band radar.

Vegetation Response

Radar waves interact with a vegetation canopy as a group of volume scatterers composed of a large number of discrete plant components (leaves, stems, stalks, limbs, etc.). In turn, the vegetation canopy is underlain by soil that may result in surface scattering of the energy that penetrates the vegetation canopy. When the radar wavelengths approximate the mean size of plant components, volume scattering is strong and, if the plant canopy is dense, there will be strong backscatter from the vegetation. In general, shorter wavelengths (2 to 6 cm) are best for sensing crop canopies (corn, soybeans, wheat, etc.) and tree leaves. At these wavelengths, volume scattering predominates and surface scattering from the underlying soil is minimal. Longer wavelengths (10 to 30 cm) are best for sensing tree trunks and limbs.

In addition to plant size and radar wavelength, many other factors affect radar backscatter from vegetation. Recall that vegetation with a high moisture content returns more energy than dry vegetation. Also, like-polarized (*HH* or *VV*) sensing penetrates vegetation more than cross-polarized (*HV* or *VH*) sensing. Likewise, more energy is returned from crops having their rows aligned in the azimuth direction than from those aligned in the range direction of radar sensing (this is especially true for like-polarized systems).

Water and Ice Response

Smooth water surfaces act as specular reflectors of radar waves and yield no returns to the antenna, but rough water surfaces return radar signals of varying strengths. Experiments conducted with the Seasat radar system (*L*-band system with a look angle of 20 to 26°, as described in Section 8.9) showed that waves with a wavelength greater than 100 m could be detected when wave heights were greater than about 1 m and surface wind speeds exceeded about 2 m/sec [23]. It was also found that waves moving in the range direction (moving toward or away from the radar system) could be detected more readily than waves moving in the azimuth direction.

Radar backscatter from sea ice is dependent on the dielectric properties and spatial distribution of the ice. In addition, such factors as ice age, surface roughness, internal geometry, temperature, and snow cover also affect radar backscatter. *X*-band radar has proven useful in determining ice types, and by inference, ice thickness. *L*-band radar is useful for showing the total extent of ice, but it is often not capable of discriminating ice type and thickness.

8.8   INTERPRETATION OF SLAR IMAGERY

SLAR image interpretation has been successful in many fields of application. These include, for example, mapping major rock units and surficial materials, mapping geologic structure (folds, faults, and joints), mapping vegetation types (natural vegetation and crops), determining sea ice types, and mapping surface drainage features (streams and lakes).

Since the spatial resolution of most SLAR images is coarser than that of low and medium altitude aerial photographs, SLAR image interpretations are seldom made at scales much larger than 1:125,000. Thus, SLAR should be considered more a tool for reconnaissance mapping than for extremely detailed mapping.

Because of its sidelighted character, SLAR imagery superficially resembles aerial photography taken under low-sun-angle conditions. However, in interpreting SLAR imagery, we must keep in mind the previous discussion pointing out the effects of wavelength versus object "roughness," the effects of water and metals, the effect of "corner reflectors," and polarization and incidence angle effects. Table 8.3 illustrates how "rough" various surfaces appear to radar pulses of various wavelengths, using the modified Rayleigh criterion described in Section 8.7 (see also Table 8.2).

As a generalization, high SLAR return signals are received from slopes facing the aircraft, rough objects, objects with a high moisture content, metal objects, and urban and other built-up areas (resulting from corner reflections). Surfaces acting as diffuse reflectors return a weak to moderate signal and may often have considerable image texture. Low returns are received from surfaces acting as specular reflectors, such as smooth water, pavements, and playas (dry lakebeds). No return is received from radar "shadow" areas (Figure 8.18).

Radar images, such as those illustrated here, contain some degree of *speckle*, a grainy or salt-and-pepper pattern. Speckle arises from the coherent nature of radar waves, causing random constructive and destructive interference and, hence, random bright and dark areas in radar imagery. Speckle can be reduced through the application of image processing techniques, but cannot be completely eliminated. One technique useful for reducing speckle is *multiple-look processing*. In this procedure, several independent images of the same area, produced by using different portions of the synthetic aperture, are averaged together to produce a smoother image. The number of independent images being averaged is called the *number of looks* and the amount of speckle is inversely proportional to the square root of this value. The size of the resolution cell of the averaged image is directly proportional to the number of looks. For example, a four-look image would have a resolution cell four times larger than a one-look image and a speckle intensity one-half that of a one-look image.

TABLE 8.3 SLAR Surface Roughness at a Local Incidence Angle of 45°

Root-mean-square surface height variation (cm)	K_a band ($\lambda = 0.86$ cm)	X band ($\lambda = 3.2$ cm)	L band ($\lambda = 23.5$ cm)
0.05	Smooth	Smooth	Smooth
0.10	Intermediate	Smooth	Smooth
0.5	Rough	Intermediate	Smooth
1.5	Rough	Rough	Intermediate
10.0	Rough	Rough	Rough

Adapted from [51].

Figure 8.20 is a SLAR image of an area of folded sedimentary rocks obtained using both *HH* and *HV* polarizations. A large synclinal mountain is seen in the upper left and center portions of the scene. Note that the slopes facing the top of the page have a lighter tone than those facing the bottom. This is because the flight line was to the top

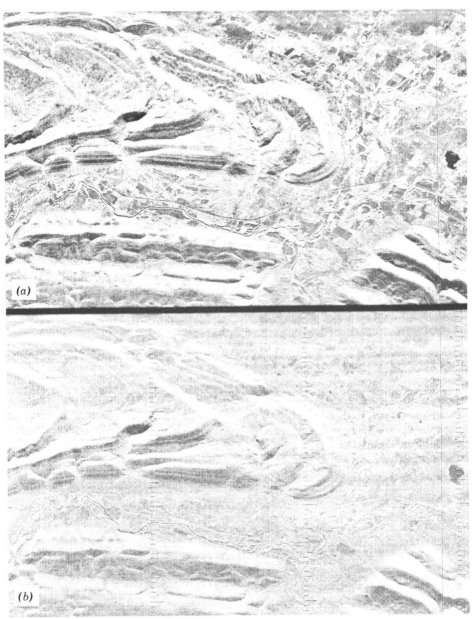

FIGURE 8.20   SLAR images, Ouchita Mountains, Oklahoma, *K* band, real aperture. 1:180,000. *(a) HH* polarization. *(b) HV* polarization. (Courtesy Westinghouse Electric Corp.)

of this image and slopes facing that direction produce a greater return signal. Despite the fact that the topography of this bedrock hill is so strikingly exhibited on this radar image, the radar signal is principally returned from vegetation surfaces. The banding that can be seen around the synclinal mountain is due to an alternation of bedrock types, principally sandstone and shale. Some of the banding results from differences in shading because of topography and some results from differences in vegetation type and vigor over the different rock formations. Note also the dark tone of the lake at right center and the various rivers in this scene caused by specular reflection of the radar signal. The cross-polarized signal (*HV*), in this case, results in an image with less image contrast, showing fewer distinctions among vegetation types, than the like-polarized (*HH*) image. Because the complex manner in which radar signals interact with and return from features is dependent on slope orientation, surface roughness, vegetation cover, and soil and vegetation water content, it is not always possible to predict whether *HH* or *HV* images will have a higher information content for a particular application. As shown in the next illustration, there can be conditions where the cross-polarized image has a greater information content than the like-polarized image.

Figure 8.21 is a SLAR image showing an area with a variety of soil and rock conditions obtained using both *HH* and *HV* polarizations. At the top of the image are dissected bedrock hills with sufficient relief to exhibit considerable shadowing. Below the bedrock hills is a light-toned area of alluvial materials washed down from the bedrock hills. Some braiding of the distributary stream channels can be seen, especially on the *HV* image. Basaltic lava flows can be seen at *C* and *D*. The "Sunshine Basalt" flow (*C*) issued from Sunshine Crater (18 mm above and to the right of the letter *C* on this image). The younger "Pisgah Basalt" flow (*D*) issued from Pisgah Crater, located just outside the lower right-hand corner of this image. The Sunshine Basalt flow has a much darker tone on the *HV* image than the Pisgah Basalt flow, whereas both have nearly the same tone on the *HH* image. The small alluvial fan at *A* has a much lighter tone than the adjacent Sunshine Basalt flow on the *HV* image but nearly the same tone on the *HH* image. This lighter tone is principally due to the greater density of vegetation on the alluvial fan than on the adjacent Sunshine Basalt flow. The contrast in tones at *B* on the *HV* image represents the boundary between the lighter-toned alluvial materials and the darker-toned Sunshine Basalt flows. Note that this boundary is not visible on the *HH* image. The large dark-toned area at lower left is a playa (dry lakebed) with a mud-cracked clay surface that acts as a specular reflector. The light-toned line running across the playa is a gravel road. Note that the playa is dark-toned on both images and the gravel road is light-toned.

Figure 8.22a is a SLAR image showing a small urban area (population 6000) adjacent to the Mississippi River. In the urban area, note the high return from the larger buildings of the central business district, which act as corner reflectors, as well as from the metallic bridges crossing the river. The river water acts as a specular reflector and has a very dark image tone. The urban area is located on a river terrace with flat topography. Note the rectangular field patterns resulting from image tone differences caused by differing amounts of diffuse reflection from different crops on this terrace. The lower left portion of the image is a dissected surface of horizontally bedded sedimentary rocks that rises 140 m above the river terrace. Note the extensive radar shadowing and irregular field patterns resulting from the relief in this part of the scene.

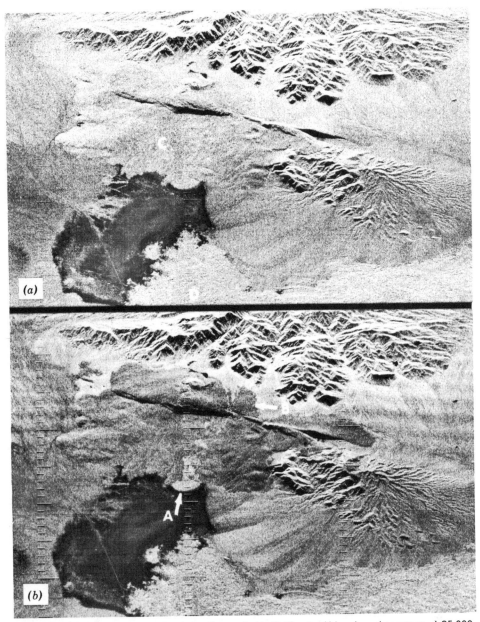

FIGURE 8.21 SLAR images, Sunshine Crater Area, California, *K* band, real aperture. 1:85,000. *(a)* HH polarization. *(b)* HV polarization. (Courtesy Westinghouse Electric Corp.)

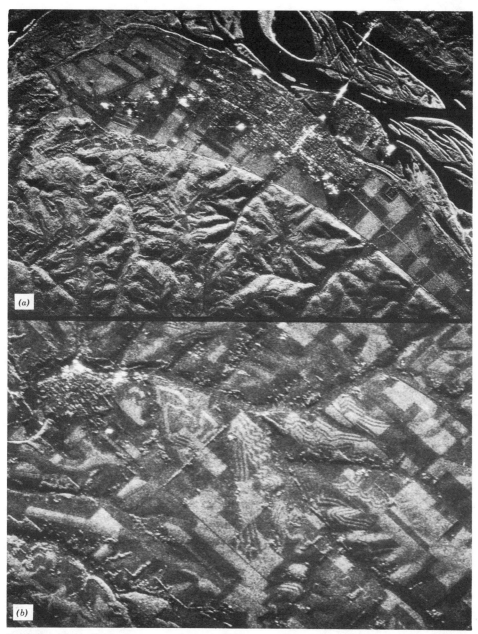

FIGURE 8.22 SLAR images, southwestern Wisconsin, September 1, 1970, X band, synthetic aperture. *(a)* Prairie du Chien and vicinity. 1:80,000. *(b)* Rural area near Prairie du Chien. 1:50,000. (Courtesy Strategic Air Command and Goodyear Aerospace.)

Figure 8.22*b* is a SLAR image showing agricultural land in an area of horizontally bedded sedimentary rocks with a loess cover having moderate relief. Because of potential soil erosion, many of the farmers in this area employ strip farming practices, which can be seen on this image as alternations of light-toned and dark-toned crops resembling contour lines. These variations in image tone result from varying amounts of diffuse reflection from the different crops. Tree lines and individual trees can be seen on this "6 m resolution" SLAR image.

Figure 8.23 shows a SLAR image of the Washington, D.C., area. This image was acquired using the IRIS (Integrated Radar Imaging System) system in its "high-resolution" mode, in which it images a 12 km wide swath with a slant-range resolution of 3 m and an azimuth resolution of 6 m. This system can also operate in a "wide swath" mode in which it images a 60 km wide swath with a slant-range resolution of 18 m and an average azimuth resolution of 10 m. In this image, the urbanized areas of Washington stand out as light tones due to high radar signal reflection from the many large buildings that act as corner reflectors. Wide streets are dark-toned due to specular reflection from flat road surfaces. "The Mall" is also dark-toned, due to low reflection

FIGURE 8.23 SLAR image, Washington, D.C., and vicinity, *X* band, synthetic aperture. 1:250,000. (Courtesy MacDonald Dettwiler and Associates Ltd., and Intera Technologies.)

from its grassy surface. The Potomac River is black, due to specular reflection from its water surface. The dark-toned, nearly rectangular area at lower right is the runway−taxiway complex at Andrews Air Force Base.

8.9 RADAR REMOTE SENSING FROM SPACE

The examples described in the previous sections have dealt with airborne radar remote sensing. Perhaps the largest single boost to the development of applications of radar imaging will be the increased availability of image data from spaceborne systems. In the case of multispectral scanning, for example, the launch of Landsat precipitated a boom in the application of MSS technology. The prospect of repetitive coverage from orbital radar systems holds considerable potential for similar advances in the application of radar imagery. The operating characteristics and geometry previously described for SLAR systems apply also to radar images from space. However, because only synthetic aperture radar systems are used for spaceborne radar remote sensing (real aperture systems would have insufficient resolution), we use the term *SAR* (synthetic aperture radar) to refer to side-looking radar systems operated from space. Also, it should be noted that the radar "look angle" and "incidence angle" with spaceborne radar are not the same because of the earth's curvature.

Seasat-1

Seasat-1 was the first of a proposed series of satellites oriented toward oceanographic research. The Seasat-1 satellite was launched on June 27, 1978, into an 800 km near-polar orbit. The satellite was designed to provide alternating day and night coverage each 36 hr. Approximately 95 percent of the earth's oceans were to be covered by the system. Unfortunately, system failure 99 days after launch limited the image data produced by the satellite.

An important "first" realized with Seasat-1 was an *L*-band (23.5 cm), SAR system with *HH* polarization. It was designed to generate imagery across a 100 km swath with a look angle of 20 to 26° and a 25 m resolution in both range and azimuth.

Although the rationale for placing the imaging radar system on board Seasat was its potential for monitoring the global surface wave field and polar sea ice conditions, the resultant images of the oceans revealed a much wider spectrum of oceanic and atmospheric phenomena, including internal waves, current boundaries, eddies, fronts, bathymetric features, storms, rainfalls, and windrows. Seasat was also operated over the world's land areas and many excellent images illustrating applications to geology, water resources, land cover mapping, agricultural assessment, and other land-related uses were obtained.

Radar images from space have revealed interesting patterns that have been shown to correlate with ocean bottom configurations. Figure 8.24a is a Seasat SAR image of the English Channel near the Straits of Dover. Here, the Channel is characterized by tidal variations of up to 7 m, and reversing tidal currents with velocities at times over 1.5 m/sec. Also, there are extensive sand bars on both sides of the Straits and along the coasts of France and England. The sand bars in the Channel are long, narrow ridges from 10 to 30 m in depth, with some shallower than 5 m. Together with the high

FIGURE 8.24   English Channel near the Straits of Dover. *(a)* Seasat SAR image, *L* band, August 19, 1978. *(b)* Map showing ocean bottom contours in meters. (Courtesy NASA Jet Propulsion Laboratory.)

volume of ship traffic, these sand bars make navigation in the Channel hazardous. By comparing this image with Figure 8.24*b*, it can be seen that the surface patterns on the radar image follow closely the sand bar patterns present in the area. Tidal currents at the time of image acquisition were 0.5 to 1.0 m/sec generally in a northeast-to-southwest direction. The more prominent patterns are visible over bars 20 m or less in depth.

Figure 8.25 shows arctic pack ice on Seasat SAR images acquired 3 days apart. In the lower right-hand portion of these images is Banks Island, a stable land mass. The remainder of the images shows ice blocks of various ages and stages. The brighter ice areas are older ice that may have rough surfaces and scattered areas of rock debris. The darker areas are either open water or recently frozen ice. In the 3 days between these two images, ice in the western part of this image moved 15 km to the south, while ice near the coast of Banks Island moved very little. The large feature with the brightest

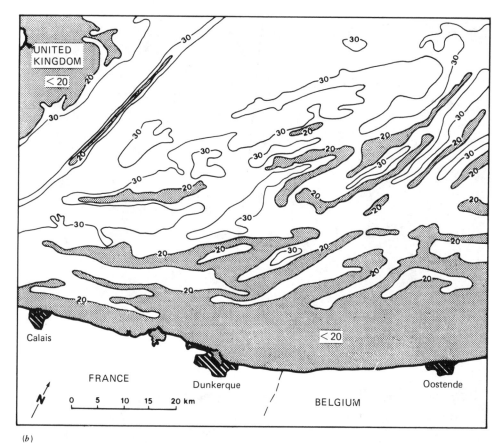

(b)

FIGURE 8.24   *(continued)*

return is Fletcher's Ice Island, a feature that was discovered in 1946. This island is a tabular block of ice 7 × 12 km in size. It was imaged by Seasat on eight separate passes during a 2 month period, during which time it traveled a distance of 157 km.

Geologists have made extensive use of radar airborne imagery in the past primarily for purposes of terrain analysis and structural mapping. A limitation of airborne imagery in such applications is the large change in incidence angle across the image swath. In these circumstances, it is often difficult to distinguish differences in backscatter caused by variations in incidence angle from those actually related to the structure and composition of the surface materials present in an image. Spaceborne radar images overcome this problem because they have only small changes in incidence angle. This makes their interpretation more definitive. In general, images acquired at small incidence angles (less than 30°), such as Seasat radar images, emphasize variations in surface slope, although geometric distortions due to layover and foreshortening in

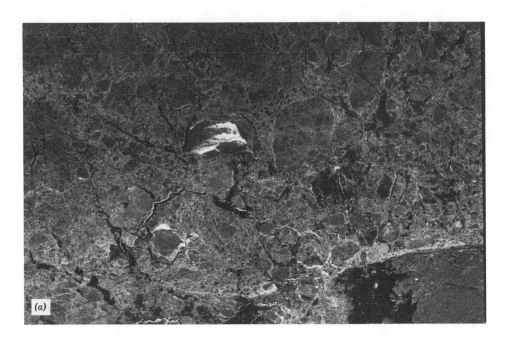

FIGURE 8.25   Seasat SAR images of pack ice in the Beaufort Sea, Canada, L band. 1:750,000. (a) October 3, 1978. (b) October 6, 1978. (Courtesy NASA Jet Propulsion Laboratory.)

mountainous regions can be severe. Images with large incidence angles, such as SIR-A radar imagery, have reduced geometric distortion and emphasize variations in surface roughness, although radar shadows increase [30].

Figure 8.26 shows a Seasat SAR image of an area of folded sedimentary rocks in the

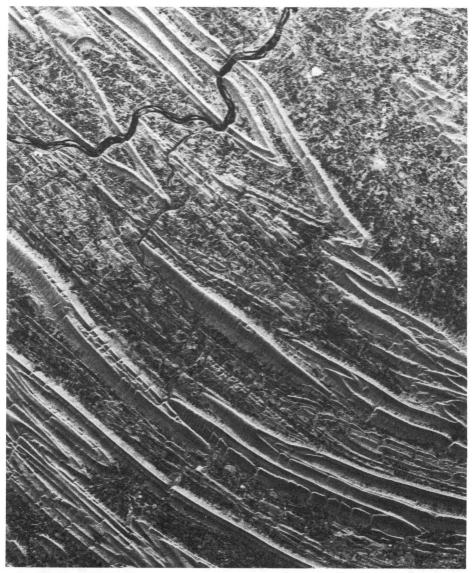

FIGURE 8.26   Seasat SAR image of Appalachian mountains of Pennsylvania, *L* band, August 19, 1978. 1:650,000. (Courtesy NASA Jet Propulsion Laboratory.)

Appalachian mountains of Pennsylvania. Here, the "sidelighting" nature of SAR imaging emphasizes the linear hills and valleys associated with the anticlines and synclines (Section 4.6) present in this area.

Shuttle Imaging Radar

A number of spaceborne radar experiments have been conducted using a series of Shuttle Imaging Radar (SIR) systems. SIR-A experiments were conducted from the Space Shuttle at an altitude of 260 km during November 1981. The SIR-A system possessed many of the same characteristics as the radar system onboard Seasat. The principal difference between these two was that the SIR-A antenna (9.4 m long) illuminated the earth's surface at a larger look angle (47 to 53°) than Seasat. As with Seasat, an L-band (23.5 cm) system with *HH* polarization was used. The swath width imaged was 50 km and resolution was 40 m in both range and azimuth. SIR-A obtained imagery over 10 million km^2 of the earth's surface and acquired radar images of many tropical, arid, and mountainous regions for the first time.

Figure 8.27 shows a Landsat MSS band 7 (near infrared) image (*a*) and a SIR-A image (*b*) of an area in the Widyan region of Saudi Arabia and Iraq. This is an area of rugged terrain composed of extensively dissected carbonate rocks (several types of limestone and dolomite). Numerous dry river channels in the area form the regional drainage network. The dry river beds are covered with smooth, dry layers of wind-deposited silt and sand that produce very low radar returns. The outcropping carbonate rocks adjacent to the river beds have rough angular surfaces that produce strong radar returns. The contrast between the light-toned carbonate rocks and the dark-toned dry river beds provides ready discrimination of the dendritic drainage pattern on the radar image. Although the Landsat band 7 image is the best available Landsat image of this area, it shows little contrast between the river beds and the adjacent carbonate bedrock.

Figure 8.28 is a SIR-A image showing villages, roads, and cultivated fields in eastern China. Each of the hundreds of white spots on this image is a village. The agricultural crops common in this area are winter wheat, kaoliang, corn, and millet. The dark linear and winding features with white lines on each side are rivers and drainageways located between levees.

Figure 8.29 shows a comparison of Landsat MSS (*a*) and SIR-A (*b*) imagery of the Sahara Desert in southeastern Egypt. The Landsat image shows the windblown sand deposits that cover this hyperarid area. The sand sheet is virtually featureless, consisting of hundreds of square kilometers of flat terrain composed of coarse sand and fine pebbles. However, the L-band (23.5 cm) radar waves have penetrated unusually far (at least 1 to 2 m) into this extremely dry material to reveal the underlying bedrock structure. The subsurface contains numerous previously unknown buried river channels and gravel terraces apparently associated with an ancient drainage system. SIR-A imagery has proven to be useful in interpreting the history of such features. Similarly, SIR-A radar images of this area have revealed a series of semirectangular features that are hypothesized to be previously unrecognized Stone Age agricultural fields or pastoral sites.

FIGURE 8.27 Widyan region of Saudi Arabia and Iraq. *(a)* Landsat MSS band 7 image (0.8 to 1.1 μm), July 14, 1973. 1:630,000. *(b)* SIR-A image, *L* band, November 1981. 1:630,000. (Courtesy NASA Jet Propulsion Laboratory.)

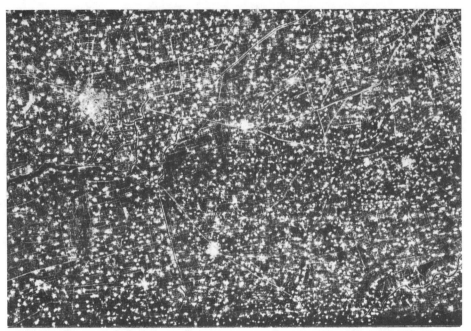

FIGURE 8.28   SIR-A image of eastern China, L band, November 14, 1981. 1:600,000. (Courtesy NASA Jet Propulsion Laboratory.)

SIR-B experiments were conducted from the Space Shuttle during October 1984. Again, an L-band system with HH polarization was used. The principal difference between the SIR-A and SIR-B radar systems is that SIR-B was equipped with an antenna that could be tilted mechanically to beam its radar signals toward the earth at varying look angles (ranging from 15 to 60°). This provided the opportunity for scientific studies aimed at assessing the effect of various incidence angles on radar returns. In addition, it provided the opportunity for the acquisition of stereo radar images. The azimuth resolution of SIR-B was 25 m. The range resolution varied from 14 m at a look angle of 60° to 46 m at a look angle of 15°.

Figure 8.30 shows a SIR-B image of Montreal, Canada, and vicinity. The most highly developed areas of the city have the highest radar returns and are light-toned in this image. The St. Lawrence River is dark-toned because of the specular reflection of the radar waves from the water surface. The numerous bridges crossing the river are linear white-toned features. In the lower right of the image are seen long, striplike patterns of agricultural fields, generally at right angles to rivers and streams, typical of the French land subdivision system.

Figure 8.31 shows SIR-B images of Mt. Shasta, a 4300 m high volcano in northern California. These images illustrate the effect of incidence angle on image layover. In 8.31a, having an incidence angle of 60°, the peak of the volcano is imaged near its

FIGURE 8.29 Sahara Desert in southeastern Egypt. *(a)* Landsat MSS image (black and white copy of color infrared composite image). *(b)* SIR-A image, *L* band, November 1981. (Courtesy NASA.)

center. In 8.31*b*, having an incidence angle of 30°, the peak is imaged near the top of the figure (the look direction was from top to bottom in this figure). Several light-toned tongues of lava can be seen on the flanks of this strato volcano—Figure 4.25 is an airphoto stereopair of the very light-toned tongue of lava that can be seen at upper left in this radar image. The surface of this young lava flow consists of unvegetated angular chunks of basalt $\frac{1}{3}$ to 1 m in size that present a very rough surface to the *L*-band radar

FIGURE 8.30 SIR-B image, Montreal and vicinity, Canada, L band, October 7, 1984. 1:330,000. (Courtesy NASA Jet Propulsion Laboratory.)

waves. The other, somewhat darker-toned, lava flows on the flanks of Mt. Shasta are older, have weathered more, and are more vegetated.

The image parallax associated with data from two different incidence angles can not only be used to generated stereopairs of radar data, it can also be used to prepare topographic maps and digital elevation models of the imaged terrain. For example, Figure 8.32 shows 12 perspective views of Mt. Shasta that were generated from a digital elevation model extracted from the radar data shown in Figures 8.31a and b. Image parallax was achieved by same-side illumination, using the same altitude but differing incidence angles (Section 8.5). Through computer modeling, perspective views from various vantage points around the mountain were calculated for this display.

Figure 8.33 shows a stereopair of SIR-B images of volcanic terrain in Chile. Again, two incidence angles (45 and 54°) were used for data collection. Although the stereo convergence angle is relatively small (9°), the stereo perception of the imagery is excellent because of the ruggedness of the terrain. The volcano near the bottom of the figure is Michinmahuida volcano; it rises 2400 m above the surrounding terrain. The snow covered slopes of this volcano appear dark-toned, because of absorption of the radar signal by the snow.

Figure 8.34 shows SIR-B images of a forested area in northern Florida and further illustrates the effect of radar imaging at multiple incidence angles on the interpretability of radar images. The terrain is flat, with a mean elevation of 45 m. Sandy soils overlay weathering limestone; lakes are sinkhole lakes. Various land cover types can be

FIGURE 8.31 SIR-B images, Mt. Shasta, California, L band, October 1984. 1:300,000. *(a)* 60° incidence angle. *(b)* 30° incidence angle. Note the severe layover of the mountain top in *(b)*. (Courtesy NASA Jet Propulsion Laboratory.)

FIGURE 8.32 Perspective views of Mt. Shasta, California, generated from the SIR-B data shown in Figures 8.31a and b. From left to right, these images correspond to successive views taken clockwise around the mountain (beginning from the right of Figure 8.31). (Courtesy NASA Jet Propulsion Laboratory).

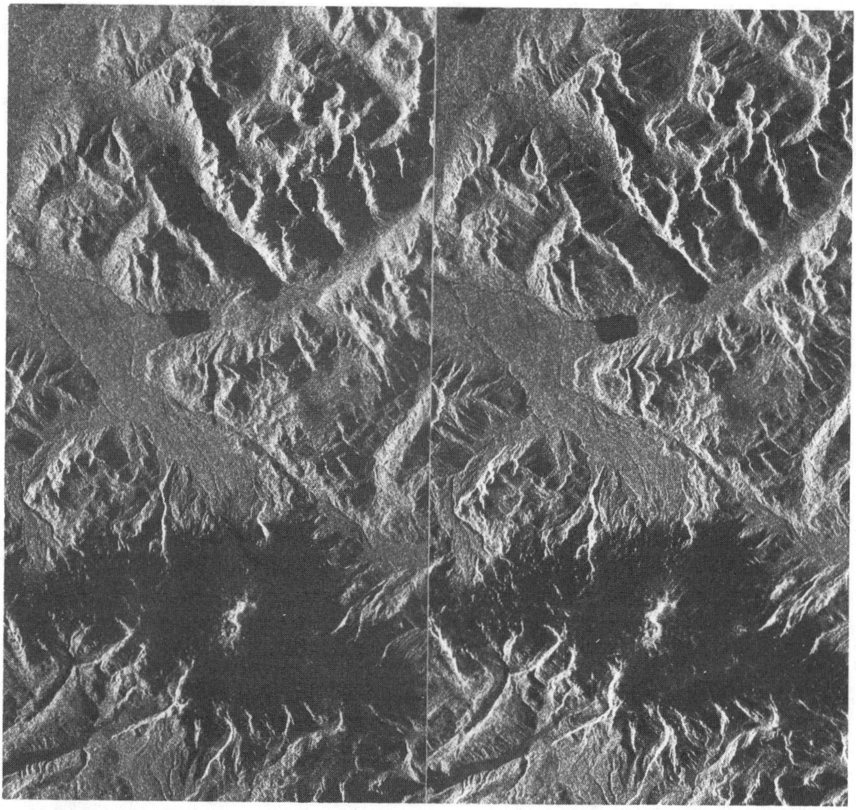

FIGURE 8.33 SIR-B stereopair, Michinmahuida Volcano, Chiloe Province, Chile, October 1984. 1:350,000. The data for this stereopair were collected at two incidence angles with same-side illumination. (Courtesy NASA Jet Propulsion Laboratory.)

identified on Figure 8.34*b* by their tone, texture, and shape. Water bodies *(W)* have a dark tone and smooth texture. Clear-cut areas *(C)* have a dark tone with a faint mottled texture, and rectangular to angular shapes. The powerline right-of-way *(P)* and roads *(R)* appear as dark-toned, narrow, linear swaths. Pine forest *(F)*, which covers the majority of this image, has a medium tone with a mottled texture. Cypress−tupelo swamps *(S)*, which consist mainly of deciduous species, have a light tone and a mottled texture. However, the relative tones of the forested areas vary considerably with incidence angle. For example, the cypress−tupelo swamp areas are dark-toned at an incidence angle of 58° and cannot be visually distinguished from the pine forest. These same swamps are somewhat lighter-toned than the pine forest at an incidence angle of 45° and much lighter-toned than the pine forest at an incidence angle of 28°. The very high radar return from these swamps on the 28° image is believed to be caused by specular reflection from the standing water in these areas acting in combination with

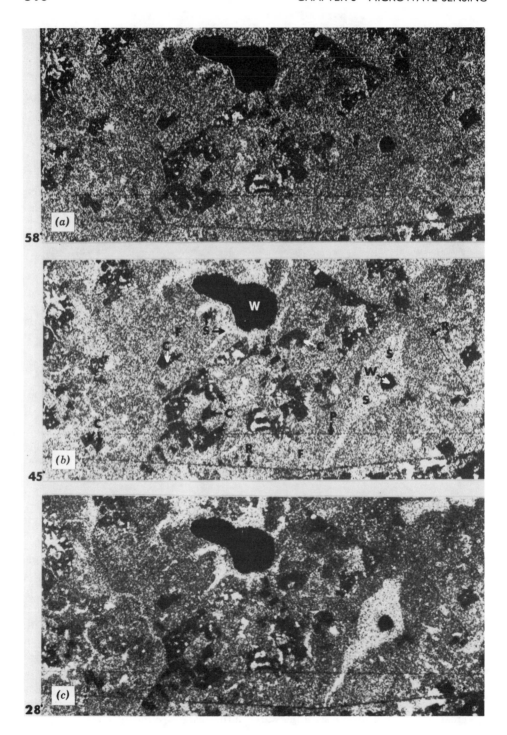

reflection from the tree trunks, resulting in a complex corner reflector effect [29]. This effect is more pronounced at an incidence angle of 28° than at the larger incidence angles because the penetration of radar waves through the forest canopy is greater at the smaller incidence angle.

SIR-C (scheduled for launch in 1989) experiments are designed to explore multiple-wavelength radar sensing from space, with simultaneous operation of L-band (23.5 cm) and C-band (5.7 cm) systems. SIR-C look angles are variable in one degree increments from 15 to 60°, and four polarizations are available (*HH, HV, VV,* and *VH*). (Tentatively, an X-band *VV* polarization system is to be added to the mission payload by the Federal Republic of Germany.)

The radar systems on board Space Shuttles are experimental systems that acquire data only for a few days per mission. Satellites planned for launch by the European Space Agency, the Canadian government, and the National Space Development Agency of Japan are designed to gather radar data on a daily basis. We briefly describe each of these systems below.

ERS-1 (European Space Agency)

Scheduled for launch in 1990 is a C-band (5.7 cm) SAR system to be placed onboard the ERS-1 satellite of the European Space Agency. This system is expected to have a look angle of 23° and a resolution of 30 m. Called *AMI* (standing for *active microwave instrumentation*), this system is intended to provide high-resolution images of coastal zones, ice areas, and land areas, together with data about sea surface conditions.

Radarsat (Canada)

The Canadian *Radarsat* satellite, scheduled for launch in 1991, is designed to gather radar data on a daily basis over an anticipated 5 to 10 year life span. This system will operate in the C band (5.7 cm) with variable look angles (20 to 45°) and a resolution of 28 m. It will circle the earth in a near-polar orbit 14 times a day. Stereoscopic coverage will be possible. Radarsat is intended primarily as a commercial rather than scientific operation with its data being marketed to specific users. One important use that is made possible by Radarsat's orbital characteristics and variable look angle is near-real-time monitoring of sea ice for use in guiding Arctic ships across Canada's Northwest

---

FIGURE 8.34   SIR-B images, northern Florida, L band. 1:165,000. *(a)* 58° incidence angle, October 9, 1984. *(b)* 45° incidence angle, October 10, 1984. *(c)* 28° incidence angle, October 11, 1984. (Courtesy Department of Forestry and Natural Resources, Purdue University, and NASA Jet Propulsion Laboratory.)

C = Clear-cut area   R = Road
F = Pine forest   S = Cypress−tupelo swamp
P = Powerline right-of-way   W = Open water

Passage. Other intended uses include crop monitoring, timber mapping, oil spill detection, snow distribution mapping, and providing ice information to personnel on offshore drilling rigs.

Radarsat is expected to have two imaging systems in addition to the radar system. One is a four-band multilinear array scanner (similar in concept to the SPOT HRV system described in Section 9.13) with a resolution of 30 m that will sense blue, green, red, and near-IR wavelengths. The other is a five-band AVHRR system (similar in concept to the NOAA AVHRR system described in Section 9.16) with a resolution of 1300 m that will sense red, near-IR, and thermal-IR (three bands) wavelengths.

JERS-1 (Japan)

Scheduled for launch in 1991 is an L-band SAR system to be placed onboard the JERS-1 satellite of the National Space Development Agency of Japan. This system is expected to have a look angle of 33° and a resolution of 25 m.

8.10   ELEMENTS OF PASSIVE MICROWAVE SENSING

Operating in the same spectral domain as radar, passive microwave systems yield yet another "look" at the environment—one quite different from that of radar. Being passive, these systems do not supply their own illumination but rather sense the naturally available microwave energy within their field of view. They operate in much the same manner as thermal radiometers and scanners. In fact, passive microwave sensing principles and sensing instrumentation parallel those of thermal sensing in many respects. As with thermal sensing, blackbody radiation theory is central to the conceptual understanding of passive microwave sensing. Again as in thermal sensing, passive microwave sensors exist in the form of both radiometers and scanners. However, passive microwave sensors incorporate antennas rather than photon detection elements.

Most passive microwave systems operate in the same spectral region as the shorter wavelength radar (out to 30 cm). As shown in Figure 8.35, passive microwave sensors operate in the low-energy tail of the 300°K blackbody radiation curve typifying terrestrial features. In this spectral region, all objects in the natural environment emit microwave radiation, albeit faintly. This includes terrain elements and the atmosphere. In fact, passive microwave signals are generally composed of a number of source components—some emitted, some reflected, and some transmitted. This is illustrated in Figure 8.36. Over any given object, a passive microwave signal might include (1) an emitted component related to the surface temperature and material attributes of the object, (2) an emitted component coming from the atmosphere, (3) a surface reflected component from sunlight and skylight, and (4) a transmitted component having a subsurface origin. In short, the intensity of remotely sensed passive microwave radiation over any given object is dependent not only on the object's temperature and the incident radiation but also on the emittance, reflectance, and transmittance properties of the object. These properties in turn are influenced by the

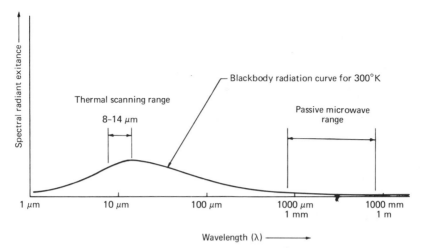

FIGURE 8.35 Comparison of spectral regions used for thermal versus passive microwave sensing.

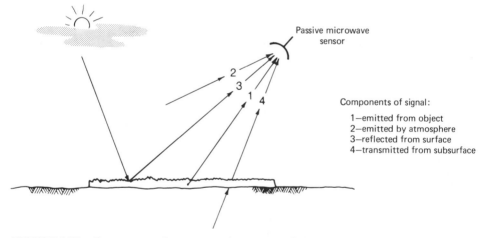

FIGURE 8.36 Components of a passive microwave signal.

object's surface electrical, chemical, and textural characteristics, its bulk configuration and shape, and the angle from which it is viewed.

Because of the variety of its possible sources and its extremely weak magnitude, the signal obtained from various ground areas is "noisy" compared to that which cameras, scanners, or radars provide. The interpretation of this signal is thus much more complex than that of the other sensors discussed. In spite of the difficulties, the utility of passive microwave systems ranges from measuring atmospheric temperature profiles on the one hand, to analyzing subsurface variations in soil, water, and mineral content on the other. These applications are briefly discussed in Section 8.12.

8.11 PASSIVE MICROWAVE SENSORS

The technology of passive microwave sensors has largely been adapted from concepts used in the field of radio astronomy. Major problem areas in the design of such systems include system sensitivity, absolute accuracy, spectral selectivity, and response directionality. Each application involves a particular set of constraints of system cost, size, weight, power, reliability, operational simplicity, and signal interpretability. Both airborne and satellite systems exist. Here, we consider the basic configuration of airborne radiometers and scanners.

Microwave Radiometers

The basic configuration of a typical microwave radiometer system is shown in Figure 8.37. Scene energy is collected at the antenna. A microwave switch permits rapid, alternate sampling between the antenna signal and a calibration temperature reference signal. The low strength antenna signal is amplified and compared with that of the internal reference signal. The difference between the antenna signal and the reference signal is electronically detected and input to some mode of readout and recording. (It should be noted that we have greatly simplified the operation of a microwave radiometer and that many variations of the design illustrated here exist.)

Common to all radiometer designs is the trade-off between antenna beamwidth and system sensitivity. Because of the very low levels of radiation available to be passively sensed in the microwave region, a comparatively large antenna beamwidth is required to collect enough energy to yield a detectable signal. Consequently, passive microwave radiometers are characterized by low spatial resolution.

Microwave radiometers, like thermal radiometers, are nonimaging, profiling devices. Their output is normally recorded on magnetic tape in either an analog or a digital format. During daylight operation, photography can be concurrently acquired to provide a visual frame of reference for the profile data. Normally, the radiometer output is expressed in terms of *apparent antenna temperature*. That is, the system is calibrated in terms of the temperature that a blackbody located at the antenna must reach to radiate the same energy as was actually collected from the ground scene.

Scanners

To afford the advantages of image output, a number of scanning microwave radiometer systems have been developed. Conceptually, a scanning radiometer operates on the same principle as a profiling system except that its antenna field of view is scanned transverse to the direction of flight. This may be performed mechanically, electronically, or by using a multiple antenna array. Thus, with the use of a synchronized film recorder, a passive microwave image can be obtained.

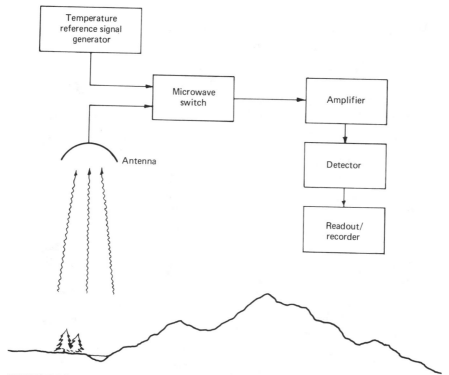

FIGURE 8.37 Block diagram of a passive microwave radiometer.

Figure 8.38 shows three segments of a strip of imagery acquired with a scanning passive microwave radiometer, or scanner. The image covers a transect running from Coalinga, California, visible at the western (left) end, to Tulare Lake (dry, now in agriculture) at the eastern (right) end in California's San Joaquin Valley. (Note that the image has the tonal and geometric appearance of thermal scanner imagery. However, in this image bright areas are radiometrically "cold" and dark areas are "warm.") Agricultural fields are visible along the length of the transect. The striping in several of the fields is due to irrigation. The darker fields are natural vegetation or dry bare soil. Density measurements made from this type of imagery have been found to relate quite systematically to the moisture content of the top 50 mm of the soil [17].

While additional verification of the overall utility of using such images to estimate near surface soil moisture is continuing, it appears that passive microwave data have a strong potential for providing soil moisture data over large inaccessible areas. Such data would greatly aid agriculturalists, meteorologists, hydrologists and other environmental scientists in that—short of exhaustive field sampling—no dependable method for gathering regional soil moisture data presently exists.

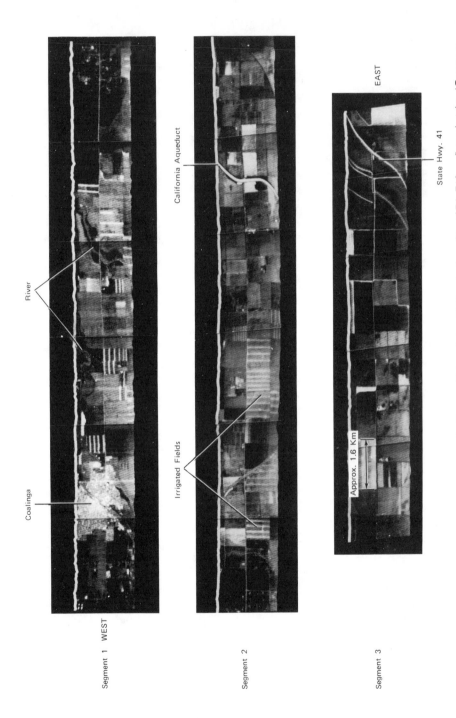

FIGURE 8.38 Passive microwave image transect, Coalinga to Tulare Lake, California, June 26, 1974, 760 m flying height. (Courtesy Geography Remote Sensing Unit, University of California—Santa Barbara, and Naval Weapons Center, China Lake, Calif.)

8.12 APPLICATIONS OF PASSIVE MICROWAVE SENSING

Like radar imaging, the field of passive microwave sensing has been developed only recently and the interpretation of passive microwave data is still not fully understood. However, there are certain very positive characteristics inherent in this form of remote sensing. As with radar, passive microwave systems can be operated day or night, under virtually all weather conditions. By the appropriate selection of operating wavelength, systems can either look *through* or look *at* the atmosphere. That is, a number of atmospheric "windows" and "walls" exist in microwave regions, principally due to selective absorption by water vapor and oxygen. Meteorologists are now using selected wavelength microwave sensing to measure atmospheric temperature profiles and to determine the atmospheric distribution of water and ozone.

Passive microwave sensing has strong utility in the field of oceanography. These applications range from monitoring sea ice, currents, and winds, to detecting oil pollution in even trace amounts. Though currently sparse in number, investigations related to the utility of passive microwave sensing in hydrology have shown potential for providing information on snow melt conditions, soil temperature, and soil moisture over large areas.

The coarse resolution of passive microwave systems does not preclude their value for synoptic surveillance of many earth resource features that occur over large areas. In fact, from satellite altitudes, the concept of gross scale worldwide resource monitoring with such systems is a present reality. Other useful applications involve the study of features that lie beneath a soil overburden. *Multispectral* microwave radiometry appears to be a means by which we can peer through this overburden. This has obvious potential implications in the field of geology in terms of delineating geologic structure, material changes, subsurface voids, and so on.

With time, passive microwave sensing, like radar sensing, will become more commonplace because of its existing and potential utility in a host of disciplinary areas.

8.13 LIDAR

The final radarlike system we wish to mention in closing this chapter is *lidar* (standing for *light detection and ranging*). As with radar, lidar systems are active remote sensing systems. They simply use pulses of laser light, rather than microwave energy, to illuminate the terrain. As with passive microwave systems, lidar systems can be operated in either a profiling or a scanning mode.

One of the principal applications of lidar data has been the accurate profiling of water depths. This is done by transmitting pulsed coherent laser light beneath an aircraft such that first a strong reflected return is recorded from the water surface, and this is followed closely by a weaker return from the bottom of the water body. The depth of the water is determined from the round-trip travel time the pulse is in the water (Figure 8.39).

Lidar remote sensing is the subject of continuing research. Among these efforts is the use of lidar systems for measuring heights within timber stands and estimating

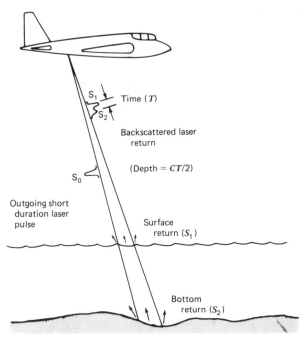

FIGURE 8.39   Principle of lidar bathymetry. (Adapted from [45].)

forest biomass. Figure 8.40 illustrates the type of data recorded by a lidar system over a forest canopy. The upper line on this graph represents the lidar return from the top of the canopy. The "×'s" correspond to individual pulses returned from the ground through openings in the canopy. They are used to define the "ground level" indicated by the lower line in the figure. Tree heights within the canopy correspond to the relative height differences between the canopy and ground returns [1, 43].

   Another application of lidar systems is their use in measuring the *laser-induced fluorescence (LIF)* properties of earth surface features. Fluorescence refers to the characteristic of various materials to absorb energy of one wavelength and then reemit energy, generally at a longer wavelength, shortly after excitation by the original energy source. Because different materials tend to fluoresce at different wavelengths, LIF can be used to discriminate among material types. *Laser fluorosensors* make use of this property. They employ a single-channel laser source to illuminate objects and multi-channel receivers to record the spectral characteristics of the resulting fluorescence emitted by the objects. Such systems have been used operationally to detect oil slicks and other water pollutants and to map the chlorophyll concentration of natural bodies of water [45]. LIF has also been shown to have promise for distinguishing several major plant groups and some species and stress conditions within each group [12]. As research in this vein continues, there will be increased application of lidar systems in the future.

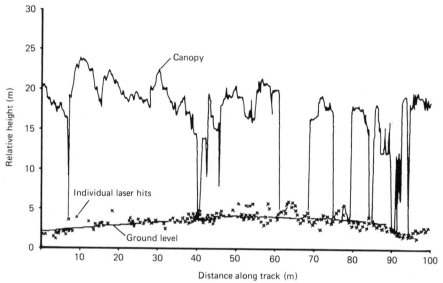

FIGURE 8.40 Lidar returns measured over a forest canopy. (Adapted from [43].)

SELECTED BIBLIOGRAPHY

1. Aldred, A.H., and G.M. Bonner, *Application of Airborne Lasers to Forest Surveys*, Information Report PI-X-51, Petawawa National Forestry Institute, Chalk River, Ontario, 1985.

2. American Society of Photogrammetry, *Manual of Remote Sensing*, 2nd ed., Falls Church, Va., 1983.

3. Arp, H., J.C. Griesbach, and J.P. Burns, "Mapping in Tropical Forests: A New Approach Using the Laser APR," *Photogrammetric Engineering and Remote Sensing*, vol. 48, no. 1, January 1982, pp. 91–100.

4. Brisco, B., and R. Protz, "Manual and Automatic Crop Identification with Airborne Radar Imagery," *Photogrammetric Engineering and Remote Sensing*, vol. 48, no. 1, January 1982, pp. 101–109.

5. Brisco, B., F.T. Ulaby, and R. Protz, "Improving Crop Classification through Attention to the Timing of Airborne Radar Acquisitions," *Photogrammetric Engineering and Remote Sensing*, vol. 50, no. 6, June 1984, pp. 739–745.

6. Bristow, M.P.F., et al., "Airborne Laser Fluorescence Survey of the Columbia and Snake River: Simultaneous Measurements of Chlorophyll, Dissolved Organics, and Optical Attenuation," *International Journal of Remote Sensing*, vol. 6, no. 11, 1985, pp. 1708–1734.

7. Bryan, M.L., "The Effect of Radar Azimuth Angle on Cultural Data," *Photogrammetric Engineering and Remote Sensing*, vol. 45, no. 8, August 1979, pp. 1097–1107.

8. Bryan, M.L., "Optically Processed Seasat Radar Mosaic of Florida," *Photogrammetric Engineering and Remote Sensing*, vol. 47, no. 9, September 1981, pp. 1335–1337.

 9. Bryan, M.L., "Analysis of Two Seasat Synthetic Aperture Radar Images of an Urban Scene," *Photogrammetric Engineering and Remote Sensing*, vol. 48, no. 3, March 1982, pp. 393–398.

10. Bryan, M.L., and J. Clark, "Potentials for Change Detection Using Seasat Synthetic Aperture Radar Data," *Remote Sensing of Environment*, vol. 16, no. 2, 1984, pp. 107–124.

11. Burke, H.K., et al., "Determination of Snowpack Properties from Satellite Passive Microwave Properties," *Remote Sensing of Environment*, vol. 15, no. 1, 1984, pp. 1–20.

12. Chappelle, E.W., et al., "Laser-Induced Fluorescence of Green Plants," *Applied Optics*, vol. 24, no. 1, January 1985, pp. 74–80.

13. Cimino, J.B., and C. Elachi, *Shuttle Imaging Radar-A (SIR-A) Experiment*," JPL Publ. 82-77, NASA Jet Propulsion Laboratory, Pasadena, Calif., 1982.

14. Curlis, J.D., V.S. Frost, and L.F. Dellwig, "Geological Mapping Potential of Computer-Enhanced Images from the Shuttle Imaging Radar: Lisbon Valley Anticline, Utah," *Photogrammetric Engineering and Remote Sensing*, vol. 52, no. 4, April 1986, pp. 525–532.

15. Daily, M., "Hue–Saturation–Intensity Split-Spectrum Processing of Seasat Radar Imagery," *Photogrammetric Engineering and Remote Sensing*, vol. 49, no. 3, March 1983, pp. 349–355.

16. deLoor, G.P. (ed.), "Radar Remote Sensing," *Remote Sensing Reviews*, vol. 1, 1983.

17. Estes, J.E., M.R. Mel, and J.O. Hooper, "Measuring Soil Moisture with an Airborne Imaging Passive Microwave Radiometer," *Photogrammetric Engineering and Remote Sensing*, vol. 43, no. 10, 1977, pp. 1273–1281.

18. Ford, J.P., J.B. Cimino, and C. Elachi, *Space Shuttle Columbia Views the World with Imaging Radar: The Sir-A Experiment*, JPL Publ. 82–95, NASA Jet Propulsion Laboratory, Pasadena, Calif., 1983.

19. Ford, J.P., et al., *Seasat Views North America, the Caribbean, and Western Europe with Imaging Radar*, JPL Publ. 80-67, NASA Jet Propulsion Laboratory, Pasadena, Calif., 1980.

20. Ford, J.P., et al., *Shuttle Imaging Radar Views the Earth from Challenger: The SIR-B Experiment*, JPL Publ. 86-10, NASA Jet Propulsion Laboratory, Pasadena, Calif., 1986.

21. Foster, J.L., and D.K. Hall, "Multisensor Analysis of Hydrologic Features with Emphasis on the Seasat SAR," *Photogrammetric Engineering and Remote Sensing*, vol. 47, no. 5, May 1981, pp. 655–664.

22. Frost, V.S., et al., "Digital Enhancement of SAR Imagery as an Aid in Geologic Data Extraction," *Photogrammetric Engineering and Remote Sensing*, vol. 49, no. 3, March 1983, pp. 357–364.

23. Fu, L., and B. Holt, *Seasat Views Oceans and Sea Ice with Synthetic-Aperture Radar*, JPL Publ. 81-120, NASA Jet Propulsion Laboratory, Pasadena, Calif., 1982.

24. Green, G.M., "Use of SIR-A and Landsat MSS Data in Mapping Shrub and Intershrub Vegetation at Koonamore, South Australia," *Photogrammetric Engineering and Remote Sensing*, vol. 52, no. 5, May 1986, pp. 659–670.

25. Haack, B.N., "L- and X-Band Like- and Cross-Polarized Synthetic Aperture Radar for Investigating Urban Environments," *Photogrammetric Engineering and Remote Sensing*, vol. 50, no. 3, March 1984, pp. 331–340.

26. Hardaway, G., G.C. Gustafson, and D. Lichy, "Cardinal Effect on Seasat Images of Urban Areas," *Photogrammetric Engineering and Remote Sensing*, vol. 48, no. 3, March 1982, pp. 399–404.

27. Henderson, F.M., "Land-Use Analysis of Radar Imagery," *Photogrammetric Engineering and Remote Sensing*, vol. 45, no. 3, March 1979, pp. 295–307.

28. Henderson, F.M., "A Comparison of SAR Brightness Levels and Urban Land-Cover Classes," *Photogrammetric Engineering and Remote Sensing*, vol. 49, no. 11, November 1983, pp. 1585–1591.

29. Hoffer, R.M., P.W. Mueller, and D.F. Lozano-Garcia, "Multiple Incidence Angle Shuttle Imaging Radar Data for Discriminating Forest Cover Types," *Technical Papers of the American Society for Photogrammetry and Remote Sensing*, ACSM–ASPRS Fall Technical Meeting, September 1985, pp. 476–485.

30. Imaging Science Radar Working Group, *The SIR-B Science Plan*, JPL Publ. 82-78, NASA Jet Propulsion Laboratory, Pasadena, Calif., 1982.

31. Jackson, T.J., A. Chang, and T.J. Schmugge, "Aircraft Active Microwave Measurements for Estimating Soil Moisture," *Photogrammetric Engineering and Remote Sensing*, vol. 47, no. 6, June 1981, pp. 801–805.

32. Jensen, H., et al., "Side Looking Airborne Radar," *Scientific American*, vol. 237, no. 4, 1977, pp. 84–95.

33. Kasischke, E.S., G.A Meadows, and P.L. Jackson, *The Use of Synthetic Aperture Radar Imagery to Detect Hazards to Navigation*, ERIM Report 169200-2-F, Environmental Research Institute of Michigan, Ann Arbor.

34. Krabill, W.B., et al., "Airborne Laser Topographic Mapping Results," *Photogrammetric Engineering and Remote Sensing*, vol. 50, no. 6, June 1984, pp. 685–694.

35. Leberl, F., *Radargrammetry for Image Interpreters*, 2nd ed., International Institute for Aerial Survey and Earth Sciences, Enschede, The Netherlands, 1978.

36. Leberl, F., "Accuracy Analysis of Stereo Side-Looking Radar," *Photogrammetric Engineering and Remote Sensing*, vol. 45, no. 8, August 1979, pp. 1083–1096.

37. Levine, D., *Radargrammetry*, McGraw–Hill, New York, 1960.

38. Lewis, A.J. (ed.), "Geoscience Applications of Imaging Radar Systems," *Remote Sensing of the Electromagnetic Spectrum*, vol. 3, no. 3, 1976.

39. Li, F.K., and M.L. Bryan, "Tradeoffs Among Several Synthetic Aperture Radar Image Quality Parameters: Results of a User Survey Study," *Photogrammetric Engineering and Remote Sensing*, vol. 49, no. 6, June 1983, pp. 791–803.

40. Long, M.W., *Radar Reflectivity of Land and Sea*, Lexington Books, Lexington, Mass., 1975.

41. Lyzenga, D.R., "Shallow-Water Bathymetry Using Combined Lidar and Passive Multispectral Scanner Data," *International Journal of Remote Sensing*, vol. 6, no. 1, 1985, pp. 115–125.

42. MacDonald, H.C., Geologic Evaluation of Radar Imagery from Darien Province, Panama, *Modern Geology*, vol. 1, no. 1, 1969, pp. 1–63.

43. Maclean, G.A., and W. Krabill, "Gross Merchantable Timber Volume Estimation Using an Airborne Lidar System," *Canadian Journal of Remote Sensing*, vol. 12, no. 1, July 1986, pp. 7–18.

44. McCauley, J.F., et al., "Subsurface Valleys and Geoarcheology of the Eastern Sahara Revealed by Shuttle Radar," *Science*, vol. 218, no. 4576, 3 December 1982, pp. 1004–1020.

45. Measures, R.M., *Laser Remote Sensing*, Wiley, New York, 1984.

46. Moore, R.K., and E. Schanda (eds.), "A Selection of Papers from the International

Symposium on Microwave Signatures in Remote Sensing," *International Journal of Remote Sensing*, vol. 6, no. 2, 1985.

47. Naraghi, M., W. Stromberg, and M. Daily, "Geometric Rectification of Radar Imagery Using Digital Elevation Models," *Photogrammetric Engineering and Remote Sensing*, vol. 49, no. 2, February 1983, pp. 195–199.

48. Nelson, R., W. Krabill, and G. Maclean, "Determining Forest Canopy Characteristics Using Airborne Laser Data," *Remote Sensing of Environment*, vol. 15, no. 3, 1984, pp. 201–212.

49. Ormsby, J.P., B.J. Blanchard, and A.J. Blanchard, "Detection of Lowland Flooding Using Active Microwave Systems," *Photogrammetric Engineering and Remote Sensing*, vol. 51, no. 3, March 1985, pp. 317–328.

50. Rosenthal, W.D., and B.J. Blanchard, "Active Microwave Responses: An Aid in Improved Crop Classification," *Photogrammetric Engineering and Remote Sensing*, vol. 50, no. 4, April 1984, pp. 461–468.

51. Sabins, F.F., Jr., *Remote Sensing: Principles and Interpretation*, 2nd ed., Freeman, New York, 1986.

52. Schultejann, P.A., "Structural Trends in Borrego Valley, California: Interpretations from SIR-A and SEASAT SAR," *Photogrammetric Engineering and Remote Sensing*, vol. 51, no. 10, October 1985, pp. 1615–1624.

53. Siegal, B.S., and A.R. Gillespie (eds.), *Remote Sensing in Geology*, Wiley, New York, 1980.

54. Ulaby, F.T., R.K. Moore, and A.K. Fung, *Microwave Remote Sensing: Active and Passive, A Three Volume Series*, Artech House, Dedham, Mass.

    Vol. I: *Microwave Remote Sensing Fundamentals and Radiometry*, 1981.
    Vol. II: *Radar Remote Sensing and Surface Scattering and Emission Theory*, 1982.
    Vol. III: *From Theory to Applications*, 1986.

EARTH RESOURCE SATELLITES

9.1 INTRODUCTION

Probably no combination of two technologies has generated more interest and application over a wider range of disciplines than the merger of remote sensing and space exploration. Although many aspects of the process are still in the developmental stage, studying the earth from space has evolved from the realm of pure research to that of worldwide, day-to-day application. Currently we depend on spaceborne sensors to assist in tasks ranging from weather prediction, crop forecasting, and mineral exploration to applications as diverse as pollution detection, rangeland monitoring, and commercial fishing. All this has happened in a very short period of time and the status of remote sensing from space continues to change as new and/or improved spacecraft are placed into earth orbit.

In this chapter we emphasize the past, present, and prospective spaceborne remote sensing systems that have earth resource observation as their primary operating objective. The *Landsat* and *SPOT* series of satellites receive the bulk of our attention, although we describe other systems that will likely expand our earth monitoring capabilities in the future.

Following our treatment of land-oriented satellite systems, we conclude this chapter with a brief introduction to the application of meteorological and ocean monitoring satellites to earth resource management.

9.2 EARLY HISTORY OF SPACE IMAGING

Remote sensing from space received its first impetus through remote sensing from rockets. As early as 1891, a patent was granted to Ludwig Rahrmann of Germany for a "New or Improved Apparatus for Obtaining Bird's Eye Photographic Views." The apparatus was a rocket-propelled camera system that was recovered by parachute. By 1907, another German, Alfred Maul, had added the concept of gyrostabilization to rocket–camera systems. In 1912, he successfully boosted a 41 kg payload containing a 200 × 250 mm format camera to a height of 790 m [5].

Space remote sensing began in earnest during the period 1946 to 1950 when small cameras were carried aboard captured V-2 rockets that were fired from the White

Sands Proving Ground in New Mexico. Over the succeeding years, numerous flights involving photography were made by rockets, ballistic missiles, satellites, and manned spacecraft. However, the photographs produced during early space flights were generally of inferior quality because early missions were made primarily for purposes other than photography [31]. But crude as they were by today's standards, the early photographs demonstrated the potential value of remote sensing from space.

In many respects, the initial efforts aimed at imaging the earth's surface from space were rather incidental outgrowths of the development of meteorological satellites. Beginning with TIROS-1 in 1960, early weather satellites returned rather coarse views of cloud patterns and virtually indistinct images of the earth's surface. With refinements in the imaging sensors aboard the meteorological satellites, images of both atmospheric and terrestrial features became more distinct. Eventually, meteorologists began intensive study of surface areas to collect data on water, snow, and ice features. The prospect of looking *through*, not just *at*, the earth's atmosphere had begun.

The exciting future for remote sensing from space became more apparent during the manned space programs of the 1960s: Mercury, Gemini, and Apollo. On May 5, 1961, Alan B. Shepard, Jr., made a 15 min suborbital Mercury flight on which 150 excellent photographs were taken. These pictures were shot with an automatic Mauer 70 mm camera. Because of the trajectory of Shephard's flight, the photographs showed only sky, clouds, and ocean, but the images did indeed substantiate Shepard's statement, "What a beautiful view." On February 20, 1962, John Glenn, Jr., made three historic orbits around the earth and took 48 color photographs during Mercury mission MA-6. The photographs were taken on color negative film with a 35 mm camera and showed mostly clouds and water, although several pictured the deserts of northwest Africa [4]. On later Mercury missions, color reversal photographs were taken with 70 mm Hasselblad cameras. A specially modified Hasselblad camera, with an 80 mm lens, soon became the workhorse for the photographic experiments conducted in the Gemini program. Mission GT-4 of this program included the first formal photographic experiment from space specifically directed at geology. Coverage included nearly vertical overlapping photographs of the southwestern United States, northern Mexico, and other areas of North America, Africa, and Asia. These images soon led to new and exciting discoveries in tectonics, volcanology, and geomorphology [5].

With the success of the Gemini GT-4 photographic experiments in geology, subsequent missions included a host of similar experiments aimed at investigating various geographic and oceanographic phenomena. Photography comparable to that of the GT-4 experiments was acquired over areas extending between approximately 32° north and south latitudes. Each image had a nominal scale of about 1:2,400,000 and included about 140 km on a side. By the end of the Gemini program, some 1100 high quality color photographs had been taken for earth resource applications and the value of remote sensing from space had become well recognized. Serious thinking began about systematic, repetitive image coverage of the globe.

The scientific community's knowledge and experience with space photography was further extended with the Apollo program. One of the Apollo earth orbit flights (Apollo 9) made prior to the lunar landings included the first controlled experiment involving the acquisition of *multispectral* orbital photography for earth resource studies. A four-camera array of electrically driven and triggered 70 mm Hasselblad cameras was used in the experiment. Photographs were produced using panchromatic film with green and red filters, black and white IR film, and color IR film. Some 140 sets of imagery were thus obtained over the course of 4 days. The imagery covered parts of the southwestern, south central, and southeastern United States, as well as parts of Mexico and the Caribbean—Atlantic area.

In 1973, Skylab, the first American space workshop, was launched and its astronauts took over 35,000 images of the earth with the *Earth Resources Experiment Package (EREP)* on board. The EREP included a six-camera multispectral array, a long focal length "earth terrain" camera, a 13-channel multispectral scanner, a pointable spectroradiometer, and two microwave systems. The EREP experiments were the first to demonstrate the complementary nature of photography and electronic imaging from space [36, 38].

Another early (1975) space station experiment having a remote sensing component was the joint *U.S.—USSR Apollo—Soyuz Test Project (ASTP)*. Regrettably—because earth resource imaging was not a primary goal of this venture—hand-held 35 and 70 mm cameras were again used. For various reasons, the overall quality of most of the images from the ASTP was disappointing. However, like Skylab, the ASTP mission demonstrated that trained crewmembers could obtain useful, and sometimes unique, earth resource data from visual observation and discretionary imaging. The results of training crewmembers to look for specific earth resource phenomena and selectively record important events crystallized the complementary nature of manned and unmanned observation systems.

9.3 LANDSAT SATELLITE PROGRAM OVERVIEW

With the exciting glimpses of earth resources being provided by the early meteorological satellites and the manned spacecraft missions, NASA, with the cooperation of the U.S. Department of Interior, began a conceptual study of the feasibility of a series of *Earth Resources Technology Satellites (ERTS)*. Initiated in 1967, the program resulted in a planned sequence of six satellites that were given before-launch designations of ERTS-A, -B, -C, -D, -E, and -F. (After a successful launch into prescribed orbits, they were to become ERTS-1, -2, -3, -4, -5 and -6.)

ERTS-1 was launched by a Thor-Delta rocket on July 23, 1972, and it operated until January 6, 1978. The platform used for the ERTS-1 sensors was a Nimbus weather satellite, modified for the ERTS mission objectives. It represented the first unmanned satellite specifically designed to acquire data about earth resources on a systematic, repetitive, medium resolution, multispectral basis. It was primarily designed as an *experimental* system to test the *feasibility* of collecting earth resource data from unmanned satellites. All data would be collected in accordance with an *"open skies"* principle, meaning there would be nondiscriminatory access to data collected anywhere in the world. All nations of the world were invited to take part in evaluating ERTS-1 data and the results of this worldwide experimentation with the system were overwhelmingly favorable. In fact, these results probably exceeded most of the expectations of the scientific community. About 300 individual ERTS-1 experiments were conducted in 43 U.S. states and 36 nations.

Just prior to the launch of ERTS-B on January 22, 1975, NASA officially renamed the ERTS program the "Landsat" program (to distinguish it from the planned Seasat oceanographic satellite program). Hence, ERTS-1 was retroactively named Landsat-1 and all subsequent satellites in the series carried the Landsat designation. As of the time of this writing (1986), five Landsat satellites have been launched and this experimental program has evolved into an operational global resource monitoring program.

Table 9.1 highlights the characteristics of the Landsat-1 through -5 missions. It should be noted that three different types of sensors have been flown in various combinations on these missions. These are the Return Beam Vidicon (RBV) camera systems, the Multispectral Scanner (MSS) systems, and the Thematic Mapper (TM). Table 9.2 summarizes the spectral sensitivity and spatial resolution of each of these systems as included on the various missions.

Because Landsat -1, -2, and -3 were so similar in their operation, as were Landsat-4 and -5, it is convenient to discuss these systems as two distinct groups.

9.4   ORBIT CHARACTERISTICS
OF LANDSAT-1, -2, and -3

Figure 9.1 illustrates the basic configuration of Landsat-1, -2 and -3. These butterfly-shaped systems were about 3 m tall and 1.5 m diameter, with solar panels extending to about 4 m. The satellites weighed about 815 kg and were launched into circular orbits at a nominal altitude of 900 km. (The altitude varied between 880 and 940 km.) The orbits passed within 9° of the North and South Poles. They circled the earth once each 103 min, resulting in 14 orbits per day. The ground track speed of the satellite was about 6.46 km/sec. Figure 9.2 shows the north-to-south ground traces of the satellite orbits for a single day. Note that they cross the equator at an angle of about 9° from normal, and successive orbits are about 2760 km apart at the equator. Because the sensors aboard the satellite imaged only a 185 km swath, there are large gaps in image coverage between successive orbits on a given day. However, with each new day the satellite orbit progressed slightly westward, just overshooting the orbit pattern of the previous day. (See orbit 15 in Figure 9.2.) This satellite orbit/earth rotation relationship thus yielded images that overlap those of the previous day. The overlap is a maximum at 81° north and south latitudes (about 85 percent) and a minimum (about 14 percent) at the equator. Figure 9.3 shows the set of orbital paths covering the conterminous United States. It took 18 days for the orbit pattern to progress westward to the point of coverage repetition. Thus, the satellites had the capability of covering the globe (except the 82 to 90° polar latitudes) once every 18 days, or about 20 times per year. The satellite orbits were corrected occasionally to compensate for orbital precession caused by atmospheric drag. This ensured that repetitive image centers were maintained to within about 37 km.

At the 103 min orbital period, the 2760 km equatorial spacing between successive

TABLE 9.1 Characteristics of Landsat-1 to -5 Missions

Satellite	Launched	Decommissioned	RBV bands	MSS bands	TM bands	Orbit
Landsat-1	July 23, 1972	January 6, 1978	1,2,3 (simultaneous images)	4,5,6,7	None	18 day/900 km
Landsat-2	January 22, 1975	February 25, 1982	1,2,3 (simultaneous images)	4,5,6,7	None	18 day/900 km
Landsat-3	March 5, 1978	March 31, 1983	A,B,C,D (one-band side-by-side images)	4,5,6,7,8[a]	None	18 day/900 km
Landsat-4	July 16, 1982	—	None	1,2,3,4	1,2,3,4,5,6,7	16 day/705 km
Landsat-5	March 1, 1984	—	None	1,2,3,4	1,2,3,4,5,6,7	16 day/705 km

[a]Band 8 (10.4–12.6 μm) failed shortly after launch.

TABLE 9.2 Sensors Used on Landsat-1 to -5 Missions

Sensor	Mission	Sensitivity (μm)	Resolution (m)
RBV	1,2	0.475−0.575	80
		0.580−0.680	80
		0.690−0.830	80
	3	0.505−0.750	30
MSS	1−5	0.5−0.6	79/82[a]
		0.6−0.7	79/82
		0.7−0.8	79/82
		0.8−1.1	79/82
	3	10.4−12.6[b]	240
TM	4,5	0.45−0.52	30
		0.52−0.60	30
		0.63−0.69	30
		0.76−0.90	30
		1.55−1.75	30
		10.4−12.5	120
		2.08−2.35	30

[a]79 m Landsat-1 to -3, and 82 m for Landsat-4 and -5.
[b]Failed shortly after launch (band 8 of Landsat-3).

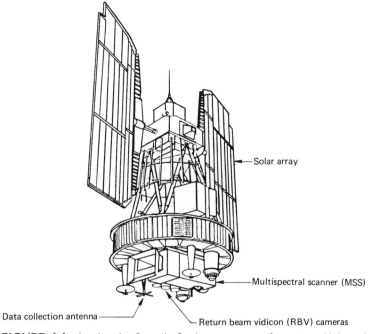

FIGURE 9.1 Landsat-1, -2, and -3 observatory configuration. (Adapted from [37].)

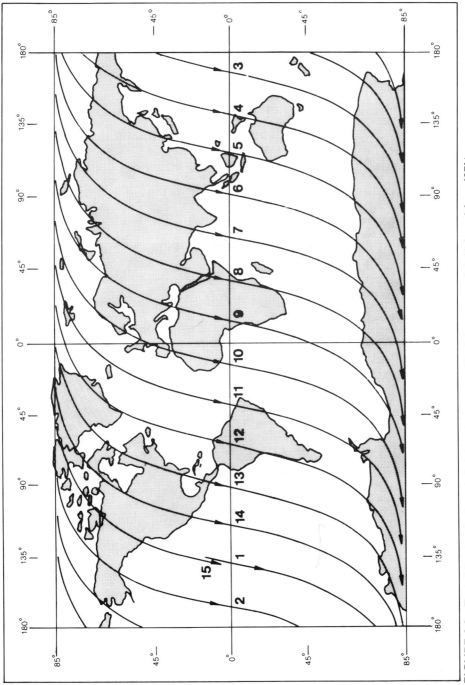

FIGURE 9.2   Typical Landsat-1, -2, and -3 daily orbit pattern. (Daylight passes only.) (Adapted from [37].)

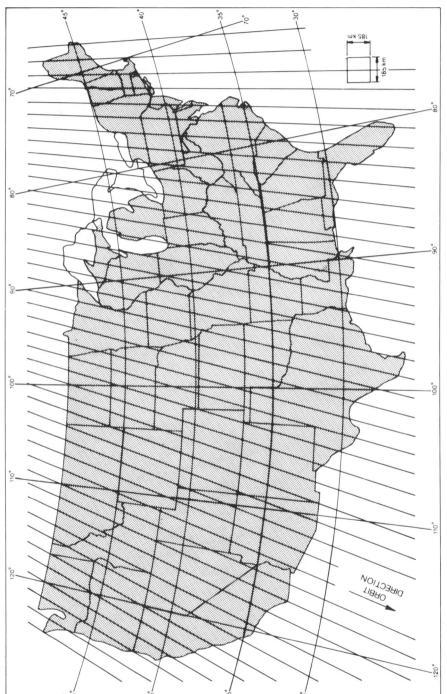

FIGURE 9.3 Landsat-1, -2, and -3 orbital passes over the conterminous United States. (Adapted from [37].)

orbits caused the satellites to keep precise pace with the sun's westward progress as the earth rotated. As a result, the satellite always crossed the equation at precisely the same local *sun* time (the local clock time varied with location within a time zone). Such orbits are referred to as *sun-synchronous.*

Landsat-1, -2 and -3 were launched into orbits that crossed the equator at 9:42 A.M. local sun time on each pass; however, orbital perturbations caused the crossing times to vary somewhat. This time was selected to take advantage of early morning skies that are generally clearer than later in the day. Because the system's orbital velocity was constant, all other points in its orbit were also passed at a relatively constant local sun time, either slightly after 9:42 A.M. in the northern hemisphere, or slightly before in the southern. The important implication of the sun-synchronous orbit is that it ensures repeatable sun illumination conditions during the specific seasons. Repeatable illumination conditions are desirable when mosaicking adjacent tracks of imagery and comparing annual changes in land cover.

Although sun-synchronous orbits ensure repeatable illumination conditions, these conditions vary with location and season. That is, the sun's rays strike the earth at varying solar elevation angles as a function of both latitude and time. For example, the sun's rays strike Sioux Falls, South Dakota, at approximately 20° in December and at 60° in July. Along a single January orbit, the solar elevation changes from 4° in Alaska to 45° near the equator. Likewise, the azimuth direction of solar illumination changes with season and latitude. In short, a sun-synchronous orbit does not compensate for changes in solar altitude, azimuth, or intensity. These factors are always changing and are compounded by variations in atmospheric conditions between scenes [54].

9.5 SENSORS ONBOARD LANDSAT-I, -2, AND -3

Landsat-1 and -2 were launched with two identical remote sensing systems onboard: (1) a three-channel RBV system, and (2) a four-channel MSS system. The RBV system consisted of three television-like cameras aimed to view the same 185 × 185 km ground area simultaneously. The nominal ground resolution of the cameras was about 80 m and the spectral sensitivity of each camera was essentially akin to that of a single layer of color infrared film: 0.475 to 0.575 μm (green); 0.580 to 0.680 μm (red); and 0.690 to 0.830 μm (near-infrared). These bands were designated as bands 1, 2, and 3. RBVs do not contain film, but instead their images are exposed by a shutter device and stored on a photosensitive surface within each camera. This surface is then scanned in raster form by an internal electron beam to produce a video signal just as in a conventional television camera.

Because RBVs image an entire scene instantaneously, in camera fashion, their images have greater inherent cartographic fidelity than those acquired by the Landsat MSS. Also, the RBVs contained a *reseau grid* in their image plane to facilitate geometric correction of the imagery. This resulted in an array of tick marks being precisely placed in each image. By knowing the observed image position versus the theoretical calibration position of these marks, almost all image distortion can be compensated for in the image recording process.

The RBV on Landsat-1 produced only 1690 scenes between July 23 and August 5, 1972, when a tape recorder switching problem (malfunctioning relay switch) forced a system shutdown. The RBV on Landsat-2 was operated primarily for engineering evaluation purposes and only occasional RBV imagery was obtained, primarily for cartographic uses in remote areas. Two major changes were introduced in the design of the RBV system onboard Landsat-3: the system sensed in a single broad band rather than multispectrally, and the spatial resolution of the system was improved by a factor of about 2.6 compared with the previous RBVs. The spectral sensitivity range of the system was 0.505 to 0.750 μm (green to near-IR). The change to a 30 m nominal ground resolution was achieved by doubling the focal length of the camera lens system, decreasing the exposure time to reduce image motion during exposure, and maintaining adequate exposure by removing the spectral filters of the previous RBVs. To compensate for the decrease in the ground area covered by doubling the focal length, a two-camera side-by-side configuration was employed. The two cameras were aligned to view adjacent 98 km square ground scenes with a 13 km sidelap, yielding a 183 × 98 km scene pair (Figure 9.4). Two successive scene pairs coincided nominally with one MSS scene. The four RBV scenes that filled each MSS scene were designated A, B, C, and D. Figure 9.5 shows one frame of RBV imagery from Landsat-3.

While not intended, the RBV systems onboard Landsat-1, -2, and -3 became secondary sources of data in comparison to the MSS systems flown on these satellites. Two factors contributed to this situation. First, RBV operations were plagued with various technical malfunctions. More importantly, the MSS systems were the first global monitoring systems capable of producing multispectral data in a digital format. The advantages in being able to process the MSS data by computer led to their widespread application during the Landsat-1, -2, and -3 era. Several tens of billions of square kilometers of the earth's surface (unique in time but repetitive in area) were imaged by the MSS systems onboard these satellites.

The MSS onboard Landsat-1, -2, and -3 covered a 185 km swath width in four wavelength bands: two in the visible spectrum at 0.5 to 0.6 μm (green) and 0.6 to 0.7 μm (red), and two in the near-infrared at 0.7 to 0.8 μm and 0.8 to 1.1 μm. These bands were designated as bands 4, 5, 6, and 7. The MSS onboard Landsat-3 also incorporated a thermal band (band 8) operating in the region 10.4 to 12.6 μm. However, operating problems caused this channel to fail shortly after launch. Thus, all three MSS systems effectively produced data in the same four bands. In fact, the identical bands were also used in the MSS systems flown on Landsats-4 and -5, but were designated as bands 1, 2, 3, and 4. In Figure 9.6 these bands of operation are compared with the spectral bands associated with color and color infrared film.

The MSS operating configuration is shown in Figure 9.7. The instantaneous field of view (IFOV) of the scanner is square and results in a ground resolution cell of approximately 79 m on a side. The total field of view scanned is approximately 11.56°. Because this angle is so small (compared to 90 to 120° in airborne scanners), an oscillating, instead of spinning, scan mirror is employed. The mirror oscillates once every 33 msec. Six contiguous lines are scanned simultaneously with each mirror oscillation. This permits the ground coverage rate to be achieved at one-sixth the single-line scan rate, resulting in improved system response characteristics. This

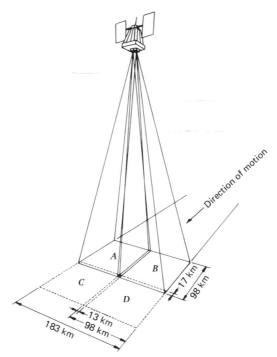

FIGURE 9.4 Landsat-3 RBV system configuration. (Adapted from [37].)

arrangement requires four arrays (one for each band) of six detectors each (one for each line). When not viewing the earth, the detectors are exposed to internal light and sun calibration sources.

The analog signal from each detector is converted to digital form by an onboard A-to-D converter. A digital number range of 0 to 63 (6 bits) is used for this purpose. These data are then scaled to other ranges during subsequent ground-based processing. (Normally, bands 4–6 are scaled to a range of 0 to 127 and band 7 is scaled to 0 to 63.)

The A-to-D converter samples the output of the detectors about 100,000 times a second, resulting in a nominal ground spacing of 56 m between readings. Because of this spacing, the image values form a matrix of 56 × 79 m cells (as shown in Figure 9.8). Note, however, that the brightness value for each pixel is actually derived from the full 79 × 79 m ground resolution cell (shaded area in Figure 9.8).

The MSS scans each line from west to east with the southward motion of the spacecraft providing the along-track progression of the scan lines. Each Landsat MSS scene is "framed" from the continuous MSS data swath so that it covers approximately a 185 × 185 km area with 10 percent endlap between successive scenes. A nominal scene consists of some 2340 scan lines, with about 3240 pixels per line or about 7,581,600 pixels per channel. With four spectral observations per pixel, each image

FIGURE 9.5   Landsat-3 RBV image, Cape Canaveral, Florida, March 14, 1978. 1:500,000.

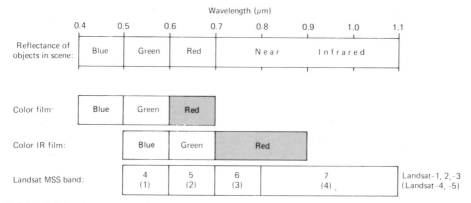

FIGURE 9.6 Spectral sensitivity of the four Landsat MSS bands compared with the spectral sensitivity of the three emulsion layers used in color and color infrared film.

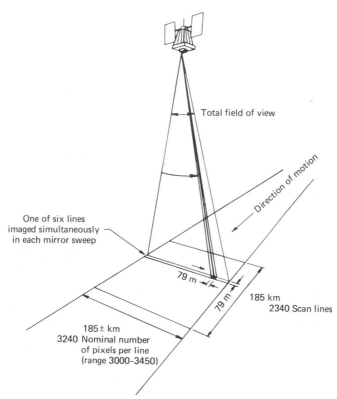

FIGURE 9.7 Landsat MSS operating configuration. (Adapted from [37].)

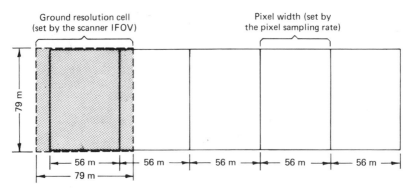

FIGURE 9.8   Ground resolution cell size versus MSS pixel size. (Adapted from [54].)

data set contains over 30 million observations. Considering that an image is collected in about 25 sec, the rate of data generation is enormous.

Figure 9.9 is a full-frame, band 5 Landsat MSS scene covering a portion of central New York. Note that the image area is a parallelogram, not a square, because of the earth's rotation during the 25 sec it takes the satellite to travel from the top of the scene to the bottom. The tick marks and numbers around the margins of this image refer to an approximate latitude and longitude (degrees and minutes) grid for the image. At the bottom of the image is a step wedge containing 15 steps corresponding to the full potential range of brightness values detected by the MSS. Not all steps are visible on this image because only a limited portion of the full scale was used in printing this scene.

Above the step wedge is an annotation block giving specific information about the acquisition of this image. For Figure 9.9, the block shows, from left to right, the date (10JUN75); the latitude and longitude of the center of the image in degrees and minutes (N43-11/W075-36); the latitude and longitude of the ground point directly beneath the satellite (the nadir) (N43-08/W075-29)—the discrepancy between this location and the center indicates a slight degree of tilt in the image; the sensor and band (MSS 5); the reception mode (D), specifying direct versus recorded; sun elevation and azimuth to nearest degree (SUN EL57 AZ117); various orbital and processing parameters (191-4668-N-1-N-D-2L); identification as Landsat satellite (NASA ERTS); and a unique scene identification number (E-5052-14562-5). The exact format of the annotation block has changed slightly through the course of the Landsat program.

In addition to black and white images of single bands, *color composites* can be generated for any MSS data set by printing three MSS bands in registration onto color film. Generally, band 4 is printed in blue, band 5 is printed in green, and band 7 is printed in red. This combination simulates the color rendition of color infrared film (Figure 9.6).

The distribution of Landsat data in the United States has gone through three distinct phases—experimental, transitional, and operational. During the experimental

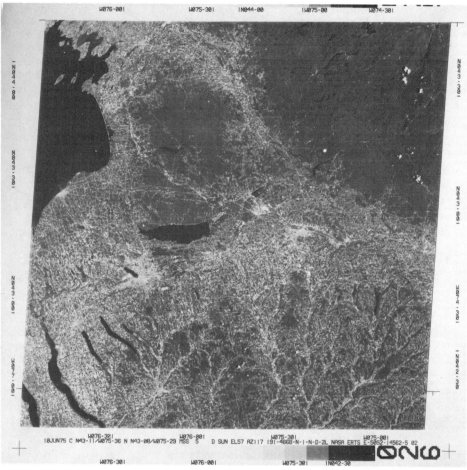

FIGURE 9.9 Full-frame, band 5, Landsat MSS scene, central New York, June 10, 1975. 1:1,700,000. Shown are portions of Lake Ontario (upper left), Adirondack Mountains (upper right), and Finger Lakes Region (lower left).

phase of Landsat-1, -2, and -3 all imagery and computer-compatible tapes were disseminated by the Earth Resources Observation System (EROS) Data Center at Sioux Falls, South Dakota. The satellites were operated by NASA and the data distribution process was operated by the USGS within the Department of Interior at that time. Gradually, all operations were assumed by the National Oceanic and Atmospheric Administration (NOAA) within the U.S. Department of Commerce during the transitional period. During this period, the operation of the Landsat program was transferred from the federal government to a commercial firm—The Earth Observation Satellite Company (EOSAT). This transfer was provided for within the Land Remote Sensing Commercialization Act of 1984. EOSAT assumed system operation on September 27, 1985. (Inquiries and orders for Landsat tapes and images can be addressed to EOSAT, 4300 Forbes Boulevard, Lanham, Maryland 20706; telephone 1-800-344-9933.)

As the above changes in the dissemination of Landsat data were being made, several technical improvements were also being made in the manner in which Landsat data were processed prior to distribution. Hence, the precise form of Landsat-1, -2, and -3 data products varied considerably over the course of time. For example, digital MSS data supplied in computer-compatible tape (CCT) format after 1979 were resampled (Section 10.2) into pixels having a nominal dimension of 57 × 57 m (compared to the 56 × 79 m size used previously).

During the Landsat-1, -2, and -3 era, several countries throughout the world established data receiving stations. The precise form of data products produced at these facilities likewise varied considerably. Accordingly, prospective users of data from these early missions are advised to closely investigate the exact form of data processing employed to produce the products they may wish to analyze. Also, prospective users of Landsat-3 data obtained between 1979 and 1983 should be aware that the MSS developed a scanning line-start synchronization problem in early 1979. This resulted in loss of all (or portions) of the data from the western 30 percent of each scene. The remaining 70 percent of each scene was normal.

Landsat-1, -2, and -3 images are catalogued according to their location within the Worldwide Reference System (WRS). In this system each orbit within a cycle is designated as a path. Along these paths, the individual nominal sensor frame-centers are designated as rows. Thus, a scene can be uniquely defined by specifying a path, a row, and a date. The WRS for Landsat-1, -2, and -3 has 251 paths corresponding to the number of orbits required to cover the earth in one 18-day cycle. Paths are numbered from 001 to 251, east to west. The rows are numbered so that row 60 coincides with the equator on the orbit's descending node. The U.S. archive of Landsat-1, -2, and -3 data contains 567,627 MSS and RBV scenes. As of 1986, the worldwide data base for MSS and RBV data contained some 1.3 million scenes. These data represent an irreplaceable resource for long-term global monitoring.

9.6   LANDSAT MSS IMAGE INTERPRETATION

The application of Landsat MSS image interpretation has been demonstrated in many fields, such as agriculture, botany, cartography, civil engineering, environmental monitoring, forestry, geography, geology, geophysics, land resource analysis, land use planning, oceanography, and water resource analysis.

As shown in Table 9.3, the image scale and area covered per frame are very different for Landsat images than for conventional aerial photographs. For example, more than 1600 aerial photographs at a scale of 1:20,000 with no overlap are required to cover the area of a single Landsat MSS image! Because of scale and resolution differences, Landsat images should be considered as a complementary interpretive tool instead of a replacement for low altitude aerial photographs. For example, the existence and/or significance of certain geologic features trending for tens or hundreds of kilometers,

TABLE 9.3   Comparison of Image Characteristics

Image format	Image scale	Area covered per frame (km²)
Low altitude USDA−ASCS aerial photographs (230 × 230 mm)	1:20,000	21
High altitude NASA aerial photographs (RB-57 or U-2) (230 × 230 mm)	1:120,000	760
Landsat scene (185 × 185 mm)	1:1,000,000	34,000

and clearly evident on a Landsat image, might escape notice on low altitude aerial photographs. On the other hand, housing quality studies from aerial imagery would certainly be more effective using low altitude aerial photographs rather than Landsat images, since individual houses cannot be resolved on Landsat MSS images. In addition, most Landsat MSS images can only be studied in two dimensions, whereas most aerial photographs are acquired in stereo.

The effective resolution (in terms of the smallest adjacent ground features that can be distinguished from each other) of Landsat MSS images is about 79 m (about 30 m on Landsat-3 RBV images). However, linear features as narrow as a few meters, having a reflectance that contrasts sharply with that of their surroundings, can often be seen on Landsat images (for example, two-lane roads, concrete bridges crossing water bodies, etc.). On the other hand, objects much larger than 79 m across may not be apparent if they have a very low reflectance contrast with their surroundings, and features detected in one band may not be detected in another.

As a line scanning system, the Landsat MSS produces images having one-dimensional relief displacement. Because there is displacement only in the scan direction and not in the flight track direction, Landsat images can be viewed in stereo only in areas of sidelap on adjacent orbit passes. This sidelap varies from about 85 percent near the poles to about 14 percent at the equator. Consequently, only a limited area of the globe may be viewed in stereo. Also, the vertical exaggeration when viewing Landsat in stereo is quite small compared to conventional airphotos. This stems from the extreme platform altitude (900 km) of the satellite compared to the base distance between images. Whereas, stereo airphotos may have a 4× vertical exaggeration, stereo Landsat vertical exaggeration ranges from about 1.3× at the equator to less than 0.4× at latitudes above about 70°. Subtle as this stereo effect is, geologists in particular have found stereoviewing in Landsat overlap areas quite valuable in studying topographic expression. However, most interpretations of Landsat imagery are made monoscopically, either because sidelapping imagery does not exist or because the relief displacement needed for stereoviewing is so small. In fact, because of the high altitude and narrow field of view of the MSS, images from the scanner contain little or no relief displacement in nonmountainous areas. When such images are properly processed, they can be used as planimetric maps at scales as large as 1:250,000.

Landsat MSS imagery has been used a great deal as a planimetric mapping tool in certain areas of the world. For example, the World Bank uses Landsat images for economic geography studies and site surveys in parts of the world where adequate maps do not exist. The USGS has published image maps and mosaics of selected areas at scales ranging from 1:1,000,000 to 1:250,000. The Defense Mapping Agency (DMA) has employed Landsat data to revise global aeronautical charts and to update hydrographic charts of shallow sea areas. The multinational petroleum companies also use Landsat images and digitally processed Landsat data as an integral part of their exploration strategy in many areas.

The most appropriate band or combination of bands of MSS imagery should be selected for each interpretive use. Bands 4[1] (green) and 5 (red) are usually best for detecting cultural features such as urban areas, roads, new subdivisions, gravel pits, and quarries. In such areas, band 5 is generally preferable because the better atmospheric penetration of red wavelengths provides a higher contrast image. In areas of deep, clear water, greater water penetration is achieved with band 4. Band 5 is excellent for showing silty water flowing into clear water (Figure 4.60a). Bands 6 and 7 (near-infrared) are best for delineating water bodies. Since energy of near-infrared wavelengths penetrates only a short distance into water, where it is absorbed with very little reflection, surface water features have a very dark tone in bands 6 and 7. Wetlands with standing water or wet organic soil where little vegetation has yet emerged also have a dark tone in bands 6 and 7, as do asphalt-surfaced pavements and wet bare soil areas. Both bands 5 and 7 are valuable in geologic studies, the largest single use of Landsat MSS data.

Figure 9.10, an enlargement of a small portion of a Landsat scene, illustrates the comparative appearance of the four Landsat MSS bands. The extent of the urban areas shown is best seen in bands 4 and 5 (light-toned). The major roads are best seen in band 5 (light-toned), clearly visible in band 4, undetectable in band 6, and slightly visible in band 7 (dark-toned). An airport is located 9 mm (on this image) above and to the right of the largest lake. It has a newly surfaced concrete runway and taxiway running vertically on the figure. To the right of this runway is a group of intersecting asphalt-surfaced runways. The concrete pavement is clearly visible in bands 4 and 5 (light-toned), very faint in band 6 (light-toned), and undetectable in band 7. The asphalt pavement is very faint in bands 4 and 5 (light-toned), reasonably clear in band 6 (dark-toned), and best seen in band 7 (dark-toned). The four major lakes and connecting river are best seen in bands 6 and 7 (dark-toned). These lakes have a natural green color in mid-July resulting from the presence of algae in the water. In the band 4 image, all four lakes have a tone similar to the surrounding agricultural land, which consists principally of green-leafed crops such as corn. The two lakes at upper left are mostly surrounding by urban development, and, therefore, their shorelines can be reasonably well detected. The two lakes at lower right are principally surrounded by agricultural land and their shorelines are often indistinct. The shorelines are more distinct in band 5, but still somewhat difficult to delineate. The surface water of all four major lakes and the

---

[1] For simplicity, we use only the Landsat-1 to -3 MSS band numbers here (4, 5, 6, and 7). They are equivalent to bands 1, 2, 3, and 4 of the Landsat-4 and -5 MSS.

connecting river is clearly seen in both bands 6 and 7 (dark-toned). The portions of this scene in agricultural use have a rectangular field pattern with different tones representing different crops. This is best seen in bands 5, 6, and 7. For purposes of crop identification and mapping from MSS images, the most effective procedure is to view two or more bands simultaneously in an additive color viewer or to interpret color composite images. Small forested areas in this scene appear dark-toned in bands 4 and 5. In regions receiving a winter snowfall, forested areas can best be mapped using wintertime images where the ground is snowcovered. On such images, the forested and shrubland areas will appear dark-toned against a background of light-toned snow.

As mentioned in Section 9.4, each Landsat satellite passes over the same area on the earth's surface during daylight hours about 20 times per year. The actual number of times per year a given ground area is imaged depends on amount of cloud cover, sun angle, and whether or not the satellite is in operation on any specific pass. This provides the opportunity for many areas to have Landsat images available for several dates per year. Because the appearance of the ground in many areas with climatic change is dramatically different in different seasons, the image interpretation process is often improved by utilizing images from two or more dates.

Figure 9.11 shows band 5 images of a portion of Wisconsin as imaged in September and December. The ground is snow covered (about 200 mm deep) in the December image and all water bodies are frozen, except for a small stretch of the Wisconsin River. The physiography of the area can be better appreciated by viewing the December image, due in part to the low solar elevation angle in winter that accentuates subtle relief. A series of stream valleys cuts into the horizontally bedded sedimentary rock in the upper-left portion of this scene. The snow covered upland areas and valley floors have a very light tone, whereas the steep, tree covered, valley sides have a darker tone. The identification of urban, agricultural, and water areas can better be accomplished using the September image. The identification of forested areas can be more positively done using the December image.

The synoptic view afforded by space platforms can be particularly useful for observing short-lived phenomena. However, the use of Landsat images to capture such ephemeral events as floods, forest fires, and volcanic activity is, to some degree, a hit-or-miss proposition. If a satellite passes over such an event on a clear day when the imaging system is in operation, excellent images of such events can be obtained. On the other hand, such events can easily be missed if there are no images obtained within the duration of the event or, as is often true during floods, extensive cloud cover obscures the earth's surface. However, some of these events do leave lingering traces. For example, soil is typically wet in a flooded area for at least several days after the flood waters have receded and this condition may be imaged even if the flood waters are not. Also, the area burned by a forest fire will have a dark image tone for a considerable period of time after the actual fire has ceased.

Figure 9.12 shows band 7 images of a portion of the Wisconsin River in July 1974 and March 1973. In the July image, the principal channels of this braided river can be seen as a very dark tone winding across the scene from right to left. The river flow on the date of this image was 200 m³/sec. The March image shows spring flood waters overtopping the stream channel banks and flowing onto the flood plain. The river flow

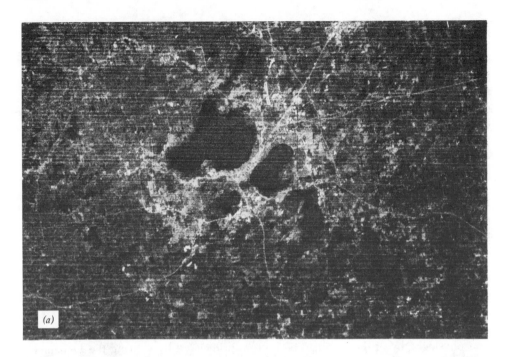

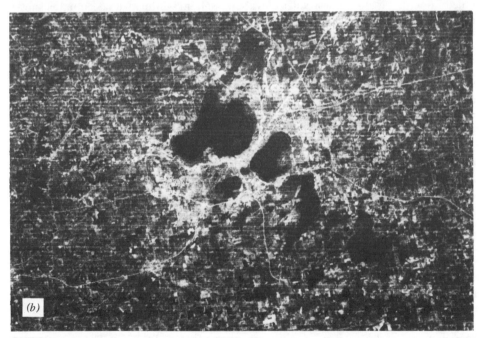

FIGURE 9.10 Individual Landsat MSS bands, Madison, Wisconsin, and vicinity, July 13, 1974. 1:400,000. (a) Band 4, green, 0.5 to 0.6 μm. (b) Band 5, red, 0.6 to 0.7 μm. (c) Band 6, near-infrared, 0.7 to 0.8 μm. (d) Band 7, near-infrared, 0.8 to 1.1 μm.

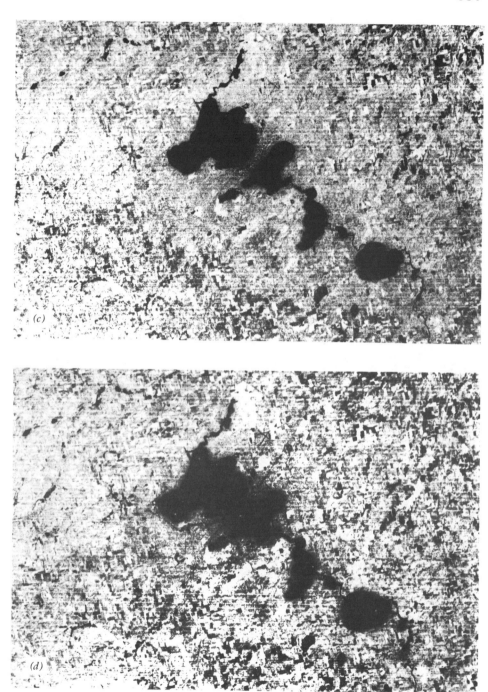

(c)

(d)

FIGURE 9.10 (continued)

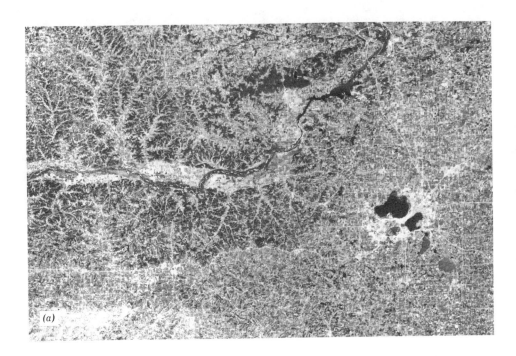

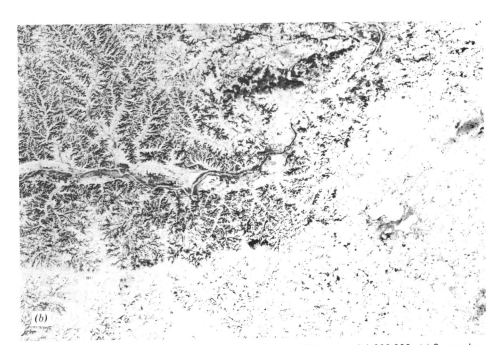

FIGURE 9.11 Landsat MSS band 5 images, southwestern Wisconsin. 1:1,000,000. *(a)* September 15, 1972. *(b)* December 14, 1972.

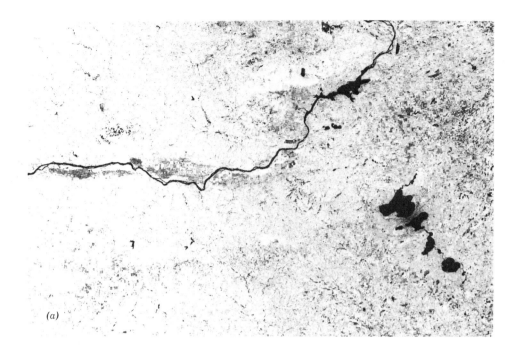

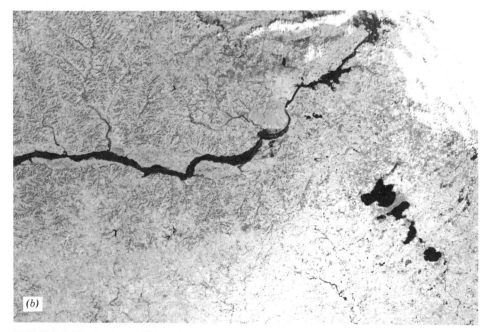

FIGURE 9.12 Landsat MSS band 7 images, southwestern Wisconsin. 1:1,000,000. *(a)* July 13, 1974. *(b)* March 14, 1973.

on this date was 1300 m^3/sec, a flood rate that can be expected once every four years on this river.

Figure 9.13a is a Landsat scene showing an area about 390 km northwest of Fairbanks, Alaska [51, 66]. A forest fire was burning at the time (note smoke in several locations) and had burned approximately 330 km^2 when this image was acquired. The black tone of the burned area contrasts sharply with the lighter tones of the surrounding unburned forest area.

Figure 9.13b is a Landsat scene showing an active volcano on the northeastern tip of Kunashir Island, USSR [51]. Two days before this Landsat image was acquired, the 1800 m tall strato volcano Tiatia, which had been dormant for 161 years, began to erupt in a series of violent explosions. A great plume of ash-laden gases, such as seen here, rose to heights of 4600 m or more. This eruption cloud is issuing from a new vent located on the south flank of the volcano (north is essentially to the top of this image). Much of the surface of the volcano on the north, east, and south faces has been covered by volcanic ash to depths exceeding 600 mm (note the dark-toned areas).

Figure 9.14 illustrates extensive geologic features that are clearly visible on Landsat images. Figure 9.14a is a band 5 Landsat image showing an area north and east of Los Angeles, California [66]. Figure 9.14b is a map of major geologic faults visible on this Landsat image along which movement is known to have occurred. The well-known San Andreas fault that bisects this image is nearly 1000 km long. The San Francisco earthquake of 1906 occurred because of movement along this fault. The six solid dots shown on this map are the centers of earthquakes of magnitude 6.0 or greater on the Richter scale which occurred on the dates shown. The movement along the San Andreas fault in 1857 is estimated to have been as great as 10 m (land on the Pacific Ocean side of the fault is moving to the north relative to the continental side).

A variety of large circular features have been observed on Landsat images. Most of these are either volcanic calderas or meteorite impact crater scars. Figure 9.15 illustrates the 66 km wide Manicouagan ring in east-central Quebec. This circular depression serves as a water storage reservoir (frozen and snow covered on this image) for hydroelectric power generation. Such broad scale features can only be observed in their entirety from orbital altitudes. This feature had been considered a volcano−tectonic structure. However, the probability that it is a meteorite crater scar has recently gained wide acceptance. The concept that the Manicouagan structure is the result of a great meteorite impact would have major implications if verified, because it is as large as many of the large lunar craters.

The two MSS images in Figure 9.16 show Mt. St. Helens, Washington, before and after its 1980 eruptions. In (a), we see the snow-capped peak of the 3000 m high volcano in the lower center. Between Mt. St. Helens and the other snow-capped peak to the north, we see dark-toned Spirit Lake. Toward the right, we see many clear-cut areas, where the dark-toned Douglas fir trees stand in stark contrast to the light-toned clear-cut areas. In (b), we see the dramatic contrasts in land cover brought about by the May 18, 1980, eruption of Mt. St. Helens. After vast quantities of ash were ejected from the summit, and large amounts of rock and pyroclastic debris slid down the north face of the mountain, the summit dropped 400 m, leaving the large crater visible in (b).

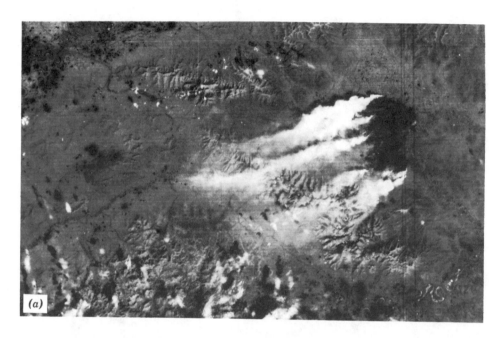

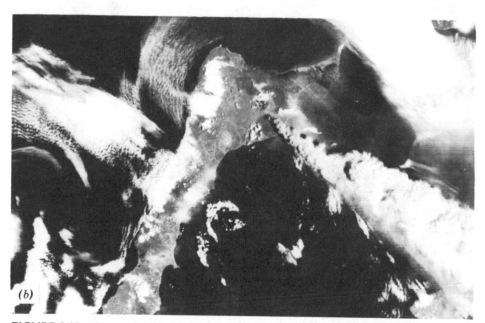

FIGURE 9.13 Observation of short-lived phenomena on Landsat MSS imagery. (Black and white reproductions of color composite images.) 1:1,000,000. *(a)* Active forest fire in Alaska, July 26, 1972. *(b)* Volcanic eruption in USSR, July 16, 1973.

FIGURE 9.14 Extensive geologic features visible on Landsat MSS imagery. *(a)* Landsat band 5 image, Los Angeles, California, and vicinity, October 21, 1972. 1:1,000,000. *(b)* Map showing major geologic faults and major earthquake sites. (Adapted from [66].)

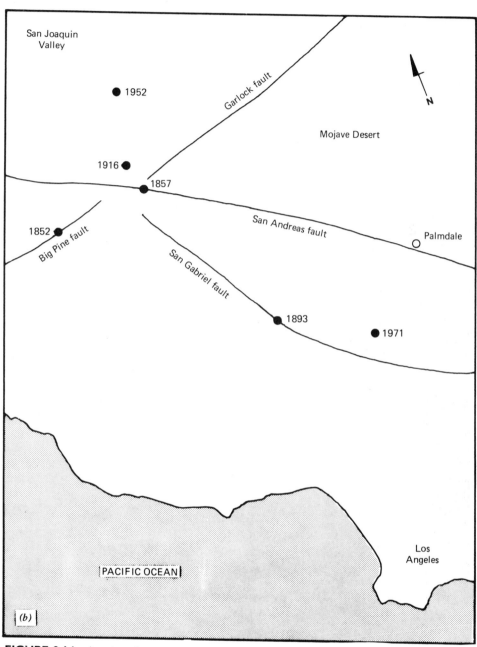

FIGURE 9.14 *(continued)*

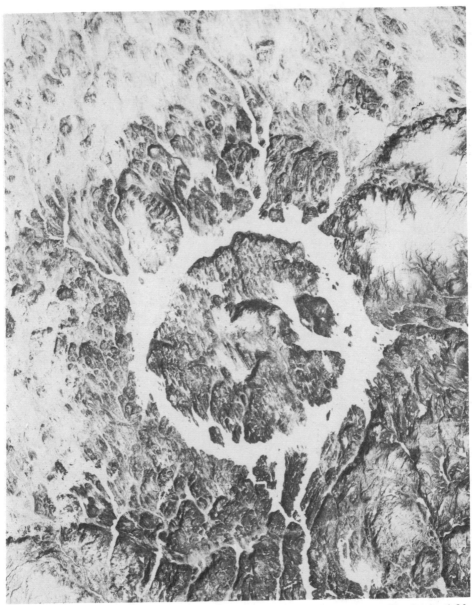

FIGURE 9.15 Landsat MSS band 6, Manicouagan ring, east-central Quebec, Canada, April 20, 1974. 1:1,000,000.

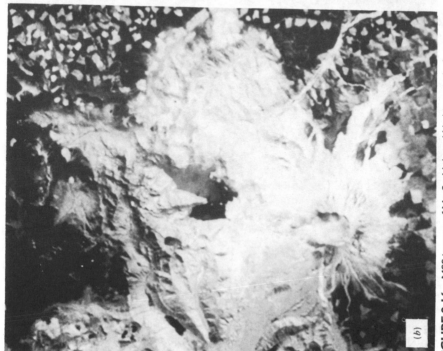

FIGURE 9.16   MSS images of Mt. St. Helens, Washington, before and after its 1980 eruptions. (*a*) July 25, 1976. (*b*) July 31, 1980. 1:240,000. North is to the top of these images. Black and white copies of false color composites. (Courtesy Conoco, Exploration Research Division.)

Several mud and debris flows and ensuing floods swept through the valleys to the west of the mountain, and large areas northward from the mountain were covered with deep deposits of airborne volcanic ash (gray tones in (b)).

Figure 9.17 is an MSS image showing part of the Province of Manitoba, Canada. The capital city, Winnipeg, can be seen at upper right as a large light-toned urban area ringed by roads. To the southwest of the city is a light-toned area of dead vegetation surrounded by a medium-toned agricultural area. This light-toned area is a tornado and hail scar resulting from a storm occurring about 2 weeks before. This MSS image was used by crop insurance companies to help settle crop loss claims.

Figure 9.18 is an MSS image showing tropical deforestation on the island of East Kalimantan, Indonesia. In response to intense population pressures on the island of Java, the Indonesian government has established a transmigration program under which tens of thousands of families per year are being relocated to less populated outer islands. The newly established transmigration sites have an area of at least 50,000 ha each, with each family being given a plot of land 2 to 5 ha. Figure 9.18 shows an extensive area of forest land being cleared for transmigration site development. The dark-toned area in the left portion of this image is forested land. Areas being actively cleared are principally to the left of the dark-toned river that runs from top to bottom in

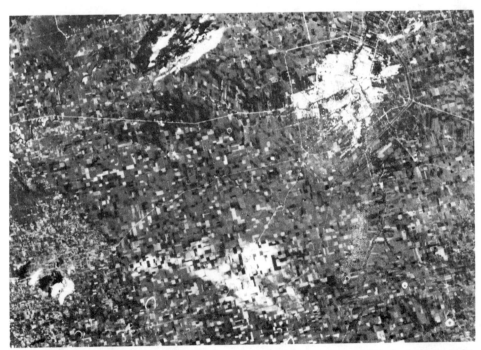

FIGURE 9.17   MSS image of Manitoba, Canada, showing tornado and hail scar, July 18, 1984. 1:900,000. North is to the top of this image. Black and white copy of false color composite. (Courtesy Canada Centre for Remote Sensing.)

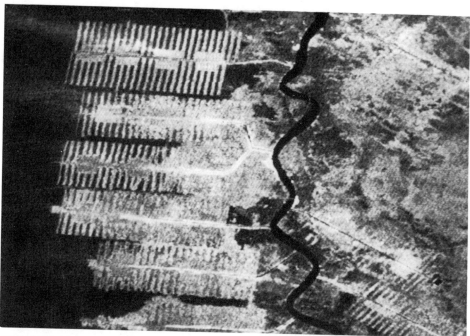

FIGURE 9.18 MSS image of East Kalimantan, Indonesia, showing tropical deforestation, August 1984. 1:225,000. Black and white copy of a band 4—5—7 (green, red, near-infrared) color composite. (Courtesy LAPAN and Institut Pertanian Bogor, Indonesia.)

this image. Each of the six tracts of land to the left of the river has a central canal with dozens of drainage ditches at right angles, forming a trellis pattern. The light-toned "fingers" cutting into the forested land are cleared areas. The indistinct lighter-toned plumes from the nearly cleared areas to the left edge of the image are smoke plumes from burning debris. The area to the right of the river has been cleared previously.

9.7 ORBIT CHARACTERISTICS OF LANDSAT-4 AND -5

Landsat-4 and -5, like their predecessors, were launched into repetitive, circular, sun-synchronous, near-polar orbits. However, these orbits were lowered from 900 to 705 km. These lower orbits were chosen to make the satellites potentially retrievable by the Space Shuttle and to aid in the improvement of the ground resolution of the sensors onboard.

As shown in Figure 9.19 Landsat-4 and -5 orbits have an inclination angle of 98.2° (8.2° from normal) with respect to the equator. The satellite crosses the equator on the north-to-south portion of each orbit at 9:45 A.M. local sun time. Each orbit takes approximately 99 min, with just over 14.5 orbits being completed in a day. Due to

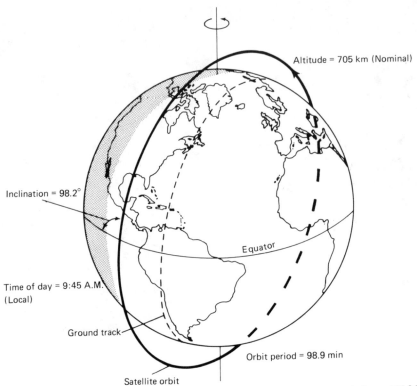

FIGURE 9.19 Sun-synchronous orbit of Landsat-4 and -5. (Adapted from NASA diagram.)

earth rotation, the distance between ground tracks for consecutive orbits is approximately 2752 km at the equator (Figure 9.20).

The above orbit results in a 16 day repeat cycle for each satellite. The orbits of Landsat-4 and -5 were established 8 days out of phase, such that when both satellites were operational an 8 day repeat coverage cycle could be maintained with alternating coverage by each satellite. As shown in Figure 9.21, the time interval between adjacent coverage tracks of the same satellite is 7 days. This coverage pattern is quite different from that of the previous three satellites, which had 18 day orbital cycles and a 1 day interval between orbits over adjacent tracks. Consequently, Landsat-4 and -5 images are catalogued according to a set of WRS paths different from those used to reference data from Landsat -1, -2, and -3. The Landsat-4 and -5 WRS is made up of 233 paths numbered 001 to 233, east to west, with path 001 crossing the equator at longitude 64°36′W. The same number of rows is used as in the previous WRS system. That is, row 60 coincides with the equator at the orbits' descending node. Row 1 of each path starts at 80°47′N latitude.

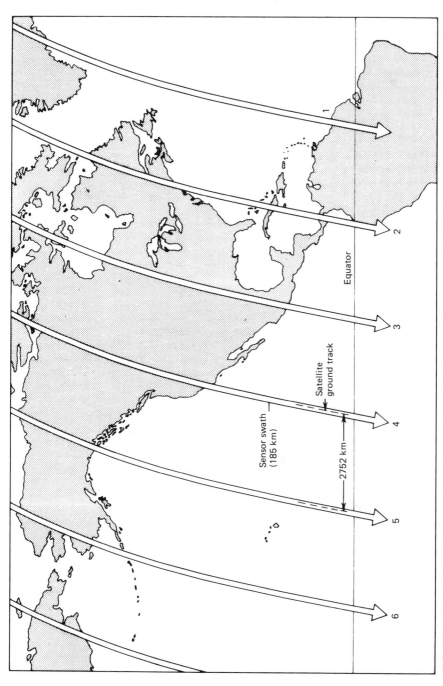

FIGURE 9.20 Spacing between adjacent Landsat-4 or -5 orbit tracks at the equator. The earth revolves 2752 km to the east at the equator between passes. (Adapted from NASA diagram.)

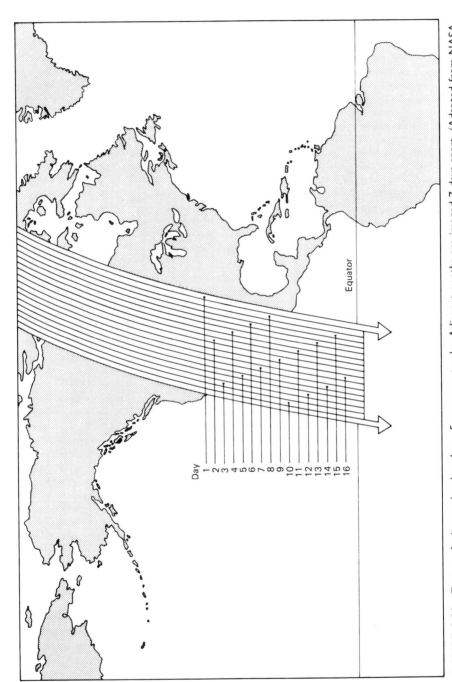

FIGURE 9.21   Timing of adjacent Landsat-4 or -5 coverage tracks. Adjacent swaths are imaged 7 days apart. (Adapted from NASA diagram.)

9.8   SENSORS ONBOARD LANDSAT-4 AND -5

Figure 9.22 shows the design of the Landsat-4 and -5 satellites which include both the MSS and the TM. This spacecraft weighs approximately 2000 kg and includes four 1.5 × 2.3 m solar panels, which are mounted to one side. The high gain antenna shown protruding above the spacecraft can be used to relay data through geosynchronous communication satellites included in the *Tracking and Data Relay Satellite System* (*TDRSS*). (Currently the only operational satellite in this system is TDRS-1, placed at 41°W longitude and providing near-complete coverage of the Western hemisphere.) Direct transmission of MSS and TM data to ground receiving stations is made possible via the X-band and S-band antennas onboard the satellite. The data transmission rates involved are substantial; the MSS transmits 15 megabits per second (Mbps) and the TM transmits 85 Mbps. (The MSS has been flown on these missions primarily to ensure continuity of data for receiving stations unable to receive and process TM data.)

The MSS onboard Landsat-4 and -5 is essentially identical to the MSS sensors on the previous Landsat satellites. The across-track swath of 185 km has been maintained at the lower orbit altitude by increasing the total field of view to 14.92° (from 11.56° on previous systems). The optics of the MSS system have also been modified to yield an 82 × 82 m IFOV to correspond essentially to the 79 × 79 m IFOV of the previous

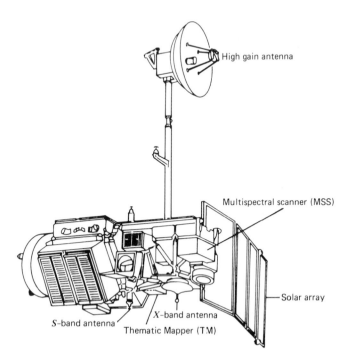

FIGURE 9.22   Landsat-4 and -5 observatory configuration. (Adapted from NASA diagram.)

systems. The same four spectral bands are used for data collection but they have been renumbered. That is, bands 1−4 of the Landsat-4 and -5 MSS correspond directly to bands 4−7 of the previous MSS systems (Figure 9.6).

The TM is a highly advanced multispectral scanner incorporating a number of spectral, radiometric, and geometric design improvements relative to the MSS. Spectral improvements include the acquisition of data in seven bands instead of four, with new bands in the visible (blue), mid-infrared, and thermal portions of the spectrum. Also, based on experience with MSS data and extensive field radiometer research results, the wavelength range and location of the TM bands (Table 9.2) have been chosen to improve the spectral differentiability of major earth surface features.

Radiometrically, the TM performs its onboard analog-to-digital signal conversion over a quantization range of 256 digital numbers (8 bits). This corresponds to a fourfold increase in the gray scale range relative to the 64 digital numbers (6 bits) used by the MSS. This finer radiometric precision permits observation of smaller changes in radiometric magnitudes in a given band and provides greater sensitivity to changes in relationships between bands. Thus, differences in radiometric values that are lost in one digital number in MSS data may now be distinguished.

Geometrically, TM data are collected using a 30 m IFOV (for all but the thermal band which has a 120 m IFOV). This represents a decrease in the lineal dimensions of the IFOV of approximately 2.6 times, or a reduction in the area of the IFOV of approximately 7 times. At the same time, several design changes have been incorporated within the TM to improve the accuracy of the geodetic positioning of the data. Most geometrically corrected TM data are supplied using 28.5 by 28.5 m pixels registered to the Space Oblique Mercator (SOM) cartographic projection. The data may also be fit to the Universal Transverse Mercator (UTM) or Polar Stereographic projections.

Table 9.4 lists the seven spectral bands of the TM, along with a brief summary of the intended principal applications of each. The TM bands are more finely tuned for vegetation discrimination than those of the MSS for several reasons. The green and red bands of the TM (bands 2 and 3) are narrower than their MSS counterparts. Also, the near-infrared TM band (4) is narrower than the combined bands of the MSS in this region and centered in a region of maximum sensitivity to plant vigor. Sensitivity to plant water stress is obtained in both of the TM mid-infrared bands (5 and 7). Plant stress discrimination is also aided by data from the TM blue band (1).

In addition to improved discrimination of vegetation, the TM has been designed to afford expanded or improved use of satellite data in a number of other application areas. Among these is the use of TM data (particularly from band 1) in the field of bathymetry. Likewise, the mid-infrared bands (5 and 7) have proven to be extremely valuable in discrimination of rock types. Band 5 is also ideal for differentiating between snow and cloud covered areas. Finally, band 6 makes TM data potentially useful in a range of thermal mapping applications. We treat the visual interpretation of TM data in the next section of our discussion and the digital processing of TM data in Chapter 10. In the remainder of this section we discuss the basic differences in the design and operation of the TM and the MSS.

TABLE 9.4 Thematic Mapper Spectral Bands

Band	Wavelength (μm)	Nominal spectral location	Principal applications
1	0.45−0.52	Blue	Designed for water body penetration, making it useful for coastal water mapping. Also useful for soil/ vegetation discrimination, forest type mapping, and cultural feature identification.
2	0.52−0.60	Green	Designed to measure green reflectance peak of vegetation (Figure 1.10) for vegetation discrimination and vigor assessment. Also useful for cultural feature identification.
3	0.63−0.69	Red	Designed to sense in a chlorophyll absorption region (Figure 1.10) aiding in plant species differentiation. Also useful for cultural feature identification.
4	0.76−0.90	Near-infrared	Useful for determining vegetation types, vigor, and biomass content, for delineating water bodies, and for soil moisture discrimination.
5	1.55−1.75	Mid-infrared	Indicative of vegetation moisture content and soil moisture. Also useful for differentiation of snow from clouds.
6[a]	10.4−12.5	Thermal infrared	Useful in vegetation stress analysis, soil moisture discrimination, and thermal mapping applications.
7[a]	2.08−2.35	Mid-infrared	Useful for discrimination of mineral and rock types. Also sensitive to vegetation moisture content.

[a]Bands 6 and 7 are out of wavelength sequence because band 7 was added to the TM late in the original system design process.

Whereas the MSS collects data only when its IFOV is traversing in the west-to-east direction along a scan line, the TM acquires data during both the forward (west-to-east) and reverse (east-to-west) sweeps of its scan mirror. This bidirectional scanning procedure is employed to reduce the rate of oscillation of the scan mirror and to increase the time an individual detector is able to dwell upon a given portion of the earth within its IFOV. The TM scans through a total field of view of 15.4° (±7.7° from nadir). It completes approximately seven combined forward and reverse scan cycles per second. This relatively slow rate limits the acceleration of the scan mirror, improving the geometric integrity of the data collection process and improving the signal-to-noise performance of the system.

Another major difference between the TM and the MSS is the number of detectors used for the various bands of sensing. Whereas the MSS employs six detectors to record data in each of its four bands of sensing (total of 24 detectors), the TM uses 16 detectors for all nonthermal bands and four detectors for the thermal band (total of 100 detectors). That is, 16 lines of each nonthermal band and four lines of thermal data are acquired with each sweep of the scan mirror. Silicon detectors are used for bands 1−4 and these are located within a primary focal plane assembly (Figure 9.23). The detectors for bands 5−7 are located in a second focal plane assembly incorporating passive radiation cooling to increase their radiometric sensitivity. Indium antimonide (InSb) detectors are employed for bands 5 and 7, and mercury cadmium telluride (HgCdTe) detectors are used for band 6.

At any instant in time, all 100 detectors view a different area on the ground due to the spatial separation of the individual detectors within the two TM focal planes. Figure 9.23 illustrates the projection of the detector IFOVs onto the ground. Accurate band-to-band data registration requires knowledge of the relative projection of the detectors in both focal planes as a function of time. This information is derived from data concerning the relative position of the individual detector arrays with respect to the optical axis, the spacecraft position and attitude, and the motion of the scan mirror during successive scan cycles. A *scan angle monitor* on the scan mirror generates signals indicating the mirror's angular position as a function of time. These signals are called scan mirror correction data and are transmitted to the ground for incorporation into the geometric processing of TM image data.

Signals from the scan angle monitor are also used to guide the motions of a *scan line corrector* located in front of the primary focal plane (Figure 9.23). The function of the scan angle corrector is illustrated in Figure 9.24. During each scan mirror sweep, the scan line corrector rotates the TM line-of-sight backward along the satellite ground track to compensate for the forward motion of the spacecraft. This prevents the overlap and underlap of scan lines and produces straight scan lines which are perpendicular to the ground track.

The TM also employs an internal radiometric calibration source consisting of three tungsten filament lamps, a blackbody for the thermal band, and a pivot mounted shutter. The shutter passes through the field of view of the instrument's detectors each time the scan mirror changes directions. The shutter permits light from the lamps to pass into the field of view of the nonthermal bands directly, and a mirror on the shutter directs energy from the thermal calibration source into the field of view of the thermal detectors. These calibration sources are used to monitor the radiometric response of the various detectors over the sensor's service life.

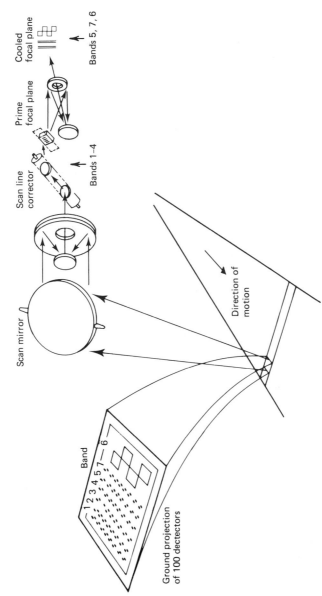

FIGURE 9.23 TM optical path and projection of detector IFOVs on earth surface. (Adapted from NASA diagram.)

Direction of spacecraft motion

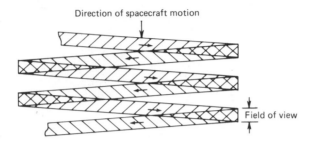

Field of view

(a) Uncompensated scan lines

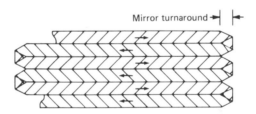

(b) Correction for satellite motion

Mirror turnaround

(c) Compensated scan lines

FIGURE 9.24   Schematic of TM scan line correction process. (Adapted from NASA diagram.)

9.9   LANDSAT TM IMAGE INTERPRETATION

Landsat TM images are useful for image interpretation for a much wider range of applications than Landsat MSS images. This is because the TM has both an increase in the number of spectral bands and an improvement in spatial resolution as compared with the MSS. The MSS images are most useful for large area analyses, such as geologic mapping. More specific mapping, such as detailed land cover mapping, is difficult on MSS images because so many pixels of the original data are "mixed pixels," pixels containing more than one cover type. With the decreased IFOV of the TM data, the area containing mixed pixels is smaller and interpretation accuracies are increased. The TM's improved spectral and radiometric resolution also aid image interpretation.

Figure 9.25 illustrates the dramatic improvement in resolution from the MSS's IFOV of 79 × 79 m to the TM's IFOV of 30 × 30 m. This figure shows the Detroit,

FIGURE 9.25 Detroit, Michigan, airport and vicinity. 1:120,000. *(a)* Landsat-3 MSS band 5. *(b)* Landsat-4 TM band 3.

Michigan, airport and vicinity as imaged on two different dates by (a) the Landsat-3 MSS and (b) the Landsat-4 TM. Many indistinct light-toned patches on the MSS image can be clearly seen as recent suburban development on the TM image. Also, features such as agricultural field patterns that are indistinct on the MSS image can be clearly seen on the TM image.

As outlined in Table 9.4, the TM has more narrowly defined wavelength ranges for the three TM bands roughly comparable to MSS bands 1–4, and has added bands in four wavelength ranges not covered by the MSS bands. Figure 9.26 shows all seven TM bands for a summertime image of an urban fringe area near Madison, Wisconsin (same geographical area as shown in center top of Figure 9.10, an MSS image). This figure shows the same excellent resolution of urban areas and field patterns as shown in Figure 9.25b. Also, the characteristic appearance of the various bands is illustrated.

For example, the blue-green water of the lake, river, and ponds in the scene has moderate reflection in bands 1 and 2 (blue and green), a small amount of reflection in band 3 (red), and virtually no reflection in bands 4, 5, and 7 (near- and mid-infrared); reflection from roads and urban streets is least in band 4; and, overall reflection from agricultural crops is highest in band 4. Note also the high band 4 reflectance of the golf courses appearing to the right-center of the river and the right-center of the lake. The distinct tonal lineations from upper right (northeast) to lower left (southwest) in these images are a legacy from the most recent glaciation of Wisconsin. Glacial ice movement from northeast to southwest left a terrain characterized by many drumlins (Section 4.10) and scoured bedrock hills. Present-day crop and soil moisture patterns reflect the alignment of this grooved terrain. The thermal band (band 6) has a less distinct appearance than the other bands because the IFOV of this band is 120 m. It has an indistinct, rather than blocky, appearance because the data have been resampled into the 30 m format of the other bands. As would be expected on a summertime thermal image recorded during the daytime, the roads and urban areas have the highest radiant temperature, and the water bodies have the lowest radiant temperature.

Plate 12 shows six color composite images of the same area as shown in Figure 9.26. Table 9.5 shows the color combinations used to generate each of these composites. Note that (a) is a "normal color" composite, (b) is a "color infrared" composite, and (c)–(f) are some of the many other "false color" combinations that can be produced. A preliminary study at the USGS EROS Data Center [41] showed an interpreter preference for several specific band–color combinations for various features. For the mapping of water sediment patterns, a normal color composite of bands 1, 2, and 3 (displayed as blue, green, and red) was preferred. For most other applications, such as mapping urban features and vegetation types, the combinations of (1) bands 2, 3, and 4 (color infrared composite), (2) bands 3, 4 and 7, and (3) bands 3, 4, and 5 (all in the order blue, green, and red) were preferred. However, a great deal of personal preference is involved in band–color combinations for interpretive purposes, and, for specific applications, other combinations could be optimum.

Figure 9.27 shows a Landsat TM band 6 (thermal) image of Green Bay and Lake Michigan (between the states of Wisconsin and Michigan). In this image, the land area

FIGURE 9.26 Individual Landsat TM bands, suburban Madison, Wisconsin, August 26, 1984. 1:115,000. *(a)* Band 1— 0.45 to 0.52 μm (blue); *(b)* band 2— 0.52 to 0.60 μm (green); *(c)* band 3 — 0.63 to 0.69 μm (red); *(d)* band 4 — 0.76 to 0.90 μm (near-infrared); *(e)* band 5 — 1.55 to 1.75 μm (mid-infrared); *(f)* band 7—2.08 to 2.35 μm (mid-infrared); *(g)* band 6 —10.4 to 12.5 μm (thermal infrared).

FIGURE 9.26 *(continued)*

FIGURE 9.26   *(continued)*

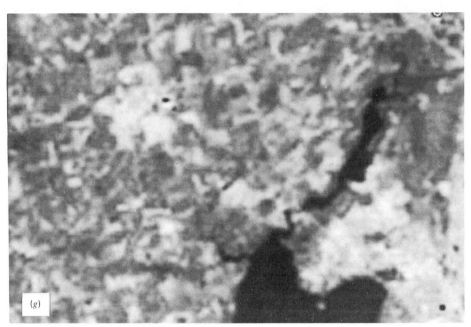

(g)

FIGURE 9.26   *(continued)*

TABLE 9.5   TM Band–Color Combinations
Shown in Plate 12

Plate 12	TM band–color assignment in composite		
	Blue	Green	Red
(a)	1	2	3
(b)	2	3	4
(c)	3	4	5
(d)	3	4	7
(e)	3	5	7
(f)	4	5	7

has been masked out and is shown as black (using techniques described in Section 10.4). Based on a correlation with field observations of water surface temperature, the image data were sliced into six gray levels, with the darkest tones having a temperature less than 12°C, the brightest tones having a temperature greater than 20°C, and each of the four intermediate levels representing a 2°C range between 12 and 20°C [29].

FIGURE 9.27 Landsat TM band 6 (thermal infrared) image, Green Bay and Lake Michigan, Wisconsin–Michigan, July 18, 1984. 1:250,000.

Figure 9.28 shows a Landsat TM band 5 image illustrating timber clear-cutting practices in the northwestern United States. Here the darker-toned areas are dense stands of Douglas fir, and the lighter-toned areas are recently cleared areas consisting of tree stumps, shrubs, and various grasses, in areas where essentially all trees have been removed during timber harvesting operations. Mottled, intermediate-toned,

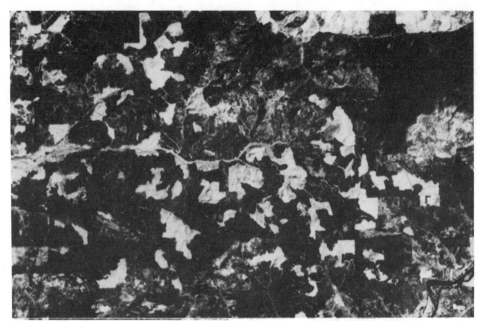

FIGURE 9.28 Landsat TM band 5 (mid-infrared) image, Cascade Mountains, Western Oregon, April 14, 1984. 1:150,000.

areas have been replanted with Douglas fir trees and are at an intermediate growth stage.

Figure 9.29a is a statewide Landsat TM band 5 image map showing the State of Illinois. Thirteen individual TM scenes acquired during a 26 day period in the fall of 1982 were mosaicked together to create this map. The mosaic was prepared through a photomechanical process that utilizes contrast-balanced film images rather than the paper prints traditionally used in mosaic preparation. This photomechanical method resulted in high geometric accuracy and optimum image resolution by using stable base films during all steps of mosaic preparation, with the resulting film composite having the appearance of a single image. (A color composite version of this image was published in 1985 at a scale of 1:500,000 by the Illinois Geological Survey, with the cooperation of the USGS and others.) Figure 9.29b is an enlargement of a small portion of this image that shows the spatial detail inherent in the mosaic. The area covered by this enlargement includes the Mississippi river flood plain and adjacent upland in eastern Iowa and northwestern Illinois. Circular field patterns associated with center-pivot irrigation agriculture can be seen on the excessively drained soils of the flood plain. The loess-covered bluff line to the left of the Mississippi river flood plain is revealed by a concentration of sharply incised stream valleys that contrast with the nearly level flood plain. Braiding of the Mississippi River is also clearly seen here.

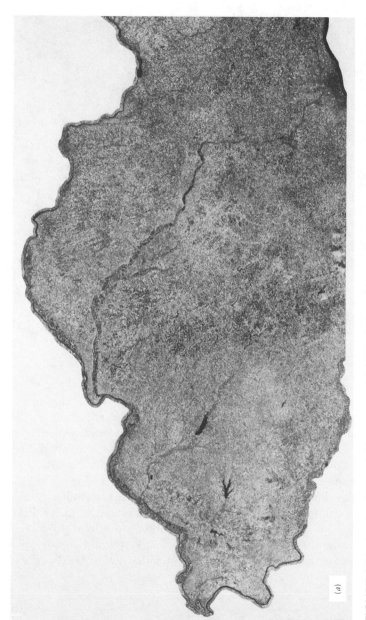

FIGURE 9.29   Landsat TM band 4 image map, Fall 1982. (a) Statewide mosaic showing the State of Illinois, 1:3,860,000. (b) Enlargement of an area in northwestern Illinois showing the Mississippi River Valley. 1:260,000. (Courtesy Northern Illinois University Laboratory for Cartography and Spatial Analysis, and Illinois State Geological Survey.)

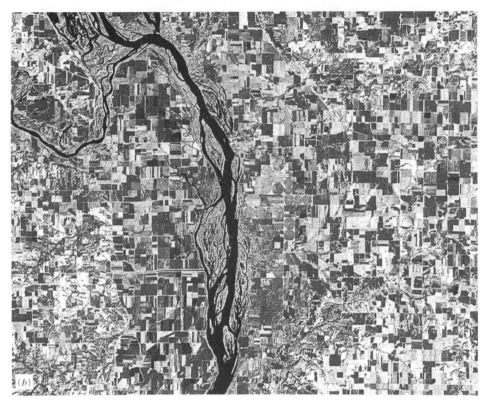

FIGURE 9.29   *(continued)*

TM data have been used extensively to prepare image maps over a range of mapping scales. Such maps have proven to be useful tools for resource assessment in that they depict the terrain in actual detail, rather than in the line-and-symbol format of conventional maps. Image maps are often used as map supplements to augment conventional map coverage and to provide coverage of unmapped areas.

As we see in Chapter 10, there are several digital image processing procedures that may be applied to the image mapping process. These include such things as large area digital mosaicking, image enhancement procedures, merging of image data with conventional cartographic information, and streamlining the map production and printing process using highly automated cartographic systems. Extensive research continues in the area of image mapping, with both Landsat and SPOT data (described below).

9.10 LANDSAT-6 AND -7

The precise plans for the Landsat-6 and -7 missions are far from certain at the time of this writing (1987). Proposals under consideration range from continued use of single mission platforms, to the concept of a multimission platform designed to be repairable, refurbishable, and retrievable from the Space Shuttle by mission specialists. The potential advantages of the multimission concept include a longer service life (up to 20 years) and the ability to provide excess capacity to fly other experiments and instruments in addition to the Landsat sensors. At the same time, repairs and design improvements could be made to the various payloads.

It is proposed that Landsat-6 will include an *Enhanced Thematic Mapper (ETM)*. This system will be similar to the previous TMs, but it will incorporate an additional "panchromatic" band (0.5 to 0.86 μm) with a ground resolution of 15 m. Possibly to be flown in tandem with the ETM is a low-resolution (500 m) instrument that would provide wider swath imaging and higher frequency ground coverage over any given area than the ETM.

Landsat-7 is proposed to carry the ETM with potentially a multiband thermal infrared sensing capability. In order to ensure global data collection, EOSAT proposes to operate both Landsat-6 and -7 with high-volume onboard tape recorders. Again, the precise payloads to be included on these missions are uncertain at this time.

9.11   SPOT SATELLITE PROGRAM

In early 1978 the French Government decided to undertake the development of the *Systeme Pour l'Observation de la Terre* or *SPOT* program. Shortly thereafter Sweden and Belgium agreed to participate in the program with the aim of launching the first of a series of SPOT earth observation satellites. From its inception, SPOT was designed as a commercially oriented program which was to be operational, rather than experimental, in character.

Conceived and designed by the French Centre National d'Etudes Spatiales (CNES), SPOT has developed into a large scale international program with ground receiving stations and data distribution outlets located in more than 30 countries. The first satellite in the program, SPOT-1, was launched from the Kourou Launch Range in French Guiana on February 21, 1986, onboard an Ariane launch vehicle. This satellite began a new era in space remote sensing, for it is the first earth resource satellite system to include a linear array sensor and employ push-broom scanning techniques. It is also the first system to have pointable optics. This enables side-to-side off-nadir viewing capabilities, and it affords full-scene stereoscopic imaging from two different satellite tracks permitting coverage of the same area. We describe these various features of SPOT-1 in the following sections.

9.12   ORBIT CHARACTERISTICS OF SPOT-1

Like the Landsat satellites, SPOT-1 has a circular, near-polar, sun-synchronous orbit. The nominal orbit of SPOT-1 has an altitude of 832 km and an inclination of 98.7°. SPOT-1 descends across the equator at 10:30 A.M. local solar time, with slightly later crossings in northern latitudes and slightly earlier crossings in southern latitudes. For example, SPOT-1 crosses areas at a latitude of 40°N at approximately 11:00 A.M. and areas at a latitude of 40°S at 10:00 A.M.

The orbit pattern for SPOT-1 repeats every 26 days. This means any given point on the earth can be imaged using the same viewing angle at this frequency. However, the pointable optics of the system enable off-nadir viewing during satellite passes separated alternatively 1 and 4 (and occasionally 5) days, depending on the latitude of the area viewed (Figure 9.30). For example, during the 26 day period separating two successive satellite passes directly over a point located at the equator, seven viewing opportunities exist (Day D and Days D + 5, +10, +11, +15, +16, and +21). For a point located at a latitude of 45° a total of 11 viewing opportunities exist (Day D and Days D + 1, +5, +6, +10, +11, +15, +16, +20, +21, and +25). This "revisit" capability is important in two respects. First, it increases the potential frequency of coverage of areas where cloud cover is a problem. Second, it provides an opportunity for viewing a given area at frequencies ranging from successive days, to several days, to a few weeks. Several application areas, particularly within agriculture and forestry, require repeated observations over these types of time frames.

9.13 SENSORS ONBOARD SPOT-1

Figure 9.31 is a schematic of the SPOT-1 satellite. The systems weighs approximately 1750 kg and the main body of the satellite is approximately $2 \times 2 \times 3.5$ m. The solar panel has an overall length of approximately 15.6 m. The SPOT platform is of modular design such that it is compatible with a variety of sensor payloads. Thus, in subsequent SPOT missions, changes in sensor design can be implemented without significant modification of the platform.

The sensor payload for SPOT-1 consists of two identical *high-resolution-visible* (HRV) imaging systems and auxiliary magnetic tape recorders. Each HRV is designed to operate in either of two modes of sensing: (1) a 10 m resolution "panchromatic" (black and white) mode over the range 0.51 to 0.73 μm, or (2) a 20 m resolution multispectral (color infrared) mode over the ranges 0.50 to 0.59, 0.61 to 0.68, and 0.79 to 0.89 μm.

The HRV employs push-broom scanning, as described in Section 2.17. The SPOT push-broom scanning system does not employ a scanning mirror, as do mirror-sweep systems. Rather, it employs a linear array of CCDs arranged side-by-side along a line perpendicular to the satellite orbit track. A line of image data is obtained by sampling the response of the detectors along the array and successive lines of coverage are obtained by repeated sampling along the array as the satellite moves over the earth. Push-broom scanning has the distinct advantage relative to mirror-sweep systems of requiring no moving parts. This not only increases the life of the system, it eliminates the geometric errors introduced in the sensing process by variations in scan mirror velocity. At the same time, linear array detectors can dwell on the area within their IFOVs longer than those employed in sweeping systems. This increases the relative signal-to-noise performance of the linear array instruments.

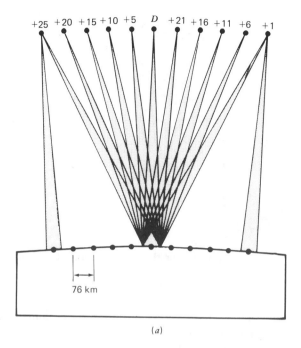

(a)

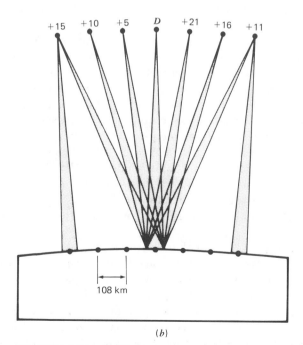

(b)

FIGURE 9.30 SPOT-1 revisit pattern. (a) Latitude = 45°. (b) Latitude = 0°.

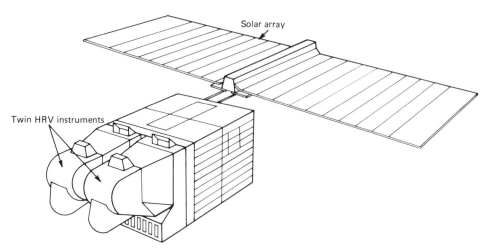

FIGURE 9.31   SPOT-1 observatory configuration. (Adapted from CNES diagram.)

Each HRV actually contains four CCD subarrays. A 6000-element subarray is used in the panchromatic mode to record data at 10 m resolution. Three 3000-element subarrays are employed in the multispectral mode at 20 m resolution. Data are effectively encoded over a 256-digital number range and are transmitted at a rate of 25 Mbps. Each instrument's field of view is 4.13°, such that the ground swath of each HRV scene is 60 km wide under nadir viewing conditions.

The first element in the optical system for each HRV is a plane mirror which can be rotated to either side by ground command, through an angle of ±27° (in 45 steps of 0.6° each). This allows each instrument to image any point within a strip extending 475 km to either side of the satellite ground track (Figure 9.32). The size of the actual ground swath covered naturally varies with the pointing angle employed. At the 27° maximum value, the swath width for each instrument is 80 km. When the two instruments are pointed so as to cover adjacent image fields at nadir, the total swath width is 117 km and the two fields overlap by 3 km (Figure 9.33). While each HRV instrument is capable of collecting panchromatic and multispectral data simultaneously, resulting in four data streams, only two data streams can be transmitted at one time. Thus, either panchromatic or multispectral data can be transmitted over a 117 km wide swath, but not both simultaneously.

Stereoscopic imaging is also possible due to the off-nadir viewing capability of the HRV. That is, images of an area recorded on different satellite tracks can be viewed in stereo (Figure 9.34). The frequency with which stereoscopic coverage can be obtained, being tied directly to the revisit schedule for the satellite, varies with latitude. At a latitude of 45° (Figure 9.30a), there are six possible occasions during the 26 day orbit cycle on which *successive day* stereo coverage may be obtained (Day D with $D + 1$, $D + 5$ with $D + 6$, $D + 10$ with $D + 11$, $D + 15$ with $D + 16$, $D + 20$ with $D + 21$,

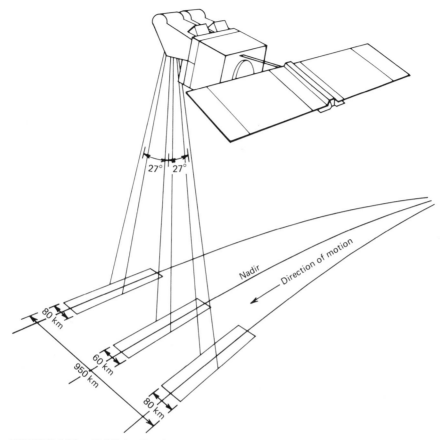

FIGURE 9.32 SPOT-1 off-nadir viewing range. (Adapted from CNES diagram.)

and D + 25 with Day D of the next orbit cycle). At the equator (Figure 9.30b), only two stereoviewing opportunities on successive days are possible (D + 10 with D + 11, and D + 15 with D + 16). The base–height ratio also varies with latitude, from approximately 0.50 at 45° to approximately 0.75 at the equator. (If stereoscopic coverage need not be acquired on a successive day basis, the range of possible viewing opportunities and viewing geometries greatly increases.)

It should now be clear that the SPOT-1 system affords a broad range of viewing conditions and spectral modes of operation. The particular observation sequence for a given day of satellite operation is loaded into SPOT-1's onboard computer by the Toulouse, France, ground control station while the satellite is within its range. The day's operating sequence for each HRV is controlled entirely independently. This includes the viewing angles of the two instruments, the spectral mode of operation

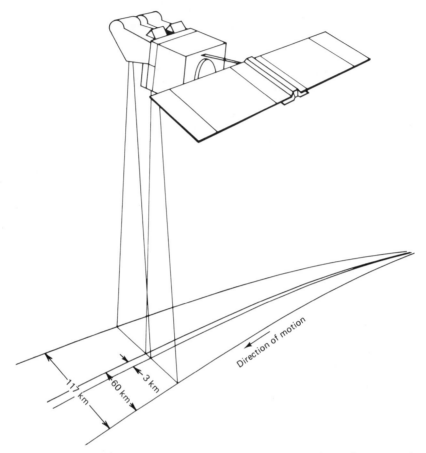

FIGURE 9.33 SPOT-I ground coverage with HRVs recording adjacent swaths. (Adapted from CNES diagram.)

(panchromatic or multispectral), the timing of image acquisition, and the modes of data transmission. Data are normally transmitted directly when the satellite is within range of a ground receiving station (approximately a 2600 km radius around the station). The onboard tape recorders are used when images are acquired over areas outside the range of a ground receiving station. In such cases, the recorded image data are subsequently transmitted to the Toulouse or Kiruna, Sweden, stations when the satellite reenters their range.

In the United States, inquiries about SPOT tapes and images can be addressed to SPOT Image Corporation, 1897 Preston White Drive, Reston, Virginia 22091-4326.

Pass on first coverage day   Pass on second coverage day

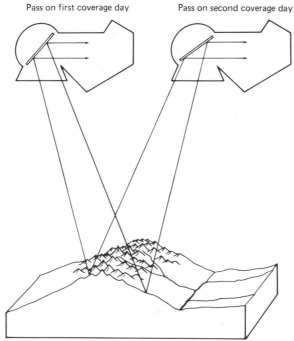

FIGURE 9.34   SPOT-1 stereoscopic imaging capability. (Adapted from CNES diagram.)

9.14   SPOT HRV IMAGE INTERPRETATION

The use of SPOT data for various interpretive purposes is facilitated by the system's combination of multispectral sensing with excellent spatial resolution, geometric fidelity, and the provision for multidate and stereo imaging.

The spatial resolution of SPOT-1 panchromatic imagery is illustrated in Figure 9.35, which shows Montreal, Canada. This scene was acquired 6 days after launch. (Note that this area is also shown in Figure 8.30, a SIR-B image.) In this image, various developmental patterns stand out as dark tones against a white snow background. The details shown in the airport runway and taxiway system at lower left illustrate the appearance of this 10 m resolution imagery as contrasted with the 30 m resolution of the Landsat TM and the 80 m resolution of the Landsat MSS that are displayed in Figure 9.25 (which shows the Detroit, Michigan, airport).

The stereoscopic imaging capability of SPOT-1 is illustrated in Figure 9.36, which is a stereopair acquired on the third and fourth days after launch. In these images of Libya, an eroded plateau is seen at the top and center, and alluvial fans are shown at the

FIGURE 9.35   SPOT-1 panchromatic image, Montreal, Canada, February 27, 1986. 1:155,000.
(Copyright © 1986 CNES. Courtesy SPOT Image Corp.)

bottom. Some vertical streaking can be seen, especially in the left-hand image. This
artifact is present in this early image from the system because the scene was processed
using preflight calibration parameters to record this "engineering data set" and the
individual detectors of the CCDs were not fully calibrated at that time.

Plate 13 is a SPOT-1 multispectral-mode false color composite image, acquired 3

FIGURE 9.36 SPOT-1 panchromatic image, stereopair, February 24 and 25, 1986, Libya 1:210,000. (Copyright © 1986 CNES. Courtesy SPOT Image Corp.)

days after launch, showing the Gran Canaria island, a periodically active volcano off the cost of Morocco. The bright red area on the north (top) side of the island is natural vegetation resulting from rainfall caused by the orographic lifting of atmospheric moisture by the prevailing northerly winds up the volcanic slopes. Many erosional valleys can be seen on the drier southern side of the volcano. Along the eastern shore, agricultural activities, as well as towns and an airport, can be clearly identified.

Even greater apparent resolution of multispectral images can be achieved through the merger of data from the panchromatic and multispectral acquisition modes. Plate 14 shows the merger of simulated SPOT data for a scene that includes a portion of the city of Sherbrooke, Quebec. To produce this image, 10 m resolution panchromatic data were digitally merged with each of the three 20 m resolution multispectral bands [16]. The resulting data consist of 10 m square pixels in each of three bands (green plus panchromatic, red plus panchromatic, and infrared plus panchromatic). These three bands were then used to produce a color composite image with the same color scheme as color infrared photographs. Plate 14a shows the original multispectral channel image with 20 m resolution. Plate 14b shows the original panchromatic channel image with 10 m resolution, and Plate 14c shows the merged image. Both the spatial and spectral resolution of the merged image approach that seen in small scale, high-altitude color infrared photographs. Such a technique could also be used with stereo color composite SPOT images to enhance image interpretability.

9.15   SPOT-3 AND -4

Like its Landsat counterpart, the SPOT program has been designed to provide long-term continuity of data through the anticipated launch of several systems. In this regard, SPOT-2 is designed to be identical in operation to SPOT-1. However, a number of design changes are proposed for SPOT-3 and -4. These include the addition of a 20 m resolution band in the mid-infrared portion of the spectrum (between 1.58 and 1.75 μm). This band is intended to improve vegetation monitoring capabilities of the data. Furthermore, mixed 20 and 10 m data sets will be coregistered onboard instead of during ground processing.

Another proposal for SPOT-3 and -4 is the inclusion of a new wide field of view (approximately 2200 km) instrument to be flown in combination with the HRVs. This instrument records 10-bit data in five spectral bands: the HRV bands currently in use; the mid-IR band described above; and a blue band (0.43 to 0.47 μm) designed for oceanographic studies. Repeat coverage of any location will be acquired once or twice per day, depending on latitude. Images will be produced with a ground resolution of 1 km for regional studies or 4 km for coverage of larger areas.

9.16   METEOROLOGICAL SATELLITES

Designed specifically to assist in weather prediction and monitoring, *meteorological satellites*, or *metsats*, generally incorporate sensors that have very coarse spatial resolution compared to land-oriented systems. On the other hand, metsats afford the advantages of global coverage at very high temporal resolution. Accordingly, metsat data have been shown to be useful in natural resource applications where frequent, large area mapping is required and fine detail is not. Apart from the advantages of depicting large areas at high temporal resolution, the coarse spatial resolution of metsats also greatly reduces the volume of data to be processed for a particular application.

Numerous countries have launched various types of metsats with a range of orbit and sensing system designs. In the remainder of this section we treat only three representative series of metsats that are operated by the United States. The first is the *NOAA* series named after the *National Oceanic and Atmospheric Administration*. These satellites are in near-polar, sun-synchronous orbits similar to those of Landsat and SPOT. In contrast, the *GOES* series of satellites are geostationary, remaining in a constant relative position over the equator. GOES is an acronym stemming from *Geostationary Operational Environmental Satellite*. The final systems we discuss are part of the U.S. Air Force *Defense Meteorological Satellite Program (DMSP)*. All three of these satellite series carry a range of meteorological sensors. We treat only the salient characteristics of those sensors used most often in land remote sensing applications.

NOAA Satellites

Several generations of satellites have been flown in the NOAA series. Germane to this discussion are the NOAA-6 through NOAA-10 missions that contained the *Advanced Very High Resolution Radiometer (AVHRR)*. The even-numbered missions have daylight (7:30 A.M.) north-to-south equatorial crossing times and the odd-numbered missions have nighttime (2:30 A.M.) north-to-south equatorial crossing times. Table 9.6 lists the basic characteristics of these missions and the AVHRR instrument. Figure 9.37 shows the 2400 km swath width characteristic of the system. Coverage is acquired at a ground resolution of 1.1 km at nadir. This resolution naturally becomes coarser with increases in the viewing angle off-nadir. NOAA receives AVHRR data at full resolution and archives them in two different forms. Selected data are recorded at full resolution, referred to as local area coverage (LAC) data. All of the data are sampled down to a nominal resolution of 4 km, referred to as global area coverage (GAC) data. Figure 9.38 summarizes the spectral sensitivity of the AVHRR relative to the Landsat MSS, the Landsat TM, and the SPOT HRV.

Figure 9.39 shows typical images (band 2) from the AVHRR. Figure 9.39*a* shows a raw AVHRR image including the northeastern U.S. coastline and extending across the region of the Great Lakes. Note the greatly increased coverage and coarser resolution of such images compared to Landsat or SPOT images. Note also the scale compression near the edges of the image. (These effects are particularly noticeable in the distorted shape of the Great Lakes and the State of Michigan.) These distortions result from the wide angle of view of the AVHRR, as well as earth curvature effects. Figure 9.39*b* illustrates the appearance of such imagery after geometric corrections are made for these distortions.

NOAA satellites provide daily (visible) and twice-daily (thermal IR) coverage. Images and digital tapes are used operationally in a host of applications requiring timely data. For example, Figure 9.40 is an enlarged portion of a visible channel NOAA image showing the snow covered Sierra Nevada Mountains on the California—

TABLE 9.6   Characteristics of NOAA-6 through NOAA-10 Missions

Parameter	NOAA-6, -8, and -10	NOAA-7 and -9
Launch	6/27/79, 3/28/83, 9/17/86	6/23/81, 12/12/84
Altitude (km)	833	833
Period of orbit (min)	102	102
Orbit inclination	98.9°	98.9°
Orbits per day	14.1	14.1
Distance between orbits	25.5°	25.5°
Day-to-day orbital shift[a]	5.5°E	3.0°E
Orbit repeat period (days)[b]	4−5	8−9
Scan angle from nadir	±55.4°	±55.4°
Optical field of view (mr)	1.3	1.3
IFOV, at nadir (km)	1.1	1.1
IFOV, off-nadir maximum (km)		
Along track	2.4	2.4
Across track	6.9	6.9
Swath width	2400 km	2400 km
Coverage	Every 12 hr	Every 12 hr
Northbound equatorial crossing (pm)	7:30	2:30
Southbound equatorial crossing (am)	7:30	2:30
AVHRR spectral channels (μm)		
1	0.58−0.68	0.58−0.68
2	0.72−1.10	0.72−1.10
3	3.55−3.93	3.55−3.93
4	10.5−11.50	10.3−11.30
5	Channel 4 repeat	11.5−12.50

[a]Satellite differences due to differing orbital alignments.
[b]Caused by orbits per day not being integers.

Nevada border. Lake Tahoe lies just above and to the left of the center of the figure. This region receives up to 18 m of snow per year, and this resource is closely monitored by hydrologists. The frequent coverage rate and large area coverage of NOAA imagery make it particularly well suited to this type of application. Analysis of satellite imagery is an integral component of operational snow monitoring programs. The different gray tones discernible in the snow fields relate to either the depth or the melting conditions of the snowpack. Also shown in this image is the distinct tonal difference between the chapparal−coniferous forest land cover southwest of the mountain range and the sagebrush cover in the arid region to the northeast.

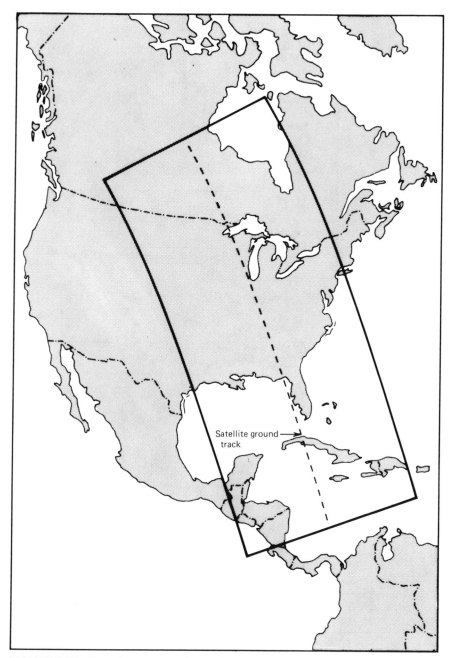

Satellite ground track

FIGURE 9.37 Example coverage of the NOAA AVHRR.

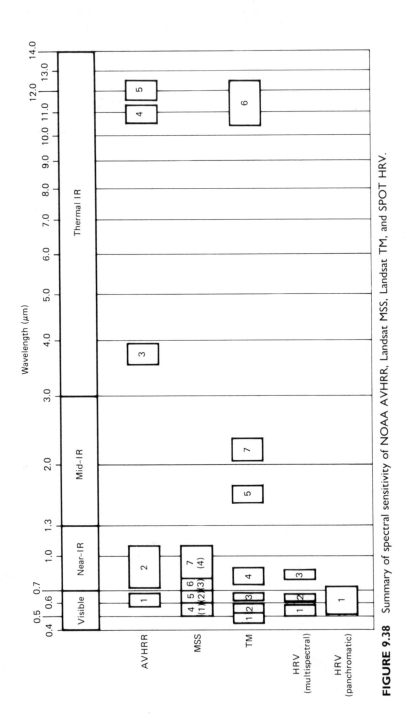

FIGURE 9.38   Summary of spectral sensitivity of NOAA AVHRR, Landsat MSS, Landsat TM, and SPOT HRV.

FIGURE 9.39 AVHRR images. (a) Raw image. (b) Geometrically corrected image.

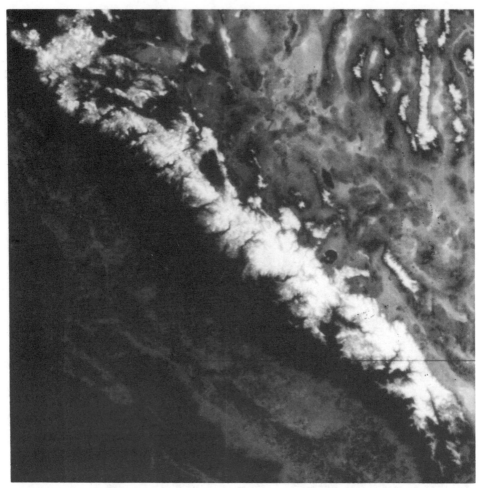

FIGURE 9.40   NOAA AVHRR image showing snow extent in the Sierra Nevada Mountains. (Courtesy NOAA/National Environmental Satellite, Data, and Information Service.)

In addition to snow cover mapping, AVHRR data have been used extensively in applications as varied as flood monitoring, vegetation mapping, regional soil moisture analysis, wildfire fuel mapping, fire detection, dust and sandstorm monitoring, and various geologic applications including observation of volcanic eruptions and mapping of regional drainage and physiographic features [42].

AVHRR images of the Mississippi River delta and vicinity are shown in Plate 15 and Figure 9.41 (see Figure 4.60 for Landsat MSS images covering much of the same area). The color composite shown in Plate 15 was produced from two channels of AVHRR data by displaying channel 1 through both blue and green filters and channel 2 through a red filter. Past and present channels and deltas of the Mississippi River, as shown in

Figure 9.41*a*, can be clearly seen in these images. In Plate 15, silt-laden water is light blue in color. Such water appears both in the river channels and in Lake Pontchartrain, as well as parts of the Gulf of Mexico that are receiving water discharged from the Mississippi and Atchafalaya Rivers. The Atchafalaya River now carries about 25 percent of the Mississippi River discharge water and many scientists believe that it will become the principal channel of the Mississippi River in the future. Along the Gulf Coast, bright red areas are higher and drier, while darker red-brown areas are lower and wetter. A few stringlike clouds appear in the image as bright white tones. As was seen in Figure 4.60, the red channel (AVHRR channel 1) emphasizes the silty materials in the water, whereas the near-infrared channel (AVHRR channel 2) fails to penetrate the water to show the silt. In Figure 9.41*b*, plumes of silty water can be seen flowing into Lake Pontchartrain from the Mississippi River and into the Gulf of Mexico from both the Mississippi and the Atchafalaya Rivers. In *(c)*, the land–water interface is emphasized as well as the wetter versus drier land areas. AVHRR channel 4 (thermal infrared) is shown in *(d)*, with the tone convention used for meteorological thermal images; that is, the cooler areas are lighter-toned and the warmer areas are darker-toned (so clouds appear white). The plumes of cooler river water flowing into Lake Pontchartrain and the Gulf of Mexico are very distinct on this image.

Plate 16 illustrates the use of AVHRR data to produce large area mosaics. This plate shows an AVHRR color composite mosaic of a major portion of the western United States. This image is a digital mosaic of five NOAA-8 AVHRR images acquired over a 5 day period. These data were resampled to a 1500 m pixel size, registered to an Albers Equal Area projection, enhanced using spatial filtering techniques (low pass, high pass, and edge enhancement), and merged with USGS digital line graph data. (Such procedures are discussed in Chapter 10.) To produce the color composite, channel 1 (red) data were displayed as both blue and green, and channel 2 (near-infrared) data were displayed as red.

AVHRR data have been used extensively for large area vegetation monitoring [35]. Typically, the spectral bands used for this purpose have been the channel 1 visible band (0.58 to 0.68 μm) and the channel 2 near-infrared band (0.73 to 1.10 μm).

Various mathematical combinations of the AVHRR channel 1 and 2 data have been found to be sensitive indicators of the presence and condition of green vegetation. These mathematical quantities are thus referred to as *vegetation indices*. Two such indices have been routinely calculated from AVHRR data—a simple vegetation index (VI) and a normalized vegetation index (NVI). These indices are computed from the equations

$$VI = Ch_2 - Ch_1$$

and

$$NVI = \frac{Ch_2 - Ch_1}{Ch_2 + Ch_1}$$

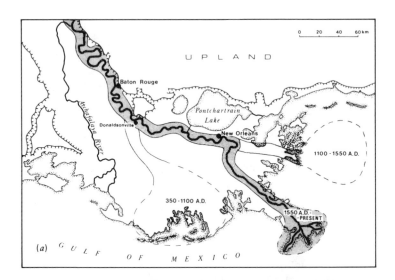

FIGURE 9.41   NOAA-8 AVHRR images and map, Mississippi River delta and vicinity. Image date May 24, 1983. *(a)* Map showing present and past Mississippi River channels and deltas. *(b)* Channel 1 image (red). *(c)* Channel 2 image (near-infrared). *(d)* Channel 4 image (thermal infrared). (Map adapted from Thornbury [58], after H. N. Fisk.) (Images courtesy USGS EROS Data Center.)

where Ch_1 and Ch_2 represent data from AVHRR channels 1 and 2. Vegetated areas will generally yield high values for either index because of their relatively high near-infrared reflectance and low visible reflectance. In contrast, clouds, water, and snow have larger visible reflectance than near-infrared reflectance. Thus, these features yield negative index values. Rock and bare soil areas have similar reflectances in the two bands and result in vegetation indices near zero.

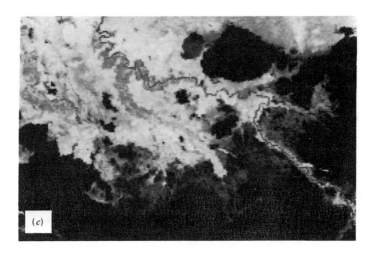

FIGURE 9.41   *(continued)*

The normalized vegetation index is preferred to the simple index for global vegetation monitoring because the NVI helps compensate for changing illumination conditions, surface slope, aspect, and other extraneous factors. In highly vegetated scene areas, the NVI typically ranges from 0.1 to 0.6, in proportion to the density and greenness of the plant canopy.

By processing AVHRR data orbit by orbit it is possible to produce global NVI image mosaics on a daily basis. A single day's mosaic consists of a composite of 14 orbit swaths in a polar-stereographic projection. Because about half the earth is obscured by clouds on any single day, a composite period of 7 days of data is normally used to produce global vegetation index maps operationally. For each composite period of 7 days, only the pixel from the daily image data sets having the greatest NVI on any day is portrayed at each location. This eliminates clouds from the composite (except in areas that are cloudy for all 7 days). Using only the maximum NVI value also reduces the atmospheric effects present in the mosaic.

Figures 9.42 and 9.43 are 7 day composite NVI mosaics for the Northern and Southern hemispheres, respectively. A gray scale relating the value of the NVI to

FIGURE 9.42   Normalized vegetation index mosaic for the northern hemisphere. (Courtesy NOAA/National Environmental Satellite, Data, and Information Service.)

FIGURE 9.43   Normalized vegetation index mosaic for the southern hemisphere. (Courtesy NOAA/National Environmental Satellite, Data, and Information Service.)

image brightness is shown in the lower portion of each figure. It can be seen that bodies of water, clouds, snow, and ice appear as white or light gray; deserts, rocks, and bare soil as light gray; and agricultural and forest land as medium to dark gray, depending on the greenness and density of the vegetation. Such images are used operationally by NOAA to assess global climate effects on vegetation and crops. (We further discuss vegetation indices in Section 10.6.)

GOES Satellites

The SMS/GOES program, like the other civilian meteorological satellite programs, is a cooperative venture between NOAA and NASA. The *Synchronous Meteorological Satellites (SMS)*, or Geostationary Operational Environmental Satellites (GOES), are part of a global network of meteorological satellites spaced about 70° longitude apart around the world. The domestic SMS/GOES program began providing image data in 1974. The program consists of multiple spacecraft orbiting the earth at 36,000 km, where they are synchronous with the rotation of the equator. Similar systems are in operation or planned by Japan, the European Space Agency, and the Soviet Union in a cooperative venture within the World Meteorological Organization.

From its vantage point, GOES sees an entire hemispherical disk (Figure 9.44). The repeat frequency is therefore limited only by the time it takes to scan and relay an

FIGURE 9.44   GOES-2 visible band (0.55 to 0.7 μm) image of hemispherical disk including North and South America, September 1, 1977. A hurricane is clearly discernible in the Gulf of Mexico. (Courtesy NOAA/National Environmental Satellite, Data, and Information Service.)

image. GOES images are generated twice an hour in a visible band and a thermal IR band. The visible band operates during daylight hours, and the IR band runs day and night. These images are scanned in a novel way: the entire satellite spins to cause the IFOV to scan parallel to the equator. Sequential scan lines are imaged by changing the angle of a stationary mirror slightly between scans.

GOES images are by now very familiar to us all. They are distributed in near real-time for use in local weather forecasting. They have also been used in certain large area analyses, such as regional snow cover mapping, when higher resolution data are not required [30].

Defense Meteorological Satellite Program

The U.S. Air Force administers its own meteorological satellite program called the *Defense Meteorological Satellite Program (DMSP)*. Some of the data produced from the two operational satellites in this program have been available to civilian users on an unclassified basis since April 1973 [13]. The DMSP satellites carry a range of meteorological sensors. Scanners onboard the satellites produce images in the 0.4 to 1.1 μm (visible and near-IR) band and the 8 to 13 μm (thermal IR) band. System resolution is on the order of 3 km and sun-synchronous polar orbits permit day and night global coverage. A unique capability of the DMSP scanner is nighttime visible band imaging. This comes about through the ability to "tune" the amplifiers of the system to obtain images under low illumination conditions. The system produces vivid images of phenomena such as the urban light patterns shown in Figure 9.45. Auroral displays, volcanoes, oil and gas fields, and forest fires have also been detected with the low light sensor [13]. Both the thermal and daytime visible images of the DMSP have been used for such civilian applications as snow extent mapping.

9.17   OCEAN MONITORING SATELLITES

The oceans, which cover more than two-thirds of the earth's surface, have important influences on global weather and climate; yet, they represent a natural resource about which comparatively little is known. Satellite imaging can provide synoptic views of the oceans over large areas and extended time periods. This task is virtually impossible to accomplish with traditional oceanographic measurement techniques.

Seasat (Section 8.9) carried several instruments dedicated to ocean monitoring that operated in the microwave portion of the spectrum. Another satellite carrying ocean monitoring sensors was the Nimbus-7 satellite, launched in October 1978. This satellite carried the *Coastal Zone Color Scanner (CZCS)* which was employed on a limited-coverage "proof of concept" mission. The CZCS was designed specifically to measure the color and temperature of the coastal zones of the oceans. Table 9.7 lists the six bands in which the CZCS operated. These included bands in the visible, near-infrared, and thermal regions of the spectrum. The system had a 1566 km swath width and an 825 m IFOV at nadir.

The first four (visible) bands of the CZCS were very narrow (0.02 μm wide) and centered to enhance the discrimination of very subtle water reflectance differences.

FIGURE 9.45   Defense Meteorological Satellite Program nighttime image of the eastern United States, April 17, 1981, 0.4 to 1.1 μm band. 1:19,000,000. (Courtesy U.S. Air Force and NOAA.)

Data from these bands have been used to successfully map phytoplankton concentrations and inorganic suspended matter such as silt. The near-infrared channel has been used to map surface vegetation and to aid in separating water from land areas prior to processing data in the other bands. The thermal infrared channel has been used to measure sea surface temperatures. In short, the CZCS has been used to successfully detect chlorophyll, temperature, suspended solids, and *gelbostoffe* (yellow substance) in the combinations and concentrations typical of near-shore and coastal waters.

TABLE 9.7 Spectral Bands of the Coastal Zone Color Scanner

Channel	Wavelength (μm)	Principal parameter measured
1	0.43–0.45	Chlorophyll absorption
2	0.51–0.53	Chlorophyll absorption
3	0.54–0.56	*Gelbostoffe* (yellow substance)
4	0.66–0.68	Chlorophyll concentration
5	0.70–0.80	Surface vegetation
6	10.50–12.50	Surface temperature

Seasat and the CZCS have vividly demonstrated the capability to measure important ocean properties from space. Based on this experience, the United States and several other countries are currently in the process of designing several satellite systems specifically designed for ocean monitoring. The ability to monitor the oceans at regional and global scales with these systems will not only lead to a new understanding of the oceans' role in the global carbon cycle but also their influence on global climate. Likewise, commercial interests such as fisheries, offshore petroleum exploration, and marine mining will be served by the information to be collected from ocean monitoring satellites. These systems will also play a key role in monitoring sources of ocean sediment and pollution—a prerequisite to preserving and enhancing the quality of oceanic environments.

9.18 CONCLUSION

We have outlined the technical form of past and present space remote sensing systems with applicability in earth resource observation. The student should recognize that we have been far from technically detailed in our treatment of this complex subject. Furthermore, we have treated aerial and space systems separately for convenience reasons alone. Most earth resource problems entail the need for *combinations* of terrestrial, aerial, and space data acquired by various sensors in various formats *and* by other methods of observation. Successful resource management and environmental monitoring requires a "systems approach" to integration of remotely sensed observations with geobased observations.

Resource inventory and analysis activities that have been and will be enhanced by remote sensing from space are too numerous and diverse to detail here. Suffice it to say that remote sensing from space has already revolutionized our understanding and activities in cartography, geology, geophysics, water resources, land use analysis, agriculture, forestry, rangeland management, environmental monitoring, evaluation of natural hazards, conservation, and oceanography. It has had an impact on our educational system, our methods of scientific investigation, our international communication, and our international cooperation. Numerous satellite systems are currently being planned by countries throughout the world (e.g., Brazil, Canada,

People's Republic of China, India, Japan, USSR, and members of the European Space Agency).

Remote sensing from space is here to stay. It is changing daily and it is replete with economic and sociopolitical implications. Yet, it is a major key to understanding the earth, its resources, and their environment.

SELECTED BIBLIOGRAPHY

1. Abrams, M.J., et al., "Geologic Mapping Using Thermal Images," *Remote Sensing of Environment*, vol. 16, no. 2, 1984, pp. 107–124.

2. American Society for Photogrammetry and Remote Sensing, Special Issue on SPOT Simulation Results, *Photogrammetric Engineering and Remote Sensing*, vol. 51, no. 8, August 1985.

3. American Society for Photogrammetry and Remote Sensing, Special Issue on Landsat Image Data Quality Analysis, *Photogrammetric Engineering and Remote Sensing*, vol. 51, no. 9, September 1985.

4. American Society of Photogrammetry, *Manual of Color Aerial Photography*, Falls Church, Va., 1968.

5. American Society of Photogrammetry, *Manual of Remote Sensing*, 2nd ed., Falls Church, Va., 1983.

6. American Society of Photogrammetry, *SPOT Simulation Applications Handbook*, Falls Church, Va., 1984.

7. American Water Resources Association, *Satellite Hydrology—Proceedings: 5th Annual William T. Pecora Memorial Symposium on Remote Sensing*, Sioux Falls, S.D., 1981.

8. Amos, C.L., and B.J. Topliss, "Discrimination of Suspended Particular Matter in the Bay of Fundy Using the Nimbus 7 CZCS," *Canadian Journal of Remote Sensing*, vol. 11, no. 1, 1985, pp. 85–92.

9. Badhwar, G.D., R.B. MacDonald, and N.C. Mehta, "Satellite-Derived Leaf-Area-Index and Vegetation Maps as Input to Global Carbon Cycle Models—A Hierarchical Approach," *International Journal of Remote Sensing*, vol. 7, no. 2, 1986, pp. 265–281.

10. Bauer, M.E. (ed.), AgRISTARS Issue, *Remote Sensing of Environment*, vol. 14, nos. 1–3, 1984.

11. Begni, G., "Selection of the Optimum Spectral Bands for the SPOT Satellite," *Photogrammetric Engineering and Remote Sensing*," vol. 48, no. 10, October 1982, pp. 1613–1620.

12. Borgeson, W.T., R.M. Batson, and H.H. Kieffer, "Geometric Accuracy of Landsat-4 and Landsat-5 Thematic Mapper Images," *Photogrammetric Engineering and Remote Sensing*, vol. 51, no. 12, December 1985, pp. 1893–1898.

13. Brandli, H.W., "The Night Eye in the Sky," *Photogrammetric Engineering and Remote Sensing*, vol. 44, no. 4, April 1978, pp. 503–505.

14. Bullard, R.K., and R.W. Dixon-Gough, *Britain from Space—An Atlas of Landsat Images*, Taylor & Francis, London/Philadelphia, 1985.

15. Chevrel, M., M. Courtois, and G. Weill, "The SPOT Satellite Remote Sensing Mission," *Photogrammetric Engineering and Remote Sensing*, vol. 47, no. 8, August 1981, pp. 1163–1171.

16. Cliche, G., F. Bonn, and P. Teillet, "Integration of the SPOT Panchromatic Channel into Its Multispectral Mode for Image Sharpness Enhancement," *Photogrammetric Engineering and Remote Sensing*, vol. 51, no. 3, March 1985, pp. 311–316.

17. Cochrane, G.R., and G.H. Browne, "Geomorphic Mapping from Landsat-3 Return Beam Vidicon (RBV) Imagery," *Photogrammetric Engineering and Remote Sensing*, vol. 47, no. 8, August 1981, pp. 1205–1213.

18. Croft, T.A., "Radiometry with Nighttime DMSP Images in Digital Form," *Photogrammetric Engineering and Remote Sensing*, vol. 47, no. 9, September 1981, pp. 1319–1325.

19. Derenyi, E.E., "Skylab in Retrospect," *Photogrammetric Engineering and Remote Sensing*, vol. 47, no. 9, September 1981, pp. 1319–1325.

20. Doyle, F.J., *Status of Satellite Remote Sensing Programs*, Open-File Report 82-237, USGS, Reston, Va., 1982.

21. Francis, P., and P. Jones, *Images of Earth*, Prentice–Hall, Englewood Cliffs, N.J., 1984.

22. Hayes, L., "The Current Use of TIROS-N Series of Meteorological Satellites for Land-Cover Studies," *International Journal of Remote Sensing*, vol. 6, no. 1, 1985, pp. 35–45.

23. Heilman, J.L., and D.G. Moore, "Evaluating Depth to Shallow Groundwater Using Heat Capacity Mapping Mission (HCMM) Data," *Photogrammetric Engineering and Remote Sensing*, vol. 48, no. 12, December 1982, pp. 1903–1906.

24. Horler, D.N.H., and F.J. Ahern, "Forestry Information Content of Thematic Mapper Data," *International Journal of Remote Sensing*, vol. 7, no. 3, 1986, pp. 405–428.

25. Irons, J.R., and R.L. Kennard, "The Utility of Thematic Mapper Sensor Characteristics for Surface Mine Monitoring," *Photogrammetric Engineering and Remote Sensing*, vol. 52, no. 3, March 1986, pp. 389–396.

26. Jensen, J.R., and D.L. Toll, "Detecting Residential Land-Use Development at the Urban Fringe," *Photogrammetric Engineering and Remote Sensing*, vol. 48, no. 4, April 1982, pp. 629–643.

27. Khorram, S., "Use of Ocean Color Scanner Data in Water Quality Mapping," *Photogrammetric Engineering and Remote Sensing*, vol. 47, no. 5, May 1981, pp. 667–676.

28. Kidwell, K.B., *NOAA Polar Orbiter Data (TIROS-N, NOAA-6, NOAA-7, and NOAA-8) Users Guide*, NOAA, Satellite Data Services Division, World Weather Bulding, Washington, D.C., 1983.

29. Lathrop, R.G., Jr., and T.M. Lillesand, "Use of Thematic Mapper Data to Assess Water Quality in Green Bay and Central Lake Michigan," *Photogrammetric Engineering and Remote Sensing*, vol. 52, no. 5, May 1986, pp. 671–680.

30. Lillesand, T.M., et al., "Use of GOES and TIROS/NOAA Satellite Data for Snow-Cover Mapping," *Photogrammetric Engineering and Remote Sensing*, vol. 48, no. 2, February 1982, pp. 251–259.

31. Lowman, P.D., Jr., "Space Photography—A Review," *Photogrammetric Engineering*, vol. 31, no. 1, January 1965, pp. 76–86.

32. Markham, B.L., and J.L. Barker, "Spectral Characterization of the Landsat-4 MSS Sensors," *Photogrammetric Engineering and Remote Sensing*, vol. 49, no. 6, June 1983, pp. 811–833.

33. Markham, B.L., and J.L. Barker, "Spectral Characterization of the Landsat Thematic Mapper Sensors," *International Journal of Remote Sensing*, vol. 6, no. 5, 1985, pp. 697–716.

34. Matson, M., and J. Dozier, "Identification of Subresolution High Temperature Sources

Using a Thermal IR Sensor," *Photogrammetric Engineering and Remote Sensing*, vol. 47, no. 9, September 1981, pp. 1311–1318.

35. Miller, W.A., and D.G. Moore, "Time-Series Vegetation Monitoring with NOAA Satellite Data," *Proceedings: International Conference on Renewable Resource Inventories for Monitoring Changes and Trends*, 1983, pp. 86–89.

36. NASA, *Skylab Earth Resources Data Catalog*, Doc. no. 330000586, U.S. Gov. Printing Office, Washington, D.C., 1974.

37. NASA, *Landsat Data Users Handbook*, Doc. no. 76SDS4258, Goddard Space Flight Center, Greenbelt, Md., 1976.

38. NASA, *Skylab Explores The Earth*, SP-380, NASA Scientific and Technical Information Office, Washington, D.C. 1977.

39. National Geographic, *Atlas of North America—Space Age Portrait of a Continent*, National Geographic Society, Washington, D.C., 1985.

40. Nelson, R., and B. Holben, "Identifying Deforestation in Brazil Using Multiresolution Satellite Data," *International Journal of Remote Sensing*, vol. 7, no. 3, pp. 429–448.

41. NOAA, "Visual Interpretation of TM Band Combinations Being Studied," *Landsat Data Users Notes*, no. 30, March 1984.

42. NOAA, *Hydrologic and Land Science Applications of NOAA Polar-Orbiting Satellite Data*, National Environmental Satellite, Data, and Information Service, Washington, D.C., 1985.

43. Price, J.C., "Satellite Orbital Dynamics and Observation Strategies in Support of Agricultural Applications," *Photogrammetric Engineering and Remote Sensing*, vol. 48, no. 10, October 1982, pp. 1603–1611.

44. Ryerson, R.A., R.N. Dobbins, and C. Thibault, "Timely Crop Area Estimates from Landsat," *Photogrammetric Engineering and Remote Sensing*, vol. 51, no. 11, November 1985, pp. 1735–1743.

45. Schnapf, A. (ed.), *Monitoring Earth's Ocean, Land, and Atmosphere from Space—Sensors, Systems, and Applications*, American Institute of Aeronautics and Astronautics, New York, 1985.

46. Schneider, S.R., D.F. McGinnis, Jr., and G. Stephens, "Monitoring Africa's Lake Chad Basin with Landsat and NOAA Satellite Data," *International Journal of Remote Sensing*, vol. 6, no. 1, 1985, pp. 59–73.

47. Sheffield, C., *Earthwatch—A Survey of the World from Space*, Macmillan, New York, 1981.

48. Sheffield, C., *Man on Earth—How Civilization and Technology Changed the Face of the World—A Survey from Space*, Macmillan, New York, 1983.

49. Short, N.M., *The Landsat Tutorial Workbook*, NASA Ref. Publ. 1078, U.S. Gov. Printing Office, Washington, D.C., 1982.

50. Short, N.M., and L.M. Stuart, Jr., *The Heat Capacity Mapping Mission (HCMM) Anthology*, NASA SP-465, U.S. Gov. Printing Office, Washington, D.C., 1982.

51. Short, N.M., et al., *Mission to Earth: Landsat Views the World*, SP-360, NASA Scientific and Technical Information Office, Washington, D.C., 1976.

52. Slater, P.N., "Survey of Multispectral Imaging Systems for Earth Observations," *Remote Sensing of Environment*, vol. 17, no. 1, 1985, pp. 85–102.

53. Snyder, J.P., "The Space Oblique Mercator Projection," *Photogrammetric Engineering and Remote Sensing*, vol. 44, no. 5, May 1978, pp. 585–596.

54. Taranik, J.V., *Characteristics of the Landsat Multispectral Data System*, Open-File Report 78-187, USGS, Sioux Falls, S.D., 1978.

55. Tarpley, J.D., S.R. Schneider, and R.L. Money, "Global Vegetation Indices from the NOAA-7 Meteorological Satellite," *Journal of Climate and Applied Meteorology*, vol. 23, no. 3, 1984, pp. 491–494.

56. Thomas, V.L. *Generation and Physical Characteristics of the Landsat 1 and 2 MSS Computer Compatible Tapes*, Doc. no. X-563-75-223, Goddard Space Flight Center, Greenbelt, Md., 1975.

57. Thompson, L.L., "Remote Sensing Using Solid-State Array Technology," *Photogrammetric Engineering and Remote Sensing*, vol. 45, no. 10, October 1979, pp. 47–55.

58. Thornbury, W.D., *Regional Geomorphology of the United States*, Wiley, New York, 1965.

59. Townshend, J.R.G., and C.J. Tucker, "Objective Assessment of Advanced Very High Resolution Radiometer Data for Land Cover Mapping," *International Journal of Remote Sensing*, vol. 5, no. 2, 1984, pp. 497–504.

60. Tucker, C.J., J.A. Gatlin, and S.R. Schneider, "Monitoring Vegetation in the Nile Delta with NOAA-6 and NOAA-7 AVHRR Imagery," *Photogrammetric Engineering and Remote Sensing*, vol. 50, no. 1, January 1984, pp. 53–61.

61. USGS, *Landsat Data Users Handbook Revised*, USGS, Sioux Falls, S.D., 1979.

62. USGS and NOAA, *Landsat 4 Data Users Handbook*, USGS, Sioux Falls, S.D., 1984.

63. Watson, K., S. Hummer-Miller, and D.L. Sawatzky, "Registration of Heat Capacity Mapping Mission Day and Night Images," *Photogrammetric Engineering and Remote Sensing*, vol. 48, no. 2, February 1982, pp. 263–268.

64. Welch, R., and S. Zupko, "Urbanized Area Energy Utilization Patterns from DMSP Data," *Photogrammetric Engineering and Remote Sensing*, vol. 46, no. 2, February 1980, pp. 201–207.

65. Welch, R., T.R. Jordon, and M. Ehlers, "Comparative Evaluations of the Geodetic Accuracy and Cartographic Potential of Landsat-4 and Landsat-5 Thematic Mapper Image Data," *Photogrammetric Engineering and Remote Sensing*, vol. 51, no. 11, November 1985, pp. 1799–1812.

66. Williams, R.S., and W.D. Carter (eds.), *ERTS-1, a New Window on Our Planet*, USGS Professional Paper 929, Washington, D.C., 1976.

CHAPTER TEN

DIGITAL IMAGE PROCESSING

10.1 INTRODUCTION

Digital image processing involves the manipulation and interpretation of digital images (Section 1.5) with the aid of a computer. This form of remote sensing actually began in the 1960s with a limited number of researchers analyzing airborne multispectral scanner data and digitized aerial photographs. However, it was not until the launch of Landsat-1, in 1972, that digital image data became widely available for land remote sensing applications. At that time, not only was the theory and practice of digital image processing in its infancy, the cost of digital computers was very high and their computational efficiency was very low by modern standards. Today, access to low cost, efficient computer hardware and software is commonplace and the sources of digital image data are many and varied. These sources range from commercial earth resource satellite systems, to the meteorological satellites, to airborne scanner data, to airborne solid-state camera data, to image data generated by scanning microdensitometers and high-resolution video cameras. All of these forms of data can be processed and analyzed using the techniques described in this chapter.

Digital image processing is an extremely broad subject and it often involves procedures which can be mathematically complex. Our objective in this chapter is to introduce the basic principles of digital image processing without delving into the detailed mathematics involved. Also, we avoid extensive treatment of the hardware associated with digital image processing. The references at the end of this chapter are provided for those wishing to pursue such additional detail.

The central idea behind digital image processing is quite simple. The digital image is fed into a computer one pixel at a time. The computer is programmed to insert these data into an equation, or series of equations, and then store the results of the computation for each pixel. These results form a new digital image that may be displayed or recorded in pictorial format or may itself be further manipulated by additional programs. The possible forms of digital image manipulation are literally infinite. However, virtually all these procedures may be categorized into one (or more) of the following four broad types of computer assisted operations:

1. *Image rectification and restoration.* These operations aim to correct distorted or degraded image data to create a more faithful representation of the original scene.

This typically involves the initial processing of raw image data to correct for geometric distortions, to calibrate the data radiometrically, and to eliminate noise present in the data. Thus, the nature of any particular image restoration process is highly dependent upon the characteristics of the sensor used to acquire the image data. Image rectification and restoration procedures are often termed *preprocessing* operations because they normally precede further manipulation and analysis of the image data to extract specific information. We briefly discuss these procedures in Section 10.2 with treatment of various geometric corrections, radiometric corrections, and noise corrections.

2. *Image enhancement.*   These procedures are applied to image data in order to more effectively display or record the data for subsequent visual interpretation. Normally, image enhancement involves techniques for increasing the visual distinction between features in a scene. The objective is to create "new" images from the original image data in order to increase the amount of information that can be visually interpreted from the data. The enhanced images can be displayed interactively on a monitor or they can be recorded in a hard copy format, either in black and white or in color. There are no simple rules for producing the single "best" image for a particular application. Often several enhancements made from the same "raw" image are necessary. We summarize the various broad approaches to enhancement in Section 10.3. In Section 10.4, we treat specific procedures that manipulate the contrast of an image (level slicing and contrast stretching). In Section 10.5, we discuss spatial feature manipulation (spatial filtering, convolution, edge enhancement, and Fourier analysis). In Section 10.6, we consider enhancements involving multiple spectral bands of imagery (spectral ratioing, principal and canonical components, vegetation components, and intensity−hue−saturation color space transformations).

3. *Image classification.*   The objective of these operations is to replace visual analysis of the image data with quantitative techniques for automating the identification of features in a scene. This normally involves the analysis of multispectral image data and the application of statistically based decision rules for determining the land cover identity of each pixel in an image. When these decision rules are based solely on the spectral radiances observed in the data, we refer to the classification process as *spectral pattern recognition*. In contrast, the decision rules may be based on the geometrical shapes, sizes, and patterns present in the image data. These procedures fall into the domain of *spatial pattern recognition*. In either case, the intent of the classification process is to categorize all pixels in a digital image into one of several land cover classes, or "themes." These categorized data may then be used to produce *thematic maps* of the land cover present in an image, and/or to produce summary statistics on the areas covered by each land cover type. Due to their importance, image classification procedures comprise the subject of half of the material in this chapter (Sections 10.7 to 10.14). We emphasize *spectral* pattern recognition procedures because the current state-of-the-art for these procedures is more advanced than for *spatial* pattern recognition approaches. (Substantial research is ongoing in the development of spatial and combined spectral/spatial image classification.) We treat both "supervised" and "unsuper-

vised" approaches to spectrally based image classification. We also describe various procedures for assessing the accuracy of image classification results.

4. *Data merging.* These procedures are used to combine image data for a given geographic area with other geographically referenced data sets for the same area. These other data sets might simply consist of image data generated on other dates by the same sensor, or by other remote sensing systems. Frequently, the intent of data merging is to combine remotely sensed data with other sources of information in the context of a geographic information system (GIS). For example, image data are often combined with soil, topographic, ownership, zoning, and assessment information. We discuss data merging in Section 10.15. In this section, we highlight multitemporal data merging, change detection procedures, and multisensor image merging. We also illustrate the integration of remote sensing data in a GIS.

We have made the above subdivisions of the topic of digital image processing to provide the reader with a conceptual roadmap for studying this chapter. Although we treat each of these procedures as distinct operations, they all interrelate. For example, the restoration process of noise removal can often be considered an enhancement procedure. Likewise, certain enhancement procedures (such as principal components analysis) can be used not only to enhance the data, but also to improve the efficiency of classification operations. In a similar vein, data merging can be used in image classification in order to improve classification accuracy. Hence, the boundaries between the various operations we discuss separately here are not well defined in practice.

10.2   IMAGE RECTIFICATION AND RESTORATION

As previously mentioned, the intent of image rectification and restoration is to correct image data for distortions or degradations which stem from the image acquisition process. Obviously, the nature of such procedures as applied to solid-state linear array camera data or multispectral scanner data is quite different from that applied to Landsat, SPOT, or meteorological satellite data. We make no attempt to describe the entire range of image rectification and restoration procedures applied to each of these various types of sensors. Rather, we treat these operations under the generic headings of geometric correction, radiometric correction, and noise removal.

Geometric Correction

Raw digital images usually contain geometric distortions so significant that they cannot be used as maps. The sources of these distortions range from variations in the altitude, attitude, and velocity of the sensor platform, to factors such as panoramic distortion, earth curvature, atmospheric refraction, relief displacement, and nonlinearities in the sweep of a sensor's IFOV. The intent of geometric correction is to compensate for the distortions introduced by these factors so that the corrected image will have the geometric integrity of a map.

The geometric correction process is normally implemented as a two-step procedure. First, those distortions that are *systematic*, or predictable, are considered. Second, those distortions that are essentially *random*, or unpredictable, are considered.

Systematic distortions are well understood and easily corrected by applying formulas derived by modeling the sources of the distortions mathematically. For example, a highly systematic source of distortion involved in multispectral scanning from satellite altitudes is the eastward rotation of the earth beneath the satellite during imaging. This causes each optical sweep of the scanner to cover an area slightly to the west of the previous sweep. This is known as *skew distortion*. The process of *deskewing* the resulting imagery involves offsetting each successive scan line slightly to the west. The skewed-parallelogram appearance of satellite multispectral scanner data is a result of this correction.

Random distortions and residual unknown systematic distortions are corrected by analyzing well-distributed ground control points (GCPs) occurring in an image. As with their counterparts on aerial photographs, GCPs are features of known ground location that can be accurately located on the digital imagery. Some features that make good control points are highway intersections and distinct shoreline features. In the correction process numerous GCPs are located both in terms of their two image coordinates (column, row numbers) on the distorted image and in terms of their ground coordinates (typically measured from a map in terms of UTM coordinates or latitude and longitude). These values are then submitted to a least-squares regression analysis to determine coefficients for two *coordinate transformation equations* that can be used to interrelate the geometrically correct (map) coordinates and the distorted image coordinates. Once the coefficients for these equations are determined, the distorted image coordinates for any map position can be precisely estimated. Expressing this in mathematic notation,

$$x = f_1\,(X,Y)$$
$$y = f_2\,(X,Y)$$

(10.1)

where

(x,y) = distorted image coordinates (column, row)
(X,Y) = correct (map) coordinates
f_1, f_2 = transformation functions

Intuitively, it might seem as though the above equations are stated backward! That is, they specify how to determine the distorted image positions corresponding to correct, or undistorted, map positions. But, that is exactly what is done during the geometric correction process. We first define an undistorted output matrix of "empty" map cells and then fill in each cell with the gray level of the corresponding pixel, or pixels, in the distorted image. This process is illustrated in Figure 10.1. This diagram shows the geometrically correct output matrix of cells (solid lines) superimposed over the original, distorted matrix of image pixels (dashed lines). After producing the

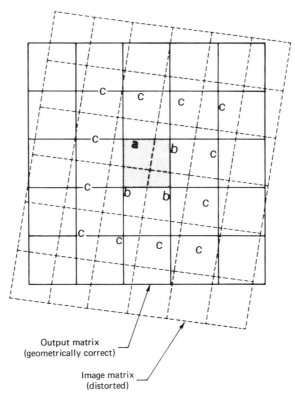

Output matrix
(geometrically correct)

Image matrix
(distorted)

FIGURE 10.1 Matrix of geometrically correct output pixels superimposed on matrix of original, distorted input pixels.

transformation function, a process called *resampling* is used to determine the pixel values to fill into the output matrix from the original image matrix. This process is performed using the following operations:

1. The coordinates of each element in the undistorted output matrix are transformed to determine their corresponding location in the original input (distorted image) matrix.

2. In general, a cell in the output matrix will not directly overlay a pixel in the input matrix. Accordingly, the intensity value or digital number (DN) eventually assigned to a cell in the output matrix is determined on the basis of the pixel values which surround its transformed position in the original input matrix.

A number of different resampling schemes can be used to assign the appropriate DN to an output cell or pixel. To illustrate this, consider the shaded output pixel shown in Figure 10.1. The DN for this pixel could be assigned simply on the basis of the DN of the closest pixel in the input matrix, disregarding the slight offset. In our example, the DN of the input pixel labeled *a* would be transferred to the shaded output pixel. This approach is called *nearest neighbor* resampling. It offers the advantage of computational simplicity and avoids having to alter the original input pixel values. However, features in the output matrix may be offset spatially by up to one-half pixel. This can cause a disjointed appearance in the output image product. Figure 10.2*b* is an example of a nearest neighbor resampled Landsat MSS image. Figure 10.2*a* shows the original, distorted image.

More sophisticated methods of resampling evaluate the values of several pixels surrounding a given pixel in the input image to establish a "synthetic" DN to be assigned to its corresponding pixel in the output image. The *bilinear interpolation* technique takes a distance-weighted average of the DNs of the four nearest pixels (labeled *a* and *b* in the distorted image matrix in Figure 10.1). This process is simply the two-dimensional equivalent to linear interpolation. As shown in Figure 10.2*c*, this technique generates a smoother appearing resampled image. However, because the process alters the gray levels of the original image, problems may be encountered in subsequent spectral pattern recognition analyses of the data. (Because of this, resampling is often performed after, rather than prior to, image classification procedures.)

An improved restoration of the image is provided by the *cubic convolution* method of resampling. In this approach, the transferred "synthetic" pixel values are deter-

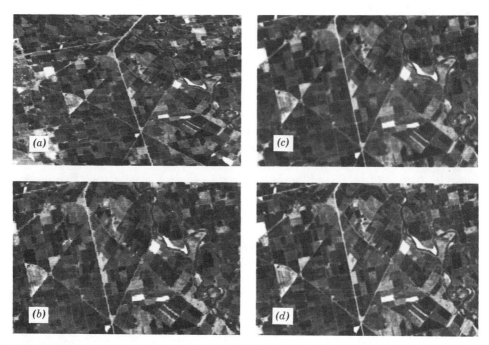

FIGURE 10.2   Resampling results. *(a)* Original MSS data. *(b)* Nearest neighbor assignment. *(c)* Bilinear interpolation. *(d)* Cubic convolution. (Courtesy IBM Corp.)

mined by evaluating the block of 16 pixels in the input matrix that surrounds each output pixel (labeled *a*, *b*, and *c* in Figure 10.1). The precise form of this neighborhood evaluation process is outside the scope of our discussion and may be found elsewhere [13, 58]. Suffice it to say, cubic convolution resampling (Figure 10.2*d*) avoids the disjointed appearance of the nearest neighbor method and provides a slightly sharper image than the bilinear interpolation method. (Again, this method alters the original image gray levels to some extent and other types of resampling can be employed to minimize this effect.)

As we discuss later, resampling techniques are important in several digital processing operations besides the geometric correction of raw images. For example, resampling is used to overlay or register multiple dates of imagery. It is also used to register images of differing resolution. Finally, resampling procedures are used extensively to register image data and other sources of data in GISs.

Radiometric Correction

As with geometric correction, the type of radiometric correction applied to any given digital image data set varies widely among sensors. Other things being equal, the radiance measured by any given system over a given object is influenced by such factors as changes in scene illumination, atmospheric conditions, viewing geometry, and instrument response characteristics. Some of these effects, such as viewing geometry variations, are greater in the case of airborne data collection than in satellite image acquisition. Also, the need to perform correction for any or all of these influences depends directly upon the particular application at hand.

In the case of satellite sensing in the visible and near-infrared portion of the spectrum, it is often desirable to generate mosaics of images taken at different times, or to study the changes in the reflectance of ground features at different times or locations. In such applications, it is usually necessary to apply a *sun elevation correction* to account for the seasonal position of the sun relative to the earth (Figure 10.3). Through this process, image data acquired under different solar illumination angles are normalized by calculating pixel brightness values assuming the sun was at the zenith on each date of sensing. This type of correction ignores topographic and atmospheric effects and simply amounts to dividing each pixel value in a scene by the sine of the solar elevation angle for the particular time and location of imaging [81]. Information on the solar elevation angle for a given scene is normally part of the ancillary data supplied on the CCT for the scene.

As discussed in Section 6.8, the influence of solar illumination is compounded by atmospheric effects. The atmosphere affects the radiance measured at any point in the scene in two contradictory ways. First, it attenuates (reduces) the energy illuminating a ground object. Second, it acts as a reflector itself, adding a scattered, extraneous "path radiance" to the signal detected by a sensor. Thus, the composite signal observed at any given pixel location can be expressed by

$$L_{\text{tot}} = \frac{\rho E T}{\pi} + L_{\text{p}} \tag{10.2}$$

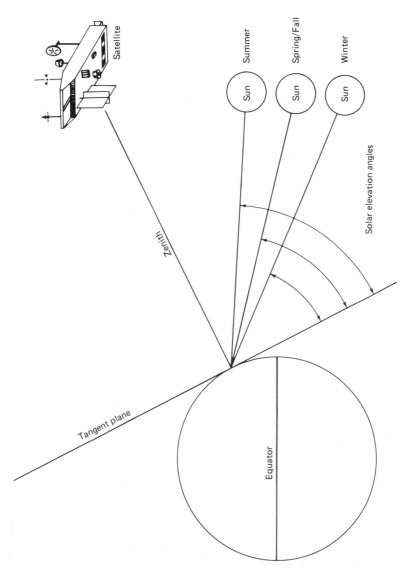

FIGURE 10.3 Effects of seasonal change on solar elevation angle. (Adapted from NASA diagram.)

where

L_{tot} = total spectral radiance measured by sensor
ρ = reflectance of target
E = irradiance on the target
T = transmission of atmosphere
L_p = path radiance

(All of the above quantities depend on wavelength.)

Only the first term in the above equation contains valid information about ground reflectance. The second term represents the scattered path radiance, which introduces "haze" in the imagery and reduces image contrast. (Recall that scattering is wavelength dependent, with shorter wavelengths normally manifesting greater scattering effects.) *Haze compensation* procedures are designed to minimize the influence of path radiance effects. One means of haze compensation in multispectral data is to observe the radiance recorded over target areas of essentially zero reflectance. For example, the reflectance of deep clear water is essentially zero in the near-infrared region of the spectrum. Therefore, any signal observed over such an area represents the path radiance and this value can be subtracted from all pixels in that band.

For convenience, haze correction routines are often applied uniformly throughout a scene. This may or may not be valid, depending on the uniformity of the atmosphere over a scene. When extreme viewing angles are involved in image acquisition, it is often necessary to compensate for the influence of varying the atmospheric path length through which the scene is recording. In such cases, off-nadir pixel values are usually normalized to their nadir equivalents.

Another radiometric data processing activity involved in many quantitative applications of digital image data is *conversion of DNs to absolute radiance values*. This operation accounts for the exact form of the A-to-D response functions for a given sensor and is essential in applications where measurement of absolute radiances is required. For example, such conversions are necessary when changes in the absolute reflectance of objects are to be measured over time using different sensors (e.g., the MSS on Landsat-3 versus that on Landsat-5). Likewise, such conversions are important in the development of mathematical models that physically relate image data to quantitative ground measurements (e.g., water quality data).

Normally, detectors and data systems are designed to produce a linear response to incident spectral radiance. For example, Figure 10.4 shows the linear radiometric response function typical of an individual TM channel. Each spectral band of the TM has its own response function and its characteristics are monitored using onboard calibration lamps (and temperature references for the thermal channel). The absolute spectral radiance output of the calibration sources is known from prelaunch calibration and is assumed to be stable over the life of the sensor. Thus, the onboard calibration sources form the basis for constructing the radiometric response function by relating known radiance values incident on the detectors to the resulting DNs.

It can be seen from Figure 10.4 that a linear fit to the calibration data results in the following relationship between radiance and DN values for any given channel:

$$DN = GL + B \tag{10.3}$$

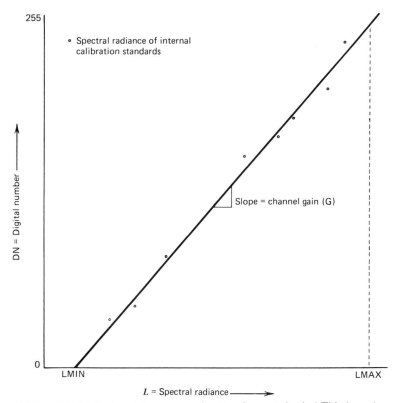

FIGURE 10.4   Radiometric response function for an individual TM channel.

where
　DN = digital number value recorded
　　G = slope of response function (channel gain)
　　L = spectral radiance measured (over the spectral bandwidth of the channel)
　　B = intercept of response function (channel offset)

Note that the slope and intercept of the above function are referred to as the *gain* and *offset* of the response function, respectively. LMIN in Figure 10.4 is the spectral radiance corresponding to a DN response of 0. LMAX is the minimum radiance required to generate the maximum DN (here 255). That is, LMAX represents the radiance at which the channel saturates. The range from LMIN to LMAX is the dynamic range for the channel.

Figure 10.5 is a plot of the inverse of the radiometric response. Here we have simply interchanged the axes from Figure 10.4. The equation for this line is

$$L = \left(\frac{\text{LMAX} - \text{LMIN}}{255}\right) \text{DN} + \text{LMIN} \tag{10.4}$$

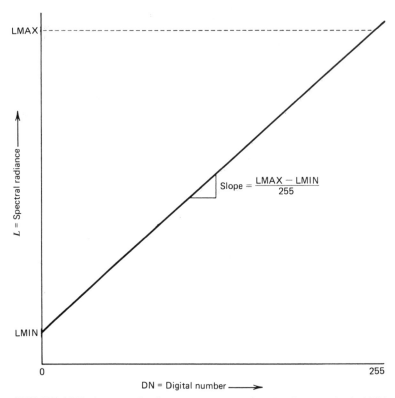

FIGURE 10.5   Inverse of radiometric response function for an individual TM channel.

Equation 10.4 can be used to convert any DN in a particular band to absolute units of spectral radiance in that band if LMAX and LMIN are known from the sensor calibration.

Often the LMAX and LMIN values published for a given sensor are expressed in units of mW cm^{-2} sr^{-1} μm^{-1}. That is, the values are often specified in terms of radiance per unit wavelength. To estimate the total within-band radiance in such cases the value obtained from Eq. 10.4 must be multiplied by the width of the spectral band under consideration. Hence, a precise estimate of within-band radiance requires detailed knowledge of the spectral response curves for each band [53].

Noise Removal

Image noise is any unwanted disturbance in image data that is due to limitations in the sensing, signal digitization, or data recording process. The potential sources of noise range from periodic drift or malfunction of a detector, to electronic interference between sensor components, to intermittent "hiccups" in the data transmission and recording sequence. Noise can either degrade or totally mask the true radiometric information content of a digital image. Hence, noise removal usually precedes any subsequent enhancement or classification of the image data. The objective is to restore an image to as close an approximation of the original scene as possible.

As with geometric restoration procedures, the nature of noise correction required in any given situation depends upon whether the noise is systematic (periodic), random, or some combination of the two. For example, multispectral scanners that sweep multiple scan lines simultaneously often produce data containing systematic *striping* or *banding*. This stems from variations in the response of the individual detectors used within each band. Such problems were particularly prevalent in the collection of early Landsat MSS data. While the six detectors used for each band were carefully calibrated and matched prior to launch, the radiometric response of one or more tended to drift over time, resulting in relatively higher or lower values along every sixth line in the image data. In this case valid data are present in the defective lines but they must be normalized with respect to their neighboring observations.

Several *destriping* procedures have been developed to deal with the type of problem described above. One method is to compile a set of histograms for the image—one for each detector involved in a given band. For MSS data this means that for a given band, one histogram is generated for scan lines 1, 7, 13, etc; a second is generated for lines 2, 8, 14, etc; and so forth. These histograms are then compared in terms of their mean and median values to identify the problem detector(s). A gray-scale adjustment factor(s) can then be determined to adjust the histogram(s) for the problem lines to resemble those for the normal data lines. This adjustment factor is applied to each pixel in the problem lines and the others are not altered (Figure 10.6).

Another line-oriented noise problem sometimes encountered in digital data is *line drop*. In this situation, a number of adjacent pixels along a line (or an entire line) may contain spurious DNs. This problem is normally addressed by replacing the defective DNs with the average of the values for the pixels occurring in the lines just above and below (Figure 10.7). Alternatively, the DNs from the preceding line can simply be inserted in the defective pixels.

Random noise problems in digital data are handled quite differently than those we have discussed to this point. This type of noise is characterized by nonsystematic variations in gray levels from pixel to pixel called *bit errors*. Such noise is often referred to as being "spikey" in character and it causes images to have a "salt and pepper" or "snowy" appearance.

Bit errors are handled by recognizing that noise values normally change much more abruptly than true image values. Thus, noise can be identified by comparing each pixel in an image with its neighbors. If the difference between a given pixel value and its surrounding values exceeds an analyst specified threshold, the pixel is assumed to contain noise. The noisy pixel value can then be replaced by the average of its neighboring values. Moving neighborhoods or windows of 3×3 or 5×5 pixels are typically used in such procedures. Figure 10.8 illustrates the concept of a moving window comprising a 3×3 pixel neighborhood and Figure 10.9 illustrates just one of many noise suppression algorithms using such a neighborhood. Finally, Figure 10.10 illustrates the results of applying the algorithm included in Figure 10.9 to an actual image.

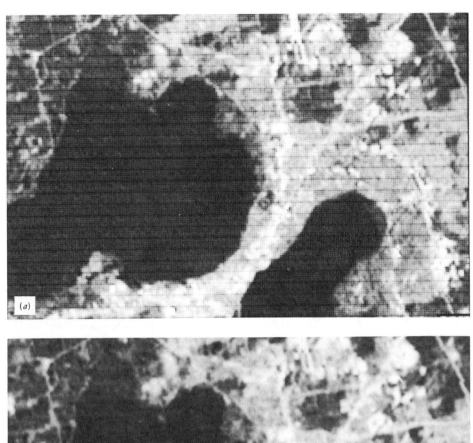

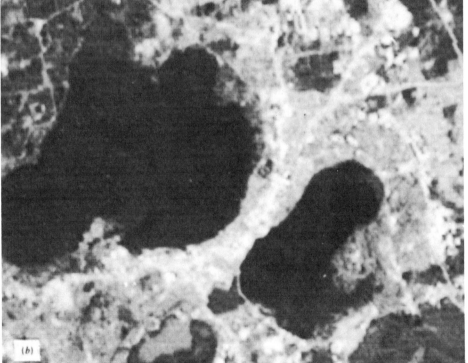

FIGURE 10.6 Destriping algorithm illustration. *(a)* Original image manifesting striping with a six-line frequency. *(b)* Restored image resulting from applying histogram algorithm.

FIGURE 10.7   Line drop correction. *(a)* Original image containing two line drops. *(b)* Restored image resulting from averaging pixel values above and below defective lines.

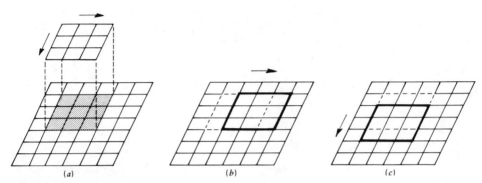

FIGURE 10.8   The moving window concept. *(a)* Projection of 3 × 3 pixel window in image being processed. *(b)* Movement of window along a line from pixel-to-pixel. *(c)* Movement of window from line-to-line. (Adapted from [74].)

DN_1	DN_2	DN_3
DN_4	DN_5	DN_6
DN_7	DN_8	DN_9

$AVE_A = (DN_1 + DN_3 + DN_7 + DN_9)/4$
$AVE_B = (DN_2 + DN_4 + DN_6 + DN_8)/4$
$DIFF = |AVE_A - AVE_B|$
$THRESH = DIFF \times WEIGHT$
IF: $|DN_5 - AVE_A|$ or $|DN_5 - AVE_B| > THRESH$
THEN: $DN_5' = AVE_B$ OTHERWISE $DN_5' = DN_5$

FIGURE 10.9   Typical noise correction algorithm employing a 3 × 3 pixel neighborhood. *Note:* WEIGHT is an analyst-specified weighting factor. The lower the weight, the greater the number of pixels considered to be noise in an image.

FIGURE 10.10 Result of applying noise reduction algorithm. (a) Original image data with noise-induced "salt and pepper" appearance. (b) Image resulting from application of algorithm shown in Figure 10.9.

10.3   IMAGE ENHANCEMENT

As previously mentioned, the goal of image enhancement is to improve the visual interpretability of an image by increasing the apparent distinction between the features in the scene. The process of visually interpreting digitally enhanced imagery attempts to optimize the complementary abilities of the human mind and the computer. The mind is excellent at interpreting spatial attributes on an image and is capable of selectively identifying obscure or subtle features. However, the eye is poor at discriminating the slight radiometric or spectral differences that may characterize such features. Computer enhancement aims to visually amplify these slight differences to make them readily observable.

The range of possible image enhancement and display options available to the image analyst is virtually limitless. Most enhancement techniques may be categorized as either point or local operations. *Point operations* modify the brightness value of each pixel in an image data set independently. *Local operations* modify the value of each pixel based on neighboring brightness values. Either form of enhancement can be performed on single band (monochrome) images or on the individual components of multi-image composites. The resulting images may also be recorded or displayed in black and white or in color. Choosing the appropriate enhancement(s) for any particular application is an art and often a matter of personal preference.

Enhancement operations are normally applied to image data after the appropriate restoration procedures have been performed. Noise removal, in particular, is an important precursor to most enhancements. Without it, the image interpreter is left with the prospect of analyzing enhanced noise!

Below, we discuss the most commonly applied digital enhancement techniques. These techniques can be categorized as *contrast manipulation, spatial feature manipulation*, or *multi-image manipulation*. Within these broad categories, we treat the following:

1. *Contrast manipulation.*   Gray-level thresholding, level slicing, and contrast stretching.
2. *Spatial feature manipulation.*   Spatial filtering, edge enhancement, and Fourier analysis.
3. *Multi-image manipulation.*   Multispectral band ratioing and differencing, principal components, canonical components, vegetation components, and intensity–hue–saturation (IHS) color space transformations.

10.4   CONTRAST MANIPULATION

Gray-Level Thresholding

Gray-level thresholding is used to *segment* an input image into two classes—one for those pixels having values below an analyst defined gray level and one for those above this value. We illustrated this procedure earlier (Section 6.7) as a means of segmenting land from water areas using the infrared sensitive layer of digitized film. Here we illustrate the use of thresholding to prepare a *binary mask* for an image. Such masks are used to segment an image into two classes so that additional processing can then be applied to each class independently.

Shown in Figure 10.11a is a TM1 image that displays a broad range of gray levels over both land and water. Let us assume that we wish to show the brightness variations in this band in the water areas only. Because many of the gray levels for land and water overlap in this band, it would be impossible to separate these two classes using a threshold set in this band. This is not the case in the TM4 band (Figure 10.11b). The histogram of DNs for the TM4 image (Figure 10.11c) shows that water strongly absorbs the incident energy in this near-infrared band (low DNs), while the land areas are highly reflective (high DNs). A threshold set at DN = 40 permits separation of these two classes in the TM4 data. This binary classification can then be applied to the TM1 data to enable display of brightness variations in only the water areas. This is illustrated in Figure 10.11d. In this image, the TM1 land pixel values have all been set to 0 (black) based on their classification in the TM4 binary mask. The TM1 water pixel values have been preserved for display.

Level Slicing

Level slicing is an enhancement technique whereby the DNs distributed along the x axis of an image histogram are divided into a series of analyst specified intervals or "slices." All of the DNs falling within a given interval in the input image are then displayed at a single DN in the output image. Consequently, if six different slices are established, the output image contains only six different gray levels. The result looks something like a contour map, except that the areas between boundaries are occupied by pixels displayed at the same DN. Each level can also be shown as a single color.

Figure 10.12 illustrates the application of level slicing to the "water" portion of the scene illustrated in Figure 10.11. Here, TM1 data have been level-sliced into multiple levels in those areas previously determined to be water from the TM4 binary mask.

Level slicing is used extensively in the display of thermal infrared images in order to show discrete temperature ranges coded by gray level or color. (See Figures 7.40b and 9.27.)

Contrast Stretching

Image display and recording devices typically operate over a range of 256 gray levels (the maximum number represented in 8-bit computer encoding). Sensor data in a single image rarely extend over this entire range. Hence, the intent of contrast stretching is to expand the narrow range of brightness values typically present in an input image over a wider range of gray values. The result is an output image that is designed to accentuate the contrast between features of interest to the image analyst.

To illustrate the contrast stretch process, consider a hypothetical sensing system whose image output levels can vary from 0 to 255. Figure 10.13a illustrates a histogram of brightness levels recorded in one spectral band over a scene. Assume that our

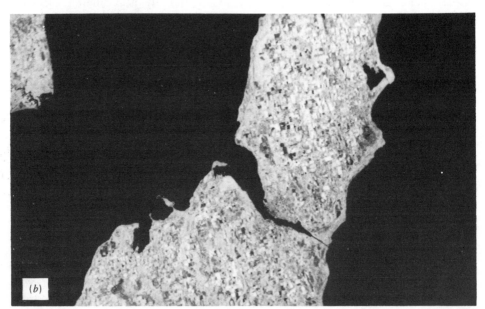

FIGURE 10.11 Gray-level thresholding for binary image segmentation. *(a)* Original TM1 image containing continuous distribution of gray tones. *(b)* TM4 image. *(c)* TM4 histogram. *(d)* TM1 brightness variation in water areas only.

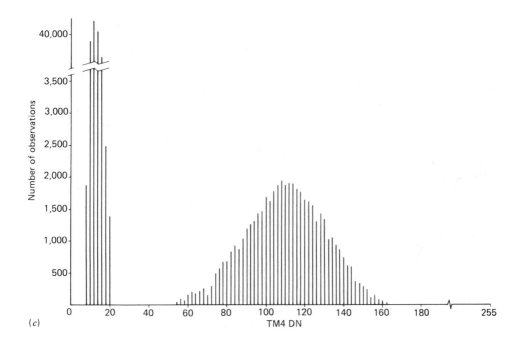

(c)

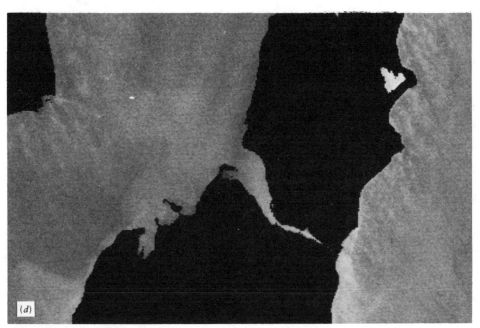

(d)

FIGURE 10.11 *(continued)*

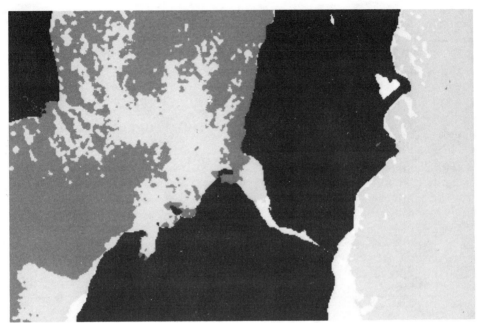

FIGURE 10.12   Level-slicing operation applied to TM1 data in areas determined to be water in Figure 10.11.

hypothetical output device (CRT, or film recorder) is also capable of displaying 256 gray levels (0 to 255). Note that the histogram shows scene brightness values occurring only in the limited range of 60 to 158. If we were to use these image values directly in our display device (Figure 10.13b), we would be using only a small portion of the full range of possible display levels. Display levels 0 to 59 and 159 to 255 would not be utilized. Consequently, the tonal information in the scene would be compressed into a small range of display values, reducing the interpreter's ability to discriminate radiometric detail.

A more expressive display would result if we were to expand the range of image levels present in the scene (60 to 158) to fill the range of display values (0 to 255). In Figure 10.13c, the range of image values has been uniformly expanded to fill the total range of the output device. This uniform expansion is called a *linear stretch*. Subtle variations in input image data values would now be displayed in output tones that would be more readily distinguished by the interpreter. Light tonal areas would appear lighter and dark areas would appear darker.

In our example, the linear stretch would be applied to each pixel in the image using the algorithm

$$DN' = \left(\frac{DN - MIN}{MAX - MIN} \right) 255 \tag{10.5}$$

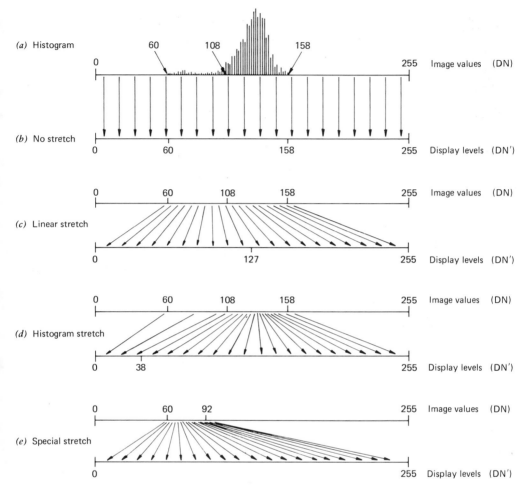

FIGURE 10.13 Principle of contrast stretch enhancement.

where

DN′ = digital number assigned to pixel in output image

DN = original digital number of pixel in input image

MIN = minimum value of input image, to be assigned a value of 0 in the output image (60 in our example)

MAX = maximum value of input image, to be assigned a value of 255 in the output image (158 in our example).

Figure 10.14 illustrates the above algorithm graphically. Note that the values for DN and DN′ must be discrete whole integers. Since the same function is used for all pixels in the image, it is usually calculated for all possible values of DN *before* processing the image. The resulting values of DN′ are then stored in a table (array). To process the image, no additional calculations are necessary. Each pixel's DN is simply used to index a location in the table to find the appropriate DN′ to be displayed in the output image. This process is referred to as a *table lookup* procedure and the list of DN′s associated with each DN is called a *lookup table* (LUT). The obvious advantage to the table lookup process is its computational efficiency. All possible values for DN′ are computed only once (for a maximum of 256 times) and the indexing of a location in the table is then all that is required for each pixel in the image.

One drawback of the linear stretch is that it assigns as many display levels to the rarely occurring image values as it does to the frequently occurring values. For example, as shown in Figure 10.13c, half of the dynamic range of the output device (0 to 127) would be reserved for the small number of pixels having image values in the range 60 to 108. The bulk of the image data (values 109 to 158) are confined to half the output display levels (128 to 255). Although better than the direct display in (*b*), the linear stretch would still not provide the most expressive display of the data.

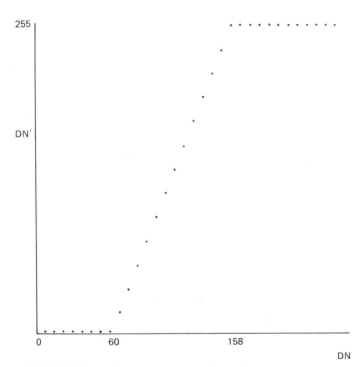

FIGURE 10.14 Linear stretch algorithm. Each point represents several discrete digital numbers.

To improve on the above situation, a *histogram-equalized stretch* can be applied. In this approach, image values are assigned to the display levels on the basis of their frequency of occurrence. As shown in Figure 10.13*d*, more display values (and hence more radiometric detail) are assigned to the frequently occurring portion of the histogram. The image value range of 109 to 158 is now stretched over a large portion of the display levels (39 to 255). A smaller portion (0 to 38) is reserved for the infrequently occurring image values of 60 to 108.

For special analyses, specific features may be analyzed in greater radiometric detail by assigning the display range exclusively to a particular range of image values. For example, if water features were represented by a narrow range of values of a scene, characteristics in the water features could be enhanced by stretching this small range to the full display range. As shown in Figure 10.13*e*, the output range is devoted entirely to the small range of image values between 60 and 92. On the stretched display, minute tonal variations in the water range would be greatly exaggerated. The brighter land features, on the other hand, would be "washed out" by being displayed at a single, bright white level (255).

The visual effect of applying a contrast stretch algorithm is illustrated in Figure 10.15. An original Landsat MSS image covering the Nile Delta in Egypt is shown in (*a*). A small portion of the Mediterranean Sea appears in the upper left portion of the scene, and the city of Cairo lies close to the apex of the delta near the center-right edge of the scene. Because of the wide range of image values present in this scene, the original image shows little radiometric detail. That is, features of similar brightness are virtually indistinguishable.

In Figure 10.15*b*, the brightness range of the desert area has been linearly stretched to fill the dynamic range of the output display. Patterns that were indistinguishable in the low contrast original are now readily apparent in this product. An interpreter wishing to analyze features in the desert region would be able to extract far more information from this display.

Because it reserved all display levels for the bright areas, the desert enhancement shows no radiometric detail in the darker irrigated delta region, which is displayed as black. If an interpreter were interested in analyzing features in this area, a different stretch could be applied, resulting in a display as shown in Figure 10.15*c*. Here, the display levels are devoted solely to the range of values present in the delta region. This rendering of the original image enhances brightness differences in the heavily populated and intensively cultivated delta, at the expense of all information in the bright desert area. Population centers stand out vividly in this display, and brightness differences between crop types are accentuated.

The contrast stretching examples we have illustrated represent only a small subset of the range of possible transformations that can be applied to image data. For example, nonlinear stretches such as sinusoidal transformations can be applied to image data to enhance subtle differences within "homogeneous" features such as forest stands or volcanic flows [17]. Also, we have illustrated only monochromatic stretching procedures. Enhanced color images can be prepared by applying these procedures to separate bands of image data independently and then combining the results into a composite display.

(a)

FIGURE 10.15 Effect of contrast stretching Landsat MSS data. Nile Delta, May 10, 1973. *(a)* Original image. *(b)* Stretch that enhances contrast in bright image areas. *(c)* Stretch that enhances contrast in dark image areas. (Courtesy IBM Corp.)

(b)

FIGURE 10.15 *(continued)*

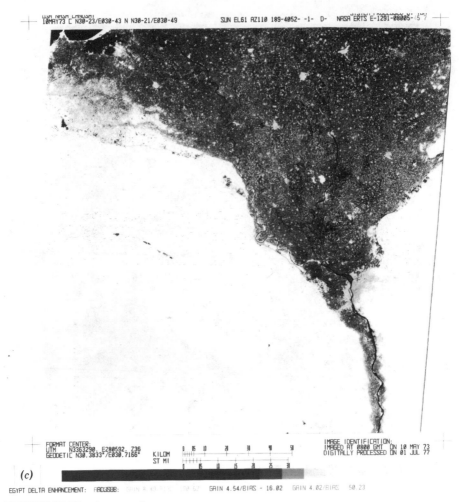

(c)

EGYPT DELTA ENHANCEMENT:

FIGURE 10.15 (continued)

10.5 SPATIAL FEATURE MANIPULATION

Spatial Filtering

In contrast to spectral filters, which serve to block or pass energy over various spectral ranges, spatial filters emphasize or deemphasize image data of various *spatial frequencies*. Spatial frequency refers to the "roughness" of the tonal variations occurring in an image. Image areas of high spatial frequency are tonally "rough." That is, the gray levels in these areas change abruptly over a relatively small number of pixels (e.g., across roads or field borders). "Smooth" image areas are those of low spatial frequency, where gray levels vary only gradually over a relatively large number of pixels (e.g., large agricultural fields or water bodies). *Low-pass filters* are designed to emphasize low frequency features (large area changes in brightness) and deemphasize the high frequency components of an image (local detail). *High-pass filters* do just the reverse. They emphasize the detailed high frequency components of an image and deemphasize the more general low frequency information.

Spatial filtering is a "local" operation in that pixel values in an original image are modified on the basis of the gray levels of neighboring pixels. For example, a simple low-pass filter may be implemented by passing a moving window throughout an original image and creating a second image whose DN at each pixel corresponds to the local average within the moving window at each of its positions in the original image. Assuming a 3 × 3 pixel window is used, the center pixel's DN in the new (filtered) image would be the average value of the 9 pixels in the original image contained in the window at that point. This process is very similar to that we described previously under the topic of noise suppression. (In fact, low-pass filters are very useful for reducing random noise.)

A simple high-pass filter may be implemented by subtracting a low-pass filtered image (pixel-by-pixel) from the original, unprocessed image. Figure 10.16 illustrates the visual effect of applying this process to an image. The original image is shown in 10.16a. Figure 10.16b shows the low frequency component image and Figure 10.16c illustrates the high frequency component image. Note that the low frequency component image (b) reduces deviations from the local average which smooths or blurs the detail in the original image, reduces the gray-level range, but emphasizes the large area brightness regimes of the original image. The high frequency component image (c) enhances the spatial detail in the image at the expense of the large area brightness information. Both images have been contrast stretched. (Such stretching is typically required because spatial filtering reduces the gray-level range present in an image.)

Convolution

Spatial filtering is but one special application of the generic image processing operation called *convolution*. Convolving an image involves the following procedures:

1. A moving window is established which contains an array of coefficients or weighting factors. Such arrays are referred to as *operators* or *kernels* and they are normally an odd number of pixels in size (e.g., 3 × 3, 5 × 5, 7 × 7).

2. The kernel is moved throughout the original image and the DN at the center of the kernel in a second (convoluted) output image is obtained by multiplying each coefficient in the kernel by the corresponding DN in the original image and adding all the resulting products. This operation is performed for each pixel in the original image.

Figure 10.17 illustrates a 3 × 3 pixel kernel with all of its coefficients equal to 1/9. Convolving an image with this kernel would result in simply averaging the values in the moving window. This is the procedure that was used to prepare the low frequency enhancement shown in Figure 10.16*b*. However, images emphasizing other spatial frequencies may be prepared by simply altering the kernel coefficients used to perform the convolution. Figure 10.18 shows three successively lower frequency enhancements (*b*, *c*, and *d*) that have been derived from the same original data set (*a*).

The influence convolution may have on an image depends directly upon the size of the kernel used and the values of the coefficients contained within the kernel. The range of kernel sizes and weighting schemes is limitless. For example, by selecting the appropriate coefficients, one can center-weight kernels, make them of uniform weight, or shape them in accordance with a particular statistical model (such as a Gaussian distribution). In short, convolution is a generic image processing operation that has numerous applications in addition to spatial filtering. (Recall the use of "cubic convolution" as a resampling procedure.)

Edge Enhancement

We have seen that high frequency component images emphasize the spatial detail in digital images. That is, these images exaggerate local contrast and are superior to unenhanced original images for portraying linear features or edges in the image data.

FIGURE 10.16 Effect of spatial filtering Landsat TM data. *(a)* Original image. *(b)* Low frequency component image. *(c)* High frequency component image.

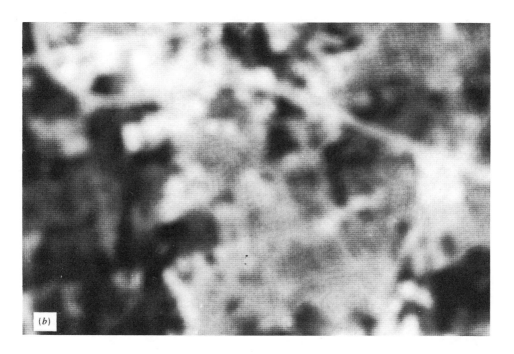

FIGURE 10.16   *(continued)*

1/9	1/9	1/9
1/9	1/9	1/9
1/9	1/9	1/9

(*a*) Kernel

67	67	72
70	68	71
72	71	72

(*b*) Original image DNs

	70	

(*c*) Convolved image DN

Convolution: $1/9(67) + 1/9(67) + 1/9(72) + 1/9(70) + 1/9(68) + 1/9(71) + 1/9(72) + 1/9(71) + 1/9(72) = 630/9 = 70$

FIGURE 10.17   Concept of convolution. Shown is a 3 × 3 pixel kernel with all coefficients equal to 1/9. The central pixel in the convolved image (in this case) contains the average of the DNs within the kernel.

However, high frequency component images do not preserve the low frequency brightness information contained in original images. Edge enhanced images attempt to preserve both local contrast and low frequency brightness information. They are produced by "adding back" all, or a portion, of the gray values in an original image to a high frequency component image of the same scene. Thus, edge enhancement is typically implemented in three steps:

1. A high frequency component image is produced containing the edge information. The kernel size used to produce this image is chosen based on the roughness of the image. "Rough" images suggest small filter sizes (e.g., 3 × 3 pixels), whereas large sizes (e.g., 9 × 9 pixels) are used with "smooth" images.

2. All, or a fraction, of the gray level in each pixel of the original scene is added back to the high frequency component image. (The proportion of the original gray levels to be added back may be chosen by the image analyst.)

3. The composite image is contrast stretched. This results in an image containing local contrast enhancement of high frequency features that also preserves the low frequency brightness information contained in the scene.

Plate 17 shows the influence of applying the edge enhancement process as part of the production of a color composite from Landsat MSS data. This scene covers the coast of Massachusetts, showing Cape Cod and the metropolitan areas of Boston (upper left) and Providence, Rhode Island (lower left). The original color composite for the image is given in *(a)*. The edge enhanced imaged *(b)* depicts cultural features much more clearly than the original. It should also be noted that due to contrast stretching, the enhancement generally manifests deeper reds over vegetated areas, lighter tones in urbanized regions, and brighter whites in the coastal dune formations. Because of the improved interpretability afforded by the combination of contrast stretching and edge enhancement, the edge enhancement process is often applied in the production of image maps.

Directional first differencing is another enhancement technique aimed at emphasizing edges in image data. It is a procedure that systematically compares each pixel in an image to one of its immediately adjacent neighbors and displays the difference in terms of the gray levels of an output image. This process is mathematically akin to determining the first derivative of gray levels with respect to a given direction. The direction used can be either horizontal, vertical, or diagonal. In Figure 10.19, a horizontal first difference at pixel A would result from subtracting the DN in pixel H from that in pixel A. A vertical first difference would result from subtracting the DN at pixel V from that in pixel A; a diagonal first difference would result from subtracting the DN at pixel D from that in pixel A.

It should be noted that first differences can be either positive or negative, so a constant such as the display value median (127 for 8-bit data) is normally added to the difference for display purposes. Furthermore, because pixel-to-pixel differences are often very small, the data in the enhanced image often span a very narrow range about the display value median and a contrast stretch must be applied to the output image.

FIGURE 10.18   Frequency components of an image resulting from varying the kernel used for convolution. *(a)* Original image. *(b–d)* Successively lower frequency enhancements.

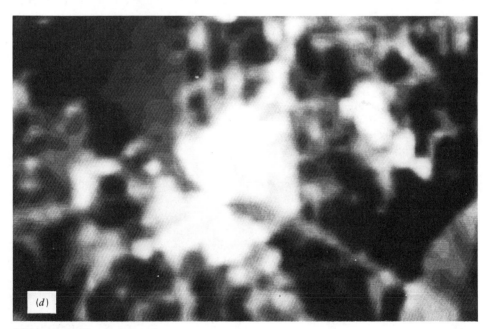

FIGURE 10.18 *(continued)*

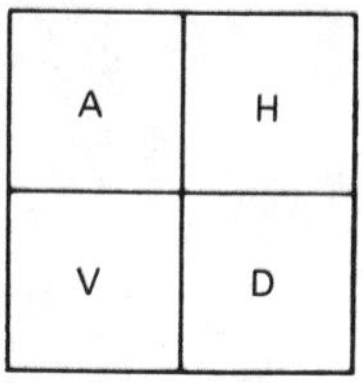

Horizontal first difference = $DN_A - DN_H$

Vertical first difference = $DN_A - DN_V$

Diagonal first difference = $DN_A - DN_D$

FIGURE 10.19   Primary pixel (A) and reference pixels (H, V, and D) used in horizontal, vertical, and diagonal first differencing, respectively.

First difference images emphasize those edges normal to the direction of differencing and deemphasize those parallel to the direction of differencing. For example, in a horizontal first difference image, vertical edges will result in large pixel-to-pixel changes in gray level. On the other hand, the vertical first differences for these same edges would be relatively small (perhaps zero). This effect is illustrated in Figure 10.20 where vertical features in the original image *(a)* are emphasized in the horizontal first difference image *(b)*. Horizontal features in the original image are highlighted in the vertical first difference image *(c)*. Features emphasized by the diagonal first difference are shown in *(d)*.

Figure 10.21 illustrates yet another form of edge enhancement involving diagonal first differencing. This image was produced by adding the absolute value of the upper left-to-lower right diagonal first difference to that of the upper right-to-lower left diagonal. This enhancement tends to highlight all edges in the scene.

Fourier Analysis

The spatial feature manipulations we have discussed thus far are implemented in the *spatial domain*—the (x,y) coordinate space of images. An alternative coordinate space that can be used for image analysis is the *frequency domain*. In this approach, an image is separated into its various spatial frequency components through application of a mathematical operation known as the *Fourier transform*. A quantitative description of how Fourier transforms are computed is beyond the scope of this discussion. Conceptually, this operation amounts to fitting a continuous function through the discrete DN values if they were plotted along each row and column in an image. The "peaks and valleys" along any given row or column can be described mathematically by a combination of sine and cosine waves with various amplitudes, frequencies, and phases. A Fourier transform results from the calculation of the amplitude and phase for each possible spatial frequency in an image.

After an image is separated into its component spatial frequencies it is possible to display these values in a two-dimensional scatter plot known as a *Fourier spectrum*. Figure 10.22 illustrates a digital image in *(a)* and its Fourier spectrum in *(b)*. The lower

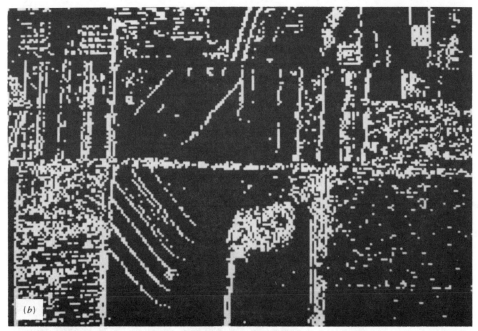

FIGURE 10.20 Effect of directional first differencing. *(a)* Original image. *(b)* Horizontal first difference. *(c)* Vertical first difference. *(d)* Diagonal first difference.

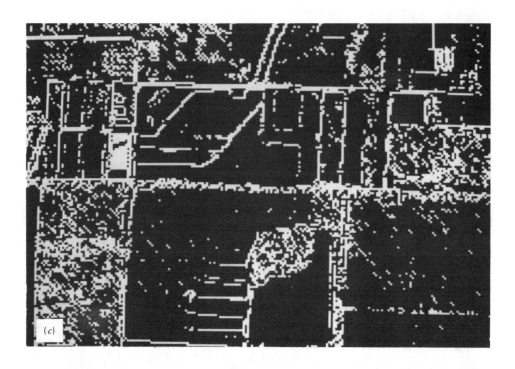

FIGURE 10.20   *(continued)*

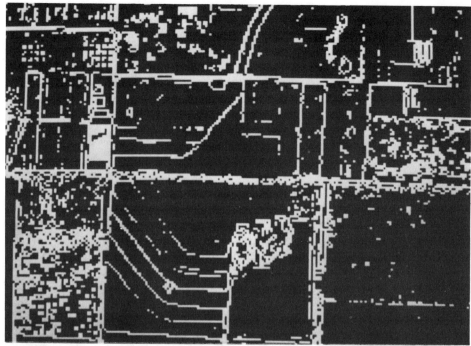

FIGURE 10.21   Edge enhancement through cross diagonal first differencing.

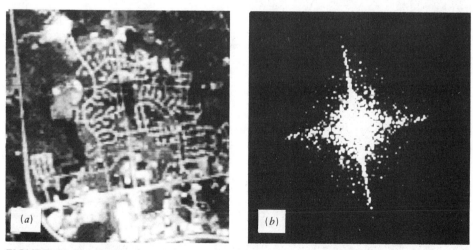

FIGURE 10.22   Application of Fourier transform. (a) Original scene. (b) Fourier spectrum of (a).

frequencies in the scene are plotted at the center of the spectrum and progressively higher frequencies are plotted outward. Features trending horizontally in the original image result in vertical components in the Fourier spectrum; features aligned vertically in the original image result in horizontal components in the Fourier spectrum.

If the Fourier spectrum of an image is known, it is possible to regenerate the original image through the application of an *inverse Fourier transform*. This operation is simply the mathematical reversal of the Fourier transform. Hence, the Fourier spectrum of an image can be used to assist in a number of image processing operations. For example, spatial filtering can be accomplished by applying a filter directly on the Fourier spectrum and then performing an inverse transform. This is illustrated in Figure 10.23. In Figure 10.23a, a circular high frequency blocking filter has been

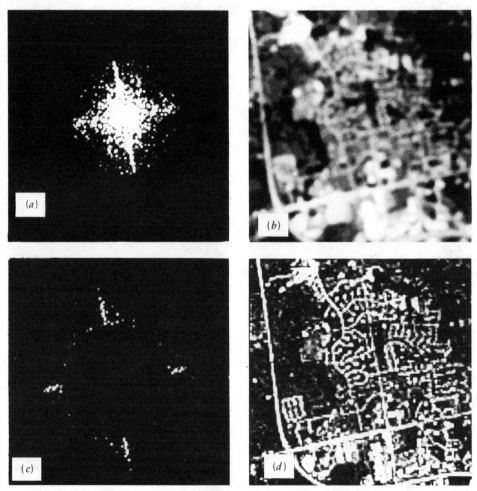

FIGURE 10.23   Spatial filtering in the frequency domain. *(a)* High frequency blocking filter. *(b)* Inverse transform of *(a)*. *(c)* Low frequency blocking filter. *(d)* Inverse transform of *(c)*.

applied to the Fourier spectrum shown previously in Figure 10.22b. Note that this image is a low-pass filtered version of the original scene. Figures 10.23c and d illustrate the application of a circular low frequency blocking filter (c) to produce a high-pass filtered enhancement (d).

Figure 10.24 illustrates another common application of Fourier analysis—the elimination of image noise. Shown in 10.24a is an airborne multispectral scanner image containing substantial noise. The Fourier spectrum for the image is shown in 10.24b. Note that the noise pattern, which occurs in a horizontal direction in the original scene, appears as a band of frequencies trending in the vertical direction in the Fourier spectrum. In 10.24c a vertical *wedge block filter* has been applied to the spectrum. This filter passes the lower frequency components of the image, but blocks the high

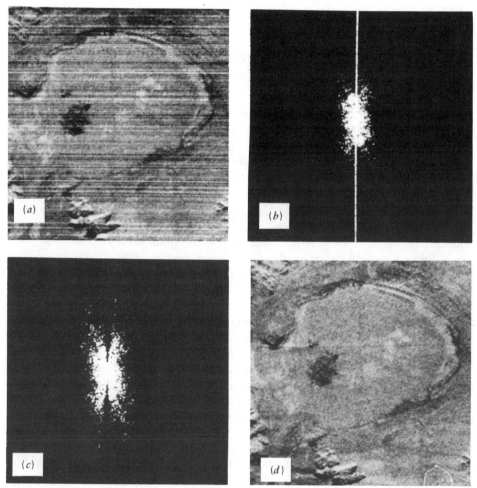

FIGURE 10.24 Noise elimination in the frequency domain. *(a)* Airborne multispectral scanner image containing noise. (Courtesy NASA.) *(b)* Fourier spectrum of *(a)*. *(c)* Wedge block filter. *(d)* Inverse transform of *(c)*.

frequency components of the original image trending in the horizontal direction. Figure 20.24*d* shows the inverse transform of *(c)*. Note how effectively this operation eliminates the noise inherent in the original image.

Fourier analysis is useful in a host of image processing operations in addition to the spatial filtering and image restoration applications we have illustrated in this discussion. However, most image processing is currently implemented in the spatial domain because of the number and complexity of computations required in the frequency domain. (This situation is likely to change with improvements in computer hardware and advances in research on the spatial attributes of digital image data.)

Before leaving the topic of spatial feature manipulation it should be reemphasized that we have illustrated only a representative subset of the range of possible processing techniques available. Several of the references included at the end of this chapter describe and illustrate numerous other procedures that may be of interest to the reader.

10.6 MULTI-IMAGE MANIPULATION

Spectral Ratioing

Ratio images are enhancements resulting from the division of DN values in one spectral band by the corresponding values in another band. Earlier we introduced the notion of spectral ratioing in the context of photographic radiometry (Section 6.10). At that time, we pointed out that a major advantage of ratio images is that they convey the spectral or color characteristics of image features, regardless of variations in scene illumination conditions. This concept is illustrated in Figure 10.25, which depicts two different land cover types (deciduous and coniferous trees) occurring on both the sunlit and shadowed sides of a ridge line. The DNs observed for each cover type are substantially lower in the shadowed area than in the sunlit area. However, the ratio values for each cover type are nearly identical, irrespective of the illumination condition. Hence, a ratioed image of the scene effectively compensates for the brightness variation caused by the varying topography and emphasizes the color content of the data.

Ratioed images are often useful for discriminating subtle *spectral* variations in a scene that are masked by the *brightness* variations in images from individual spectral bands or in standard color composites. This enhanced discrimination is due to the fact that ratioed images clearly portray the variations in the *slopes* of the spectral reflectance curves between the two bands involved, regardless of the absolute reflectance values observed in the bands. These slopes are typically quite different for various material types in certain bands of sensing. For example, the near-infrared to red ratio for healthy vegetation is normally very high. That for stressed vegetation is typically lower (as near-infrared reflectance decreases and the red reflectance increases). Thus a near-infrared to red (or red to near-infrared) ratioed image might be very useful for differentiating between areas of the stressed and nonstressed vegetation. This type of ratio has also been employed extensively in vegetation indices aimed at quantifying relative vegetation greenness and biomass.

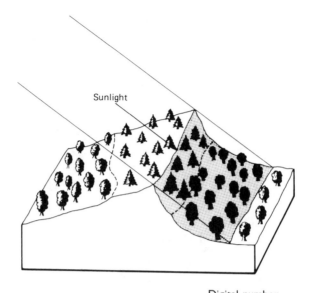

Land cover/illumination	Digital number		
	Band A	Band B	Ratio (band A/band B)
Deciduous			
Sunlit	48	50	0.96
Shadow	18	19	0.95
Coniferous			
Sunlit	31	45	0.69
Shadow	11	16	0.69

FIGURE 10.25 Reduction of scene illumination effects through spectral ratioing. (Adapted from [71]).

Obviously, the utility of any given spectral ratio depends upon the particular reflectance characteristics of the features involved and the application at hand. The form and number of ratio combinations available to the image analyst also varies depending upon the source of the digital data. The number of possible ratios that can be developed from n bands of data is $n(n - 1)$. Thus, for Landsat MSS data, $4(4 - 1)$ or 12 different ratio combinations are possible (six original and six reciprocal). For the six nonthermal bands of Landsat TM data there are $6(6 - 1)$ or 30 possible combinations.

Figure 10.26 illustrates four representative ratio images generated from TM data. These images depict higher ratio values in brighter tones. Shown in (a) is the ratio TM1/TM2. Because these two bands are highly correlated for this scene the ratio image has low contrast. In (b) the ratio TM3/TM4 is depicted so that features such as water and roads which reflect highly in the red band (TM3) and little in the near-infrared band (TM4) are shown in lighter tones. Features such as vegetation appear in darker tones because of their relatively low reflectance in the red band (TM3) and high reflectance in the near-infrared (TM4). In (c) the ratio TM5/TM2 is shown. Here,

FIGURE 10.26 Ratioed images derived from Landsat TM data collected on July 18, 1984, near Sturgeon Bay, Wisconsin. Higher ratio values are displayed in brighter image tones. (a) TM1/TM2. (b)TM3/TM4. (c)TM5/TM2. (d) TM3/TM7.

(c)

(d)

FIGURE 10.26   (continued)

vegetation generally appears in light tones because of its relatively high reflectance in the mid-infrared band (TM5) and its comparatively lower reflectance in the green band (TM2). However, note that certain vegetation types do not follow this trend due to their particular reflectance characteristics. They are depicted in very dark tones in this particular ratio image and can therefore be discriminated from the other vegetation types in the scene. Part (d) shows the ratio TM3/TM7. Roads and other cultural features appear in lighter tone in this image due to their relatively high reflectance in the red band (TM3) and low reflectance in the mid-infrared band (TM7). Similarly, differences in water turbidity are readily observable in this ratio image.

Ratio images can also be used to generate false color composites by combining three monochromatic ratio data sets. Such composites have the twofold advantage of combining data from more than two bands and presenting the data in color, which further facilitates the interpretation of subtle spectral reflectance differences. Choosing which ratios to include in a color composite and selecting colors in which to portray them can sometimes be difficult. For example, excluding reciprocals, 20 color combinations are possible when the 6 original ratios of Landsat MSS data are displayed 3 at a time. The 15 original ratios of nonthermal TM data result in 455 different possible combinations.

Various quantitative criteria have been developed to assist in selecting which ratio combinations to include in color composites. The Optimum Index Factor (OIF) is one such criterion [18]. It ranks all possible three-ratio combinations based on the total variance present in each ratio and the degree of correlation between ratios. That combination containing the most variance and least correlation is assumed to convey the greatest amount of information throughout a scene. A limitation of this procedure is that the best combination for conveying the *overall* information in a scene may not be the best combination for conveying the *specific* information desired by the image analyst. Hence, some trial-and-error is often necessary in selecting ratio combinations.

Certain caution should be taken when generating and interpreting ratio images. First, it should be noted that such images are "intensity blind." That is, dissimilar materials with different absolute radiances, but having similar slopes of their spectral reflectance curves, may appear identical. This problem is particularly troublesome when these materials are contiguous and of similar image texture. One way of minimizing this problem is by using a *hybrid color ratio composite*. This product is prepared by displaying two ratio images in two of the primary colors, but using the third primary color to display an individual band of data. This restores a portion of the lost absolute radiance information and some of the topographic detail which may be needed to discriminate between certain features. (As we illustrate later, intensity–hue–saturation (IHS) color space transformations can also be used for this purpose.)

Noise removal is an important prelude to the preparation of ratio images since ratioing enhances noise patterns that are uncorrelated in the component images. Furthermore, ratios only compensate for multiplicative illumination effects. That is, division of DNs or radiances for two bands cancels only those factors that are operative equally in the bands and not those that are additive. For example, atmospheric haze is an additive factor that might have to be removed prior to ratioing to yield acceptable results. Alternatively, ratios of between-band differences and/or sums may be used to improve image interpretability in some applications (see Section 6.10).

The manner is which ratios are computed and displayed will also greatly influence the information content of a ratio image. For example, the ratio between two raw DNs for a pixel will normally be quite different from that between two radiance values computed for the same pixel. The reason for this is that the detector response curves for the two channels will normally have different offsets, which are additive effects on the data. (This situation is akin to the differences one would obtain by ratioing two temperatures using the Fahrenheit scale versus the Celsius scale.) Some trial-and-error may be necessary before the analyst can determine which form of ratio works best for a particular application.

It should also be noted that ratios can "blow up" mathematically (become equal to infinity) in that divisions by zero are possible. At the same time, ratios less than one are common and rounding to integer values will compress much of the ratio data into gray level 0 or 1. Hence, it is important to scale the results of ratio computations somehow, and relate them to the display device used. One means of doing this is to employ an algorithm of the form

$$DN' = R \arctan \left(\frac{DN_X}{DN_Y} \right) \tag{10.6}$$

where
 DN' = digital number in ratio image
  R = scaling factor to place ratio data in appropriate integer range

$\arctan \left(\dfrac{DN_X}{DN_Y} \right)$ = angle (in radians) whose tangent is the ratio of the digital numbers in bands X and Y; if DN_Y equals 0, this angle is set to 90°

In the above equation the angle whose tangent is equal to the ratio of the two bands can range from 0 to 90°, or 0 to approximately 1.571 radians. Therefore, DN' can range from 0 to approximately $1.571R$. If an 8-bit display is used, R is typically chosen to be 162.3, and DN' can then range from 0 to 255.

Principal and Canonical Components

Extensive interband correlation is a problem frequently encountered in the analysis of multispectral image data. That is, images generated by digital data from various wavelength bands often appear similar and convey essentially the same information. Principal and canonical component transformations are two techniques designed to remove or reduce such redundancy in multispectral data. These transformations may be applied either as an enhancement operation prior to visual interpretation of the data or as a preprocessing procedure prior to automated classification of the data. If employed in the latter context, the transformations generally increase the computational efficiency of the classification process because both principal and canonical component analyses may result in a reduction in the dimensionality of the original data set. Stated differently, the purpose of these procedures is to compress all of the information contained in an original n-channel data set into fewer than n "new channels" or *components*. The components are then used in lieu of the original data.

A detailed description of the statistical procedures used to derive principal and canonical component transformations is beyond the scope of this discussion. However, the concepts involved may be expressed graphically by considering a two-channel image data set such as that shown in Figure 10.27. In (*a*), a random sample of pixels has been plotted on a scatter diagram according to their gray levels as originally recorded in band A and band B. Superimposed on the band A/band B axis system are two new axes (axis I, axis II) that are rotated with respect to the original measurement axes and that have their origin at the mean of the data distribution. Axis I defines the direction of the *first principal component* and axis II defines the direction of the *second principal component*. The form of the relationship necessary to transform a data value in the original band A/band B coordinate system into its value in the new axis I/axis II system is

$$DN_I = a_{11}DN_A + a_{12}DN_B$$
$$DN_{II} = a_{21}DN_A + a_{22}DN_B$$

(10.7)

where
$$DN_I, \ DN_{II} = \text{digital numbers in new (principal component) coordinate system}$$
$$DN_A, \ DN_B = \text{digital numbers in old coordinate system}$$
$$a_{11}, a_{12}, a_{21}, a_{22} = \text{coefficients (constants) for the transformation}$$

In short, the principal component data values are simply linear combinations of the original data values.

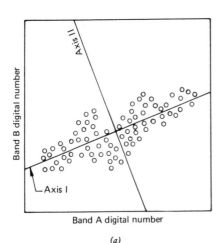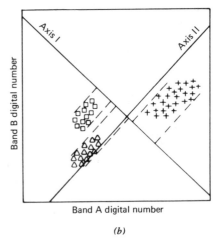

(*a*)   (*b*)

FIGURE 10.27   Rotated coordinate axes used in principal component (*a*) and canonical component (*b*) transformations.

It should be noted in Figure 10.27a that the data along the first principal component (axis I) have a greater variance or dynamic range than the data plotted against either of the original axes (band A, band B). The data along the second principal component have far less variance. This is characteristic of all principal components. For channels of multispectral data, the first principal component (PC1) includes the largest percentage of the total scene variance and succeeding components (PC2, PC3, . . . , PCn) each contain a decreasing percentage of the scene variance. Furthermore, because successive components are chosen to be orthogonal to all previous ones, the data they contain are uncorrelated.

Principal component enhancements are generated by displaying contrast stretched images of the transformed pixel values. We illustrate the nature of these displays by considering the Landsat MSS images shown in Figure 10.28. This figure depicts the four MSS bands of a scene covering the Sahl al Matran area, Saudi Arabia. Figure 10.29 shows displays of the principal component values for this scene. Some areas of geologic interest labeled on Figure 10.28 are (A) alluvial material in a dry stream valley, (B) flat-lying quaternary and tertiary basalts, and (C) granite and granodiorite intrusion.

Note that in Figure 10.29, PC1 expresses the majority (97.6 percent) of the variance in the original data set. Furthermore, PC1 and PC2 explain virtually all of the variance in the scene (99.4 percent). This compression of image information in the first two principal components of Landsat MSS data is typical. Because of this, we refer to the *intrinsic dimensionality* of Landsat MSS data as being effectively 2. Also frequently encountered with Landsat MSS data, the PC4 image for this scene contains virtually no information and tends to depict little more than system noise. However, note that both PC2 and PC3 illustrate certain features that were obscured by the more dominant patterns shown in PC1. For example, a semicircular feature (labeled C in Figure 10.28), is clearly defined in the upper right portion of the PC2 and PC3 images (appearing bright and dark, respectively). This feature was masked by more dominant patterns both in the PC1 image and in all bands of the original data. Also, its tonal reversal in PC2 and PC3 illustrates the lack of correlation between these images.

As in the case of ratio images, principal component images can be analyzed as separate black and white images (as illustrated here), or any three component images may be combined to form a color composite. If used in an image classification process, principal component data are normally treated in the classification algorithm simply as if they were original data. However, the number of components used is normally reduced to the intrinsic dimensionality of the data, thereby making the image classification process much more efficient by reducing the amount of computation required.

Principal component enhancement techniques are particularly appropriate where little prior information concerning a scene is available. *Canonical component analysis*, also referred to as multiple discriminant analysis, may be more appropriate when information about particular features of interest is known. Recall that the principal component axes shown in Figure 10.27a were located on the basis of a random, undifferentiated sample of image pixel values. In Figure 10.27b, the pixel values shown are derived from image areas containing three different analyst-defined feature types (the feature types are represented by the symbols △, □, and +). The canonical component axes in this figure (axis I, axis II) have been located to maximize the

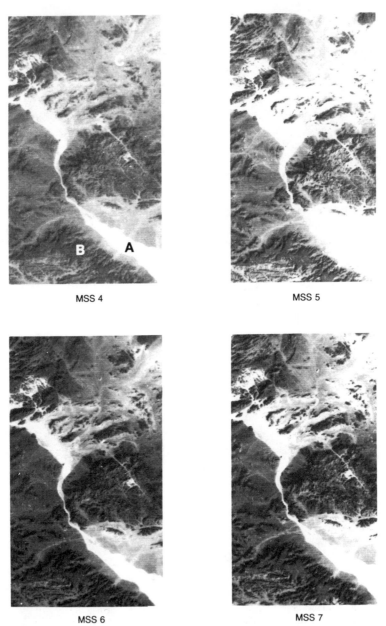

FIGURE 10.28 Four MSS bands covering the Sahl al Matran area of Saudi Arabia, July 15, 1973. 1:943,400. Note the redundancy of information in these original image displays. (Courtesy NASA.)

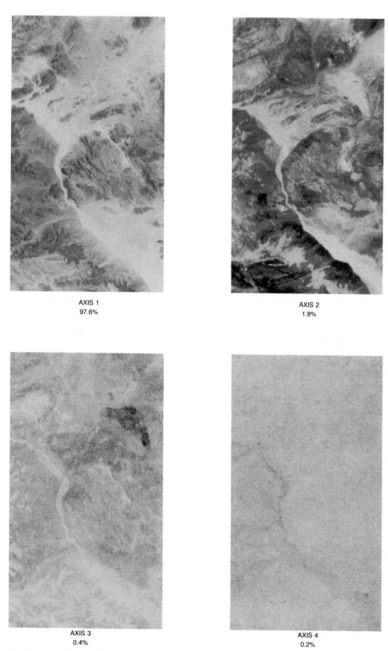

AXIS 1
97.6%

AXIS 2
1.8%

AXIS 3
0.4%

AXIS 4
0.2%

FIGURE 10.29 Transformed data resulting from principal component analysis of the MSS data shown in Figure 10.28. The percentage of scene variance contained in each axis is indicated. (Courtesy NASA.)

separability of these classes while minimizing the variance within each class. For example, the axes have been positioned in this figure such that the three feature types can be discriminated solely on the basis of the first canonical component (CC1) values located along axis I.

In Figure 10.30, canonical component images are shown for the Landsat MSS scene shown in Figure 10.28. Once again, CC1 expresses the highest percentage variation in the data with subsequent components representing lesser amounts of uncorrelated additional information. These displays, as in cases such as feature *C*, may enhance subtle features not evident in the original image data. Like principal component data, canonical component data can also be used in image classification. Canonical components not only improve classification efficiency but they also can improve classification accuracy for the identified features due to the increased spectral separability of classes.

Vegetation Components

Previously (Section 9.16), we introduced the concept of vegetation indices and the use of between-band differences and ratios to produce vegetation index images from AVHRR data. Here we wish to point out that numerous other forms of linear data transformations have been developed for vegetation monitoring, with differing sensors and vegetation conditions dictating different transformations [42, 64, 89]. For example, Kauth and Thomas derived a linear transformation of the four Landsat MSS bands that established four new axes in the spectral data that can be interpreted as *vegetation components* useful for agricultural crop monitoring [47]. This "tasseled cap" transformation rotates the MSS data such that the majority of information is contained in two components or features which are directly related to physical scene characteristics. Brightness, the first feature, is a weighted sum of all bands, and is defined in the direction of the principal variation in soil reflectance. The second feature, greenness, is approximately orthogonal to brightness and is a contrast between the near-infrared and visible bands. Greenness is strongly related to the amount of green vegetation present in the scene. Brightness and greenness together typically express 95 percent or more of the total variability in MSS data and have the characteristic of being readily interpretable features generally applicable from scene to scene (once illumination and atmospheric effects are normalized).

Crist and Cicone extended the tasseled cap concept to Landsat TM data and found that the six bands of reflected data effectively occupy three dimensions, defining planes of soils, vegetation, and a transition zone between them [22]. The third feature, called wetness, relates to canopy and soil moisture.

Figure 10.31 illustrates the application of the tasseled cap transformation to TM data acquired over north central Nebraska [93]. The northern half of the area is dominated by circular corn fields that have been watered throughout the summer by center-pivot irrigators. The southern half of the area is at the edge of the Nebraska Sand Hills which are covered by grasslands. Lighter tones in these images correspond to larger values of each component.

Plate 18 illustrates another vegetation transformation, namely, the *transformed*

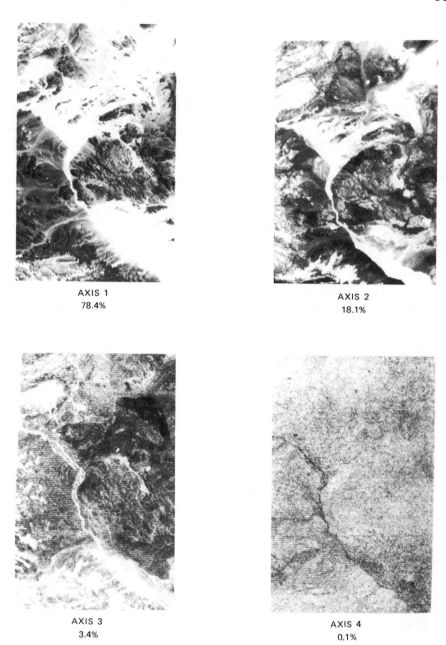

FIGURE 10.30 Transformed data resulting from canonical component analysis of the MSS data shown in Figure 10.28. The percentage of scene variance contained in each axis is indicated. (Courtesy NASA.)

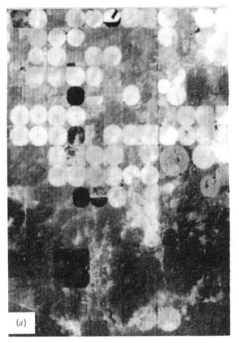

(a)

(b)

(c)

FIGURE 10.31 Tasseled cap transformation for a TM image of north-central Nebraska. The image was collected on September 24, 1982. The three components shown here illustrate relative greenness (a), brightness (b), and wetness (c). (Courtesy Institute of Agricultural and Natural Resources, University of Nebraska.)

vegetation index (TVI), applied to the same data set shown in Figure 10.31. The TVI is computed as

$$\text{TVI} = \left[\frac{\text{DN4} - \text{DN3}}{\text{DN4} + \text{DN3}} + 0.5 \right]^{1/2} \times 100$$

where DN3 and DN4 correspond to the DNs in bands TM3 and TM4, respectively. A false color composite of the scene is shown in *(a)* and the TVI image for the scene is shown in *(b)* of Plate 18. Ground reference data collected in such areas have shown the TVI to be proportional to the amount of green biomass present within each pixel. In fact, such scenes can be calibrated by relating ground-based biomass measurements from several corn fields and pastures located in the scene to the corresponding TVI values. Separate calibration relationships must be established for each cover type and these become the quantitative basis upon which to depict the biomass present in similar fields and pastures throughout the scene. The relative biomass levels present in a series of analyst-defined corn fields is shown in *(c)*. In *(d)* the biomass present in 10 selected pastures is shown. In each case, high TVI levels are coded as green, intermediate values are yellow, and low values are red. Such information can be valuable to the individual farmer or rancher managing such lands. For example, the spatial variation in the various corn fields could provide the basis for differential spatial applications of irrigation water, fertilizers, herbicides, and so on, to individual fields to optimize crop yields [19]. Similarly, ranch management decisions can be based on the estimated level of forage present in each pasture [55].

Intensity–Hue–Saturation (IHS) Color Space Transformation

Digital images are typically displayed as additive color composites using the three primary colors: red, green, and blue (RGB). Figure 10.32 illustrates the interrelation among the RGB components of a typical color display device (such as a CRT). Shown in this figure is the RGB *color cube*, which is defined by the brightness levels of each of the three primary colors. For a display with 8 bit per pixel data encoding, the range of possible DNs for each color component is 0 to 255. Hence, there are 256^3 (or 16,777,216) possible combinations of red, green and blue DNs that can be displayed by such a device. Every pixel in a composited display may be represented by a three-dimensional coordinate position somewhere within the color cube. The line from the origin of the cube to the opposite corner is known as the *gray line* since DNs that lie on this line have equal components of red. green, and blue.

RGB displays are used extensively in digital processing to display normal color, false color infrared, and arbitrary color composites. For example, a normal color composite may be displayed by assigning TM bands 1, 2, and 3 to the blue, green, and red components, respectively. A false color infrared composite results when TM bands 2, 3, and 4 are assigned to these respective components. Arbitrary color composites result when other bands or color assignments are used. Color composites may be

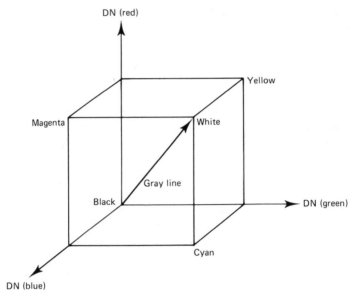

FIGURE 10.32   The RGB color cube. (Adapted from [74].)

contrast stretched on a RGB display by manipulating the contrast in each of the three display channels (using a separate lookup table for each of the three color components).

An alternative to describing colors by their RGB components is the use of the *intensity—hue—saturation (IHS)* system. "Intensity" relates to the total brightness of a color. "Hue" refers to the dominant or average wavelength of light contributing to a color. "Saturation" specifies the purity of a color relative to gray. For example, pastel colors such as pink have low saturation compared to such high saturation colors as crimson. Transforming RGB components into IHS components *before* processing may provide more control over color enhancements [74].

Figure 10.33 shows one (of several) means of transforming RGB components into IHS components [21, 29, 74]. This particular approach is called the *hexcone model* and it involves the *projection* of the RGB color cube onto a plane that is perpendicular to the gray line and tangent to the cube at the corner farthest from the origin. The resulting projection is a hexagon. If the plane of projection is moved from white to black along the gray line, successively smaller color *subcubes* are projected and a series of hexagons of decreasing size results. The hexagon at white is the largest and the hexagon at black degenerates to a point. The series of hexagons developed in this manner define a solid called the *hexcone* (Figure 10.34a).

In the hexcone model *intensity* is defined by the distance along the gray line from black to any given hexagonal projection. Hue and saturation are defined at a given intensity, within the appropriate hexagon (Figure 10.34b). *Hue* is expressed by the angle around the hexagon and *saturation* is defined by the distance from the gray point at the center of the hexagon. The farther a point lies away from the gray point, the more

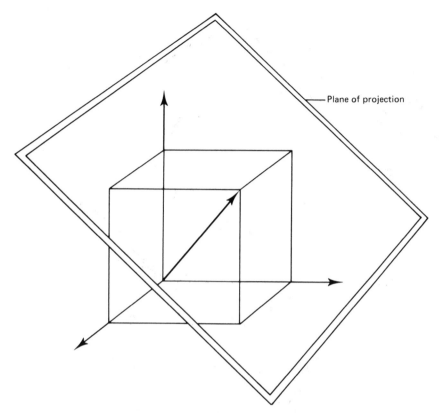

FIGURE 10.33 Planar projection of the RGB color cube. A series of such projections results when progressively smaller subcubes are considered between white and black.

saturated the color. (In Figure 10.34b, linear distances are used to define hue and saturation, thereby avoiding computations involving trigonometric functions.)

At this point we have established the basis upon which any pixel in the RGB color space can be transformed into its IHS counterpart. Such transformations are often useful as an intermediate step in image enhancement. This is illustrated in Figure 10.35. In this figure the original RGB components are shown transformed first into their corresponding IHS components. The IHS components are then manipulated to enhance the desired characteristics of the image. Finally, these modified IHS components are transformed back to the RGB system for final display.

Among the advantages of IHS enhancement operations is the ability to vary each IHS component independently, without affecting the others. For example, a contrast stretch can be applied to the intensity component of an image and the hue and saturation of the pixels in the enhanced image will not be changed (as they typically are in RGB contrast stretches). The IHS approach may also be used to display spatially registered data of varying spatial resolution. For example, high-resolution data from

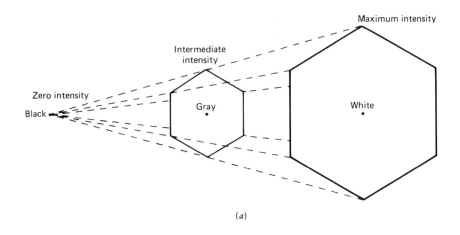

(a)

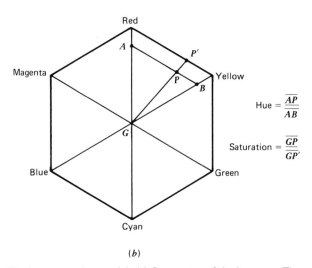

(b)

FIGURE 10.34   The hexcone color model. (a) Generation of the hexcone. The size of any given hexagon is determined by pixel intensity. (b) Definition of hue and saturation components for a pixel value, P, having a typical, nonzero intensity. (Adapted from [74].)

one source may be displayed as the intensity component and low-resolution data from another source may be displayed as the hue and saturation components.

Plate 19 illustrates the use of IHS processing to display a color ratio composite. This scene includes the southwestern part of the Sinai Peninsula and the northern part of the Eastern Desert of Egypt flanking the Gulf of Suez. In (a) a Landsat MSS false color infrared composite (bands 4, 5 and 7) is shown. Even though this image has been

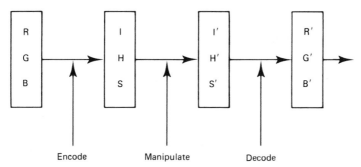

Encode   Manipulate   Decode

FIGURE 10.35   IHS/RGB encoding and decoding for interactive image manipulation. (Adapted from [74].)

contrast stretched and edge enhanced, relatively little color variation is interpretable. The dark-colored crystalline rocks can be readily distinguished from the light-toned alluvial areas along the Gulf of Suez. However, little differentiation can be seen within the alluvial or bedrock areas. To enhance the subtle color differences that are actually present, ratioing can be applied. However, recall that ratio processing suppresses the textural details of an image because it is "intensity blind." Hence, scene information associated with the interaction of scene brightness, illumination, and topography is diminished.

Plate 19*b* illustrates the solution to the above problem through the combination of IHS and ratio processing. To produce this illustration Landsat MSS bands 4, 5, and 7 were transformed into intensity to preserve the texture information in the original scene. The MSS 5/4 ratio was assigned to hue, and the 5/6 ratio to saturation. The resulting IHS enhancement was then transformed back to the RGB system for display. The improved separability of lithologic units is evident in this enhancement, as is the differentiation of the alluvial materials. The reddish areas within the crystalline rock are pink granitic bodies with a relatively high red spectral component compared with their green component. Bluish areas represent the reverse color situation. Note also the correlation between the colors of the alluvial fan materials and their source rocks. The coding scheme used to produce this image was such that as the MSS 5/4 ratio varies from high to low, hues vary from red to yellow, green, blue, and purple. High 5/6 ratios relate to saturated colors and vice versa. With an interactive display, all three types of input data can be evaluated in concert or independently [34].

The development and application of various IHS encoding and enhancement schemes are the subject of continuing research. An interesting project in this regard has been the use of IHS transformations to display two bands (bands 1 and 2) of raw AVHRR data in a three-color composite. In such composites, the sum of bands 1 and 2 is used to represent intensity. The band 2/1 ratio is used to define hue and the difference between bands 1 and 2 is used to define saturation. The resulting image looks very similar to a standard color infrared composite.

10.7   IMAGE CLASSIFICATION

The overall objective of image classification procedures is to automatically categorize all pixels in an image into land cover classes or themes. Normally, multispectral data are used to perform the classification and, indeed, the spectral pattern present within the data for each pixel is used as the numerical basis for categorization. That is, different feature types manifest different combinations of DNs based on their inherent spectral reflectance and emittance properties. In this light, a spectral "pattern" is not at all geometric in character. Rather, the term pattern refers to the set of radiance measurements obtained in the various wavelength bands for each pixel. *Spectral pattern recognition* refers to the family of classification procedures that utilizes this pixel-by-pixel spectral information as the basis for automated land cover classification.

Spatial pattern recognition involves the categorization of image pixels on the basis of their spatial relationship with pixels surrounding them. Spatial classifiers might consider such aspects as image texture, pixel proximity, feature size, shape, directionality, repetition, and context. These types of classifiers attempt to replicate the kind of spatial synthesis done by the human analyst during the visual interpretation process. Accordingly, they tend to be much more complex and computationally intensive than spectral pattern recognition procedures.

Temporal pattern recognition uses time as an aid in feature identification. In agricultural crop surveys, for example, distinct spectral and spatial changes during a growing season can permit discrimination on multidate imagery that would be impossible given any single date. For example, a field of winter wheat might be indistinguishable from bare soil when freshly seeded in the fall and spectrally similar to an alfalfa field in the spring. An interpretation of imagery from either date alone would be unsuccessful, regardless of the number of spectral bands. If data were analyzed from both dates, however, the winter wheat fields could be readily identified, since no other field cover would be bare in late fall and green in late spring.

As with the image restoration and enhancement techniques we have described, image classifiers may be used in combination in a hybrid mode. Also, there is no single "right" manner in which to approach an image classification problem. The particular approach one might take depends upon the nature of the data being analyzed, the computational resources available, and the intended application of the classified data.

In the remaining discussion we emphasize spectrally oriented classification procedures for land cover mapping. (As stated earlier, this emphasis is based on the relative state-of-the-art of these procedures. They currently form the backbone of most classification activities.) First, we describe *supervised classification*. In this type of classification the image analyst "supervises" the pixel categorization process by specifying, to the computer algorithm, numerical descriptors of the various land cover types present in a scene. To do this, representative sample sites of known cover type, called *training areas*, are used to compile a numerical "interpretation key" that describes the spectral attributes for each feature type of interest. Each pixel in the data set is then compared numerically to each category in the interpretation key and labeled with the name of the category it "looks most like." As we see in the next section, there are a number of numerical strategies that can be employed to make this comparison between unknown pixels and training set pixels.

Following our discussion of supervised classification we treat the subject of *unsupervised classification*. Like supervised classifiers, the unsupervised procedures are applied in two separate steps. The fundamental difference between these techniques is that supervised classification involves a training step followed by a classification step. In the unsupervised approach the image data are first classified by aggregating them into the natural spectral groupings or *clusters* present in the scene. Then, the image analyst determines the land cover identity of these spectral groups by comparing the classified image data to ground reference data. Unsupervised procedures are discussed in Section 10.11.

10.8 SUPERVISED CLASSIFICATION

We use a hypothetical example to facilitate our discussion of supervised classification. In this example, let us assume that we are dealing with the analysis of five-channel airborne MSS data. (The identical procedures would apply to Landsat MSS, TM, or SPOT HRV multispectral data.) Figure 10.36 shows the location of a single line of the MSS data collected over a landscape composed of several cover types. For each of the pixels shown along this line, the MSS has measured scene radiance in terms of DNs recorded in each of the five spectral bands of sensing: blue, green, red, near-infrared, and thermal infrared. Below the scan line, typical DNs measured over six different land cover types are shown. The vertical bars indicate the relative gray values in each spectral band. These five outputs represent a coarse description of the spectral response patterns of the various terrain features along the scan line. If these spectral patterns are sufficiently distinct for each feature type, they may form the basis for image classification.

Figure 10.37 summarizes the three basic steps involved in a typical supervised classification procedure. In the *training stage* (1), the analyst identifies representative training areas and develops a numerical description of the spectral attributes of each land cover type of interest in the scene. Next, in the *classification stage* (2), each pixel in the image data set is categorized into the land cover class it most closely resembles. If the pixel is insufficiently similar to any training data set it is usually labeled "unknown." The category label assigned to each pixel in this process is then recorded in the corresponding cell of an interpreted data set (an "output image"). Thus, the multidimensional image matrix is used to develop a corresponding matrix of interpreted land cover category types. After the entire data set has been categorized, the results are presented in the *output stage* (3). Being digital in character, the results may be used in a number of different ways. Three typical forms of output products are thematic maps, tables of full scene or subscene area statistics for the various land cover classes, and digital data files amenable to inclusion in a geographic information system (GIS). In this latter case, the classification "output" becomes a GIS "input."

We discuss the output stage of image classification in Section 10.12. Our immediate attention is focused on the training and classification stages. We begin with a discussion of the *classification* stage because it is the heart of the supervised classification process—during this stage the spectral patterns in the image data set are evaluated in the computer using predefined decision rules to determine the identity of each pixel.

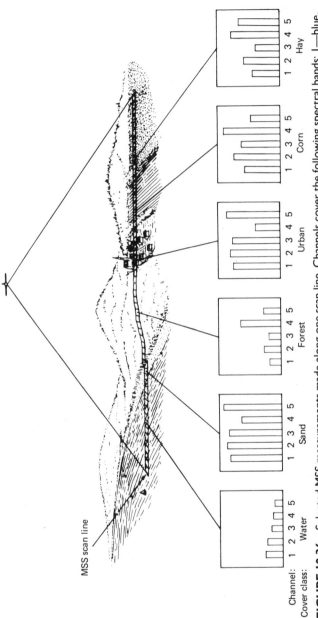

FIGURE 10.36   Selected MSS measurements made along one scan line. Channels cover the following spectral bands: 1—blue, 2—green; 3—red, 4—near-infrared, 5—thermal infrared.

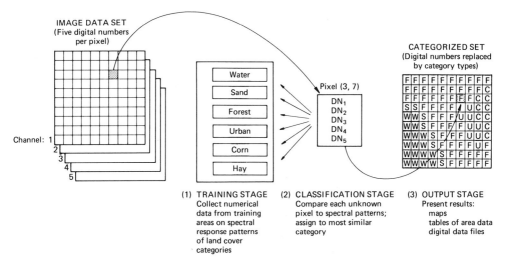

FIGURE 10.37 Basic steps in supervised classification.

Another reason for treating the classification stage first is because familiarity with this step aids in understanding the requirements which must be met in the training stage.

10.9 THE CLASSIFICATION STAGE

Numerous mathematical approaches to spectral pattern recognition have been developed and extensive discussion of this subject can be found in the various references found at the end of this chapter. Our discussion only "scratches the surface" of how spectral patterns may be classified into categories.

Our presentation of the various classification approaches is illustrated with a two-channel (bands 3 and 4) subset of our hypothetical five-channel MSS data set. Rarely are just two channels employed in an analysis, yet this limitation simplifies the graphic portrayal of the various techniques. When implemented numerically, these procedures may be applied to any number of channels of data.

Let us assume that we take a sample of pixel observations from our two-channel digital image data set. The two-dimensional digital values, or *measurement vectors*, attributed to each pixel may be expressed graphically by plotting them on a *scatter diagram*, as shown in Figure 10.38. In this diagram, the band 3 digital numbers have been plotted on the y axis and the band 4 digital numbers on the x axis. These two digital numbers locate each pixel value in the two-dimensional "measurement space" of the graph. Thus, if the band 4 DN for a pixel is 10 and the band 3 DN for the same pixel is 68, the measurement vector for this pixel is represented by a point plotted at coordinate (10, 68) in the measurement space.

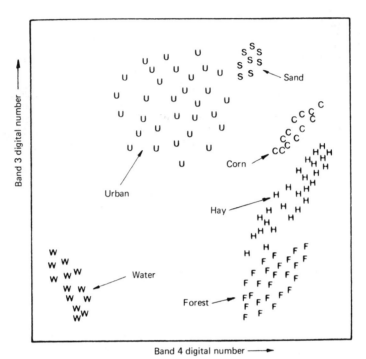

FIGURE 10.38   Pixel observations from selected training sites plotted on scatter diagram.

Let us also assume that the pixel observations shown in Figure 10.38 are from areas of known cover type (that is, from selected training sites). Each pixel value has been plotted on the scatter diagram with a letter indicating the category to which it is known to belong. Note that the pixels within each class do not have a single, repeated spectral value. Rather, they illustrate the natural centralizing tendency—yet variability—of the spectral properties found within each cover class. These "clouds of points" represent multidimensional descriptions of the spectral response patterns of each category of cover type to be interpreted. The following classification strategies use these "training set" descriptions of the category spectral response patterns as interpretation keys by which pixels of unidentified cover type are categorized into their appropriate classes.

Minimum-Distance-to-Means Classifier

Figure 10.39 illustrates one of the simpler classification strategies that may be used. First, the mean, or average, spectral value in each band for each category is determined. These values comprise the *mean vector* for each category. The category means are indicated by +'s in Figure 10.39. By considering the two-channel pixel values as positional coordinates (as they are portrayed in the scatter diagram), a pixel of unknown identity may be classified by computing the *distance* between the value of the un-

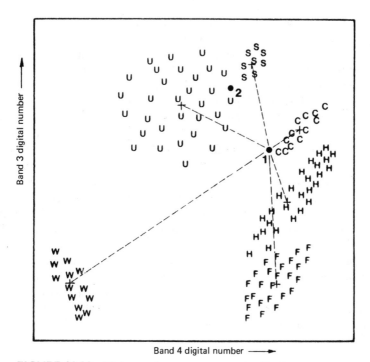

FIGURE 10.39   Minimum distance to means classification strategy.

known pixel and each of the category means. In Figure 10.39, an unknown pixel value has been plotted at point 1. The distance between this pixel value and each category mean value is illustrated by the dashed lines. After computing the distances, the unknown pixel is assigned to the "closest" class, in this case "corn." If the pixel is farther than an analyst-defined distance from any category mean, it would be classified as "unknown."

The minimum-distance-to-means strategy is mathematically simple and computationally efficient but it has certain limitations. Most importantly, *it is insensitive to different degrees of variance in the spectral response data.* In Figure 10.39, the pixel value plotted at point 2 would be assigned by the distance-to-means classifier to the "sand" category, in spite of the fact that the greater variability in the "urban" category suggests that "urban" would be a more appropriate class assignment. Because of such problems, this classifier is not widely used in applications where spectral classes are close to one another in the measurement space and have high variance.

Parallelepiped Classifier

We can introduce sensitivity to category variance by considering the *range* of values in each category training set. This range may be defined by the highest and lowest digital number values in each band, and appears as a rectangular area in our two-channel scatter diagram, as shown in Figure 10.40. An unknown pixel is classified according to the category range, or *decision region*, in which it lies, or as "unknown" if it lies outside all regions. The multidimensional analogs of these rectangular areas are called *parallel-epipeds*, and this classification strategy is referred to by that tongue-twisting name. The parallelepiped classifier is also very fast and efficient computationally.

The sensitivity of the parallelepiped classifier to category variance is exemplified by the smaller decision region defined for the highly repeatable "sand" category than for the more variable "urban" class. Because of this, pixel 2 would be appropriately classified as "urban." However, difficulties are encountered when category ranges overlap. Unknown pixel observations that occur in the overlap areas will be classified as "not sure" or be arbitrarily placed in one (or both) of the two overlapping classes. Overlap is caused largely because category distributions exhibiting *correlation* or high *covariance* are poorly described by the rectangular decision regions. Covariance is the tendency of spectral values to vary similarly in two bands, resulting in elongated, slanted clouds of observations on the scatter diagram. In our example, the "corn" and "hay" categories have positive covariance (they slant upward to the right), meaning that high values in band 3 are generally associated with high values in band 4, and low values in band 3 are associated with low values in band 4. The water category in our example exhibits *negative covariance* (its distribution slants down to the right), meaning that high values in band 3 are associated with low values in band 4. The "urban"

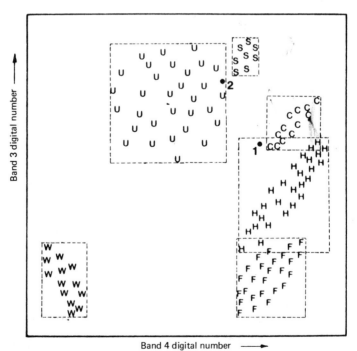

FIGURE 10.40   Parallelepiped classification strategy.

class shows a lack of covariance, resulting in a nearly circular distribution on the scatter diagram.

In the presence of covariance, the rectangular decision regions fit the category training data very poorly, resulting in confusion for a parallelepiped classifier. For example, the insensitivity to covariance would cause pixel 1 to be classified as "hay" instead of "corn."

Unfortunately, spectral response patterns are frequently highly correlated and high covariance is often the rule rather than the exception. The resulting problems can be somewhat alleviated within the parallelepiped classifier by modifying the single rectangles for the various decision regions into a series of rectangles with stepped borders. These borders then describe the boundaries of the elongated distributions more specifically. This approach is illustrated in Figure 10.41.

Gaussian Maximum Likelihood Classifier

The maximum likelihood classifier quantitatively evaluates both the variance and covariance of the category spectral response patterns when classifying an unknown pixel. To do this, an assumption is made that the distribution of the cloud of points forming the category training data is Gaussian (normally distributed). This *assumption*

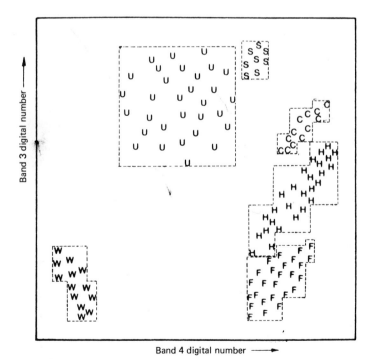

FIGURE 10.41 Parallelepiped classification strategy employing stepped decision region boundaries.

of normality is generally reasonable for common spectral response distributions. Under this assumption, the distribution of a category response pattern can be completely described by the *mean vector* and the *covariance matrix*. Given these parameters, we may compute the statistical probability of a given pixel value being a member of a particular land cover class. Figure 10.42 shows the probability values plotted in a three-dimensional graph. The vertical axis is associated with the probability of a pixel value being a member of one of the classes. The resulting bell-shaped surfaces are called *probability density functions* and there is one such function for each spectral category.

The probability density functions are used to classify an unidentified pixel by computing the probability of the pixel value belonging to each category. That is, the computer would calculate the probability of the pixel value occurring in the distribution of class "corn," then the likelihood of its occurring in class "sand," and so on. After evaluating the probability in each category, the pixel would be assigned to the most likely class (highest probability value), or labeled "unknown" if the probability values are all below a threshold set by the analyst.

In essence, the maximum likelihood classifier delineates ellipsoidal "equiprobability contours" in the scatter diagram. These decision regions are shown in Figure

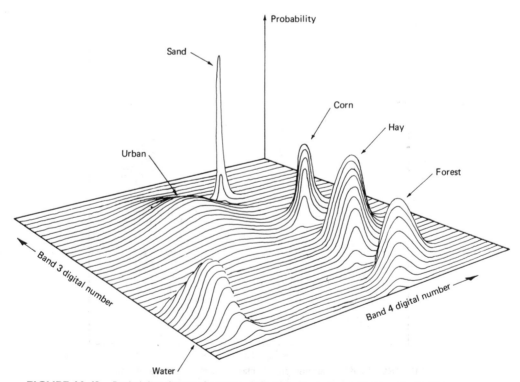

FIGURE 10.42   Probability density functions defined by a maximum likelihood classifier.

10.43. The shape of the equiprobability contours expresses the sensitivity of the likelihood classifier to covariance. For example, because of this sensitivity, it can be seen that pixel 1 would be appropriately assigned to the "corn" category.

An extension of the maximum likelihood approach is the *Bayesian classifier*. This technique applies two weighting factors to the probability estimate. First, the analyst determines the "a priori probability," or the anticipated likelihood of occurrence for each class in the given scene. For example, when classifying a pixel, the probability of the rarely occurring "sand" category might be weighted lightly, and the more likely "urban" class weighted heavily. Second, a weight associated with the "cost" of misclassification is applied to each class. Together, these factors act to minimize the "cost" of misclassifications, resulting in a theoretically optimum classification. In practice, most maximum likelihood classification is performed assuming equal probability of occurrence and cost of misclassification for all classes. If suitable data exist for these factors, the Bayesian implementation of the classifier is preferable.

The principal drawback of maximum likelihood classification is the large number of computations required to classify each pixel. This is particularly true when either a large number of spectral channels are involved or a large number of spectral classes must be differentiated. In such cases, the maximum likelihood classifier is much slower computationally than the previous techniques.

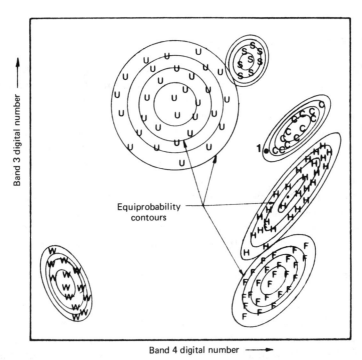

FIGURE 10.43 Equiprobability contours defined by a maximum likelihood classifier.

Several approaches may be taken to increase the efficiency of maximum likelihood classifiers. In the table lookup implementation of such algorithms, the category identity for all possible combinations of digital numbers occurring in an image is determined in advance of actually classifying the image. Hence, the complex statistical computation for each combination is only made once. The categorization of each pixel in the image is then simply a matter of indexing the location of its multichannel gray level in the lookup table.

Another means of optimizing the implementation of the maximum likelihood classifier is to use some method to reduce the dimensionality of the data set used to perform the classification (thereby reducing the complexity of the required computations). As stated earlier, principal or canonical component transformations of the original data may be used for this purpose.

Decision tree, stratified, or layered classifiers have also been utilized to simplify classification computations and maintain classification accuracy. These classifiers are applied in a series of steps, with certain classes being separated during each step in the simplest manner possible. For example, water might first be separated from all other classes based on a simple threshold set in a near-infrared band. Certain other classes may require only two or three bands for categorization and a parallelepiped classifier may be adequate. The use of more bands or the maximum likelihood classifier would then only be required for those land cover categories where residual ambiguity exists between overlapping classes in the measurement space.

10.10 THE TRAINING STAGE

Whereas the actual classification of multispectral image data is a highly automated process, assembling the training data needed for classification is anything but automatic. In many ways, the training effort required in supervised classification is both an art and a science. It requires close interaction between the image analyst and the image data. It also requires substantial reference data and a thorough knowledge of the geographic area to which the data apply. Most importantly, the quality of the training process determines the success of the classification stage and, therefore, the value of the information generated from the entire classification effort.

The overall objective of the training process is to assemble a set of statistics that describe the spectral response pattern for each land cover type to be classified in an image. Relative to our earlier graphical example, it is during the training stage that the location, size, shape, and orientation of the "clouds of points" for each land cover class are determined.

To yield acceptable classification results, training data must be both representative and complete. This means that the image analyst must develop training statistics for all *spectral* classes constituting each *information* class to be discriminated by the classifier. For example, in a final classification output, one might wish to delineate an information class called "water." If the image under analysis contains only one water body and if it has uniform spectral response characteristics over its entire area, then only one training area would be needed to represent the water class. If, however, the same water body contained distinct areas of very clear water and very turbid water, a minimum of two spectral classes would be required to adequately train on this feature. If multiple water bodies occurred in the image, training statistics would be required for each of the other spectral classes that might be present in the water covered areas. Accordingly, the single information class "water" might be represented by four or five spectral classes. In turn, the four or five spectral classes would eventually be used to classify all the water bodies occurring in the image.

By now it should be clear that the training process can become quite involved. For example, an information class such as "agriculture" might contain several crop types and each crop type might be represented by several spectral classes. These spectral classes could stem from different planting dates, soil moisture conditions, crop management practices, seed varieties, topographic settings, atmospheric conditions, or combinations of these factors. *The point that must be emphasized is that all spectral classes constituting each information class must be adequately represented in the training set statistics used to classify an image.*

The location of training areas in an image is normally established by viewing *windows,* or portions of the full scene, in an enlarged format on an interactive color display device. The image analyst normally obtains training sample data by outlining training areas using a reference *cursor.* The cursor may be controlled by any of several means (e.g., a track ball, joy stick, digitizer, "mouse," or keyboard strokes). Figure 10.44 shows the boundaries of several agricultural training site polygons that have

FIGURE 10.44 Training area polygons delineated on a computer graphics display.

been delineated in this manner. Note that these polygons have been carefully located to avoid pixels located along the edges between land cover types. The row and column coordinates of the vertices for these polygons are used as the basis for extracting (from the image file) the digital numbers for the pixels located within each training area boundary. These pixel values then form the sample used to develop the statistical description of each training area (mean vector and covariance matrix in the case of the maximum likelihood classifier).

When using any statistically based classifier such as the maximum likelihood method, the theoretical lower limit of the number of pixels that must be contained in a training set is $n + 1$, where n is the number of spectral bands. In our two-band example, theoretically only three observations would be required. Obviously, the use of fewer than three observations would make it impossible to appropriately evaluate the variance and covariance of the spectral response values. In practice, a minimum of from $10n$ to $100n$ pixels is used since the estimates of the mean vectors and covariance matrices improve as the number of pixels in the training sets increases. Within reason, the more pixels that can be used in training, the better the statistical representation of each spectral class.

When delineating training set pixels, it is important to analyze several training sites throughout the scene. For example, it would be better to define the training pattern for a given class by analyzing 20 locations containing 40 pixels of a given type than one location containing 800 pixels. Dispersion of the sites throughout the scene increases the chance that the training data will be representative of all the variations in the cover types present in the scene.

The fine line to be walked in the development of training data sets is that of having sufficient sample size to ensure the accurate determination of the statistical parameters used by the classifier and to represent the total spectral variability in a scene, without going past a point of diminishing returns. In short, one does not want to omit any important spectral classes occurring in a scene, but one also does not want to include redundant spectral classes in the classification process from a computational standpoint. During the process of *training set refinement* the analyst attempts to identify such gaps and redundancies.

As part of the training set refinement process the overall quality of the data contained in each of the original candidate training areas is assessed and the spectral separability between the data sets is studied. The analyst carefully checks to see if all data sets are essentially normally distributed and spectrally pure. Training areas that inadvertently included more than one spectral class are identified and recompiled. Likewise, extraneous pixels may be deleted from some of the data sets. These might be edge pixels along agricultural field boundaries or within-field pixels containing bare soil rather than the crop trained upon. Training sets that might be merged (or deleted) are identified, and the need to obtain additional training sets for poorly represented spectral classes is addressed.

One or more of the following types of analysis is typically involved in the training set refinement process.

1.   *Graphical representation of the spectral response patterns.*   The distributions of training area response patterns can be graphically displayed in many formats.

Figure 10.45 shows a hypothetical histogram printout for the "hay" category in our five-channel MSS data set. Histogram output is particularly important when a maximum likelihood classifier is used, since it provides a visual check on the normality of the spectral response distributions. Note in the case of the hay category that the data appear to be normally distributed in all bands except band 2, where the distribution is shown to be bimodal. This indicates that the training site data set chosen by the analyst to represent "hay" is in fact composed of two subclasses with slightly different spectral characteristics. These subclasses may represent two different varieties of hay or different illumination conditions, and so on. In any case, the classification accuracy will generally be improved if each of the subclasses is treated as a separate category.

Histograms illustrate the distribution of individual categories very well, yet they do not facilitate comparisons between different category types. To evaluate the spectral separation between categories, it is convenient to use some form of *coincident spectral plot*, as shown in Figure 10.46. This plot illustrates, in each

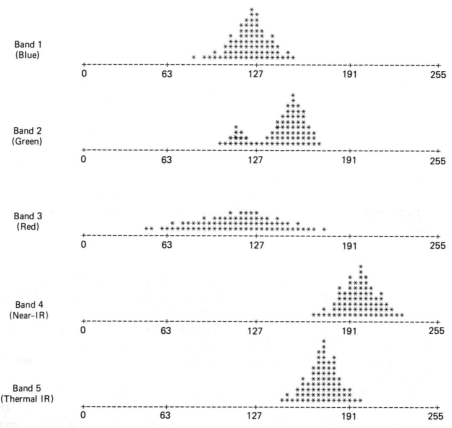

FIGURE 10.45 Sample histograms for data points included in the training areas for cover type "hay."

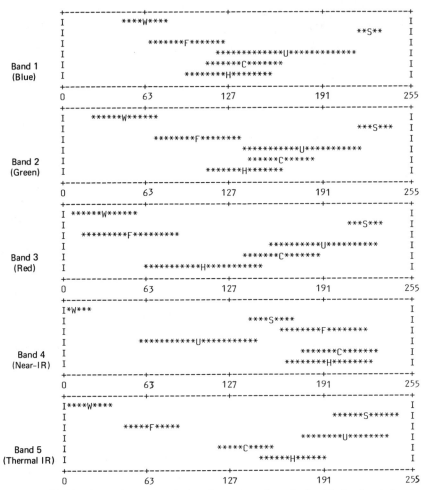

FIGURE 10.46 Coincident spectral plots for training data obtained in five bands for six cover types.

spectral band, the mean spectral response of each category (with a letter) and the variance of the distribution (±2 standard deviations shown in asterisks). Such plots indicate the overlap between category response patterns. For example, Figure 10.46 indicates that the hay and corn response patterns overlap in all spectral bands. The plot also shows which combination of bands might be best for discrimination because of relative reversals of spectral response (such as bands 3 and 5 for hay/corn separation).

The fact that the spectral plots for hay and corn overlap in all spectral bands indicates that the categories could not be accurately classified on any *single* MSS band. However, this does not preclude successful classification when two or more bands are analyzed (such as bands 3 and 4 illustrated in the last section). Because of this, two-dimensional scatter diagrams (as shown in Figures 10.38 to 10.41) provide better representations of the spectral response pattern distributions. By illustrating the multivariate distribution of the data, the scatter diagram depicts between-category overlap more accurately. Unfortunately, only two bands can normally be illustrated on a single scatter diagram. (Certain display devices permit depiction of the training data in three-dimensional perspective.)

2. *Quantitative expressions of category separation.* A measure of the statistical separation between category response patterns can be computed for all pairs of classes, and presented in the form of a matrix. One statistical parameter commonly used for this purpose is *divergence*, a covariance-weighted distance between category means. Many mathematical expressions of divergence exist. In general, the larger the divergence, the greater the "statistical distance" between training patterns and the higher the probability of correct classification of classes. A sample matrix of divergence values is shown in Table 10.1. In this example, the maximum possible divergence value is 2000 and values less than 1500 indicate spectrally similar classes [85]. Accordingly, the data in Table 10.1 suggest spectral overlap between the "sand" and "urban" classes, as well as between the "corn" and "hay" classes.

3. *Self-classification of training set data.* Another evaluation of spectral separability is provided by a *contingency table* (sometimes called a *confusion matrix*) as shown in Table 10.2. This table is prepared by classifying the training set pixels. The known category types of the pixels used for training are listed versus the categories chosen by the classifier. From this information, classification errors of omission and commission can be studied. In an ideal case, all nondiagonal elements of the contingency table would be zero, indicating no misclassification. Commission errors are represented by nondiagonal elements of the table where pixels are classified into a category to which they do not actually belong (e.g., 5 pixels of "forest" are misclassified as "water" in Table 10.2). Omission errors represent the reverse type of situation (16 pixels that should have been classified as "sand" were not). If more than an acceptable percentage of the pixels in a class is

TABLE 10.1 Divergence Matrix Used to Evaluate Training Class Spectral Separability

Class[a]	1	2	3	4	5	6
1	0					
2	1998	0				
3	1996	1994	0			
4	1953	898	1882	0		
5	1997	1938	1812	1823	0	
6	1992	1976	1628	1938	1362	0

[a]1—Water, 2—sand, 3—forest, 4—urban, 5—corn, 6—hay.

TABLE 10.2   Contingency Table Resulting from Classifying Training Set Pixels

Known category type[a]	Number of pixels	Percentage correct	Number of pixels classified into category					
			1	2	3	4	5	6
1	480	100	480	0	0	0	0	0
2	68	76	0	52	0	16	0	0
3	356	88	5	0	313	0	0	38
4	248	51	0	20	40	126	38	24
5	402	85	0	0	0	0	342	60
6	438	82	0	0	0	0	79	359

[a]1—Water, 2—sand, 3—forest, 4—urban, 5—corn, 6—hay.

misclassified, that category may warrant further inspection and retraining. For example, Table 10.2 again suggests that the "corn" and "hay" categories are not spectrally separable and may have to be combined into one class (perhaps "agriculture"). Likewise, retraining in the "sand" and "urban" classes may be necessary.

It is important to avoid considering a contingency table based on training set values as a measure of *overall* classification accuracy throughout an image. For one reason, certain land cover classes might be inadvertently missed in the training process. Also, the contingency table simply tells us how well the classifier can classify the *training areas* and nothing more. Because the training areas are usually good, homogeneous examples of each cover type, they can be expected to be classified more accurately than less pure examples that may be found elsewhere in the scene. Overall accuracy can be evaluated only by considering *test areas* that are different from, and considerably more extensive than, the training areas. This evaluation is generally performed after the classification and output stages (as discussed in Section 10.14).

In general, the training set refinement process cannot be rushed with the "maximum efficiency" attitude appropriate in the classification stage. It is normally an iterative procedure in which the analyst revises the statistical descriptions of the category types until they are sufficiently spectrally separable. That is, the original set of "candidate" training area statistics is revised through merger, deletion, and addition to form the "final" set of statistics used in classification.

Training set refinement for the inexperienced data analyst is often a difficult task. Typically, an analyst has little difficulty in developing the statistics for the distinct "nonoverlapping" spectral classes present in a scene. If there are problems, they typically stem from spectral classes on the borders between information classes— "transition" or "overlapping classes." In such cases, the impact of alternative deletion and pooling of training classes can be tested by trial-and-error. In this process the sample size, spectral variances, normality, and identity of the training sets should be rechecked. Problem classes that occur only rarely in the image may be eliminated from the training data so that they are not confused with classes that occur extensively. That is, the analyst may accept misclassification of a class that occurs only rarely in the scene in order to preserve the classification accuracy of a spectrally similar class that appears over extensive areas. Furthermore, a classification might initially be developed assuming a particular set of detailed information classes will be maintained. After studying the actual classification results, the image analyst might be faced with aggregating certain of the detailed classes into more general ones (for example, "birch" and "aspen" may have to be merged into a "deciduous" class, or "corn" and "hay" into "agriculture").

One final note to be made here is that training set refinement is usually the key to improving the accuracy of a classification. However, if certain cover types occurring in an image have inherently similar spectral response patterns, no amount of retraining and refinement will make them spectrally separable! Alternative methods, perhaps including visual interpretation or field checking, must be used to discriminate these cover types. Multitemporal or spatial pattern recognition procedures may also be applicable in such cases.

10.11 **UNSUPERVISED CLASSIFICATION**

As previously discussed, unsupervised classifiers do *not* utilize training data as the basis for classification. Rather, this family of classifiers involves algorithms that examine the unknown pixels in an image and aggregate them into a number of classes based on the natural groupings or clusters present in the image values. The basic premise is that values within a given cover type should be close together in the measurement space, whereas data in different classes should be comparatively well separated.

The classes that result from unsupervised classification are *spectral classes*. Because they are based solely on the natural groupings in the image values, the identity of the spectral classes will not be initially known. The analyst must compare the classified data with some form of reference data (such as larger scale imagery or maps) to determine the identity and informational value of the spectral classes. Thus, in the *supervised* approach we define useful information categories and then examine their spectral separability; in the *unsupervised* approach we determine spectrally separable classes and then define their informational utility.

We illustrate the unsupervised approach by again considering a two-channel data set. Natural spectral groupings in the data can be visually identified by plotting a scatter diagram. For example, in Figure 10.47 we have plotted pixel values acquired over a forested area. Three groupings are apparent in the scatter diagram. After comparing the classified image data with ground reference data, we might find that one cluster corresponds to deciduous trees, one to conifers, and one to stressed trees of both types (indicated by D, C, and S in Figure 10.47). In a supervised approach, we may not have considered training for the "stressed" class. This highlights one of the primary advantages of unsupervised classification: the *classifier* identifies the distinct spectral classes present in the image data. Many of these classes might not be initially apparent to the analyst applying a supervised classifier. Likewise, the spectral classes

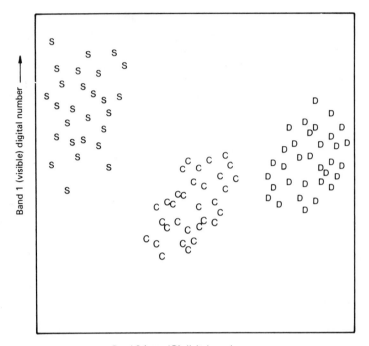

FIGURE 10.47   Spectral classes in two-channel image data.

in a scene may be so numerous that it would be difficult to train on all of them. In the unsupervised approach they are found automatically.

There are numerous *clustering* algorithms that can be used to determine the natural spectral groupings present in a data set. One common form of clustering, called the "K-means" approach, accepts from the analyst the number of clusters to be located in the data. The algorithm then arbitrarily "seeds" or locates that number of cluster centers in the multidimensional measurement space. Each pixel in the image is then assigned to the cluster whose arbitrary mean vector is closest. After all pixels have been classified in this manner, revised mean vectors for each of the clusters are computed. The revised means are then used as the basis to reclassify the image data. The procedure continues until there is no significant change in the location of class mean vectors between successive iterations of the algorithm. Once this point is reached the analyst determines the land cover identity of each spectral class.

Because the K-means approach is iterative it is computationally intensive. Therefore, it is often applied only to image subareas rather than to full scenes. Such subareas are often referred to as *unsupervised training areas* and should not be confused with the training areas used in supervised classification efforts. Whereas supervised training areas are located in regions of homogeneous cover type, the unsupervised training areas are chosen to contain numerous cover types at various locations throughout the scene. This ensures that all spectral classes in the scene are represented somewhere in the various subareas. These areas are then clustered independently and the spectral classes from the various areas are analyzed to determine their identity. They are subjected to a pooled statistical analysis to determine their spectral separability and normality. As appropriate, similar clusters representing similar land cover types are combined. Training statistics are developed for the combined classes and used to classify the entire scene (e.g., by a minimum distance or maximum likelihood algorithm). Because this approach involves elements of both unsupervised and supervised analysis it is termed *hybrid* classification.

Hybrid classifiers are particularly valuable in analyses where there is complex variability in the spectral response patterns for individual cover types present. These conditions are quite common in such applications as vegetation mapping in mountainous areas. Under these conditions, spectral variability within cover types normally comes about both from variation within cover types per se (species) and from different site conditions (soils, slope, aspect). The hybrid classification approach helps the analyst deal with such variability.

Another common approach to unsupervised classification is the use of algorithms that incorporate a sensitivity to image "texture" or "roughness" as a basis for establishing cluster centers. Texture is typically defined by the multidimensional variance observed in a moving window passed through the image (e.g., a 3 × 3 window). The analyst sets a variance threshold below which a window is considered "smooth" (homogeneous) and above which it is considered "rough" (heterogeneous). The mean of the first smooth window encountered in the image becomes the first cluster center. The mean of the second smooth window encountered becomes the second cluster center, and so forth. As soon as an analyst-specified maximum number of cluster centers is reached (e.g., 50), the classifier considers the distances between all previously defined cluster centers in the measurement space and merges the two closest clusters, combining their statistics. The classifier continues through the image combining the closest two clusters encountered until the entire image is analyzed. The resulting cluster centers are then analyzed to determine their separability on the basis of an analyst-specified statistical distance. Those clusters separated by less than this distance are combined and their statistics are merged. The final clusters resulting from the analysis are used to classify the image (e.g., with a minimum distance or maximum likelihood classifier).

Data from supervised training areas are sometimes used to augment the results of the above clustering procedure when certain land cover classes are poorly represented in the purely unsupervised analysis (another hybrid approach). Roads, and other linear features, for example, may not be represented in the original clustering statistics if these features do not happen to meet the smoothness criteria within the moving window. Likewise, in some unsupervised classifiers the order in which different feature types are encountered can result in poor representation of some classes. For example, the analyst-specified maximum number of classes may be reached in an image long before the moving window passes throughout the scene.

Before ending our discussion of unsupervised classification, we reiterate that the result of such efforts is simply the identification of spectrally distinct classes in image data. The analyst must still use reference data to associate the spectral classes with the cover types of interest. This process, like the training set refinement step in supervised classification, can be quite involved.

Table 10.3 illustrates several possible outcomes of associating spectral classes with information classes for data from a scene covering a forested area. The ideal result would be outcome 1, in which each spectral class is found to be associated uniquely with a feature type of interest to the analyst. This outcome will occur only when the features in the scene have highly distinctive spectral characteristics.

A more likely result is presented in outcome 2. Here, several spectral classes are attributable to each information category desired by the analyst. These "subclasses" may be of little informational utility (sunlit versus shaded conifers) or they may provide useful distinctions (turbid versus clear water and upland versus lowland deciduous). In either case, the spectral classes may be aggregated after classification into the smaller set of categories desired by the analyst.

Outcome 3 represents a more troublesome result in which the analyst finds that several spectral classes relate to more than one information category. For example,

TABLE 10.3   Spectral Classes Resulting from Clustering a Forested Scene

Spectral class	Identity of spectral class	Corresponding desired information category
Possible Outcome 1		
1	Water ⟶	Water
2	Coniferous trees ⟶	Coniferous trees
3	Deciduous trees ⟶	Deciduous trees
4	Brushland ⟶	Brushland
Possible Outcome 2		
1	Turbid water ⟶	Water
2	Clear water ⟶	
3	Sunlit conifers ⟶	Coniferous trees
4	Shaded hillside conifers ⟶	
5	Upland deciduous ⟶	Deciduous trees
6	Lowland deciduous ⟶	
7	Brushland ⟶	Brushland
Possible Outcome 3		
1	Turbid water ⟶	Water
2	Clear water ⟶	
3	Coniferous trees ⟶	Coniferous trees
4	Mixed conif./decid. ⟵	
5	Deciduous trees ⟶	Deciduous trees
6	Decid./brushland ⟶	Brushland

spectral class 4 was found to correspond to coniferous trees in some locations and deciduous trees in others. Likewise, class 6 included both deciduous trees and brushland vegetation. This means that these information categories are spectrally similar and cannot be differentiated in the given data set.

As with supervised classification, access to efficient hardware and software is an important factor in determining the *ease* with which an unsupervised classification can be performed. The *quality* of the classification still depends upon the analyst's understanding of the concepts behind the classifiers available and knowledge about the land cover types under analysis.

10.12   THE OUTPUT STAGE

The utility of any image classification is ultimately dependent on the production of output products that effectively convey the interpreted information to its end user. Here the boundaries between remote sensing, computer graphics, digital cartography, and geographic information system management become blurred. A virtually unlimited selection of output products may be generated. Three general forms that are commonly used include graphic "map" products, tables of area statistics, and digital data files.

Graphic Products

Since classified data are in the form of a two-dimensional data array, graphic output can be easily computer generated by displaying different colors, tones, or characters for each cell in the array according to its assigned land cover category. A broad range of peripheral equipment can be used for this purpose, including color monitors, printers, film recorders, and large format laser scanners. Plate 23*a* illustrates a classification photographed from a color monitor. Such displays portray classification results very effectively and the analyst can choose to interactively display only subsets of the original file, or easily change color assignment, class groupings, and so forth. When inexpensive hard copy output is desired for such data, an electrostatic or ink jet printer can be used. Printouts can be prepared either in black and white or in color. Alternatively, a color film recorder or laser scanner can be used to produce reproducible hard copy output of high color fidelity and geometric precision.

Tabular Data

Another common form of classification output is a table that lists summary statistics on the areal extent of the cover types present in a scene or in user-defined subscene areas. It is a simple task to derive area statistics from the grid-based interpreted data file. First, the boundary of a region of interest, such as a watershed or a county, is digitized in terms of its image matrix coordinates. Within the boundary, the number of cells in each land cover class is tabulated and multiplied by the ground area covered by a single cell. This process is considerably simpler than manually measuring areas on a map and represents a major advantage of processing land cover data in a digital format.

Digital Information Files

The final general class of output is interpreted data files containing the classification results recorded on some type of computer storage medium (e.g., CCT or disk). As we illustrate in Section 10.15, the interpreted data in this form may be conveniently input to a GIS for merger with other geographic data files.

10.13 POSTCLASSIFICATION SMOOTHING

Classified data often manifest a salt-and-pepper appearance due to the inherent spectral variability encountered by a classifier when applied on a pixel-by-pixel basis (Figure 10.48a). For example, several pixels scattered throughout a corn field may be classified as soybeans, or vice versa. In such situations it is often desirable to "smooth" the classified output to show only the dominant (presumably correct) classification (Figure 10.48b) Initially, one might consider the application of the previously described low-pass spatial filters for this purpose. The problem with this approach is that the output from an image classification is an array of pixel locations containing numbers serving the function of *labels*, not *quantities*. That is, a pixel containing land cover 1 may be coded with a 1. A pixel containing land cover 2 may be coded with a 2, and so on. A moving low-pass filter will not properly smooth such data because, for example, the averaging of class 3 and class 5 to arrive at class 4 makes no sense. In short, postclassification smoothing algorithms must operate on the basis of logical operations, rather than simple arithmetic computations.

One means of classification smoothing involves the application of a *majority filter*. In such operations a moving window is passed through the classified data set and the majority class within the window is determined. If the center pixel in the window is not the majority class its identity is changed to the majority class. If there is no majority class in the window, the identity of the center pixel is not changed. As the window progresses through the data set the original class codes are continually used, not the labels as modified from the previous window positions. (Figure 10.48b was prepared in this manner, applying a 3 × 3 pixel majority filter to the data shown in Figure 10.48a.)

Majority filters can also incorporate some form of class and/or spatial weighting function. Data may also be smoothed more than once. Certain algorithms can preserve the boundaries between land cover regions and also involve a user-specified minimum area of any given land cover type that will be maintained in the smoothed output.

One way of obtaining smoother classifications is to integrate the types of logical operations described above directly into the classification process. This involves the use of spatial pattern recognition techniques that are sensitive to such factors as image texture and pixel context. Compared to purely spectrally based procedures, these types of classifiers have received only limited attention in remote sensing in the past. However, with the continued improvement in the spatial resolution of remote sensing systems, and the increasing computational power of image processing systems, such procedures will likely become more common.

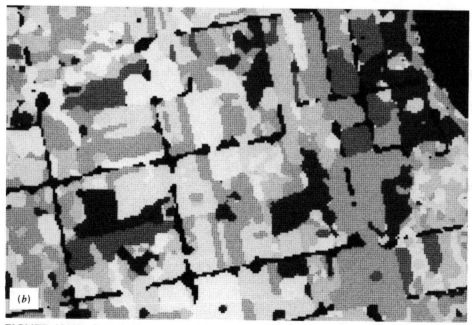

FIGURE 10.48   Postclassification smoothing. *(a)* Original classification. *(b)* Smoothed classification—note the decreased definition of the roads in this image.

10.14 CLASSIFICATION ACCURACY ASSESSMENT

Another area that is continuing to receive increased attention by remote sensing specialists is that of classification accuracy assessment. Unfortunately, to date the ability to produce digital land cover classifications far exceeds the ability to meaningfully quantify their accuracy. In fact, this problem sometimes precludes the application of automated land cover classification techniques even when their cost compares favorably with more traditional means of data collection.

There is no simple, standardized, generally accepted methodology for determining classification accuracy. Below we briefly describe two of the most commonly employed approaches. They both involve comparing the results obtained from a digital classification to the "known" identity of land cover in test areas derived from reference data. The test areas are typically represented by one, or combinations, of the following:

1. Homogeneous test areas selected by the analyst.
2. Test pixels or areas selected randomly.

Previously (Section 10.10) we introduced the concept of using a contingency table to aid in assessing *training* area classification accuracy. It should be remembered that such procedures only indicate how well the statistics extracted from these areas can be used to categorize the same areas! If the results are good it means nothing more than the training areas are homogeneous, the training classes are spectrally separable, and the classification strategy being employed works well in the training areas. This aids in the training set refinement process but it indicates little about how the classifier performs elsewhere in a scene. One should expect training area accuracies to be overly optimistic, especially if they are derived from limited data sets. (Nevertheless, training area accuracies are sometimes used in the literature.)

Test areas are areas of representative, uniform land cover that are different from, and considerably more extensive than, training areas. They are often located during the training stage of supervised classification by intentionally designating more candidate training areas than are actually needed to develop the classification statistics. A subset of these may then be withheld for the postclassification accuracy assessment, again using a contingency table to express the results (see Table 10.4). The accuracies obtained in these areas represent at least a first approximation to classification performance throughout the scene. However, being homogeneous, test areas might not provide a valid indication of classification accuracy at the individual pixel level of land cover variability.

One way that would appear to ensure adequate accuracy assessment at the pixel level of specificity would be to compare the land cover classification at every pixel in an image with a reference source. While such "wall-to-wall" comparisons may have value in research situations, assembling reference land cover information for an entire project area is expensive and defeats the whole purpose of performing a remote sensing-based classification in the first place.

Random sampling of pixels circumvents the above problems, but it is plagued with its own set of limitations. First, collection of reference data for a large sample of

TABLE 10.4 Contingency Table Resulting from Classifying Test Area Pixels[a]

Known category type[b]	Number of pixels	Percentage correct	Number of pixels classified into category					
			1	2	3	4	5	6
1	5325	97	5165	0	42	44	53	21
2	328	66	0	216	0	108	4	0
3	4284	84	0	0	3599	16	482	187
4	945	42	12	92	228	397	132	84
5	2380	80	0	9	28	78	1904	361
6	3048	72	8	0	48	18	779	2195

[a]Overall classification performance: 82.6% (total correct pixels/total pixels). Average performance by class: 73.5% (average of category accuracies).
[b]1—Water, 2—sand, 3—forest, 4—urban, 5—corn, 6—hay.

randomly distributed points is often very difficult and costly. For example, travel distance and access to random sites might be prohibitive. Second, the validity of random sampling depends on the ability to precisely register the reference data to the image data. This is often difficult to do. One way to overcome this problem is to sample only pixels whose identity is not influenced by potential registration errors (for example, points at least several pixels away from field boundaries).

Another consideration is making certain that the randomly selected test pixels or areas are geographically representative of the data set under analysis. Stratified random sampling, where each land cover category may be considered a stratum, is frequently used. Clearly, the sampling approach appropriate for an agricultural inventory would differ from that of a wetlands mapping activity. Each sample design must account for the area being studied and the cover type being classified.

One common means of accomplishing random sampling is to overlay classified output data with a grid. Test cells within the grid are then selected randomly and groups of pixels within the test cells are evaluated. The cover types present are determined through ground verification (or other reference data) and compared to the classification data. The results are then normally summarized in a contingency table (similar to Table 10.4).

In interpreting classification accuracies it is important not only to note the percentage of correctly classified pixels, but also to determine the nature of errors of omission and commission on a class-by-class basis. Further, it should be understood that even a completely random classifier will produce percentage correct values in a contingency table. In fact, in order to compensate for this, several investigators have suggested that the use of an index which adjusts percentage correct values for random agreement [20]. This *kappa* or *KHAT* index ranges between 0 and 1 and expresses the proportionate reduction in error achieved by a classifier as compared with the error of a completely random classifier. Thus, a value of 0.75 would indicate that the classifier was avoiding 75 percent of the errors that a totally random process would have produced.

Sample size should also weigh heavily in the development and interpretation of classification accuracy figures. It has been shown that more than 250 test pixels are necessary to estimate the mean accuracy of a class to within ±5 percent. When fewer test pixels are sampled the confidence limits on the observed accuracy widen substantially. For example, if 49 pixels are used to estimate a classification accuracy figure of 89.8 percent, the 95 percent confidence interval for this figure would range from 79 to 95 percent [74]. In short, the number of points to sample depends on the sample procedure being used, the desired accuracy of the estimate, the number of pixels occurring in a category, and an estimate of the classification accuracy.

There are two other facets of classification accuracy assessment that we wish to emphasize before leaving the subject. The first relates to the fact that the quality of any accuracy estimate is only as good as the information used to establish the "true" land cover types present in the test sites. To the extent possible, some estimate of the errors present in the reference data should be incorporated into the accuracy assessment process. The second point to be made is that the accuracy assessment procedure must be designed to reflect the intended use of the classification. For example, a single pixel misclassified as "wetland" in the midst of a "corn" field might be of little significance in the development of a regional land use plan. However, this same error might be intolerable if the classification forms the basis for land taxation or for enforcement of wetland preservation legislation.

10.15   DATA MERGING

Many applications of digital image processing are enhanced through the merger of multiple data sets covering the same geographic area. These data sets can be of various forms. For example, in Section 9.14 we illustrated the utility of merging *multiresolution data* acquired by the same sensor (SPOT 10 m panchromatic and 20 m multispectral data). In the remainder of this chapter, we briefly discuss the following additional data merging operations: multitemporal data merging, change detection procedures, multisensor image merging, merging of image data and ancillary information, and integration of remote sensing data into geographic information systems.

Multitemporal Data Merging

Earlier in this chapter we introduced the concept of *multitemporal data merging* as a means of improving image classification. In such operations, two or more images acquired by the same sensor on different dates are registered and all (or a subset) of the image data from the various dates are used in the classification process.

Plate 20 illustrates the value of multitemporal data merging in the context of agricultural crop classification. Plate 20*a* is a Landsat MSS false color composite of the Toledo, Ohio, region acquired during the spring (May). This image has been geometrically corrected and resampled into a 50 m UTM grid. Light tones in the image are fields of bare soil that will probably be planted in corn or soybeans. The red fields in this image represent winter wheat or hay. Plate 20*b* shows the identical area during the summer (August) of the same growing season. Substantial changes in the appearance of the crops present in the scene can be observed between the two dates. Like the spring image *(a)*, the summer image, *(b)* has been geometrically corrected and resampled into a 50 m UTM grid. Hence, the two images can be precisely registered, pixel-by-pixel, on this common geographic base. The composite data set can then be used for automated classification or for generating a range of multidate composite images. Plate 20c illustrates one such composite, which results from the following color assignments:

Blue	Visible green (band 4, May)
Green	Near-IR (band 6, May)
Red	Near-IR (band 6, August)

The various land cover categories occurring in the composite image can be discriminated using the following interpretation key:

Urban	Dark blue, black
Residential	Dark green
Tended grass, hay fields	Yellow
Wheat fields, cut hay	Green
Corn fields	Light blue or purple
Soybean fields	Pink or red
Forests	Brown
Water	Dark blue
Wetlands	Dark red
Quarries	White

When the single-date and multidate data sets shown in Plate 20 were used in independent maximum likelihood classifications of the scene, the multidate approach yielded an average classification accuracy approximately 13 percent greater than either of the single-date classifications. Even greater improvements in classification accuracy than this are possible through the merger of multidate data. However, such increases in accuracy are clearly a function of the particular land cover types involved and both the number and timing of the various dates of imagery used.

One of the more effective means of dealing with multitemporal data for crop classification has been the *multitemporal profile* approach [7]. In this approach, classification is based on physical modeling of the time behavior of each crop's spectral response pattern. It has been found that the time behavior of the greenness of annual crops is sigmoidal (Figure 10.49), whereas the greenness of the soils (G_0) in a given region is nearly constant. Thus, the greenness at any time t can be modeled in terms of the peak greenness G_m, the time of peak greenness t_p, and the width σ of the profile between its two inflection points. (The inflection points, t_1 and t_2, are related to the rates of change in greenness early in the growing season and at the onset of senescence.) The features G_m, t_p, and σ account for more than 95 percent of the information in the original data and can therefore be used for classification instead of the original

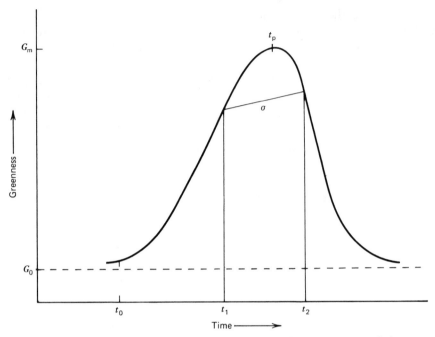

FIGURE 10.49 Temporal profile model for greenness. Key parameters include spectral emergence date (t_0), time (t_p) of peak greenness (G_m), and width of the profile (σ). (Adapted from [11], after [7]).

spectral response patterns. These three features are important because they not only reduce the dimensionality of the original data, they provide variables directly relatable to agrophysical parameters [11].

Change Detection Procedures

Change detection involves the use of multitemporal data sets to discriminate areas of land cover change between dates of imaging. The types of changes that might be of interest can range from short-term phenomena such as snow cover or flooding to long-term phenomena such as urban fringe development or desertification. One way of discriminating changes between two dates of imaging involves independently classifying each image, registering the results, and locating those pixels that have changed their land cover classification between dates. Another procedure is to simply register two images and prepare a *temporal difference image* by subtracting the DNs for one date from those of the other. The difference in areas of no change will be very small (approaching zero) and areas of change will manifest larger negative or positive values. Alternatively, a *temporal ratio image* can be used with data from two dates being ratioed, rather than subtracted. Ratios for areas of no change tend toward one and areas of change will have higher or lower ratio values. In either case, the analyst must find a meaningful "change—no change" threshold within the data. This is done either interactively by viewing areas of known change on a display monitor or statistically by estimating the threshold [4].

In lieu of using raw DNs to prepare temporal difference or ratio images, it is often desirable to correct for illumination and atmospheric effects and to transform the image data into physically meaningful quantities such as radiances or reflectances (Section 10.2). Also, the images may be prepared using transformations such as principal components or vegetation components. Likewise, linear regression procedures may be used to compare the two dates of imagery. In this approach a linear regression model is applied to predict data values for date 2 based on those of date 1. Again, the analyst must set a threshold for detecting meaningful change in land cover between the dates of imaging [43].

Multisensor Image Merging

Plate 21 illustrates yet another form of data merging, namely, the combination of image data from two different types of sensors. This plate shows a Landsat TM color composite image (a), a radar image (b), and a Landsat—radar combination image (c). The area shown is just south of the Detroit—Windsor area and includes suburban Detroit (Michigan) on the left, the Detroit River, and suburban Windsor (Ontario) on the right. The TM data were acquired on July 25, 1982, and the radar data on October 4, 1984. The TM data are displayed as a "color—infrared" combination. That is, band 2 data are shown as blue, band 3 as green, and band 4 as red. The radar data are aircraft data acquired using the STAR-1 system jointly developed by the Environmental Research Institute of Michigan and Intera Environmental Consultants, Ltd. of Canada. The STAR-1 system is an X-band, synthetic aperture, side-looking radar system, with HH polarization and a resolution of 6 × 6 m. The Landsat data were resampled into a 6 × 6 m cell size for the purpose of registration with the radar data. This data combination takes advantage of the spectral resolution of the Landsat TM data and the spatial resolution and "sidelighting" characteristics of the radar data to produce a composite image that offers potentially greater interpretability than an image from either sensor alone.

Merging of Image Data with Ancillary Information

Probably one of the most important forms of data merger employed in digital image processing is the registration of image data with "nonimage" or ancillary data sets. This latter type of data set can vary, ranging from soil type, to elevation data, to assessed property valuation. The only requirement is that the ancillary data be amenable to accurate geocoding so that they can be registered with the image data to a common geographic base. For example, digital elevation model (DEM) data can be readily combined with image data for a number of different purposes. Plate 22 illustrates the merger of DEM and image data to produce *synthetic stereoscopic images*. Shown in this plate is a synthetic stereopair generated by introducing simulated parallax into a Landsat MSS image. Whereas standard Landsat images exhibit only a fixed, weak stereoscopic effect in the relatively small areas of overlap between orbit passes, the synthetic image can be viewed in stereo over its entirety and with an analyst-specified degree of vertical exaggeration. These images are produced in a manner similar to the process used to produce stereomates for orthophotographs (Section 5.10). That is, the elevation at each pixel position is used to offset the pixel according to its relative elevation. When this distorted image is viewed stereoscopically with the original scene, a three-dimensional effect is perceived. Such images are particularly valuable in applications where landform analysis is central to the interpretation process. The technique is also useful for restoring the topographic information lost in the preparation of spectral ratio images.

Plate 23 illustrates the merger of DEM data and thermal scanner data. This plate shows volcanoes located on Miyake Island, 180 km south of Tokyo, Japan. On the afternoon of October 3, 1983, Mt. Jinanyama (located on the flank of Mt. Oyama) began an eruption that resulted in tongues of lava flowing downslope from source vents toward the ocean. As this lava moved across the ground surface, it cooled and solidified. On the evening of October 5 (7:00 P.M.), thermal imagery of the island was obtained when the tongues of lava were no longer flowing, but were still very hot. A perspective view of the island, created from the DEM, is shown in *(a)*. Here, the bands of color represent different elevation ranges. In *(b)*, the elevation data have been merged with the thermal data to display a perspective view of the island. The relief has been magnified three times in this view and a 10° elevation angle has been used. In *(c)*, the elevation angle has been increased to 20°. In *(d)*, contour lines have been added to the perspective view shown in *(c)*. Other views from other apparent vantage points could also be created. In *(e)*, the thermal and elevation data have been merged to create a stereopair.

Merging topographic information and image data is often useful in image classification. For example, topographic information is often important in forest type mapping in mountainous regions. In such situations, species that have very similar spectral characteristics might occupy quite different elevation ranges, slopes or aspects. Thus, the topographic information might serve as another "channel" of data in the classification directly or as a postclassification basis upon which to discriminate between only the spectrally similar classes in an image. In either case, the key to improving the classification is being able to define and model the various associations between the cover types present in a scene and their habitats.

Obviously, topographic information is not the only type of ancillary data that might be useful in a given image classification. Information as varied as soil type and land ownership might be useful.

Integration of Remote Sensing Data in Geographic Information Systems

As discussed earlier (Section 3.15), remote sensing data can be readily merged with other sources of geocoded information in a GIS. This permits the overlapping of several layers of information with the remotely sensed data, and the application of a virtually unlimited number of forms of data analysis. On the one hand, the data in a GIS might be used to aid in image classification. On the other hand, the land cover data generated by a classification might be used in subsequent queries and manipulations of the GIS data base.

Plate 24 illustrates the use of classified TM data in the context of soil erosion potential mapping. Shown in (a) is a land cover classification of a portion of Dane County, Wisconsin. Water is shown as blue, row crops as red, meadow and grassland as yellow, trees as dark green, and urban and other areas as gray. (This classification was generated using the TM data previously illustrated in Figure 9.26 and Plate 12.) To assess the soil erosion potential in this area, the land cover data were merged with information on the intrinsic erodibility of the soil present and land surface slope information. These latter forms of data were already resident in a GIS covering the area. Hence, all data could be resampled into a compatible base (30 m UTM grid) for comparison. Thus, the land cover data (a) were combined with the soil erodibility data (b) and the slope information (c) to develop the soil erosion potential map (d). In (b), areas of high potential soil erosion are shown in red, other land areas in tan, and water in black. In (c) areas of increasing steepness of slope are shown as blue, green, yellow, pink, and red; water is black. The soil erosion potential map (d) shows five colors depicting five levels of potential soil erosion. Nominal 1 square mile (1.61 km square) sections of land, as defined by the Public Land Survey System, are shown as a white grid overlay. Areas having the highest erosion potential are shown in red. These areas are represented by row crops growing on erodible soils on steep slopes. Areas of decreasing erosion potential are shown in orange, pink, and yellow. Green is assigned to areas of little to no erosion potential. These include nonagricultural regions in the scene and areas where continuous cover crops are growing on nonerodible soils and/or less steep slopes. Water is blue on this map.

When the increasing availability and sophistication of geographic information systems are coupled with the increasing availability of high-resolution multispectral data, the outlook for utilizing remote sensing data as an integral component of the land management process is indeed a bright one.

10.16 CONCLUSION

In concluding this discussion, we must reiterate that this chapter has only been a brief and general introduction to digital image processing. This subject is extremely broad and the procedures we have discussed are only a representative sample of the types of image processing operations useful in remote sensing. The scope of digital image processing in the generic sense is virtually unlimited.

SELECTED BIBLIOGRAPHY

1. Adeniyi, P.O., "Digital Analysis of Multitemporal Landsat Data for Land-Use/Land-Cover Classification in a Semi-arid Area of Nigeria," *Photogrammetric Engineering and Remote Sensing*, vol. 51, no. 11, November 1985, pp. 1761–1774.

2. American Society for Photogrammetry and Remote Sensing, *Proceedings: 10th William T. Pecora Memorial Remote Sensing Symposium*, Fort Collins, Colo., 1985.

3. American Society for Photogrammetry and Remote Sensing, Special Issue on Landsat Image Data Quality Analysis, *Photogrammetric Engineering and Remote Sensing*, vol. 51, no. 9, September 1985.

4. American Society of Photogrammetry, *Manual of Remote Sensing*, 2nd ed., Falls Church, Va., 1983.

5. Aronoff, S., "The Minimum Accuracy Value as an Index of Classification Accuracy," *Photogrammetric Engineering and Remote Sensing*, vol. 51, no. 1, January 1985, pp. 99–111.

6. Avery, T.E., and G.L. Berlin, *Interpretation of Aerial Photographs*, 4th ed., Burgess, Minneapolis, 1985.

7. Badhwar, G.D., "Classification of Corn and Soybeans Using Multitemporal Thematic Mapper Data," *Remote Sensing of Environment*, vol. 16, 1985, pp. 175–181.

8. Barzegar, F., "Rock Type Discrimination Using Enhanced Landsat Imagery," *Photogrammetric Engineering and Remote Sensing*, vol. 45, No. 5, May 1979, pp. 605–610.

9. Batson, R.M., K. Edwards, and E.M. Eliason, "Synthetic Stereo and Landsat Pictures," *Photogrammetric Engineering and Remote Sensing*, vol. 44, no. 4, 1978, pp. 503–505.

10. Bauer, M.E. (ed.), AgRISTARS Issue, *Remote Sensing of Environment*, vol. 14, nos. 1–3, 1984.

11. Bauer, M.E., "Spectral Inputs to Crop Identification and Condition Assessment," *Proceedings of the IEEE*, vol. 73, no. 6, June 1985, pp. 1071–1085.

12. Baxes, G.A., *Digital Image Processing*, Prentice–Hall, Englewood Cliffs, N.J., 1984.

13. Bernstein, R., et al., *Digital Image Processing for Remote Sensing*, Wiley, New York, 1978.

14. Blodget, H.W., F.J. Gunther, and M.H. Podwysocki, *Discrimination of Rock Classes and Alteration Products in Southwestern Saudi Arabia with Computer-Enhanced Landsat Data*, NASA Technical Paper 1327, U.S. Printing Office, Washington, D.C., 1978.

15. Buchanan, M.D., and R. Pendergrass, "Digital Image Processing: Can Intensity, Hue, and Saturation Replace Red, Green, and Blue?" *Electro-Optical Systems Design*, vol. 12, no. 3, March, 1980, pp. 29–36.

16. Carnahan, W.H., and G. Zhou, "Fourier Transform Techniques for the Evaluation of the Thematic Mapper Line Spread Function," *Photogrammetric Engineering and Remote Sensing*, vol. 52, no. 5, May 1986, pp. 639–648.

17. Chavez, P.S., Jr., G.L. Berlin, and W.B. Mitchell, "Computer Enhancement Techniques of Landsat MSS Digital Images for Land Use/Land Cover Assessments," *Remote Sensing of Earth Resources*, vol. 6, University of Tennessee Space Institute, Tullahoma, 1977.

18. Chavez, P.S., Jr., G.L. Berlin, and L.B. Sowers, "Statistical Method for Selecting Landsat MSS Ratios," *Journal of Applied Photographic Engineering*, no. 8, 1982, pp. 23–30.

19. Cheng, T.D., *Canopy Biomass Measurement of Individual Agricultural Fields with Landsat Imagery*, Ph.D. thesis, Department of Forest Science, Texas A&M University, College Station, 1985.

20. Congalton, R.G., R.G. Oderwald, and R.A. Mead, "Assessing Landsat Classification Accuracy Using Discrete Multivariate Statistical Techniques," *Photogrammetric Engineering and Remote Sensing*, vol. 49, no. 12, pp. 1671–1678, 1983.

21. Conrac Division, *Raster Graphics Handbook*, Conrac Corp., Covina, Calif., 1980.

22. Crist, E.P., and R.C. Cicone, "Application of the Tasseled Cap Concept to Simulated

Thematic Mapper Data," *Photogrammetric Engineering and Remote Sensing*, vol. 50, no. 3, pp. 343–352, 1984.

23. Crist, E.P., and R.J. Kauth, "The Tasseled Cap De-mystified," *Photogrammetric Engineering and Remote Sensing*, vol. 52, no. 1, January 1986, pp. 81–86.

24. Curlis, J.D., V.S. Frost, and L.F. Dellwig, "Geological Mapping Potential of Computer-Enhanced Images from the Shuttle Imaging Radar: Lisbon Valley Anticline, Utah," *Photogrammetric Engineering and Remote Sensing*, vol. 52, no. 4, April 1986, pp. 525–532.

25. Dubayah, R.O., and J. Dozier, "Orthographic Terrain Views Using Data Derived from Digital Elevation Models," *Photogrammetric Engineering and Remote Sensing*, vol. 52, no. 4, April 1986, pp. 509–518.

26. Ekstrom, M.P., *Digital Image Processing Techniques*, Academic Press, New York, 1984.

27. Eyton, J.R., "Landsat Multitemporal Color Composites," *Photogrammetric Engineering and Remote Sensing*, vol. 49, no. 2, February 1983, pp. 231–235.

28. Fleming, M.D., J.S. Berkehile, and R.M. Hoffer, *Computer-Aided Analysis of Landsat-1 MSS Data: A Comparison for Three Approaches, Including a Modified Clustering Approach*, LARS Information Note 072475, Purdue University, West Lafayette, Ind., 1975.

29. Foley, J.D., and A. Van Dam, *Fundamentals of Interactive Computer Graphics*, Addison–Wesley, Reading, Mass., 1983.

30. Ford, G.E., and C.I. Zanelli, "Analysis and Quantification of Errors in the Geometric Correction of Satellite Images," *Photogrammetric Engineering and Remote Sensing*, vol. 51, no. 11, November 1985, pp. 1725–1734.

31. Fox, L., III, J.A. Brockhaus, and N.D. Tosta, "Classification of Timberland Productivity in Northwestern California Using Landsat, Topographic, and Ecological Data," *Photogrammetric Engineering and Remote Sensing*, vol. 51, no. 11, November 1985, pp. 1745–1752.

32. Gurney, C.M., and J.R.G. Townshend, "The Use of Contextual Information in the Classification of Remotely Sensed Data," *Photogrammetric Engineering and Remote Sensing*, vol. 49, no. 1, January 1983, pp. 55–64.

33. Hay, A.M., "Sampling Designs to Test Land-Use Map Accuracy," *Photogrammetric Engineering and Remote Sensing*, vol. 45, no. 4, April 1979, pp. 529–533.

34. Haydn, R., G.W. Dalke, J. Henkel, and J.E. Bare, "Applications of the IHS Color Transform to the Processing of Multisensor Data and Image Enhancement," *Proceedings: International Symposium on Remote Sensing of Arid and Semi-arid Lands, Egypt, 1982*.

35. Hixson, M., et al., "Evaluation of Several Schemes for Classification of Remotely Sensed Data," *Photogrammetric Engineering and Remote Sensing*, vol. 46, no. 12, December 1980, pp. 1547–1553.

36. Holm, T.M., *Canonical Analysis: The Use of Transformed Landsat Data for Crop Type Discrimination*, USGS, Sioux Falls, S.D., 1982.

37. Holm, T.M., "Canonical Analysis of Crop Type Discrimination," *Proceedings: 9th International Symposium on Machine Processing of Remotely Sensed Data*, Purdue University, West Lafayette, Ind., 1983.

38. Hord, R.M., *Digital Image Processing of Remotely Sensed Data*, Academic Press, New York, 1982.

39. Horler, D.N.H., and F.J. Ahern, "Forestry Information Content of Thematic Mapper Data," *International Journal of Remote Sensing*, vol. 7, no. 3, 1986, pp. 405–428.

40. Hutchinson, C.F., "Techniques for Combining Landsat and Ancillary Data for Digital Classification Improvement," *Photogrammetric Engineering and Remote Sensing*, vol. 48, 1982, pp. 123–130.

41. Imhoff, M.L., et al., "Digital Overlay of Cartographic Information on Landsat MSS Data for Soil Surveys," *Photogrammetric Engineering and Remote Sensing*, vol. 48, no. 8, August 1982, pp. 1337–1342.

42. Jackson, R.D., "Spectral Indices in N-Space," *Remote Sensing of Environment*, vol. 13, no. 5, 1983, pp. 409–421.

43. Jensen, J.R., "Urban Change Detection Mapping Using Landsat Digital Data," *The American Cartographer*, vol. 8, no. 2, 1981, pp. 127–147.

44. Jensen, J.R., *Introductory Digital Image Processing: A Remote Sensing Perspective*, Prentice–Hall, Englewood Cliffs, N.J., 1986.

45. Jensen, S.K., and F.A. Waltz, "Principal Component Analysis and Canonical Analysis in Remote Sensing," *Proceedings: 45th Annual Meeting*, American Society of Photogrammetry, Falls Church, Va., 1979.

46. Jupp, D.L.B., and K.K. Mayo, "The Use of Residual Images in Landsat Image Analysis," *Photogrammetric Engineering and Remote Sensing*, vol. 48, no. 4, April 1982, pp. 595–604.

47. Kauth, R.J., and G.S. Thomas, "The Tasselled Cap—A Graphic Description of Spectral–Temporal Development of Agricultural Crops as Seen by Landsat," *Proceedings: 2nd International Symposium on Machine Processing of Remotely Sensed Data*, Purdue University, West Lafayette, Ind., 1976.

48. Kolm, K.E., and H.L. Case, "The Identification of Irrigated Crop Types and Estimation of Acreages from Landsat Imagery," *Photogrammetric Engineering and Remote Sensing*, vol. 50, no. 10, October 1984, pp. 1479–1490.

49. Kowalik, W.S., R.J.P. Lyon, and P. Switzer, "The Effects of Additive Radiance Terms on Ratios of Landsat Data," *Photogrammetric Engineering and Remote Sensing*, vol. 49, no. 5, May 1983, pp. 659–669.

50. Knepper, D.H., Jr., and G.L. Raines, "Determining Stretch Parameters for Lithologic Discrimination on Landsat MSS Band-Ratio Images," *Photogrammetric Engineering and Remote Sensing*, vol. 51, no. 1, January 1985, pp. 63–70.

51. Lo, T.H., F.L. Scarpace, and T.M. Lillesand, "Use of Multitemporal Spectral Profiles in Agricultural Land-Cover Classification," *Photogrammetric Engineering and Remote Sensing*, vol. 52, no. 4, April 1986, pp. 535–544.

52. Lyon, R.J.P., "Mineral Exploration Applications of Digitally Processed Landsat Imagery," *Proceedings: 1st William T. Pecora Memorial Symposium*, USDA Paper 1015, U.S. Govt. Printing Office, Washington, D.C., 1977.

53. Markham, B. and J.L. Barker, "Spectral Characterization of Landsat Thematic Mapper Sensors," *International Journal of Remote Sensing*, vol. 6, no. 5, 1985, pp. 697–716.

54. Markham, B.L., et al., "Temporal Spectral Response of a Corn Canopy," *Photogrammetric Engineering and Remote Sensing*, vol. 48, no. 11, November 1981, pp. 1599–1605.

55. Miller, L.D., et al., "Assessing Forage Conditions in Individual Ranch Pastures Using Thematic Mapper Imagery and an IBM Personal Computer," *Proceedings: 10th William T. Pecora Memorial Symposium*, American Society for Photogrammetry and Remote Sensing, Fort Collins, Colo., 1985.

56. Miller, W.A., and D.C. Johnston, "Comparison of Fire Fuel Maps Produced Using MSS and AVHRR Data," *Proceedings: 10th William T. Pecora Memorial Remote Sensing Symposium*, pp. 305–314, American Society for Photogrammetry and Remote Sensing, Ft. Collins, Colo., 1985.

57. Miller, W.A., and M.B. Shasby, "Refining Landsat Classification Results Using Digital Terrain Data," *Journal of Applied Photographic Engineering*, vol. 8, 1982, pp. 35–40.

58. Moik, J.G., *Digital Processing of Remotely Sensed Images*, NASA SP-431, U.S. Govt. Printing Office, Washington, D.C., 1980.

59. Muller, J-P, ed., *Digital Image Processing in Remote Sensing*, Taylor & Francis, London/Philadelphia, 1986.

60. Nelson, R., "Reducing Landsat MSS Scene Variability," *Photogrammetric Engineering and Remote Sensing*, vol. 51, no. 5, May 1985, pp. 583–593.

61. Newcomer, J.A., E.H. Horvath, and R.H. Haas, "A Spectral Stratification Approach to Classifying and Mapping Natural Vegetation," *Proceedings: Eighth International Symposium for Machine Processing of Remotely Sensed Data*, Purdue University, West Lafayette, Ind., 1982.

62. Pratt, W.K., *Digital Image Processing*, Wiley, New York, 1978.

63. Prieto, A., J. Bescos, and J. Santamaria, "Spatial Frequency Pseudocolor Filters," *Photogrammetric Engineering and Remote Sensing*, vol. 48, no. 11, November 1982, pp. 1701–1708.

64. Richardson, A.J., and C.L. Wiegand, "Distinguishing Vegetation from Soil Background Information," *Photogrammetric Engineering and Remote Sensing*, vol. 43, no. 12, 1977, pp. 1541–1552.

65. Ripple, W.J., "Asymptotic Reflectance Characteristics of Grass Vegetation," *Photogrammetric Engineering and Remote Sensing*, vol. 51, no. 12, December 1985, pp. 1915–1921.

66. Rohde, W.G., J.K. Lo, and R.A. Pohl, "EROS Data Center Landsat Digital Enhancement Techniques and Imagery Availability," *Canadian Journal of Remote Sensing*, no. 4, 1978, pp. 63–76.

67. Rosenfeld, A., and A.C. Kak, *Digital Picture Processing*, 2nd ed., Academic Press, New York, 1982.

68. Rosenfield, G.H., "Analysis of Thematic Map Classification Error Matrices," *Photogrammetric Engineering and Remote Sensing*, vol. 52, no. 5, May 1986, pp. 681–686.

69. Rosenfield, G.H., and K. Fitzpatrick-Lins, "A Coefficient of Agreement as a Measure of Thematic Classification Accuracy," *Photogrammetric Engineering and Remote Sensing*, vol. 52, no. 2, February 1986, pp. 223–227.

70. Ru-Ye, W., "An Approach to Tree-Classifier Design Based on Hierarchical Clustering," *International Journal of Remote Sensing*, vol. 7, no. 1, 1986, pp. 75–88.

71. Sabins, F.F., Jr., *Remote Sensing: Principles and Interpretation*, 2nd ed., Freeman, New York, 1986.

72. Satterwhite, M., W. Rice, and J. Shipman, "Using Landform and Vegetative Factors to Improve the Interpretation of Landsat Imagery," *Photogrammetric Engineering and Remote Sensing*, vol. 50, no. 1, January 1984, pp. 83–91.

73. Schowengerdt, R.A., "Reconstruction of Multispatial, Multispectral Image Data Using Spatial Frequency Content," *Photogrammetric Engineering and Remote Sensing*, vol. 46, no. 10, October 1980, pp. 1325–1334.

74. Schowengerdt, R.A., *Techniques for Image Processing and Classification in Remote Sensing*, Academic Press, New York, 1983.

75. Schreier, H., L.C. Goodfellow, and L.M. Lavkulich, "The Use of Digital Multi-date Landsat Imagery in Terrain Classification," *Photogrammetric Engineering and Remote Sensing*, vol. 48, no. 1, January 1982, pp. 111–119.

76. Sheffield, C., "Selecting Band Combinations from Multispectral Data," *Photogrammetric Engineering and Remote Sensing*, vol. 51, no. 6, June 1985, pp. 681–687.

77. Shih, E.H., and R.A. Schowengerdt, "Classification of Arid Geomorphic Surfaces Using Landsat Spectral and Textural Features," *Photogrammetric Engineering and Remote Sensing*, vol. 49, no. 3, March 1983, pp. 337–347.

78. Short, N.M., *The Landsat Tutorial Workbook*, NASA Ref. Publ. 1078, U.S. Govt. Printing Office, Washington, D.C., 1982.

79. Siegal, B.S., and A.R. Gillespie (eds.), *Remote Sensing in Geology*, Wiley, New York, 1980.

80. Smith, J.A., T.L. Lin, and K.J. Ranson, "The Lambertian Assumption and Landsat Data," *Photogrammetric Engineering and Remote Sensing*, vol. 46, no. 9, September 1980, pp. 1183–1189.

81. Slater, P.N., *Remote Sensing Optics and Optical Systems*, Addison–Wesley, Reading, Mass., 1980.

82. Story, M., and R.G. Congalton, "Accuracy Assessment: A User's Perspective," *Photogrammetric Engineering and Remote Sensing*, vol. 52, no. 3, March 1986, pp. 397–399.

83. Stow, D.A., and J.E. Estes, "Landsat and Digital Terrain Data for County-Level Resource Management," *Photogrammetric Engineering and Remote Sensing*, vol. 47, no. 2, February 1981, pp. 215–222.

84. Strahler, A.H., T.L. Logan, and N.A. Bryant, "Improving Forest Cover Classification Accuracy from Landsat by Introducing Topographic Information," *Proceedings: 12th International Symposium on Remote Sensing of Environment*, Environmental Research Institute of Michigan, Ann Arbor, 1978.

85. Swain, P.H., and S.M. Davis (eds.), *Remote Sensing: The Quantitative Approach*, McGraw–Hill, New York, 1978.

86. Taranik, J.V., *Principles of Computer Processing of Landsat Data for Geologic Applications*, Open-File Report 78-177, USGS, Sioux Falls, S.D., 1978.

87. Tom, C.H., and L.D. Miller, "An Automated Land-Use Mapping Comparison of the Bayesian Maximum Likelihood and Linear Discriminant Analysis Algorithms," *Photogrammetric Engineering and Remote Sensing*, vol. 50, no. 2, February 1984, pp. 193–207.

88. Townsend, F.E., "The Enhancement of Computer Classifications by Logical Smoothing," *Photogrammetric Engineering and Remote Sensing*, vol. 52, no. 2, February 1986, pp. 213–221.

89. Tucker, C.J., "Red and Photographic Infrared Linear Combinations for Monitoring Vegetation," *Remote Sensing of Environment*, vol. 8, 1979, pp. 127–150.

90. Tucker, C.J., J.H. Elgin, Jr., and J.E. McMurtrey III, "Temporal Spectral Measurements of Corn and Soybean Crops," *Photogrammetric Engineering and Remote Sensing*, vol. 45, no. 5, May 1979, pp. 643–653.

91. USGS, *20th International Remote Sensing Workshop, Quantitative Remote Sensing*, EROS Data Center, Sioux Falls, S.D., 1983.

92. Welch, R.A., T.R. Jordan, and E.L. Usery, "Microcomputers in the Mapping Sciences," *Computer Graphics World*, no. 6, pp. 33–39, 1983.

93. Yang, Y.K., *Microcomputer Techniques for the Creation and Analysis of 7½' Image Map from Landsat MSS, RBV, and Thematic Mapper Images*, Ph.D thesis, Department of Forest Science, Texas A&M University, College Station, 1985.

94. Zobrist, A.L., N.A. Bryant, and R.G. McLeod, "Technology for Large Digital Mosaics of Landsat Data," *Photogrammetric Engineering and Remote Sensing*, vol. 49, no. 9, September 1983, pp. 1325–1335.

IMAGE SOURCES

Listed below are the major sources of remote sensing data in the United States. Also listed are the images included in Chapter 4 of this book. The following tabular information specifies the agency that originally obtained the image and also the image identification numbers. Note that the figure captions contain additional information on location and date of image acquisition, which may be helpful when placing an order.

Order information and current prices may be obtained from the following:

NASA, NHAP, and USGS photographs
   EROS Data Center
   Sioux Falls, SD 57198

ASCS and NHAP photographs
   Aerial Photography Field Office
   ASCS–USDA
   P.O. Box 30010
   Salt Lake City, UT 84125

Large Format Camera photographs
   Chicago Aerial Survey, Inc.
   2140 Wolf Road
   Des Plaines, IL 60018

Landsat images and digital products
   EOSAT Corporation
   4300 Forbes Boulevard
   Lanham, MD 20706

SPOT images and digital products
   SPOT Image Corporation
   1897 Preston White Drive
   Reston, VA 22091

NOAA meteorological satellite images and digital products
   Satellite Data Service Branch

NOAA/National Environmental Satellite, Data, and Information Service
World Weather Building, Room 100
Washington, DC 20233

Information on cartographic data throughout the United States, including maps,
charts, airphotos, space images, geodetic control, digital elevation and planimetric
data, and related information from federal, state, and some private sources, may be
obtained from:

National Cartographic Information Center
U.S. Geologic Survey
507 National Center
Reston, VA 22092

Figure no.	Agency	Image ID no.
4.5a	ASCS	BWI-1BB-27-28
4.5b	ASCS	BMO-1T-125-126
4.5c	ASCS	BRT-IFF-155-156
4.6	ASCS	BWI-1BB-29
4.7a	ASCS	WW-1R-49
4.7b	ASCS	BWI-1BB-29
4.8	USGS	GS-WI-12-146-147
4.9	ASCS	DIC-8AA-14-15
4.10	ASCS	APL-4V-98-99
4.11	USGS	GS-WI-36-68-69
4.12	ASCS	CMY-1DD-33-34
4.13	ASCS	RF-2AA-97-98
4.15	USGS	GS-VBGD-1-89-90
4.16	USGS	GS-VBGD-1-10-11
4.17	ASCS	APU-1V-156-157
4.20	USGS	GS-IE-5-107-108
4.21	ASCS	II-6BB-90-91-92
4.23	USGS	GS-CMA-32-88-89
4.24	ASCS	BOI-5CC-210-211
4.25	ASCS	DDC-10P-90-91
4.26	ASCS	EKL-14CC-6-7
4.27	ASCS	EKN-1CC-197-198
4.28	ASCS	CVP-5W-193-194
4.29	ASCS	EKM-3CC-55-56

(continued)

Figure no.	Agency	Image ID no.
4.31	ASCS	YR-5T-178-179
4.33	USGS	GS-VID-1-96-97
4.35	USGS	GS-RR-5-118-119
4.36	ASCS	ABN-14W-21-22
4.37	ASCS	CXN-3AA-117-118
4.38	ASCS	CWQ-1P-08-09
4.39	NASA	1296-17023
4.40	ASCS	CBD-7N-37-38
4.42	ASCS	BKP-1GG-34-35
4.44	ASCS	BXR-4V-63-64
4.45	ASCS	BWI-3BB-95-96
4.46*b*	ASCS	AX-5R-85-86
4.47	ASCS	BIC-1V-37-38
4.48	ASCS	XB-3R-98-99
4.49	ASCS	XA-2R-65-66
4.50	ASCS	BRT-9V-38-39
4.52	ASCS	ZY-1CC-53-54
4.53	ASCS	ARE-2V-108-109
4.54	ASCS	BHQ-3AA-244-245
4.56	USGS	"California A,B"[a]
4.57	ASCS	Photo Index Sheet #3, Knox Co.
4.58	ASCS	QQ-1V-74
4.59	ASCS	ARU-1EE-74-75
4.60	NASA	1177-16023
4.61	ASCS	WV-5R-187-188
4.62	ASCS	WV-4R-91-92

[a]Order "California A,B" from the National Cartographic Information Center (NCIC).

INDEX

709